margins

Road to Guildford

W. B. Andrews

A. H. Stone

W. T. Graham

P. Brown

Claise Cr.

Lake

P. Brown

Church Site

Swamp

Burial Ground

Georges Terrace

R i v e r

Pt Fraser

Perth in 1894
(Barrack Street looking south from Wellington Street)

On a Saturday afternoon in summer on the eve of the great gold rushes, Perth looks to be a town at one with itself. A man walks at ease with his neighbour. A working class family walks purposefully in the direction of Barrack Street Jetty. A boy investigates the contents of his father's hands. A carter lazily wends his way down the street. Behind him a horse-carriage, with more picnic trippers, passes over the lip of the ridge. A dog side-steps towards one of the new telephone poles. If the sea breeze is in, it is wafting lightly. The bike parked outside the cycle agency is quite safe. The Town Hall, Governor Hampton's gift to the people of Perth, is still the dominant building. The telephone wires, not more than five years old, strike a discordant note to modern eyes, but to the people of Barrack Street they are a sign of progress; and in any case, the moment of excitement about their construction has passed.

A successful quest for 'internal peace'? The photograph suggests so. Yet facades do not tell all. It was only a short time ago that the poor sweated labourers in the Rev. Traylen's City Press and General Printery had protested about their working conditions, a protest which had become a catalyst in the struggle for an eight-hour working day. And in Phineas Seeligson's loan office, minor and major human tragedies were experienced every day, and some tormented people of Perth were moved to steal from the office when they had nothing left with which to 'raise the wind' for rent. Men had bought and sold the street since 1829, and within five years of our photograph being taken, scarcely a building in it would be left standing. The heap of bricks on the corner block portended the construction boom of the later 1890s. The unknown photographer had captured a moment of equipoise in the history of the people of Perth.

Front endsheet: A modified version of the '1833 plan of Perth'. The original plan was used as an inset on a map of Western Australia, drawn by the renowned cartographer, John Arrowsmith, based on information supplied to the Colonial Office, London, by Surveyor-General J. S. Roe.

to Maria

A tune beyond us as we are,
Yet nothing changed by the blue guitar.

Wallace Stevens,
'The man with the blue guitar', **The Collected Poems,**
Faber and Faber, 1955.

The People of Perth

C.T. Stannage

The People of Perth

A Social History
of Western Australia's
Capital City

Published by the Perth City Council
Perth, Western Australia.

Published in Western Australia by the Perth City Council

First Published August 1979

Copyright © C. T. Stannage

National Library of Australia **Cataloguing-in-Publication Data**

Stannage, Charles Thomas
   The People of Perth

Index
Bibliography
ISBN O 909994 86 2
ISBN O 909994 85 4 Limited ed.
ISBN O 909994 87 0 Softcover

1. Perth — History.   2. Perth — Social Life and customs.   I. Perth City Council.   II.   Title

994'.1 [1]

Text designed by Max J. McNamara

Phototypeset by Fastype Photosetting, WA Turf Club Building, 30 The Esplanade, Perth
Negatives and plates by Donalds Platemaking Service Pty Ltd, 87 Brown St, East Perth
Printed by Dix Print Pty Ltd, 10 Wittenoom St, East Perth
Bound by Printing Trade Services, 20 Sutherland St, West Perth

Publishing Consultants: Ⓜ **Carroll's Pty Ltd, 566 Hay St, Perth**

Foreword

Six years ago the City Council commissioned Dr Tom Stannage, a West Australian, to produce the history of Perth for publication in 1979 during the State's 150th celebrations.

This book is now the result of his intensive research into what happened in the early days of the colony and beyond.

It portrays history as I would have liked it to have been taught to me. It is history as it occurred to our grandfathers and fathers but perhaps its sheer honesty will not win it universal approval.

It is not only a story of success and progress but a story of struggle, the struggle of ordinary people to survive under extraordinary conditions. It is the story of the people that gave us and our State our future.

THE HON. F. C. CHANEY, CBE, AFC.
Lord Mayor of Perth

Acknowledgements

A local history like *The People of Perth* cannot be written without the co-operation of the local community, and I am extremely grateful to the many people of Perth who have given me assistance and support. The book was commissioned by the Perth City Council during Sir Ernest Lee Steere's Lord Mayoralty; it was completed under the present Lord Mayor, Fred Chaney. The Councillors and ratepayers of the City of Perth granted me twelve months' paid research in 1976. The hard-working staff of the Perth City Council have been unfailingly helpful. Not to mention some names would be to do less than justice to the assistance given: G. O. Edwards, Reg Dawson, Russell Elsegood, Milton Rundle, Kieran Woods, Kathy Pawluk, Elaine McFarling, Mrs Mollie Jones and Pat McCarthy. They, and the rest of the staff, would understand why I acknowledge here an especially great debt to Irene Mills, Ernest Polis, and Di Hope-Johnstone.

I wish also to acknowledge the assistance of the following people and institutions:

Ms Ruth Allender, to whom I owe an especially great debt of gratitude.

The Master of the Supreme Court of Western Australia, Mr G. T. Staples; the Registrar of the Court, Mr Ward; Don Cunningham and Judy Salinger.

At the Battye Library of Western Australian History—the Principal Librarian, Ms Margaret Medcalf; also Wendy Sobon, Paul Malone, Robin South, and the junior assistants.

At the Art Gallery of Western Australia—the Senior Curator, Lou Klepac; also Ms Barbara Chapman and Jan Moore.

At the library of the Royal WA Historical Society—the former Honorary Secretary, Ms Gwen Dalton; also the Librarian, Mr Ian Heppingstone.

For greatly valued research assistance: Lee Wheeler, Elspeth Douglas, and Jan Brazier.

Ian Elliott, Merredith Thomas, Debbie Robinson, Margaret Pitt-Morison, Margaret Brown, Sally Kennedy, Mrs Rica Erickson, Sandra Taylor, Ian and Helen Alexander, Rob Pascoe, Ian Crawford, Lynne Stevenson, Margaret Grellier, Lenore Layman, Bob and Joan Manning, Bill and Glenys Walker, Tom Jenkins, the Rev. McNair, the late Father Moynihan, the late Dom William, OSB, Neville Green, Geoff Shaw, David Hutchison, Don Garden, Mrs M. W. White, Mrs Jones, Raelene Davidson, Mrs A. D. McGeorge, Brian Stoddart, Laaden Fletcher, Keith Sinclair, and Suzanne Welborn. I am grateful to still others who loaned me material or answered queries.

My friends and colleagues in the Department of History at the University of Western Australia offered the priceless gift of 'growling' (as the late Walter Murdoch would have put it). I am especially grateful to Mrs Phyllis Langley, Di Hollis, and Barbara Williamson. It was on the recommendation of Professor Peter Reeves that the University of Western Australia granted me leave of absence in 1976, on secondment to the Perth City Council.

Geoffrey Bolton suggested that I should tackle *The People of Perth*, and kindly commented on the manuscript. He is not, of course, responsible for the views expressed in the book.

My research was aided by a grant from the Australian Research Grants Committee. Writing deadlines could not have been met without the aid of a research fellowship in the Department of History in the Research School of Social Sciences at the Australian National University. My colleagues there have been unfailingly kind and supportive. Jean Dillon, Sandra Young, Janice Aldridge and Lois Simms typed the manuscript.

I am grateful to the Grolier Society of Australia Pty Ltd for permission to reprint in substance my entry on 'Perth', in *Australian Encyclopaedia* 1977 and later editions. The entry forms part of the Overview.

Finally, a community history is also a family affair. My grandparents were 't'othersiders' who became Westralians. In their old age they shared with me some of the dreams and the realities of their lives. My father and mother fostered, by example, my interest in literature and history. My sister's paintings, wayward and always inspiring, are now part of the history of the people of Perth. *The People of Perth* is dedicated to my wife, Maria. Our children, Chris and Kate, sorted papers, helped to choose some of the illustrations, and cheerfully accompanied us through Perth's history, whether in old houses, or in art galleries, or on demolition sites.

Contents

Abbreviations

ABC	:	Australian Broadcasting Commission
ADB	:	*Australian Dictionary of Biography*
ANUP	:	Australian National University Press
CSO	:	*Colonial Secretary's Office, Letters and Memoranda*
Early Days	:	Journal of the Royal Western Australian Historical Society (RWAHS in Bibliography)
HRA	:	*Historical Records of Australia*
MUP	:	Melbourne University Press
OUP	:	Oxford University Press
PCC	:	Perth City Council
SRP	:	*Swan River Papers*
UQP	:	University of Queensland Press
UWA	:	University of Western Australia
UWAP	:	University of Western Australia Press
WA	:	West Australia or Western Australia
WAPD	:	*Western Australian Parliamentary Debates*

Conversion Table: weight, liquid volume, measure and area

Imperial	Metric
one ounce (oz)	28.35 grams (g)
one pound (lb)	0.454 kilograms (kg)
one ton	1.016 tonnes (t)
bushell	36.74 bushells to one tonne (t)
one gill	0.142 litre (l)
one gallon	4.546 litres (l)
one inch	2.54 centimetres (cm)
one foot (feet or ft)	0.305 metre (m)
one yard	0.914 metre (m)
one chain (66 feet)	20.117 metres (m)
one mile	1.609 kilometres (km)
one acre	0.405 hectare (ha)

Monetary (pre 1966 Australian currency)

£ (pounds)
s (shillings)
d (pence)

Overview

History

The site of Perth was discovered in 1697 by the Dutch navigator, de Vlamingh, who named Swan River after the black swans he saw there. Perth was founded in August 1829 by Captain James Stirling, a sea-captain who wanted a picturesque setting well out of range of naval bombardment. The colony survived early vicissitudes, and by the 1860s the physical and social shape of Perth had largely been determined. The administrative, political, business, and military centre was the immediate vicinity of the old domain, on the corner of Barrack Street and St George's Terrace. Hay Street was developing as a lesser commercial and shopping precinct; while farther north the Wellington Street area contained artisans' workshops, cottages and stockyards. Perth's 'port' was at the foot of William Street, and it provided the people of Perth with trading links with the greater port settlement of Fremantle and the inland village port of Guildford. Indeed by the 1860s Perth was also becoming more accessible to its regions by overland routes, thanks to those reluctant colonists, the convicts, the first shipload of whom arrived in 1850.

The convict era is a notable one in Perth's history. Convict labour provided the colony with a hospital, a new Government House, a Town Hall, and the Cloisters, as well as aiding colonial spiritual improvement by helping to construct Trinity Church and the first stage of the Roman Catholic Cathedral. But the convicts also constructed other monuments to British civilisation, namely a gaol and court-house (which they themselves frequently revisited), and a barracks for their overseers, the Enrolled Pensioner Guard. The free people of Perth learnt to live with the brutalising presence of convicts, though many carried guns by day and few ventured far afield in the evenings. When transportation ceased in 1868 the spiritual and social effects of convictism lingered and even today few people of convict descent would openly acknowledge their family's past. In general the people of Perth successfully erased from the collective memory of their community much of the experience of convictism, preferring to remember and celebrate the material benefits of that experience while forgetting the lacerated backs which were its essence.

By one of history's ironies Perth was proclaimed a City by Queen Victoria at the height of convictism (1856). City status meant increased local responsibility for good government, and when in 1858 the Perth City Council settled down to its work it was clear to all that Perth was now a well-established part, if not perhaps a jewel, in the British Empire; that it was indeed another province for England's gentry.

The 1870s and the early 1880s were years of consolidation. In January 1871 the City of Perth was incorporated and several other municipal councils and road boards were established. One striking change in the lives of the people of Perth was that from the 1880s they could travel by rail from Perth to Guildford and from Perth to Fremantle. Business was expedited, and for the ladies the train journey proved far less arduous than the former means of travel, particularly in the winter season. Evening strolls became more common after the installation of lighting in the mid-1870s, and late evening shopping seems to have played a greater part in the lives of the citizens than previously. And from the mid-1880s river reclamation led to the creation of the Esplanade for recreation purposes. While economically there was a loss of impetus, and while the failure to discover gold was worrying, life in Perth was fairly comfortable, particularly for the affluent and the well-connected, and particularly for the men. An excellent club was established in the 1870s (named after Governor Weld). Located in St George's Terrace near the commercial and social centre of the city, it provided men of substance an opportunity to meet and discuss the affairs of the day, to read the latest British and colonial newspapers, and to try their hand at billiards. For the workers too there was a club, but it was safely tucked away in Wellington Street and conveniently sited near the city gaol in case moral enlightenment should falter before the vices of drink and rowdyism, much associated with life in the northern quarter from the beginnings of the settlement to the present day. In these years Perth became a mayoralty, the first incumbent being George Shenton, described by a political opponent as 'Warwick the Kingmaker', so powerful a figure was he in the business and political life of the community. With Shenton began a tradition of the mayoralty being held by eminent businessmen and social leaders, a tradition rarely broken in the last one hundred years. Shenton would learn with great pleasure that in the mid-1970s a descendant of his colleague, Sir James Lee Steere, was running the affairs of the city.

In the 1890s Perth underwent great structural and social changes, due to the influx of population following the discovery of gold in the Murchison and the eastern goldfields. In this decade Perth retained its supremacy as the colony's major centre, though not without considerable effort on the part of the Government of the day led by Sir John Forrest, and the Perth City Council, led on two occasions by his brother Alexander. The Government established a colony-wide railway system centred on Perth, and by upgrading the Port of Fremantle and making it suitable for deep-sea liners it enabled that port to overtake Albany, its keenest rival. The Perth City Council had to meet vastly increased demands for such services as drainage, sewerage, lighting, road construction, and so on. The city's population spilled out of the old residential areas into the bushlands to the north, east and west where new suburbs were established with links (sometimes tramways) back into the city centre. From this period Perth became less a walking city than a public transport city. Many of the buildings which today are the concern of preservation bodies—such as His Majesty's Theatre and the Palace Hotel—date from the goldrush period. In general the period left Perth with rather imposing neo-classical facades, of neighbourly proportions still, if less intimate than the structures demolished to make way for them; and the city centre began to lose much of its residential character: 'community' began to mean localised suburban communities rather than a single Perth community.

In the twentieth century, Perth has undergone many changes. Many of these can be identified with W. E. Bold, Town Clerk extraordinary for 44 years to 1944. It was Bold who, from before World War I, promoted the idea of 'Greater Perth' or an amalgamation of several suburban municipalities under the aegis of the Perth City Council. The idea was attractive from planning and financial points of view, and during World War I the suburbs of North Perth, Leederville and Victoria Park surrendered their sovereignty to the Perth City Council. The 'Greater Perth' movement was not without its critics, and Subiaco held out against it, while the Perth Roads Board successfully retained control over the Mount Lawley and Inglewood districts despite their efforts to join the City Council. In the same period the Perth City Council acquired the 'Lime-kilns' Estate area west of the city. This enabled Bold to fulfil a dream, which was to create a garden suburb. Well before his retirement the suburb of Floreat Park was established. Other citizens, like the architect/planner Harold Boas, joined with Bold in providing Perth with an orderly development, to some extent along garden-city lines. From 1928 development was subject to a Town Planning Act. In the course of the 1920s the appearance and character of Perth were confirmed rather than altered dramatically, though late in the 1930s the construction of the several-storey Colonial Mutual Life building in St George's Terrace foreshadowed the dramatic changes of the 1960s.

In other respects the lives of the people of Perth were changed. In the 1920s horse carriages almost disappeared and motor taxis were in almost universal use. While trams and railways continued to carry many passengers, there was a distinct trend towards the use of buses and motorcars. The economic life of the city faltered and then collapsed during the Depression of the 1930s, and even well-established professional firms were forced to retrench valued and faithful employees. In times of hardship in the nineteenth century the people of Perth had traditionally protested outside the gates of Government House; but by the 1930s power and responsibility rested squarely with the State Government, and the dispossessed and unemployed on occasion demonstrated outside the Treasury Buildings in central Barrack Street. The Perth City Council did much to alleviate distress in the city, though its efforts were hampered by a decreased revenue. However, it was able to carry out extensive river reclamation projects which resulted in the creation of the sports area known as Langley Park, and a fine city by-pass road appropriately named Riverside Drive.

During and immediately after World War II there were very few major building developments in the city, though an increasing number of city-users were travelling to work in motorcars and the city was beginning to lose its 'public transport' character. Turning into the 1960s this trend gathered momentum and was accompanied, particularly in the later 1960s and early 1970s, by a drastic alteration to the city's skyline as massive blocks were constructed. More than at any other time in the city's history, planning was now a controversial and public matter. The city has by no means lost its reputation for orderly development; nor has it completely lost its 'local' character.

Modern Perth

The city block of Perth is in the shape of an elongated rectangle, with St George's Terrace, Murray and Wellington Streets running from east to west, and Milligan, King, William, Barrack and Pier Streets from south to north. St George's Terrace ('the Terrace') is flanked by a mixture of buildings, some dating from the nineteenth century, but many more having been built since the late 1960s. At the eastern end it continues into Adelaide Terrace and towards the Causeway which crosses the Swan over Heirisson Island. Proceeding on the south side of 'the Terrace' one passes the new Australian Government offices, the city's new concert hall (1973), the Tudor-like nineteenth-century Government House, and the City Council's glassy office block. In the same block on the northern side can be seen the Deanery (1850s), St George's Anglican Cathedral, and the Treasury Buildings, with their fine nineteenth-century colonnades. West of Barrack Street lie the banks, insurance offices, and Stock Exchange. The block contains some of the highest buildings in the city, including the Allendale and AMP towers. Among the old buildings which remain are Trinity Church, Perth Boys' School, the Cloisters and the Palace Hotel. At the western end of 'the Terrace' all that remains of the convict-built Pensioner barracks which once dominated the street is the arch, retained after much public controversy, and now a rather forlorn-looking object of curiosity to visitors.

Hay and Murray Streets are the city's retail arteries, and are joined together by several fine shopping arcades. As supermarkets have mushroomed in the suburbs, a feature of the city's retail developments in recent years has been the increase in number and quality of specialist shops, many of which occupy premises which had become run-down and tatty. In brief, Perth's shopping centre is bright, modern and extensive. Hay Street central and Forrest Place are now pedestrian malls. The old Town Hall still stands. Murray Street east is characterised by St Mary's Roman Catholic Cathedral, and the Royal Perth Hospital.

The pattern of arterial roads round Perth has been revolutionised by the construction of the Mitchell Freeway. This crosses the city at its western end, and at its southern point joins the Narrows Bridge and Kwinana Freeway through South Perth to the Canning River. It has caused the reclamation of part of Perth Water.

Perth is a garden city. In the heart of the city are Stirling Gardens and Supreme Court Gardens. The former was once the city's botanical gardens, and even today some ancient pines have survived the Gardens' transformations; on weekdays it serves as a lunchground for thousands of city workers. Supreme Court Gardens is a venue of the city's annual 'Carols by Candlelight', a Christmas celebration of pop-concert proportions. Tucked away in the eastern end of the city is a serene English-style park—Queen's Gardens. It is a water garden of great beauty, developed on the site of old clay-pits, from which came materials for the construction of many of Perth's notable buildings in the nineteenth century. The park is a haven from the bustle of city traffic and, to the delight of generations of Perth children, contains a statue of Peter Pan. Other open parklands adjacent to the city include Hyde Park, Boas (Delhi) Square, Lake Monger, and Langley Park. But the city's most celebrated open space is King's Park (400 hectares), a bushland heritage overlooking the city. A unique blend of native trees, wildflowers, shrubs, landscaped botanical gardens, rolling lawns, and family picnic areas, 'the Park' has won popularity with generations of Western Australians and visitors.

Among the many sporting facilities of the city are Beatty Park for swimming and Perry Lakes Stadium for athletics and soccer. Several of the Australian Rules football clubs have grounds within the City of Perth. Swimming and surfing at metropolitan beaches are regular summer pastimes, as is yachting on the Swan. Rottnest, the island of 'sin, sun, and sand', remains a popular holiday resort with teenagers and young families. Cricket, trotting, and horseracing have their headquarters on the banks of the Swan not far from the centre of the city, which now also boasts a greyhound track.

Perth has two universities. The University of Western Australia with its river setting on Matilda Bay, now has 10 000 students; and Murdoch University (named after the celebrated essayist Walter Murdoch), south of the river, first took students in 1975. The largest of the tertiary education institutions is the Western Australian Institute of Technology. Since the first teachers' college (Claremont) was founded in 1902, Perth has seen the establishment of several more. In common with the other Australian cities, Perth has a number of co-educational high and primary schools and several private schools and colleges. The metropolitan area has many fine kindergartens, but child-care and play facilities suffer from inadequate public financing, and depend largely on voluntary workers, including mothers' co-operatives.

The State Public Library is a reference library which maintains a lending service to local municipal libraries. The Public Library also houses the Battye Library (Western Australian history) and State Archives. The Art Gallery, which contains a fine collection of nineteenth-century English paintings and several excellent Australian paintings (notably McCubbin's 'Down on his Luck'), is to move into much-needed new quarters by 1980, as part of a proposed cultural complex. The adjacent Museum houses splendid displays of Aboriginal culture in a fine new building. Culture of a more popular sort can be had nightly in the new colosseum-like Entertainment Centre which dominates the city west of the railway station.

Perth is an industrialised city. Secondary industries, particularly manufacturing, building, and transport, employ about 35 per cent of the workers, while tertiary concerns such as shops, schools, banks, and hospitals employ about 63 per cent, with the remainder engaged in primary industries like mining and market gardening. Industrial works have largely moved away from the centre of the city, even from East Perth, a traditional location for industry. The Welshpool/Kewdale industrial area, a few kilometres east of the city, has expanded greatly, as has Osborne Park to the north-west of Perth. The older industrial areas of Subiaco/Jolimont and Bassendean/Midland continue to function as such, though they contain fewer new developments. The State's major industrial area is south of Fremantle at Kwinana, where there is a steel rolling mill and Australia's largest oil refinery. The City of Perth remains the administrative and financial centre of Western Australia.

Geography of Perth

Perth, the capital city of Western Australia, lies in lat. 31°57′ S., long. 115°50′ E., on the banks of the Swan River, with its lake-like expanses Perth Water and Melville Water. It is 16 kilometres from the mouth of the Swan, which forms the inner harbour of the Port of Fremantle. The name Perth may be applied to the central city area (including some blocks north of the railway line which bisects the city); to the City of Perth (the land extending from the Indian Ocean at City Beach to the Swan River and beyond and including Victoria Park and Carlisle); or to the greater metropolitan area, which houses nearly three-quarters of the State's population and which extends for about 65 kilometres from north to south and 40 kilometres from west to east. In the early 1970s the metropolitan area had a population of about 642 000, and the City of Perth, 97 500.

The Perth area extends over three parallel strips of land, which run north to south. On the west are the coastal reefs and dunes, heavily eroded on the outer fringe, of which Rottnest Island, Carnac Island, and Garden Island are striking remnants. The coast is sandy, broken by numerous limestone reefs. The coastal strip is about 6.5 kilometres wide. The Swan is the only river to traverse the strip. Farther east is a sandy coastal plain about 14.5 kilometres wide. Most of the population of Perth live on the coastal plain and strip. Farther east again the Perth area reaches the foot of the Darling Scarp, covered with fertile clays. The range itself averages about 300 metres in height. The climate of Perth is congenial, with a mean temperature of 29.8°C. in February and 17.3°C. in July. Average rainfall varies from 8 millimetres in January to 185 millimetres in June, with a total of 879 millimetres spread over about 120 days of the year.

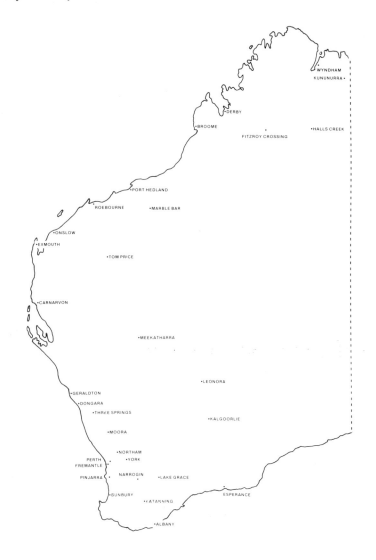

Introduction

'Swan River Colony was designed to foster agricultural settlement by attracting middle class investors who were offered generous land grant terms as an incentive for their migration and as compensation for the high risks they undertook.'[1] It was scarcely surprising therefore that Captain Stirling chose as the capital of the new settlement a site midway between the known limits of likely agricultural development and the harbour town of Fremantle, and on the colony's first commercial line, the Swan River itself. Western Australia was founded as a colony of individual private enterprise, and all early decisions concerning it, including the siting of the capital, reflected and embodied this motivating force. The 250 or so investors (including Captain Stirling) who took out land grants in the first decade of settlement shaped the physical contours of town and rural development and established the community's moral, social, spiritual and legal characteristics, not for that decade alone but for subsequent generations of Westralians of all classes. Visiting Perth in 1891 Gilbert Parker, a seasoned traveller, was strongly reminded of 'the days of William IV';[2] and R. E. N. Twopeny's 1880s observation 'It cannot be too thoroughly understood that Australia is before everything a money-making place'[3] echoes George Fletcher Moore's belief, expressed in 1835, that in Perth money can make money.[4] Money—brought out from England or acquired in the colony—gave power and status to men who possessed it; and the men who possessed it in Perth for much of the nineteenth century were deeply conservative about social relations and the nature of politics. As one of them wrote to the *Perth Gazette*[5]

> It was ordained from the beginning of the world that there should be different denominations and classes of people, in order that each nation should preserve its own internal peace. It was ordained from the beginning that there should be masters and servants . . .

The quest for 'internal peace', whether pursued in the market place, the church, the courts, the legislature and local councils, or the general intercourse of everyday life, helped to shape Perth physically and socially. It was never achieved completely, for the dreaded 'levelling principles of the age'[6] touched even the Swan River Colony, and men, by inclination and the opportunities provided by migration, occasionally resisted their placement in the 'natural' and ordained order of things. But perhaps the quest was more successful in Perth than elsewhere in Australia, although it is not a purpose of this book to argue that it was so. Its purpose is to study the people of Perth: to follow, however inadequately, Fustel de Coulanges' challenge to know how societies are constituted; the forces of cohesion, unity and disunity; to study the organs by which people have lived, including their government and law,

---

[1] J. M. R. Cameron and E. K. G. Jaggard (eds.) *Western Australian Readings*, (Churchlands College, 1977) p.19: Cameron, 'James Stirling's Examination of Swan River'.

[2] Gilbert Parker, *Round the Compass in Australia*, 1892, p.387

[3] R. E. N. Twopeny *Town Life in Australia*, 1883, p.32.

[4] George Fletcher Moore *Diary of Ten Years Eventful Life of an Early Settler in Western Australia*, 1884, p.274.

[5] *Perth Gazette*, 10 July 1847.

[6] *Perth Gazette*, 11 September 1847.

their public economy, their habits of mind, their material habits and all their concepts of existence.[7]

Fustel also described a society as a living being. The historian's task, he asserted, was to describe its life. But how? The history of Western Australia, including the history of Perth, is usually broken up into short chronological periods, each of which is structured internally along an economic history, political history, social history continuum and which gains coherence from the dominance of a set of experiences or events. Thus the period to 1850 is described as 'Pioneering' or 'Early Settlement' and is described largely in terms of the experience of struggle and survival in the new environment. A second period, 1850 to 1870, is dominated by the importation of British capital and convicts; and so on through to the boom years of the goldrushes, and the subsequent twentieth century experiences of war, boom, depression, recovery, war, reconstruction, and boom again. This is an orderly mode of presenting the past and corresponds well enough to the time-scale of public events in Perth's history: it is not abandoned in this book, and each period has its locational (physical), demographic, institutional (and organizational), and behavioural aspects. But periodization, especially for brief spans of years, tends to disguise underlying or fundamental patterns of social experience, and it tends to set on one side the private time scales and the rhythms of individual lives. In this book an attempt is made to reconcile the several uses to which time can be put. It is recognized that in all periods people of all ages bought, rented, and sold goods and land; in all periods there were masters and servants, or employers, self-employed and employees; in all periods men and women fell in love, made love, married or remained single, even celibate; that they constructed and lived in low lodging houses or near-palaces and all shades of housing in between; that in all periods children played, worked, went to school or didn't; that in all periods people grew old and worried themselves about ailments, Poor Houses, their children, their estates, and the afterlife. In all periods men founded institutions and clubs, bashed their womenfolk and each other and were tender to both. In all periods women coped with the recurrent experience of childbirth, raised families and ran a domestic economy, enjoyed neighbourly conversation and suffered grievously from *anomie*. In all periods people drank heavily or little, acted ignobly or nobly. In all periods some people killed themselves, died violently from external causes, stole and murdered or raped or thought of doing some or all these things. In all periods the Aborigines were slaughtered, enslaved, reduced to mendicant refugees in their own land, were loved and gave love, clung to traditional ways, fought back with spear and petition. In all periods men and women lied and were truthful, were consumed by ambition's fire and achieved or failed to achieve goals on their own and others' reckoning. In all periods friendships were forged and were broken by death, dispute and disaster. In a single day or a lifetime a person might experience many of these things and much else besides—with transient and long term effects.

The challenge in writing a history of Perth lies not so much in getting 'right' the broad patterns of urban growth, stagnation, or decline, although this must be done with some care. Rather it lies in placing life experiences in a meaningful social context, defined in this

---

[7] Fustel de Coulanges, *La Gaule Romaine: L'Alleu et le domaine rural*, iv-v, 1889, cited in H. E. Hallam 'Social History'; *Historicus*, 1966.

book largely in terms of the distribution of power within Perth. In short, a major theme of this history of Perth is the acquisition, maintenance, and exercise of power, and the social consequences of its distribution. It is present for all periods and it affects all people. It is the bonding agent which helps to enable us to make sense of Perth's past. The past is not inert. It moves as the focus of the historian shifts. There are as many histories of Perth as there are people writing or talking about it. All are time-bound; all encapsulate an individual world-view. That is how it should be. That is how it can only be. There will even be another 'official' history of Perth.

*The **Foundation of Perth** by George Pitt-Morison: 'It was ordained from the beginning of the world that there should be different denominations and classes of people, in order that each nation should preserve its own internal peace.'*

Chapter One: 'A Sense of Place' — Gentryism

The walls of Perth: Gentryism 1979.

The Founders

On 12 August 1829 Mrs Helen Dance, wife of the commander of H.M.S. *Sulphur*, drove an axe into a tree on the site of the British Empire's newest town. In this way was Perth christened. It was a scene which one hundred years later was to become well known to Western Australian schoolchildren, for it inspired one of the colony/State's few history paintings, 'The Foundation of Perth', by George Pitt-Morison, prints of which were distributed to and hung in government schools from 1929 onwards. The painting was also reproduced in school history and social study texts up to and including the 1970s, thereby becoming part of the mythology of the early history of Western Australia.[1] In the painting some figures are named, others are identified only as the 'military guard', while two men, dressed neither in suits nor uniforms, are not labelled in any way. They are workers, dressed as such with shirt sleeves rolled up to the elbows. They are placed apart from the main body. One man stands with his hands resting on an axe, ready to receive orders to begin clearing the land; the other is on his knees removing food and drink from a picnic basket, so that the officers might eat and drink the health of His Majesty the King, George IV, whose proclamation is being read aloud by Governor James Stirling. As represented by the artist 'The Foundation of Perth' is a symbol of the ordered society, that 'internal peace', which Stirling and his friends hoped to create at Swan River, and which generations of Western Australians have been taught to believe actually came into being. The painting then is in some ways a paradigm of early colonial life; it was also an affirmation of the continued relevance of the social values of those times.

The central figure in Pitt-Morison's painting is Captain Stirling. In August 1829 Stirling received part of his library. The books listed offer clues to the character of the new colony, and help explain the activities of the colonial administration. There was a Bible and Prayer Book, for Swan River was to be a decent, God-fearing and Christian society, dominated by Anglicans. There was Sir William Blackstone's *Commentaries on the Laws of England*, which stressed the rights of property owners:

> Necessity begat property: and, in order to insure that property, recourse was had to civil society, which brought along with it a long train of inseparable concomitants; states, government, laws, punishments, and the public exercise of religious duties. Thus connected together, it was found that a part only of society was sufficient to provide, by their manual labour, for the necessary subsistence of all; . . . and leisure was given to others to cultivate the human mind, to invent useful arts, and

[1] See Sir H. Colebatch *A Story of a Hundred Years*, 1929, p.350; A. E. Williams and A. B. Jones *Western Wakening*, 1975, p.19.; *Swan River Settlement*, a Western Australian Education Department publication, undated c. 1969, p.19.

to lay the foundations of science... And thus the legislature of England has universally promoted the grand ends of civil society, the peace and security of individuals, by steadily pursuing that wise and orderly maxim, of assigning to everything capable of ownership a legal and determinate owner.

In addition there was Pope's *Laws of the Customs*, Burns's five volumes on *Justice*, and a law dictionary, for Swan River was to be a colony rooted firmly in British law practice. There was also Louden's *Gardening*, and one of Cobbett's less polemical works, *Cottage Economy*, for Swan River was to be another province for Britain's gentry. There was Nicholson's three volume *Architecture*, for the new towns and houses must be designed according to the best precepts of British architecture. There was also Crawford's *Indian Archipelago*, for Stirling had told his Downing Street superiors that Swan River would play an important role in the economy and trade of the Indies and Far East. And as there was an ancient belief that the latitudes within which Swan River fell might be an el dorado, there was Jameson's *Minerology* to identify the wealth-producing ores. And as a governor must know everything, there was a set of the *Encyclopaedia Britannica*, with proper advice and example for all occasions.[2] Missing from the library was Edmund Burke, for Burke was a Whig and Swan River was to be stolidly Tory. Missing too was Tom Paine, for Swan River was to be an organic society based on rank and status, not a class society thriving on social dialectic. Missing too were the writings of Mary Wollstonecraft, for Stirling and his youthful wife, Ellen (née Mangles), moved in more polite circles than did that fiery feminist. But the books brought out by Stirling reflected accurately enough his social values and hopes for the colony. Their meaning was understood also by Stirling's officials and leading settlers, among them John Septimus Roe and Commander F. C. Irwin, both of whom appear in Pitt-Morison's painting, and whose governance of Swan River, together with that of George Fletcher Moore, W. H. Mackie, and the Rev. John Burdett Wittenoom, extended to the 1850s. The object of the colony was to let money make money; and the legal, religious, and production manuals were directed to this end.

The senior officials and leading settlers of Swan River were men of means, not mendicant refugees from the old world. And economic success in the colony depended as much on affluence on arrival and family connections as it did on possession of a talent for business matters. This was recognized in the booster literature of the 1830s, including Commander F. C. Irwin's *State and Position of Western Australia* (1835) and Nathaniel Ogle's *The Colony of Western Australia: a manual for emigrants* (1839), though of course the possibility of economic advancement of a limited kind was held out to thrifty and hardworking labouring men. Others were even more forthright. George Fletcher Moore, writing privately to his father in Britain, confided his relief that he had not been responsible for encouraging people to emigrate to Swan River. He was insistent that

> there must be—money. I mean for one who sets up for himself, and not as the servant or steward of another. I think few situations could be much more trying than that of a person arriving here now (1835) with but a small capital, unless his ideas were proportionately adjusted.[3]

Moore himself arrived in 1830 with goods, cash and labourers to the

A shaper of Perth: George Fletcher Moore.

2   *CSO* Vol. 1, 1829, p.143.   3   Moore, *Diary*, pp.274–5.

value of £800,[4] that is, sufficient to net 12 000 acres in the fertile Upper Swan district. He held well-paid government offices, including those of civil commissioner and advocate general, thereby enjoying a stable cash income which enabled him to ride out difficult seasons and the loss of stock as well as retain his servants and employ seasonal labour as required. His family at home provided him with farm equipment, clothing, and the like. By the time Moore returned to England, in 1852, he had amassed 24 000 acres of good farming land not only on the Swan but also in the important agricultural York area 'over the hills' and a large house in the town of Perth.

Moore's career was paralleled by those of other officer-farmers. Governor Stirling was a naval officer and a gentleman. He was connected by marriage to one of the biggest traders of the British Empire, James Mangles, a director of the East India Company, and from the outset he viewed Swan River as a commercial speculation, at least in part because the family business had suffered a partial collapse in the financial crisis in Britain in 1825. At Swan River he took fine land near the town of Guildford, calling his estate, Woodbridge, after the family seat in Surrey. He was also granted over 50 000 acres in the south-west as well as several smaller properties in other parts of the colony. In time his business dealings were severely criticised by many colonists:

> The name 'Stirling' appears in so many places on the Maps . . . that people . . . begin to suspect they have been duped by a Company of mere speculators.[5]

James Stirling

Two shapers of Perth

John Septimus Roe

In time too his rapaciousness won him the censure of the Imperial Government. But he profited greatly from his speculations, selling part of his Woodbridge estate for £2000 in 1833 and his Collie River estates for £11,500 in 1840. From 1839 until his death in 1865 he lived comfortably in England.

Perhaps those who grieved most when Stirling left Swan River were gentry officers like Moore who had profited from Stirling's patronage. Among this group were the Colonial Secretary, Peter Broun, the Commandant, Frederick Chidley Irwin, and the Surveyor General, John Septimus Roe. Broun enjoyed the patronage not only of Stirling but also of the Secretary of State for Colonies, Sir George Murray. He received an annual salary of £400, and as he had brought out goods and servants worth £500, he was granted nearly 10 000 acres which he took up on the Upper Swan. Despite some financial setbacks and persistent ill-health Broun lived well in Perth, where he built a large house in the early 1830s. Unlike Stirling and Moore he died in office.[6] John Septimus Roe, a naval man well acquainted with Australian waters, also took up a several thousand acre property on the Upper Swan which he called Sandalford.[7] He brought with him his wife and two servants. In January 1830 he complained to Stirling that his salary of £300 a year was 'very inadequate to meet my expenses, where labour and the common necessaries of life are not to be obtained but at very high rates'. He sought and was granted an additional £100 a year in order to keep up two establishments: the Upper Swan farm and a substantial brick house in Perth.[8] On his death

---

[4] *CSO* Vol. 10, 1830, p.33.
[5] *Swan River Guardian*, 5 January 1837, cited Cameron, in L. Hunt (ed.) *Westralian Portraits*, 1979.
[6] *ADB* Vol. 1—entry for Brown.   [7] *CSO* Vol. 12, 1831, pp.35–6.
[8] *CSO* Vol. 4, 1830, p.106; Vol. 7, 1830, p.12.

in Perth in 1878 he bequeathed a large estate to his family.[9]

Irwin was a professional soldier sent to Swan River in the course of his duties. With a salary of £400 a year and independent resources as well he purchased an Upper Swan property called Henley Park which became the cultural centre of gentry life, especially after 1836 when Irwin married the sister of the colony's Registrar-General. Like Moore and Stirling, Irwin eventually returned to England where he died in comfort at Cheltenham in 1860. Irwin's cousin, William Henry Mackie, the son of an East India Company surgeon, came out to Western Australia in 1829 as a private settler with £550 and two servants, hoping, like George Fletcher Moore, to secure a judicial appointment. It was probably Irwin who influenced Stirling to appoint Mackie as Chairman of the Courts of Petty and Quarter Sessions in December 1829 on an annual salary of £200, rising to £300 in 1834. Mackie was to be the colony's principal law officer until his retirement in 1857. He and Irwin jointly owned Henley Park as well as 7000 acres on the Avon between Beverley and York. He also owned a large house in Perth, Whitehall, situated in William Street near the river jetty. Mackie's colleague on the bench in the early years was the Rev. Wittenoom, formerly headmaster of Newark Grammar School, and the colony's sole Oxford graduate. In July 1829, shortly after the death of his wife, Wittenoom was appointed chaplain to the civil establishment at Swan River, with a stipend of £250 and the promise of a house. On arriving at Perth with his mother, sister, and four sons, Wittenoom took up land near York and bought or was granted two allotments in Perth close to the river with valuable frontages on St George's Terrace near the Governor's residence. These he sold at great profit some time later. The York property was farmed by his sons. Wittenoom remained Colonial Chaplain until his death in Perth in 1855. All these men came from county society, whether in Scotland, Ireland or England. Their *milieu* was that of Jane Austen: indeed all of them could have walked out of her novels.[10] They valued above all things 'respectability and comfort', and lacking an independent income in England sufficiently large to ensure this, they sought placement in a society which they could shape in their own image.[11]

Many more of the early settlers of Perth held official positions which were either salaried or which allowed for the collection of fees. Others held government contracts of various kinds. Still others held honorary positions such as magistracies. All were dependent on the goodwill and patronage of Stirling and his senior officials, though some, like the Samsons and the Tanners, grew affluent enough to stand outside the immediate and compelling influence of the governing group. Those who arrived wealthy stayed that way. George Leake, a merchant, brought out £2000 in cash and goods. He also brought out a carpenter, a gardener, a domestic servant and two agricultural labourers. This enabled him to take up 15 000 acres on the Upper Swan, to which he added a further 10 000 acres before the mid-1830s, by which time it was thought that if he foreclosed on his loans he would ruin nearly two-thirds

[9]   Will—Supreme Court of Western Australia.
[10]   O. MacDonagh 'Highbury and Chawton: Social Convergence in "Emma"', *Historical Studies* Vol. 18, No. 70, April 1978.
[11]   See *CSO* Vol. 12, 1831, p.179: A letter from Isaac Jecks of Guildford to Colonial Secretary Broun. Jecks was to receive £100 a year as Superintendent of Public Improvements. The salary, he wrote, was 'sufficient to enable me (with other small resources of my own) to live with respectability and comfort'.

of the settlers.[12] He was one of the founders of the first WA Bank, and from 1839 until his death in 1849 he was an unofficial member of the Legislative Council. He bequeathed to his family an estate worth many thousands of pounds, easily the largest in the early history of the colony.[13] His daughter's family and his nephews built on George's fortune and became magistrates and politicians and city councillors with influence in Western Australia up to the Great War.

Others who arrived early and established family dynasties were the Samson brothers, the Shentons, the Stones, the Brockmans, the Barrett Lennards, and the Bussells. Lionel and William Samson arrived with cash reserves and several domestic servants. Lionel was a friend of George Leake even before they left England, and they seem to have co-operated in the colony. Lionel held the government position of postmaster general and auctioneer which netted him fees, but he made most of his money by merchandising, partly by keeping the price of flour high through the 1830s.[14] In 1839 he built a huge house with store and auction rooms attached on his St George's Terrace allotment. It was believed to have cost £3000. At a 'house-warming ball and supper' no less than 150 people attended, including the Governor.[15] In the 1850s the Samsons removed almost entirely to Fremantle, and there a family dynasty remained powerful for more than a hundred years.

There were also the Stone brothers, George Frederick and Alfred Hawes, both lawyers with cash reserves. Each held government offices from the early 1830s, each married advantageously, each married off his children 'sensibly', and each possessed valuable urban real estate. Neither died until the 1870s, by which time their children were holding important positions in Perth society. As important to the history of Perth was the Shenton family. William Kernot Shenton arrived in 1829 and established a mill opposite the town of Perth. His cousin George, a pharmacist, arrived in 1833. By 1838 George had built up a flourishing merchandising firm with large premises in Hay Street. He held agencies for several companies and was poised to become one of the wealthiest men in the colony. In the mid-1840s when many colonists floundered in the economic recession, Shenton expanded his operations, pioneering the export of sandalwood, investing in mining ventures, and developing agricultural interests in the Greenough area three hundred miles north of Perth. His large St George's Terrace home, Rosehall, backed on to warehouses and offices at the edge of the river. On his death in 1867, his son, also George, stepped straight into the father's public offices, remaining a power in the land to beyond the goldrush years. There was also William Locke Brockman, aged only 28 years, with a young wife and 2-year-old infant, when he arrived at Swan River in January 1830. But he came with labourers, bricklayers, carpenters and domestic servants, and goods and cash to the value of £1500. Like Roe, Irwin, and other leading settlers, Brockman was the son of an Anglican clergyman, and was himself a pillar of the church. His property at Upper Swan, Herne Hill, became a showplace farm, so well was it managed. Brockman bred blood horses and pedigree sheep; in fact he pioneered the export of fine horses to India for the British army. Even before the coming of the convicts he was one of the largest landowners in the colony, with estates in most districts, but particularly in the Avon Valley.

[12] *ADB* Vol. 1—entry for Leake.   [13] Will—Supreme Court, No. 47, 1848.
[14] *Perth Gazette*, 14 March 1835.   [15] Moore *Diary*, p.399.

He was a member of the Legislative Council and took a prominent role at public meetings in Perth on a variety of subjects. On his death in 1872 his sons, both parliamentarians, inherited his vast estate.[16]

While Brockman's influence on the affairs of the city persisted through the activities of his children, William Tanner's influence ceased when in 1853 his family sold his estates and returned to England in protest against the presence of convicts in Western Australia. Tanner arrived in 1829 with goods valued at £2500 and a staff of twenty adults. He took up one of the largest properties in the Swan Valley and was generally regarded as a power in the land, even though he was sometimes at odds with Stirling and his successors. He worked closely with Moore, Mackie, and Irwin throughout the 1830s and 1840s. A more compliant settler of means was Captain Richard Goldsmith Meares who arrived with goods worth £1000.[17] Even Captain William Shaw and his wife Elizabeth, whose personal history has been so movingly recorded by Mary Durack,[18] arrived with over £600 and took up fine farming land in the Upper Swan district. Even in their difficult times the Shaws could draw on friends in high places for assistance, for they were a couple of substance and refinement. Like the Shaws, James Purkis brought with him over £600 and some servants.[19] Purkis rapidly became one of Perth's leading merchants and politicians. All the people discussed here were household names in Western Australia: most knew each other well, and played, even prayed together. They all came as investors and as men of some means; most enjoyed back-up resources in England and benefited from gentry and official connections 'back home'. In short, very few settlers who arrived with this sort of background and resources failed to become prominent citizens of Perth and its hinterland.

Some did however, and any portrait of Perth society in these years which did not mention this would be presenting a false picture. Usually, however, when a man of means failed it was at least in part because the Governor and senior officials declined to assist him, and this could happen for personal, political, and religious reasons. In October 1829 a 39-year-old retired army officer, Thomas Hester, arrived in Swan River with his wife Sophia and their five children, whose ages ranged from 2 years to 11 years. He brought a servant with him, and he was granted 3000 acres on the Canning River to the south-east of Perth.[20] Within four years Hester was in grave difficulties. His wife Sophia died in 1830. One of his labourers had also died and another had absconded. Floods had destroyed his crops and the Aborigines had taken his sheep. He did not know how he was going to provide for his children.[21] Hester estimated his cash loss to be £1000, which was extremely galling to him as he had given up his soldier's half-pay when he emigrated to Swan River. By October 1834 his plight had worsened. His children, he wrote, were 'in a state of nudity around me wanting bread'. He pleaded for assistance:

> I have been obliged to dispose of our musical instruments as our last resource . . . any place of profit of the smallest consideration would be

[16] Various official sources and *ADB* entries; also wills in Supreme Court: Shenton (No. 157, 1867), Brockman (No. 426, 1872), and A. H. Stone (No. 437, 1873).

[17] *CSO* Vol. 11, December 1830, p.140.   [18] *To Be Heirs Forever*, 1976.

[19] *CSO* Vol. 5, 1830, p.99; also Supreme Court Will No. 65, 1853. Purkis' daughters married W. H. Drake, Alfred Hillman, and Francis Lochee, all of whom were prominent in the economic and social life of Perth.

[20] He had £455 in property—*HRA* Series 3, Vol. VI, Stirling to Murray, 30 January 1830, enclosures 1a and 2a.

[21] *CSO* Vol. 31, April 1834, p.147, Hester to Acting Governor Daniell.

better than being exposed upon the road with my children where I should be subject to the insults of disgarded servants.[22]

Hester received no assistance from the Government. He seems to have struggled on until 1838 when he once more sought Government aid, again unsuccessfully.[23] Eventually Hester, with his boys coming of working age, and a pretty daughter of marriageable age,[24] managed to revive the family fortunes a little, but not in the immediate vicinity of the capital. Hester, and others like him, had lost the treasured experience of 'respectability and comfort'. But what of those men and women in the colony who had known nothing of respectability and comfort in the old country, those who would seek to heap insults on masters who fell on hard times?

Social Relationships

The nature of class relationships was defined by legal contracts, government directives, and social experience. On 30 May 1829 Frederick Friend signed a 'Contract of Servitude' with Henry Camfield—the bond to be good wherever Camfield might go and for a period of seven years. In return for his labour, and that of his wife and child; Frederick Friend, an illiterate 33-year-old Kentish labourer, would receive shelter, clothing and wages of £3 a year. In time he must repay his master the cost of the family's passage from England to Swan River.[25] Frederick Friend and his family were slaves. With many others in similar circumstances they were intended to form a helot class round whose frail frames the new society would be constructed. Of course Friend had chosen to indenture himself to Camfield and go to Swan River, but what was the alternative open to him? To stay in rural Kent in the 1830s would mean, as it had meant in the 1820s, uncertain employment, shelter in hovels, disease, poor relief, and perhaps bread riots—an iron circle of poverty.[26] Enslavement overseas seemed preferable, if only because it offered security of employment and shelter, and the possibility after seven years of a fresh start in a place asserted to be free of the ills of the old world. Of the 1500 or so settlers who came to Swan River before the end of 1830, half were labourers and servants and their families, many, like Friend, bound by 'Contracts of Servitude'. They came from urban and rural poor houses and villages from most parts of England and Scotland, and some from Ireland.

Within six months of the foundation of Perth the Government had had to regulate master and servant relationships. The earliest grumbles came from some literate servants and tended to be ignored by the Governor, despite the eloquence of the plea: 'I crave the redress which under such circumstances as an Englishman I have the right to Expect'.[27] But then the grumbles came thick and fast from the masters and Stirling

---

22 *CSO* Vol. 35, October 1834, p.41. 23 *CSO* Vol. 59, January 1838, pp.60–1.
24 R. Erickson 'T. N. Yule Esq: Gentleman of Misfortune', *Early Days* Vol. 7, Pt. III, 1971, pp.15–16, citing Yule to Wright, 21 August 1840: 'Old Hester is getting on much better. Miss Hester is the prettiest and altogether the finest girl in the colony.'
25 *CSO* Vol. 1, 1828–29, p.38.
26 J. D. Chambers and G. E. Mingay *The Agricultural Revolution 1750–1880*, 1966, Chapter 5.
27 *CSO* Vol. 2, October 1829–30, p.118, Charles Chapman, seeking redress from his master, Isaac Jecks, for failing to provide him with grog as agreed in the terms of employment.

of _Ripley_ .... of the age of _twenty one_ years and upwards,

in the County of _Kent_

of the one part, and _Henry Ampfield_ .... of

Shelohurst in the County of _Kent_ .... of the other part,

Witnesseth, that in consideration of the Covenants hereinafter entered into by the said _Henry Ampfield_ .... the said _Richard Smith_

doth by these presents contract and bind himself with and to the said

Henry Ampfield .... faithfully to serve the said

Henry Ampfield .... or his Agent

and his Executors, Administrators, and Assigns,

as a _Carpenter & Labourer_ on the Settlement on the Swan and Canning Rivers, or King George's Sound, or in the Colony of Van Diemen's Land, or New South Wales, and to make himself generally useful in the Service of the said _Henry Ampfield_ .... his Executors, Administrators, and Assigns, as he or his Agent may direct, for the Term of _five_ Years, to be computed from the _twenty eighth_ Day of _November_ next. **AND** the said _Richard Smith_ doth hereby covenant, promise, and agree with and to the said _Henry Ampfield_ ....

his Executors, Administrators, and Assigns, ~~or the Agent of the said~~ _Richard Smith_ by these Presents in manner following (that is to say),

That he the said _Richard Smith_ .... shall and will during the said Term of _five_ Years, to the best and utmost of his Skill and Power, employ his whole time in or about the proper Business and Employment of a _Carpenter & labourer_ and otherwise as aforesaid, in the Service of the said _Henry Ampfield_ .... or in the Service of such other person as he or the said Parties shall from Time to Time direct; and generally shall and will conduct himself during the said Term as a dutiful Servant in the capacity hereinbefore mentioned AND in Consideration of the Covenants entered into by the said _Richard Smith_ the said _Henry Ampfield_ .... doth promise and agree to provide a passage for the said _Richard Smith_ .... his Wife and Children, from the Port of London to the said Colony or Colonies or Settlement, together with proper and sufficient .... Voyage. AND shall during the said Term of _five_ years pay or cause to be paid unto the said _Richard Smith_ the clear annual sum of _Ten_ pounds of lawful Money of Great Britain; the Wages or Salary to commence .... estate in Van Diemen's Land, New South Wales, or the Settlement on the Swan and Canning Rivers AND shall during the said Term of _five_ Years _find_ .... for the said _Richard Smith_ .... his Wife and Children, to commence from the arrival of the said _Richard Smith_ .... in either of the said Colonies AND also to provide for the said _Richard Smith_ .... and his said Wife and Children, such Fuel and Food as are by the existing Regulations of the Government of the said Colony or Colonies .... cases, required to be provided AND the said Parties hereto mutually bind themselves to the ... . the due performance of this Contract, and of the respective Covenants herein contained and agreed to be performed on their respective parts, in the Sum of _three hundred_ Pounds of lawful Money of Great Britain, to be recovered by Action of Debt or otherwise, in any Court of the Colony or elsewhere, duly authorized to take cognizance of the same. In Witness whereof the said Parties to these Presents have hereunto set their Hands and Seals the Day and Year first above written.

Signed, Sealed and Delivered, }
in the presence of }

Wm Rodgers

Henry Ampfield

Richd Smith

I, the said _Richard Smith_ .... do further agree for myself, my Wife and Children, (named in the Margin) to bind myself responsible that each and all of them separately do serve the Party or Parties, or them or their Agents as aforesaid (named in the accompanying Indenture,) faithfully and diligently, as their services may be required, during the _five_ Years I have bound myself and them to serve the said Party, to be computed from the _twenty eighth day of_ _November next_, in Return for which _he_ agrees to provide my Wife and said Children with such Board and Fuel as are by the existing Regulations of the Government of the said Colony or Colonies required to be furnished AND the said Parties mutually bind themselves to each other for the due performance of the above Agreements, in the Sum of _three hundred pounds_ of lawful Money of Great Britain, to be recovered by Action of Debt or otherwise, in any Court of the Colony or elsewhere, duly authorized to recover the same. Witness their Hands this _twentieth_ Day of _May_ 182 _9_

Mary Smith

Robert Smith

September next

Contract of Servitude: _Richard Smith and family, 1829._

18

acted promptly. In a Despatch sent to the Secretary of State for Colonies on 20 January 1830 Stirling reported that:

> Among the settlers who arrived, there were many indentured servants, who had been recommended to their employers by parish officers, and whose habits were of the loosest description. To control these and to protect their masters in their just rights, as well as to secure the safety of persons and property, I was obliged before the conclusion of the year to appoint a magistracy and a body of constables; the first from among the most wealthy and prudent of the settlers; the latter including the steady and most respectable part of the working class.

As a rider Stirling observed that

> as part have commenced agricultural labour, drunkenness and similar evils will be less frequent than when the people congregated in one or two towns with little to do.[28]

The law then was introduced to Swan River to contain the servants; and the administration of the law was to be in the hands of the masters, the respectable investors. Those who arrested and imprisoned recalcitrant servants would come from the serving class, but would be distinguished by their temperance and thrift. Stirling's rider was important too, for the men of the investing class tended to view the towns as likely sources of evil, as Genesis and the literary tradition of England had taught them to believe,[29] and as their own eyes had witnessed in the towns and cities of Great Britain in the post Napoleonic War years. They believed in an arcadia, that middle world between the wilderness and the city where peace and harmony could prevail.[30] But for the moment sanction had to be imposed on those who transgressed.

In March 1830 'in consequence of frequent disputes having lately arisen between servants and their masters', the chief judicial officer, W. H. Mackie, established ration rates and hours of work, and penalties. Servants could not leave a master's 'premises or location without leave'. Servants could not work for another master in their spare time unless they had the consent of the master to whom they were contracted. Where a servant absented himself from his master's service

> without leave, or incapacitated himself for labour by drunkenness, the Master shall be allowed to charge such Servant the current wages of the colony for the lost time.

If he complied with these conditions a servant was eligible to receive daily 1 lb of beef, ¾ lb of pork, 1 lb of biscuit, flour or bread, and ½ gill of spirits (rum was mentioned). A female servant would receive the same ration except that 2 ozs of tea and ½ lb sugar a week was substituted for the spirits. For the children of labourers there would be a proportion of the male servants' rate: 50% for a child 10 to 14 years; 33⅓% for a child 7 to 10 years. All other articles were labelled 'indulgences' and could be withdrawn at will. As these included vegetables, it is not surprising that scurvy was widespread among labourers and their families in the first years of settlement. To be eligible for rations a mechanic or husbandry labourer would have to work eight hours a day, six days a week, between mid November and mid February; and nine hours a day, six days a week,

[28] *HRA* Series III, Vol. VI, p.616.
[29] See G. R. Strange 'The Victorian City and the Frightened Poets', *Victorian Studies* Vol. 11, 1967–68 Supplement. The first city, Enoch, was founded by a murderer and a vagabond, one expressly forbidden to till the soil.
[30] See L. Marx *The Machine in the Garden*, 1964.

between mid-February and mid-November.[31] Disputes between masters and servants would be settled by Mackie and his fellow magistrates.

But the Governor, the Colonial Secretary, and the magistrates were masters who had devised a law based on a desire to protect private property and to ensure the existence of a quiescent and industrious serving class. A servant could appeal to the Governor for assistance, but how could a poor illiterate man like Frederick Friend prepare his case? Literate masters were unlikely to write his appeal for him. The few lawyers in the colony were masters and, in any case, they would require the payment of fees from clients whose grievance might well be the non-payment of wages. It would seem from the files of the Colonial Secretary's Office that sometimes Mackie took oral evidence from those servants who could get to Perth or Fremantle to state their case, while the few literate servants expressed their grievances in letters addressed to the Colonial Secretary who passed the complaints on to Mackie. In these circumstances it would seem that the cases known from the records represent but a small sample of those who experienced hardships at the hands of masters in the early history of Perth.

A servant's best chance of the law acting in his favour was when the masters fell out among themselves, and perhaps fought over the right of ownership of his labour, or if some masters were seen to be acting against the best interests of a harmonious society. One master who transgressed in this way was Thomas Peel, the colony's largest private employer of labour. In April 1830, within four months of the arrival of the first of his emigrant ships, the *Gilmore*, Peel's establishments south of Fremantle and on the Murray were in disarray. His tenants and servants began to apply to Stirling to leave the colony, some of them describing their present living conditions in harrowing terms.[32] By mid winter, through maladministration and misadventure,[33] Peel's establishment was the scene of a major catastrophe. Dr Alexander Collie, the Colonial Surgeon, found to his horror that no less than twenty-eight of Peel's people had died, mostly of dysentery and scurvy. Many more of the 450 people allegedly in Peel's care were sick with the same diseases. Collie reported that

> proper food for the sick was not to be procured from the Store, and the sick had not money to purchase it elsewhere.

Collie was not at all keen to criticise Peel for this state of affairs. Indeed he attributed much of the disaster to the 'irregular habits', especially drunkenness, among Peel's servants. But he also concluded that some settlers were poorly housed, that bad quality flour and salt meat was provided, and that neither lime juice nor fresh vegetables were being distributed.[34] By July 1830 Peel's servants were arriving in Fremantle and Perth where they sought release from Peel's establishment. They complained that Peel refused to pay their wages and did not allow from the stores 'sufficient Food to support our Familys'. Others charged Peel with threatening to have them put in custody if they protested about their conditions, 'yet we are without one shilling and our last loaf in the Oven'. By October, so many of Peel's men were unemployed and destitute in Perth that the Government agreed to employ some of them

---

[31] *CSO* Vol. 5, 1830, pp.92, 184, 1 and 25 March 1830.
[32] *CSO* Vol. 6, 1830, p.72, 15 April 1830.
[33] See *ADB* Vol. 2—entry for Solomon Levey; also A. Hasluck *Thomas Peel of Swan River*, 1965.
[34] *CSO* Vol. 8, 1830, p.39, Collie's Report is dated 25 July 1830.

Thomas Peel of Swan River:
gentleman.

for general labouring work round the town, at the same time making it known that it had not entered into an agreement with Peel to take over his responsibilities. Nevertheless Stirling and his magistrates, especially Thomas Bannister, George Leake, and Mackie, were now recommending to Peel that in some cases he ought to acquiesce in the requests being made. In the terrible case of Robert Robinson who, with his wife and child, almost perished of thirst and hunger on the long walk from the Murray to Fremantle, and who arrived at Fremantle 'without bedding or any other comforts', Stirling urged Leake to 'contact' Peel about the matter.[35] Throughout 1831, 1832 and 1833 servants left Peel for the settlements of Fremantle, Perth, and Guildford, usually without their few possessions which were detained by Peel. As late as May 1833 the

[35] *CSO* Vol. 8, 1830, pp.125, 211; Vol. 10, 1830, p.38; Vol. 12, 1831, p.61.

Civil Court was still hearing cases involving Peel's servants, sometimes finding in Peel's favour—in one case after Mackie had appeared as a witness for Peel; sometimes in favour of the servants, if narrowly: 'This is a hard case, but I must look at the peculiarity of Mr Peel's establishment'.[36] In June 1834 Peel released the last of his servants. He informed the Colonial Secretary: 'I am now without any servant . . . My only wish now is to get my family away'.[37] Some of Peel's servants also got away, but most could not and stayed in Fremantle, Perth, and the country to battle it out.

From the foregoing it might seem that most cases involving relations of master and servant were brought before the Court by the servants. But the 'peculiarity of Mr Peel's establishment' should not disguise the fact that for the colony as a whole far more cases were initiated by masters than by servants, and in most instances the Court found in favour of the plaintiff. By July 1830, of the twenty-seven prisoners held in the wreck of the *Marquis of Anglesey*, twelve had been convicted for breaking their labour indentures.[38] A typical judgment, delivered by Mackie and Wittenoom, reads:

> We have the honour to inform you that John Woods, a farm servant indentured to Dr John Whatley of Hones Green, Swan River, was on Monday last convicted before us of wilful and repeated disobedience of orders, neglect of work, and three several acts of desertion.[39]

Woods was sent to prison for 15 days, long enough to allow him to ponder on the error of his ways, but not so long as to remove him from the workforce to the disadvantage of either Whatley's or the colony's economy. In another case W. T. Graham, whose own social activities were already the subject of discussion in polite society, sought to claim £125 from his indentured maidservant, Ann Tew, for quitting his service some two years before her contract expired: 'the servant in question has used my family so *exceedingly* ill that I am determined to do all that I legally can to indemnify myself for the great trouble and expense she has put me to.' Stirling must have acceded to Graham's request to prevent Tew from leaving the colony, for Tew, harassed yet alone, was to become one of the many derelict women of Perth from the mid-1830s onwards.[40] As it happened Graham too was to die in Perth lacking dignity and respectability.[41] In that all masters strove to harness a quiescent and hardworking labour force, neither of these cases distorts the nature of class relationships in Swan River.

The preparedness of masters to pursue their servants can be seen clearly in the following case involving Richard Goldsmith Meares. Meares, a distinguished Waterloo veteran, had sold his commission and given £500 to Peel to be repaid in land and materials after their arrival at Swan River colony. Diddled by Peel he nevertheless had reserves of capital and labour, including seven servants, to take up substantial grants of land on the Murray and at Guildford.[42] In 1831 Meares not only fell out with Peel; he also attempted to squeeze £1 a week from a

36   *Perth Gazette*, 18 May 1833.
37   *CSO* Vol. 32, 1834, p.229; Peel to Broun, 17 June 1834.
38   *CSO* Vol. 7, p.114, 1830.   39   *CSO* Vol. 7, 1830, p.85, 24 June 1830.
40   *CSO* Vol. 13, 1831, p.40; Graham to Broun, 24 February 1831.
41   See E. P. Joske 'Captain Graham: Colonist and Coroner of Fremantle' *Early Days* Vol. 7, Pt. VI, 1974, pp.49–59.
42   *ADB* Vol. 2—entry for Meares; *CSO* Vol. 11, 1830, p.145; Property estimated at £1000. Meares died a very wealthy man: Supreme Court Will No. 117, 1861.

discharged servant, Richard Powell, who, like Meares himself, had a family to support. As with many of the labourers in Perth Powell was in ill-health and worrying about his sick wife and their three small children. For a time Powell was employed as a day labourer on the construction of Perth's gaol, for which work he received 8 shillings a day. When it rained, work ceased on the gaol and Powell received no income. To get his discharge from Meares, Powell had agreed to pay him 3 shillings a day. Inevitably he fell behind with his repayments and was taken by Meares before Mackie. Mackie, worried by some apparent irregularities in Powell's discharge, and realizing that Powell could not meet the 3 shillings a day, reduced the repayment to 2 shillings a day. Powell pleaded for still greater relief: 'he saw nothing but starvation awaiting himself and his family', but Mackie upheld the master's law. Nevertheless Mackie was a man not without compassion. He gave Powell a little of his own money, presumably to allow Powell to meet a debt on bread purchases. Meares felt that Mackie had let him down and foolishly said so, though he later apologised abjectly when severely reprimanded. Mackie had found that Powell had sought work honestly, but that the family could neither feed themselves nor meet their medical expenses, and that the children were inadequately clothed and sheltered. This limited protection of the law did not save the Powells. As they had been casualties of the old world, so they became casualties in the new. Mrs Powell died in the mid-1830s, and in December 1837 the Colonial Surgeon reported to Broun that

Richard G. Meares: 'his only object was to secure the repayment of Powell's passage money'.

> The patient Rd Powell recommended to my care is I am afraid past recovery. Consequently will be considered by me as an outdoor patient. I do not know whether his son is able to provide for him or not. If not, ordinary diet will be sufficient.

Powell died shortly after and was given a pauper's funeral.[43]

In 1842 the Legislative Council passed a Master and Servant Act. Drafted by Mackie, it was the product of the experience of labour relations in the 1830s. It was, as F. K. Crowley has written,[44] 'the rich man's law'; indeed, if anything, it strengthened the power of masters. Not until 1892 was this law altered to make the courts less places of punishment and more places of justice.

One in three of the early settlers granted land took up fewer than 1000 acres on an investment of £70 or less, even to as low as £15. Perhaps six in ten of them had left the colony by the late 1830s. Another group, mostly free artisans, took up town allotments in Perth and Fremantle.[45] This latter group found their trade skills in great demand. They tended to stay in the colony, although few did better than keep their heads above water through the 1830s. Most of them had to relinquish the first of their town allotments (many were along St George's and Adelaide Terraces) and take up less desirable allotments under Mt Eliza to the west of the town. A few prospered and in time came to hold positions of some authority in society, without ever penetrating Government House society—but 'respectability and comfort' were theirs. One such man was

Richard Powell and family: 'they saw nothing but starvation awaiting'.

43   *CSO* Vol. 13, 1831, pp.84–6; *CSO* Vol. 14, 1831, p.5; *CSO* Vol. 69, December 1837, p.30 approx—the volume is wrongly numbered: it should probably be No. 58.
44   See F. K. Crowley 'Master and Servant in Western Australia' *Early Days* Vol. 4, Pt. VI, 1954, pp.15–32.
45   J. M. R. Cameron and E. Jaggard *Western Australian Readings*, 1977, pp.122–3; Map of Perth allotments 1838; also Lands and Survey Department material 'Town Lot Description Books', Battye Library Acc. No. 660.

Bayley Maycock, a young carpenter from Folkstone, who had an allotment between Hay Street and St George's Terrace west of King Street. Maycock worked on Government buildings in the 1830s, became a builder by calling, and eventually became a member of the Perth City Council. So too did John Chipper who had arrived as one of Mr Henty's labourers.[46] These were the respectable working class men on whom governors and senior officials could rely. They enhanced the possibility of 'internal peace' in Perth for they were neither drunken wastrels who were a cost to the community, nor critics of the social and political values of the leading settlers. They did not speak of 'combination' and 'the levelling principles of the age'. In early Perth they were few in number.

The Swan River gentry believed that in their natural condition labourers and domestic servants were morally dissolute and given to drunkenness. The gentry's mission, in the interests of social order and economic efficiency, was to 'save' them from themselves. Even imprisonment, as has been shown, could be used as a means to this end. As Peel put it: if 'his people . . . persevere in regularity of conduct . . . their labour will ultimately turn to their own greatest advantage'. But, alas, too many of them continued to 'dissemminate mischief and corrupt others', and he knew that 'ultimately'

> if any Individuals of such a class can meet with encouragement in any quarter there will be no end to the injury we must sustain.[47]

'no end to the injury we must sustain'—that was the crux of the matter for Peel and his fellow investors. John Bateman understood this when he notified Colonial Secretary Broun that when the new tavern was opened

> Our intentions are not to allow any tippling or give any encouragement to the lower class, but to keep it as select and respectable as possible.[48]

As Broun, Mackie, Leake and Wittenoom formed the Licensing Board, Bateman did well to write as he did; and he gained his licence. But the labourers of Perth insisted on drinking to excess; indeed they insisted on drinking before working. Eventually Stirling decided that for the present it might be more expedient to have drunken workers than fractious ones. From 1833 employers could pay workers up to one-third of their wage in grog—many did, for it saved cash reserves and the grog could be over-valued. At the same time it was thought desirable to establish a temperance society and to imprison totally inebriated workers. So a splendid double standard developed in Perth, with the rhetoric of salvation co-existing happily with the practice of collusion. If one could not wean labourers from their 'natural condition', then in the interests of economic advancement (and after all, the tax on imported grog constituted the colony's principal source of revenue), the leading settlers must make the best of that condition and harness the law to meet that need.[49]

The investors believed that the serving class was given not only to drunkenness but to loose moral behaviour as well, and that they lacked the social feelings of the investing class. The following incident shows this clearly. One evening in late May 1829, as *Parmelia* heaved to off

---

46 These stories have to be pieced together from newspaper, *CSO* and PCC material.
47 *CSO* Vol. 6, 1830, p.72.   48 *CSO* Vol. 9, 1830, p.48.
49 *Perth Gazette* 15 February 1834. Urban employers were not encouraged to do this under the new Licensing Act, but it was general practice nevertheless. See also J. A. Backhouse *A Narrative of a Visit to the Australian Colonies*, 1843, pp.538, 544. Backhouse described it as a 'pernicious law'. He was in Swan River in January 1838.

Fremantle, and the Stirlings and Roes dined and wined in the State-room, a maidservant and the ship's boatswain made love in some quiet corner between decks. In February 1830 the maidservant, Elizabeth Gamble, was heavy with child, but in respect to baby linen she made no preparations for the arrival of the infant. When upbraided for this by her mistress, Mrs Drummond, Elizabeth exclaimed:

> Ma'am, if I had a pair of shoes, or even slippers, I would no longer be bothered with the child, but would take it down to Fremantle and throw it on the deck of the ship of the father of it.

One week after the birth of the child the hut in which Elizabeth lived (some one hundred yards distant from the Drummond house) was burnt to the ground, the fire having begun, apparently, on the kitchen side. When people reached the hut

> the remains of the infant were clearly distinguishable, and tho' reduced to a cinder, retained the form and outline of the body and limbs—but the ashes were soon blown away by the strong breeze.

Elizabeth Gamble then faced the ordeal of a Coroner's Court and its suspicion that she had deliberately set fire to the hut and killed her infant child. Mrs Drummond deposed in Court that Elizabeth was 'remarkably fond of dress and careful about her clothes', and that the clothes too had been burnt in the fire. Commissioner Mackie therefore ruled that had arson been intended then Elizabeth would have first removed the clothes from the cottage. Indeed Mrs Drummond further deposed that Elizabeth seemed far more concerned about the loss of her clothes than the loss of her infant. This led Mackie to comment:

> The neglect shown by the suspected party toward her child arose more from a blindness of parental feeling too common among persons of her class, than from any evil design.

Furthermore, it seems that Mrs Drummond, who was a kindly mistress, had told Elizabeth that she would not be dismissed from service as a result of her pregnancy. Mackie observed that

> The usual motive of infanticide, namely the dread of losing a situation and of being unable to provide for the child

was absent in this case. His recommendation to the Governor was that no further action be taken in the matter and that the child's death be recorded as a misadventure. But however compassionately explained by Mackie, the beliefs held by the gentry were these: women of 'that class' were of loose morals; women of 'that class' lacked the true 'parental feeling' of women of the investing class; women of 'that class' often committed infanticide and were punished for so doing. That all these ascribed characteristics of working class women were the product of power relationships was not Mackie's concern. For he, and his gentry colleagues, accepted unquestioningly that infanticide, like drunkenness and violence among labouring men, was an integral part of the natural condition of the lower orders. In this way too were roles ascribed to individuals and classes in colonial society and contributed to the shaping of Perth.[50]

*William Henry Mackie: 'the Law of the Colony in all its branches seems to be completely Mackiefied'. (**Swan River Guardian**, 24 November 1836.)*

---

[50] *CSO* Vol. 5, 1830, p.65ff.

'They seemed angry at our invasion of their Territory: Swan River in 1827'. (Clause?, artist.)

Aborigines and Settlers

The cultural baggage of the settlers who came to Swan River included popular notions of racialism. The Catholic Irish or 'bogmen' were regarded as an inferior sort of human being. But even lower in the 'Chain of Being' than the Irish were the Australian Aborigines.[51] This was not the official attitude towards the Aborigines, for Stirling hoped, as had Phillip in New South Wales forty years earlier, to civilise and Christianise them and mould them into a serving class for white settlers. Some of the settlers still subscribed to the Enlightenment view that the Aborigines were noble savages, whose pristine condition was to be admired; but few maintained that view for long. It rapidly became clear that the Aborigines cared little for white men's theories of their place in the order of things. The believers in noble savagery were shocked by Aboriginal acts of barbarism and theft. The believers in Aboriginal inferiority found that firepower was required to buttress the natural order of things. On the 'Credible testimony' of the grasping engineer, Henry Reveley, the first punitive expedition was mounted by Captain Irwin in May 1830 (before that time there had only been sporadic and individual violent encounters between whites and Aborigines). With a detachment of soldiers Irwin attacked an Aboriginal encampment north of Fremantle in the belief that it contained men who had 'broken into and plundered the house of a man called Paton' and killed some poultry. According to the 'Credible testimony' it seems that Paton called together some more whites who, armed with muskets, set after the Aborigines and came upon them not far from the house. 'The tall savage who appeared the Chief showed unequivocal Gestures of defiance and contempt', and was accordingly shot. He rose once, but fell again and was carried away by his friends. Irwin's course was now clear:

> This daring and hostile conduct of the Natives induced me to seize the opportunity to make them sensible to our superiority, by showing how severely we could retaliate their aggression.

In the raid which followed over the next few days, more Aborigines were killed and wounded, for their terrible moans were heard coming from the reedy lagoons, as the Report put it.[52] Three soldiers were wounded, including Ensign Dale who was twice stabbed by spear thrusts while trying to secure an Aborigine. Dale hadn't done very well in the circumstances, as his victim had already been shot in the face, 'his jaw being seen to hang'. But Irwin was pleased with the raid and reported to Stirling that

> Considering the object I had in view as now fully accomplished; of impressing a salutary dread of our superiority and arms; while we shewed them we did not wish to injure them, after getting them and their families completely in our power, we left them at sunset, apparently on terms as friendly as usual.

But the object of the raid was not 'fully accomplished', for the Aborigines went back to Paton's place and many more besides, and time and again the muskets were presented; and repeatedly punitive parties set out to accomplish once and for all what Irwin had failed to do. The Aborigines had not read Blackstone's *Commentaries on the Laws of*

---

[51] See H. Reynolds 'Racial Thought in Early Colonial Australia', *Australian Journal of Politics and History* Vol. 20, 1974, pp.45–53.
[52] *CSO* Vol. 6, 1830, pp.146–7.

England, nor the literature of racialism which placed them at the foot of the human pile. They coped with invasion as best they could—by engaging in guerilla warfare, by helping themselves to stock-piled food supplies, by arguing their case with sympathetic invaders like Fletcher Moore and interpreters like Francis Armstrong, and by holding together an ancient and familiar culture wherever possible. They suffered horribly whether resisting openly or by appearing to acquiesce in invasion, for appearances occasionally to the contrary, the Aborigines refused to put themselves and their families 'completely in our power'. Stirling's first report on the Perth Aborigines, made in March 1827 as he sighed over a 'rich and romantic country', was prophetic: 'They seemed angry at our invasion of their Territory'.[53]

The Perth Ball 1831

On 3 September 1831, in the company of no less than 180 ladies and gentlemen, most of whom believed with Mr Lyon that they 'moved in the first circle of society at home',[54] George Fletcher Moore, himself a son of Byron and the romantic movement, danced at the Governor's Ball in Perth from early evening to 5 in the morning. Gallopades and quadrilles, fine dress, cheerful and polite conversation, superb decorations, and a splendid supper—truly life in Swan River was worth singing about, and with joy in his heart Moore rose and before that gay and distinguished company sang a grand new song of his own composing, the title and refrain of which was 'Western Australia for Me':

> From the old Western World we have come to explore
> The Wilds of this Western Australian shore.
> There's good wood and good water, good flesh and good fish,
> Good soil and good clime, and what more could you wish
> Than we live without trouble and stealth Sirs,
> Our currency's all sterling wealth, Sirs,
> So here's to our Governor's health, Sirs,
> And Western Australia for Me![55]

And in that beautiful moment the elegant 180 set to one side their worries about the market-place, unruly servants, and the intimidating presence of Aborigines: 'Happiness and good feeling, one towards another, seemed to have taken possession of all and no ill will or ill nature dared even to shew their noses in Perth'.[56] Perhaps the dreams of 'internal peace' were coming true after all. Perhaps indeed Western Australia was for them.

Perth as Arcadia, 1830s. (C. D. Wittenoom, artist.)

[53] *HRA* Series III, Vol. VI, pp.556, 558.   [54] *CSO* Vol. 13, 1831, pp.24–8.
[55] Moore *Diary*, p.64; I have made a single stanza from several.
[56] M. Durack *To Be Heirs Forever*, 1976, p.89; Letter written by Eliza Shaw.

Chapter Two: Shaping Perth — 1829 to 1851

A site for a Capital

On 30 December 1828 Stirling received a despatch from his friend, the new Secretary of State for Colonies, Sir George Murray. Murray, a fellow Scot, commissioned Stirling 'to assume the Title of Lieutenant Governor' and to attend to the 'wants and prospects of the settlement'.[1] Stirling was instructed to determine

> The most convenient site for a Town to be erected as the future Seat of Government. You will be called upon to weigh maturely the advantages, which may arise from placing it on so secure a situation as may be afforded on various points of the Swan River, against those which may follow from establishing it on so fine a port for the reception of Shipping, as Cockburn Sound is represented to be; and more effectually to guard against the evils to be apprehended from an improvident disposal of the land in the immediate vicinity of the Town, you will take care that a square of three miles (or 1920 acres) is reserved for its future extension; and that the land within this space is not granted away (as in ordinary cases) but shall be held upon leases from the Crown for a term not exceeding 21 years. You will from the commencement of the undertaking be observant of the necessity of marking out and reserving for public purposes all those peculiar positions within or in the vicinity of the projected Town, which from natural advantages or otherwise will probably be essential to the future welfare of the Settlement. In laying the foundation of any such Town, care must be taken to proceed upon a regular plan, leaving all vacant spaces, which will in future times be required for thoroughfares and as the Sites of Churches, Cemeteries, and other Public Works of utility and general convenience.[2]

Stirling, a naval captain sensible to the dangers of naval bombardment, chose a river site in preference to Cockburn Sound. In addition, Cockburn Sound was too far from the area of expected farming development. But the reasons why he chose as the main site of the town the strip of land between Point Lewis and Point Frazer are less clear. When he and Frazer explored the Swan River in March 1827, both men were impressed with Point Heathcote which stood on Melville Water. The site possessed a supply of fresh water, and a 'Garden' had been planted there. In addition, Lieutenant Belches had discovered the Canning River nearby. Stirling may have put this view to the Colonial Office. Certainly late in 1831 the Under Secretary to the Colonial Office, R. W. Hay, specifically asked Stirling why he had not selected Point Heathcote as the capital. In reply Stirling expressed his surprise at the importance Hay seemed to attach to the matter. Nevertheless he offered the following explanation:

---

[1] Stirling must have been pleased to receive his commission before the end of the year; had it been sent on 1 January 1829 or after he would have lost his half-pay as a naval officer, as would Harbour Master Currie, Storekeeper Morgan and several others.

[2] *HRA* Series III, Vol. VI, pp.600–1.

On our arrival here with the expedition the imperfect knowledge which I had of the country was of course soon extended and it was found in consequence that a Town at the mouth of the Estuary would be requisite for landing goods and as a Port Town, while another sufficiently high on the River to afford easy communication between the Agriculturalists on the Upper Swan and the Commercial Interest at the Port would tend much to the speedy occupation of that useful District. In selecting a site for this purpose, the present position of Perth seemed to be so decidedly preferable in building materials, streams of water and facility of communication, that I was induced on these grounds to establish the Town there.

Point Heathcote had probably been considered as a dual purpose site: port and agricultural entrepot. When Stirling realized that, contrary to his 1827 opinion, the rock bar across the mouth of the Swan was indeed a severe obstacle to deep-draft shipping, he was left with no alternative but to create a port town at the point where goods would have to be unloaded. It then made some sense to push the capital as close to the agricultural lands of the Upper Swan as he could manage, beyond Point Heathcote to the point beyond which cutters and the like could not readily go. This was Perth, for north of Point Frazer the mud flats made the river impassable for all but gigs and flat bottomed barges. Later he learnt that with canalization larger craft could negotiate the mud flats north of Perth, but by that time Perth was well-established and as Stirling observed to Hay:

Perth has hitherto been considered the Capital, and I see no reason for supposing that it will cease to be so.

Lest this should seem to be put a little too firmly to so powerful a figure as Hay, Stirling added that 'if the course of events pointed out sufficient motives for a change' then he would indeed move the seat of government.[3]

On 27 July 1829, following a further exploratory trip by soldiers and others up to the Point Frazer area, Captain Stirling posted a 'Government Notice' at his Garden Island headquarters:

Notice is hereby given that on the 12th August, the anniversary of the day on which His Gracious Majesty was born, the first stone will be laid of a New Town, to be called Perth, near to the entrance of the Estuary of the Swan River. After that date the Public Business in the several Departments of the Government will there be transacted and all applications for land and other subjects received.

Captain Fremantle, of HMS *Challenger*, left this description of the auspicious occasion:

The Lieutenant Governor having made up his mind to establish a Town up the Swan River to be called Perth and to lay the first Stone of it on the King's birthday, the 12th August 1829, I offered to render him any assistance with boats, and to convey him up. We proceeded a large party on the 9th but could not pass the bar, therefore hauled the boats over the neck of the land and then proceeded up ... On the 12th our Party increased and there being no stone contiguous for our purpose, to celebrate the commencement of the new Town, Mrs Dance cut down a tree; fired Volleys and made speeches and gave several cheers; named the Town Perth, according to the wishes of Sir George Murray.

'Who ever heard of such a place', exclaimed William Leake to Under

---

3   *HRA* Series III, Vol. VI, pp.549–640, August 1831; January 1832; see also M. Uren *Land Looking West*, 1948, p.99.

Secretary Horace Twiss, when he heard the news in February 1830. He added that

> a vast number already declare against Swan River because they now consider it a place where Scotch interests will only prevail.[4]

With a town named after a Scot's birthplace and constituency, a Governor who was Scottish by birth and upbringing, and in Thomas Peel a Scot who was the largest landowner, the new colony certainly bore a Scottish stamp. Leake could also have grumbled that the new Colonial Secretary, Peter Broun, and the Government Botanist, James Drummond, were also Scots. By one of history's ironies, William Leake's son George became a Chairman of the Perth Town Trust and a leading citizen, presumably in defiance of the Scots' interest so disliked by his father. In November 1830 the Wellington Ministry fell, but Perth retained its name, and Murray Street too had by then been named, as had Wellington Street. Perhaps one street name was changed before it had gained local currency. It may be that the town's principal street was first called King George's Terrace, after King George IV, the reigning monarch at the time of settlement—certainly the Colonial Secretary, Peter Broun, wrote of the street as 'King George's Tce' as late as December 1834.[5] And after all the town was founded on George's birthday. But George IV died in June 1830 and it might be the case that a decision to alter the street name to St George's Terrace was taken shortly after. The extension of St George's Terrace was named Adelaide Terrace after the new King William IV's wife; and King William was honoured by having a major north-south road named after him, though gradually the 'King' was lost, and the street was known by the more democratic 'William'. Other streets were named after leading officials in Swan River and at home—for example, Stirling, Mackie, Irwin and Howick Streets.

Peter Broun: Colonial Secretary, 1829–1846.

Some thought that Stirling had chosen his site wisely. One such was Captain Fremantle, who may have had a hand in the decision. Fremantle recorded in his diary

> I think the situation of Perth well adapted for a town, certainly preferable to any other spot I have yet seen.

But even Fremantle could see that the site was by no means ideal:

> Unfortunately the Islands stop up all direct communication by water, but the distance to convey goods will not exceed a mile and ultimately perhaps a Canal will be cut which will render communication direct with the sea from the Source of the River.

He added, however, 'I wish the Soil immediately in the Neighbourhood of Perth was a little better . . .'[6] Fremantle wrote as a friend to the site. Others were still more emphatic in their criticism. In November 1829 a visitor to Perth, Samuel Taylor, was moved to write for the benefit of Tasmanian readers:

> I have just returned from the headquarters (Perth) . . . where you have one of the most delightful demi-panoramic views, I suppose, in the world; but this is all that can be said of it. Not a blade of grass to be seen—nothing but sand, scrub, shrubs, and stunted trees, from the verge of the river to the tops of the hills.[7]

---

4   Cited Uren *Land Looking West*, p.124. Fremantle's description comes from Ann Parry (ed.), *The Admirals Fremantle*, 1971, p.147.
5   *CSO* Vol. 36, 1834, p.31.
6   Cited Parry *The Admirals Fremantle*, p.148.
7   *Colonial Times*, 12 February 1830, cited Cameron *op. cit.* p.58.

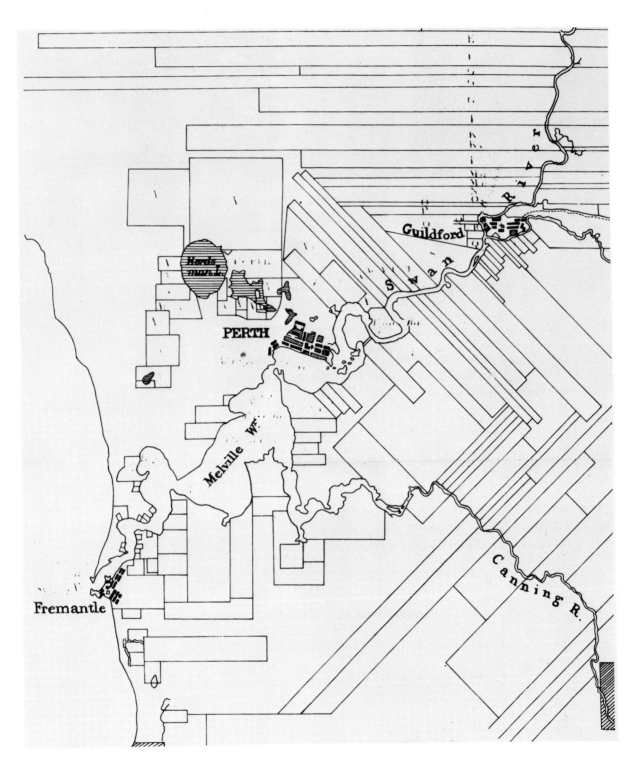

Perth and its hinterland, 1830s:
land grants as marked.

Taylor added, somewhat over-pessimistically, that

> I may say with certainty, that the soil is such, on which no human being can possibly exist. Indeed, so palpable and unpardonable a delusion is not to be met with in the whole annals of Gullism.

Another wrote, this time for Sydney readers:

> We had an excursion to Perth . . . and returned last night heartily glad to get back from such a comfortless hole . . . the miserable huts are built in a wood on a soil of dark-coloured sand, swarming with fleas and mosquitos; in fact a more perfect purgatory cannot be devised.[8]

Still another, the ship's surgeon, T. B. Wilson, perhaps mindful of the health risks of swamps and mud-flats, wrote that 'It seemed to Captain Barker and myself that the situation of the town was not judiciously chosen'.[9] Could this be the same site as that described by another surgeon, Clause, in March 1827, as 'the most healthy part of the Globe I have visited'? In its Irish way the whirligig of time would prove that both observers were right.

Stirling's determination to found Perth in August had been prompted in part by the arrival of still more settlers at Fremantle and the need to get them to the farming lands of the Swan as quickly as possible. Moving his administration to Perth would, he hoped, accomplish this. Accordingly, the day after the foundation of the town, Surveyor General Roe began laying out the townsite in accordance with the directions laid down by Sir George Murray. He surveyed the likely Government land and town allotments along the front street, which became St George's Terrace. He was then recalled to Fremantle where he surveyed urban lots from 24 August until 10 September. But on 15 September Stirling began to locate settlers on the Perth allotments, thereby throwing the Survey Office into confusion. From October to December 1829 the surveying of allotments scarcely kept ahead of the leasing of the blocks, each of which was nine-tenths of an acre. In December a plan of the district of Perth was drawn up and a register of allotments prepared. Late in December Roe and Hillman marked out the burial ground to the east of the townsite.[10] By then a number of dwellings had been erected along St George's Terrace, mostly of wood, some prefabricated, but more usually of wattle and daub. Tents were still in use also. By the beginning of 1830 three hotels were in the course of erection: Lewis Mayo's Perth Hotel, James Kenton's Swan Hotel, and Thomas Dent's most inaptly named The Happy Emigrant. All these buildings had primitively thatched roofs. From 1830 the wealthy settlers, including the Governor, began to build homes and business establishments in brick, though this really only proceeded rapidly after December 1830 when a house made of wood burnt down. Stirling had been correct in believing that the clay deposits to the east of the town would be suitable for brickmaking, but for much of the 1830s the bricks used were imported. In time however, most of the houses of Perth would have walls made of local bricks, while Fremantle would develop with stone as the important building material. Perhaps the earliest buildings of substance in Perth were the Government offices, situated on the south side of St George's Terrace. They were small and difficult to work from; perhaps the largest was the Civil Engineer's

---

8 Uren *Land Looking West*, p.139.
9 T. B. Wilson *Narrative of a Voyage Round the World*, 1835, p.221-4.
10 *CSO* Vol. 4, 1830, p.2ff—Survey Department monthly report: Vol. 3 is missing.

office, measuring as it did 18 feet by 9 feet,[11] and in 1832 more substantial premises were erected on the northside. Their construction provided work for skilled tradesmen, especially Henry Trigg and Bayley Maycock, both of whom were to gain affluence and status in Perth society over the next thirty years.[12]

But while some building was taking place in 1830 and 1831 more people lived in tents and modified Aboriginal *mias*, or reed and brush constructions with attendant risks of fire, poor sanitation and ill-health. By 1832 Fremantle had developed the faster of the two towns, containing over 400 people compared with Perth's 360, and there were twice as many houses.[13] Captain Fremantle, on a return visit to Perth in September 1832, commented on the relative growth of the two towns:

> I was much disappointed at the appearance of the Capital as it does not appear to have made much progress, very few houses having been built and many of those scarcely worth the name being mostly of wood and very small . . . Perth has not kept pace with Fremantle.[14]

A year later another visitor, the botanist Karl von Haegel, found 'about 100 houses and cottages in rows, with broad streets between them.'[15] Indeed, from 1833 Perth began to overhaul Fremantle, though the growth of both was sluggish.

The Religion of the People

In matters of religion the State served the Anglican Church and the Anglican Church served the State. Swan River in the 1830s was as conservative in religion as it was Tory in politics. The Anglican Church in Western Australia was founded by Archdeacon Scott, a redoubtable figure who had first come to the Australian colonies in 1819 as secretary to T. H. Bigge, a Royal Commissioner sent out by the Imperial Government to conduct an investigation into the state of the convict system, agriculture and administration of Macquarie's New South Wales. As an aristocratic Tory, Bigge found much in New South Wales that was distasteful to him; indeed he was a straitener, a cold, humourless man who revelled in chastising that man of great compassion, Governor Macquarie. Bigge's relation and secretary was rather like the Commissioner. Scott's father had been chaplain ordinary to King George III, and his sister was the wife of the Earl of Oxford. At the conclusion of Bigge's inquiry in New South Wales Scott had returned to England where he was ordained priest in 1822. From 1824 to 1829 he was Archdeacon of New South Wales, the principal churchman in that colony and a member of the Legislative Council. Like his political masters Scott believed that Church and State were one. As a Tory, a friend of John Macarthur, and a supporter of the unpopular Governor Darling, Scott was persistently abused by progressives in New South Wales. He was also constantly in dispute with non-conformists and Roman Catholics. In November 1829 the ship in which he was returning

---

[11]   See illustration in *CSO* Vol. 13, 1831, pp.45–7. For general 1830s development see D. Markey *More of a Symbol than a Success*, Mt Lawley Teachers' College, 1976.
[12]   Trigg correspondence, 1829–30, Battye Library HS/591.
[13]   Stirling to Goderich, 2 April 1832, *Swan River Papers* Vol. 9, pp.36–7, Battye Library. The value of Perth's buildings was £10,000; those of Fremantle, £15,000.
[14]   Fremantle's 'Diary', cited Parry *The Admirals Fremantle*, p.161.
[15]   Kathleen D. Napier 'New Holland in Europe', *Early Days* Vol. 7, Pt. VII, 1975, p.59.

to England struck a reef off Carnac Island and was forced into Fremantle for repairs. Scott was to remain in Perth for a year. It was a social environment entirely to his liking.[16]

Prior to Scott's unexpected arrival in Swan River, prayers had been read to the gentry each Sunday by that pious soldier, Commander F. C. Irwin. On Friday 25 December 1829 there gathered in Stirling's house eighty members of the respectable classes to celebrate the birth of Christ and to share in the Holy Sacrament for the first time since leaving home. In the little rush-walled and thatched church nearby, which had been hastily erected by the reluctant soldiers of the 63rd at Scott and Irwin's direction, the believers took bread and wine. It was a moving occasion. For once the soldiers, who seemed to find more comfort in the consolations of the bottle than the exordiums of religion, were not unruly. Scott's church would remain in use for seven years: it was, as Stirling put it to his patron Sir George Murray, 'a decent place of worship' and was owing to 'the zeal and energy of the venerable Archdeacon Scott'.[17] One of the church's builders, Private Phillip Corrigan, also tried to build his own house—not a house of God, to be sure, but a shelter for one of Simon's lambs—but he stole some timber and was sent to gaol. With his house eventually built Corrigan lived in it for less than one year when he was moved to steal some cut-glass belonging to the Colonial Secretary, Peter Broun. For this more serious crime Corrigan was transported for seven years, the life of the little rush church he had built for Scott.[18]

'In the Beginning . . .': The Rush Church, Perth, 1830s. Soldiers' tents at left, Government offices at right, and the Rush Church at centre.

Scott was still officiating in Perth after the arrival in January 1830 of the Colonial Chaplain, the Rev. J. B. Wittenoom. Indeed Wittenoom benefited from Scott's patronage, for it was at Scott's bidding that Stirling agreed to subsidise Wittenoom for house rent over and above his

16 *ADB* Vols. 1 and 2—entries for Bigge and Scott.
17 *HRA* Series III, Vol. VI, p.616.
18 Supreme Court Criminal Court Record Book, Case 70, October 1833; also *Perth Gazette*, 4 October 1834.

The Rev. J. B. Wittenoom: a 'high and dry' churchman and magistrate.

salary. Scott and Wittenoom were similar in temperament and training; both were High Churchmen and High Tories. The transition from the one to the other was smooth, and the Anglican Church in Western Australia remained locked within the Establishment of Perth society for many years thereafter. Both Scott and Wittenoom had grown up in county society, the one in Oxfordshire and the other in Nottinghamshire. Wittenoom had taken out his BA at Brasenose College, Oxford in 1810, and Scott his BA from St Alban's Hall, Oxford, in 1817. Oxford religious experience in these years has been described as 'high and dry', so sterile was its Anglicanism. Most of the Colleges accepted uncritically the alliance of Church and State. A few Colleges were favourable to Evangelicanism and Methodism, but St Alban's and Brasenose were not among them. 'The Oxford high churchmen supported good causes; but their inviolable conservatism of mind made them suspicious of social and political as well as religious radicalism.'[19] This 'inviolable conservatism of mind' is an apt description of Wittenoom's ministry in Swan River.[20] Even his colleague from 1841 onwards, the Rev. John Ramsden Wollaston, himself a Peelite conservative and no friend of Whiggism and Reform, found Wittenoom to be of the 'old High Church Tory Party', and his churchmanship utterly cheerless.[21] But Wollaston had been to Cambridge not Oxford, and had experienced there a more latitudinarian or eclectic approach to Anglicanism, though he too was by no means an Evangelical or in any way kindly disposed towards Dissenters and Roman Catholics.

Until 1837 the little rush church doubled as a courthouse; after 1837, and until the construction of the imposing St George's Church in 1840-42, the new courthouse doubled as a church. In part this dual usage was a reflection of the lack of capital available for the construction of single use buildings in Perth. But there can also be no doubt that the leading colonists thought of the church and the courthouse as two sides of the same coin. There was in fact little difference between Anglicanism and the Law: both served the investing class and both sought to inculcate in the 'inferior class' a respect for private property, an obedience to governors, and a fear of punishment for wrong-doing. And of course the law and religion were administered by the same people—Wittenoom, Irwin, Mackie and Moore. In a community which was by no means 'immaculate', the weekly practice of the religious few could call to all the recollection of the duties of their holy religion. And when example failed and men erred in their ways—'not having the fear of God before their eyes but being moved and seduced by the instigation of the Devil'—the Court dispensed British justice, tempered by Christian mercy, in a building designed to turn men's eyes and thoughts to the Great Deliverer, the High Judge of all men.[22]

Wittenoom's Anglicanism and the needs of the State helped produce a society in which intolerance was a way of life. When Picton Beete was sworn in as Lieutenant Governor in October 1834, like others before and after him he repeated the words

19   V. H. H. Green *Religion at Oxford and Cambridge*, 1964, p.260.
20   *ADB* Vol. 2—entry for Wittenoom; also Canon Burton *Church Beginnings in the West*, 1941.
21   *Wollaston's Picton Journal 1841–44*, edited by Burton and Henn, reprinted University of WA Press, 1975, p.51.
22   *Perth Gazette*, 8 June 1833; Supreme Court Register, June 1830.

Perth's Court House, 1837: for those 'seduced by the instigation of the Devil'.

> I abhor detest and abjure as unpious and heretical, that damnable doctrine and position that princes excommunicated or deprived by the authority of the see of Rome may be deposed or murdered by their subjects or any other whatsoever. And I do declare that no foreign prince person prelate State or potentate hath or ought to have any jurisdiction power superiority prominence or authority, ecclesiastical or spiritual within the realm of England or any of the dominions thereunto belonging.

To this was added the following:

> I do solemnly and sincerely in the presence of God testify and declare, on the true faith of a Christian, that I will never exercise any power authority or influence which I may possess by virtue of my office and truth as Lieutenant Governor and Commander in Chief of this Colony of Western Australia to injure or weaken the Protestant Church as it is by law established in England.[23]

Here too was an 'inviolable conservatism of mind' which helped to shape Swan River Colony for many years. There was not yet a Roman Catholic Church with which to contend. But would the Anglican Church be weakened by the presence in Swan River Colony of dissenters? In Britain during the 1820s and 1830s some Tory leaders were severely critical of the unreformed Church of England and the subject status of other churches. In 1829, the year of Swan River's foundation, the Tory Government of Wellington repealed the Test and Corporation Acts and passed the Catholic Relief Act, thereby enabling dissenters and Catholics greater freedoms and opportunities to engage in political life. By the terms of the Dissenters' Marriage Act of 1835, dissenters were no longer obliged to marry in Anglican churches. In 1835 too it was Peel's Conservative

23 *CSO* Vol. 32, 1834, pp.3–5.

Joseph Hardey, Wesleyan preacher and farmer: 'May I come out of the fire as gold purified seven times'.

administration which created an Ecclesiastical Commission to reform the Church of England. But in Swan River, Wittenoom, Irwin, Mackie, and Moore, as well as Governor Stirling, had been moulded by the unreformed Church of England. Like many senior members of the Anglican Church in England, they were utterly out of sympathy with the reform movement at home and had no intention of importing it to Swan River. But if they did not encourage the migration of Catholics and dissenters, they did not actively seek to prevent the migration of the latter, especially the more conservative of the Wesleyan groups.

While it is possible that some of the indentured labourers may have been dissenters, the first well known contingent of Wesleyans came to Perth in 1830. Led by Joseph and John Wall Hardey, a group of Yorkshire Wesleyans, their families and servants, chartered the ship *Tranby* and, on arrival at Swan River, took up land on fertile flats four miles upstream from Perth and later in the York area. They lived and worked as a religious community following the tenets of John Wesley, and they prospered at Swan River. Joseph Hardey had been born and raised in Lincolnshire, a county noted for its religious enthusiasm.[24] As a young man he moved to Yorkshire, a centre of dissent, where he farmed for some time before marrying in August 1829 at the age of twenty-five years. Six years before, he had become a lay preacher. He had heard with Wesley that 'God is holy: I am unholy. God is a consuming fire: I am altogether a sinner meet to be consumed'. 'Yet I heard a voice (and is it not the voice of God?) saying "Believe and though shalt be saved. He that believeth is passed from death into life"'. Man was a miserable sinner, but God's grace would be freely bestowed, and man pardoned of his sin, and thereby sanctified or made without the capacity for sin. And this salvation was open to all men, not Calvin's chosen few, and could be experienced by man while he was still on earth. As Wesley had taken the old cannon foundry at Moorfields in London and made a chapel of it, so Joseph Hardey took a warehouse at Fremantle and preached there to his flock until the move to Perth. And there in 1834 he built the first Wesley Church.[25]

As part of his rejection of the unreformed Church of England, Wesley had ordered that there should be no pews in chapels and that the classes of people should be intermingled and not, as in Anglican churches, with masters in the front pews and servants at the back of the church. Hardey did use pews rather than backless benches, but pews could not be bought by the affluent as they were in the Anglican church. In the warehouse, in the Perth chapel, and in the fields and the cottages of the Peninsula Farm, Joseph Hardey and his followers sang the great hymns of Charles Wesley, reiterating daily the important truths of their most holy religion. They did not sing as though they were half asleep or half dead; they sang without weariness

> Still the fountain of thy blood
> Stands for sinners open'd wide
> Now, even now, my Lord and God
> I wash me in thy side.[26]

Wesley had been no political radical: he was an ardent monarchist; he

24 J. Obelkevich *Religion and Rural Society: South Lindsey 1825–75*, 1976, Chapter 4.
25 W. Lutton *The Wesley Story*, 1970; also *ADB* Vol. 1—entry for Hardey.
26 See Anthony Armstrong *The Church of England, the Methodists and Society 1700–1850*, 1973, p.78.

opposed 'John Wilkes and Liberty'; and he deplored the revolt of the American colonists. Nonetheless he had little time for an effete and corrupt aristocracy, and he bore a genuine concern for working class people—many of his early preachers were skilled artisans and small farmers. Wesley's successor, Jabez Bunting, wrote that 'Methodism hates democracy as much as it hates sin'.[27] Hardey and his people did not come out to Swan River to effect a socio-political revolution, and, when their hope of religious toleration was realized, and as prosperity followed godly observance, they worked within the lines of social and political development mapped out by the Anglicans Wittenoom, Irwin, Mackie, and Moore. Hardey, like Wesley before him, attended Anglican services sometimes, and welcomed Anglicans to his own. Stirling had permitted him to build a chapel, and Stirling's successor, the evangelical Clapham sect member, John Hutt, a Whig, an advocate of the reformed Anglican Church and a member of the Aborigines Protection Society, even gave the Wesleyans a small grant from the Government, rather to the consternation of the Anglican clergy. The Wesleyans built a fine new church in 1840. John Wall Hardey became a member of the Legislative Council. Thus the Wesleyans became collaborators in the great enterprise of letting money make money. They co-operated and quarrelled with other farmers, merchants, and labourers; they took part in public meetings on political and economic matters; they hammered the Government and worked with it. In fellow Wesleyan George Shenton they had a powerful ally in the affairs of town and country. And in George Lazenby, Henry Trigg, and James Inkpen, they had men prominent in the life of the town. No group worked harder to achieve that 'internal peace', so desired by the Anglican masters of Swan River. They even set the pace for the christianising and civilizing of Aboriginal children. They were the perfect colonists. In 1830 Joseph Hardey had written: 'May I come out of the fire as gold purified seven times'.[28] He died in September 1875, a wealthy old man knowing the answer to his prayer.

But what of disturbance within Anglicanism itself? Could this too be contained? One of the first Anglican priests to assist Wittenoom in Swan River was a convert from Roman Catholicism, the Rev. Giustiniani. Giustiniani came from a princely line of Italians. He had been recruited in England by Irwin for the WA Missionary Society which had been established during Irwin's visit in 1834–35. Giustiniani arrived in Perth in July 1836, to be met by George Fletcher Moore who observed: 'he is animated with zeal, and full of hope for success among the natives'.[29] His 'zeal', and his hope for success among the natives, were to be his undoing, because they carried him beyond the defined parameters of acceptable behaviour in Swan River Colony. Shortly after arriving at Guildford where he was to build a church, Giustiniani travelled across the ranges to York. There he fraternised with the Aborigines and learnt of atrocities committed against them by white settlers; he seems to have confirmed these with sympathetic whites. His experiences on the Swan at Guildford and York led him to the conclusion that the settlers were acting in defiance of the expressed intention of the Imperial

---

[27] E. P. Thompson *The Making of the English Working Class*, 1968 (ed.), p.430.
[28] 'Diary 1830–39', mss Battye Library 566A2; also part-published by Canon Burton in *Journal of the Royal WA Historical Society* Vol. 1, Pt. VI, 1929, pp.17–28. The entry was for 31 July 1830.
[29] Moore *Diary*, p.303.

Government, especially that of the noted protector of native peoples, Lord Glenelg, Secretary of State for Colonies, and that the local Government in fact condoned and even promoted the 'system of cruelty, oppression, and injustice to which the aboriginal inhabitants were exposed' in Swan River. To the horror of the 'respectable classes' Giustiniani allied himself with Nairne Clark, editor of the radical *Swan River Guardian*, who defended working men against brutal masters and who, in an unceasing war on officialdom, took the part of the Aborigines. In October 1837 Giustiniani became the first white man to defend Aborigines (rather than interpret their evidence as Armstrong and others had done) in the Perth Courthouse. The charge against the two Aborigines was theft, but the bench in fact tried Giustiniani, though it found the Aborigines guilty of the crimes as charged. The bench was composed of the Rev. Wittenoom, who completely disassociated himself from his colleague's activities, W. H. Mackie, and the York Government Resident, D. McLeod; the crown prosecutor was George Fletcher Moore. In Court Giustiniani was ridiculed and censured, and shortly after, the Missionary Society, probably at Irwin's bidding, dismissed him from office. He left Swan River in February 1838. In London he brought his accusations against the settlers to the notice of the Secretary of State for Colonies, Lord Glenelg, who was sufficiently impressed to instruct the new Governor of Swan River, John Hutt, to investigate the charges. But Hutt's advisers were the men who had contained and eliminated Giustiniani and the matter lapsed. Perhaps he would have prosecuted the matter more vigorously had he been able to read Lieutenant Bunbury's letter of 10 July 1836, with the following comment on contact with the Aborigines: 'I shot a few of them one night'.[30]

As it happened, Giustiniani's successor at the Upper Swan, the Rev. William Mitchell, did little to ameliorate the condition of the Aborigines once he found that, unlike the Indians he had worked among in Bombay, they could not be readily trained for domestic service. The Mitchells floated in a Jane Austenish society at Guildford.[31]

A letter from Dr Giustiniani to Lord Glenelg, Secretary of State for Colonies, 16 July 1838.

Aborigines and Settlers

In his letters to Lord Glenelg, the banished Dr Giustiniani had named a number of people guilty of atrocities against the Aborigines and he had described in detail the nature of the offences. The offences included placing an armed white servant in a shed with one door left open and flour clearly visible from the outside—the unsuspecting Aborigine would enter the shed and be fired on by the servant armed with a shotgun. Another offence was what was known throughout the colony as 'the shot of mercy', that is, killing a wounded Aborigine as one would finish off a writhing bullock. A third was simply to kill Aborigines

[30] See W. S. Bunbury and W. P. Morrell (eds.) *Early Days in Western Australia, being the Letters and Journal of Lieutenant H. W. Bunbury*, 1930, p.27; for Giustiniani, see A. Burton *Church Beginnings in the West*, 1941, pp.28–9; for his connection with the *Swan River Guardian* see B. Smith 'Early Western Australian Literature', *University Studies in History*, 1961–62, p.31; see also *CSO* Vol. 61, 1838, pp.106–13, and 160 for Giustiniani's letters to Lord Glenelg, and Glenelg's memorandum to Governor Hutt; for the courthouse scenes see *Perth Gazette*, October–November 1837.

[31] See Burton *Church Beginnings in the West*, p.65; also Mrs Mitchell's 'Diary', Mitchell Library, 5-82A, B1148-B1149.

for the sport of it, as Bunbury did, or as the Perth butcher and landowner, Mr Knight, was alleged to have taken part in: 'They met a native and his wife and took them prisoners, although no crime was laid to their charge, and a man named Sydney George, a servant of Mr Knight's, without any provocation, shot the man in the head, and the party left him for dead in the Forrest'. In the town of Perth there was plenty of contact between the Aborigines and the settlers: in fact the town was on a traditional line of movement for Aborigines, and the shallows were traditional fishing waters. For years after the foundation of the town more than 100 Aborigines could be present at any one time, though more frequently they were present in smaller numbers. The Government had appointed a Superintendent of Aborigines who was to arrange for the distribution of bread and biscuits, which the Aborigines liked 'very good', as the *Perth Gazette* reported it.[32]

By early 1833 the Aborigines were becoming more of a threat to the settlers in Perth than they had hitherto been (as indeed was the reverse case). In March 1833 the Government Resident for Perth, John Morgan, publicly drew attention to the fact that

> there are always in my Office, sixty stand of arms, with a full supply of ammunition, for those who may require it, ready to inflict a prompt and heavy punishment on the natives, should their conduct at any time be considered to deserve it, by those whose duty it is to judge and to act in such matters—

men like himself, in short.[33] This drew a rebuke from the editor of the *Perth Gazette*, who was an evangelical; but MacFaull also deplored the policy of handing out rations to the Aborigines, at least in the town, and he noted that

> it is true that they are extremely importunate, and are becoming most accomplished beggars.[34]

But Morgan was not without supporters in the town. One wrote that 'The deceit and impertinence of the natives are daily complained of by the inhabitants of Perth at this very moment'.[35] Three weeks later two servants were speared by the Aborigines on the Canning. This led to Yagan, Midgigooroo, and Munday being declared to be outlaws, even though there was some doubt that all three were present at the scene.[36] That same week another Aborigine was shot dead at Fremantle, by Mr Chidlow: 'the ball lodged in (Domjum's) head, and although the brains were exuding from the cavity, he lingered for three days before he expired'. Yagan avenged this murder,[37] but in July he was lured into a trap and was murdered, along with his friend Heegan, who 'was shot through the head and his brains were running out, one of the party put him out of his misery'.[38] In the interim old Midgigooroo had been captured and was sentenced to death in Perth. On the appointed day volunteers of the besotted 63rd, under the direction of John Morgan, brought out Midgigooroo, pinioned and blind-folded, and tied him to the outer door of the gaol. He was shot at six paces. The *Perth Gazette* reported that 'A great number of persons were assembled on the occasion'. There was 'general satisfaction and, in some instances, of loud and vehement exaltation'.[39]

[32] *Perth Gazette*, 16 February 1833.   [33] *Perth Gazette*, 2 March 1833.
[34] *Perth Gazette*, 2 March 1833.   [35] *Perth Gazette*, 13 April 1833.
[36] *Perth Gazette*, 4 May 1833.   [37] *Perth Gazette*, 1 June 1833.
[38] *Perth Gazette*, 13 July 1833.   [39] *Perth Gazette*, 25 May 1833.

Nor did relations between Aborigines and Perth's white settlers improve after this 'example' had been experienced. Indeed by mid-1834, on his return from England, Stirling found his settlers in an embattled position. In April 1834 a group of thirty Aborigines attacked the mill on the point opposite the town of Perth. While some of them took flour from the mill, others held down young George Shenton, without harming him. The Superintendent of Natives, Captain Ellis, set off after the Aborgines and succeeded in killing one, wounding others, and capturing three who were brought back to Perth. Yeydong and Gummol, both teenagers, received 15 and 25 lashes respectively at the Perth whipping post. Galute, a little older,

> received 60 lashes with a knotted rope, and although he uttered but few exclamations, the exhausted state in which he fell from the post, when the order was given for the flogger to desist, was an earnest to the extent of his suffering.[40]

In his official report to the Colonial Secretary, Captain Ellis noted that

> Several of the working class who assembled appeared disappointed that they were not to witness an execution and behaved in a disorderly manner calling out to shoot him or hang him.[41]

This was only to be expected, for far more servants than masters were speared by the Aborigines, and the racist views of the masters were held in still more primitive and even virulent form by those influenced by them. This was also true of New South Wales at about the same time.[42] Stirling returned in August 1834 to be met with an almost unanimous demand from the settlers to have done with the Aborigines once and for all. Even the men of moderate opinion like Charles MacFaull and George Fletcher Moore now believed that a punitive war was necessary. In November Stirling launched the offensive known as the battle of Pinjarrah, in which fourteen Aborigines were killed and twenty wounded. The only casualty among the raiders was the Superintendent of Aborigines, Captain Ellis, who died of wounds and complications a few days after the raid. Stirling believed that this and subsequent punitive expeditions prevented the 'extermination of the whites'. He seems to have convinced himself that 'if they (the Aborigines) had the inclination and the power to combine their efforts, it would be useless to attempt to maintain our conquest with our present numbers'.[43] Within the next five years all major resistance to white settlement of the Perth region had been broken. Perhaps 200 of the Swan and Murray River Aborigines had been killed, and half this number wounded. Others died of white-introduced diseases. By 1840 MacFaull was expressing his surprise at the high quality of the work being done by the Aborigines clearing the square behind the Government Offices.[44] By 1840 too the Native School of Francis Armstrong was doing well; indeed Armstrong had just placed one of his pupils with MacFaull at the offices of the *Perth Gazette*.[45] The Aborigines came into the town not only for their own festivals, but also for the anniversary celebrations of the foundation of the colony. On June 1 each year after 1835, the Aborigines would give exhibitions of spear throwing at a loaf of bread stuck on a spear, or

---

[40] *Perth Gazette*, 3 May 1834.   [41] *CSO* Vol. 32, May 1834, p.90.
[42] See R. H. W. Reece *Aborigines and Colonists*, 1974.
[43] Cited by Green, in C. T. Stannage (General Editor) *A New History of Western Australia*, 1979.
[44] *Perth Gazette*, 18 April 1840.   [45] *Perth Gazette*, 24 October 1840.

engage in displays of boomerang throwing, or attempt to catch a greasy pig, much to the entertainment of white observers.[46]

Nor were they ever accepted as equals by the white settlers of Perth. In 1838 James Purkis complained bitterly about his neighbour, Francis Armstrong, who allowed Aborigines to congregate at his house

> not only destroying the peace and comfort of my family and home, but must ultimately annihilate the value of my property altogether.

It was true that the Aborigines continued to carry out tribal killings in St George's Terrace, and this too was a source of dismay to Purkis and his fellow allotment owners:

> myself and family have been deprived of rest for five successive Nights from the hideous mournful chaunting . . . 30 Natives . . . with five or six blazing fires, were from their cookeries by day most noisome smells and smoke arise contaminating the air, so that at intervals it is scarcely possible to open our back windows for ventilation.

Later the same month Stirling received a petition from some of the people of Perth. It had been drafted by the builder, Henry Trigg:

> I do earnestly intreat you as a Father of a family—and by every tie that holds you dear to that family—as well as by every bond that connects you to decent—Civilized—and Christian Society to urge on the prayer of the memorialist. I am fully aware of the ticklish ground on which His Excellency stands as to interfering with the Natives, but when our feelings are outraged—our families contaminated—our laws broken—and our lives endangered, surely this is ground sufficiently solid on which to take footing, to stay their outrages at least in our streets.[47]

The Memorial to which Trigg attached a covering letter read in part:

> That the Inhabitants be empowered to destroy all spears found in the hands of the other Natives within the limits of the Town. And that they be not allowed to appear in a state of nudity.

The memorial was signed by Trigg, Samuel Kingsford, John Chipper, Peter Broun, William Samson, George Fletcher Moore, Henry Reveley, Charles MacFaull, Robert Habgood, A. H. Stone, G. F. Stone, John Septimus Roe, Lionel Samson, Bayley Maycock, William Leeder, William Cook, Edward Barron, George Johnson, Rev. J. B. Wittenoom, H. C. Sutherland, Samuel Cox, Thos W. Mews (senior and junior), George Leake, T. Rogers, George Shenton, Thomas Helms, J. Nairn, and W. B. Andrews.[48] This high-powered memorial could not fail to impress the Governor. Shortly after, Stirling authorised closer policing of Aborigines in the town; they seem also to have been prevented from congregating in large numbers at Armstrong's house in St George's Terrace.

By the 1840s several Perth Aborigines were in domestic employment; others were used as bush guides and trackers. Of course the Aborigines continued to be provided with liquor and were often convicted of drunkenness. Indeed as late as 1847 the Legislative Council passed legislation making it possible to 'summarily convict and punish native offenders' rather than go to the expense of having them tried at Quarter Sessions.[49] In January 1849 the *Perth Gazette* commented on

---

46 See, for example, *Perth Gazette*, 6 June 1835; 5 June 1841—on this occasion the spear-throwing became more general and for several years after 1841 the Aborigines seem to have played little part in what was once described as the white man's 'corroborra'.

47 *CSO* Vol. 32, October 1838, pp.32–3, p.40.

48 *CSO* Vol. 62, October 1838, p.77.   49 *Perth Gazette*, 25 March 1848.

the frequent occurrence of cases of intoxication among the Aborigines frequenting Perth . . . it is certain that since the foundation of Perth, the tribe inhabiting the locality has gradually been dwindling away, until at present there are but about half-a-dozen left who will soon follow.[50]

In the early 1830s about 400 Aborigines inhabited the Swan area, and up to double this number visited Perth for great gatherings—from the Murray to the south and the Avon to the north-east as well as the Perth people.[51] In the early 1830s the Aboriginal leaders were known by name. By the late 1840s there were perhaps 100 in the Swan area, and perhaps about 25 in Perth itself. There were now fewer great gatherings of Aborigines in the Swan area. The great chief, Yallagonga, had been drowned in 1843. The leaders no longer bore proud historic names, but carried names given them by their white masters and white labouring men, at least in white company. The battle of St George's Terrace was over; the enemy had been routed, indeed decimated, and a 'decent—Civilized—and Christian Society' had been established. The quest for 'internal peace' was proving successful.

Social Dissidents

The bond between the Anglican Church and the Perth gentry, the commonalty of purpose and method, had first contained and then eliminated the dissident clergyman, Louis Giustiniani. What the Church itself did to Giustiniani, the Churchmen did to citizens who moved outside the parameters of acceptable behaviour in Perth, through use of the Court. Among *Parmelia*'s passengers were several unmarried men, described as artificers. One of them was John McKail, a carpenter-turner aged 22 years. McKail was one of those who did not accept that it was ordained from the beginning that good order in society depended on the working class cheerfully conceding a 'becoming deference' to the upper class.[52] He understood with Francis Place that the law and its administrators saw no distinction between cutting and trampling furze bushes and cutting down and trampling upon the people.[53] He had witnessed the upsurge of unionism in London in the early 1820s and the reintroduction of the Combination Act in 1825. He was almost twenty years old when the economic boom broke and he experienced the return of popular politics which was to reach its climax in the long agitation for a Reform Bill. He had lived out his short life during the Napoleonic Wars and their aftermath, including the suppression of civil liberties. He was twelve when the Manchester radicals were massacred at Peterloo. In the making this Deptford apprentice was one of those of whom Lord Grey asked in 1819: 'Is there one among them with whom you would trust yourself in the dark?'. The England of his formative years had seen the beginnings of the Mechanics' Institute movement and of the Society for

50 *Perth Gazette*, 13 January 1849.
51 Hallam's and Green's chapters in C. T. Stannage (General Editor), *A New History of Western Australia*, 1979.
52 *Perth Gazette*, 25 September 1847 'We do think, with many others, that two classes are indispensable, and that a becoming deference should be cheerfully conceded by the lower, not as an acknowledgement of inferiority, exactly, but as a mark of respect, to the upper: Not as from the obsequious serf to the supercilious noble, but as from the operative to his superior.'
53 Asa Briggs *The Age of Improvement*, 1959, p.213.

the Diffusion of Useful Knowledge. McKail was a literate man of the urban artisan class. In peacetime conditions the future for young naval dockyard turners was not bright, so early in 1829 McKail joined Stirling on the Swan River venture.

On arrival in Swan River, McKail worked under the direction of Reveley on the construction of the first Government offices, but he resigned in February 1830, already nursing a grievance against local governors. It seems that he had left his tools in the care of John Morgan, the Government Storekeeper, who had dumped them on the mainland beach from where they had been stolen. This was a terrible blow to an enterprising artisan. In June 1830 he sought compensation for his loss. Stirling offered him £5. McKail showed his mettle by returning the £5: 'allow me to state the contents of the chest were worth considerably more than twenty pounds'. He enclosed a full list of the tools, which included a lathe and other turning tools, an auger, jack plane, and bolts. Neither Stirling nor Broun minuted McKail's letters and it seems that his request for full compensation was never met. Over the next couple of years McKail did contract work at King George Sound and in Perth, for a short time working on Irwin's house in St George's Terrace. In Perth he had had to forego his allotment in St George's Terrace as he had not been able to meet improvements conditions. On 28 September 1833, at about 9 p.m., some thirty to forty labourers gathered in St George's Terrace near the barracks. It seems clear that they had been drinking for a longish time at Dent's, The Happy Emigrant, nearby. In the midst of their revelry someone suggested that as Lieutenant Governor Irwin was soon leaving the colony he should be given a proper send-off by the workers of the town. A stuffed figure of Irwin was duly set on fire, to the accompaniment of jeers and cheers.[54] The authorities were not amused, and John Morgan, the Government Resident, clapped some of the revellers in gaol, including the fiery John McKail. As was his way McKail appealed against his imprisonment, but Justice Mackie upheld Morgan's action. McKail, he said, had gathered for the purpose of 'creating a disturbance'. He added that McKail and his friends were fortunate that the military did not avenge the dishonour done to the regiment and its distinguished leader.

Irwin, who prayed daily for all men and for peace on earth, would have been deeply upset by these events, but he knew that the Lord moved in mysterious ways and that his faith in God and in his own mission in the wilderness would not be without its rewards. He left for England to renew his faith and to encourage like-minded people, especially good Anglican clergymen, to go and settle in Western Australia, whose 'state and position' he was to define for them. For despite McKail and the town and country troublemakers, Swan River would be a Christian place where harmony prevailed.

Some time later John McKail too left Perth. For weeks the Aborigines had been taking precious flour from his hut under Mt Eliza. Coming upon them on one occasion McKail shot and killed a fleeing Aborigine. As with most settlers so charged, he told the Court that he had fired to frighten the Aborigine, not to kill him. Had he been a Bussell he would have been believed, but he was John McKail and that

*Perth's Christian Soldier: Frederick Chidley Irwin, author of **The State and Position of Western Australia, 1835**. John McKail was an artisan who refused to accept his 'state and position' in Perth.*

---

[54] This was a traditional working class 'ritual of justice'. See A. E. Green and T. Wales (eds.), H. Burstowe *Reminiscences of Horsham*, 1911, reprinted with Introduction, 1975, pp.xxviii–xxx.

made quite a difference. Even Mackie could not bring himself to hang a white man for this crime, but McKail had delivered himself into the hands of his enemies and their course was clear. He was banished from Perth. How Irwin must have rejoiced when the news of McKail's banishment reached him: by whose Almighty will was Perth purged of this sower of discord and evil? Mackie, his cousin, friend, and the Lord's servant in this and in all things—didn't they pray together and share the Holy Sacrament?—had done a good thing.[55]

In 1835 too Perth's investing class contained and frustrated another follower of Francis Place—the tailor Joseph Mead. Mead had advertised his hostility to the existing order in a pamphlet addressed to 'mechanics and labourers' in which he advocated combination. Others too had spoken of combination, as George Fletcher Moore had noted uneasily in his diary in 1831:

> Great visitings among the neighbouring servants; seven or eight of them patrolling about; and all this is sure to end in drunkenness and mischief—they talk of forming a *club!*[56]

But little had come of this. A Union Society had been formed in August 1833 but by mid-1834, perhaps because of unemployment in Perth and elsewhere, it foundered.[57] Mead not only advocated combination, he proposed to open an evening school for youth, no doubt to instil in them these and other radical doctrines; but there is no record of the school ever opening. Mead also seems to have written a novel *The Wanderers*, which bore an ominous-sounding sub-title, *A Tale from Real Life*. Unfortunately this two volume tract was either never published or has since been lost. One night in mid-1835 this little man gave up the struggle. He succumbed to drink and was gaoled for riotous behaviour. Swan River had snapped his mind—had broken him as it had removed McKail.[58] The workers of Swan River would not 'make themselves' a class as they were doing in Britain. Blackstone, not Wooler, or even Cobbett, was king.

One who believed otherwise was the editor–solicitor William Nairne Clark. Clark had arrived in Swan River as early as 1831 and practised there as a notary public. A hot tempered man, Clark was involved in a duel at Fremantle in August 1832 in which he shot and killed a merchant, George Johnson. The jury acquitted him of manslaughter and, undeterred, he continued to make assaults on those to whom he took a

55   For McKail see *CSO* Vol. 1, June 1829, p.57; Vol. 5, 1830, p.94; Vol. 7, 1830, p.36; Vol. 2, December 1830, p.147; Perth Description Book, Lands and Survey Department, for 1829–40; *Perth Gazette*, 12 October 1833; *CSO* Vol. 34, 1834, p.201; *Perth Gazette*, 30 May 1835; *CSO* Vol. 61, 1838, p.259; *CSO* Vol. 62, 1838, pp.111–4.
Note on McKail's later career. Banished from Perth he took up residence at Albany. In February 1836 he was imprisoned for refusing to pay a fine of £20 for illegally landing spirits. In 1837 he won the contract to build Albany's first jetty. In 1840 he married Henrietta Jenkins, a sixteen-year-old daughter of one of Sir Richard Spencer's servants. In 1843 he was Albany's post master, and from this time to 1847 he taught Aboriginal children in a local school. In the late 1840s his enterprise in the export of sandalwood and kangaroo skins made him comfortably off. By the early 1850s he had taken up pastoral land. In 1856 Henry Camfield, the resident magistrate, who had arrived in Swan River in 1829, recommended that McKail be made a magistrate, as he was a respectable storekeeper and shipping agent. In the mid-1860s he purchased his own ship and was consul for German States and then the Empire. In 1870 he became MLC for Albany and returned to Perth to take his seat in the Legislative Council, close to the spot where 37 years previously he had burnt the Lieutenant Governor in effigy. McKail died in August 1871, leaving a will so complicated that it was still before the court thirty years after his death. His three daughters married into polite society. (Information: Don Garden.)
56   Moore *Diary*, p.91.   57   *Perth Gazette*, 10 August 1833, 24 May 1834.
58   For Mead see *Perth Gazette*, 17 May 1834, 6 June 1835.

dislike. One target was Charles MacFaull, Whiggish journalist and viticulturalist, with whom Clark formed a business relationship which ended in a case for libel. MacFaull went on to found the *Perth Gazette*, the colony's premier journal from 1833 to the present day. Clark responded by founding a journal in the interests of the artisan and yeoman class, called the *Swan River Guardian*. Unlike the *Perth Gazette*, the *Guardian* did not receive paid Government advertisements, and without this subsidy it collapsed in 1838, less than two years after it began. Clark consistently attacked Governor Stirling and those whom he described as 'the Elite of Swan River'. He strongly supported the formation in 1836 of a short-lived Mechanics' and Labourers' Agricultural Company, and also the Sons of Australia Benefit Society in 1837. And in return he received some support from those whom he championed. He claimed that two hundred people of the labouring classes each subscribed 2s 6d per week to keep the *Guardian* in print. Even allowing for exaggeration (after all the *Perth Gazette* had a circulation of only 100 or so), it seems clear that artisans and farm labourers did use his newspaper, particularly to air their grievances in the 'Letters' columns; also, through him they petitioned the Legislative Council not to pass legislation which would restrict the freedom of the press. And he articulated their desire not so much as to convulse society as to succeed in it. The country's strength, he wrote, resides in

> a bold peasantry . . . and not in mercantile speculators who abandon the place where their objects are attained, not in those who care for nothing except the monthly payment of their salaries, not in Honourables and Esquires who never had the presumption to claim these titles at home; but in men who resolutely put their shoulders to the wheel and endeavour by the sweat of their brows whether as agriculturalists, artisans, carpenters, etc. to earn an honest independence for themselves and posterity. These are the men who will one day be the esquires of Swan River.

Clark shared not only their desire to succeed as 'esquires' but also their belief that Swan River was the best place to live and work, and that Britain was a place to visit when successful. He printed verse with titles like 'A Swan River Melody' and 'A Song for Swan River'.

In 1838, overcome by financial difficulties, and without the comfort of 'society' when his wife was seduced by his former confrère, Captain W. T. Graham, Clark was unable to continue publishing the *Guardian*. He remained active on the court circuit, particularly at York where he exposed abuses in the court, there presided over by a persecutor of servants, the Magistrate, Captain Richard Goldsmith Meares. Clark also seems to have played a part in the formation of the Shepherds Club and Mutual Protection Society at York in 1843. But Perth society was too much for him, and as it had overcome Joseph Mead and exiled John McKail, so in 1848 it overcame Clark who left Swan River to settle in Van Diemen's Land where he died several years later. He had sought to widen the parameters of acceptable political behaviour and he had failed. Wittenoom, Irwin, Mackie and Moore were too much for him. His legacy in Perth was that inspiration and moral support which gave the artisan and labouring classes the strength to form associations for the defence and furtherance of their own interests.[59]

[59] See B. Smith 'Early Western Australian Literature', *University Studies in History* Vol. 4, No. 1, 1961–62, pp.24–101; *Swan River Guardian*, 1836–38; *Perth Gazette*, 28 January 1843; Supreme Court Criminal Case File, 1832; Civil Court Case, 1839—Clark versus Graham; *ADB* Vol. 1, 1966—entry for Clark.

'Sir,

We will feel great pleasure if you can insert the following lines in the "Guardian".

About 12 months ago labour in Perth was very scarce and great number (sic) being out of Employment and we were obliged to apply to the Hon. Peter Brown for work under the Government who told us that he understood there was a combination amongst the labourers of this colony and that they would not go up to Harvesting under a certain price. On that account he refused us work many of us having large families to maintain and also said if we could not get work we might starve. We now wish to show the Public where the Combination lies. Having been sent for for a few days ago (sic) up the Country to assist in reaping for the Harvest we went but could not agree for price we however walked on a few miles and were invited by a friend to stay the night; and during our conversation in the evening the Devil upon Two Sticks popped in at the window and showed us the following which is a copy of a Note picked up by Paul Pry not far from a Magistrate's residence on the Swan. Mr—

"I am not in want of hands myself. I send you these three men the price will be from £1 to £1 5s per acre, one half in cash, the other in meal at 2¼d per lb. I am sir, etc".

Now Mr Editor I wish to ask the Public whether or not they consider that there was a combination between those parties to lower the price of labour. Mr Editor, we hope we have not intruded in your columns this time as we have more intended for you in the future.

We are Sir, with respect,
TRIO.'

'Sir . . .': a letter of grievance from labourers in Perth. (**Swan River Guardian**, 1837.)

Property and Position

During the 1830s and 1840s the investing class learnt not only the rudiments of survival and how to contain dissidents, but also how to prosper in the new land, within the lines of development laid down by Governors Stirling and Hutt, as well as by the formidable four—Wittenoom, Mackie, Irwin and Moore. They learnt the importance of possessing an income from Government service, as base capital from which investments could grow. The Stones, Septimus Roe, and Peter Broun prospered in this way, as did less well known men like W. H. Drake, the Commissary General, and H. C. Sutherland, the Collector of Revenue, and Charles Leroux, the Auditing Clerk. The Government officials formed a socio-political elite in Perth which sustained itself through to the convict period, though making concessions to colonial conditions where necessary.[60]

From the very beginning there was hostility towards the propertied officials from landowners like W. L. Brockman and William Tanner, who felt that the officials governed in their own interests and not in those of the colonists as a whole, or at least those belonging to the wider investing class. They felt excluded from decision-making in Swan River, and, lacking that guaranteed annual income from Government, they believed that officials had an unfair advantage in the acquisition of wealth. When in early 1835 the Government sought to recover debts due to the Crown, it was William Tanner who convened a meeting in Perth to protest against this unfair act.[61] The officials also faced hostility from men engaged primarily in trade—large merchants like the Samsons, William Lamb (who had stores and land in Perth), and George Leake,[62] and from the late 1830s, the redoubtable George Shenton as well as the several smaller traders. Initially some of these men did not belong to the inner circle of Swan River officialdom and were specifically excluded from a Union Club, created by the officials, ex-army officers, some large agriculturalists and 'investors', for 'trade' was still thought of as the domain of men who were not gentlemen.[63] And not until the late 1830s did one of their number receive nomination for the Legislative Council, and even then there was little they could do about legislation which affected them adversely. But the conditions of colonial life militated against the preservation of such fine social distinctions. The Union Club took in big merchants like William Lamb, and in this way seems to have kept going to at least the end of 1838.[64]

In Swan River a man like George Leake, who could buy and sell most of the officials, could not be excluded from 'society'. Despite the fine and socially meaningful traditional distinctions between trade and landed officialdom, for women as well as men, the quarrels were essentially of a family character and the distinctions too often blurred to persist for too long. Samson, for instance, held pecuniary positions under the Crown, and Leake and Shenton held large tracts of farming land. Often it was the merchants who excited the anger and envy of gentry officials like Fletcher Moore because of the control they enjoyed

[60] *Perth Gazette*, 10 February 1849. [61] *Perth Gazette*, 21 February 1835.
[62] *Perth Gazette*, 5 January, 2 February 1833.
[63] *Perth Gazette*, 23 August, 13 September 1834; 29 August 1835.
[64] *CSO* Vol. 62, October 1838, p.54: Wittenoom, Secretary of Union Club, to the Colonial Secretary, seeking fee simple for land held by the Club, even though the usual improvement requirements had not been met: 'The objects of the Society are more of a public than a private nature'.

over the importation of goods into the colony,[65] especially the necessaries of life like grog and flour. But other officials seem to have co-operated with the merchants. In March 1835, for instance, Captain Hay, master of the ship *Jess*, tried to sell his cargo direct to the Commissariat, but his offer was refused. He then sold his consignment at a reduced rate to Lionel Samson, 'a Fremantle merchant', who succeeded in reselling it to the Commissariat at a price far higher than that originally asked by Captain Hay.[66] A final twist was given to the incident (thought to be only one instance of a general practice) when some of the flour was returned to the *Jess* for reshipment, on a commission basis, to King George Sound. By the time the flour was made available to the general public through the Commissariat, its cost had escalated by up to 100%, occasioning some hardship and much annoyance. Certainly the merchant benefited for the Government would have paid him in cash, with which he could buy further ships' cargoes. Probably too a Commissariat official benefited from the deal, although the public records are silent on the subject. Of course, the 'petty enmities' of economic life persisted; masters foreclosed on masters and the truth of the 'bundle of sticks' was sometimes ignored,[67] but rarely so in relation to the labouring classes.

In general, labourers and their families ate less well than did the families of the masters, though in the early history of Perth all groups suffered from inadequate supplies of basic foods. Many masters kept their own vegetable gardens and planted fruit trees, which were usually cared for by servants who themselves had little time to develop gardens of their own. Some vegetables were sold commercially, usually the excess from masters' gardens, though increasingly from commercial market gardens. The first of these tended to be further up the Swan: in 1833 a Mr Waters was congratulated in the press for sending a regular supply of vegetables down to Perth. By the end of the first decade there were commercial gardens in Perth itself, both along the foreshore under Mt Eliza, and on swampy land behind the town, where Thomas Mews had partially drained a lake for the purpose of growing vegetables.[68] The vegetables were sold by hawking, by direct sale off the property, or by sending them to the town market place, first situated near the old jetty, (hence Bazaar Street) and then closer to the site of the later Town Hall. The first two were the most popular means of sale, for as the *Perth Gazette* commented 'The whole producing industry of the colony are too independent to sit like a Dutch frau at a market place'.[69] In good times a labourer could feed a family of four for a shilling's worth of cabbage, carrots or Knole Cole; in bad times it would cost him twice this much.

Nor was milk plentiful and cheap, 'to the great scandal of the farmer' as a critic put it.[70] But from the mid-1830s, as a town herd was built up, Jane Barron, the proprietor of the Wheat Sheaf Inn in Murray Street, seems to have been able to supply milk on a regular basis, as indicated by advertisements in the *Perth Gazette*. The supply of fresh meat was also haphazard. Even as late as 1840 there was no well-established butchery, though several men had tried to make a living from slaughtering and selling meat in the town. It was claimed that the farmers demanded too high a profit margin; but in any case 'the public pay and

[65] Moore *Diary*, p.272: '. . . merchants who thrive in proportion to their exactions'.
[66] *Perth Gazette*, 14 March 1835.
[67] *Perth Gazette*, 28 September 1849.
[68] See *Perth Gazette*, 22 August 1835, 10 October 1840.
[69] *Perth Gazette*, 21 March 1840.   [70] *Perth Gazette*, 9 February 1833.

bleed freely'.[71] Even Walter Padbury, who died a colonial philanthropist, battled for a time as a butcher in Perth after 1845. Not until the early 1850s, when he won Government contracts for the provision of meat for the Convict Establishment, was he able to do better than keep his head above water. And as early as 1847 the slaughterhouses in the centre of town were causing concern over public health, and in time they would be removed to the town boundaries. This popular pressure also inhibited the growth of butcheries.[72]

Throughout the 1830s flour and bread were extremely expensive. Indeed there were times when the standard 4 lb loaf of bread cost as much as 2s6d, though 1s6d was more usual. This represented a very high proportion of a labourer's day wage, and has to be taken into account when comparing the living standards of labourers in the old world and the new. By the late 1840s the price of a 4 lb loaf of bread had sunk to 10d, putting it within reach of many labouring families. Bread could be purchased from Wood's bakery or from Mary Hodge's Hotel and Bakery, and Jane Barron's Wheatsheaf Inn, as well as from several smaller establishments. Throughout this period flour tended to be purchased direct from the Commissariat Store or from the several millers of Perth, including Reveley (when his costly machinery was functioning, which was rarely), Kingsford, and, on the South Perth side, Shenton. But for much of this period the price of flour was kept artificially high and caused great hardship to many of the poorer colonists. Even when they were paid in wheat, they had to meet the miller's costs—they were squeezed each way and suffered accordingly.

This was less true of drink. Good drinking water was to be had from several wells put down by the Government, and from the private wells also. There was in addition the spring at the foot of Mt Eliza near the settlement there. Sometimes the water was polluted, when wells were placed too close to cess-pits. But the health of even the labourers benefited from the absorbant character of Perth's sandy soil which reduced the amount of soakage. The settlers required more than water however, as temperance visitors like the Rev. Backhouse noted to their dismay.[73] The importation of spirits provided the Government with its principal source of revenue. Most settlers of substance imported large quantities of rum, as well as hogsheads of ale, and even bottled beer. This was used by themselves or as wages for workers. Rum and ale were also available from the numerous taverns and inns in Perth.[74] Some settlers brewed their own beer, without license. But by 1840 Perth had two breweries, the best known of which was Stoke's Albion (later Stanley) Brewery, under Mt Eliza, on the site of the present Emu Brewery. It was well received by the people of Perth: 'A wholesome beverage produced in the colony is far better than the trashy stuff generally imported'.[75] The other brewer in these years was Henry Strickland (1842) in St George's Terrace. Colonial beer was a boon to the working men of Perth.

*James Stokes advertises his new Albion Brewery. (**Perth Gazette**, 2 May 1840.)*

BREWERY.—Mr. Stokes' brewery presents a very businesslike appearance, and, we are informed, will soon be fully at work. The arrangements for facilitating a great extent of business are equal to the object contemplated, and we expect we shall have, before long, a supply of malt liquor from this establishment. The undertaking is one which claims every encouragement, and from the persevering manner in which it has been prosecuted, will no doubt meet its reward. A wholesome beverage produced in the colony is far better than the trashy stuff generally imported.

71 *Perth Gazette*, 18 January 1840.
72 See Cara Cammilleri 'Walter Padbury 1820-1907', *Early Days* Vol. 7, Pt. III, 1971, p.52; also *Perth Gazette*, 28 August 1847, 10 June 1848.
73 J. A. Backhouse *A Narrative of a Visit to the Australian Colonies*, 1843, p.536: 'Spirit drinking, and avarice in obtaining grants of large extent, have paralysed the country.' He also ascribed drinking as the cause of many deaths in Swan River.
74 See Trevor Tuckfield 'Early Colonial Inns and Taverns', *Early Days* Vol. 7, Pt. III, 1971, pp.65-83.
75 *Perth Gazette*, 11 April 1840.

If the gentry-officials were somewhat inconvenienced by the trading and market system, the labouring class were almost ruined by it. Labourers were often paid in kind, usually grog, clothing, and flour, the value of which was calculated at what the masters paid out to the merchants, and sometimes higher. What did it avail a labourer to receive a higher wage than he would have received in Britain for the same work, if his costs were even greater than at home and the 'wage' in any case paid in goods calculated at even higher than market rates? On 10 August 1833 MacFaull reported that

> The high retail prices we are exposed to, and the constant fluctuations in the market, which fall so heavy on the labouring classes, has led to the formation of a Union Society in Perth, which will strike at the root of monopoly and prove a salutary check on the extortionate.

He was pleased to report that the co-operative society

> at this moment . . . is saving 20% in the article of bread alone, a strong incentive to further combination. The method they have adopted is, to subscribe a certain sum weekly, which places funds in the hands of the Treasurer, with which he makes purchases, directly from the ship.

MacFaull had hoped that the Society's action would cause merchants to reduce their prices, but in March 1834 he was again grumbling about the high price of flour as a result of 'stock being confined to a very few hands'.[76] In May 1834 MacFaull refuted rumours that the Society had been beaten by the merchants:

> The saving thus occasioned with economy and frugality, places in the hands of a most deserving class of men (namely mechanics), the means of a further increase in their store and provision for the casualties of life, which the extravagant, not to say extortionate, prices of the present day, can leave them but little hope of acquiring.[77]

The standard 4 lb loaf of bread, which in March cost a high 1s6d, had suffered a 75% increase by June, reaching 2s6d. By June, MacFaull was losing patience with the artisans. Noting some of them doing Government sustenance work clearing ground between the Commissariat Store and the new jetty, he wrote

> How they have been reduced to require this assistance, unless by extravagance and intemperance, we are at a loss to conjecture. It is true that the prices of the necessaries of life have for some time back been extremely high, but these could not run away with the 5s or 6s per day . . . Surely some trifle might have been laid aside to provide against the winter season; but no![78]

He added that Mr J. R. Phillips of the Canning was prepared to pay men £1 per month with food but without grog: 'the latter proviso, we suspect, will be a bar to the entertainment of the proposition on the part of the labourers'. The Society folded shortly after. MacFaull felt let down. The fact of the matter was that men in uncertain employment and paid part in kind, could not save money even if they wanted to, and some at least did want to.[79] The artisans and labourers lacked the cash reserves to bid successfully against the merchants on the wharf or to charter supply ships. Their experience in 1833 and 1834 gives one level of meaning to the old settler's observation that 'the labourer lies wholly at the mercy of his master'.

ON SALE
AT THE
STORES OF THE UNDERSIGNED,
At Perth and Fremantle,
FOR CASH ONLY,
AT THE ANNEXED PRICES,

	Wholesale	Retail
CAPE Wines, 4s 6d. per gal.		5s per gal
Ditto beef, 4½d per lb.		6d per lb.
Ditto butter, 10d per lb.		1s. per lb.
Irish, Indian Pork, £11 per tierce.		10½d per lb
American ditto, £5 per barrel		8d per lb
Sydney beef. 4½d. per lb.		6d per lb
Ditto tongues,		2s each.
Ditto bacon, 10½d per lb.		1s per lb
Ditto ditto heads and pieces,		11d per lb
Ditto soap, 8d per lb.		10d per lb
Ditto dip candles, 10d per lb.		1s per lb
Ditto mould ditto, 1s per lb.		14d per lb
Ditto cheeses,		1s per lb
Ditto soap, 9d per lb.		1s per lb
English hops, 4s. per lb.		5s per lb
Black pepper, 9d per lb.		1s per lb
Segars, 25s per 1000.		3s per 100

A variety of Sydney slippers, shoes and ankle boots, from 2s. per pair and upwards
London ladies' shoes, 7s and 8s. per pair
Ditto gentlemen's ditto, and boots, various
Ditto ditto black beaver hats, 20s to 30s. each
Ditto best gin, bottled, 25s. per dozen
A variety of tinware, consisting of lamps, lanthens, candlesticks, candle boxes, tea kettles, wash basins, dishes, spirit drawers, lamp-feeders, slop pails, funnels, saucepans, sets of Imperial measures, quart and pint pots and pannicans
Common knives and forks, .. 5s. per doz
Superior ditto ditto, .. 20s
Seine twine, .. 2s6d per lb.
Cut glass tumblers, wine glasses, &c., various.
Three-inch deal planks, 11d per foot
Coir rope, 1s per lb.
London mustard, pickles, salad oil, &c, &c.
Wheat, .. 13s. per bushel
Oats .. 8s.
A variety of iron-ware, consisting of ploughs, spades, hoes, axes, pickaxes, nails, &c, &c.
Corks, .. 4s. per gross
Dutch cheese, .. 1s per lb.
Crockery ware, (plates, cups and saucers, basins &c, &c.), various
Slop clothing, linen drapery, haberdashery, and hosiery
A number of panneled deal doors, 25s & 30s. each
Deal frames for window sashes, 6s. each
Raisins and other dried fruits
Westphalia hams, .. 1s 6d per lb.
Iron in bar and rod, .. 3d. per lb.
Ash oars, .. 9d per foot
White, black, and green paint
A quantity of pewter plates and basins, various
A variety of stationery
New four bushel sacks, .. 4s each
Window glass of various dimensions.
&c, &c., &c. G. LEAKE.
February 4, 1834.

'The extravagant, not to say extortionate, prices of the present day': the making of George Leake's fortune?

76 *Perth Gazette*, 15 March 1834.
77 *Perth Gazette*, 24 May 1833.   78 *Perth Gazette*, 7 June 1834.
79 See letter from 'Old Settler' in *Perth Gazette*, 14 June 1834.

Even for the investing-class the exchange system in Swan River was chaotic. But the attempts to make it less so underline the 'family' character of investing class relationships. When in 1835 the merchant William Lamb planned a private note issue of 500 £1 notes, he lodged his security repayment with the Stone brothers 'whose standing was unquestioned'.[80] But schemes such as this were less successful than a natural or informal system of barter which demanded considerable co-operation among the investors. For example, a house owner advertised that for rent 'stores will be taken at the market price'.[81] Marshall MacDermott, who owned land in Perth and on the Swan, and who was to become a banker in Perth and Adelaide, recalled that

> If you required a team of horses, the person desirous of selling one did not want what you could offer in exchange but wished for sheep. You then applied to an owner of sheep who desired something you did not possess; and frequently two or three exchanges were necessary before you could procure the articles you wanted.[82]

Buttressing the barter system was a promissary note system, and when the Civil Court was established in 1832 it dealt with hundreds of petty disputes arising from both exchange systems, indeed 250 in 1832 alone. Early in 1833 the *Perth Gazette* wrote that

> The establishment of a Court of Civil Judicature in this Colony was hailed with general satisfaction, but has tended to the diffusion of a spirit of litigation amongst us, which it is painful to see growing with our growth. The list last Court day, comprised 22 unimportant cases . . . In so small a community, it is a lasting reflection upon us.[83]

But by the late 1830s more than 2000 cases had been heard by the Court, the records of which form as important a source of early economic history of Western Australia as the *Government Gazette*, Lands records, and private papers. In fact nearly every employer in the colony, including the gentry officials, appeared in court as defendant and plaintiff.[84] The leading men knew that all this was not in their own interests, but as long as they had to pay 25% or more interest on cash loans, the chaotic exchange system with court action as its concomitant must continue. The high rate of interest was of course another reason why so few labourers and artisans were able to acquire and develop property in Swan River. Plans for a bank had been floated since the early 1830s, and a public meeting in Perth in February 1835[85] had called for the immediate establishment of a bank. But none of the eastern colonial banks were interested in establishing a branch in Perth.

By 1837, however, despite the unsatisfactory exchange system, the investing class in Swan River had begun to export wool, whale oil, timber and horses. In this general period of optimism and progress it was estimated by Marshall MacDermott that it was at last possible to accumulate sufficient cash to make a bank reserve. In January 1837 a small meeting of leading merchants and officials, presided over by Governor Stirling, established the Bank of Western Australia.[86] The capital was set at £10,000 in shares of £10 each. Notes of £1 were to be

---

[80] This and much of the following is drawn from S. J. Butlin *Foundations of the Australian Monetary System*, 1953, p.383ff.
[81] *Perth Gazette*, 10 August 1833.
[82] MacDermott's Autobiography, cited Butlin *Foundations*, p.386.
[83] *Perth Gazette*, 13 April 1833.
[84] Civil Court Record Book, held in the Supreme Court of Western Australia.
[85] *Perth Gazette*, 21 February, 1835.   [86] *Perth Gazette*, 7 January 1837.

issued, and loans were to bear an interest rate of 12½%. The creators of the Bank, the first director and first shareholders, included the Colonial Secretary Peter Broun; the Assistant Commissary General John Lewis; the merchant and Government Auctioneer, Lionel Samson and his brother William; the merchants George Leake and William Habgood; the farmer-merchant and secretary of the colony's most important pressure group, the Agricultural Society, Sam Moore; the pastoralist W. L. Brockman; Dr Hinds and Marshall MacDermott. Initially the bank had sixty-four shareholders, a fair indication of the concentration of wealth in Perth after nearly ten years of settlement.[87]

Directors and shareholders of the first Bank of Western Australia.

---

[87] See *Perth Gazette*, 4 July 1840; there is a list of the 'partners' of the WA Bank in *CSO* Vol. 61, 1838, p.76.

The new Bank of Western Australia was operated by the investing class in its own interest: it was one of those institutions whereby the gentry were enabled to maintain and extend their power in the decision-making processes of the colony and to determine the proper relationships of classes within it. The directors decided that they would not release cash if a ship was known to be due in port. They themselves could purchase the ship-load of goods, and then release the Bank's money at favourable rates to the general public. The recipients of the Bank's money would then have to turn to the merchandising bankers for the purchase of their goods.[88] In part this was of course the system which the artisans had tried to introduce as a co-operative society in the mid-1830s; the difference was that they had sought to protect their own interests, while the banker merchants extended theirs and exploited others. The bankers also sought to increase the pool of investable money by inculcating habits of thrift among the more respectable members of the working class; and to this end they offered an interest of 5% on savings deposits. But the optimism and progress which was enabling the investing class to set its monetary affairs in some order had not extended down to the lower orders, other than some builders and contractors, and few deposits were made. Once again the workers had let down MacFaull, the well-intentioned Wakefieldian editor of the *Perth Gazette*:

> It is to be presumed that the laboring classes are not aware of the fact of this institution (the savings bank) being established by the promoters of the West Australian Bank as a preventive of improvidence, and the extravagant expenditure of the sums they acquire from steady application and labour . . . Savings Banks are not instituted for the wealthy and learned members of society.[89]

Some of the labourers would not have accepted the validity of the last sentence; but in any case, most of them earned too little and had high expenditures on rent and food and clothing, as well as the 'extravagant' expenditures that made life in Swan River bearable, to have anything left for deposit in a savings bank.[90]

By 1841 the Bank of Western Australia was returning a handsome dividend to its shareholders. Western Australia still did not have a convict population to provide very cheap labour; nor did it have the large expenditure of public money which characterised penal establishments. But it seemed to be prospering, and the imperial Bank of Australasia reversed an earlier decision and opened a branch at Swan River in 1841. It entered the field with dramatic effect, for it caused the closure of the Bank of Western Australia, recruited local directors like Peter Broun, George Leake, and Lionel and William Samson, and appointed Marshall MacDermott as manager. The shareholders of the old Bank of Western Australia divided fairly evenly (57 to 51) over the disposition of funds, some wishing to invest in the Bank of Australasia and others keen to form a new WA Bank.[91] Indeed a new local bank came into being. Called the Western Australian Bank, its strongest supporters initially were William Tanner, Dr Hinds, G. F. Stone, Sam Moore from the old bank, the Surveyor General Septimus Roe, and Perth businessmen T. R. C. Walters and W. J. Laurance, as well as a wealthy landed newcomer,

[88] *Perth Gazette*, 8 August 1846, 1 August 1840.
[89] *Perth Gazette*, 17 October 1840.
[90] Note Moore *Diary*, p.406—even his labourers were talking of striking for higher wages.
[91] Butlin *Foundations*, p.395; also *Perth Gazette*, 24 March, 24 April 1841.

Edward Hamersley, who had recently purchased Spring Park from the former Governor, Stirling.[92]

The existence of the two banks helped to cushion the effect on WA of the depression in the eastern colonies, at least to 1844. But by the mid-1840s the competition had become so fierce that the Bank of Australasia, which may also have been in trouble elsewhere, decided to pull out of Western Australia, and its cashier, John Lewis, committed suicide. Certainly the Western Australian Bank had done well. In fact in its first year of trading it had reported a gross profit of just over 40%. MacDermott had countered with an expansionary lending programme, but it seems clear that he took too many risks with suspect borrowers, and eventually the Western Australian Bank had been able to undercut him with discounted rates of interest. The Leakes and Samsons came back to the fold and the investing class once again co-operated to further their own ends, and through their influence in the Legislative Council ensured that there were few Government controls over the operation of the Bank. Not until 1927 was the Western Australian Bank taken over by a larger bank. Thus for nearly one hundred years of the history of Perth it was a major institution for the maintenance and exercise of power.

The early 1840s also saw the beginnings of insurance in Perth. In 1841 the London-based Australian Colonial and General Life Assurance and Annuity Coy, with Sir James Stirling and Charles Mangles as directors, appointed Sam Moore (George Fletcher's farmer/merchant brother) its Swan River agent. He was succeeded in 1850 by A. H. Stone, the agency's first policy holder. Roe and the WA Bank also handled the agency's business which remained solely the province of the gentry/officer class for many years. The Company enjoyed a monopoly in insurance until 1860.[93]

Roads and Bridges

The more prosperous years of 1837 and 1838 had brought into existence not only the colony's first bank, but also its first local government councils. The early allotment and building regulations had been promulgated by Stirling, who had also advised lot owners that the

> conservation of the roads, paths and plantations will be committed to the charge of the commissioners of crown lands, who will assess on each house its proportion of the expense.[94]

As the first land commissioners were the Government officials Septimus Roe and George Fletcher Moore, there is little to suggest that they functioned full-heartedly as a commission. In 1834 they authorised the construction of a narrow clay-based road for St George's Terrace, and in 1836 and 1837 they managed to spend £501 and £330 on sundry improvements for the colony as a whole. In 1837 Stirling reported to the Secretary of State for Colonies that

> At the present time it can scarcely be said that any roads exist, although certain lines of communication have been improved by clearing them of timber and by bridging streams and by establishing ferries in the

WESTERN AUSTRALIAN BANK.
_____
ESTABLISHED 23rd JUNE, 1841.

PRESENT CAPITAL, £20,000, IN 2,000 SHARES OF £10

DIRECTORS:—

W. Knight, Esq.	Robt. deBurgh, Esq.
J. G. C. Carr, Esq.	G. F. Stone, Esq.
I. S. Leake, Esq.	Alfred Hillman, Esq.
George Shenton, Esq.	

FRANCIS LOCHEE, Esq., Cashier and P.O.

Agents in London.—The Bank of South Australia, 54, Old Broad Street, E.C.
" South Australia.—The Bank of South Australia.
" New South Wales, Victoria, and Queensland.—The Bank of New South Wales.
" India, Mauritius, and Singapore.—The Oriental Bank Corporation.
" New Zealand.—The Bank of New South Wales.
" Hobart Town.—The Commercial Bank.
" Batavia.—The Chartered Bank of India, Australia, and China.

Fremantle Agency.—W. D. Moore, Esq.
Geraldton Agency.—C. Crowther, Esq.

The Bank purchases Bills on England and other countries, issues Drafts on its several Agents, and transacts every description of Banking business.

---

92   _Perth Gazette_, 28 November 1840.
93   E. S. Whiteley 'The Birth and Progress of Insurance', _Early Days_ Vol. 10, 1947, pp.41–7.
94   _CSO_ Vol. 4, 1830, p.2.

broader parts of the Swan River... The funds available for this purpose are appropriated to the removal of these inconveniences which press most heavily upon the Settler.[95]

It was scarcely surprising therefore that the state of the roads of Perth and Fremantle and the connecting lines between them and Guildford were a constant source of grievance to landowners and labourers. When, for instance, the respected merchant Lionel Samson was 'heavily thrown from his horse' while travelling along the Fremantle road, his misadventure was attributed by the *Perth Gazette*[96]

to the want of proper caution on the part of the Commissioners of Roads and Bridges.

Many a horseman had taken a tumble while travelling along the Fremantle road. But it was a tribute to Samson's standing in the community that one week after his encounter with a tree stump the Government invited tenders for

a new and more direct route between Perth and Fremantle to be opened up 15 ft wide by rooting up and clearing away all trees, brushwood, fallen timber and stumps.[97]

Tenders were also called for 'some improvements to the footpaths in the main street of Perth', and the construction of a pathway of clay and rubble stones from Pier Street to the Court house and the Commissariat. Moore and Roe continued to act as Commissioners until mid-1838. As late as February 1838 they were

engaged all day in visiting the 'flats or shallows', about Perth, for the purpose of reporting upon the practicability of making a passage across by rampart and bridge. We were obliged to walk about in our shirts through the water, under the burning sun, so that the skin has come off my face and legs.[98]

It was virtually their last, and easily their most strenuous, activity as Commissioners, for Stirling had decided, and the Commissioners concurred, that the colony was now in a state of prosperity and possessed enough 'fit and proper' persons to form town trusts. (Stirling had sought Moore's advice on this in 1836, but at that time Moore believed that the colony had too few affluent men with leisure to take part in the work of a trust).[99] Legislation to create a town trust and a general road trust was drawn up in March 1838, introduced into the Legislative Council on 19 May, and enacted a month later.[100] The Act provided for the appointment of Trustees who were to be justices of the peace and proprietors of land held in fee simple within the proclaimed limits of Perth. The Bill further provided for quarterly meetings and an annual general meeting in January, and the collection of monies from tolls and voluntary subscriptions and Government grants; and an amendment early in 1839 empowered the Trustees to make rate assessments for town improvements.[101] With a bank and a town trust it seemed that Perth was coming of age.

95 *SRP*, 1837, Report; now available as separate document in Battye Library.
96 *Perth Gazette*, 12 August 1837.   97 *Perth Gazette*, 19 August 1837.
98 Moore *Diary*, p.337.   99 Moore *Diary*, p.298.
100 *Perth Gazette*, 1838, 1 Vic. No. 2: 'An Act to provide for the Management of Roads, Streets and other Internal Communications within the Settlement of Western Australia.'
101 *Perth Gazette*, 4 April 1839; 1839, 2 Vic. No. 5: 'An Act to enable the Inhabitants of any Township to Assess Themselves for the Improvement of the Town.'

But the first public meeting of men qualified to become Town Trustees was so poorly attended that the business could not be proceeded with; the meeting was adjourned for a week. George Fletcher Moore, who had chaired the first meeting, printed an advertisement in which he urged landed townsmen to 'sign a Declaration of Qualification and to exercise their right of voting in the choice of Officers'. The same issue of the *Perth Gazette* editorialised:

> It is a matter of some moment that all those who hold allotments in fee simple should make a point of attending... as they are individually interested in the appointment of their chairman and local directors, who will be chosen by ballot.[102]

It was also true that, as Moore put it in his *Diary* (p.357) at this time, 'everybody wishes to have the roads made, but nobody wishes to pay for them'. At the adjourned meeting George Leake was elected first chairman; most of his fellow directors were paid Government officials, including Septimus Roe and Henry Reveley. There was also Henry Trigg, for whom, thanks to Government contracts, Swan River had become a place of plenty; and Charles MacFaull, editor of the *Perth Gazette*, an occasional critic of Tory rule, but who was heavily dependent on Government advertisements to keep his head above water. The Trust attempted to initiate a programme of activity for the next year, but it immediately ran into difficulties. Firstly, the Civil Engineer, Reveley, resigned prior to his departure from Swan River. Henceforth the work of the Trust was bedevilled by lack of continuity in personnel. Then the Trust was faced with a revolt over its plan to upgrade St George's and Adelaide Terraces. Some of the Perth traders wanted money spent creating a road on the river's edge instead—the so-called Bazaar Terrace line. This proposal in turn alarmed some of the landowners of Bazaar Terrace, for they had privately extended their boundaries southwards to include a river frontage. Indeed some of these had actually built houses directly on the line of road as surveyed in 1829–30. It transpired that only the Secretary of State for Colonies could resolve Perth's Bazaar Street controversy, so the matter was shelved for some time. The Trust then decided to proceed with the St George's Terrace plan, but this too was abandoned when leading landowners refused to allow themselves to be taxed the full £1000 required for the work.

In fact the newly appointed Clerk of Works, Mr Charles Brown, seems to have had so little to do that he resigned after six months. The first rate struck was for 10s per allotment (June 1839), but little of this was collected, even though it was payable in two instalments of 5s each.

At the annual general meeting held in January 1840, only seven ratepayers troubled to attend. With a cheering optimism they increased the size of the Directorate from five to seven and then elected themselves to it. George Leake remained as Chairman. But a missing face was Charles MacFaull. Always suspicious of Government officials, MacFaull had been incensed by the recent appointment of Henry Trigg as Government Superintendent of Works, which position was popularly regarded as a sinecure. MacFaull retired to become a vitriolic critic of the Trust and all its works, or rather its lack of them.[103] Leake again courted the displeasure of his fellow investors when a charge of £1 11s 6d was put on each allotment to pay for a new footpath along the north side of St George's Terrace. The newly appointed rate collector, Mr Strudwicke,

[102] *Perth Gazette*, 28 July 1838.   [103] *Perth Gazette*, June 1839; 25 January 1840.

battled hard for a month and then resigned, having collected nothing from the intransigent landowners. In July 1840 John Chipper, a man made of sterner stuff, was appointed not only rate collector, but the impounder of stray cattle (of which there were plenty in the town), the licensee for wood cutting and stone quarrying within the town boundaries; he could also levy taxes on people bringing cartloads of firewood and clay into the town, and lay charges against horsemen who insisted on riding along the town's precious footpath. Chipper was decidedly busy, but he too had to live with the landowners' unrelenting hostility to all forms of taxation. As MacFaull put it in an editorial inciting tax evasion: 'Will it be credited that in the midst of a forest we have to pay duty for our few logs of fuel'.[104] Hampered by lack of funds the Trust yet succeeded in reconstructing the St George's Terrace footpath, only to see its new clay surface washed away by the first winter rains, causing MacFaull to comment acidly:

> The footpaths . . . have been tried by the late rains and the plan for their formation . . . is shamefully defective. It seems that we have nothing better to do with our money, but must needs pour it into the sand.[105]

In 1841 a new survey of St George's Terrace reduced its width from 93 feet to 66 feet, but even so, the best that the Trust could do was to lay a 15 feet strip of rubble and clay down the middle. This crumbled badly at the unsecured edges and won the Trust further disapproval.

Another issue with which the Trust grappled in 1840 and 1841 was the provision of a town jetty on the Swan. Since the foundation of Perth goods and people had been landed down by the flats or on the 'beaches' below the town. Often the mud was so deep that craft were moored off-shore, with the following results:

> The present practice of landing passengers 'pick a pack', the boatman being obliged to wade through mud for the extent of thirty or forty yards, is hazardous and unpleasant . . . those who have suffered as we have done, by two or three falls in the mud, we are convinced will as strenuously urge some improvement.[106]

In November 1841 the Trust issued £10 debentures to pay for the construction of a jetty at the foot of (King) William Street. The debentures would return 10% interest, and seem to have been taken up by some of the Trust's directors and Government officials. But others in the town were also seeking to benefit from increased trading, and on 24 November 1841 the *Inquirer* wrote that

> A sudden rage would appear to have sprung up in Perth on the subject of jetties. Until this week . . . it was somewhat doubtful whether we should have even one, and now we are promised three, within a quarter of a mile of each other—namely the Perth Town Trust jetty at the end of William St; the second, projected by a public company, at the end of Mill St; and the third, a private one, at the end of Barrack St to be run by our enterprising townsman Mr H. L. Cole.

The Town Trust jetty was to be opened officially on 1 June 1842 with a thirteen gun salute (it being the colony's 13th birthday). The jetty workmen were to be provided with old English brown ale or stout, and plum buns made from colonial flour—they were expected to drink success to the jetty and to give three hearty cheers for the town of Perth and the colony of Western Australia. It was to be a memorable day. But

---

[104] Cited Uren *Land Looking West*, p.55.
[105] *Perth Gazette*, 6 June 1840.   [106] *Perth Gazette*, 2 March 1833.

The Causeway or Perth Bridge, 1840s. (Photograph taken after a flood in 1862.)

work on the jetty proceeded slowly, and not until November would it be opened—'the ale is now sour and the cakes are musty'.[107] As the *Perth Gazette* commented: 'The affairs of the Town Trust are thrown into the most admired confusion'.[108] The Perth merchant James Purkis took over the chairmanship until the Annual General Meeting early in 1842, when W. B. Andrews, one of the colony's first landowners, took over from him. The directorate included Peter Broun, George Leake and Lionel Samson. In January 1842 the Trust's balance sheet showed a working capital of £22 4s 6d, lodged with the Western Australian Bank. The election had revealed an anomaly regarding the eligibility of voters. Under the 1838 Act only freehold owners of an entire allotment were eligible to vote. This did not matter much until allotments came to be subdivided on a relatively large scale. By the early 1840s several St George's Terrace frontages, as well as Hay Street blocks had been subdivided. This meant, for example, that at the 1842 election only four of the Hay Street houseowners could exercise a vote. The anomaly was removed later in the year when the Act was amended.[109]

One of the most important town developments in these years took place outside the ken of the Town Trust. This was the construction of the causeway bridge across the river flats to the east of the town, built between 1840 and 1843 under the direction of the General Road Trust.[110] The bridge was easily the most ambitious construction undertaken in the colony, and when completed it considerably expedited travel between Perth and Guildford and the Canning area. Users were charged a toll (the tollkeeper was John Crane) with double rate at night. Indeed it led to a major upgrading of the left bank road through Belmont, and the construction of the South Guildford Bridge over the Helena River.[111] In the mid and late 1840s the Perth Road Trust accomplished very little. In 1846 it discussed the possibility of laying a wooden-block road along St George's Terrace, but not even the Government's offer of the use of prison labour could tempt the Trust, led by Purkis for most of the 1840s, into committing itself to such a large expenditure. Instead H. L. Cole's tender for yet another stone and clay road was accepted, despite the

---

[107] *Perth Gazette*, 30 April, 5 November 1842.
[108] *Perth Gazette*, 18 December 1841.   [109] *Perth Gazette*, 1844, 8 Vic. No. 2.
[110] Minutes of the General Road Trust, 28 February 1839; 27 May 1840; 5 January 1842, Battye Library Acc. No. 491.
[111] See P. Hasluck 'Guildford and the Swan', *Early Days*, Vol. 1, Pt. II, 1928.

likelihood of it too being swept away by the winter rains. Shortage of money was always the problem for the Trust. In 1849, in a desperate attempt to raise money, it threatened to sue absentee landlords through their local agents, and a list of defaulters was published in the *Government Gazette*. But the cost of collection was as great as the income so gained, and the short-term problem was not resolved. This was largely because the colony as a whole was in the grip of a severe depression from about 1844 onwards, and even such vital entrepreneurs as George Leake, Lionel Samson, and George Shenton, all directors, had little stomach for large-scale Trust projects.[112]

By 1847 it was clear to the Government that neither the General Road Trust nor the Perth Town Trust was meeting the colony's needs. It therefore created a Central Board of Works, the funds for which were to come from a tax on the export of sandalwood. This change produced a torrent of abuse from the businessmen, including some of the Perth Trust directorate, who were profiting from the sandalwood trade. They became especially abusive in mid-1848 when the price of sandalwood per ton fell to only £13, but the tax was retained.[113] Even before this the Central Board of Works had won for itself an unenviable reputation for the poor construction of roads and its neglect of necessary works—there was still no clay section in Adelaide Terrace down to the causeway, and daily one heard 'the tearing and straining of teams, dragging heavy loads of farm produce from the country, up the sandy hill from the tollgate'.[114] The Perth merchants offered to pay a subscription into a road fund if the tax on sandalwood was lifted,[115] but Acting Governor Irwin, who was not engaged in the sandalwood trade, held firm against them.

By mid-1848 the matter of viable local government through the trusts, and the role of the Central Board of Works, had become inextricably bound up with general criticism of the Government and a growing interest in the introduction of convicts. The *Perth Gazette* commented, with reference to the impending arrival of the new Governor:

> Verily Captain Fitzgerald will need a strong besom to sweep away the rotteness which prevails among us.[116]

In August it compiled a list of needed public works: a new road from Perth to Guildford; a new road from Guildford to Fremantle via the Canning; a bridge over the Canning; a bridge over the Swan at Fremantle; and a hard road through Perth (Cole's road had survived a few winters but had been cut up by the town's herd of cattle). All this in addition to a new gaol, a new schoolhouse, the draining of the lakes behind Perth (the floods of 1842 and 1847 had covered the town north of Hay Street with a single sheet of water from Lake Kingsford to Claise Brook, while the runoff down to Perth Water had damaged St George's Terrace premises and road), the removal of the rocky bar across the mouth of the Swan, and a new Government House (for white ants had made the existing one unsafe).[117] In 1849 the Central Board of Works was about to be abolished; but the Trust went its unhappy way through

---

[112] *Perth Gazette*, 24 August, 10, 17 October 1846, 23 January 1847: 'We however struggle against all reverses, and living in hope, we trust the colony will not die of despair'; also 7 April, 17 November 1849.
[113] *Perth Gazette*, 13 May 1848. [114] *Perth Gazette*, 12 February 1848.
[115] *Perth Gazette*, 4 September 1847. [116] *Perth Gazette*, 13 May 1848.
[117] *Perth Gazette*, 5 August 1848; 12 October 1849.

to the late 1850s. The major change in these years was the decrease in officer-gentry representation on the Trust and the emergence of men whose interests were bound even more intimately to the town of Perth—George Lazenby, Bernard Smith, and Bayley Maycock being typical examples.

Buildings and Builders

By the late 1840s a pattern of settlement had been clearly established in Perth. In general the regulatory changes of the 1830s and 1840s led to a consolidation of property ownership in a few hands. Originally, for instance, a number of labourers had been granted leases on lots on Adelaide Terrace. But early in 1833 new 'Regulations relative to Town and Suburban Allotments in Western Australia' required that owners of lots in St George's Terrace and Adelaide Terrace must build houses to the value of £200. Inevitably few labourers were able to meet this requirement and from September 1834 when the lots could be purchased freehold (at a minimum price of £5) they were resumed and sold to more affluent men. As the same regulations required that houses to the value of £100 should be built on Bazaar Terrace and other streets of Perth, it is clear that the lesser men would buy (when they could) these properties. In 1835 Perth contained seventy houses valued at more than £150 each. It was a fair indication of the concentration of wealth in the town.

By 1840 there was a housing shortage in Perth. Rents were very high (for example, Francis Armstrong let a four-room cottage with cellar and river views for £30 a year), and allotments under Mt Eliza were selling from £30 to £60 each unimproved. With heavy demand, some of the wealthier landowners began to subdivide their properties. One who did so was the Rev. J. B. Wittenoom who in September 1840 sold the top half of L1 and L2 (south-west corner of Barrack Street and St George's Terrace) for £400. This block was further sub-divided in 1841. The process of sub-division was facilitated by the Government's decision to relax a provision that building could only take place in the middle of a block and 30 feet from the street boundary. Henceforth (from March 1841) buildings could be constructed up to the footpath line and right across the block. When the street width was reduced from 93 feet to 66 feet (March 1841), and buildings were brought forward to the new line, there was still, however, a sense of spaciousness to the physical appearance of the town. It was also in 1841 that Governor Hutt cracked down on absentee landlords and others who had not met the improvements regulations. He resumed a great number of blocks which were sold at auction mostly to the merchants, officers, and gentry (who by then had a local bank from which to borrow cash), for the limit on the number of blocks an individual could own had also been relaxed. In other ways, too, ownership of town land was consolidated in the hands of the ruling group. The town perimeter to the north had been divided into suburban lots of varying size but all in excess of an acre. They could be bought only by men who already possessed freehold land in the colony in excess of 1000 acres. The land so bought became a tremendously valuable asset as the town developed northwards in the convict period and after. Undoubtedly some of the purchasing was of a speculative character. For instance, the Leakes bought up lots in James Street on the

The prefabricated (imported) house of Perth townsman, Thomas Helms. (Constructed before 1850; photographed 1860s.)

61

Perth as Pastoral Myth: *early testimony by Horace Samson, 1847.*

north side of the town, though they lived in a more salubrious part. And when the decision was taken to construct the Causeway over Perth flats, and to upgrade the main road through the town, a number of prominent Perth men bought lots in the east and west ends of the town, believing that they would rapidly increase in value, as indeed they did, especially during the convict years. In all these ways the serving class was driven to take up land in unhealthy parts of the town—especially low lying Murray and Wellington Streets—or in streets some distance from the town centre, as in the settlement under Mt Eliza. Of the 400 or so houses in Perth in 1848 perhaps 250 were made of brick and belonged to the gentry officers and merchants, as well as affluent artisan/builders like Trigg and Maycock. Some were rented by working men. The rest of the houses were made of wood—often reeds and bushes, crudely constructed and extremely vulnerable to fire. (Perth did not possess a fire brigade until 1848, and given the thatched and shingled character of many cottages, so conducive to the rapid spread of fire, it was of limited utility.)[118]

By 1850 Perth possessed some solid buildings. The Georgian-style Anglican St George's Church was built on the central square in the 1840s. The Wesleyans too had built a towered church (in William Street) in 1840. The three-storey Commissariat Store, built in 1834, remained a

The Anglican Church of St George, central Perth, 1840s. (Photographed 1860s.)

prominent landmark on the river side. Mews' boatsheds under Mt Eliza and Kingsford's brick mill nearby bore testimony to the enterprise of their owners. The public buildings tended to be rather ramshackle. Indeed Government House, which bore 'more the appearance of a Lunatic Asylum than the residence of the representative of the Queen', was in danger of falling down so badly had it been ravaged by Perth's infamous white ants. Nor were the buildings on the public square particularly sound. The mud-walled Perth gaol was a source of public ridicule, so readily did Aboriginal inmates escape from it. And the old Colonial Hospital was an eyesore. When in 1848 it was decided to enlarge

[118] *Perth Gazette*, 20, 27 April 1833; 20 September 1834; 21 March 1835; 8 February, 28 March, 25 April, 9 May, 12 September, 28 December 1840; 13 March, 10 April, 26 June, 12 September 1841; 16 September 1848; *Census of WA*, 1848.

'More the appearance of a Lunatic Asylum than the residence of the representative of the Queen.': old Government House, 1830s–60s.

the Hospital, a cry of indignation from the citizenry ensured that it would be relocated away from the centre of town—indeed up near the Roman Catholic quarter to the east. The Roman Catholics had built there 'a great ornament to the Town of Perth'—The 'Holy Cross' Convent of the Sisters of Mercy.[119]

In the following one hundred years Perth would gain an enviable reputation for its open spaces and parks. The first of these was the square opposite the Government offices and St George's Church, the land which later became known as Stirling Gardens. From the beginning of settlement this block had been used for horticultural purposes, at first by the Colonial Botanist, James Drummond, and then on a leasehold basis to residents of Perth. It was cleared partly by Aboriginal prison labour, though Aborigines were not allowed to use the land. Along with the umbrageous mulberry trees planted along St George's Terrace outside the Anglican Church, the public gardens were a source of health and recreation to the class which used it. A contemporary record reads as follows:

> On warm summer days, the tired official may be allured from the monotonous avocations of his musty office, to saunter away an hour in this prettily situated garden . . . what can contribute more to resusitate the frame, exhausted by the scorching days, than this promenade, which commands the pleasing perspective of our beautiful Perth water.

To which was added:

> A few European trees judiciously planted about other open parts of the town, would contribute alike to the gratification of the eye, and the relief of the body . . . the invigorating sea breeze must not be obstructed: it should have uninterrupted play throughout every part of the town, so as to disperse the damp exhalations which are so injurious to health.[120]

This advice too was heeded for the next one hundred years.

119 *Perth Gazette*, 8 April, 6, 20 May 1848.
120 *Perth Gazette*, 24 April, 28 August 1847.

The Poor and the Dispossessed

While by the late 1830s the power relationships imported into Swan River were enhancing the gentry's quest for 'internal peace', their consequences for the labouring population were less happy. A George Fletcher Moore could see his life in Swan River as one long romp or adventure in the wilderness; but the employed classes were constrained in ways which rendered romanticism impossible. Few, if any, of them enjoyed a table such as the gentry made merry with at Leeder's Hotel on the occasion of the King's birthday celebrations in August 1833, with nine types of meat and a choice of three desserts.[121] Caught in a vicious cycle of poverty, bare subsistence, social and personal despair, and poverty again, the labouring classes were driven to act in ways which the gentry believed were central to their natures: they drank excessively, they bloodied each other and Aborigines and Lascars, they beat their womenfolk, they stole from all and sundry, and proportionately more of them committed suicide. Others endured their hardships in proud silence. These were among the ones held up by the gentry as the 'deserving poor'. Silence should not be taken as a sign that the sufferer acquiesced in his condition; for some, perhaps most, the cost of making a complaint or otherwise protesting was very high—so high indeed that one's condition could be worsened rather than bettered. As in the Great Depression one hundred years later, so throughout the history of Perth, labourers were told that if they stayed silent then things would get better for them. But in their silence they left few records of their condition. The historian must piece together their life experiences from evidence not usually of their own making, or at least not made by them with an eye on posterity. Even using court records, newspaper reports, statistical returns and the like, we see their lives as through a glass darkly. But the question must still be put: what was it like to live the life of the 'lower orders of society', those described as 'morally deformed'.[122]

On the *Caroline*'s voyage to Swan River in 1829 a carpenter/servant to Mr Henty, Charles Gee, composed and sang a song about the horrors of old England and the fine prospects of New Holland. The song went in part:

> Come all you English lads that have a mind to go
> Into some foring contery I would have you for to know
> Come join along with Henty and all his joiful crew
> For a set of better fellows in this world you never knew.

> Coris

> So is here is of to New Holland if God will spear our lifes
> All with littel families, hower sweethearts, and hower wifes
> Now all you I leves in England, I hope you may do well
> But allow me for one moment your fourchoen for to tell
> You must unto your Parish go to get small relife
> Weare you will be flounced and bounced about as if you weare a thif.

When Henty later went on to the eastern colonies Gee and his family stayed in Swan River, where for a time he found employment in Perth with Dr Milligan. Perhaps New Holland would still be good for those with 'littel families'.

---

[121] *Perth Gazette*, 24 August 1833.
[122] *Perth Gazette*, 8 March 1833.

Early in 1833 Charles Gee left the service of Dr Milligan in order to find work which would pay him sufficient to keep his wife and children in more comfort than the doctor had thought necessary. Fortune did not smile on him and one day in late autumn he returned to his former employer's house and stole from it a few bars of soap, intending, no doubt, to sell it in the town for the few shillings needed for a loaf of bread and a measure of ale. As he left the house he was seen by Milligan's new maid servant who, on finding soap missing from the storeroom, ran to tell the doctor that he had been robbed. (Had she not done so it is probable that she herself would have been charged with the theft, for masters turned on their servants with impunity.) The incensed Dr Milligan set off in the direction of the town centre, and on coming up to the Gees found the soap lying on the ground, rolled up in Mrs Gee's apron. After chastising Gee for acting so reprehensively towards a former employer, Milligan had him charged with theft. Placed in custody and hauled before the magistrate, Gee was imprisoned for three months. Mrs Gee and her small children were left to fend for themselves as best they could. She became vulnerable to the advances of men with money, while her young son William took to thievery, including the theft of potatoes. When released from gaol in due course, Gee found that he could not cope with his family's circumstances and his own ignominy. In court he had deposed that his wife was a good woman and 'as innocent as a child unborn, of the whole matter'. But by the spring of 1833, with the wildflowers coming beautifully into bloom and being so described by the gentry women, Gee was beating his wife with a rope. He was unable to pay a fine for this offence and found his way back to gaol on this and other occasions. His son embarked on a career of crime which led him to be described at twelve years of age as 'an old and hardened offender' and 'an incorrigible rogue'. Ditched by Mr Henty, persecuted by Dr Milligan, imprisoned by Mackie and Moore, the Gees were rendered useless as founders of the new society. The marriage broke up and the older children fended for themselves. A Charles Gee was transported in 1837 for the theft of a turkey. One of the five sons, also Charles, eventually won respectability as a policeman; two sons lived into the 1890s, each owning a four-room cottage in working class Wellington and Stirling Streets. Who could say that the family had done better in Perth than it would have done in the old country? Dr Milligan lived to see a street named after him, very close to the spot where he had shattered the fragile life of Charles Gee. And when Mrs Milligan was sued by an auctioneer for her failure to pay for goods she had purchased, the civil commissioner and high ball-room dancer, George Fletcher Moore, gently observed: 'I am afraid Mrs Milligan has fallen into a mistake'; he suffered her to pay merely the difference owing. For one family a single lapse was recoverable; for the other it spelt social disaster and the forbidding stench of criminality.[123]

One morning late in 1841, with sunshine on his shoulder, William Holmes left his hut and walked the short distance to the Mill Street jetty, where he was to commence three months' work for Mr Henry Laroche ('King') Cole, at the excellent rate of £3 cash per week for work on land.

[123] *Perth Gazette*, 1 June 1833, 30 November 1833; Supreme Court Record Book, Case 64, 1833, and Case 172, 1837; *Perth Gazette*, 10 August 1833, 15 February 1834, 24 January 1835, 16 January 1841, and City of Perth Rate Books for 1880s and 1890s; *Historical Records of Australia* Series III, Vol. VI, p.635; also M. Bassett *The Hentys*, 1954, pp.53–4 for Gee's song.

Colony of
Western Australia
to wit.

Deposition, taken before the
undersigned justices at Perth in
the said Colony the 29 day of
May 1833.

William Milligan of Perth aforesaid
Doctor of Medicine being duly sworn saith
Yesterday evening about half past eight
while myself and Mrs Milligan were
at Mr Wells' house, our female servant
came, ~~to her~~ and told her mistress
that some soap had been taken
out of our kitchen, and, as she
suspected, by the Prisoner Gee, who
had been seen running out of the
kitchen, a few minutes before the
soap was missed. I sent a message
to my nephew Francis Milligan
to follow Gee, and I also followed
on overtaking Gee, whose wife was
in company with him, I saw the
soap at the feet of Gee's wife

*Charles Gee: 'flounced and
bounced about' in New Holland.
(Section of Dr Milligan's Court
deposition, 1833.)*

A strong young man and a trained mason, he had won steady employment in the recent past, and now he had just married. As he came lightly down the hill to the jetty, the sunshine on Perth Water looked lovely. It was a moment for dreaming. Cole's foreman greeted him on the jetty. He was told that he must dress the stone as agreed, but that this could be done best with Holmes standing in the water alongside the jetty, rather than the water being carted to him on land. And so he began work. Each day, for the six days of his first working week, he dressed the stone for eight hours while standing waist-deep in the river. At the end of the week he collected his wages. To his surprise he was given only £2 in cash; the other £1 came in goods, valued by Mr Cole. Three weeks later Holmes was seriously ill. He had severe chilblains, respiratory and circulation problems, and migraine. The walk to the jetty became more painful each morning, and evening fell hard for him. The salt water ate at his legs and lower trunk, while the sunshine of Perth Water beat down unrelentingly on his head and shoulders. He wanted medicine, but the doctor would not accept goods as payment, so he went without. One morning he was unable to make the walk to the jetty. On this and several other days he stayed in his hut. He had sought a higher wage for high-risk work; he had sought agreement for the work to be done on land. Both were denied him. His master, Henry Laroche Cole, countered by taking the matter to the Court, which, despite evidence in his favour given by fellow artisans, found that Holmes was guilty of breaking his contract. He was ordered to return to work or go to gaol for a month. He would be there tomorrow, but his dreams would not. Crippled physically and financially, the Holmes' could not soar like a George Fletcher Moore. And when darkness came and pain was all around, who eased their minds?[124]

Lacking the comforts of religion and their lack of means denying them news of home and old friends (so important a source of social reassurance to the investing class), the servants, labourers, and soldiers of the 63rd and later regiments turned in on themselves for physical and spiritual sustenance, and released among themselves the frustrations of their condition. In the 1830s and 1840s they crowded into pubs like Thomas Dent's The Happy Emigrant, Edward and Jane Barron's The Wheat Sheaf Tavern, James Ougden's Jetty Tavern and Louis Mayo's Perth Hotel—all were off St George's Terrace which contained the fashionable United Services Tavern (owned by Cole from 1844 to 1854).[125] Mayo's Perth Hotel was a place which, as one investor, John Butler, put it, 'one didn't like to mix with the company that was there'.[126] The 'company that was there' would sing lewd variations of 'The Merry Month of May' and 'The Glasses Sparkle on the Board'; it would roar with laughter at the public rows of Thomas Davis and his drunken wife; it would talk of 'politics' and 'combination'; it would argue, even brawl, over whether or not Hunt and Foulkes had been sent to NSW and Van Diemen's Land 'for their country's good'; it would curse George Leake for bringing charges against Thomas Walsh for stealing a pair of boots; and it would earn the epithet 'drunken idlers' by deciding to fire off guns, on the pretext of celebrating the Battle of Waterloo, 'spreading a complete panic through the town'. 'The company that was there' would

124 *Perth Gazette*, 29 January 1842.
125 See T. Tuckfield 'Early Colonial Taverns and Hotels', *Early Days* Vol. 7, Pt. III, 1971, pp.102–3.
126 *Perth Gazette*, 18 May 1833.

do all this and much more.[127] The pub was the centre of an informal economy, where goods and cash (earned and stolen) exchanged hands, often through the mediation of the publican and his wife. It continued to be this through the convict years and beyond. At the pub also men could play bagatelle and such games. At the pub also men engaged in still coarser activities.

On Christmas eve 1832, John Velvick, servant to Mr J. R. Phillips on the Canning, was drinking at Mayo's in the company of thirty or so other men and women. A black Muslim, Samud Ali by name, came into Mayo's to get some grog to take back to his hut a short distance away in Murray Street, where he lived with other Lascars. Velvick said to him 'Black man, give me a glass of grog'. When Samud Ali refused, Velvick yelled at him: 'Oh you black bugger, if you do not give me a glass of grog I will kick your arse'. A scuffle then broke out, in the course of which Velvick received a slight blow from a stick wielded by Samud Ali or a companion, who then fled. Arming themselves with heavy sticks Velvick and his mates lurched around the back of Mayo's to where the black men were seated around their open fire in front of their hut. There about twenty white men beat the blacks until they were covered in blood. In court the next day Velvick had little to say about the incident except that he was there with others 'and we thrashed the black men because they had before thrashed some of our people'. The attack had its warped side for one of the participants, wielding a belt, had 'exulted that the blood of a black was on his body'. The court witnesses for the prosecution came from the investing class. One was James Purkis, merchant and later chairman of the Perth Town Trust; another was John Wittenoom, son of the Rev. J. B. Wittenoom. Both deposed in favour of the Lascars. In part at least they were motivated by a concern for the physical well-being of the Lascars, though not perhaps for altruistic reasons. The Lascars, perhaps forty of them, had been stranded in Swan River, when a ship on which they had been working was wrecked off Fremantle.[128] They were employed as cheap domestic servants by people like the Stones, the Barrett Lennards, William Tanner, Peter Broun, Richard Morrell and other investors. The plain fact of the matter was that blacks with broken heads would be inefficient servants, and should therefore be protected with the full force of the law. Another witness, David Paterson, was concerned about the black men's hut, for he was agent to the absentee investor, Hugh MacDonald, on whose lot the hut was located. Paterson deposed that on several occasions he had heard the whites who 'frequented Mayo's threaten to pull down the hut'. When cheap labour and private property were so endangered, the investing class chorused their fears to their colleagues on the bench. Velvick was sentenced to three months' imprisonment. By one of history's ironies he and his brother were speared to death by Aborigines a few months later.

In time too his host, Louis Mayo, left Perth. In September 1833 he almost lost his licence for keeping the pub open after hours. And around this time he took to abusing his wife Sarah, saying that he would 'suck her blood and eat her liver' for, he alleged, she provoked him by 'saying that she wished him dead, and such kind of language'. At his best he was a wild sort of fellow; drunk he was a demon who belted his wife mercilessly. He was forced to sell out to J. H. Monger and respectability,

---

[127] *Perth Gazette*, 24 January, 8, 18 June 1835; 6 July 1833; 22 August 1835.
[128] *CSO* Vol. 5, 1830, pp.112 and 133.

No	Defendant	Crime or Offence charged	Day of Com.t	Day of Trial	Judgment	Sentence	Rem...
1	George Balguison	Larceny		1st Octr 1830	Guilty	14 Days Imprist & to one publicly whip? 50 lashes	whipped a... in Fre...
2	Tom Brown	Simple Larceny		10th Jany 1831	Not Guilty	— — —	forthwith
3	Paul Lockyer	Simple Larceny		Same	Guilty	1 Cal. Viet Imprt with H.L.	
4	Robert No-ell	Larceny on River		4th April 1831	Not Guilty	— — —	forthwith
5	Mahomed a Lascar	Larceny		Same	Not Guilty	— — —	forthwith
6	William Harrison	Simple Larceny		Same	Guilty	4 Cal. Viet Imprt with H.L.	
7	Charles Spencer	Larceny		Same	Guilty	2 Cal. Viet Imprt with H.L.	
8	John Philip	Burglary		Same	Not Guilty	— — —	convicted ... an off? ... to 4 Cal. Viet with H.L. Remanded
9	Richard...	...		Same	Not Guilty		...

First page of the Western Australian Criminal Court Record Book No. 1, 1830–87.

and seems eventually to have cleared out of Perth leaving his family to survive on their wits.[129] But, 'for the company that was there', Mayo's had been a source of companionship and the cheering cup: for some at least it made life bearable in Swan River.

As for the battered Lascars, their story too is an integral part of the early history of Perth. They were not ideal or very docile servants. In fact, along with the privates of the 63rd and the 51st they were among the most unruly and troublesome of pioneers. One of them, Balquoizon, had the distinction of being the first-named in the colony's Criminal Court Record Book, for in September 1830 he committed a petty theft and was given 50 lashes at the Cart's Tail in Fremantle, where he spent fourteen days in gaol. A year later he was gaoled for theft again, this time for six months with hard labour. In February 1830 A. H. Stone, Clerk to the Civil Court and later first Master of the Supreme Court, sent his Lascar servant to prison for 14 days with six dozen lashes to be delivered publicly at the whipping post in front of the Perth Gaol. Carnow had had the audacity to steal no less than 10 gallons of wine from his thirsty master. It was not only the white labourers of Perth, therefore, who whipped the backs of servant blacks. In July 1833 the enterprising Habib stole some money from his master Richard Morrell, as he lay drunk and insensible on the floor of his house, having been reduced to that state by a raging toothache. Habib hid the money in the thatch of the black men's hut, but as that was usually the first place searched, it was found and Habib went to gaol for six months. Sylvester Dias, also a 'man of colour', stole from James Solomon's store a bottle of aniseed and a pudding, which he took to Mark Read the sawyer's hut to 'enjoy with Philip (Fernando), Captain McDermott's servant'. Dias was caught and went without aniseed and pudding for some time after. Some years later Fernando too went to gaol for a two year stretch. Oppressed, misused, and misunderstood, the Lascars of Perth formed an unhappy helot class during the 1830s and 1840s.[130]

The Lascars' lives intersected not only with those of white masters and white servants, but also with the lives of girls in Perth. Girls, indeed women generally, were at risk in a frontier environment with a preponderance of males. There were undoubtedly many more cases of assault and rape than were heard by the court, for such cases were difficult to prove to the satisfaction of a male jury, and in any case were too expensive for many labouring families to bother bringing them to the notice of the court.[131] The gentry also regarded it as a degrading public exposure of a personal and tragic occurrence. In this way assaults by Aborigines on white women and children were usually concealed from public knowledge.[132] One case which did come before Mackie concerned Robert Collins' servant, Nassip. Collins was a boatman who lived on the flats above Perth on the south side of the river. Collins' daughter was sometimes left at the house while her father worked nearby. One day Nassip came to the house and asked her to give him some grog, which she did. He fastened the door and put a fork in the fire. 'He then said, if I

129 For the Velvick and Mayo incidents see *Perth Gazette*, 5 January 1833; Supreme Court Criminal Court Record Book and Case File 52, 1833; *Perth Gazette*, 18 May, 6 November 1833.
130 *Perth Gazette*, 6 July 1833; Supreme Court Criminal Record Book Cases 1, 5, 13, 17, 26, 28, 32, 57, 61, 89, 93, 95, 96 and 100, to 1834 alone; *Perth Gazette*, 4 January 1840, 9 April 1842.
131 See Supreme Court Case File 57, April 1833—Martha Withnell case and £20 deposit.
132 See *Perth Gazette*, 13 September 1834.

did not comply with what he wished, he would run the fork into me, taking it out of the fire at the same time. He then unrolled his bed, took off his trowsers, took me up and laid me upon it . . . he then lay himself upon me'. The terrified girl was saved from further assault by the sudden and unexpected return of her father. Collins' daughter was only eight years old. She was motherless and already was doing most of the domestic chores for her father. Nassip had seemed sober and trustworthy. Collins had had to keep at his work or the family would have starved. He had come to Swan River to farm; but he lacked the capital to take up good land. He had hoped to raise a large family; but his wife Georgiana had left shortly after their arrival in Perth. There were no relatives and no Government patronage to ease the pain. In October 1833 Robert Collins foolishly stole a gun. At the October quarter sessions Nassip was sentenced to gaol for two months for assaulting Collins' daughter; Collins was sentenced to three months imprisonment for stealing the gun. It is not known what became of the little girl during her father's imprisonment; nor is the family's later history known. But in Perth in 1833 Robert Collins, his daughter, and Nassip were caught in a web of life spun by others.[133]

Nassip, a sick man, assaulted another child eighteen months later, and was sentenced to six months gaol and five dozen lashes. The little girl whom he assaulted in 1835 had had a life more trying than anything experienced by the children of the Roe, Drummond, and Wittenoom families. Her father, Thomas Dent, who had once described himself as a farmer, ran a pub in Barrack Street called The Happy Emigrant. Never was a pub more inaptly named. Situated close to the military barracks it was the drinking house of the unhappiest of pioneers, the privates of the 63rd. When Dent occasionally refused a sodden private another drink, the soldiers threatened to 'burn the bloody tent over my head'. By 1832 the pub was no longer a tent but a thatched wattle and daub establishment; and one of the soldiers, J. Rahill, did set fire to the thatch after he'd been refused a drink after hours. The rough and ready Rahill was later gaoled for assaulting another publican's wife. Mrs Dent, however, was by then being assaulted by her own husband. In mid-1832 Dent had suffered at the Rev. Wittenoom's hands. Wittenoom's pigeons had been eating his precious garden seeds, and the enraged Dent had killed the offending birds, only to be hauled into court and fined and gaoled. After this he seems to have gone more or less permanently berserk. Time and again neighbours witnessed his unprovoked assaults on Mrs Dent. They became so frequent and so severe that their youngest child was taken away to stay with kindly Mrs Bourke nearby. Mrs Dent said that 'The moment my husband entered the house on his return from gaol he knocked me down . . . He treats me more like a slave . . . I swear that I am in fear of being murdered by my husband'. But Thomas had not always been like this: he had loved and been loved in return. In court Mrs Dent had deposed that he had been a good husband before they came to Swan River. Swan River snapped his mind, as it did others. To the Court he roared 'Gag me and be damned' and went to gaol again for a three months' spell. The pub was leased, and later the land was sold to the respectable James Solomon. Mrs Dent recovered from her battering, and worried, as did all colonial mothers, about her daughter's safety in

[133] Supreme Court Criminal Case Files 69 and 75, 1833; also *Perth Gazette*, 5 October 1833.

Perth. In June 1835 this desperate woman experienced the still greater horror of having her little daughter assaulted and raped by the deranged Nassip. Mrs Dent's dream of freedom and independence, of plenty within the bosom of her family—a dream which possessed other Elizabeths, like Captain Will Shaw's wife—had been lost in a nightmare of domestic and personal trauma. Nearly twenty years later, an unthinking master, A. H. Stone, described his aging domestic servant, the same Mrs Dent, as a 'stupid old thing'.[134]

The Children of Perth

Perhaps nothing indicates better the gulf between the life experiences of the investing class and the serving class than a study of children. It is true that in a frontier environment like Swan River the children of monied parents went without the privileges available to them in the old world—witness Eliza Shaw's dismay as she observed her son Nat's progress from boyhood to manhood.[135] But it does not follow from this that the new society 'levelled' children's experiences. In the first place the children of the serving class, even of tender years, had to supplement their own and the family's fare in ways alien to the children of investors. Too often they had to steal or lie their way through childhood, sometimes in concert with members of their family, sometimes in defiance of their parents, and sometimes independently of any family. As a result many of them reached manhood bearing the scars of the lash which rarely, if ever, curled around the shoulders of officer/gentry children. Still more were mentally scarred by the experience of 'wrong-doing'—girls as well as boys—even though they escaped conviction. Francis Williams was one boy who was caught. An orphan, he had been sent out to Swan River by the London Society for the Suppression of Juvenile Vagrancy. Williams frustrated the charitable intentions of the Society; of Stirling, who had agreed to take the lads and work them into decency and godliness; and of Mr St A. Ward, the storekeeper master from whom he stole soap and cigars. Francis Williams was fourteen years of age when he joined Lascars, soldiers, Aborigines, and poor 'free' whites in gaol. He was not the only one of the 'official' vagrant boys to break stones under supervision.[136]

By the mid-1830s the Government, on the recommendation of Mackie and the Rev. Wittenoom, had installed in Perth a public whipping post and public stocks. Both were to remain in use for many years. The idea, as expressed by Mackie and Wittenoom, was to 'speedily and effectually' reduce vice 'by a degrading exposure'.[137] In November 1833 two urchins were caught robbing the Government Garden of grapes and peas. Mr Drummond, the botanist, preferred charges, and the two children were placed in stocks and their parents were ordered to flog them publicly.[138] In February 1835 a young Aborigine was flogged at the

---

[134] The events of this paragraph have been reconstructed from Supreme Court Criminal Case File 27, 1832; Case File 55, 1833; Supreme Court unregistered case, May 1832; *Perth Gazette*, 5 January 1833; *CSO* Vol. 32, May 1834; *Perth Gazette*, 10 August 1833; *Perth Gazette*, 11 April 1835; Supreme Court Case File 124, 1835; 'The Diary of Alfred Hawes Stone', *Early Days* Vol. 1, Pt. VI, 1929, p.33.
[135] Mary Durack *To Be Heirs Forever*, 1976, pp.97, 207-8.
[136] *Perth Gazette*, 22 November 1834.
[137] *CSO* Vol. 35, October 1834.
[138] *Perth Gazette*, 30 November 1833.

post for stealing vegetables from Mr Armstrong's garden: 'A native named Garbel inflicted the punishment, under the direction of Mr Armstrong'. Mr Armstrong, prosecutor and supervisor of the whipping, was the colony's official interpreter for and protector of the Aborigines of Perth.[139] Casual loungers of all classes watched these performances. For the serving class the sight of the stocks and post was a daily reminder of their fate should they not aspire to 'respectability and comfort'. For the children of the serving class the sight (and the experience) was part of the educational process designed for them by men like Stirling, Mackie, Wittenoom and Moore. So too was the story which young William Glover brought back with him from Fremantle Gaol. Glover had stolen some gun-powder and silver coins from Charles Leroux's store. Mr Leeder's well-groomed little girl spied young Will entering the back of the store empty-handed and emerging holding goods. Will was challenged by a policeman but denied the crime: 'His father then took hold of a rope and flogged him till at last the prisoner confessed'. Will was carted down to Fremantle Gaol, given two dozen lashes before entering, and, after serving fourteen days imprisonment, received another two dozen lashes before being released. William Glover was ten years of age.[140] And Ann Ryan was only 14 years of age when she went to gaol for one month's hard labour for stealing clothes from A. H. Stone.[141] In this way did the gentry seek to shape and harness a quiescent labouring force. In this way did it conduct its quest for 'internal peace'.

It was not simply their appearances on the whipping post and in gaol which distinguished the children of the serving class from more affluent children. They were also more vulnerable to diseases induced by poor diet and lack of hygiene. Even supposedly democratic epidemics like whooping cough and influenza struck harder among the poorer children, who had to fend off disease in the ill-ventilated and noisome huts—or even while sleeping on straw in the open—scattered round the town and under Mt Eliza.[142] And despite the heroic work of the Colonial Surgeon, too often the children of the poor went without medical aid. Perhaps one in fifteen babies died before reaching one year in the pre-convict years; for the poorer classes the death-rate was still higher.[143] And when they were well they ran around barefooted, unlike the children of the gentry. Indeed their parents tended to do the same. As the *Perth Gazette* commented in relation to a reported death from tetanus: 'the habit of the lower classes in this colony, of going about without any protection to the feet is much to be reprehended, particularly in the towns'.[144] But there was also play. The older children swam in the Swan, fished in the Swan, caught gilgies in the swamps at the back of the town, or just strolled along the waterside under Mt Eliza.

When the gentry and press discussed the need for schools in Perth, they thought primarily of the children of the investing class. As Charles MacFaull put it in an editorial

> The difficulty generally felt in a new colony of obtaining suitable
> instruction for the youths of the higher classes of the community, has

---

139 *Perth Gazette*, 7 February 1835. 140 Supreme Court Case File 38, 1832.
141 *Perth Gazette*, 4 January 1840. 142 *Perth Gazette*, 18 May 1833.
143 Census of WA, 1848; E. J. P. Joske 'Health and Hospital: a Study of Community Welfare in Western Australia 1829–55'. In 1845, for example, one in three deaths was of an infant under one year. MA thesis, University of WA, 1973; see also *Inquirer*, 16 October 1844 for birth/death tables 1841–44.
144 *Perth Gazette*, 2 January 1847.

been experienced here . . . Many families of respectability . . . are deterred from emigrating in consequence of their reflecting that their children must of necessity run wild in the trackless woods of a new settlement.[145]

But he rejoiced that from now on all would be well, for that great shaper of men's lives, the Rev. J. B. Wittenoom, was establishing a private seminary in Perth for the children of gentlemen. In fact all was not well for, despite the efforts of Wittenoom, by 1836 less than 100 of the colony's 600 school-age children were being educated in a school, partly because many parents kept their children at home doing what a critic described as 'trifling services'.[146] In the late 1830s Wittenoom did as he had had to do at Newark Grammar before he came to Swan River, namely attempt to increase his school's enrolment by introducing a second stream of pupils, drawn from the 'inferior classes', who would be taught the three Rs but not the classical education of their betters.[147] But the illiterate children of Perth still did not come to school, and by 1841 a newspaper correspondent was warning that without better education the Western Australians were in grave danger of becoming a 'degraded race'.[148] Not until the late 1840s did the Government grapple seriously with the problem, and then it did so only because the extraordinary success of the Roman Catholic schools, founded in 1846, threatened to undermine the Protestant ascendancy in Perth.[149] Bishop Brady and his energetic band of Sisters of Mercy rapidly won popular approval among the lower orders, for they educated boys and girls at little cost to the parents and with little concern for class distinctions. In 1848, the Government, prompted by the Rev. Wittenoom, set up a rival elementary school system administered by a central committee dominated by Anglicans and using a curriculum based on the teachings of the Anglican Church. It was organized on Wittenoomian lines with three divisions: rich; yeomanry; and poor. It lasted for 23 years. A year later, under pressure from the Secretary of State for Colonies, the Government gave a grant of £20 to the Catholics: it was a poor enough reward, as by then nearly 50% of the children at school attended Catholic schools.[150] Thus were the unsuspecting children of Perth drawn into one of the most torrid wars of the modern world, pawns in a power game without end. In this, as in all things, the children of the serving class fared worse than those not caught in the cross fire.

Self Help and Social Control

Wittenoom also had a hand in the education and self-improvement of the fathers of artisan-class children—the 'respectable' working men of Perth. In 1837 a group of artisans met in Perth to form the Sons of Australia Benefit Society for the mutual protection of 'mechanical and handicraft tradesmen'. A subscription of 2s 4d per month would be sufficient to relieve an artisan of the financial worry of ill-health and

[145] *Perth Gazette*, 2 March 1833.   [146] *Perth Gazette*, 1 June 1833.
[147] D. Mossenson *State Education in Western Australia*, 1972, p.5.
[148] *Inquirer* 14, 21 July, 4 August 1841—cited by L. Fletcher 'Educating the People', in C. T. Stannage (General Editor) *A New History of Western Australia*.
[149] P. McCarthy 'The Foundations of Catholicism in Western Austraia', 1829-1911, *University Studies in History* Vol. 2, No. 4, 1956, pp.20-3; also Mossenson *State Education in Western Australia*, pp.12-18.
[150] M. Newbold 'The Sisters of Mercy', *Early Days* Vol. 7, Pt. VI, 1974, pp.26-35.

To THE WORSHIPFUL His Majesty's Jus
tices of the Peace for the Colony of Western
Australia, commonly called Swan River, in
New Holland, in the General Quarter Sessions of the Peace assembled—

The Humble Memorial and Petition
of Charles Foulkes, William Holmes, Robert
Minson, John Dudley, Charles Farmer, John
Tichbon, Edward Flaharty, John Flaharty,
William Nairn, William Heard, John Spen-
cer, James Dobbins, Henry Rice Bond, John
Thompson, Launcelot Taylor Cook, Robert
Ferris, Robert Bell, Robert Moore, William
Glover, Joseph Joyce, William Ward, Wil-
liam Rogers,— Sheweth

That your Memorialists are desirous
of forming themselves into a friendly Society
to provide by Contribution for the maintain-
ance or assistance of the Members thereof in
Sickness, Old Age, and other Infirmities un
der the authority, and subject to the Provisions of a certain act of Parliament made and
passed in the 59th year of the reign of His late
Majesty George the Third,—Intituled an Act
for the further protection and encouragement
of Friendly Societies, and for preventing
Frauds and Abuses therein, and we propose
that——

William Nairn of Perth, William Rogers
the Elder of Perth, and John Tompson of Perth, all
Substantial Householders and whose names are hereto
Subscribed and set, be the Trustees of such Society,
and that the said Society be Governed by the Rules
Orders, and Regulations following.

costs associated with death. The title of the society was a self-conscious statement of their belief that Western Australia was their home and that like-minded men in other colonies were forming similar institutions. It implied a rejection of Britain only in material terms, in the exigencies of day to day living. It did not imply a rejection of the values of the motherland as represented in Swan River by men like Wittenoom, Irwin, Mackie, and Moore. The members met in the fashionable United Services Tavern, in St George's Terrace, only a stone's throw from Government House and the Anglican Church. Following their meetings the forty or so members, led by stewards Charles Foulkes, Nairn, Tomson, and Robert Moore, the sawyer, would march to the Church and there attend divine service conducted by the Rev. Wittenoom. Because it was comprised of youthful, thrifty, and hardworking artisans, the Society had few outgoings for many years. With its savings put at the disposal of their employers, through the WA Bank, the Society flourished financially and socially, lasting throughout the nineteenth century.[151]

The success of Sons of Australia fostered the belief that before too long its members would form a Mechanics' Institution.[152] This in fact occurred early in 1842 when the enterprising Charles Foulkes, a painter by trade, called mechanics to a meeting at his own house. By March the new Institute had acquired a library from either the Perth Book Society or the WA Book Society, both gentry-run clubs which foundered at this time.[153] Unlike the Sons of Australia Society, the new Mechanics' Institute does not seem to have received very much encouragement from the gentry: for example, it does not seem to have been offered land by the Government. Perhaps the chord of independence was being struck a little too hard by Foulkes and his friends. Whether because of this, or for lack of support from artisans, the Institute failed within a few months. When it was revived a decade later, the initiative came less from the artisans than from the gentry, in yet another attempt to preserve the social distinctions so necessary for the achievement of 'internal peace'.

More successful was the establishment in 1840 of another association, known variously as the Perth Club and the Western Australian Club. This club had rooms in Hay Street and for a time was run by a full-time manager, and former publican, George Embleton. It was financed by the issue of fifty shares of £10 each, with subscribers paying £3 per year. It provided some accommodation, a reading room, and, much to the chagrin of the hoteliers, it served meals and drinks as well. It seems to have been patronised by lesser merchants and more affluent artisans like builders. Despite newspaper concern that the Club might foster class divisions, it seems not to have done so, at least insofar as it organized cricket matches with 'Gentlemen' rather than combating them economically. It may also have assisted the gentry with the annual Tradesmen's Ball, held usually in conjunction with the Foundation Day celebrations. It was still active in 1847, but does not seem to have survived into the convict period.[154] The same men fraternised with the Anglican gentry in masonic lodges, such as the Perth Assembly, the

151 The Supreme Court of WA holds the Rule Book of the Sons of Australia for the late 1830s and early 1840s; Perth Gazette, 4 January 1837, 11 January 1840, 23 January 1841, 21 January 1843.
152 Perth Gazette, 23 January 1841.
153 See Perth Gazette, 18 January, 18 July, 29 August 1840.
154 Perth Gazette, 10 October, 19 December 1840; 24 December 1842; 1 May 1847.

Good Templars, St John's and St George's, all of which were active in Perth in the 1840s.[155] So too with the Temperance Society which, after false starts in 1835 and 1839, was established on a firm footing in September 1846.[156]

The most influential institution established in these years was the York Society, founded in August 1840.[157] For many years the WA Agricultural Society, which met in Perth and Guildford, had been the principal forum of unofficial gentry opinion in the colony. Its membership included not only land-owning Government officials, but also prominent farmers like William Tanner of the Upper Swan who believed that the Government impeded rather than assisted rural development, and that men like himself should have more say in the government of the colony. By 1840 he was on the Legislative Council and a vocal critic of Hutt and his policies. It was Tanner who in 1840 established the weekly journal the *Inquirer* (8 August 1840) with a view to putting forward opinions contrary to those of the *Perth Gazette* and the Government generally. But by 1840 the Avon Valley had become an important farming region, particularly around York. Families like the Meares, the Mongers and the Burges' had prospered at York, and it was scarcely surprising that by 1840 they had come to feel that their interests could be served best by creating a new society rather than working through the WA Agricultural Society. If anything, the York Society was even more suspicious of the Government than was the old Society; certainly it believed that its members should have a much more active role in government than they had under Hutt. As importantly, the new Society had stronger views on the general morality of Perth and Fremantle than had the old Society, and therefore its formation is an important stage in the development of town–country relations in 19th century Western Australia. The old WA Agricultural Society was wound up in 1846.[158]

'The Convicts are Coming'

The importance of the York Society in Western Australian history rests chiefly on the desire of its members to possess a cheap and plentiful labour force. From its inception the Society strove to influence the Imperial and colonial governments to send out rural labourers from the mother country. The cry for cheap labour was an old one, but it gathered momentum in the 1840s and was loudest in the eastern districts, though the *Perth Gazette* too was fairly sympathetic early in the decade. It wrote: 'The colonists are retarded in their agricultural operations from the want of good hands'.[159] The *Gazette* believed then that part of the problem was that rural labourers too rapidly became landowners themselves: 'The majority here have their own freehold property', and again, 'If there be an evil, it is that the continued and unchecked advance to a state of general prosperity has converted into independent proprietors and masters a greater portion of the operative classes than

---

[155] See *ADB* Vol. 2—entry for Lochee; *Perth Gazette*, 11 April 1840; 4 September 1841; 18 March 1848.

[156] Backhouse *A Narrative of a Visit*, p.537; Moore *Diary*, p.251; *Perth Gazette*, 9 January 1841; 4 September 1846—the 'revival' was spearheaded by William Tanner and other prominent gentry figures.

[157] *Perth Gazette*, 15 August 1840.

[158] *Perth Gazette*, 3 October 1846.   [159] *Perth Gazette*, 4 January 1840.

the limited state of our population can spare without inconvenience.'[160] By April 1842, following the failure of Mr Samson's scheme to bring out 50 labourers,[161] and the partial failure of Robert Schoales' ambitious plan to bring several hundred emigrants of all classes to WA,[162] it was calculated that the colony required about 200 labourers if the economy was to function efficiently, and this was despite the acquisition of some labourers from the Australind experiment in the south-west.[163]

For a year or so the effects of the depression in Britain and the eastern colonies were not felt at Swan River, but in 1843 they struck with considerable force. Trade dwindled, there was a marked reduction in capital inflow, and masters found difficulty in meeting wage commitments. Some investors went to the wall and left the colony altogether 'after . . . a number of years of toil and fearful expenditure of capital . . . their hopes blighted . . .';[164] but others were made of tougher fibre or were luckier and stayed on to harass their servants and labourers and squeeze their livelihood by demanding the introduction of more cheap labour. From the foundation of the colony they had had their indentured servants, black Lascars, orphaned and delinquent children, Hindoos from India, and Chinese from Singapore—all to occupy the role of the helot class in Swan River Society; but still they were dissatisfied. Depressions do not distribute their dire effects equally and their worst effects bore more heavily on the labouring class who were without savings and credit to help them through, and who were without property to sell. The demand for labour temporarily slackened, but by early 1847 Swan River was beginning to pull out of the depression and there was again a strong demand for cheap labour. But then a strange thing happened. As the labourers of York won a little cash from their masters they left the district and headed coastwards to Fremantle, from where they took passage to the eastern colonies. They had had enough of the fierce masters of the Avon Valley. They had endured low wages, in many cases not provided in cash, but almost entirely in clothing (pre-depression costing) and grog, and some provisions. As the economy picked up still further so too did the exodus of rural labourers increase apace. By mid-1847 even the *Perth Gazette* was moved to write: 'Surely something must be wrong or the working class would not be seized with a mania for emigrating from a colony where work is so plentiful and bears so remunerating a price'.[165] So wrote Elizabeth MacFaull, more radical than her late husband, the former editor Charles.

For weeks a debate raged in the pages of the *Inquirer* and the *Perth Gazette*, but despite the protestations of fair treatment to labourers from the Burges family and other big York farmers, the weight of evidence told against them. Small farmers joined with labourers in exposing the evils of the York masters. The main grievance concerned poor accommodation, sometimes described as 'more suitable for a dog than a Christian', and payment in kind. Even when cash was paid, Monger the storekeeper charged exorbitant prices for his goods.[166] He wasn't known as the 'Duke' for nothing. Indeed it may have been the case that Mr Monger's family fortune was built on the profits accruing from the

[160] *Perth Gazette*, 11 January, 24 October 1840.
[161] *Perth Gazette*, 4 January 1840.
[162] See Ray Oldham 'The Reminiscences of William Wade', *Early Days* Vol. 6, Pt. II, 1963.
[163] *Perth Gazette*, 23 April 1842.   [164] *Perth Gazette*, 21 November 1846.
[165] *Perth Gazette*, 19 June 1847.   [166] *Perth Gazette*, 3 July 1847.

depression years, both from flock masters and labourers. On the general problem one labourer wrote of the 'relentless talons of our irascible York gentry'.[167] This description was even less heartless than might seem to be warranted, for certainly the gentry had a keen sense of ranking in society and the consequences of that ranking. As one of their number wrote:

> It was ordained from the beginning of the world that there should be different denominations and classes of people, in order that each nation should preserve its own internal peace. It was ordained from the beginning that there should be masters and servants, but it was not so ordered that the servant should take for his hire his master's substance, and until our colony has, like all other countries and colonies its full supply of labour, these errors will exist—these evils will come to pass.[168]

It seems likely that this letter writer was one of the big farmers who throughout 1847 sought to have convicts introduced to Western Australia. Even the arrival of a shipload of Chinese labourers failed to meet their demands.[169] On a generous estimate made by a small York farmer in July 1847 it was thought that perhaps only 100 new shepherds would be quite sufficient for the colony's needs; any more would lead to unemployment, it was argued.[170]

But the big farmers of York insisted on the need for a reservoir of cheap labour, and by 1847 they had made up their minds that it had to be convict labour. Even the *Perth Gazette* would not countenance the introduction of convicts as domestic servants and rural labourers. Indeed Elizabeth MacFaull barely countenanced the presence of convicts for the purpose of erecting public works. The colony, she wrote, would receive British capital while the convicts built roads, bridges and buildings, and by the time their work was done, and they were sent away, then the colony would be in a prosperous state.[171] But capital, Elizabeth MacFaull knew, was not of primary concern for the half yearly report of the WA Bank revealed all too clearly the existence of a large pool of unused capital.[172] But plagued by uncertainty ('much as want of labour was before felt, it was nothing to what is now experienced')[173] Elizabeth MacFaull, like others in Swan River, was vulnerable to 'the humbugging manoeuvres of the convict agitators'.[174]

And the convict agitators in 1848 found support where support was most needed—not among the people, for power did not lie there, but from the new Governor, Captain Fitzgerald, who arrived at Swan River in August of that year. Unlike Captain Irwin who had governed Western Australia from February 1847 to August 1848, Fitzgerald was closely in tune with Imperial thinking about transportation. He knew that the cessation of transportation to NSW in 1840 had in fact created problems for the Home Government about the placement of British criminals. He knew that ticket-of-leave experiments in parts of England, particularly London, had brought down on the Government the wrath of the populace and had brought about a partial suspension of the programme, thereby overloading the gaols still further. He knew also that increased pressure on British gaols had caused the Government to resume transportation to the eastern colonies of Victoria and New South Wales; and by the time he landed in Swan River he knew that those eastern

'Convict Agitator': William Burges, farmer of York.

[167] The *Perth Gazette* wrote of the condition of labourers as 'serfdom in perpetuity'. *Perth Gazette*, 21, 28 August 1847.   [168] *Perth Gazette*, 10 July 1847.
[169] *Perth Gazette*, 16 May, 6 November 1847.   [170] *Perth Gazette*, 3 July 1847.
[171] *Perth Gazette*, 17 April 1847.   [172] *Perth Gazette*, 3 July 1847.
[173] *Perth Gazette*, 6 November 1847.   [174] *Perth Gazette*, 28 August 1847.

colonists had risen up against the convict transport *Hashemy* (8 June 1848) and prevented her from landing her human cargo.[175]

Knowing what his superiors required, Fitzgerald took the seed of convict agitation he found in Swan River among the half dozen or so big farmers of York, nurtured it, and eventually brought it into full bitter fruit. He first proposed (in October 1848) that 300 specially selected convicts and their families be sent out to Swan River. These were the so-called 'Pentonville Exiles', usually impoverished men gaoled for minor crimes against property who had almost completed their sentences. In Swan River the brave 300 would labour in the fields and on the roads and from their wages would be deducted their passage money which, when pooled, would finance the emigration of free settlers. And so the bait was dangled temptingly before the colonists of Swan River, and the little as well as the big fish began to nibble: some labour was required—the Pentonvillians would provide the labour in the requisite numbers and no more to follow; the Pentonvillians were not 'real' criminals, but able workers fallen on hard times; they would not be bestial and violent for they would have their families with them. And a little Imperial capital would come with the Pentonvillians. Perhaps the opportunity was too good to pass up. And here was a new Governor who seemed ready to help them rather than hinder them as Irwin had done, and who ought to be encouraged and even trusted. In York the big farmers, emboldened by Fitzgerald's statements, called public meetings of district men. What did it matter if one-third of the farmers who attended the meeting refused to sign the petition to the Secretary of State urging him to make Western Australia a penal settlement, for now two-thirds were on-side where twelve months previously there had been but a handful.[176] The Burges', the Parkers, and the Meares were coming of age in colonial affairs. In January 1849 the petition was presented to Sheriff Stone for consideration by his Excellency the Governor. It was signed not only by William Burges and the men of York, but also by some Perth and Fremantle merchants, among them Lionel Samson, Robert Habgood, Phillip Marmion, as well as by some publicans like Devenish and J. G. C. Carr and the brewer James Stokes, who knew one thing, namely that British labourers, bond or free, drank heavily and were a source of great profit to the seller and maker of grog.[177]

By now it was well known that Fitzgerald had not spoken from his own initiative; that the October statement about the Pentonvillians was a calculated one, delivered by order of Her Majesty's Imperial Government. Around the time that Fitzgerald made his proposal the Under Secretary of State for Colonies, Mr Hawes, received a deputation of investors in Swan River properties. Messrs Louis Samson, C. Barrett Lennard, E. W. and H. Landor, Davey and Strudwicke had addressed Mr Hawes on the subject of the procurement of cheap labour for Swan River. Could he not foster free emigration to Swan River? No, Mr Hawes said, he could not; but as the disappointed investors were about to withdraw Mr Hawes turned back to them and asked politely if convict labour would be acceptable, Pentonville men of course. Light of heart now the deputation sang its way out of Whitehall to write excitedly to friends in Swan River that the Pentonvillians were coming.[178]

'Convict Agitator': James Stokes, brewer of Perth.

175 See A. G. L. Shaw *Convicts and the Colonies*, 1966, Chapters 14 and 15.
176 *Perth Gazette*, 2, 9 December 1848.
177 *Perth Gazette*, 27 January, 10 February 1849.   178 *Perth Gazette*, 16 February 1848.

But the final decision had not yet been taken. What had become clear to West Australians was that regardless of their feelings on the subject the Imperial Government was going to transport some criminals to Swan River. The question they now had to resolve was whether it was more or less advantageous to be a convict settlement; that is receiving Pentonvillians but without a proper military establishment and a large injection of British capital, or become a penal settlement, receiving not only Pentonvillians but other classes of criminals (still 'good' ones of course) backed by a military establishment and large-scale British capital. The Legislative Council had sought the latter, and so too, after some considerable debate, did a public meeting in Perth in late February 1849. The irrepressible Lionel Samson contended loudly that with Parkhurst boys and Pentonvillians, Swan River was in effect a convict colony but 'without protection or the concomitant advantages of a large expenditure'.[179] And the Burges', George Shenton, Charles Wittenoom, Mr Lukin and Mr Will Shaw, among others, chorused their agreement. The meeting was not large; nor was the resolution passed unanimously. And some Swan River men in England had still not given up hope that WA might yet receive free emigrants, for the year witnessed the creation of the Western Australian Land and Labour Association.[180] And perhaps there is an irony in the fact that the period June 1848 to June 1849 brought more free emigrants than the previous four years; also that exports were well up.

'Convict Agitator': George Shenton Snr, merchant of Perth.

Yet none of this mattered much for late in April 1849 the Imperial Government decided to print an Order in Council of Her Majesty's Government by which Western Australia was proclaimed to be 'one of the places to which convicts may lawfully be sent from the United Kingdom'.[181] The humbugging manoeuvres of the convict agitators, perhaps especially the Burges' and the Samsons, had enabled the Imperial Government to press on Western Australia what it had been thwarted from doing in New South Wales. Aided and abetted by the *Inquirer* newspaper in Perth, the big farmers of York, and the big merchants and publicans of Perth and Fremantle, had demonstrated clearly whose voice dominated the counsels of Swan River, and this fact more than anything else showed how different Swan River was from New South Wales and even Van Dieman's Land, then on the threshold of divesting itself of transportation. The *Perth Gazette* articulated the views of many Swan River settlers when it wrote feelingly of 'the degradation and infamy the convict party and their organ have procured for their adopted country'. And as was the custom, a colonial versified:

The Convicts are coming—what capital sport,
The road to the gallows made easy and short,
And long will the Swanites remember the day,
When the convicts were sent to their shores
    by Earl Grey.[182]

The decision taken without the concurrence of the colonists... surely the colonists of Swan River would rise up as had their compatriots in New Zealand, South Africa, and New South Wales and prevent the arrival of convicts. There must be public meetings, for 'admit one cargo and it will speedily be followed by others, and no long time will elapse before you will groan beneath the chain you will have fastened upon

---

[179] *Perth Gazette*, 24 February 1849. [180] *Perth Gazette*, 14 April, 29 June 1849.
[181] Despatch dated 1 May 1849; *Government Gazette*, 6 November 1849.
[182] *Perth Gazette*, 16 November 1849.

From Croft's house in St George's Terrace, looking across to Mt Eliza, 1850. (A. Taylor, artist.)

yourselves'. The question could be put squarely: 'Are our 5000 inhabitants so sunk in listlessness . . . that they are ready quietly to look on while the Home Government pours out upon their coasts the outcasts, the very dregs of the British Isles?'[183] One impassioned voice cried 'No!' It belonged to that Wesleyan preacher and farmer J. W. Hardey who likened the decision to an earthquake. Hardey knew, along with others, that Fitzgerald and the Imperial Government had deceived and were now brutalising the majority of the settlers of Swan River. Hadn't Fitzgerald incited support for his Pentonville scheme: 'The farmers did not apply for the men; but were applied to'.[184] But the short answer to the question posed by the *Perth Gazette* was 'Yes', the colonists of Swan River were sunk too deeply in listlessness to protest with strength and conviction. Those who cared greatly, on either side, were few. The labouring population, drunken and ground down, and having lost some men of enterprise and independence through emigration to the eastern colonies, and without a powerful investing class spokesman like Robert Lowe to mobilise them, accepted the decision resignedly, mouthing their objections and fears in the pubs and grog shops and rarely if ever in the company of masters.[185]

The ultimate deceit was worked out in the symbolically important month of June in the year 1850. In June the colonists of Swan River traditionally celebrated two great events in their past. The first was the anniversary of the Battle of Waterloo, the victory of freedom and honour over the tyrant of France. Labourers drunkenly fired off their guns round the streets of Perth alarming the governors of Swan River, who dined and wined the event with equal feeling but with greater decorum. In June too each year the settlers celebrated the anniversary of the foundation of the colony, usually with old English sports and a Tradesmen's Ball or the like. Essentially it was an attempt to make the labourers of Swan River grateful for working out their lives in Swan River rather than in the poorhouses and slums of the old country. Certainly the sports organized by the gentry were popular and the balls usually well patronised. Interest in foundation day flagged occasionally, and especially during the depression years and the mid-1840s and their aftermath. Nevertheless even in 1849 the *Perth Gazette* commented that 1 June was 'a day which many of our settlers have cause to regret, but we believe a far greater number have reason to rejoice at'.[186] But on the first of June 1850 there were no public celebrations and no public rejoicing for on that day the transport ship *Scindian* dropped anchor in Gage Roads and spewed out its human cargo on to the mainland of Swan River Colony. Thereafter 1 June 1850 bore a different meaning for the colonists, and not until the 1870s, well after the cessation of transportation, was 1 June celebrated again in a full-hearted way. In 1854 the *Perth Gazette* observed that: 'The anniversary of the foundation of the colony was passed over yesterday in Perth without the slightest demonstration of rejoicing'.[187] It became more usual to forget about the meaning of 1 June and celebrate instead the Queen's Birthday which fell on 24 May, a day unencumbered by feelings of doubt and sorrow. And of course even the Queen's Birthday could not be celebrated too full-heartedly for the colonists of Swan River had learnt that

---

[183] *Perth Gazette*, 30 November 1849.
[184] *Perth Gazette*, 14 December 1849.   [185] *Perth Gazette*, 28 December 1849.
[186] *Perth Gazette*, 1 June 1849.   [187] *Perth Gazette*, 2 June 1854.

SEVENTH ANNIVERSARY OF THE ESTABLISHMENT OF THE COLONY CELEBRATED ON THE 1ST JUNE, AT PERTH—The entertainments on this occasion were not of so striking a character as those of last year, owing to the absence of previous arrangement; taking this disadvantage into consideration, which may be a matter of regret, the day passed off very pleasantly. The usual rustic sports—foot-racing, jumping in sacks, gingling matches, &c., for small prizes, with a horse-race—comprised the amusements of the day. Several booths were erected on the ground,—a cleard space at the back of the town,—affording refreshment for the visitors. His Excellency Sir James and Lady Stirling, with a party of friends, and all the respectable inhabitants in the neighbourhood, attended. We had wished, and, indeed, expected that the amusements would have been more extended, growing with our growth; but we have found ourselves disappointed. That they have obtained a national character, may be inferred from the great encouragement given to the natives, who had assembled from the various remote districts, conscious that on this day the *white men* were to hold a " corroborra," or rejoicing. The occasion of this rejoicing, they were acquainted with, and entered into the sport of spearing loaves of bread, and racing, with as much glee as any persons on the ground. The most successful in this exercise proved to be those who are known to us as prominent characters—Munday, Migo, &c. Two or three good marksmen firing at a target might have been introduced with good *moral* effect, as the natives would have witnessed and felt their great inferiority.

An anniversary not worth celebrating in 1850: the Perth Gazette report of the Foundation Day celebrations, 1836.

labourers and ex-convicts must not be allowed to congregate together in large numbers else they might rise up and riot against their grievances. This too was a response to the convict presence. But this was in the future. The twelve hundred people of Perth (a quarter of Swan River's population) faced with intermingled hope, uncertainty, and doubt the next phase of their quest of 'internal peace'.

Chapter Three: 'conservative in everything' — Perth 1851 to 1884

Perth in 1884

In 1884 Western Australia was still a small and isolated outpost of the British Empire. Compared to the eastern colonies its total population of 33 000 was minuscule. Perth, with 6500 people, was three times smaller than Brisbane, the next smallest Australian capital city; and its nearest neighbour, Adelaide, with 95 000 people was fifteen times larger. In fact Perth was about the same size as Albury, a country town in the Riverina district of New South Wales.[1] As for the colony's isolation, it was proverbial. As one visitor wrote: 'you feel yourself more out of the world in Perth than in Siberia'.[2] Visitors who travelled no further than across Victoria Harbour to the township of Albany were usually delighted with Western Australia, for Albany was both pretty and busy, reminiscent of the seaside towns of the Kentish coast.[3] But the great P. and O. ships steamed on to Adelaide and Melbourne, and few passengers stayed in Western Australia to travel the wearisome 250 miles north-west to the town of Perth. Even seasoned travellers like Trollope, Twopeny and Cornish complained about the sparsely inhabited countryside, the long staging runs, and the uncomfortable rest houses. Colonial politicians en route to England invariably declined the resident Governor's invitation to dine with him at Government House in Perth. It was one of the disappointments of an appointment to Perth; it was one of the petty vexations endured by the people of Perth. On the rare occasions when a dignitary did visit Perth, as the Duke of Edinburgh did in 1868, the people of Perth wagged their tails happily and won for themselves an enviable reputation for old-world hospitality, which was not lost in the next one hundred years.

In some ways the colony was less insulated from the rest of the world than it had been in the 1840s. The steam passage from England took about 45 days or less in 1884, whereas the journey by sail had taken 90 days or longer. Increasing intercolonial trade brought almost weekly news of events in Sydney and Melbourne, for most of the eastern colonial newspapers were read in the West. And the coming of the telegraph line in 1877–78 gave Perth merchants and newspaper proprietors a link with the wider world's experiences of a day or two before. The impact of the telegraph should not be exaggerated, for the cable was expensive, the news coming down it was highly selective and sketchy, and the local newspapers continued their long-established practice of reprinting fuller accounts from British and colonial journals

---

[1] J. W. McCarty 'Australian Capital Cities in the Nineteenth Century', in C. B. Schedvin and J. W. McCarty (eds.), *Urbanization in Australia*, 1974; G. L. Buxton *The Riverina 1861–91*, 1967.

[2] R. E. N. Twopeny *Town Life in Australia*, 1883, p.169.

[3] Henry Cornish *Under the Southern Cross*, 1880, p.38.

and newspapers. Nor were the benefits of speedier travel and information spread evenly throughout the population. The principal beneficiaries were the merchants, financiers, and investors. Indeed early access to information was one of the means by which the men of high status and the men of enterprise distanced themselves still further from the life chances of the labouring population. The telegram had not been invented to enable the poor to inherit the earth or even to enable them to exchange seasonal greetings.[4]

While convictism had provided many new public works and the economic infrastructure of roads and bridges, and while it had also provided a temporarily viable local market, it could not be said in 1884 that Western Australia was economically prosperous. The major agricultural regions of the Greenough and the Avon Valley provided only half the food requirements of the colony, thereby giving merchants and South Australian farmers a handsome return on their enterprise; the high price of the necessaries of life was still as much a source of grievance to the people of Perth as it had ever been in the old days. Nor had farming techniques improved much. Trollope was shocked to discover that farmers 'continue to crop the same ground with the same crops year after year without manuring it, and when the weeds come thicker than the corn, they simply leave it.' He even saw some farmers thrashing their corn 'with flails out on the road after the old Irish fashion'.[5] The major advances in agricultural production date from the 1890s.

From the mid-1860s a pastoral industry of significant proportions had developed along the banks of the de Grey, Fortescue, Ashburton and Murchison rivers in the north-west of the colony; indeed wool was the colony's principal money-earner. Local capital and local men had played the major role in this development, though Victorian finance and South Australian men were not without significance. The families who prospered from the development of the region were often the children of the families who had prospered in the 1840s; and all were intimately linked to the financing and servicing centre of Perth, where merchants like Padbury and the Shentons, and clever lawyers like the Burts and Leakes fanned commercial speculation and invested their own and others' capital to good effect. In the south-west the old families continued to hold sway in agricultural and political matters, though there was now also a flourishing timber industry, for the housing needs of the towns and the opportunities for exporting jarrah offered a good return for enterprise and investment. In Perth there was little manufacturing activity other than a traditional sort, like tanning, coachbuilding, and brewing. Manufactories were small. There were a few furniture shops, but most furniture was imported from Britain and the eastern colonies. This was true also of clothing, for so few people were engaged in the making and repair of clothes that it could not be said that Perth possessed a textile industry. Perth's was a highly dependent economy. But there were those who predicted a great future for the colony. Among the most optimistic was the Governor, Napier Broome, who in 1884 addressed the Royal Colonial Institute on the subject.[6] Others were more pessimistic. The promise of convictism had not been fulfilled. Perth's

[4]   Telegraph rates are printed in the *WA Year Book* for 1883.
[5]   A. Trollope *Australia and New Zealand: South Australia and Western Australia*, 1873, p.128.
[6]   'Western Australia' *Proceedings of the Royal Colonial Institute* Vol. 16, 1884–85, pp.180–214.

population had risen from 5000 to just under 6000 between 1870 and 1881, an annual increase by immigration and natural means of less than 200 a year. In the 1850s men had written 'God save us from a gold discovery in Western Australia' and 'the discovery of gold would prove the greatest evil that could possibly befall us for it would excite passions and habits of excess'. But by the 1870s it was the opinion of many that nothing but gold could turn the scale, could bring 'joy out of despondency', could fill the land with towns, and crowd the streets with men. 'The one thing wanted is population. Gold, if really found in paying quantities, would be a panacea for all evils in the colony'.[7]

Government House was the centrepiece of social life in Perth in 1884 as it had been since the foundation of the town: 'a bow from his Excellency, or a word from the Governor's Lady, stamps the happy recipient as one of the elite'.[8] To be snubbed by the Governor's Lady was to bring discomfort and dismay to the conduct of social relations in Perth, as even the Stones and the Prinseps were to find on occasion. It was in Government House that the leading officials and gentry enjoyed balls, musical evenings (especially if the Governor himself played a musical instrument or had a flair for composition), cards, charades, or simply a morning 'call' on the Governor's family. But from the early 1870s there was also the exclusive Weld Club, situated in St George's Terrace. Patronised by retired and active members of the gentry and Government officials with high social standing, the Club served as an informal stock exchange, reading and billiards room, and a place of temporary residence for countrymen. It was only a short walk from the Club to the Legislative Council in Hay Street or to friends' houses or one's own down the Terrace. For the town's lesser professional and commercial men there was the Perth Club, situated in Hay Street which by 1884 had become the town's shopping heart. There was also the Working Men's Institute, hard up against the railway line in Wellington Street, where the 'aristocracy' of the working men met for moral and spiritual improvement under the guidance of a sober and conscientious upper class leadership. Social relations were still coloured by the proximity of convictism. By and large the workers were socially inhibited and legally intimidated by the Master and Servant Act; to the casual observer they seemed to accept uncritically their 'ordained' position in colonial society. It seemed to some that rhetoric and reality were as one in Western Australia:

> Brave young master!' (says the labourer) 'I'd as lief
> Have died myself or broken every limb
> As see him suffer.[9]

Each large farm contained at least one 'faithful retainer'; each large town household contained at least one 'faithful domestic servant'. But still others knew that 'the seed of crime lies in the flower of aristocracy' and were prepared to set class against class. In Perth they were few in number. And in any case, neither group ever played charades at Government House.[10]

---

[7]   *Perth Gazette*, 14 July 1851, 6 February 1852; Trollope, 1873, p.98.

[8]   Anton Helmich in *Perth Gazette*, 18 April 1873.

[9]   Henry Clay *Two and Two: a Story of the Australian Forest, with Minor Poems of Colonial Interest*, Perth, 1873, cited B. Smith 'Early Western Australian Literature', *University Studies in History* Vol. 4, No. 1, 1961–62, p.59.

[10] J. B. O'Reilly *Moondyne*, 1879, Seal Edition, 1975, p.93; also the *Morning Herald*, any number from 2 February 1867 to its demise in 1886.

Parliamentary politics was the prerogative of the Imperial officialdom, the landed gentry, and the leading town merchants. In Britain, Mr Disraeli had taken his 'leap in the dark'; and in 1884 Gladstone was steering through the Third Reform Act which enfranchised still more labouring men. But in Perth the franchise was restricted to men of substance only. The decorum of colonial politics was symbolised by the person of Luke Leake, the Member for Perth from 1870 to 1886. Merchant, landowner, and gentleman, Leake was honoured with the colony's first knighthood. At election time he would stroll through the streets, 'personally acquainted with almost every elector, (speaking) to each as an old friend, knowing his history, knowing his views, and certain at any rate of a friendly reception'.[11] In the Legislative Council the gentlemen would discuss

> whether settlers should be bound to pay half the value of the fences a neighbour has erected or wishes to erect between them; whether the railway should be allowed to go through a certain square in the township of Guildford, whether police protection, at the expense of the whole colony, should be afforded to settlers in the outlying districts who are exposed to attacks of natives.[12]

They also discussed the governance of Perth and the nature of social relationships in the colony. Politics was a leisurely affair, even though young Stephen Henry Parker had a bee in his bonnet about the need for responsible government and was occasionally very rude to his elders and betters: he was, after all, old Stephen Stanley's boy.

The Case of Henry Haynes, expiree

Late in 1883 George Shenton was elected Mayor of the City of Perth. It was the eighth time he had been elected by his fellow ratepayers to chair the Perth City Council. The wind blew fair for him as it had done from birth. In 1883 also he caught a fresh breeze and became a shareholder in the newly formed Perth Gas Company, just as his father had taken up shares in companies floated locally forty years earlier.[13] The enterprise which had launched the family successfully into the nineteenth century would be carried by George into the twentieth century. Capital accumulation can be learned, and the best teacher for a young man may be a successful father or near relative. This was true of the Leake, Burt and Britnall families, all of whose lives intersected in 1883–84 with one who sought 'respectability and comfort' but lacked their precious inheritance. In January 1884 Henry Haynes' quest for 'internal peace' came to an end when he was hanged by the neck in the execution yard of Perth Gaol.

In 1859, when he was twenty-one years of age, Haynes killed a man for which crime he was sentenced to life imprisonment. In 1861 he was transported to Western Australia. For a time he worked on Government public works and then in 1864 he received a ticket-of-leave which enabled him to seek work in private enterprise. In gaol he had learnt the trade of tailor, but in his ticket-of-leave period he seems to have been employed mainly as a domestic servant. It was in this period (9 August 1865) that he married one of Governor Hampton's domestic servants, Ann Clough, one of 46 serving girls who arrived per *Hastings* in 1864. In 1866 Ann and

---

[11] *Western Mail*, 19 May 1888.   [12] Twopeny, p.170.
[13] Minute Book of Perth Gas Company 1883–93, Battye Library Acc. No. 476A.

Henry Haynes began their family with a daughter, Mary Ann. Henry was then aged 28 years. In 1870, having served out his ticket-of-leave honourably, he was granted a conditional pardon, and round this time he settled in Goderich Street, moving later to the north side of Wellington Street between Mackie and Lord Streets, at the Mackie Street end. In the small rented cottage he set up a tailoring work room and recommenced his trade. In 1868 and 1870 two boys were added to the family. Apart from an illness in 1874 which put him in the Colonial Hospital for a spell, the 1870s seem to have been moderately good to Haynes. The family did not prosper, but they kept their heads above water. They could not afford to buy the house in which they lived, but they met the rates and rental when they fell due. They could not afford to educate their children, who all went to work at an early age. To their friendly ex-convict artisan neighbours the Haynes' seemed to live happily together. She was said to be a pleasant, hardworking, woman; and he was thought to be a quiet and inoffensive man. Indeed it seems to have been a love match. He spoke of her as a good and dear wife, and she of him as being always kind to her and the children.

But Haynes was a man with a past which haunted him and a present which tied him to the ground. He had not wanted his lovely Ann to know about the crime for which he was sent to Western Australia, but 'that' Governor Hampton had told her, and the knowledge that she knew hurt him deeply. In his mind it became an explosive which she alone could trigger; and the longer she refrained from detonating it, the larger and more potentially destructive it became to him. There had been a time too when self-pity had driven him to drink; but his loving wife's home-brewed sugar beer had kept at bay the seductions of the Horse and Groom nearby, and had kept him temperate at his workbench. But being temperate at his workbench had not produced enough income to keep the household financially secure. Ann had opened a store in the front room of the house, and from her shop she sold fresh cakes—usually in 'penniworths' to local children and mothers—and ginger beer, and kerosene which she bottled herself from drums. In more desperate times she took in needlework as well. In mid-1883, when he was 45 years of age, Haynes found his way once more to the Horse and Groom. He knew and feared the consequences: indeed he asked his friend Constable Connor to lock him up for a day or so, which Connor refused to do. He knew that he was risking his wife's sorrowful censure, more humiliating even than overt anger. Perhaps to avoid a scene over money, perhaps in one last desperate fling to win life's lottery, Haynes stole and sold a roll of cloth belonging to his landlord Thomas Britnall. It was the beginning of the end. He was caught and sentenced to one month's imprisonment in Perth Gaol. He had lived in its shadow for twenty years.

The month in gaol focussed his mind. There was nothing he could do about Governor Hampton. Nor dare he further antagonise his landlord-customer, Thomas Britnall. The policeman was his friend. Absorbed in self-analysis and self-pity, Haynes annoyed his fellow prisoners by asking simple questions on points of tailoring which they knew to be second nature to him. Or so it seemed to them. It may also have been a manifestation of his loss of confidence in himself as a tailor. When he spoke directly on his troubles, however, it was to blame his wife 'for getting his month'. To a visitor he complained that 'it was owing to his wife being obstinate and keeping a shop contrary to his wishes that he had been drinking'. Even as he turned in on his family as the source of his ills, Ann visited him and he was happy and joyful to see her. When she had gone he spoke affectionately of her and said that 'he would try and lead a better life and keep from drink when he came out'. That was the only day on which he was composed and happy.

Haynes was released from prison on Monday 8 October at 7.30 a.m. He reached his front door fifteen minutes later. As he came into the house he caught Ann by the throat and said 'You put me in prison'. She countered by saying 'No, I've done all I can to keep you from there'. She then calmed him down:

> Come and get some breakfast—I've got a nice bath ready for you . . . if you don't feel inclined to begin work today you can rest a day and begin work in the morning.

As he sat down to breakfast Haynes asked her: 'Ann, how do you think I shall go on now?', to which she replied 'Well Henry if you keep steady you'll get your work all back again'. She agreed that he could have a pint of beer each night with his supper. For the rest of the day he worked at his bench, making a suit for Mr Octavius Burt, the Resident Magistrate for Newcastle, whose brother Alfred took an interest in the Haynes' family. During the day Haynes asked Ann if she had had any men about the place while he was in gaol, which charge she denied. Haynes asked his daughter, Mary Ann, the same question and received the same answer. In the evening he had his pint of beer. The following day he worked on the suit until evening, when he again had a beer with his supper. However on Wednesday morning at about 10 a.m. he said that he would like a beer. Ann gave him 2*d* and he went for his beer. He was back in five minutes and worked on the suit for the rest of the day. He did not taunt or annoy Ann on Wednesday. On Thursday he worked till 10 and then asked again for a beer. This time Ann's fears surfaced and she said 'Well Henry you're getting as bad as ever'. She offered him a cup of coffee; but at 12 he took 2*d* and went off for a beer. On his return he worked again, but in the afternoon he taunted Ann about sending him to prison and having men around the house. She refused to quarrel with him and walked out of the room. In the evening Haynes went out for a walk and to see a newspaper. He had a late supper at home, including his customary pint of beer. That night he and Ann slept together.

The next morning Haynes rose early and worked till 10 when he again wanted a pint of beer. This time Ann refused to give him any money. He turned to his daughter who gave him 1*s* of her own money. He went out and returned shortly after with a jug of beer and, after returning the 8*d* change to his daughter, he asked Ann to join him for a drink. When she refused to have a drink he grew cross with her, so she took a small glassful. He then worked until 3 in the afternoon when he wanted another pint which Ann would not let him have. He said that he felt quite nervous and would like a drink. Ann reiterated that she could not work so hard for money and let him go and spend it. Haynes then turned again to his daughter who gave him 6*d*. He spent 4*d* on the beer and gave the change to Mary Ann. After tea that evening he went out for a walk. When he returned to the house at 8 p.m. he was not quite sober but he could walk straight. He was also a little cross. He told Ann that 'only for you I might have been worth hundreds of pounds'. Ann retorted that 'If it had not been for me I don't know where the children would have been years ago'. At 10, Mary Ann coaxed Haynes to go to bed.

On the Saturday morning Haynes rose early. After breakfast he went into his workshop and made out the bill for the completed suit of clothes. The nervousness about finishing the job and the need for assurance that all was well prompted Haynes to ask 'Well Ann do you think my writing is the same I used to make out the Bills?' Ann said 'Yes Henry I think its just the same'. He then made up the clothing in a parcel and came into the kitchen where he said 'Well Ann I'm going now', and he went away cheerful and happy down to Adelaide Terrace where Alfred Burt lived. Burt took the bill for £1 14s and listened while Haynes talked to him about his imprisonment and how his wife had done everything for the best in that time. He told Burt that he had not been drinking since being released from prison. Burt noticed nothing strange in Haynes' manner. Haynes then called in on Frederick Spencer, Chief Clerk in the Audit Office, who lived a few doors away from Burt. Spencer gave him a coat and waistcoat to clean and repair. Haynes said to him 'I suppose I'll get over this', apparently alluding to his term of imprisonment; and Spencer advised him to take the red ribbon badge to help keep him from drinking. As he was taking leave of Spencer, Haynes added 'It's not altogether my fault my wife is so contrary, she is mad upon keeping a little shop which does not pay'.

It was about twenty to nine when Haynes left Spencer to return home, which he reached round 9. Ann was in the kitchen where she had been bottling ginger beer and sugar beer, and was about to start bottling the kerosene, after which she intended to go to town. She agreed to clean the coat with hot water and soda before she went to town. Haynes then said that the long walk down to Alfred Burt's had made him thirsty for a glass of beer. Ann replied that she had a 'kettle of water boiling and I'll make you some coffee—don't have the beer'; but when he insisted she gave him 2d. This time Haynes was not satisfied and demanded a shilling. Ann retorted that she could not afford to give him so many shillings for beer, and that he had spent several on Friday. As she said this Haynes was sitting on the kitchen sofa: Ann herself was stooping over a kerosene tin and holding a hammer with which to open it. A moment later Haynes rose to his feet, snatched the hammer, and as she screamed he smashed the hammer down on her head, not once but several times, and to the cheek and temple as well, until her brain protruded and she fell to the kitchen floor and lay speechless in a pool of her own blood. As his daughter rushed in on the terrible scene, Haynes was standing against the fireplace with the hammer in his hand. Mary Ann threw herself down on her mother and called to her 'what is the matter?' But Ann did not reply. Mary Ann turned to her father and said 'what have you done to mother?' But he too did not answer her. Instead he lay the hammer on the sofa. Mary Ann ran screaming from the house and with a neighbour stood in the street and watched Haynes leave the house, putting on his coat as he did so. He did not respond to his daughter's charge of 'Oh you brute you've murdered my poor mother'. Haynes walked towards town. He walked to the Horse and Groom. There he quickly and silently drank a pint of beer and was on his way back to his home when Constable Connor came up to him and went with him into the house where the arrest was formally made. Haynes looked on his wife once more and then was taken to the police station. Later that afternoon he was transferred to the lockup at the waterside. He asked Connor how she was and did he think that she would get 'over it', but Connor could not say. Ann died in the Colonial Hospital at 5 that afternoon. It was Monday before Haynes learnt that she was dead. He wanted to know who paid the funeral expenses and whether or not she had been buried from the deadhouse or from her own house. Connor told him. Haynes then said: 'She aggravated me to do that, and, that Governor Hampton had told her for what he (Haynes) was sent to this colony'. G. W. Leake took the depositions of witnesses. Ten weeks later, in January 1884, Haynes too was killed. At his request he was buried alongside Ann. For Ann and Henry Haynes the history of Perth had come to an end. In their lives they had given it a sad sound; in their deaths perhaps its saddest sound.[14]

The case against Henry Haynes, tailor of Perth, January 1884.

(note: as shown in the Information Document presented to the Court, the name of the victim has been incorrectly entered as **Mary** Ann Haynes. Records show that: Registration of death No. 1207/1883 **Ann** Haynes. 47, wife of Henry Benjamin Haynes died 13-10-1883.)

This has been a story about social relationships in Perth, a story centred not on a Governor or Mayor or a leading politician or merchant or lawyer or builder but on a poor ex-convict tailor and his family. Haynes did not live apart from such people; rather, in the company of shoemakers, barmen and labourers, he lived out his life within their embrace. They sustained him and they frustrated him. They put him within sight of 'respectability and comfort' but kept him from realizing this ideal. It was his quest for 'internal peace' of their defining which led him to kill his loving Ann. Sweet and caring Ann. Prompted and aided by governors and officials she carried her family to the brink of success. She was the perfect wife, the perfect mother, and the perfect citizen. In that one mad moment Haynes knew that she *was* the world which was destroying him and must itself be destroyed. It remains to explore the rhythms of that world as it evolved from 1850 to the execution of Henry Haynes.

[14] *West Australian*, 16, 20 October 1883; 3, 8, 10, 22, 24 January 1884; Supreme Court Case File 1063, January 1884; *WA Biographical Index*, Vol. 4, 'Free Settlers 1850–70'.

Convicts and Convictism

The Westralian world which evolved between 1850 and 1884 was largely the product of the arrival of nearly 10 000 male convicts, nearly 2000 serving girls, the Pensioner Guard and their families, the free artisan families, and the responses of the older settlers to their presence. Convictism was first and foremost an economic system introduced by men who had prospered mightily in the foundation years: it was consonant with the purposes for which the colony was founded. As long as the big landowners, merchants and storekeepers perceived that some economic gain might accrue from the importation of British capital and convict labour then convictism would survive, and even flourish, in Swan River, always allowing that the Imperial Government would need colonial repositories for its criminals. Some men made or increased their fortunes from the fixed capital investment of the Imperial Government, especially by means of Establishment contracts; more benefited from the sale of their produce to the vastly enlarged market. But the economic benefits of convictism were spread unevenly and could not prevent recessions in the mid to late 1850s and the mid-1860s, while the 1870s were grim years for many. There was also the labour system. On arriving in Western Australia a convict usually worked for a time within the Establishment and on public works, sometimes for the Perth City Council (after 1858), and more usually for the Government. Then, providing he was not disorderly, he would be given a ticket-of-leave and with this he could seek employment among the free settlers or even, under rigorously policed circumstances, begin work on his own account. A ticket-of-leave employee remained subject to summary jurisdiction; and, apart from private provision of wages and food, he also remained a charge on the Imperial rather than the Colonial Government. When he moved or changed jobs he had to report to the local magistracy and police. In the goodness of time the ticket-of-leave man would receive a conditional pardon, which gave him most of the rights of a free man. But as such he was a less tractable employee. Unlike the ticket-of-leave man he could not be returned to the depot if he misbehaved; and if he suffered at the hands of his master it was legally possible for him to take his grievance before a local magistrate. Furthermore, a conditional pardon man, if he fell ill or became pauperised, became a charge on the Colonial Government, which in practice meant a charge on the masters who paid duties to the government.

In these circumstances it was scarcely surprising that masters preferred to employ ticket-of-leave men, and usually did so when they had a choice. And they had taken steps to ensure that they did have a choice. They had won agreement from the Imperial Government to a system whereby the holder of a conditional pardon could leave Western Australia for other colonies (though he could not return to England).[15] The masters of Swan River seem to have encouraged him to leave, and perhaps 1500 did so before transportation ceased in 1868. Not until 1861 was this system queried by the Imperial Government. Then during the sittings of the House of Commons' Select Committee on Transportation, which sat that year, the commissioners said in amazement:

> You are now pumping in 300 men at one end, and getting rid of 300 men at the other!

A convict at work in the Governor's garden, late 1860s.

---

[15] See J. S. Battye *History of Western Australia*, 1924, Chapter 7, and Appendix 3.

The answer to this charge, given by the distinguished landowner and Surveyor General of Swan River, John Septimus Roe, was a sheepish and equivocal, yes![16] But the facts were plain. As long as there was a steady inflow of ticket-of-leave-men, and as long as a goodly number of conditional pardon men could be 'bundled' out of the colony, then the masters of Swan River were content. But when in 1864 the Imperial Government, partly in response to eastern colonial grumbles about undesirable immigrants from Western Australia, insisted that conditional pardon men must henceforth serve out their full sentences at Swan River, even the sturdiest supporters of convictism began to lose interest. And while there were pockets of concern, it seems that by and large the masters of Swan River did not lament the cessation of transportation in 1868.[17]

Another reason for employer discontent with convictism seems to have been a belief that the character of convicts sent to Western Australia worsened through time. Even though the colony did not receive female convicts, the 'crowning iniquity' of the eastern colonial experience, as Battye put it,[18] and even though there were proportionately fewer Irish in the Western Australian contingent, it was evident that as the 1850s wore on, the British officials began to send to Western Australia men convicted of serious crimes, men 'least fit to be discharged at home', as an 1862 report expressed it.[19] To some it seemed that the rot set in as early as 1853, when two boatloads of Irish convicts reached the colony, in direct contravention of what the colonists believed was a compact with the Imperial Government.[20] That this was indeed the case has been proved by Sandra Taylor in an analysis of all convicts arriving in Western Australia in the base years 1850–51, 1861–62, and 1866–68.[21] Analysis of a different kind, namely a one in eight study of an alphabetical listing of all the convicts sent to Western Australia, suggests that not only was there a worsening of character through time, but that overall the convicts sent to Western Australia were as 'disreputable' a lot, perhaps even more so, than that sent to New South Wales and Van Diemen's Land. Certainly proportionately more had committed serious crimes against persons and property.[22]

Making sense of the colonial experience of convictism necessarily involves questioning the myth that by and large the convicts were absorbed happily into Westralian society. It seems to be generally agreed that under the enlightened administration of the Controller General, Captain Henderson, there was little human misery in the gaols and on the public works. It seems also agreed that 'a considerable number of convicts . . . did make good, acquire property, marry and melt into the community',[23] and that 'the settlers and their servants seem to have led a contented life'.[24] It may be a matter of regional perspective, though one

16   House of Commons, Select Committee on Transportation, 1861, British Parliamentary Papers, No. 286, p.43, 22 March 1861.
17   Valuable information on the convict system is contained in C. J. Gertzel 'The Convict System in Western Australia', honours dissertation, UWA, 1949; also P. Anderson 'Economic Aspects of Transportation to Western Australia', honours dissertation, UWA, 1950.
18 and 19   Battye *History of Western Australia*, p.465.
20   For a comment on this see Alexandra Hasluck *Unwilling Emigrants*, 1959, Appendix C.
21   Sandra Taylor 'The Convicts of WA 1850–68', honours dissertation, UWA, 1978.
22   The source of the analysis is the *Western Australian Biographical Index, Volume 3, 'The Convicts'*, published by UWAP, 1979. There is a full discussion of this in C. T. Stannage 'Introduction', in K. McPherson and P. Simpson (eds.) *Bibliography of Convictism in Western Australia*, 1979.
23   Hasluck *Unwilling Emigrants*, p.109.   24   Crowley *Australia's Western Third*, p.52.

doubts that this would be so. But for Perth it seems a less than accurate picture of social relations and social experience during the convict years, and even after, as the story of Henry Haynes shows. There were times indeed when Perth seemed to be a society under siege, with strengthened doors, fitted locks, restricted personal movement (especially for women and children), and over and above this nervousness and concern, the actual felt experience of personal violence, alienation, and degradation.

After a honeymoon year or so, in which the newspapers reported that even with more than one thousand ticket-of-leavers at large all was well within Swan River society, the mood of the free population changed dramatically to one of concern. In September 1851, a numerously signed petition seeking police protection was forwarded to the Government by Thomas Helms and J. W. Hardey. And by December 1851 there were letters to the press from 'Johnny Newcombe' expressing fears for his family in Perth, with one in three of the adult population a ticket-of-leaver. In January 1853 the *Perth Gazette* wrote worriedly of the 'daily plunderings which are taking place', and 'the constant state of anxiety in which the good matrons of Perth every night go to rest'. In 1853 polite society in Perth suffered from the depredations of the audacious escapee, Jevan, who with his gang robbed houses at will 'to the very serious alarm of the inhabitants'. He was given refuge in Crane's pub down near the Causeway and in workers' huts under Mt Eliza. Twice he escaped from Fremantle prison, once on the Police Magistrate's horse. When caught finally after a shoot-out with police he was sentenced to an extra five years' gaol, 'seasoned' with 100 lashes and fed on bread and water for three weeks. There was another lot in 1854, and so on.[25] More than ever before the free men carried guns by day, and even in the stifling hot summer evenings few citizens left windows open or ventured out of the house. When the convicts escaped, as they did frequently, the settlers made 'the usual precautions' as 'a feeling akin to fear crept over us at the intelligence received, that the armed runaways were approaching this neighbourhood'. The precautions were usually the posting of armed guards at the entrances to the town, mooring boats together, hobbling the horses, and the placing of women and children in a central spot. In 1927 Mrs J. B. Roe, who before and after her marriage in 1866 lived in Adelaide Terrace, remembered vividly the fear experienced with escaped convicts at large, entering houses with impunity. She also remembered how the house was locked up for the night and the silver taken up to bed.[26] The court depositions of the mothers of assaulted children reveal only too clearly that Western Australia from 1850 to the 1870s was not a 'contented society'. Respected families began to leave the colony in protest against the convict presence: as Archdeacon Wollaston put it in 1853

> Respectable people of the Upper Class are moving away . . . They now dread the prospect of leaving [their children] in a penal colony . . . and they are right.[27]

But the tougher men—the Roes, Habgoods, Meares, the Shentons, the Samsons, and the Burges'—stayed to harness the convicts and did so as fully as the law would permit. 'The old rural settlers', as Kimberly was to

---

[25] *Perth Gazette*, 5 September, 19 December 1851; 22 October 1852; 28 January, 5 August, 2 December 1853; 24 February 1854.

[26] *Perth Gazette*, 7 June 1867; 'Some Old Time Memories', *Early Days* Vol. 1, Pt. I, 1927.

[27] Canon Percy U. Henn (ed.) *Wollaston's Albany Journals 1848–56*, Paterson, 1955, p.146.

write some years later, 'became conservative in everything',[28] and this was to be of the greatest political, economic, and social importance to Western Australia through to the goldrushes and beyond.

Battye, Crowley, and Hasluck did not examine the structure of colonial society and hence could not assess the impact of convictism on a range of groups of people. But it seems clear that the life experiences of many people were changed drastically by the presence of convicts. Perhaps this was most true of the Aborigines who, already suffering from the fatal impact, were still further degraded by the brutalised white convicts in ways which serious research is only beginning to reveal, especially in the areas of drunkenness and sexual abuse.[29] Those free white labourers who had survived the depression years of the 1840s and had begun to benefit from a perceived shortage of labour in the colony found that the arrival of convicts caused their wages to slump by up to 60%.[30] For a brief period a battle was enjoined between bond and free labour, with the masters determining the outcome in favour of the bond class. Many 'old colonial hands', as the free labourers were called, left Western Australia to seek freedom and independence in the gold-rich eastern colonies. In time some masters would learn to regret their departure, for convict labour though cheaper was usually less efficient. Free artisans too were affected by the massive inflow of convicts leading to an oversupply of skilled labour. Mechanics wrote of their 'not so certain six and thirty shillings a week'; others left the colony for Victoria. In the debates of the Mechanics' Institute such men would deplore the continuation of transportation; supported by their powerful leader, the Surveyor General Septimus Roe, they would also not permit ex-convicts to join the Institute, thereby opening yet another fissure in the social fabric of Western Australia.[31] In time the ex-convicts gave notice of their increasing respectability by establishing a rival working men's association. In these ways were social distinctions institutionalised.[32]

The impact of convictism on the churches was considerable. The Anglicans sought to contain and channel convictism in the Wittenoomian mould. The Roman Catholic Church increased its membership greatly and became a powerful pressure group for the first time in the colony's history, and an increase in sectarianism flowed from this. One Roman Catholic prison chaplain described the Protestant chaplain as 'an agent of the Devil' and his congregation as 'infidels who would be eternally damned', an outburst which won him suspension from office. And, despite the fact that less than one thousand Irish convicts were sent to Swan River, they were sufficiently numerous and vocal for the historian to observe that convictism imported the Irish problem to Western Australia. It will also be possible to comment on the experiences of the immigrant girls, over one thousand of whom arrived

[28] W. B. Kimberly *History of West Australia: a Narrative of her Past together with Biographies of her Leading Men*, F. W. Niven, 1897, p.193.

[29] See, for example, a report written by the Protector of Aborigines for York, Mr W. Cowan, in *Perth Gazette*, 10 February 1854.

[30] *Perth Gazette*, 19 November 1852.

[31] *Perth Gazette*, 6 February, 5 March 1852. Minute Book of the Swan River Mechanics Institute (held in the PCC), 4, 11 September 1854; also 7, 14 December 1857; and 4 April 1864, when Roe attended after hearing of a move to allow ex-convicts to join the Society; also *Perth Gazette*, 30 March 1864. A debate on transportation was held on 29 October 1866, while debates on the future development of the colony, held in 1855 and 1858, turned in part on the convict question.

[32] See B. Smith 'Early Western Australian Literature, a Guide to Colonial Life', *University Studies in History* Vol.4, No. 1, 1961–62, pp.47–73.

in Swan River from Ireland and the poor London parishes of St Giles and St George's, and the cotton mills of Lancashire. Some of them married convicts and free settlers and lived well; others fell still further and found their way to low lodging houses, the numerous brothels which sprang up in this period, or to the Poor House. The life experiences of the Pensioner Guards who accompanied the convict transports to Swan River have been partly charted; but much more needs to be known of the ways in which they coped with the unrelenting hostility of the convicts, as well as the fate of their womenfolk who were usually shunned by polite society. For some, certainly, the promise of independence in the golden lands of Australasia turned into a nightmare.[33]

Still another group deeply affected by the convict presence was the police force. The masters of Swan River expected working class policemen to keep the peace and to protect life and property, yet underpaid them (even with assistance from the Imperial Government), under-equipped them, and opposed increases in the size of the force. Consequently the police were often unable to carry out their duties efficiently, thus incurring the wrath of the free population. As the editor of the *Perth Gazette* put it:

> There is no body or class of men against whom people generally have so much prejudice as to the police. The prejudice is no doubt vulgar, but yet it is real and deeply rooted.[34]

And the police suffered terribly at the hands of the convicts. They and their families were sometimes poisoned with strychnine; they were knifed; they were shot; they were bludgeoned ('the unfortunate constable was found lying speechless and senseless . . . a long jagged wound on the crown of his head'); and they suffered the verbal abuse which only brutalised working men heap on one another. Their womenfolk were constantly at risk and fearful, as the reminiscences of one of them, Mrs Anne Morrison, testifies. The following exchange was not atypical. One night Constable O'Hara arrested George Johnstone, a ticket-of-leaver, drinking after hours (10 p.m.) in Tom Cleverley's Liverpool Arms lodging house. For Johnstone the offence meant that his ticket would be revoked.

> Johnstone: 'I am a poor man and you want to get me into trouble . . . let me go you bloody swine'.
> O'Hara: 'You've stabbed me'.
> Johnstone: 'Yes you bloody swine. I'll cook you before I let you take me to the Station.'

In these experiences lie the origins of strongly held and persisting popular attitudes towards the police, as well as that prickliness, that defensiveness, which is so characteristic of the Western Australian police force.[35]

---

[33] The quotation comes from *Perth Gazette*, 13 January 1854. On all these topics W. B. Kimberly *History of Western Australia* remains the best secondary source. See also F. H. Broomhall 'The Veterans: a History of the Enrolled Pensioner Force of Western Australia', mss Battye Library, 2 vols., 1975.

[34] *Perth Gazette*, 25 November 1870. Three years earlier (*Perth Gazette*, 27 September 1867), several policemen were dismissed from service, allegedly for cowardice. Also *WA Times*, 4 April 1879—commentary on a bystander being charged with failing to render assistance to a policeman. For the first of the grumbles about low pay see *Perth Gazette*, 30 April 1852.

[35] *Perth Gazette*, 1 March 1867; Supreme Court Case File 650, October 1874; 'The Reminiscences of Mrs Annie Morrison, 1853–1942', *Early Days*, February 1945, pp.10–14. Between 1874 and 1876 Mrs Morrision lived at the police station near the Causeway in Adelaide Terrace. The Anglican Orphanage was next door; there were labourers at work in the brick fields nearby; and the *Cricketers' Arms* was well patronised by what Mrs Morrison called 'suspicious characters'.

For the convicts themselves life was often nasty, brutish and short. While conditions in Fremantle Gaol may never have been as bad as those of the secondary penal settlements of New South Wales or Van Diemen's Land, they were almost certainly less pleasant than they have been portrayed to date. Even under the reforming hand of Henderson, the ball and chain, the lash, the triangle and the dark cell were well used. And Hampton's regime was so vicious that it earned him the censure of the Imperial Government; he had, after all, learnt his trade in Van Diemen's Land and on Norfolk Island. Battye, Hasluck and Crowley have contended that conditions were better in Western Australia partly because there was no assignment system. But this is rather misleading for one could equally contend that Western Australia had a unique ticket-of-leave system which was as unpredictable in its effects as was the old assignment system. As Kimberly wrote: 'Cases are chronicled where a ticket-of-leave man laboured under a hard inhuman taskmaster'. And in a letter published in *Cornhill Magazine* in 1866 an ex-convict wrote of 'hardwork, irregular meals, [and] contemptuous treatment'.[36] Many men, allegedly free, eked out semi-pauperised existances in an inhospitable physical and social environment; some died as 'official' paupers in Government institutions set up in Perth to receive them. Others went mad and were locked in 'barbarous and inhuman places'[37] until the Government built a grand new Asylum for them at Fremantle. More attempted to and succeeded in committing suicide, usually in the most appalling and bloody manner:

> He first cut himself about the legs apparently with a design of bleeding himself to death, but we suppose that this appeared to be too lingering for him, and he then cut his throat directly under the chin, severing the gullet and cutting into the jugular arter.[38]

Indeed so common did suicide become that in June 1858 the Mechanics' Institute held a debate on the subject. Still others, overcome by the lack of women or the frustrating presence of an inaccessible few, committed crimes of violence, bestiality, sodomy, and rape: 'The Devil had tempted him . . . marks of the ruffian's fingers on her neck and shoulders . . . hair torn from her head'. Indeed, 'the peculiar circumstances in which this colony was placed' induced Justice Mackie to retain rape as a capital offence after it was removed as such from the statutes of England.[39] In these years too Perth was a besotted community as the ex-convicts drank their problems away and stoutly resisted (often with illicit distilling) the attempts of the zealous temperance governor, Arthur Kennedy, to deny them what was rightfully theirs. It was in this period that Ferguson and Mumme's brewery (the 'Stanley', later 'The Swan') developed rapidly.

Still others turned to crime, both petty and great. Far from convictism not leading to a marked increase in crime,[40] it can be shown that between 1850 and 1860, 40% of the cases heard before the Court of Quarter Sessions involved convicts and ex-convicts as defendants; this

[36] Kimberly *History of Western Australia*, p.174; Anon 'A letter from a Convict in Australia to a Brother in England', *Cornhill Magazine* Vol. 13, January-June 1866, pp.489–512.

[37] *Perth Gazette*, 25 September 1857: 'God help the poor madmen for in Western Australia they have none other to help them'.

[38] *Perth Gazette*, 29 December 1854.

[39] The first quotation comes from *Perth Gazette*, 9 January 1857; the second from *Perth Gazette*, 8 July 1853.

[40] Hasluck *Unwilling Emigrants*, p. 109: 'The fact that after the influx of convicts there was not a great deal of added crime in the community shows either that the impulse, or the incentive, was not there'.

rose to 72% of cases heard by the Supreme Court between 1861 and 1870; 65% between 1870 and 1880; and as late as 1880 to 1890 still 40%. Charges heard, per head of population, doubled after 1850. Not until 1891 did the Supreme Court cease to distinguish between bond and free.[41] In the single year 1867, the Court of Petty Sessions heard no less than 3408 cases, all but 800 of which involved 'unwilling emigrants'; and in 1881 Western Australia had the highest crime rate of all the Australian colonies.[42] These years saw the emergence of a criminal sub-culture in colonial Perth: low lodging houses, pubs (one for every seventy-five male adults in the colony), brothels, and men with names like 'the Thief', 'Crankey Dan', 'Monkey Mick', 'Steam-up' and 'Shakey'. Crowley's assertion that 'there were not more than half a dozen convicts whose exploits could be described as "bushranging" '[43] cries out for revision. Even the most tentative listing would include Mick Nolan, James Lilley, James Fry, William Graham, William Scott, Jevan, Duffy, Brooks, Robert Palin, Phillip Dixson, George Williams, Gray of York, Rogers of Victoria Plains, Bernard Wootton, John Thomas, and Martin, not to mention thugs like Edward Bishop, John Lloyd, and William Norton. Most of these men were very unlike Moondyne Joe who thieved lightly, went unarmed, and rarely resisted arrest. While at the time they enjoyed a measure of support from among the lower orders, they have been suppressed in folk memory and edited out of WA historical writing. Some of the most desperate men committed murder and were sentenced to be hanged from the gallows outside Perth Gaol. In 1856 John Scott was conveyed in an open waggon through the streets of Perth, exciting the 'morbid and idle curiosity' of the crowd which followed him across to Beaufort Street for the hanging.[44] Morton, Thomas, Lewis and others followed Scott. Executions were carried out in Perth until the late 1880s. In 1867 one of the most infamous escapees, Bernard Wootton, who had cracked open the skull of a policemen, asked the Court: 'Would you not have done it to get your liberty?' Sentenced to death, Wootton

> continued hardened to the last, rejecting all offers of religious ministrations. On the scaffold his last words were a shout for the Irish Republic.[45]

Perhaps more typical were men like Samuel Williams. In the 1850s, as a young man, he was charged several times for vagrancy. Then in 1861 he was transported to Western Australia for theft. In 1863-64 he cut his irons and escaped and while at large frightened a good many people. He was recaptured, given 100 lashes, and sent back to prison. Freed in the early 1870s he earned a living by collecting sponges from the beach and selling them in the town. Sometimes he pretended to be blind and begged in the streets of Perth. He lived with a fish hawker to whom he paid rent of 1s a week. When he couldn't meet his rent he slept on open land near the house. One day in 1874 he stole goods and cash from William Knight, Registrar General and Church of England warden. The next day he treated his friends Francis, James Budd and Fanny Essex to plenty of

[41]   These percentages are based on an analysis of the Criminal Court Record Book, Vol. 1, 1830-87, held in the Supreme Court of Western Australia. I am grateful to the Master of the Supreme Court for permission to use the records in his care.
[42]   WA Blue Book, 1867; H. H. Hayter Victorian Year Book, 1881-82, pp.368-75. In 1878, ten years after the cessation of transportation, WA's crime rate was seven times that of neighbouring South Australia.
[43]   Crowley Australia's Western Third, p.36.
[44]   Perth Gazette, 18 January 1856.
[45]   Perth Gazette, 11 October 1867.

WESTERN AUSTRALIA.

Form 22A.

Printed at H. M. Convict Prison,
Brixton, Surrey. 200 1—72.

Reg. No.	Name	Crime and Sentence	Date of Conviction	Date of Ticket-of-leave	Remarks
7309	Saml Williams	Burglary & Pre Conviction 7 years P.S.	9th Decr 1861	18th June 1870	Expiree

Subsequent Re-convictions.

31.7.63. Absconding 2 years H.L. 31.7.63. Horse stealing 3 years H.L. 30.9.64. Absconding 7 mos Sol: confт 6 mos in Irons and to receive 50 Lashes. 30.9.64. Using obscene language 50 Lashes. 22.6.65. Cutting his Irons & boring through his cell window 100 Lashes. 17.2.68. Receiving stolen property 12 mo H.L. 19.2.68. Absconding 12 mo H.L. in Irons. 6.12.70. Absconding 3 mos H.L.

Previous Convictions

1855. Stealing 6 mos. 1860. Fraud 6 mos. 1860. Fraud 6 mos. 28.4.55. Vagrancy 1 month. January 1853. Vagrancy 1 month.

pro. Acting Comptroller General,
Perth 18th March 1874.

The record sheet of Samuel Williams, expiree, 1874.

grog. Someone informed on him,[46] and he went back to prison for ten years.[47]

Of course this is not the whole story. Certainly many convicts did settle down comfortably as teachers, artisans, small farmers (especially in the Avon Valley where by 1859 a quarter of the properties were held by ex-convicts, though much less than a quarter of the land actually being farmed),[48] builders, and so on. Many married and raised children, though until research currently being undertaken is concluded the exact number will remain unknown.[49] Many convicts stayed in the metropolitan area where most of them subsisted at the bottom of the

46 Ex-convicts often gave evidence—sometimes false—against each other, usually because the Court paid them to attend, thereby helping to 'raise the wind' for rent. See an article on this subject in *Perth Gazette*, 26 March 1858.
47 Supreme Court Case File No. 630, March 1874.
48 Information provided by Ms Margaret Grellier, whose MA in progress 'Family and Society in Western Australia in the Mid Nineteenth Century', University of WA, is based in part upon an analysis of the individual householder census schedules for York in 1859. Ms Grellier is writing a chapter on this subject in C. T. Stannage (General Editor), *A New History of Western Australia*, University of WA Press, 1979.
49 Work in progress, Mrs R. Erickson, 1 Boronia Avenue, Nedlands, Western Australia.

100

social pile.[50] Perhaps up to one-third of the Western Australian convicts left the colony to better their condition in the eastern colonies. But even those who stayed and made good carried the mark of their shame with them to the grave. They were not allowed to join agricultural societies, mechanics' institutes, or attend gentry-run dances. One of them wrote:

> every day of his life, every house he enters, wheresoever, and by whomsoever he is employed, he is the recipient of that cool look, that luke-warmness, which makes him feel his condition in a manner no words can express.

And with great feeling he added:

> There has been no Thomas Wright, no moral physician, no authoress of a *Mary Barton*, no Henry Mayhew to labour for Britain's erring sons in Western Australia.[51]

The Family: Ideal and Reality

In the world which evolved in Perth to 1884 when Henry Haynes killed his wife, the 'family' was a central institution in the quest for 'internal peace'. The gentry accepted full-heartedly the family ideal as espoused by Victorian writers like Tennyson and Ruskin and the countless writers of *Sunday at Home* and other journals. The home was seen as a 'vestal temple', impenetrable to terror, doubt and division—a 'Place of Peace'. The married mother was an angel, the father a 'Father in Heaven'; and in this way the moral authority of the Anglican Church was transferred to the family home.[52] In Perth the press printed articles on 'Home and Its Pleasures'. It dwelt on the 'Serene Highness' of the home, where 'dear domestic love and gentleness are the presiding angels'. The 'dear domestic love' of home transcended class boundaries and was found in the 'thatched cottage through which the hollow wind whistles, as well as in the gorgeous palatial pile'. If the father was a 'Father in Heaven', the wife and mother was at one and the same time subordinate and holy: 'Man to command, and woman to obey', as Tennyson put it; yet divine also. The *Perth Gazette* often printed articles with titles like 'The Value of Good Wives', and 'A Little Lesson for Well-disposed Wives', and it wrote of women as the principal guardians of future generations and the most powerful humanizing agents.[53] In short, the ideal of home and family appealed powerfully to the leading colonists as a way of ordering their own lives and of securing stability and humanity in the lives of the serving classes. Adherence to the institution of marriage would not only humanize the lower orders, but would make decent, God-fearing and industrious citizens who would carry the peace of the home into their daily occupation within their ordained station in life.

In Western Australia the ideal of marriage and the family was promoted very vigorously at least in part because of the enormous social disequilibrium produced by the presence of thousands of single male convicts drawn from the lower orders of society. In 1850 the gentry thought that the Imperial Government had agreed to send out free

Emma Thomson (née Roe): a marriage testament, 1856.
Domestic Happiness

Why has God filled the earth with these little bands of united individuals called families, if He had not in this arrangement, designed to promote the virtue and happiness of mankind? If there be anything which will soothe the agitating passions of the soul, which will calm that turbulence of feeling which the din and bustle of the world do frequently excite, it is the soothing influence of a cheerful fireside. (A man) 'goes out into the world to discharge his duties, and returns to his quiet home for happiness and repose'.

from the diary of
Emma Thomson (née Roe)

---

50 The author is comparing the convict lists with the rate book lists for Perth in 1879–80 and 1889.
51 'Justus', in *Perth Gazette*, 14 May 1858.
52 W. E. Houghton *The Victorian Frame of Mind 1830–70*, 1957, Chapter 13.
53 *Perth Gazette*, 18 July 1851; 5 May 1854; 4 February 1859; 13 June 1865; some cited from M. Grellier's pioneering chapter 'Family and Society', in C. T. Stannage (General Editor) *A New History of Western Australia*, 1979.

A. H. Stone: arch-recorder of
gentry domesticity.

female immigrants in numbers sufficient to match the incursion of male
convicts. They also thought that the Government had agreed to send out
the wives of married convicts, who formed nearly 20% of the total
number.[54] In the event very few wives of convicts came to Swan River,
mainly because the married men found it difficult to establish contact
with families, and found also that the cost of repayment of their passages
would be beyond them. Most gave up and sought the more temporary
comforts of what women were available in the colony, black or white.
Some formed more lasting bigamous arrangements,[55] unless detected and
prevented from so doing by zealous policemen and clergymen, for as the
Rev. David Shearer wrote on one occasion: 'Now I think such a thing
should be punished and that Ministers should thus be protected from
being imposed upon'.[56] But such things occurred nevertheless. In the
event also, the rate of free female immigration fell well behind that of
male convict importation, although close to 2000 poor girls and young
women did enter the colony from Ireland and England, to service gentry
mistresses and convict masters. For the first two years of convictism all
seemed well for there was a high marriage rate of convicts and immigrant
women.[57] But thereafter the numerical gap between married and single
men grew markedly and led to expressions of concern about the future of
the colony. In Perth in 1870, 60% of the adult males were single; there

54   *WA Biographical Index, Volume 3, 'The Convicts',* published by the University of WA
      Press, 1979.
55   Millett *Australian Parsonage,* p.4.
56   Supreme Court Criminal Court File No. 1076, July 1884.
57   *Perth Gazette,* 22 October 1852.

were nearly three single men for each single woman in the town. These proportions had altered slightly for the better by 1881, the date of the next census.[58] Put another way, in 1870 and again in 1881 the adult population of Perth contained about 45% unmarried men and women. This in itself was a sufficient reason for promoting the family ideal with great vigour.

The deficiency of eligible partners could have been overcome by agreeing to the introduction of female convicts. Some settlers, notably the Fremantle merchant Lionel Samson, prepared and signed petitions in favour of female convicts being brought to Swan River; but other members of the gentry, particularly leading Methodists like Shenton and the Hardeys, strongly opposed the move, as did the Anglican Bishop of Perth, Mathew Hale. The *Perth Gazette* put their viewpoint succinctly:

> With all our respect for the fair sex, we cannot but consider a bad woman as likely to do more mischief than a bad man; a woman must be very bad indeed to get transported.[59]

When in 1858 the Imperial Government decided once and for all that female convicts would not be sent to Swan River, the news was greeted with relief by most men and women of 'respectability and comfort';[60] the views of the male convicts in Swan River were not sought.

The exemplars of the familial ideal were the Governor's wife and the wives of the gentry. Government House and the Governor's Lady were to Swan River society what Queen Victoria and Buckingham Palace were

The Familial Ideal of the Empire: *Queen Victoria, Prince Albert, and the infant Duke of Connaught, receive homage from the Duke of Wellington. (Winterhaler, artist.)*

to the British Nation and Empire. If ever a governor exchanged cross words with his wife, not a syllable was breathed out of Government House. Mrs Hampton, Lady Robinson, and the rest, cultivated the arts,

[58] Censuses of Western Australia, 1870, 1881.
[59] *Perth Gazette*, 17 March 1854.   [60] *Perth Gazette*, 21 May 1858.

engaged in charitable activities, ran a domestic economy, and appeared in public with their husbands. Above all they and their families appeared in church on Sunday mornings. There they sat in the front pews and forgave those who trespassed against them, some of whom sat in the pews behind. The wives of the gentry did likewise. One such was Josephine Prinsep (née Bussell) who in 1868 had married Henry C. Prinsep, then a landowner in the south-west of the colony. The Prinseps' courtship had been idyllic, rather like those in the popular romantic novels of the day by James, Ainsworth and others. Josephine and Henry met at an 'At Home' on the Bussell estate. They went sailing and riding together, though always in company. He admired her skill in the saddle and how charmingly she played the piano and sang. One afternoon, about a month after they had met, they fell behind the others while out riding. Henry declared his love for her, and although Josephine said that it was too early to speak of such things, he knew he had cause to be happy. One evening, not long after this, he held her hand, even though a Bussell auntie was watching. Soon they were betrothed. Eighteen months later they were married in the local Anglican church.[61]

Josephine Prinsep was nineteen years of age when she gave birth to their first child, a daughter whom they named Carlotta. Then in April 1873 Josephine experienced the horror of giving birth to a still-born baby; indeed so heavily did she bleed that she almost lost her own life. There had been nothing about this in the literary ideal of the family, although in Western Australia in these years one in ten babies died within twelve months of being born. The timely arrival of the doctor saved Josephine; and Henry, her family, their servants and neighbours, rallied around her and aided her recovery. In 1874 the Prinseps removed to Perth where they lived happily for many years. Henry had lost his estates, and indeed seems glad to have done so; but he had won respectable employment in the Lands and Survey Department and the couple were *persona grata* in polite society and at Government House. In Perth, Josephine had other children: Emily in 1875 and a third daughter in 1880. On one occasion Josephine complained that Henry did too little work around the garden of their house in Howick Street, but Henry soon rectified that and in all other respects their family life went smoothly. They attended church regularly. They enjoyed their daughters' birthdays—for her sixth birthday Carlotta received a red scarf, a skipping rope, a copybook, a magenta ribbon, a puzzle, a packet of jujubes and a doll. Perhaps not all these presents came from her family for Carlotta had had a birthday party, girls only. Her diarist father recorded that Carlotta 'screamed with delight' when given her presents.[62] Carlotta's thoughtful parents had also opened in her name a savings bank account into which they had deposited £3. Birthdays came and went and the family enjoyed Perth to the full. The work around the house was done by Isaac, Joseph, or Mr Jones, while Mary attended to most of the cooking and house-cleaning. Henry read Tennyson's 'Lady of the Lake' to his daughters, and Carlotta and he agreed that *Alice in Wonderland* was the 'funniest book ever'. And the fashionable photographer, Chopin, took family photographs, some of which were sent back to England for the enjoyment of relatives there—a perfect and

Josephine

J ust at the hour when dusky twilight fades,

O n me the dearest eyes of love incline,

S erenely calm above the darking shades,

E ach peeping star on my delight doth shine,

P indaric ode or Spenser's flowing line

H as not the voice to sing the joys I mean:

I ne'er can tell how sweet a lot is mine,

N o words for me can ever paint the scene.

E nchanted, I can utter naught but Josephine.

---

[61]   Prinsep 'Diary', Battye Library, entries for 11 October, 6, 7, 8, 13, 16 November 1866; there is also A. C. Staples 'Henry Charles Prinsep', *Early Days* Vol. 5, Pt. I, 1955, pp.31–52, in which he quotes Prinsep's delightful love poem, called simply 'Josephine'.

[62]   Prinsep 'Diary', 17 June 1874.

irrefutable statement of domestic harmony in Swan River. In Spring the family would go shopping in the early evening or call in on friends at mutually convenient times. There were visits from Bussell relatives, visits to the Brockmans and other friends on the Upper Swan, and balls at Government House where Tennyson's new Anthem was sung. For Henry there were painting lessons to be given to Lady Robinson, billiards to be played at the Weld Club, the races to attend with lively friends like James Roe and George Vincent, books to read (from Fenimore Cooper to the Colenso controversy), theatre sets to be designed and painted, and time to dream of writing an autobiography. Josephine and he could deprecate the habits of the 'low living' woman who had taken a house behind them; but Josephine accepted it as her duty to take the daughter of one of their own labourers to the Colonial Hospital for treatment for an ulcerated mouth. In the rhythms of the Prinseps' life the ideal and reality of the Victorian family were fused. They gave to the history of Perth its characteristic image of a relaxed and harmonious community.

In Perth in these years marriage was a normal condition for 90% of the women in their mid-twenties and above. In the mid-1850s almost five in ten women had married in the old country and had emigrated with their families to Swan River; but by the early 1880s seven in ten marriages had taken place in the colony. Many of the free families who came to Swan River in the late 1840s and 1850s aspired to and achieved respectability and comfort, though the path to prosperity was rarely

William Buggins: *builder of a church and a family.*

smooth. Such families included the Snowballs, the Sherwoods, the Churchyards, the Courthopes, the Brittains, the Britnalls, the Summers, the Christies, the Letchs, the Hallidays and the Buggins, names far less well known today than in their own times. These men won Government, Council, and private building, construction, and communication contracts. Others became publicans and storekeepers. None entered the Legislative Council, but several, as 'fit and proper' persons, played prominent roles in the Perth City Council and institutions like the Mechanics' Institute and the Perth Building Society (founded in 1862). They were mostly good churchmen, whether Anglicans (St John's in Melbourne Road rather than the Cathedral, except on grand occasions), Wesleyans, Congregationalists, and Roman Catholics. Their wives worked harder than the Josephine Prinseps of Perth. Washing the family clothes usually took a full day: the tub, often a hogshead cut in half, was heavy and awkward to handle; and the water had to be drawn from a well by windlass and then heated over the open fire, an exhausting task at the best of times but awesomely so during the summer months. A second day was spent ironing. Some clothes, such as crinoline dresses, with their several yards of material, had to be starched and ironed, for the wives of these families kept to the fashions set by the gentry, and especially by one of Perth's great beauties, Mrs Hora, wife of Dr Hora. Perhaps a third day would be spent making and repairing clothes, for the wives in these families tended to buy clothes for very special occasions only, and even then to buy the material to be made up by a dressmaker and milliner. And on all days there was the food to be cooked, usually for no less than seven people. Only with increased prosperity was it possible to retain a serving girl to assist with the chores. Probably never more than 25% of the households of Perth in these years had servants. Like Josephine Prinsep most of these women lost at least one child in infancy; many also suffered a miscarriage. Very few of the younger children in a family reached marriageable age with both parents alive, for often they were the eighth to the twelfth child and born to a mother who was in her mid-thirties and a father in his forties. Influenza, 'colonial fever' and smallpox, not to mention accidental drownings in river, swamp and well, swelled the death rate in any one family. Family bereavements were always painful and deeply felt experiences; but central to the rituals of death was a belief in the heavenly family and an affirmation of the value and necessity of family and home on earth. The Bible was a 'Family Bible', and the hymn and prayer books were valued sources of spiritual and moral sustenance.[63] In all respects they shared the familial ideal of the gentry, just as they shared the gentry's vision of an ordered society. Respectability and comfort were theirs.

The children of such families in Perth had plenty to do to occupy their time. They all went to primary school, paying 3*d* a week for the privilege. A few boys went to Bishop Hale's school, many more went to Perth Boys' School, the Roman Catholic and Wesleyan schools, and the several private schools like Mr Letch's 'Commercial School' in St George's Terrace. The girls went to private church schools run by Miss Leonard, Miss Knight, the Sisters of Mercy, and others, while nearly half attended the State Girls' School in Pier Street, just off St George's Terrace. The non-Catholic private schools came and went with some

At school in the 1870s and 1880s: *Mr Letch's Commercial School.*

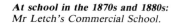

[63] J. E. Hammond 'The Builders of Perth' *Early Days* Vol. 1, Pt. XI, 1931, pp.58–64; interview Mrs M. Riley, September 1975; Grellier 'Family and Society'; W. Lutton *The Story of Wesley Church*, 1970.

A playground for the children of Perth: Hay Street in the 1870s.

rapidity, and some pupils certainly went to three or four schools before leaving to begin work, usually from twelve years upwards, and most often to apprenticeships or junior clerical work in the case of boys, and quasi-domestic service and shop assistance for girls. From the 1870s a handful of boys and girls attended high school.[64] Most of the schools had a religious base. Even in Perth Boys' School, run by the Government, the boys recited daily from a wall-chart:

> A Christian should endeavour, as the Apostle Paul commands, to live peaceably with all men.

And, as often as not, the school prizes were books on the adventures of missionaries like Dr Livingstone or the verse of Christian poets like Montgomerie.[65]

For all time and in all places: a boy and his dog.

But every schoolday had a lunchtime and a period of free play after school hours. For the boys at Perth Boys' there was the old mill pond behind the school; there was always the gleaming Swan River for fishing and crabbing; there were the vacant grants for bird-nesting and for playing marbles; there were bull frogs to catch behind Lee Steere's house; there were sham native battles to be fought. For the children of the town there was always the open grant behind Haysom's Horse and Groom, between Murray and Hay Streets. There the boys would organize themselves into foot-races, hop-step-and-jump competitions, and they would play Red Rover, cricket, and prisoner's base. There were also sham native wars with homemade weapons. In Haysom's yard too they would watch in amazement the feats of the stars of Stebbings' Circus. Along the streets the children would poke fun at 'Old Mother Kate, 28', a shabbily dressed old lady with a red and white handkerchief round her neck. And when the spirit moved them they would gather near the widow Dalton's house and marvel at the old recluse and throw stones onto her roof to see if she would come out. She never did. But it was fun anyway.

The children liked playing in the public gardens, Stirling Square, in the heart of the town. Some of them had first come to the Gardens in

---

[64] D. Mossenson *State Education in Western Australia*, 1972, p.61; L. Fletcher 'Educating of People', in C. T. Stannage (General Editor) *A New History of Western Australia*, 1979; *Perth Gazette*.

[65] *Western Mail*, 14 February 1935: a letter from Albert Mason, nephew of Ben Mason, well-known businessman in Perth in the 1870s.

prams, pushed by older sisters, mothers and, less frequently, by nursemaids. There they would have heard the Volunteer Band (largely the Bryan family) playing on the much treasured patch of cooch grass, the only plot of green earth in the town. But the Gardens had other attractions, notably the fruit trees which were fair game for the young and nimble. And quick they had to be, because old Enoch Barratt, the ex-convict caretaker, carried a large knobbed stick which he had been known to use (or so it was said) on some luckless children. To the north behind the town lay the swamps where gilgies could be caught with only a piece of string and a small lump of red meat, picked up from a butcher's yard. For the really adventurous there was tobogganing down Mount Street, past where Mr Gresswell, the jeweller, lived. The toboggans were crudely constructed, and tobogganing on Perth's black sand was a cheerful and very dirty occupation. When a little older, the boys, or at least some of them, would retrace their steps to Mount Street, not for tobogganing, but to call in on Mr Gresswell and buy a wedding ring from him, for in those years he and Mr Glaskin, back down the Terrace, had a monopoly on the sale of such items.

If the children required pennies, and they always did, then they could gather leaves from the mulberry trees of the town (especially from the 'Twelve Apostles' outside St George's Cathedral) for Mr Beauteaux, the dentist, would buy them for his silkworms. (Mr Beauteaux made fine silk, but it did not win him a fortune.) If climbing was forbidden, then scavenging for old bones could be profitable, as they returned a 1 d per lb at the foundries of Solomon Cook and Harry McGlew in Murray Street. And by the early 1860s some enterprising boys had become the first of a new breed—sellers of newspapers in the streets of Perth. Other boys earned money by looking after the cows of the town, though they had to reckon with Joe Perry, the official town herdsman. Joe, illiterate but shrewd, had begun as a cow-boy, taking 6 d per week per head from the cow-owners. In his spare moments he caught wild ponies out Wanneroo way and sold them for £1 each to the gentry families. Each time he accumulated £5 he bought an allotment in or around the town. On his death in 1920 his estate was valued at £250,000.

One doubts if Joe ever bought a lolly, but certainly many of the pennies earnt by the boys in this period found their way to old Tom Rollins who owned a lolly shop on the corner of Murray and William Streets. The children believed firmly in the message of the sign over his door:

> I don't care who tries them,
> I don't care who buys them,
> They're the best in town,
> And the most for the money.

Rollins' chief rival for the custom of the young was an ex-convict called affectionately 'Old Churchy'. Churchy lived in one of Joe Perry's whitewashed cottages in Murray Street, but his toffee-making practices were anything but hygienic for he used to spit on his hands to ease the rolling of the black goo. Not to worry. Many a penny destined for the service of the Lord found its way to Churchy's shop on a Sunday afternoon.

If Churchy's lollies were the stuff of life, there were also the grand formal occasions in a child's life. Queen Victoria's birthday was a day the two cannons near the corner of Barrack Street and St George's Terrace would be fired, and there was always a chance that a soldier

would misfire and disable himself. And having sung 'God Save the Queen', the children would sing with equal fervour:

> The 24th of May,
> Queen Victoria's birthday,
> If you won't give us a holiday,
> We'll all run away.[66]

They had plenty of these songs, some of the utmost particularity to Western Australia:

> The Governor's son has got the pip,
> The Governor's got the measles.
> But Moondyne Joe has give 'em the slip,
> Pop goes the weasel.[67]

There were also grand funerals like that of Colonel Bruce, who died in 1870. Bruce, a former acting governor of the colony, was buried with full military honours, after the pall-bearers had struggled with the coffin uphill along sandy Cemetery Road to St Bartholomew's in the east of the town. Much to the children's delight the cortège had been accompanied by the Volunteer Band which played the 'Dead March'. A decade later the children witnessed the opening of the Perth railway station, a celebration which coincided with the colony's golden jubilee. They were lined up opposite the station and each received a new 1 shilling coin. The Aborigines, including children, had also been lined up for the occasion, but they seem not to have received silver coins. But all could enjoy the roast bullock, provided by Mr Eichborn, and wrapped by him in a Union Jack in a quite extraordinary gesture of patriotism. Another well-remembered day in the lives of Perth children was the arrival of the explorer Ernest Giles and his party. To the amazement and delight of the children Giles' camels clambered up the steps of the Town Hall, apparently with the intention of joining the civic dignitaries inside.[68]

Christmas was another festival which these children looked forward to. From the late 1850s, the stationer and printer, Arthur Shenton, advertised Christmas presents for children and adults. In 1864 the *Perth Gazette* carried its first Christmas supplement which contained articles and stories of interest to children, and on 29 December 1871 the same journal printed an editorial on the meaning of the festival. Christmas cards were on sale in the 1870s.[69] Christmas was one of those festivals which reminded the young of the motherland: 'it is becoming fashionable and we, at this antipodean distance from the mother country, are determined to do Christmas in Western Australia . . . family gatherings, large puddings and a profusion of Christmas flowers'.[70] Even a main meal of hot roast beef made practical sense in an era without ice

A Christmas card for Mrs Venn (née Shenton), 1883.

---

[66] See *WA Times*, 24 May 1878 for a sober editorial on the value of the monarchy.

[67] *Sunday Times*, 27 May 1928, cited in I. Elliot *Moondyne Joe*, 1978, p.96.

[68] Many of the incidents related in the paragraphs above come from the files of the *Western Mail*, which in the 1920s and 1930s printed letters and articles on the early days, written by aging men and women who grew up in Perth before the goldrushes. 'Hugh Kalyptus' wrote 'Old Time Memories' in 1919 and 1920; 'Cygnet' contributed many articles and replies to correspondents' queries in the 1930s, and occasional papers were contributed by 'Historicus', 'P. H.', a young journalist, 'C. J. S.' and 'Sandgroper'. Particularly useful issues include 23 October 1919; 27 May 1920 (Perry); 17 December 1925; 6 September 1934 (camels), 11 October 1934 (Stebbins' circus), 11 November 1934 (Berteaux's silkworms); 21 March 1935 (toboggans), 16 May 1935 (Old Mother Kate, 28), 30 May 1935 (gilgie-ing), 20 June 1935 (Churchy). In this book I have been able only to scratch the surface of the ore-laden pages of the *Western Mail*. Also valuable is James Kennedy, born 1848, 'Perth in my Boyhood', *Early Days* Vol. 1, Pt. I, 1927.

[69] See e.g. *Perth Gazette*, 23 December 1879.

[70] *Perth Gazette*, 26 December 1873.

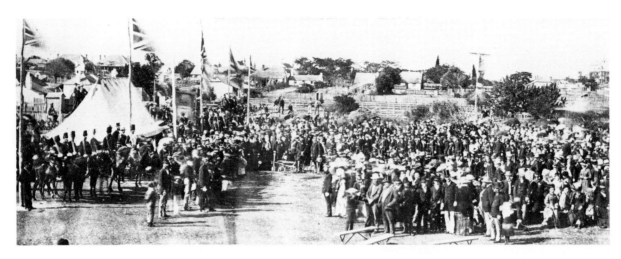

'It is not often that we see a Governor handling a spade':
Governor Ord turns the first sod of Perth's railway station, 1879.

boxes, especially if a servant could be employed to do the cooking. The festival was also used to teach the children about charity—whether for lunatics[71] or Aboriginal children: in 1873 the Church of England Native Mission had a Christmas tree laden with presents given by white children for black children, 'children of the most powerful and most civilized nation in the world to those of, we will not say the most, but we may say one of the most degraded'.[72] Of course Christmas was not for the children only. Fred Sherwood brewed 'a fine old Swan Ale . . . expressly for Christmas use—double the strength of imported ales'.[73] Perhaps he directed this advertisement more to Boxing Day when the serving families exchanged gifts and enjoyed a Sports Carnival put on for them by the gentry.[74] Alas, too often Christmas was a commercial and social success and a religious failure. As the pious owners of the *West Australian* lamented in 1881:

> Looked at from a religious point of view the Christmas festival, in Australia, is—speaking generally—a failure. . . To our unfortunate settlers, Christmas tide often means a saturnalia of drunken servants, lost sheep, bush fires and of every imaginable worry and trouble . . . the way we keep up the Feast of the Nativity is a disgrace to our civilization.[75]

Perhaps the children and the lower orders thought otherwise.

Some grand occasions were planned especially for the children, like the following:

> Tuesday last was a great day for the little folk in Perth, being the feast of the Sunday School Union. Shortly after 9 o'clock the various schools moved in procession from the Boys School, accompanied by their ministers and teachers, and headed by the excellent Royal Engineers Band. About 270 children formed an interesting sight, marching through the town with banners flying, to the recreation ground at Claise Brook, where they were soon joined by many more . . . no less than 400 engaged in various sports. A substantial dinner at 1 o'clock seemed to impart to the youngsters a fresh animus for enjoyment during the afternoon, not lessened by the distribution of enormous quantities of grapes and melons, then tea and plum cake.[76]

71 *WA Times*, December 1863.
72 *Perth Gazette*, 26 December 1863. 73 *Perth Gazette*, 17 December 1858.
74 e.g. *Perth Gazette*, 11 December 1868; 30 December 1870.
75 *West Australian*, 27 December 1881. 76 *Perth Gazette*, 19 February 1858.

The day finished with a rousing rendition of 'God Save the Queen'. It does not seem to have been as well remembered by the children of Perth as its promoters might have wished, but a day away from the classroom was a source of pleasure in itself.

Sunday school picnics and the like sometimes brought together the children of the town gentry, the artisan/contractor class, and the poor. Later, some of the poor children came from the Anglican orphanage down near the Causeway or Perth Bridge as it was usually called. By the early 1870s the Perth Orphanage housed over fifty children, drawn largely from the Poorhouse or Workhouse in Goderich Street. It was when such parties broke up therefore that the differing social experiences of the young most clearly manifested themselves—some to the Terraces and the higher parts of Hay/Howick Street and William Street; some to Hay and Murray Streets, and some to the more ragged quarters of Wellington Street and 'new town' over near the gaol, or back to the orphanage. There were other children in Perth who did not attend the party. They were the Roman Catholic children, many of whom were poor and some of whom were cared for in the Catholic Orphanage.

From whence the serving girls came: an Irish soup kitchen, 1840s.

The lives of these children were far from being idyllic. Indeed they had been crippled from birth. Nearly one in four children had been born less than eight months after the mother had married; others were born to single women; some had come into the world only because a self-abortive practice (taking Holloways Pills was one of the less crude methods) had failed, or even because a 'professional' abortionist had been inefficient or had demanded too high a fee.[77] The mothers of these children had mostly lived out their entire lives in desperate circumstances. Often they themselves had been orphans, survivors of the holocaust of the Irish Famine or the slums of inner London parishes like St George's and St Giles.[78] When institutionalised some of these girls had been taught a useful skill like needle-work, but nearly all were illiterate and remained so for the rest of their lives. In the 1850s and 1860s, under the aegis of

[77] On this point see Grellier 'Family and Society', in C. T. Stannage (General Editor) *A New History of Western Australia*, 1979.
[78] See O. MacDonagh 'Irish Overseas Emigration', in R. D. Edwards, T. Des Williams (eds.) *The Great Famine*, New York University Press, 1957, pp.352-9, 388; also British Parliamentary Papers, Emigration Commission Reports, 1848-65.

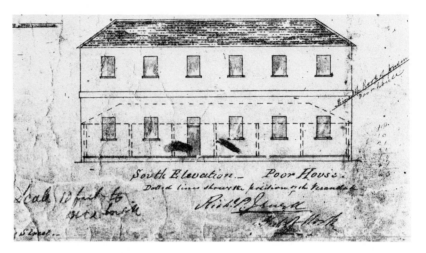

South Elevation — Poor House

For the 'unlucky exports': The Perth Poor House and Servants' House, 1860s.

various governments and emigration societies, they were rounded up and transported to the eastern colonies of Australia and to Swan River, mere bargaining counters in the hard game of convictism—for and against; and necessary acquisitions for self-respecting middle class households. On board an emigrant ship they fended for themselves as best they could, welcoming or fighting off the attentions of the sailors and passengers. On arrival in Perth the women were placed in the 'temporary' quarters of a house down in Bazaar Terrace, formerly used as a female lunatic asylum,[79] or in a building in Goderich Street which served as an Immigrant Depot, a Servants' Home, and a Poor House. In a community which had always grumbled about the dearth of domestic servants, the arrival of the immigrant women was a bonanza. Alerted by the press, masters and mistresses would apply, usually in person, to the Depot and seek out the most promising looking woman and engage her services. Some of the tougher girls held out for a reasonable wage, but most went to the first bidder and were glad to do so in order to escape from the Depot, which was constructed and administered for this purpose.[80] Even after Governor Hampton's 'humane' extensions the Depot itself was basically a long room divided off into separate spaces, likened by one visitor to a stable loosebox. It was often badly overcrowded[81] and on occasion the inmates were forced to change their clothes in the open yard, visible to passersby and loungers in the street.[82] Sometimes the girls and women broke down and wept. Others were sullen and unco-operative. And there were those who hit out against all those who helped and frustrated them, often choosing the most accessible target, namely the Poor House and its matron. In December 1868, for instance, one woman ran amuck and smashed the windows of the Home. Another threatened to take the matron's life; indeed she threw a brick-bat at the matron's head and swore that if she ever got the matron back in Tipperary she'd knock 'the daylights out of her'.[83]

A girl thought herself lucky to be engaged quickly, but her pleasure could as quickly turn to pitch, for the ex-convict servant sent to collect

[79] *Perth Gazette*, 25 June 1852.
[80] Stone Diary—entries for October 1851, in 'The Diary of Alfred Hawes Stone', *Early Days* Vol. 1, Pt. VI, 1929, p.40.
[81] Sanford Letters, Mitchell Library, mss 759; Millett *Australian Parsonage*, p.33.
[82] *Perth Gazette*, 25 November 1853.   [83] *Perth Gazette*, 18 December 1868.

her might succumb to the dual temptation of her presence and the loneliness of the road and assault her. Such incidents rarely came to the notice of the Courts. One of these 'unlucky exports' (as Mrs Millett described them) was Joanna Fennell. Joanna had arrived on, the *Travancore* late in January 1853, along with 114 other Irish girls. She was engaged by Mr Davis, a farmer on the Canning; but on the open road outside Perth she was raped by young George Thomas, the servant who had been sent to bring her to her new home. Justice Mackie could not bring himself to pass sentence of death on Thomas, even though he had ordered that this penalty for rape should be kept on the colonial statute books. Thomas won his ticket-of-leave in 1861 and received a pardon in 1868. Perhaps Joanna's story had not been fully believed—perhaps, after all, because she was only a serving girl and not the daughter of a gentry family. Certainly her chances of becoming a 'powerful humanizing agent' and 'the principal guardian of the future generation' were diminished by the experience. She returned to the Servants' Home, where a year later she suffered the further pain of being robbed of a silver coin. The thief, another girl in the Home, was sent to Perth Gaol for three months with hard labour. Joanna Fennell also served time in the Servants' Home.[84] (The irony lay in the title of Servants' 'Home', the word 'Home' having been specially chosen by Lady Fitzgerald.[85]) A year later Joanna married a whaling hand from Bunbury, where as late as the 1870s she was working as a laundress.

Many of the English and Irish immigrant girls were not told by the Emigration Commissioners that they were being sent to a penal colony; nor were they told that Swan River was thousands of miles distant from better known towns like Adelaide, Melbourne, Hobart and Sydney. Consequently they were often distressed to learn on arrival that their fellow servants were convicts and that the prospects of marriage offered nothing better than a selection from the same class. Sometimes a girl married a convict who unbeknown to her already had a wife and children back in Britain.[86] Some of the more enterprising servant girls worked hard for their mistresses, avoided entanglements with fellow servants and young masters[87] and saved sufficient money to clear out from Swan River to the eastern colonies. They were the fortunate few, very like those free male labourers who had fled from Swan River in the late 1840s. Those who stayed found that the much complained of shortage of servants was justified far less frequently than might have been thought from lines like 'Anything in female attire, undertaking servants' duties, is immediately engaged, and the rate of wages both asked and given is ridiculous in the extreme'.[88] In the early 1850s the Colonial Secretary stated that the colony was oversupplied with female servants. Indeed in the mid-1850s Earl Grey refused to maintain the flow of free emigrants to Swan River because they were not being absorbed by the colonists and were a financial burden on the Imperial Government. He and the Emigration Commissioners believed that wages were so low in Swan River that only Irish labourers were likely to improve their position, and

[84] *Perth Gazette*, 8 July 1853, *WA Biographical Index* Vol. 4, 1850–70—entry for Fennell; Supreme Court Case File No. 587, January 1854.

[85] *Perth Gazette*, 23, 30 April 1852.

[86] Millett *Australian Parsonage*, pp.33, 332–3.

[87] Always a threat. For the English experience see W. Houghton *The Victorian Frame of Mind*, 1957, p.360ff; Divorce Case File No. 11, 1873, Supreme Court of WA; also *Perth Gazette*, 24 January 1862.

[88] *Perth Gazette*, 25 April 1856; see also 9 January 1874.

even then they would not be able to support a wife and four children.[89] In the years of economic recession, like the late 1850s, the mid-1860s and most of the 1870s, unemployment was high and wages were extremely low. Certainly many girls languished for long periods in the Home, despite the disincentives to stay; and the wages of those in employment were not higher than in England, and because of the hot summers and the absence of home conveniences the work was much harder and rougher than at home. Mrs Millett, herself an employer of labour and by no means a hostile critic of life at Swan River, concluded that for the domestic servant the change of country was for the worse in nearly all respects.

Perhaps the gulf between the ideal of family life and the reality of the lives of many of the poorer women of Perth can be shown in the following series of social experiences. When a Josephine Prinsep or a Mrs Brittain lost a child in infancy, the pain, fear, and horror experienced was intense and often long-lasting in its effects. But it is also true that it took place within their own home, attended by a doctor who was often a family friend, and with husband and family close by to ease the pain and aid recovery. This was qualitatively different from the experience of a Catherine Kelly. Catherine Kelly arrived at the Servants' Home in 1862, having come out on the *Mary Harrison* with 150 other girls. Catherine became pregnant. Knowing that pregnancy would reduce her chances of gaining employment she did her best to conceal her condition. Her fellow inmates 'suspected that she was in the Family way', but it was just talk among the women, for Catherine herself never said a word. On Tuesday 16 September, just after 2 o'clock in the afternoon, having cooked and eaten lunch and feeling ill, Catherine crossed the yard to the privy. As she sat over the pit-hole her baby slid out and down into the cess-pit. When the cord had reached its full length it strained against and then tore from her body, causing the baby to sink into the pit where it died. Catherine dealt with the afterbirth as best she could, and pushed the blood-soiled skirt and rag into the pit also. She looked out from the closet and saw that some male prisoners were working in the yard. Only when they had moved away did she leave the closet and stagger with Mary Haggerty's support across to the cookhouse where she slumped down. One of the other girls ran to Matron Annear who came quickly and asked Catherine what the matter was. The girl replied that 'Nothing was the matter'. Matron Annear asked her what she had done. Catherine said that she had done nothing. She hung her head and began to cry.[90]

Catherine Kelly was first charged with the wilful murder of her child. She faced the Coroner's Court which found evidence only for a charge of concealment of the birth, on which charge whe was indicted to appear before the Supreme Court of Western Australia in January 1863. Found not guilty, she was set free to return to the Servants' Home. Here then was a life experience within the embrace of the investing class yet apart from them. It was always the same for the Catherine Kellys of Perth.

Some girls married and were fairly happy, despite a low family income. There were a good number of Ann Haynes' in Perth. By 1881

[89] Sanford Correspondence, Mitchell Library, mss 759, W. A. Sanford to his father, 12 July 1853; *Perth Gazette*, 20 June 1856.
[90] *Perth Gazette*, 19 September 1862, 9 January 1863; Supreme Court Case File No. 76, January 1863.

Kate O'Toole came and told me that Kate Kelly was ill in the closet and told me to bring her out of it as quick as possible. I went straight to the closet and found Kate Kelly in the children's closet and asked her what made she be there. She said she did not like to come out before the men in the yard. There were prisoners working in the yard. She came straight with me to the cook house and remained there until the Matron came. The Matron asked me to go over with her to the closet and we both went over. Kelly did not tell me anything that had happened. She never told me a word. In the early part of the day she got our breakfast and dinner. That is she lighted the fire and cooked. I had not the slightest idea from her appearance or otherwise that she was going to be confined at the time she was

Mary
her
+
mark
Haggerty

'Nothing was the matter', or the agony of Kate Kelly: Mary Haggerty's evidence.

there were about 50 milliners and dressmakers in Perth—while the evidence is slight (the Almanacks list only men) it seems that most of these women were married. This was probably true also of the 20 or so manglers, washerwomen and laundresses in Perth. Most would not have lived better than Ann Haynes.[91] Some lived worse. Many of the women of the poorer classes were beaten regularly and severely by their brutalised and often unemployed and drunken husbands. Indeed in these years Perth had an unhappy reputation for being a town of wife-beaters. One visitor in 1878 quoted at length a newspaper report on the subject:

> It was but the other day that the Chief Magistrate of the city directed attention . . . to the prevalence of the offence (wife beating). We believe that scarcely a week passes without charges of abuse on the part of ruffianly husbands on their wretched wives in the solitude of domestic privacy, coming to the notice of the police. The length to which the offence is extending is positively humiliating. And no man with the slightest respect for the female sex, or with a spark of manliness left in his soul, can fail to arrive at the conclusion that to allow this sort of thing to continue, to practically wink at the offence any longer, is to do a gross wrong to woman, and to connive at a crime which has a tendency to demoralise the whole community.[92]

Wife-beating among the gentry and the trading and artisan groups undoubtedly took place; but as there were greater social pressures on such families to keep the matter privatised and outside the ken of the magistrates, the extent of the suffering is impossible to gauge accurately. Several of the worst cases resulted in judicial separation following the passing of the Matrimonial Causes Act in 1863,[93] and as amended in 1879. In one such case a pregnant woman was beaten so savagely that she delivered the baby three months prematurely and it died a few days later. It was only after further beatings over a several month period, during one of which she had her arm broken, that she left him and subsequently filed a petition for judicial separation.[94] But divorce was a solution open to a mere handful of beaten wives: a divorce hearing was expensive; and a case against a husband was more difficult to prove than a case against a wife. Furthermore, the judges and magistrates were too inclined to urge the women to put up with their sufferings and try to hold the family together,[95] even after the Act was amended in 1879 to give the courts power to grant a separation order with maintenance to a wife whose husband had been convicted of aggravated assault upon her.[96]

Some of the free immigrant women, married and single, took to the bottle and were often found lying insensible in the streets of Perth and incapable of taking care of themselves. A few of the most wretched became 'posted drunkards' which meant that landlords were forbidden by law to serve them. Women comprised up to 25% of drink cases heard by the Police Magistrate in these years.[97] But there were always the low grog shops like Vagg's and Smith's and Molloy's, and Radley's Hope Hotel, from which to obtain liquor, so the disorderliness and misery continued. On any night of the week in Perth the ticket-of-leavers, the

---

91 Census of WA, 1881.
92 Quoted in H. Cornish *Under the Southern Cross*, 2nd ed., 1880, p.48.
93 *Perth Gazette*, 10 July 1863.   94 Supreme Court, Divorce Case Files, 1874.
95 For this last point see Grellier 'Family and Society'.
96 The prevalence of crimes of violence in England working class districts, especially in the case of men against their wives, is discussed in O. R. McGregor *Divorce in England*, 1957, pp.18–24. The WA legislation was based on the British Matrimonial Causes Acts of 1857 and 1878.
97 *Perth Gazette*, 24 January 1862.

*A month in the life of Perth's Police Magistrate. (**Perth Gazette**. September 1853).*

expirees, the Pensioner Guard and their wives, and the servants and housekeepers, played cards and sang, and brawled and drank their way to oblivion or the lockup. Each night saw a desperate search for companionship, even love: 'the prisoner's indiscretion was caused by his strong attachment to the fair complainant'—case dismissed; or 'desirous of cultivating an intimate acquaintance with a Pensioner's wife . . . but being disdainfully rejected, he vented his spleen against her by knocking at the door and throwing bricks on the roof'—three months' gaol.[98]

As the easiest way of coping with their condition some of the women became predators. Many a countryman visiting Perth was propositioned and then robbed by women keeping what the police described as 'bad houses'—women described as 'companions of thieves'.[99] Other women, some of whom had escaped the battering of home and family, found their way to Mrs Godfrey's, Mrs Timewell's or Mrs Dyson's, or any of the several brothels along Murray, Wellington, James and Stirling Streets. Mary Ann Timewell was a widow who cared for her young daughter in their 'disorderly house'. Other young girls worked from the premises:

> I am a single woman. I am on the streets. Mrs Timewell [?] my dresses and washes for me. I do not live with her. I have a slight recollection of inciting a gentleman outside Mrs Timewell's last Thursday afternoon. He came inside. I said to him come on Ducky and pay Mrs Timewell what I owe her. He asked me how much it was and I cannot say what took place.[100]

Mrs Timewell was strongly defended by another widow, Susan Cleverley, who ran a rough boarding house across the street. Mary Jackson was

---

98   *Perth Gazette*, 9 May 1862.
99   *Perth Gazette*, 3 July 1857; Supreme Court Case File No. 1062, January 1884.
100 Supreme Court, unnumbered case, July 1884.

Murray Street west of Barrack Street, 1870s and 1880s: a mixture of respectable artisans and those who turned their backs on 'moral enlightenment'.

another who ran a lodging house which seemed to specialise in robbing gullible countrymen and other transients.[101]

A number of the wives of the Pensioner Guard were also on the game. Indeed it was thought that quite a few of these women had only narrowly escaped being transported to Van Diemen's Land before coming to Swan River. Many spoke coarsely, chewed tobacco, expectorated freely, and made up their eyes to look like traditional black-eye-Susies of cartoon fame. In general the Pensioners formed a depressed minority group in Perth. They lived on what was described as a 'most wretched miserable pittance',[102] yet

> Strange to say that poverty fails to make him a sober man; his few shillings are often squandered in drink. The wife ... ultimately comes to do the same, or else yields to temptations of another kind, to compensate herself ... for the ill-usage she gets at the hands of a drunken reckless husband, and in some cases to avoid starvation.[103]

There were also, however, the prudent Pensioners who formed a Benevolent Society in 1855. The Society owned seven cottages which it rented out at a low rate of £12 a year. It made loans to subscribers (170 in 1863) and paid cash to widows and orphans.[104] The children of these thrifty Pensioners went to the Pensioner school in the Barracks; the rest ran wild around Perth eking out a living as best they could.

Some of the women of Perth were deserted by their husbands. One such was Jane Dyson who, with her young daughter Anna, found employment with the wealthy butcher John Liddelow at his establishment on the corner of Barrack and Murray Streets. Dyson was a cook earning £2 a month and board. But she forfeited the board to live with 'Jack the Flat', also known as 'the thief', in a row of cottages in Stirling Street. Over a four month period Jane stole from Liddelow goods and cash to the value of £58. Some of the stuff she passed on to her neighbours Ann and Herbert Davis. for there had developed in Perth in these years an informal economy among the lower classes which did

101 Supreme Court Case File No. 1062, January 1884.
102 *Perth Gazette*, 29 April 1853.
103 *WA Times*, 28 January 1864.   104 *Perth Gazette*, 26 January 1863.

not appear in Blue Book statistics. All these people were illiterate. Jane Dyson was sentenced to imprisonment for five years. On her release she became one of Perth's best known madams with a popular establishment in Stirling Street. The fate of her daughter Anna is only to be guessed at.[105]

Many of these women with young families suffered in proud silence the bitterest pangs of poverty before succumbing to the relative security of a brothel or the lesser security of a State institution. Stanton's store in William Street was one of the landmarks by which the people of Perth oriented themselves. Stanton had prospered from merchandising. He boosted his income further by renting out cottages nearby. Frances Huckle lived in one of Stanton's houses. She worked to maintain herself and her four-year-old boy. After a time she fell behind with her rent. Stanton had her furniture removed. She was fined 6s or was to serve a four-day gaol sentence; in fact she was sent to gaol for seven days when she used violent language in court. It seems that Frances Huckle tried on several occasions to get the magistrate to put her four-year-old son in the Poor House, but on each occasion her application was rejected. Six weeks after her first stint in gaol she was back in court for beating her boy and threatening to kill him.[106] In another case Johanna McLarty was charged with 'wandering abroad having no means of subsistence and seeking charitable relief'. She pleaded that her husband had gone to Champion Bay to seek work, leaving her with three children and no means of support. On several occasions she had sought admission to the Poor House, but Dr Ferguson had turned her away each time. This time, however, the presiding magistrate, E. W. Landor, solved the problem by sending Johanna to gaol for a month, after which she could go into the Poor House.[107] To protect themselves and their children some of these women cohabited with another man, risking a divorce petition if the husband found out. Domestic happiness under such circumstances was well nigh impossible.

So bad had this problem become by the late 1860s that the police and the magistrates were commenting on the amount of time they were having to devote to it.[108] Husbands were gaoled for not supporting their families; and the wives and children were swelling the ranks of applicants to the Poor House. The cost to the community was becoming prohibitive, a social and financial consequence which lessened the enthusiasm for convictism. One consequence for the children was that their condition enabled a caring and childless philanthropist, who had profited greatly from convictism, to suggest the need for a reformatory for juvenile delinquents and an industrial school. Walter Padbury offered the Government £100 and 200 acres of land to assist the project to get off the ground. As the editor of the *Perth Gazette* wrote, the task was to 'make the social waifs useful members of our social system'. At the same time it was recommended with equal vigour that Western Australia should follow the lead of the South Australians and introduce a law for the birching of 'larrikins'.[109] In Perth in 1881 more than one in five children between the ages of four and sixteen years received no education at all; 27% could neither read nor write.[110] And what did they think when they looked through the windows of Mr Arthur Shenton's

105 Supreme Court Case File No. 1067, April 1884.
106 *Perth Gazette*, 22 August, 3 October 1862.
107 *Perth Gazette*, 26 June 1868.   108 *Perth Gazette*, 2 October 1868.
109 *Perth Gazette*, 7 February 1873.   110 Census of Western Australia, 1881.

store at the India rubber air balls, the building bricks, the drums, puzzles, music boxes, alphabets in boxes, calico dolls and the range of toys displayed there? It told a story of life chances as meaningful to them as was the portico of George Shenton's house to their parents.[111]

Aborigines and Settlers

In this period Perth's Aboriginal families did not die out, as the theorists and commentators believed would happen. But their numbers did decrease, and hostility towards them remained characteristic of many of the white people of Perth. In 1860-61 a measles epidemic swept through the town killing 20 white people (mainly nursing mothers and children) and an indeterminate number of Aborigines, but enough for the 1870 census taker, William Knight, to write of them being 'wiped out'. In fact some survived only to die in 1864 when a severe epidemic of whooping cough hit the town. In this decade too the Aboriginal girls whom Salvado sent down from New Norcia to the Subiaco monastery to work as domestic servants for the nuns all died.[112] Knight estimated that since 1829 the numbers of Aborigines in the Swan, Murray, and Avon districts had fallen by two-thirds:

> the cause of this rapid decrease is easily accounted for by the periodical occurrence of diseases not previously known amongst them, such as Measles and Whooping Cough, and more especially from the evil habits they have acquired from their contact with the white man, not only in drunkenness and other debasing habits, but in the gross immorality of their women. In the earlier period of the Colony's history these evils were not much heard of, but since the arrival of Convicts, and their dispersion about the Country, the immorality of the women has become a constant custom, and the early age at which the young native girls are debauched by shepherds and labourers at outstations, is attended by lamentable consequences.

This assessment by the Registrar General, himself the namesake of a man whose party had shot and killed Aborigines in the York district, was as compassionate as any made by the gentry, though less so than by Anthony Trollope, a visitor.[113] In it the blame for the 'rapid decrease' was shifted on to historical accident—namely the inevitable and irresistible course of epidemic disease; the debauched character of the white labourers, especially the ex-convicts; and the sexual promiscuity of the Aboriginal women. But even as Knight wrote of these things with an eye to posterity, his friends were gunning down Aborigines in the north-west, just as Mr Knight's friends had gunned them down 'In the earlier period of the Colony's history, (when) these evils were not much heard of'. Men and women of his own class set the standards of behaviour towards Aborigines, male and female, for not all the growing number of half-caste whites were the progeny of labouring men and Aboriginal

---

[111] *Perth Gazette*—many numbers for these years contained Shenton's advertisements for toys and books; see, for example, 10 April 1857 and April 1870. An unnamed bookseller's account book for 1882–84, lodged in the Supreme Court of Western Australia, contains much information on books, journals, music books etc. sold in this period. The name of the purchaser is also given.

[112] G. Russo 'Bishop Salvado's Mission to Christianize and Civilize the Aborigines', MA thesis, 1974, University of WA.

[113] 'Introduction' to Census of 1870. While Trollope, *Australia*, 1873, p.87, believed that 'Their doom is to be exterminated; and the sooner that their doom be accomplished—so that their can be no cruelty—the better it will be for civilization,' he also regarded Yagan and Midgigooroo as 'brave patriots, defending their country and their rights'.

women.[114] And Knight's fascination with the alleged 'gross immorality' of the Aboriginal women had psychological roots far deeper in European history than he could ever know. As for the 'debasing habits' of the white labourers, there were some people who knew that many labourers were victims of a vicious social system, victims who sought the comforts of bottle and body when either or both were within reach.

The surviving Aborigines coped with their social environment as best they could. Between fifteen and twenty found employment as domestic servants in Perth, at least they are so recorded in the censuses of 1870 and 1881. Some may have entered into legal contracts of servitude, such as were becoming commonplace in the north-west pastoral districts and in the pearling industry. As such the Aborigines were slaves, for the lawmakers framed the law with an eye to the white settlers' quest for 'internal peace'. Sometimes the Aboriginal servants were leased out by their owners, as when in February 1884 Winthrop Hackett, lawyer and journalist, leased out Nunda (or Jerry) to his friend Charles Harper, pastoralist, politician, and owner of the *West Australian*, 'until such time as I desire him to return to me'.[115] But even after the ravages of the epidemics of the early 1860s, about fifty Aborigines lived on the periphery of Perth society, fishing in the traditional ways in the shallows of the Swan below Lord Street, and cooking their catch over fires on vacant town lots, to the habitual consternation of white adults and the fascination of white children, at least one of whom, Alexander Forrest, 'dressed' as an Aborigine for a masquerade ball.[116] A 'visitor' to Perth in the mid-1860s, J. Walsh, painted tranquil river scenes of Aborigines fishing. But he also painted scenes of the Aborigines drinking grog. Indeed drunken brawls among Aborigines along St George's Terrace occurred,[117] though perhaps less frequently than the gentry home owners of the Terrace asserted. From the death of Yagan in 1833 to the present day no historian has yet traced the life story of a single Aborigine in Perth. Some aspects of the 'fatal impact' could be quickly forgotten by the people of Perth. After the 'successful' establishment of the Rottnest Prison for Aborigines, the people of Perth no longer witnessed 'the melancholy exhibitions . . . of these unfortunate creatures working in irons'.[118] And there were few if any in the 1860s who wished to remember the sight of chained native prisoners attending divine service at St George's Church in the company of the Governor, and the ladies and gentlemen of Perth.[119] This and much else was edited out of the story of the Aborigines' decline and fall, as told by Knight and his contemporaries, and by the historians following them.

But before the sound of silence was heard the Aborigines had had their uses, especially on grand occasions. Late in 1867 when it was believed that the Duke of Edinburgh was to visit Perth, the Reception Committee planned to include the Perth Aborigines in the celebrations:

> On the 1st October, a large muster of natives is expected in Perth, that being the day on which the Committee proposes to commence feeding them in return for the exhibition of their lovely forms and most odoriferous persons. They are to be the first sight presented to the view

[114] See N. Green's chapter, in C. T. Stannage (General Editor) *A New History of Western Australia*, 1979. The problem of half-caste children was becoming acute. Trollope, visiting in the early 1870s, found 14 half-caste children among the 22 children in Hale's Native School in Perth. Trollope, *Australia*, 1873, p.86.
[115] Harper Papers, Battye Library, 1973A/7.   [116] *Western Mail*, 27 June 1935.
[117] *Perth Gazette*, 29 January 1858; 31 January 1862, for example.
[118] *Perth Gazette*, 29 January 1858.   [119] *Perth Gazette*, 7 May 1852.

Aborigines fishing in Perth Waters, 1860s. (J. Walsh, ex-convict, artist.)

of His Royal Highness upon his entrance into Perth, and a novel sight it will be to him; the Committee should pick out the best looking girl of the lot to be specially presented to the Prince, and of course he could do no less than offer the *fair* one a chaste salute.[120]

'these unfortunate creatures': a contemporary portrait, Perth 1860s. (J. Walsh, artist.)

As it happened the Duke's ship sailed clean past Swan River Colony, and by the time he reached Perth he had visited most of the eastern colonies and seen Aborigines by the score. In June 1879 when Perth celebrated the golden jubilee of its foundation, about thirty Aborigines were lured into marching in the procession through the streets of Perth. They carried their traditional weapons. After the march each Aborigine was provided with a small pannikin of beer and a new blanket: 'so that altogether it must be said that the 'oldest inhabitants' received their full share of attention at the hands of the authorities'.[121]

It was in the late 1860s that the tormented Bishop Hale reprinted from the *Melbourne Church News* an article by 'R.M.L.' on the ill-treatment of Aborigines by the early settlers of Western Australia. R. M. Lyon had been in Perth in the 1830s. His article, as reprinted by Hale in the *WA Church of England Magazine*, caused an outcry among the gentry. William Burges and Seymour Meares wrote of the 'atrocities' committed by Yagan and others. It was Hale who was routed in the exchange.[122] But he had opened an historical fight which was sufficiently meaningful to the community to be waged at intervals right up to the eve of the sesquicentennial celebrations of the foundation of the colony.[123] In 1870 the conscience-stricken Bishop Hale tended his resignation to Governor Weld and resolved to go to King George Sound to work in the Native Institution there.[124] Although persuaded to stay on as bishop,

120 *Perth Gazette*, 27 September 1867.
121 *WA Times*, special jubilee issue, 6 June 1879.
122 See *Perth Gazette*, 10 July 1868.
123 See the *West Australian*, 19, 24, 25 October 1978 for correspondence from Sir Paul Hasluck and Sylvia Hallam. Unlike the debate in the 1860s, the late 1970s debate was contested by the Aborigines, led by Ken Colbung, who had already portrayed Yagan in a film.
124 *Perth Gazette*, 21 June 1870.

Mathew Blagden Hale: 'the good bishop' of Perth.

Hale was a pale shadow of the man who had established the successful mission at Poonindie in South Australia. When Justice Archibald Paull Burt sentenced one of the Burges' family to gaol for five years for the murder of an Aborigine, and the leading settlers sought to have the decision set on one side and the judge removed from his office, Bishop Hale seems to have remained silent. Lockier Burges was an Anglican. He had worshipped in Hale's churches. Yet he had slaughtered an Aborigine. For whom should Hale pray? Who was most in need of the church's mission? In 1875 the good bishop left Perth. The wild men of the colony had proved too much for him.[125]

One issue which was widely debated in Perth in these years was whether or not an Aborigine should be hanged for murdering another Aborigine. From 1851 it was the usual practice of the Criminal Court to condemn tribal killers to death, though the sentence was not always carried out. (There were approximately 20 such judicial killings before 1884.) This was justified in British law, and some at least found a justification in Levitical and Mosaic Law; as one person put it:

> it is in agreement with the Scripture, reason and humanity to hang or otherwise remove from amongst us such lawless desperados.[126]

There were others (Joseph Chester, in the same debate) who deplored such hangings, contending that whites had no right to interfere in native customs, and that if there were now more tribal murders it was because of the pernicious influence of white men. In resolving that it was 'in accordance with reason and humanity to execute aborigines of any country living in a state of barbarism for murders committed on each other' the Mechanics' Institute debaters mirrored the values of Perth society.

Organizing an Economy

The Aborigines were not among those people in Perth who during the convict years and after 'gained fast hold of the shores of prosperity'.[127] Such successful white people did so despite economic recessions in the mid and late 1850s, from 1863 to 1865, and from 1867 through most of the 1870s. A few of these men controlled the town's financial institutions. The directors of the Western Australian Bank included Luke Leake, William Knight, J. S. Roe, George Shenton (father and son), and James Dyer, all landowners, merchants or Government officials. The Bank prospered in these years. In 1863, for example, the directors were able to declare a dividend of 30%.[128] In 1876, when 8000 £2 shares were issued, the directors took no less than 6000. By that date the WA Bank had a capital of £100,000.[129] In short the WA Bank went from strength to strength, despite competition from the National Bank of Australasia, the Union Bank of Australasia (1878) and the Bank of New South Wales (1883). Among the WA Bank's largest clients was the Perth City Council which, from 1882, borrowed heavily from the Bank, and before that time it acted for the Council as its savings bank.

[125] *Perth Gazette*, 28 February 1873; A. de Q. Robin *Mathew Blagden Hale: the Life of an Australian Pioneer Bishop*, 1976, p.150.
[126] George Lazenby, Methodist layman and PCC councillor, in the debate on this subject in the Mechanics' Institute in 1855. Minute Book Vol. 1, August/September 1855.
[127] *Perth Gazette*, 21 June 1867.
[128] *WA Times*, 7 January 1864. [129] *Western Mail*, 18 August 1921.

Community deposits in the savings bank grew erratically over this period. Most depositors were mechanics, builders, and prudent Pensioners, rather than the unskilled labourers and domestic servants,[130] which was a source of regret to the bankers and to the press who wished to expand the proportion of the population defined as 'thrifty and respectable'. But the distribution of power in society militated against this, as the life story of Henry Haynes' family indicates. It was the same with the Post Office Savings Bank which first opened its doors in 1863. In the first year of its operation the Post Office Savings Bank won 224 depositors. By 1882 this had risen to only 1654, an annual growth rate of less than 75 new depositors. Perhaps one-third of the depositors were Perth people.[131]

There were also the fire, marine, and life insurance companies. Between 1850 and 1884 their number increased from two to eleven. Two were home grown. In 1884 the West Australian Company was founded by Septimus Burt, a lawyer/pastoralist; Marmion, a merchant and pastoralist; Thomas Britnall, a builder and urban real estate owner (and landlord to Henry Haynes); and Dr Edward Scott, a Perth City councillor. The other was the merchant/pastoralist William Dalgety Moore's West Australian Marine Insurance Company. Moore was the son of Sam Moore, one of the large owners of property in the Upper Swan in the 1840s; his uncle was George Fletcher Moore, then in retirement in England. But the largest marine insurance company in Swan River was Lloyds of London, the local agent for which was George Shenton, sometime Mayor of the City of Perth. Three of the largest general insurance companies were the National Mutual Life Association (established in WA in 1869), the Colonial Mutual Life Assurance Society (1873), and the Australian Mutual Provident Society (1884). The establishment of these branches owed more to the development of pastoralism in the north-west from the 1860s than to convictism *per se*. Most of the Western Australian agents were Fremantle and Perth merchants and officials, like A. H. Stone, Alfred Hillman, J. W. Bateman, George Shenton, and Daniel Congdon. None of the local insurance companies did as well in competition with the intercolonial companies as did the WA Bank, and at least one local effort, the West Australian Fire Insurance Company, founded in 1870 by O'Grady Lefroy, Luke Leake, J. G. C. Carr, Alfred Hillman, George Glyde, James Dyer, Thomas Smith, and Bernard Smith, under the Chairmanship of Edmund Birch, seems not to have survived beyond 1871. Insurance was one area of financial activity where Westralian groups found it more profitable to act as agencies for larger extra-Westralian companies, but as so often in Western Australia's history, there were times in this period when local initiative seemed justified. Certainly in insurance as in banking, it was the larger merchant and pastoralist, Government official and lawyer, and contractor, who had access to cash for investment purposes. Life insurance, even home insurance against fire, was limited to only a few related groups in colonial society—perhaps as little as 15% of the population.[132]

In 1853, largely out of dissatisfaction with Governor Fitzgerald's protectionist economic policy, the merchants of Perth resolved to form a

---

[130] *Perth Gazette*, 18 April 1873.   [131] *WA Year Book*, 1887.
[132] See *Australian Handbook 1881*, p.354; E. S. Whiteley 'The Birth and Progress of Insurance', *Early Days* Vol. 9, December 1947, pp.41–7; *Perth Gazette*, April 1854, on high premiums.

Chamber of Commerce. There may also have been an intercolonial incentive as well for it was about this time that Chambers of Commerce were established in Sydney and Melbourne.[133] Those present at the first meeting of the Western Australian Chamber of Commerce were George and Arthur Shenton, Lionel Samson (who in 1852 had removed most of his business to Fremantle), R. M. Habgood, Mark Dyett, B. Lyon, Frederick Croft, Luke Leake and Robert King.[134] Thereafter until its demise several years later it acted as an extra-parliamentary pressure group as an advocate of free trade.[135] It also concerned itself with the upgrading of communication facilities, especially roads and mail services.[136] While Samson, Shenton, Leake and King remained prominent, the chairmanship in 1856 went to another of Perth's big merchants, Robert M. Habgood, son of Robert Habgood.[137] It seems to have been wound up in the late 1850s. Perhaps it lost too many members in the recession of 1857–58. But a more likely explanation is that experience taught the merchants that more informal means of pressure, through representation in the Legislative Council and through the pressure some of them were able to exert from within the Perth City Council, produced more satisfactory results.

Another financial institution created in the convict years was the Perth Building Society. It was founded in 1862 in the belief that by that time there had developed a sizeable respectable working and lower middle class population, inculcated with the values of self-help and independence so necessary for a successful quest for 'internal peace'. The foundation directors were the lawyer and Attorney General, G. F. Stone, Mark Dyett, R. R. Jewell, George Glyde, Edmund Birch, Ben Mason, William Ryan, Bernard Smith, Terrence Farrelly, J. Farmaner, A. B. Middleton, and Thomas Allmond. Others at the first meeting were J. G. C. Carr, J. T. Reilly, and Henry Wakeford. Stone, Wakeford and Jewell were senior Government officials, while Smith, Farrelly, Ryan and Allmond, were storekeepers and clerks. They were also leading members of the Mechanics' Institute, in whose hall the meeting was held. It was hoped that the Society would

> do much towards promoting prudent and careful habits among those classes for whom it is chiefly designed, ameliorating their condition, and establishing a barrier against the misfortunes of indigence.[138]

By 1884 the Society had many members and shareholders, and had disbursed £30,750 for the construction of 184 buildings in Perth. Like the WA Bank, the Society had the field to itself for many years, and was able to withstand the competition of intercolonial and other local building societies when these were established in the 1890s. Like the Perth City Council, the Building Society was an alliance of the gentry and the middling groups of Perth's social structure, including the few affluent Roman Catholics. It was one of those institutions like the savings banks, the Mechanics' Institute, and the Working Men's Association, by which power was kept in as few hands as possible, and its exercise directed to the acceptance of and dependence on the values of those wielding power. That it did not reach the greater part of the labouring population, who remained tenants rather than home owners, suggests strongly that either

133 See J. A. La Nauze 'Mechanics in Action', *Economic Record* Vol. 31, May 1955, pp.77–89.
134 *Perth Gazette*, 20 May 1853.
135 *Perth Gazette*, 11 July 1853.   136 *Perth Gazette*, 3 March 1854.
137 *Perth Gazette*, 14 March 1856.   138 *Perth Gazette*, 24 October 1862.

the goal was unattainable, as with the Haynes family, or that the values were not shared, or both.[139]

The men who formed the Chamber of Commerce and were prominent in other financial institutions, also formed several major companies in this period. Among them were mining and pastoral companies and, in 1870, the Electro Magnetic Telegraph Company. The first telegraph line in the colony—between Perth and Fremantle—had been established by Edmund Stirling and J. Cumming in 1869. But the directors of the new company were George Shenton, Luke Leake, J. G. C. Carr, Edmund Birch, George Glyde, Robert King, James Lee Steere, and Monger. Alfred Hillman, who held several clerical positions connected with finance, was the secretary. With a capital of £12,000 and support from the Government, the Company rapidly established telegraphic communication throughout the settled parts of the colony, including the north-west where the directors, among others, had substantial pastoral interests.[140] Directors and shareholders did well out of the Company and in 1872 sold it at a good profit to the Government. Another company formed in these years (and which was also sold to the Government after 1884) was the Perth Gas Company. This company was formed in 1883 and succeeded or rather took over the City of Perth Gas Company which had lasted shakily for a year or so. Among the shareholders were George Shenton, Lee Steere, H. C. Prinsep, the Stones, and Edward Scott, as well as some of the prominent storekeepers and tradesmen like Liddelow, Glaskin and Elsegood, who also had been or were Perth City councillors. In short its social composition was not unlike that of the Perth Building Society.[141]

The men who formed the companies and financial societies determined much of the rate of growth and general character of life in Perth. From 1859 to 1881 the number of houses in Perth doubled—from 500 to 1083. This represented an annual increase of only about thirty houses, about half of which were of three rooms or less; but with the additional construction of outbuildings, stores, and public buildings, it was enough to attract one-third of the colony's artisans, even though Perth district contained only one-fifth of the colonial population. As nearly 90% of the houses in Perth were built in brick, while 90% of the houses in Fremantle were built of stone, it was scarcely surprising that half the colony's brickmakers and bricklayers lived in the capital. Outbuildings like stables (there were at least 1250 horses in Perth in 1881) and worksheds tended to be constructed of wood, hence nearly two-fifths of the colony's sawyers worked from Perth for most of this period, though there was a decline in absolute numbers between 1870 and 1881, brought about by a consolidation of employment in builders' 'firms' and the rapid expansion of steam-driven milling in the Canning area where Ben Mason had a large mill. Another disproportionately large occupational group in Perth were the general labourers—at any time in the 1860s and 1870s there were from 250 to 180 general labourers in

[139] For the history of the Perth Building Society see R. M. C. Lourens 'The Perth Building Society: A Study in Institutional Growth', PhD thesis, University of WA, 1973. The figures cited are drawn from Lourens' thesis.

[140] See J. S. Battye (ed.) *Cyclopaedia of Western Australia* Vol. 1, 1912, p.383; see also H. Stirling 'The Telegraph in WA', *Early Days* Vol. 1, Pt. II, pp.30–3.

[141] See Minute Book of the Perth Gas Company, 27 April 1883—December 1893, Battye Library 476A; see also *Inquirer*, 27 July, 7 December 1881; 15 March 1882; and *West Australian*, 24 January 1882; 16 February 1883. A brief history of the provision of gas in Perth appeared in the *Sunday Times*, 6 May 1962.

Perth from The Old Gaol, 1860s:
workers' homes in the foreground.

George Shenton's home in St
George's Terrace, 1860s.

Perth, one-third of the general (non-agricultural) labouring population of the colony. These men were rarely in regular employment, but they picked up piecemeal work in the building and carrying industries, and some of the noxious industries such as tanning. This area of economic activity was the 'exclusive' preserve of the ex-convicts.

Between 35% and 40% of the colony's domestic servants were employed in Perth. They were not employed in the 45% of houses with three rooms or less. Indeed they were found usually in the houses of five or more rooms—perhaps 30% of houses over the period, with an increase between 1870 and 1881. For most of the period from the 1860s to the 1880s there were between 300 and 350 domestic servants in Perth, approximately 250 to 275 of whom were female. Like the labourers they faced uncertain and irregular employment, especially in recession years; but at times they accounted for up to one-third of the town's workforce, a demographic base for much of the human misery experienced in Perth in these years.

With a population which increased nearly five-fold between 1850 and 1884 Perth needed a vastly increased supply of food and drink. This accounts for the big increase in the number of market gardeners in the town—even between 1870 and 1881, when population increase was sluggish and due almost entirely to natural increase, the number of families making a living from market gardening increased from 63 to 97, at which latter number they comprised 50% of the colony's gardeners. This growth was possible only with the draining of the swamps behind the town. While there were some winters when the drainage system failed and the gardens were inundated with water, and while the drains had to be cleared of debris regularly, by the 1870s Perth was surrounded by gardens in a fan which spread out from Cole's garden in the east to Leeder's in the west. Competition between the gardeners was keen, but they also constituted a 'garden' lobby in the Perth City Council. Even when they won a separate ward for the northern section of the town, they had to fight hard to win Council approval for the construction of roads and drains in the area. Some of the larger gardeners, like Richard Gallop, Frederick Backshall, James Leeder, and Oriel (a former Spanish Benedictine novice) became substantial landowners in the town proper. None of the larger gardeners was an ex-convict, though ex-convicts were undoubtedly employed as seasonal labourers on the gardens.[142] Some

142 William Smith, who described himself as a 'gardener of Nedlands', died in 1873 leaving £17 in the Post Office Savings Bank. The rest of his estate was a fruit and garden crop valued at £20, some beehives, a sow and some pigs, and a couple of cows—total value £150. Letters of Administration Files for Intestate Cases No. 199, 1873, in Supreme Court of Western Australia.

vegetables were sold on site. A few of the gardeners took stalls under the arches of the Town Hall but street deliveries were the usual means of selling the produce. One vegetable which made its first appearance in Western Australian kitchens in these years was the Spanish tomato. This, and other vegetables, were grown also in home garden plots, but by the 1870s there were probably few households which were self-sufficient. Indeed by 1884 the market economy of gardening had been firmly established. In time the Chinese would take over much of the gardening activity of the town, but until the 1890s there were few Chinese in Perth.[143]

While bread continued to be baked in many family and lodging house kitchens, no less than 24 bakers managed to make a living from the trade in the 1870s, some 40% of the bakers in the colony. Bread was not a cheap food in Perth. Indeed flour was always expensive, for at least half the colony's needs, and perhaps three-quarters of Perth's requirements, had to be imported from South Australia—to the great profit of merchants and shipowners. A Government tax on imported flour helped to put bread outside the reach of some of the poorer people of Perth and caused at least one newspaper correspondent to call for a Sir Robert Peel to solve the situation.[144] Perhaps the bakers of Perth were not dependent on bread sales, for they also sold pies, cakes, and fancy breads. Many of them were located in Howick and Goderich Streets which suggests that sales came from both the affluent people of the Terraces and Howick and Hay Streets and the poorer people of the northern streets, though the latter also bought their cakes from small housewife-shops like Mrs Haynes' in Wellington Street. Among the better known bakers by the 1870s were Thomas Molloy, Dennis Metherington (whose hot pies with gravy were very popular), James Glen, James Dyson, John Scollard, G. Marfleet, John Liddelow, John Veryard and David Cameron (whose buns, on sale from 12 noon, were a

Richard Gallop in genteel old age: thrift and sobriety made him a successful market gardener; the Government's need for urban railway land made him his fortune.

Caporn's family store, Hay Street, 1860s.

[143] *Western Mail*, 20 June 1935; PCC Minute Book; *WA Almanac* for 1870s; and Censuses of WA, 1859, 1870, 1881, are the important sources for the above paragraphs.
[144] For the debate between protectionists and free traders see *Perth Gazette*, 5 December 1856.

George Green's mill: corner
Hay/William Streets, 1860s.

source of delight to the students of Perth Boys' School). Metherington, Glen, and Scollard were ex-convicts. Scollard rented his work premises from the Samsons, but in the 1880s he built his own house in Howick Street. Metherington and Glen seem never to have done well enough to own a home. One of the bakers, Thomas Molloy, who began with a single shop and house in Goderich Street (Q6), rented, bought and sold urban real estate, until by the 1890s he was one of the largest landowners in the town, and could be described by the rate clerk as of 'independent means'. In 1884 he entered the Perth City Council; in the early 1890s he was the Member for Perth in the Legislative Council; and in 1908–09 he was Mayor of Perth. The last of the well-known bakers of that period, John Veryard, also prospered if on a less spectacular scale than Molloy. One of his descendants, also a baker, became Lord Mayor of Perth in the 1960s.[145]

Many, though by no means all, residents of Perth who owned or rented homes kept poultry (there were 13 500 fowls in Perth in 1881), a cow and a pig—the cow for milk, and the pig for rubbish disposal and, ultimately, for bacon. Each day the town herd of cows would be driven through the streets of Perth out to the Commonage well to the west of the town-site. But milk could also be bought from professional dairymen. It was believed that the finest milk came from the Manning Bros dairy under Mt Eliza. Another source was Johnston's dairy in Murray Street. Johnston had built a brick room under his house and there the milk was strained and set in two gallon flat tin dishes on benches. A dairy girl skimmed the milk every few hours. In those days almost all families churned their own cream and butter. Some men made a hard living by delivering milk. Most days of the week in the 1870s Dan Malan left Backshall's garden and dairy in West Perth (Duke Street), with characteristic straps round his trouser legs and carrying his yoke and pails. With this load he walked through the sand until he reached the corner of Hutt (William) and Roe Streets, after which the going was easier on a made road surface. He wended his way up past Ranford's house and tannery in Pier Street and eventually reached his destination—the Colonial Hospital in Goderich Street. Another man who carted milk in this fashion was an ex-convict, Patrick Murphy, who walked in from a dairy in Bulwer Street on the northern fringe of the town.[146] The quality of the milk and the cleanliness or otherwise of the dairies were always of concern to the Colonial Surgeon and the City Council's Inspector of Nuisances, but in fact there were very few outbreaks of illness from these sources. Perhaps the area of greatest concern to the Colonial Surgeon was the use of cow's milk for feeding babies, a practice which he thought was linked causally to the appallingly high mortality rate among the infants of the colony. Despite his appeals for its retention, breast-feeding declined significantly through this period, perhaps faster among the poorer classes than among the gentry, although the evidence for this is fragmentary and imperfect.[147]

Also of concern to the Council and the Government were the

[145] Biographical information: Rate Books of the City of Perth; *WA Biographical Index*, 1979, Vols. 2, 3, 4; *WA Almanac*, various issues 1860s and 1870s; Bolton and Mozley *WA Legislature 1870–1930*, 1961; *Western Mail*, 27 June, 11 July 1935.

[146] *Perth Gazette*, 19 June 1857; *Western Mail*, 20 June 1935, 'The Reminiscences of Ben. S. Ranford'.

[147] The Prinsep diary suggests that Josephine breast-fed all her daughters, while the Colonial Surgeon's reports seem to be directed towards the more numerous lower class families.

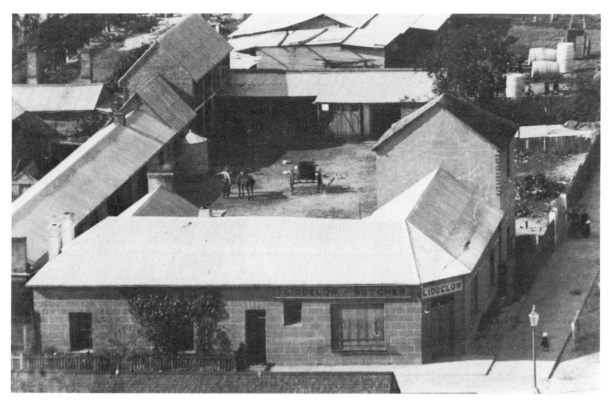

John Liddelow's butchery: corner Murray/Barrack Streets, 1860s–80s.

butchers of Perth. The biggest butchers were H. and S. Birch, John Liddelow and (in the 1850s) Walter Padbury. By 1870 there were twelve men engaged in butchering, in four or five establishments. In 1881 twenty-one men identified themselves as butchers or butchers' assistants. In the 1840s and early 1850s most butchers slaughtered sheep and cattle within the limits of the town, but in November 1852 legislation was enacted which prevented them from killing animals within six miles of the town centre.[148] In an era without refrigeration,[149] conditions at the slaughterhouses were usually unhygienic, and sickness was rife among the men who worked in them. They could however slaughter beasts at the Government's slaughterhouse at Claise Brook, and some did so for a time until the high costs drove them away. Others like Padbury continued to risk fines by slaughtering sheep near the lime kilns to the west of the town but within the six mile limit.[150] But Padbury could afford to pay fines, for in 1852 he won the contract to provide the Government with meat. The contract was for 500 lb of meat daily, costed at 6½ d per lb. Thus the annual contract, which he won again in 1853, 1854 and 1855, was worth a minimum of £3400.[151] The profits from these contracts helped to launch him on a career as merchant and pastoralist equal in wealth to George Shenton. From the mid-1850s the Perth contract was won by Liddelow and other butchers, but keen competition resulted in a lowering of the contract price. Among the smaller butchers

[148] *Perth Gazette*, 19 November 1852.
[149] Right at the end of this period Charles Harper began to experiment with meat refrigeration—Harper Papers, Battye Library Acc. No. 1973A.
[150] *Perth Gazette*, 24 June 1853.
[151] *Perth Gazette*, 30 December 1853; 24 November 1854.

was Thomas Jeffcott, an ex-convict. Saturday was the usual sale day, but during the week butchers' boys delivered ordered meat in baskets. Some butchers, like Birch and Osborne, formed close links with Toodyay and Victoria Plains farmers like Donald McPherson of Glentrommie, thereby ensuring a regular supply of stock.[152] But meat was not an inexpensive item for consumers. Even in comfortably-off artisan and carrying industry families only cheap cuts were eaten on a daily basis, with a leg or shoulder of mutton for Sunday dinner,[153] while it was generally believed that an ex-convict labourer in Perth ate meat less frequently than when he worked within the Establishment at Fremantle or in Perth Gaol.

Throughout the period 1850 to 1884 food prices were too high for labouring men to feed themselves and their families at all adequately. Poor diet may well explain why the investing classes and employers of labour so often complained of slothfulness and malingering among the ex-convict labourers. The high cost of the necessaries of life in Perth was an important factor in the high rate of emigration to the eastern colonies. For example, in observing that

> An inspection of the outward passenger lists from our Ports shows a general tendency of the laboring classes of this Colony to escape from our shores,

the *Perth Gazette* (24 January 1868) stated specifically that the departing labourers were not enamoured of Victoria, nor were they intent on escaping from Swan River convictism; rather, the high cost of living was driving them out. Artisans complained that pork, butter and eggs were 'not to be had or only at fabulous prices'.[154] In the decade of the 1870s Perth would have suffered a net loss of population if there had not been an excess of births over deaths. And of course there were those people who stayed in Perth and made do as best they could only because they could not afford the fare from Albany to the eastern colonies. In the 1850s the fare was about £15 in steerage; this had dropped to about £5 by the 1880s.[155] The claim of rhetoricians and colonial boosters that labourers in Swan River lived better than their counterparts in the old country should not be accepted uncritically. And it should also be remembered that there were some men in Swan River who were pleased to see the departure of people they regarded as little better than animals. Always the gentry wanted a better working class than they got. They wanted

> English and Scotch ploughmen and shepherds, instead of Irish spademen, and some decent English and Scotch single women for domestic servants, instead of our usual assortment of the sweepings of Irish poorhouses and English brothels which it has been the pleasure, for some years past, of Mr Walcott and his brother Emigration Commissioners to send us.[156]

The judgment was less than fair to the Commissioners and to the servants who came, but it reflected accurately enough the colonists' perceptions of social reality.

---

152 *Perth Gazette*, 2 May 1873.
153 Interview in 1975 with Mrs Riley, a member of the Caporn family which owned large river boats; also *Western Australian Times*, 9 January 1864.
154 See also *Perth Gazette*, 2 May 1873, which reports the departure of the *Wild Wave*, which was crowded with disillusioned labourers heading for Melbourne; see also Minute Book of Swan River Mechanics' Institute for debate on free trade versus protection in 1874.
155 *WA Almanacs* and *Australian Handbook 1881*.   156 Perth Gazette, 24 July 1868.

A lesser problem for the labourers of Perth was ease of transport. Most Perth workmen and workwomen walked to their places of employment, sometimes across the town, sometimes a block away, and sometimes next door or to the front or back of their own places. Once they ventured off the main streets, however, they were ankle deep in sand in summer and mud in winter. The few shell-footpaths tended to run as far as the front doors of houses belonging to members of the Perth City Council, or so it was alleged, and as a glance at the works' programmes of the period tends to confirm. Pushing a pram through the streets of Perth was extremely exhausting for mother or serving girl or daughter, and extremely hazardous for the baby. It was hardly surprising that the gentry pram pushers tended to gather on the pleasantly grassed area near the Government Domain, where at least the dust was less troublesome and where horsemen were forbidden to ride. Civil servants, too, walked to work, but usually along the better made roads. It was very much a walking town. Probably less than half the families of Perth owned a horse, though there were over 1200 horses stabled in the Perth district. For those who needed to hire a horse or horse and carriage the town had several liveries. Two of the largest—A. D. Letch's and Harry Ogborne's—were in St George's Terrace west of Barrack Street, while James Nicholls had a large livery in Murray Street. For most of this period Letch had the contract to run the mails between Perth and Fremantle, and at least two of his drivers, H. Shean and Harry Chipper, were celebrated horsemen in the town. These years also saw the emergence of Western Australia's most famous horseman, George Towton. As a young lad in the back-streets of Perth, Towton used to spend all his spare time with an old veterinary surgeon, Bob West, who taught him a great deal about horses. Towton grew up to be a hotelier (one time licensee of the No Place Inn and the Freemasons' Hotel), a livery owner, and an owner and trainer of race horses in the days after the WA Turf Club was established (1852). Another livery man was Harry Pratley who from the 1880s ran a hansom cab out to Highgate Hill, when that northern suburb first began to develop. The first hansom cab in the

Perth's mail coach, St George's Terrace, 1870s.

133

A hearse for the people of Perth.

town was made and run by John Christie who was better known as a bootmaker. It was said of Christie that his boots became to Perth what Bostock's were to London; and indeed this enterprising Perthian's boots won prizes at the Colonial and Indian Exhibitions in the 1880s. John Summers, a Perth City councillor and coachbuilder, built a less lively carriage—the town's first hearse. Summers' hearse was a very much appreciated innovation, for it was a hard walk from the town to the cemetery. The last town call for pall bearers and coffin was traditionally the John Bull Hotel, east of Barrack Street in Howick Street, popularly known as the 'funeral cockpit'. Perhaps the pall bearers were less in need of 'one for the road' after Summers' hearse came into use.[157]

Among those in Perth who ate well and rode comfortably were the civil servants, at least those whose incomes were above £200 a year. Over the period from 1854 to 1881 the number of civil servants in Perth increased from about 75 to over 140. In the late 1860s they showed their collective strength by forming the Perth Co-operative Society. The most senior of their number, namely the Colonial Secretary Frederick Barlee, heard out the complaints of the town's traders that they were being undersold by the Society, and then dismissed them, saying that the Society was like the London Co-operative Society of Civil Servants and was therefore acceptable to him. With savings of up to 40% on some food lines, the 2000 £2 shares were quickly taken up by civil servants.[158] To the civil servants should be added the clerks and accountants, whose numbers increased steadily over the years to reach about 55 by 1884. The censuses suggest strongly that Perth was the 'clerical' or 'book-keeping' capital of the colony, for in no other district did the number of 'clerks' exceed five. Professional bodies were not formed in these years, for there were simply too few professional men in town. Schoolteachers came and went with bewildering speed. Even in the early 1880s there were only six lawyers (assisted by 10 law clerks) practising in Perth, and three or four doctors. There were only nine midwives and sick nurses, and only four chemists and two dentists in Perth in 1881.

Stanley Brewery: *Spring Street, Perth.*

[157] *Western Mail*, 8, 22 November, 6 December 1934.
[158] *Perth Gazette*, 13, 20 September 1872.

Builders and Buildings

The early 1850s saw a considerable amount of building in the public sector. The two best known buildings from this period are the Perth Boys' School in St George's Terrace, and the huge gaol in the northern part of the city off Beaufort Street. Even as late as 1851 it seemed that all new public buildings would be squeezed on to St George's Square; but in 1852 it was decided to decentralise the construction of some buildings. At considerable expense a block of land at the western end of St George's Terrace was purchased for a new Government School. It was apparently designed by the Colonial Secretary, W. A. Sanford, who introduced to Perth the gothic architecture of early Victorian Britain. While at Cambridge Sanford had been a member of the Camden Society which was dedicated to the encouragement of historical and religious study of mediaeval times and the need to inculcate a high morality into contemporary life. In the gothic style the Society found an appropriate vehicle for the values it hoped to inject into British society. The Society was part of a wider movement of which Augustus Pugin was the high priest in architecture. Pugin and others built gothic churches, gothic houses, gothic railway stations and gothic public offices. Sanford was probably shocked to discover that Perth had only classical or Georgian style churches, but of course the men who built them as recently as the early 1840s had been moulded by an architectural-cum-social tradition of an earlier generation. So Sanford built the town's first gothic edifice. No doubt he would have wished for greater decoration on his building, but it was costly enough as it was, being constructed of stone rather than of bricks, and having a steeply pitched roof and many narrow windows in the gothic tradition. When a tower was added, it looked for all the world like a church, which was what was intended by the architect. It was a symbol of Sanford's aspirations for Swan River. Perth needed such a building. Daily contemplation of it made good governance more possible; it allowed men to soak up godliness and goodness; it offered the pupils lessons in citizenship equal in value to instruction from gothic text

Perth Boys' School, 1850s: *the gothic style as an agent in the quest for 'internal peace'.*

135

books. In such a building the children 'felt' the need to be dutiful, to be attentive, and to be obedient. It would be the perfect environment for the creation of a harmonious society, a powerful weapon in the quest for 'internal peace'. Alas for Sanford there were philistines in Perth who were untouched by the new mood and who spoke unceasingly of the cost of things and the absurdity of his roof and lofty tower. There were even those who thought that ventilation was necessary and that hoppers should be added to the windows. But to break a window-line to heaven was something the Colonial Secretary would not brook, so the hoppers were not put in and the first generation of pupils found that godliness was a stuffy condition. Mercifully Sanford left the colony in 1855, too early to bear the brunt of the grumbles of the schoolmasters. It was left to that practical man Richard Roach Jewell, Clerk of Works and Superintendent of the Towns of Fremantle and Perth from 1853 to 1884, to put in the hoppers and to find more meaningful ways of achieving the ends desired by Sanford and by himself and all those who strove to bring a harmonious society into being.[159]

One way was to ensure that those who refused to be morally enlightened should be punished for their sins and incarcerated in a gaol which would foster respect for governors. In 1854 Perth lacked such a place. There was the Convict Depot under Mt Eliza for the well-behaved criminals. There was also the Perth lock-up off St George's Terrace in the centre of town; but it was small and in any case the inmates escaped from it with impunity. And the gentry were disinclined to befoul the central square with a still larger gaol. What was required was an open piece of ground within sight of the cottages, lodging houses, hotels and institutions of the town's working class, including the ticket-of-leavers and conditional pardon men, but out of sight of the gentry of St George's Terrace.[160] The site chosen was perfect. It was on rising ground between low-lying Mews Lake and the equally low-lying Murray and Wellington Streets district, and was adjacent to the 'new town' being built by the working men of Perth to the east of Beaufort Street. The Hay Street and eastern Murray Street ridge concealed it from the gentry.[161] Work on the gaol commenced in November 1854. Convicts supplied most of the unskilled labour, but their deployment was erratic, and it was not until 1856 that the gaol was ready to house some of its builders. When completed the gaol was large, solid, squat and ugly, not unlike a toad in shape. But with the perverse humour of those times the entrance was an impressive Georgian portico complete with pediment and fan lighting, reminiscent of the stately homes of the Empire through whose halls the workers of Perth were never likely to walk as owners. The hallmark of distinction had been turned into a mocking gate of dishonour. In the psychological battle for the minds of the men of Perth, Jewell, with his vast experience of prison and fortification construction in the old country, had served his masters well. For the next thirty years the gaol was a daily reminder to workers of the fate of those who transgressed against the ordained nature of things or who hindered the

Richard Roach Jewell: *design and construction at the service of the gentry's quest for 'internal peace'.*

---

159 William Sanford Letters 1851–55, Mitchell Library 6-241B. In January 1852 Sanford found the situation of Perth 'most beautiful': 'Our climate is magnificent . . . the flowers are most beautiful in the neighbourhood of Perth . . . The vegetation is beautifully delicate in its appearance . . . the birds are beautiful and more numerous than I expected to find them'; but there was also the Governor, the Legislative Council, and the local press, and by mid 1853 he could not 'bear the slightest fatigue' and was feeling knocked up; also R. and J. Oldham *Western Heritage*, 1961, pp.35 and 36; also *Perth Gazette*, 22 October 1852; 8 April, 1 July, 23 December 1853.
160 Mrs Millett *Australian Parsonage*, p.31.   161 *Perth Gazette*, 22 September 1854.

Perth Gaol, 1850s–80s: *for men who transgressed against the ordained order of things.*

quest for 'internal peace'. As such it complemented Sanford's vision for the Perth Boys' School; indeed it was the coercive arm of the gothic.[162]

Of course the working of the gaol did not preclude furtherance of the wider objectives of spiritual and moral enlightenment. Indeed even the men condemned to be hanged could read books from the library and the chaplain's office. The gaol library had two sections: Protestant and Roman Catholic. From the latter could be taken *The Garden of the Soul* and the *Key to Heaven* and an unabridged edition of Butler's *Lives of the Saints*; from the former, the Holy Bible, the Book of Common Prayer, and various Religious Tract Society publications. The evidence suggests that they were little read, if only because most of the inmates, including male and female white offenders and Aborigines (children among them), were illiterate. But in any case it was more fulfilling to heap verbal abuse on the warders, in the case of the whites, or to greet the attentions of warders with silence, in the case of the Aborigines, than to discourse on the nature of heaven and hell. That was the province of the churches, the schools, the Mechanics' Institute, and the Working Men's Association.[163]

In January 1851, less than one year after the arrival of the first convicts, the free artisans and builders of Perth sought to distance themselves from the bond men by creating a Mechanics' Institute. In this they were mightily encouraged by the Government, leading officials, and the clergy of all denominations except perhaps the Roman Catholic. 'Like similar institutions in England and the other colonies it aimed to provide facilities for the improvement and recreation of mechanics and young men. It was to consist of a museum and a reading room; and lectures, classes of instruction and literary meetings were to be organized. The Regulations required that the topics chosen for discussion in literary meetings should carefully exclude all questions "of controversial theology, party politics, or of an immoral tendency".'[164] The Colonial Government provided free a block of land on the central

---

[162] R. and J. Oldham *Western Heritage*, pp.36–9; *ADB* Vol. 4—entry for Jewell; *Perth Gazette*, 24 November 1854; 11 January, 29 February, 13 June 1856; 9 April 1858.

[163] See *Your Museum* Vol. 4, No. 3, September 1976, which contains a brief history of the gaol and quotes extracts from the *Inquirer* for April 1884.

[164] B. Smith 'Early Western Australian Literature', *University Studies in History* Vol. 4, No. 1, 1961–62, p.47.

The Swan River Mechanics' Institute, Howick Street, Perth, 1850s: 'diffusing a love of order, sobriety, industry, and good conduct' among free artisans and clerks, but not among the Henry Haynes' or the Aborigines.

square, on the corner of Howick and Pier Streets, next to the Freemasons' Lodge. St George's Church was on the same block. By the end of 1852 a library, hall and discussion rooms had been erected on the site with a handsome facade proclaiming the nature and function of the Institution.[165] A few years later the building lost its symmetry when a museum was added. At the same time the Institute began to lose its artisan character, and although attracting more than 100 members, it became less a debating society than a reading room for gentlemen, where *Blackwoods Magazine, Punch*, the *Illustrated London News*, and some colonial papers could be read, and books borrowed. It lost the balance of personnel and interest which characterised its activities for the first eight or so years. It was Richard Roach Jewell who designed the museum and extensions in 1859–60. Even allowing for the handful of radicals in the Institute, Governor Fitzgerald's farewell assessment in 1855 was not far from the mark:

> The Institute has so far extended its sphere of usefulness as to be instrumental in diffusing a love of order, sobriety, industry, and good conduct within the large circle of its influence, acquirements so essential to the well-being of society and the progress of Civilization.[166]

The early 1850s also saw the construction of a Temperance Hall. This too was a response to the convict presence. In 1852 the Total Abstinence Society, organized by the gentry with artisan assistance, seems to have produced a journal called the *WA Monthly Journal and Total Abstinence Advocate*. Described as a periodical for the working classes, it contained articles on the dignity of labour, and the value of thrift and sobriety.[167] Arthur Shenton, the editor of the *Perth Gazette*, took subscriptions, and as he was one of the founders[168] of the short-lived WA Friendly Institute and Benefit Society for ticket-of-leavers, he may have edited the *Journal* as well. In June 1852 a group of 40 or so ticket-of-leavers sought Government assistance to run a boarding home

[165] *Perth Gazette*, 14, 28 May 1852.
[166] Mechanics' Institute Minute Book Vol. 1, 4 June 1855.
[167] *Perth Gazette*, 16 April, 14 May, 11 June 1852.
[168] A co-founder was T. N. Yule, the Police Magistrate—a cheery soul who enjoyed his glass of ale and who once found 'not guilty' a drunkard who claimed to be as sober as the magistrate. See R. Erickson 'T. N. Yule: A Gentleman of Misfortune', *Early Days* Vol. 7, Pt. III, 1971, p.20.

(non-alcoholic) and meeting place. This act of independence met with the approval of neither Shenton nor the Government.[169] When in June 1854 the new Temperance Hall was opened, the movement was as firmly in the hands of the gentry as was the Mechanics' Institute. At the opening Mrs Fitzgerald, well known for her charitable works, was present, as were 'several of the upper class of society'.[170] And it stayed that way with men like Bernard Smith as administrators. The Hall was open for tea between 7 a.m. and 10 p.m. and public lectures and sober entertainments were held regularly. Its greatest appeal lay to those who were already temperate in all things, for many of the labouring class were without institutionalised religion[171] and certain that grog made life in this world bearable. Some, like Henry Haynes, hovered on the brink but did not join or take the pledge, even after the great revivalist meetings of the Rev. Mathew Burnett in 1883. Burnett was a great preacher: at several of the meetings he told a packed town hall of Flasher Nugent and 'How he won 40 000 for the Pledge', and of 'Successful Colonists and the Secrets of their Success'. He spoke movingly on the theme of 'Advance Western Australia' and fifty people came forward to be invested with the red-ribbon badge.[172] Despite these successes; despite the financial success of Burnett's Coffee Palace;[173] and despite occasional reports that the temperance movement had helped to produce less drunkenness than usual on St Patrick's Day, the habit of 'shouting' defied eradication.[174] For some men, perhaps even many, like Joseph Chester in the Mechanics' Institute, drinking grog was an act of personal and social defiance of an order of things which resisted change.[175] For others, like Haynes, it simply offered a privatised solace which prayer and tea meetings could never equal.

The increased flow of willing and unwilling migrants to Swan River in the early 1850s also necessitated the construction of a new hospital in Perth. At first it seemed that the new hospital would replace the existing hospital on the central square site; but the residents and principal users of St George's Terrace and Hay Street wished to see a new hospital placed as far away from them as possible. After all the hospital was not usually patronised by the gentry and officials, the 'fit and proper' persons of the town, who tended to be treated in their homes by the few doctors available. Indeed one almost had to demonstrate one's destitution to gain admittance to the Hospital. Accordingly it was decided to build the new hospital close to where the Roman Catholic Church had established itself, in the east end of Murray Street (then known as Goderich Street), well away from the more salubrious parts of the town. Not that the site itself was an unhealthy one. Indeed, placed as it was on one of the highest points of the town it caught the afternoon sea breeze which has had such a beneficial effect on Perthians from the earliest days to the present. Designed by Richard Roach Jewell it was erected between 1853 and 1854. There was some delay late in 1853 when

[169] *Perth Gazette*, 11, 18 June, 3 September 1852.   [170] *Perth Gazette*, 9 June 1854.
[171] For one of many reports on this subject see *Perth Gazette*, 4 June 1852: 'The lower orders are totally ignorant of religion'. This was probably not true of the Roman Catholics among the 'lower orders'.
[172] *West Australian*, 15, 18 May, 1, 5 June 1883.   [173] *Western Mail*, 16 August 1934.
[174] For a note on 'shouting' see *WA Times*, 4 April 1879; for the claim about St Patrick's Day, see *WA Times*, 21 March 1876.
[175] See Minute Books of the Swan River Mechanics' Institute, 25 August 1856: 'He was entirely opposed to any law that would allow the rich man to get drunk and not the poor.'

the Army Medical Board decreed that the roof should not be made of imported galvanized iron but of locally made shingles which required a different pitch. At nearly £2000 the three-storey hospital was one of the costliest buildings ever erected in Perth to that time. It was part of the price the free colonists had to pay for the introduction of convicts and the Pensioner families and serving girls who came in their train.[176]

The link between hospitalization, immigration and pauperism, can be seen from the close proximity of the Colonial Hospital to the Servants' Home/Poor House, half a block away. The Servants' Home served as an immigrant depot and a hostel for vagrant women. During the 1850s the building, which seems to have been erected late in Stirling's time, was unable to cope with the influx of both sorts of inmates. Paupers, male and female, were often bundled out of their quarters and sent up the road to the basement of the Colonial Hospital. In the early 1860s Governor Hampton extended the building.[177]

The last of the important Government and public buildings constructed in the early 1850s was the slaughterhouse at Claise Brook. Even before the coming of the convicts the Government was concerned by the potential hazard to the health of the citizenry of the several small slaughterhouses within the town boundaries. Then with the arrival of the convicts the need for a central slaughterhouse became still more pressing. The Claise Brook site was chosen because it was well away from the town centre and the populous districts, yet not so far away as to pose delivery problems.[178] But it did not attract much custom. Just as the earlier attempt to create a central market had failed, so too with the abattoir the people of Perth stayed with their traditional ways. Indeed when in 1854 the lakes behind the town were being drained and so vast a quantity of water poured through the drain to Claise Brook as to endanger the Slaughterhouse, the *Perth Gazette* gleefully looked forward to the day that it would topple into the creek.[179] It had been thought to be a wasteful use of public money. It could not even be used as a convict depot because it was far too damp. In short it deserved the epithet 'Fitzgerald's folly'.

Building activity in the early 1850s was not confined to works of a public nature. With the draining of the lakes behind the town centre new allotments were taken up, some by workers, others by investors with a view to renting or leasing properties. New cottages, mostly made of brick, now the cheapest building material in Perth, sprang up in the northern and western parts of the town. There was still further development under Mt Eliza, and the first houses were erected in the area which later became known as East Perth. Infill development in the central area also continued. St George's Terrace and Hay Street buildings began to have decorated facades, as the following press note indicates:

> Our Perth street architecture appears lately to have taken a more decorative turn, and the houses and shop-fronts now in course of erection or lately completed exhibit a more pleasing appearance than

176 B. Cohen *A History of Medicine in Western Australia*, 1965; *Perth Gazette*, 22 October 1852; 1 July, 11 November, 23 December 1853; Colonial Surgeon's Annual Reports in *Votes and Proceedings of the Legislative Council of Western Australia*.

177 Sandra Taylor 'An Investigation of the concept of pauperism among women in mid nineteenth century Western Australia, with particular emphasis on the Institution of the Perth Poor House 1862–68', unpublished research essay, cited by permission of the author.

178 *Perth Gazette*, 5 April 1852.   179 *Perth Gazette*, 18 August 1854.

the plain brick edifices of former years. Of ornamental frontages we have something quite new to the colony in the building just completed by Mr B. Mason in Hay Street.

This building was designed by the assistant surveyor, Mr Phelps, of whom little is known. He also designed a large building for Henry Laroche Cole at about the same time. Nor was Jewell inactive. In his spare time he designed a new store-front for the merchant Mark Dyett. The *Perth Gazette* commented that these buildings

> bid fair to give as altered an appearance to the middle portion of St George's Terrace, as the very handsome portico to the residence of Mr G. Shenton has to the western end.[180]

Things proceeded slowly in Perth. Growth came in fits and starts. It happened that the early 1850s was one such growth period. But in the mid-1850s Perth was still a little town, lacking the 'poisoned courts' and 'typhus-tainted alleys' of England's cities, an open town where one decorated facade was newsworthy and a new public building could evoke a sense of wonder that it was happening in Perth. It was a trait that the people of Perth retained throughout their history.[181]

Thereafter the physical development of the town was less dramatic. Governor Fitzgerald, who had become increasingly keen to spend money, was replaced in 1855 by Arthur Kennedy who carried a brief to spend none. Even the Gaol budget was stripped of £1000. Not until about 1860 did Kennedy slacken his tight hold over the public purse, but it was his good housekeeping which enabled his successor, Hampton, to recommence the construction of important public works.

If the public purse was closed temporarily in the late 1850s, the private purse of the wealthy Anglican Bishop of Perth, Mathew Blagden Hale, was not. Hale had first visited the colony in 1848 when he was Archdeacon of the Diocese of Adelaide which then embraced Perth. On that visit he married Sabina Bussell. He called in again in 1856 en route to England for consecration as Bishop of the new Diocese of Perth. In 1858 Hale returned to Perth. The son of a wealthy landowner in Gloucestershire who has died in 1855, Hale was as affluent as George Shenton and the Leake family. Within three years he had built an impressive residence for himself off Spring Street and west St George's Terrace overlooking Perth Water; a cottage in the same grounds for the use of visiting clergy; a secondary boys' school; and a residence near St George's Church for the first Dean, George Purvis Pownall. Hale was a deeply conservative churchman, well within the tradition established by Wittenoom (who had died in 1855); and Pownall, like the former Colonial Secretary, Sanford, was a graduate of Trinity, and a member of the Camden Society. Pownall had even dallied with tractarianism. They approved of Sanford's school, and in 1859–60 they designed and had built a two storey 'parsonage' in the gothic style: 'a series of subsidiary gables, placed so as to emphasise the fenestration. These are decorated, like the end gables, with a carved wooden valance'. Like the Anglican Church itself, the building had its gentle and harsh lines, the latter being particularly evident in the formal and authoritative entrance, an echo of the new Perth Gaol and of Mr Shenton's house at the other end of the Terrace.

[180] *Perth Gazette*, 11 April 1856.
[181] *Perth Gazette*, 5 October 1849: 'A Voice From Australia'—'From poisoned air ye breathe in courts, and typhus tainted alleys, Come forth and dwell where health resorts, in fertile hills and valleys.'

A deanery for the Rev. Pownall, St George's Terrace, 1859.

Both Pownall and Hale would have seen work on the construction of the Deanery in the way they viewed their role in the Mechanics' Institute, where Pownall in particular lectured often on self help and a Christian-based morality.[182] For both men were colonial improvers, Samuel Smiles' in clerical garb. They abhorred convictism (Hale wrote a pamphlet attacking the system and he clashed often with Governor Hampton),[183] but they believed passionately that a moral force system would foster reformation. Perhaps with this in mind they employed ticket-of-leavers on the construction of the Deanery and Bishop's House. Something of the purpose and style of the houses, something of the daily intercourse with high-minded men like Hale and Pownall might help to bring such fallen men closer to godliness and decency and show them the way to independence in this world and salvation in the next. Perhaps it worked with some men. But occasionally even Hale's nerve failed. When one of his ticket-of-leave labourers, a fellow passenger on the hell-ship *Nile*, faced a charge of assaulting a little girl in the scrub on high ground behind Bishop's House, Hale did not testify on the man's behalf even though the evidence against him was slight. The incident was an index to the concern, even paranoia, of a society under siege. The man was hanged. Hale's house faced Perth Water. There would be other souls to save.

Perhaps Hale had more than his fair share of disappointments in Perth. In 1858 he financed and built a secondary school for boys. It had two storeys and was enclosed by a cloistered verandah on the northern and a smaller cloister on the southern front. The roofline was as a battlement. It was not unlike part of the Court of Trinity College, Cambridge, where Hale himself had imbibed education and religion; but the immediate inspiration was St Peter's School in Adelaide. His school attracted the children of the gentry and officials of Perth and the country: Wittenoom, Samson, Brockman, Shenton, Burt, Lee Steere, Parker, Stone, Roe and Burges. Perhaps the most humble in origin were the Forrest boys whose father was a pious and affluent miller near Bunbury, although Fred Liddelow's father was a prosperous butcher in Perth. Trained by the experienced Rev. Sweeting and the able Rev. Hare, the pupils of Bishop Hale's School formed the nucleus of the governing

Facing Perth Water: Bishop's House, 1860s.

182 e.g. Mechanics' Institute Minute Book, 29 April 1861, lecture on 'self-help'.
183 See *Perth Gazette*, 9 July 1858.

group in Western Australia to the turn of the century and beyond—an informal Anglican establishment. But in 1872 the Bishop's School had so few enrolments that it was closed down. Hale was disappointed, but the cause of the closure was less dissatisfaction with the school itself and the indifference of parents towards education, than the demography of the investing class. He had wanted to create a refined society in Swan River. At least in part this objective would be judged by the lives of his former students. They, in any case, would be the ones to remember him as 'the good bishop' after his departure in 1875.[184]

A nursery of gentry politicians and administrators: 'The Cloisters' or Bishop Hale's School, 1858-72.

From February 1862, until the arrival of the last convict transport in 1868, the Governor of Swan River was Dr John Hampton. Hampton had been Comptroller General of Convicts in Van Dieman's Land from 1846 to 1857, from which position he resigned suddenly in the midst of a crisis over allegations against him of inhumanity and corruption. He drifted round the Empire on private business until 1861, when the Duke of Newcastle sought his services for Swan River—a tough man for a tough job. On his arrival in Swan River, Hampton received an earnest prayer from the Chairman of the Perth City Council that during His Excellency's period of office a happy unanimity would prevail amongst all classes of the Colony and that a merciful Providence would bless and prosper all his undertakings.[185] In Swan River he set to one side Colonel Henderson's moral force system: floggings became commonplace, solitary confinement for petty offences was reintroduced, a convict's right of appeal against punishment was abolished, and tickets-of-leave were withheld. He was detested by the convicts and at least one attempt was made on his life.[186] Hampton alienated free labourers and contractors because he insisted that public works should be carried out by the Convict Establishment. He also alienated some members of the gentry when he appointed his son as Acting Comptroller General of

[184] Deanery description from R. and J. Oldham *Western Heritage*, pp.42-50; also *ADB* Vol. 4—entry for Hale; Canon A. Burton *Church Beginnings in the West*, 1941, Chapters 13, 14; also B. Wilson 'The First Bishop', in F. Alexander (ed.) *Four Bishops and their See*, 1958; *Perth Gazette*, 5 October 1860; Supreme Court of Western Australia, Case File 840, 1860.

[185] *Perth Gazette*, 7 March 1862.

[186] *Perth Gazette*, 1 May 1863, 16 March 1867, and 25 October 1867; *ADB* Vol. 1—entry for Hampton.

Perth as Pastoral Myth: the testimony of J. Walsh, ex-convict, 1865.

Convicts, though perhaps the outrage was more feigned than real, for nepotism and patronage were at the heart of colonial administration.

Hampton had a passion for building. He had one look at Stirling's old Government House which, despite much extension and repair, leaked like a sieve in winter, and set to to hurry along the construction of a new one. Instead of Kennedy's rate of 'a brick per man per diem'[187] the large building was erected speedily, and by 1864 the Hampton family was in occupation.[188] The Londoners would have noticed the close resemblance the new building bore to the notorious Tower of London and the equally powerful symbol of ancient authority—Hampton Court. The similarities were not accidental, for Jewell and the military designers knew almost by instinct how best to inculcate feelings of deference alongside a healthy respect for the coercive power of the State. Some citizens of Perth thought that the new Government House was altogether too grand for the colony, and a waste of money and labour.[189] But for others, its 'imposing and palatial appearance, replete with every convenience and accommodation' was a sign that Swan River could match the eastern colonies of Australia. They needed such reassurances.[190]

Government House in the late 1860s: the photographer has composed his picture as a paradigm of social order in convict Perth—convict workers at bottom of picture, the gentry above them, and Government House set high as a symbol of Imperial authority in Perth.

Hampton had just begun. At the same time as he housed himself more comfortably, he authorised the construction of a barracks for the families of the Enrolled Pensioner Force. Since 1858 when several hundred convicts had been moved to Perth Gaol, the Pensioner families had been lodged in James Ougden's hotel and elsewhere in the city: there were probably eighty to one hundred families at any one time. (In all, about five hundred Pensioner families came to Swan River). Work proceeded more slowly than it had on Government House. In fact it seems that over twelve months was required to clear the land at the west end of St George's Terrace preparatory to constructing a two- (subsequently three) storey building, which formed three sides of a quadrangle. When completed in the mid-1860s, it provided accommodation for sixty Pensioners and their families, as well as a guard

187 *Perth Gazette*, 7 March 1862.
188 *Perth Gazette*, 13 March 1863, reported the completion of the north front.
189 Mrs Millett *Australian Parsonage*, p.28.
190 Census of Western Australia, 1870—Introduction.

The Barracks at the western end of St George's Terrace, 1860s: Mr Knight's house at left, and the Pensioner Guard's school and hospital at right.

room, cookhouse and work shed. A military hospital and school was built nearby.[191] By 1880, when the Pensioner force was disbanded, most of the families had moved out to the several Pensioner 'villages', one of which was on Melville Water, and another in Aberdeen Street in the northern part of the town. Some Pensioners, however, remained in the barracks until it was taken over by the Public Works Department in 1904.[192] The barracks were impressively large and occupied a commanding position overlooking the town. With a military barracks set high at one end of the town, a huge gaol dominating the northern sector, and a turreted Government House commanding the southern and eastern entrances to the town from the river, the people of Perth understood well enough the nature of their society.

In the winter of 1862 the colony experienced severe flooding—the worst since 1830, according to the oldtimers. The gardens behind Perth reverted less to a series of lakes than to one vast lake from Murray Street north to Brisbane Street, leaving only the Gaol and one or two other buildings clear of water. The foreshore and Bazaar Street were under the swollen river; indeed the steamer *Lady Stirling* was able to drop her passengers alongside the Pier Hotel some distance up William Street. The water flooded over the Causeway, rendering it impassable, and the soldiers had to move the powder from the magazine nearby.[193] Hampton at once declared his intention to build a Causeway which would withstand such flooding. The huge task was completed with convict labour by 1866. Hampton himself officially opened the bridge.[194] There were some people at the opening, including Septimus Roe, who remembered when the first bridge was opened nearly twenty-five years previously. In 1867 a 1000-foot bridge over the Swan at North Fremantle was completed. So too was the Perth–Fremantle road, constructed this time with jarrah blocks from trees hewn down along the way—Hampton's 'cheeses', they were called. No longer need the aging Lionel Samson fear that his horse would hit an uncleared stump. And when he trotted down St George's Terrace to visit friends, he would note that Hampton had had the Terrace levelled and that the deep ravine

---

[191] *Perth Gazette*, 11 July 1862, 16 January 1863. The exact date of its completion is something of a mystery. The Census of Western Australia for 1870 suggests that the building was in occupation in the mid 1860s; but Mrs Millett stated firmly that it had not been completed when she left the colony late in 1868. Mrs Millett *Australian Parsonage*, p.27.

[192] F. H. Broomhall 'The Enrolled Pensioner Force', mss, Battye Library.

[193] *Perth Gazette*, 11 July 1862. [194] *Perth Gazette*, 15 November 1867.

The new Causeway at Perth, built by Governor Hampton, mid-1860s.

opposite Government House, which they used to call 'The Hollows', had been filled in.[195] And the roads out to the north-west—Wanneroo way—and to the north-east—Guildford and York—were also now well made and a boon to the waggoner and his team. For men like Roe, Shenton, Samson, Brockman, and other survivors from the foundation years, knew now that Perth was indeed a jewel in the British Empire, if not a particularly precious one.[196]

By now Hampton was in full flight. Early in 1867 he informed the Perth City Council that he intended to build a town hall and present it to the city. On Sunday 19 May 1867 the ministers and congregations of all the churches in Perth offered prayers to the Almighty for rain to break up the disastrous drought in the country. On Thursday 23 May preparations were finalised for the dual celebration of the Queen's birthday and the laying of the foundation stone of the new Town Hall. Over Barrack Street a triple arch had been erected, on which was written 'The Citizens Thanks'. By late afternoon the clouds were gathering, and that evening there was a great downpour which continued unabated all night. Not for the first time and nor for the last were the townsmen pleased for the farmer and sorry for themselves:

> Many were the faces exhibiting dire disappointment to be seen on Friday morning, notwithstanding that an hour or two's sunshine after breakfast gave some hopes, that proved to be lost in the clouds.

At 11.30 a.m. the combined military defence of Western Australia, already formed in line, scattered before a heavy downpour. With some difficulty Captain Finnerty got them into line again just in time to greet Governor Hampton in the Domain. Hampton congratulated them on their appearance, reviewed the 'march past', and stood through the birthday salute from the twenty-one great guns, and three volleys by the infantry. Then down came the rain again, and the Pinjarrah Rifles' dashing charges uphill at the big guns had to be cancelled. Hampton returned to Government House, while the soaking soldiers marched round to the site of the new town hall where they found that

> the flags hung mournfully from the poles, the ground was wet and sloppy, the public scared from venturing out to see the sight, and even the green arch over the roadway bore token to the general regret for the

A Hall for a city: Hampton's gift to the people of Perth.

[195] Mrs J. B. Roe 'Some Old Time Memories', *Early Days* Vol. 1, Pt. I, 1927, pp.5–7.
[196] C/f Carnarvon mss PRO, W. A. Ross to Sir John Hay: 'Western Australia is a half-civilized place', 24 November 1866. Reference provided by Mr Bruce Knox. Oddly enough Ross was seeking the governorship of Western Australia.

Governor Hampton: a builder who constructed in all weathers.

untoward weather, the inscription over it of 'The Citizens Thanks' literally dissolving itself in tears of doleful colour.

That afternoon, shortly after 1 o'clock, the dignitaries moved off in procession from Government House—members of the Perth City Council, clergymen, magistrates, and members of the Executive and Legislative Councils. The Governor and his officials brought up the rear. When the dignitaries and townsmen had gathered on the site, Archdeacon Brown read a long prayer:

> Almighty God who hast pleasure in the prosperity of Thy servants, at the commencement of this our enterprise we make our humble supplication before Thee. We most thankfully acknowledge our asbolute dependence upon Thee, and Thy great goodness and mercy to us, and all Thy Creatures. Under Thy favor, let the foundation stone of this edifice now be laid; in carrying forward this work let Thy protection never be wanting; and when, in Thy good Providence, its gates are set up, may Thy blessing crown the undertaking, and abide upon the persons and occupations of those who, age after age, shall profit by its uses.

Some British coins were placed in the mortar and then the foundation stone was laid with Mr Millar's silver trowel. J. G. C. Carr, the Chairman of the Perth City Council, thanked Governor Hampton for his gift to the city, and, with a keen sense of occasion, expressed the wish that before too long the City Council would attain the dignity of a municipality with corporate privileges. In his reply Hampton skirted round this issue, but he gracefully accepted the thanks of the city. After listening to another prayer, the crowd gave three cheers for the Governor and dispersed quickly as the rain poured down again. The soldiers dashed to the Guard House nearby, where they enjoyed a hogshead of English ale. They had deserved it.[197]

Hampton's term of office was drawing to a close. Before he left, however, he drew up plans for a building to house the Legislative Council. Situated next to the Town Hall, this last of Hampton's buildings was opened in 1870, just in time to usher in a new phase in Swan River's constitutional history, namely representative government, something which Hampton, a high Tory autocrat to the last, was not enthusiastic about. Hampton died in England in 1869. In his long career as a servant of the Queen he had learned to survive in all weathers. He seems even to have lived comfortably with the unrelenting hatred of the convicts, whose lacerated backs and broken spirits were as much his monuments in Perth as the buildings he erected with their labour.

Perth was not a secular society. Church attendance probably equalled, or even bettered, that of England (about 55%), and church festivals like Lent and Easter were widely observed.[198] Perhaps the Roman Catholics enjoyed a higher weekly turnout than did the Anglicans. Certainly in the 1860s and 1870s there was a flurry of church building activity. In February 1863 Bishop Salvado laid the foundation stone of a Roman Catholic cathedral, to be built on the 'best and most commanding position in our metropolis'.[199] The design of the cathedral is something of a mystery, for at the time it was ascribed to Bernard Smith, a prominent Catholic layman and Perth city councillor, but later

[197] *Perth Gazette*, 24, 31 May 1867; *Inquirer*, 29 May 1867.
[198] See *WA Times*, 23 March 1877, 26 April 1878 for comments on church going and the meaning of church festivals.
[199] *Perth Gazette*, 6, 20 February 1863.

research has suggested that Bishop Serra brought back from England plans drawn up earlier by the eminent British architect and champion of the Gothic Revival, Welby Augustus Pugin.[200] For two years the Benedictine brothers walked daily from their monastery in Subiaco to build their gothic cathedral. When finished, St John's Cathedral (later renamed St Mary's) was popularly regarded as the noblest and most spiritual building in Perth. It was also a sign of the growing strength of Roman Catholicism in the town. In 1848 fewer than one in five Perthians was a Roman Catholic. By the late 1860s Catholics were nearly one in three of the population of Perth. In 1880 a weekly Catholic journal, *Record*, was founded. This represented a formidable challenge to Anglicanism and led to increased sectarianism in the town, which manifested itself in elections for the Legislative Council.[201] Even the new Cathedral was the envy of the Anglicans. As Mrs Millett, wife of an Anglican clergyman, put it:

> One cannot but hope that . . . an effort may be made . . . to erect a building a little less barn-like than [the] present cathedral, which must, I fear, present but a poor contrast to the new tower of the Roman Catholic Church.[202]

Anglicanism had indeed lost ground. In 1848 nearly 70% of Perth's population belonged to the Church of England; by 1870 this had slumped to 53%; and ten years later it was down to 48%. In 1871, to the dismay of Bishop Hale, a Roman Catholic Governor, Frederick Weld, disestablished the Church of England and introduced greater State aid to Catholic schools. All this was an unexpected consequence of convictism, which had been so fervently pressed for by some leading Anglicans. In absolute numbers, however, the Church of England grew in the 1850s and 1860s. The Church rather divided over its response to increased numbers. Some like Dean Pownall wished to build a new church in the north of the town where many ex-convicts lived; but at a public meeting Hale opposed this proposal, partly on the grounds that a congregation of ex-convicts, unleavened with gentry, could lead to undesirable consequences.[203] Nor was there much enthusiasm for a new Cathedral, so the decision was taken to enlarge the existing one, however 'architecturally poor and unchurchlike', to accommodate up to 2000 people—hence Mrs Millett's reference to its barn-like character.[204] Only in 1880 was the foundation stone of a new cathedral laid; and not until 1888 were the Anglicans able to worship in the more spiritual environment of the gothic.

The Congregationalists were never more than 5% of the population, but they were an energetic lot. In 1863 they bought Mr Barnett's allotment in central St George's Terrace, and commenced clearing the land for a new church 'with a handsome architectural frontage to the street'.[205] Designed by the ubiquitous Jewell, the new Trinity Church was in the colonial gothic style. At the opening service the prayers were led by old Henry Trigg, whose career was an inspiration to all Independents in Perth, for most of the congregation were artisans, storekeepers and others of the middling orders of colonial society, though one, George

200 *Perth Gazette*, 20 February 1863; R. and J. Oldham *Western Heritage*, pp.65–7. Still later research (as yet unpublished) by Drs Joan and Jim Kerr disputes the claim for a Pugin design.
201 Censuses of Western Australia, 1848, 1870, 1881; *Perth Gazette*, November 1870.
202 Mrs Millett *Australian Parsonage*, p.37.   203 *Perth Gazette*, 2 May 1862.
204 *Perth Gazette*, 29 May 1863; Mrs Millett *Australian Parsonage*, p.37.
205 *Perth Gazette*, 7 August 1863.

Trinity Congregational Church, St George's Terrace, 1860s.

Randell, a steamship proprietor, would eventually be a member of John Forrest's cabinet. The new building would serve the community as church, Sunday school, hall, and child care centre for the next 115 years. Congregationalism in Perth, as in England, did not reach the unskilled working class.[206]

The Wesleyans had always been strong in Perth, rarely accounting for less than 10% of the population. Without increasing their flock as spectacularly as did the Roman Catholics, the Wesleyans maintained their strength through to the 1880s, and in the life of the community their influence was disproportionately great. They ran the town's largest Sunday school (housed in the first Wesleyan Church); they ran its most successful native institution; and for most of the period nearly one-third of the members of the Perth City Council belonged to the Wesleyan congregation. And they spearheaded the temperance movement in Perth. Perhaps too, the Wesleyans reached out to the ex-convicts more successfully than the Anglicans and Congregationalists: certainly they were zealous in bringing about marriages of ex-convicts, not always with the happiest results.[207] In 1866 the close-knit community decided to build its third church in thirty years. Aided by a donation of £1000 from the Shenton family, the Rev. Lowe authorised the construction of the church in 1867. The new church was designed by Jewell. Jewell was a member of Wesley Church; indeed he was a circuit steward. There can be little doubt that the church he designed for the Rev. Lowe was his finest achievement. When opened in 1870, Jewell's church, with a tall and elegant spire, rivalled Reed's work in Melbourne in its architectural beauty and spirituality. It was and remains the supreme gothic building in a town notable for its gothic revival character.[208] But something of Wesley's methodism was being lost, for the excellent new pews built by

[206] G. Kitson Clark *The Making of Victorian England*, 1962, p.163.

[207] Nearly one-third of all divorce cases heard by the Supreme Court from 1864 to 1900 involved parties married in Wesley Church. The divorce case files are lodged in the Supreme Court.

[208] *Perth Gazette*, 22 February 1867, 15 April 1870; W. Lutton *The Wesley Story*; R. and J. Oldham *Western Heritage*, pp.68–70.

150

Mr Cutting were to be occupied according to class rank: donors of £50 and above were to have first choice of pews; then the Trustees; and then back through the church according to a scale as to the amount contributed. Few ex-convicts would ever have made the middle of the church. Yet hadn't the Rev. Laurance said when the foundation stone was laid:

> Beautiful as was the Crystal Palace—sparkling like a gem in Heaven's sunlight—more beautiful in God's sight is a temple of Grace, a material structure erected for His worship; but most beautiful before Him is a converted man, devoted to His service—a living temple consecrated by the indwelling Jehovah?

The Shentons and the Hardeys sat in the front pews. Old Joseph Hardey had lived on to see the new gothic church and its fine spire. He fully understood its message. After all he had first preached in Perth in the shade of a tall gum tree which reached upward to heaven.

Thus by 1870 Perth had several very large churches. They did not dominate the town like a mediaeval city; rather were they integrated with the larger secular buildings, especially those of the State. It gave to the town what visitors called 'a pleasing appearance'. Relations between Church and State had been complicated however by the growing strength of Roman Catholicism, a faith whose quest for 'internal peace' seemed on occasions to seek too much for the poor and disinherited and to threaten disruption to the ordained society. But the prominent lay Catholics like Bernard Smith were anything but disruptive particles, and Bishop Griver lacked John Brady's fire. Perhaps all would be well.

Four more buildings erected before 1884 indicate aspects of the growth of Perth in this period. The first was the Working Men's Institute, built in 1864 on a site in Wellington Street at the foot of Barrack Street. It represented an attempt on the part of the Governor and the gentry to inculcate in working men, habits of thrift, temperance, and self help: 'to elevate and enoble the men of toil'.[209] The building was subsidised by the Government, and several colonial officials and clergymen were on the Organizing Committee which drew up the

The third Wesley Church, consecrated 1870: the second Wesley Church is in the background.

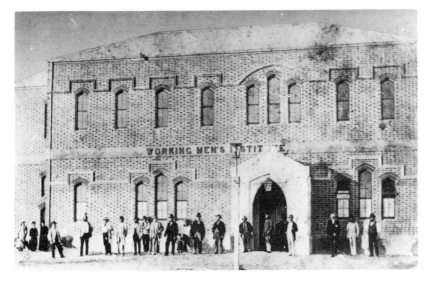

The Working Men's Institute, Barrack Street, opened 1864.

[209] See *Perth Gazette*, 25 March, 8 April 1864, for an account of formation of the Association—the meeting was chaired by Bishop Hale: 30-40 'of the working class' attended.

Books for the people of Perth:
Arthur Shenton's advertisement.

Institute's constitution, despite the protests of some of the workmen. For a time ex-convicts were not permitted to become members, but this rule was relaxed sometime in the late 1860s. Members could use the hall for entertainments, public meetings and lectures on subjects like 'Character', while there were discussion rooms and a library for the earnest few. The hall and its environs were occasionally the scene of rowdiness, for the Institute was located in the working class part of town, close to several hotels. To the regret of the Committee, the Institute's financial membership rarely exceeded 100.[210] However its influence may have been wider than this would suggest. Certainly an association with it would have helped working men to keep out of the huge gaol just up the road.[211]

The spread of settlement in these years caused the Government to locate a new Girls' School well to the north of the town centre. Previously the girls had attended a school in Pier Street on the old central square, and some continued to do so until the 1880s when it was closed down. The new building was in James Street. It attracted girls from as far west as Fitzgerald Street and as far north as Brisbane Street—indeed from Highgate Hill when that suburb began to develop in the 1880s.[212]

In 1879 the legal firm of Stone and Bush decided that Perth was large enough to have a theatre. Called St George's Theatre it was located on the north side of Howick Street, slightly to the east of the Mechanics' Institute. It had an imposing facade, with huge decorated Greek columns and a pediment, very similar in appearance to the famous Haymarket Theatre in London. In the 1880s it was well used by visiting and local performers. It was very much an institution for the 'respectable classes'; indeed it was a clear sign that there were now in Perth enough people with leisure time to enjoy such a cultural life.[213]

In 1880 the construction of the Perth railway station heralded a different kind of change in the lives of the people of Perth. From the late 1880s commercial river traffic began to decline significantly in relation to rail and road, and Perth began to lose something of its inland port character. Jobs lost in the river trade were not compensated for by an increasingly large labour demand of the railway, for Fremantle rather than Perth benefited in this way; in fact very few new employment categories were added to the town's occupational structure.[214] In the early years very few workers used the train, except for occasional weekend excursions to Greenmount or to Fremantle. The cost of tickets was high until the 1890s.

Administering Perth: men, drains, cess-pits and roads

The 1850s was a critical decade in the history of the administration of the city of Perth. The decade opened as the 1840s had finished, namely, with stagnation as the city's principal characteristic. Henry Cole

210 *WA Times*, 17 April 1879—200 members, but many in arrears.
211 *WA Blue Book* 1860s; B. Smith 'Early Western Australian Literature', *University Studies in History* Vol. 4, No. 1, 1961–62; *Perth Gazette*, 21 June 1867; 13 January 1871; 18 April, 2 May 1873.
212 R. and J. Oldham *Western Heritage*, pp.72–3.
213 R. and J. Oldham *Western Heritage*, p.73; also 'Prinsep Diary'—entries from 1870s to late 1880s.
214 1881 Census of WA: there were only 8 railway employees in Perth; the number of boatmen fell from 59 in 1870 to 25 in 1881, a decline due more to better road transport than to the introduction of rail.

continued as Chairman, although by 1853 he was embroiled in a serious dispute with the Governor over the latter's determination to resume compulsorily the former's land in Wellington Street, known as Lot Q1. This dispute was also of significance for relations between the people of Perth and the Imperial administration, for it was one of several issues which led to the Government being charged with tyrannical behaviour and to the first serious attempts to gain some sort of representative government for the colony.[215] In the early 1850s the Town Trust was (from 1851) again denied access to prison labour, and road works suffered accordingly.[216] In addition, the Governor interfered with the Trustees' choice of a Chairman—indeed he overruled their choice of Austin. As the *Perth Gazette* commented:

> The Governor appears to desire to ride roughshod over the Trust, but we rather think that he will find the townsmen can be as obstinate as himself, more particularly when they have commonsense on their side.[217]

On this issue the views of the Governor prevailed however, and after an abortive attempt to install the aging Surveyor-General, Septimus Roe, the Trust elected George Shenton to the Chairmanship, which position he was to hold until 1858,[218] despite the fact that on several occasions he headed attacks on the Governor's administration of the colony. The Trust as a whole was now composed less of officer-gentry personnel than of men even more closely identified with town life: Bernard Smith, George Lazenby, J. Chipper, Terrence Farrelly, George Haysom (publican), Bayley Maycock and Robert Habgood.[219]

In the mid-1850s the Government decided to discontinue the Central Board which had had considerable control over road servicing, but which in fact had accomplished little. It invited the Perth Town Trust to resume this responsibility. In a rider to the 'offer' it was insisted that a regular supply of finance would be necessary for the discharge of this duty, and that it would therefore be required of the Trust that it institute a valuation or rating system similar to that in England. This was a drastic alteration to the *status quo*. The Trust had always made assessments and collected rates for specific projects: it had never levied and collected general rates. It was thought by some people that a general levy would bear too heavily on owners of properties which had been improved—too heavily, that is, in relation to the more numerous owners of unimproved property.[220] The debate broadened still further when in September 1856 the Government proposed to take over all local services and to levy a rate in the British way. The Perth Town Trust was by now deeply divided over the issue, indeed over the general direction and purpose of municipal endeavour.[221] George Shenton resigned and was replaced as Chairman by Luke Leake. In October the Trust decided to remain intact and to resist the Government's attempt to abolish it.[222] It also desired to reform itself. It resolved to divide the town into four wards, each ward to be represented by two members elected by the ratepayers. A Chairman would be elected by the members from among their own number. It was

George Lazenby as The Townsman: builder, Wesleyan teacher, valuer for and member of the Perth Town Trust and City Council, debating member of the Mechanics' Institute. Flor. 1840s–70s.

[215] See *Perth Gazette*, 23 September, 11 November 1853.
[216] *Perth Gazette*, 28 January 1853.
[217] *Perth Gazette*, 13 May 1853.
[218] *Perth Gazette*, 26 August 1853.
[219] *Perth Gazette*, 28 January 1853; 6 January 1854.
[220] *Perth Gazette*, 14 March 1856.
[221] *Perth Gazette*, 19 September 1856.   [222] *Perth Gazette*, 10 October 1856.

also resolved that henceforth the Trust ought to bear the title 'City Council', and that the Council ought to have

> . . . sole control and management of the city; property to be valued and assessed according to its letting value; all unimproved allotments to be specially assessed.

The resolution was not without effect, though in the short-term it seemed otherwise, for in January 1857 Shenton was again elected as Chairman and the usual project assessment was made.[223] Then in July 1857 the resolution of the previous year was again taken up, but on this occasion the resentment at the Government's 1851 emasculation of its ability to meet its obligations took the form of despair:

> . . . that it is the opinion of this (special) meeting that, with the means at the disposal of the Trustees of the Town of Perth under the 14th Vict. No. 15, the said Trustees are unable to keep in repair the streets and pathways of the town, or to undertake the other necessary improvements such as drainage connected therewith. Under these circumstances, it becomes expedient to request the Local Government to repeal the above-named Ordinance and at once take the repairs of the streets with the general improvement of the Town by convict labour under its management and control.[224]

It was further resolved that all assessments be levied in the principle of valuation: 6*d* per £1 for all occupied allotments, 1*s* per £1 for unimproved allotments. Acting on these resolutions George Shenton approached the Government, but he was told that even if the Government was willing to consider the matter, it certainly could not 'take over' the town's affairs until the Ordinance was repealed. By the end of the month the Government had decided to act on Shenton's proposal and to have the Ordinance repealed.[225] In the meantime the Colonial Government agreed to provide the Trust with prison labour, 'The Trust defraying the cost of the cartage of material'. To do this latter, the Trust had to collect the assessment agreed to the previous January. It could then temporarily repair St George's Terrace and proceed to lay down a macadamised road from the jetty in William Street to its junction with St George's Terrace, and at the same time a second party would begin the same works from the Causeway, working up the hill into St George's Terrace. (The stone would be quarried at the Mt Eliza Depot.) With some difficulty this work was commenced, but the larger issue of municipal government was still unresolved. When the Government introduced legislation into the Legislative Council in April 1858, it was clear that while taking upon itself 'the sole direction and execution of what is to be done',[226] the Government also intended to defray costs by imposing special taxes on the inhabitants of Perth and Fremantle. The debate raged in the Legislative Council and outside for the remainder of 1858. By August 1858 Governor Kennedy was expressing the view that he had no wish to force his Bill into law against the wishes of the citizens; indeed that he was anxious to satisfy their desires. In late August a public meeting objected again to taxation without representation. It also objected to the Governor's high-handed behaviour in the past.[227]

Eventually the Government set aside its controversial Bill and introduced a more temperate one which created the Perth City Council,

---

[223] *Perth Gazette*, 16 January 1857.
[224] *Perth Gazette*, 24 July 1857.   [225] *Perth Gazette*, 31 July 1857.
[226] *Perth Gazette*, 9 April 1858.   [227] *Perth Gazette*, 27 August 1858.

thereby ensuring that the local inhabitants had control over assessments made in their names.[228] In selecting the first Council, the Governor overlooked the claim of George Shenton to be appointed its Chairman, probably because of Shenton's leadership of the 'no taxation without representation' movement, which had so embarrassed the Governor since the mid-1850s. Instead he appointed as Chairman, Henry Laroche Cole, proprietor of the United Service Tavern and a building contractor. Shenton received an appointment as councillor, as did Bernard Smith, Thomas Smith, Terrence Farrelly, Charles King and Joseph Farmaner. All these men were merchants and storekeepers, with the exception of Charles King who was a builder. They were all townsmen, though Shenton also had well-established country interests; and, again with the exception of Shenton, none was *persona grata* at Government House, but nor would they have been seen in the town's lesser taverns. They were men of substance, though not wealthy. Most were churchmen, including Farrelly and Bernard Smith, the two Roman Catholics. In short they could be recorded safely as 'fit and proper persons' to conduct the affairs of the city. At elections held late in December for two vacancies, Ben Mason and J. Gresswell, the first a publican, the latter a goldsmith, were elected, while Farrelly resigned to take up the part-time appointment of Supervisor and Town Clerk at a salary of £50 a year.[229]

An occupation of a 'fit and proper' person: Councillor Farmaner's premises in Pier Street, Perth.

In January 1859, technicalities concerning the legality of raising and expending monies agreed to by the old Town Trust had been resolved, and the Council could settle down to the business of coping with numerous requests from citizens to upgrade the major roads. It also established working relations with the Imperial Royal Engineers, who at that time were independently beginning the levelling of St George's Terrace and the reconstruction of Bazaar Terrace on the waterfront. The two issues were closely connected. A petition from merchants had noted that

> The present unfinished state is completely ruining the Town Trade in this particular street and destroying all confidence in the Government as to their intentions. The street at present is in a most unsafe and dangerous state.[230]

But the Perth City Council forwarded the petition to the Government for consideration, rather than grappling with the matter itself. This in turn led Chairman Cole to:

> . . . request to be informed as to the extent of the control the City Council may exercise over convict labour, appropriated for the use of the City of Perth, that I may be enabled to apply a portion of such labour to the necessary repairs of the streets and footpaths in the different parts of the City.[231]

Indeed it could be fairly said of Perth in the first six months of 1859 that the issue of greatest concern to the property-owning residents was the condition of St George's Terrace roadway and footpath. Eventually agreement was reached with Captain Sim of the Royal Engineers to construct a cut-away footpath on the north side of the Terrace, with a slope up to the Barracks and the space in front of the Anglican Cathedral. The soil dug out on the north side would be wheeled across to the south side which would be raised and the Terrace itself thereby

228 City of Perth Improvement Ordinance, 22 Vict. No. 10.
229 PCC Minute Book, 22 December 1858.
230 PCC Minute Book, 14 January 1859.
231 PCC Minute Book, 7 February 1859.

levelled. Eventually, too, Cole was given 20 prisoners to employ on work for the city, though he had been promised 30 and had made do for a time with 10. Of course the residents of the Terrace also had to pay out, for they were asked to construct stone front fences 'for the protection of the public footpaths now in the course of formation'.[232] But this seems to have caused them no great discomfort, for at the half-yearly general meeting of ratepayers Cole was praised for 'his able management of, and indefatigable exertions in promoting the general improvements required in the city'.[233] Cole's energy was further rewarded when in October the Government granted his request for the city to resume the track 'now known by the name "Mill Street"', thereby providing a third road running up from the river.[234]

If Cole was pleased to be re-elected Chairman for 1860, his pleasure would have been short-lived. In January the Government took away their wagons, leaving a huge pile of sand in St George's Terrace. It was some time before the roadway was clear again.[235] Then, in February, the City Treasurer, Bayley Maycock, resigned because

> . . . finding as I do that the proceedings of the Council are carried out in such an imperfect manner and altogether inconsistently with the provisions of the Act, I cannot consent to allow my name to be mixed up with the censures and reflections which are very properly made against the existing system.[236]

The problem in fact was two-fold. Ratepayers were not paying their rates, and the Government was withholding convict labour for tasks considered to be the responsibility of the Council. Among the defaulters was George Glyde, later to be a Chairman of the Council! Cole decided to overhaul the rating system, indeed to make new valuations of the city 'for the purpose of levying a rate of 2½% in accordance with the provisions of 22 No. 10'.[237] Even this proved to be difficult to accomplish for Henry Trigg, Thomas Salkeld, John Snowball and James Ougden all at one time or another agreed to act as 'valuator' and then renegged, and it was not until after the June meeting of ratepayers that John Chipper and John Churchyard actually revised the assessments made by Jewell three years previously. There was still strife over the levelling of St George's Terrace, though a commitment was made to macadamise the street to a width of 25 feet, from Barrack Street to the Bridge, at a cost of £250.[238] This was not simply a triumph for the property owners of Adelaide and St George's Terrace, although it was they who would most benefit. The road would also serve the people of the Canning, Swan and York districts and would make it easier for the wool drays to reach Perth's port. Yet the levy would fall on the residents and property owners of Perth alone, which was to be a source of grievance to them and to later generations for the next 120 years. By December 1860 Cole had had enough and resigned from Council.

The December 1860 elections saw the return of Farmaner, Shenton and Bernard Smith from the first Council, and John Chipper and Bayley Maycock from among the 'officials'. The two newcomers were both publicans—George Haysom commanded the Horse and Groom in Murray Street, and J. G. C. Carr had begun his illustrious career as owner of the Freemasons Hotel on the corner of William Street and St

[232] PCC Minute Book, 7 May 1859.   [233] PCC Minute Book, 6 June 1859.
[234] PCC Minute Book, 23 September, 20 October 1859.
[235] PCC Minute Book, 10 January 1859.   [236] PCC Minute Book, 25 February 1860.
[237] PCC Minute Book, 19 March 1860.   [238] PCC Minute Book, 26 November 1860.

George's Terrace. The councillors voted Carr into the Chair for 1861.[239] Carr in fact enjoyed a fairly quiet period in 1861 and 1862. The increased development of the city led to more requests for road development as far north as Murray Street and as far east as Lord Street; and the residents of Murray Street protested with vigour about

> . . . the clouds of dust raised in the summer months by the town herd of Cattle passing and repassing such as to blind the passerby and actually to leave a coat of sand over the floors of the houses.[240]

J. G. C. Carr: Perth City Council Chairman in the 1860s, and Member of the Legislative Council.

As to this latter problem, Council responded by directing the herdsman to take the cattle through Wellington Street, the inhabitants of which were ill-placed economically and socially to protest about such things, or indeed about anything which might discomfort their lives. But as usual it was St George's Terrace which most occupied Council's deliberations. The £250 allocated to the task of maintaining the Terrace was proving to be insufficient. Council importuned the Governor for a grant from the local exchequer. This was graciously acceded to in March 1861, though as the road ran past the Governor's house the gift was not totally altruistic.[241] It did however establish the right of Council to expect assistance in matters which were of importance to the city as the centre of a region and not only internal in implication and importance. Later in 1861 the Royal Engineers commenced construction of a major roadway under Mt Eliza. (In seeking outside assistance, Carr took a further bold step. He accepted the offer of a loan of £100 at 10½% interest per annum from a private citizen, Dr Arden.)[242] By the end of 1862 not only was St George's Terrace macadamised, but work had also commenced on the macadamization of Hay/Howick Street from Pier Street to William Street and along Barrack Street down the hill to Murray Street.

While Council was most occupied with the roadways and footpaths of the town it was also beginning to take an interest in the creation of leisure facilities for the people. In April 1862, for instance, Council agreed to allow clay in Bazaar Street to be used for a practice wicket for the town's cricket club, recognizing as it did so that 'The City Council ought to encourage moral amusements and manly sports.'[243]

By this time Carr was dealing with Hampton, a Governor who shared his belief in getting on with city improvement, though not necessarily in tandem. In the course of 1863, Carr sought permission to tax the allotments owned by Pensioner Guards. He also sought and gained permission for the Perth City Council to take over the Fee Simple of suburban Lot C, known as the cricket ground, thereby committing it even more firmly to a wider community role than the provision of roads and footpaths.[244] At the same time the Council opened discussions with the Colonial Secretary about the possible filling-in of the ground at the waterside between the two jetties at William and Barrack Streets, with a view to using the reclaimed land as a 'Public Recreation Ground'. While this proposal languished for a time as a result of a shortage of convict labour, the seed had been sown for future development. Towards the end of 1863 things began to go a little sourly for Carr. In September he had to write to the Colonial Secretary grumbling about the lack of stone available at the Government Quarry at Point Resolution for PCC

239 PCC Minute Book, 3 December 1860.
240 PCC Minute Book, 18 January 16 April 1861.
241 PCC Minute Book, 18 March 1861.   242 PCC Minute Book, 20 September 1861.
243 PCC Minute Book, 25 April 1862.   244 PCC Minute Book, 5 June 1863.

purposes. This had forced him to lay off workmen who had been macadamizing William and Pier Streets, the latter street being then 'in a dangerous state'.[245] At the annual general meeting, however, the Council encountered little criticism, despite a high turnout and vote. Carr and Bayley Maycock finished well on top of the Poll. The others elected were J. Ougden Jnr, Edmund Birch, Walter Padbury, John Chipper and Mark Read.[246] A feature of the meeting was a petition from the residents of the rapidly developing Stirling Street for a 'clayed' footpath past Bulwer Street to Lot 22.

The year 1864 was one of the most tumultuous in the history of the City Council. Early in the year the new Council took the unprecedented step of setting on one side the annual estimates prepared by the outgoing Council in December 1863 and accepted by the Annual General Meeting in that month. This was not done lightly and two leading members of the Council, Carr and Birch, resigned in protest. Following a petition from ratepayers a Special General Meeting was convened for 6 June 1864. At this meeting Bernard Smith led the attack on the Council. On examining the estimates he

> ... found that for the extension of the Macadamised Road in Hay Street, from William Street to King Street the sum of £50 was placed on these estimates, and strange to relate the Council continued that work on to Milligan Street, paying no attention to former estimates, and using all the funds in a locality the immediate neighbourhood of the Members' own property—in fact making the whole city contribute to the improvement most suitable to their own personal views.

Several ratepayers supported Smith in the lively debate which followed. It was finally proposed by Hillman and seconded by Smith, 'that a vote of censure on the remaining Members of the City Council be passed, for their unauthorised and extravagant expenditure of the Public Funds during the passed half-year'. This was carried unanimously. Thereupon Mr Chipper stepped down from the Chair and other censured councillors refused to take the Chair. Mr Hillman was then voted into the Chair and the former discussion was 'resumed and continued at considerable length'. It emerged that the amount of unauthorised money expended was £150. Hillman was rewarded for his efforts by being elected to replace one of the resigned councillors. George Haysom was also elected from a large field of 12 candidates. This did not conclude proceedings however, for ratepayers were still concerned that Council could direct expenditure on works in one part of the city to the exclusion of others. It was proposed by the resigned councillor, Carr, that

> The City be divided into districts or wards, Eastern, Western and Central and bounded by the following streets, viz, The Western District to be bounded on the East by William, Hutt and Lake Streets and on the West by the Western boundary of the City; the Central District to be bounded on the West by William Street, Hutt Street and Lake Street on the West, and on the East by Lord Street and the Guildford Road. The Eastern District to be bounded on the West by Lord Street and the Guildford Road, and on the East by the River.

This resolution was carried unanimously. It was further agreed that

> The City Council to be elected on all future occasions shall as at present be elected by the whole body of the Ratepayers assembled at the Annual Public Meeting in the month of December in each year, and that they

[245] PCC Minute Book, 8 September 1863.
[246] PCC Minute Book, 7 December 1863.

shall be chosen in the following order, viz, For the Central District (3) three members, and two members for each of the other two districts, who when elected shall (as at present) choose their own chairman from amongst the seven councillors so elected. And further that no member shall be elected for a district in which he is not a Resident Ratepayer.

This resolution seems to have been put to the meeting and carried, though the Minutes do not record that this was done.[247] Within a few days of this meeting Mr G. F. Stone, ratepayer and Solicitor-General, drafted a Government Ordinance which divided the city into three wards, each having three members. The Ordinance also required that the Chairman of Council should be elected by the whole body of ratepayers. This Ordinance was proclaimed shortly after.[248]

Hillman was an energetic chairman. He brought rate defaulters before the Court of Requests and by August he had collected £99 in arrears. He also wished to impose a second levy of 2½% for the remainder of the year, but this proposal was rejected by a special meeting of electors in August convened by J. G. C. Carr.[249] By the end of August Hillman had moved to dismiss the Supervisor, Terrence Farrelly. Farrelly was offered a subordinate clerkship which he declined at a stormy meeting of Council on 30 August. Farrelly made quite a scene and refused to retire from the room in the Mechanics' Institute where the meeting was being held. He pointed out that as Chairman of the Mechanics' Institute he had a greater right to be there than any other person. The Council then adjourned to Haysom's Hotel where the meeting was continued. In September however the lively Hillman resigned from the Council in protest against what was later described as 'a conspiracy of the disbursement of the monies'.[250] At a public meeting held shortly after, H. L. Cole defeated George Shenton 10 votes to 8 for the vacant seat.

Nor did this end the turbulence of the year. In November, Cole prepared a most comprehensive works programme for the city, necessitating an outlay of nearly £900—mainly for the macadamizing of Barrack Street, Goderich Street and the west part of St George's Terrace. To finance this expenditure he intended to levy an assessment of 5% (the maximum allowed under the Act) which would net Council £700 or seven times the amount collected in 1864. These and other matters were discussed at a well attended Annual General Meeting on 5 December 1864. This meeting was in danger of breaking up in disorder until George Shenton intervened to say that:

The Ratepayers were not assembled to cavil over trumpery nonsense, but to elect those men who they thought would do the most work for the least money and watch over the interests of the Ratepayers honestly . . .[251]

The meeting quietened down to pass the accounts. Then Walter Padbury, still smarting over the censure motion of June (he had property at the east end of Hay Street where the new road was heading), sought to clear his name from the imputation of impropriety. In clearing Padbury it was observed sarcastically that he rarely attended meetings and could not therefore have voted for the unauthorised expenditure. The meeting

[247] PCC Minute Book, 6 June 1864; also *Perth Gazette*, June 1864.
[248] PCC Minute Book, 17 June 1864; *Government Gazette*, 22 November 1864, p.223.
[249] PCC Minute Book, 1 August 1864.
[250] Report of Ratepayers' Meeting; PCC Minute Book, 30 October 1864.
[251] PCC Minute Book, 5 December 1864.

G. F. Stone's residence: *gentry participation in City Council affairs was high.*

then got bogged down in a detailed discussion of the yard-by-yard costs of macadamizing Hay Street. Surfacing from that, George Shenton declared that he did not want the new Council to be bound by the estimates prepared by the out-going Council. It was pointed out to him that the

> . . . outgoing Council were supposed to be better acquainted with the work necessary to be done during the next year than the new Council, on account of the experience they had gained whilst in office.

Shenton replied, somewhat irrelevantly, that 'the time had come when the ratepayers should act for themselves'. G. F. Stone confirmed the validity of the Chairman's interpretation of the Ordinance on this question, but the resolution put by the deposed Supervisor, Farrelly, namely

> . . . that the Estimates now before the meeting be not received as they are calculated to embarrass the incoming Council, who are to be selected representatives of the Ratepayers in each Ward

was carried. The new Council was to have a free hand.

In accordance with the new Ordinance the meeting went on to elect a Chairman for 1865. On a high poll J. G. C. Carr beat George Haysom by 76 votes to 12. From 16 candidates Edmund Birch, Ben Mason and Charles King were elected to represent central ward; from 11 candidates James Dyer, George Shenton and Walter Padbury were elected to represent west ward; and from seven candidates Bernard Smith, T. Armstrong and George Glyde were elected to represent east ward. In declaring the meeting closed George Haysom had a parting shot at Carr, who had resigned as Chairman early in 1864. Haysom expressed the hope that the new Chairman would 'stand for the year and not throw it up when he got into a little difficulty'.

The events of 1864 were immensely meaningful for the 100 or so ratepayers of the city of Perth. They had emerged from the turmoil with an open voting system for the Chairmanship of Council; a new ward-based Council election system; and a release from the obligation to accept *in toto* the estimates prepared by an outgoing Council.

The next four years were fairly stable ones for the Perth City Council. Under Carr's Chairmanship the changes made in 1864 seem to have appeased all but the most alienated individuals. The main work of the Council in these years (1865–69) was to extend the macadamizing of the streets of central Perth as far west as Melbourne Street and as far east as Lord Street, as well as Cemetery Road, long the bane of pall-bearers for its sandy condition.[252] In addition many of the newer streets on the north side received clay paths. Mill Street was up-graded to become, with St George's Terrace and Adelaide Terrace, the principal thoroughfare for colonists travelling between Guildford and Fremantle, via the city. It had been hoped to do the Mill Street upgrading with convict labour but once again the city was disappointed by 'the lack of support it received in this from the Government'. The ward system worked well in that local members reported to Council on the most necessary works required in their parts of the city. Throughout these years stability was gained from a low turnover of Council personnel. George Shenton (to 1867) and Walter Padbury represented west ward, Birch and Haysom for central ward, and in east ward all three councillors elected in 1864, Glyde, Armstrong

---

[252] The Cemetery Road macadamization proceeded slowly and was not complete at the time of Colonel Bruce's funeral in 1870.

and Smith, stayed in office. The estimates for expenditure and revenue topped £1000 in October 1867, the first time since 1861.

In the years 1865 to 1869 the collection of rates was far more efficient than before. Penalties for defaulters were imposed rigorously and revaluations were also carried out and new valuations made.[253] In this way the revenues were generally close to the estimates. Valuations were carried out by the Supervisor and by Mr J. K. Churchyard, a respected builder. The Supervisor was T. Smith, a former councillor. He was both Town Clerk and City Engineer. Smith's resignation in mid-1869 led to the creation of a schedule of duties for the Supervisor, for it was apparent that the position deserved a higher salary.[254]

Perhaps one of the most important initiatives in the city came not from the City Council but from the Government. In December 1866 Council endorsed the Government's proposal to construct a market house and town hall. Council also gave Richard Roach Jewell a vote of thanks for 'his zeal in forwarding and completing the plans' for the new building.[255] In December 1867 the Council again responded to a Government initiative when it took over the running of a recently erected crane on the William Street jetty. Council now controlled all Government cranes on the three jetties. This was seen as an enhancement of the role of the city, but later returns from the hire of the cranes suggested 'that the government had shrewdly rid itself of a liability'.[256] In one other regard relations between Government and Council were cordial. In December 1868 the Government accepted yet again the Council's plea that the upkeep of St George's and Adelaide Terraces was a colonial responsibility rather than a city one alone. Council had argued that

> traffic passing between the Eastern Districts and Fremantle is very great and the wear and tear considerable, the expense of keeping the road in repair falls entirely on the ratepayers of the City. As the road is used by the Colonists generally, this expense should be paid from the general revenue.[257]

Council also co-operated with voluntary bodies and residents, as with the construction of a footpath to the summit of Mt Eliza. This had been required by the Defence Volunteers who persuaded Council of the 'large number of citizens [who] would use such a path in pursuit of recreation'.[258] On this occasion Council voted a sum equal to that raised by the Volunteers, whose shooting range was on Mt Eliza. In these ways did Council begin to play a more positive role in the life of the community.

In June 1869 the Chairman of the City Council congratulated the Chairman of the Fremantle Town Trust 'on the opening of Telegraphic Communication' and expressed his hope that it might promote commercial and social intercourse between the two towns.[259] It was a notable occasion. Carr was not the Chairman, however, for he had resigned again in a huff in May 1869 when his plans for the stone paving of footpaths in Perth had been opposed by Councillor Jewell and others. He had had much to offer the city, but he was perhaps too sensitive to criticism for his and the city's good. Since 1867 he had also been a

253 PCC Minute Book, 7 February 1868.   254 PCC Minute Book, 1 July 1869.
255 PCC Minute Book, 14 December 1866, 3 April 1867.
256 PCC Minute Book, 11 December 1862.
257 PCC Minute Book, 27 November 1868.
258 PCC Minute Book, 24 September 1868.   259 PCC Minute Book, 22 June 1869.

nominated member of the Legislative Council and perhaps was less able to persuade councillors to this point of view than in 1864–67. For the next four years the Chairman was to be the wealthy city merchant, George Glyde.

Glyde defeated the young George Shenton by 120 votes to 41 in the 1869 election. He also had an almost entirely new Council. West ward was now represented by James Dyer, James Dyson and Fred Backshall. Central ward was represented by Snowball, Vincent and J. K. Churchyard. East ward was represented by J. B. Roe, B. Smith and W. Atkinson. Only Smith had long experience of Council, though others like Snowball, Churchyard and Backshall had served Council in one capacity or another or had held contracts for Council work.

One of Glyde's first actions was to prepare an address of welcome to Governor Weld, Commander-in-Chief in and over the Colony of Western Australia, and Vice-Admiral of the same. 'He assured Weld of the inhabitants' heartfelt loyalty to their Most Gracious Majesty the Queen. He expressed the city's pleasure that Her Majesty had appointed as her Representative in this Colony a gentleman whose antecedants would appear to peculiarly qualify him for the high and responsible position of governor.' Glyde noted that His Excellency had commenced his administration at a very critical period in the history of the Colony. The cessation of transportation and the consequent decrease of Imperial expenditure would necessitate energetic measures for the development of those resources with which Providence had so bountifully blessed Western Australia. Glyde told Weld that he had been 'appointed to the Government of a Territory of great extent, with a population sparsely scattered over hundreds of miles, but that he would find throughout it the existence of one feeling of devoted loyalty to Her Majesty, and that peace and good order were everywhere prevalent'. Weld received this address 'with no ordinary sense of gratification'. He was convinced that the true interests of the colonists were identical to those of the Mother Country. He hoped by the blessings of Providence that the difficulties looming ahead would be overcome, and that, as rapidly as 'our means will permit', those natural resources may be developed, which he was assured were destined to lead the country to prosperity. It was a pleasing start to the careers of both men. The new Governor was conveyed beneath two triumphal arches, the one erected near G. F. Stone's house bearing the sign 'The Citizens Welcome Governor Weld'; the other near the entrance gates of the Legislative Council, bearing the provocative title 'Advance Australia'.[260]

These events being concluded, Glyde settled down to the business of government. In November he had to deal with the Report of the Inspector of Nuisances, William Dale (first appointed in September 1868), who insisted that Perth in the last few years 'had witnessed a great deal of sickness, with many cases of local fever occurring, some of them fatal'. He was pleased to report that in the past six months there had been less sickness in the city, perhaps due to his own activities. But the drainage of the city was very defective: 'so long as bad drainage exists we are liable to periodical attacks, more or less severe, of sicknesses'. Not only was the city's drainage defective, but the inhabitants lived in houses with defective cess-pits or no cess-pit at all. Dale believed that cess-pits should be constructed to a uniform scale and that they should be cleaned

---

[260] *Perth Gazette*, 30 September 1869.

An avenue of sand: Lord Street in the 1860s, with members of the Stone family in the foreground.

once a month. If this was not done the city's health would continue to be in need of 'constant repair'. He hoped that this was sufficient excuse for troubling Council with his observations.[261]

Dale's Report highlighted the problems which were emerging as the town grew in size. By the late convict period there were settlements on the northern, western and eastern fringes of the central area. Council was about to begin clearing tracks along Beaufort Street as far north as Brisbane Street, as well as parts of James Street, Short Street and Nash Street, where a large ex-convict population was congregated. The shanties thrown up in these years lacked, as Dale found, adequate drainage, cess-pits, wells and so on. But pressure to reform this aspect of city life would not come from those most damaged by it. Only when the gentry and merchants complained of unwholesomeness was something done about drainage, for instance. But that was in the future.

Late in 1870 Glyde won Council approval to revalue city property and revise the assessment book. The last general valuation had been made in 1860. It was Glyde who saw clearly that the changes which had taken place in the second decade of convictism were indeed dramatic and that a fresh start should be made. In December 1870 Glyde comfortably defeated the aging former Supervisor and councillor, Terence Farrelly, by 80 votes to 28.[262] From January 1871 the Council met in the newly opened Perth Town Hall. Despite the recognition of likely economic difficulties subsequent to the withdrawal of Imperial capital, there was an air of optimism in Council discussions. The new Municipalities Bill, shortly to be enacted in the Legislative Council, enhanced the city's status and gave legislative underpinning to the optimism of Glyde and his Council.

261 PCC Minute Book, 8 November 1869.
262 PCC Minute Book, 2 September, 5 December 1870.

Perth waterfront in the 1860s and 1870s.

In 1871 Council dealt with several important issues. It gave the Electro-Magnetic Telegraph Company permission to erect telegraph poles in Adelaide and St George's Terraces, close to the beautiful lilac trees then gracing the town. Each pole was 17 feet high and was set four chains from the next. As it happened, in June 1871 several of the lilac trees died and were replaced by mulberry trees which thereafter provided the townspeople, especially the children, with fruit in season.[263] In other parts of the town more stately trees had been planted. In the late 1860s, for instance, blue gums had been planted on the north side of the city and along Cemetery Road, presumably to provide shade for the pall-bearers. The Council seems to have been extremely tree-conscious for on one occasion it refused the Volunteers' request to hack down an old tree near the waterfront—some councillors remembered when it was used as a sighting by boats coming up the Swan to Perth. In support of their stand, they quoted the old song, *Woodman Spare that Tree.*[264]

Throughout 1871 the Council co-operated with the Government over the use of labour on road and path construction. The Government loaned Council a stone-crusher, for Council could no longer use Government convicts for the purpose. Blue granite was now being brought down from a quarry at Greenmount, fifteen miles to the north-east of the city. Excess stone was sent to the Invalids' Depot at Mt Eliza, there to be broken up by the inmates. The clay pits in Howick Street east of the city were still in the Government's hands, but Council had access to the clay. The Colonial Secretary also agreed to allow Council to use the labour of Government paupers, mostly ex-convicts, for street-clearing. Council also now controlled the waterfront lands between the jetties along Bazaar Street, and extracted rents from merchants and traders like George Shenton and George Randell for use of the land.[265]

In 1870 Council had been given the responsibility for administering the Town Hall. This proved to be a burdensome task. Firstly there was the extra cost of its maintenance. Of course the Hall brought in money as well—some of its rooms were let to respectable tenants like the lawyer Septimus Burt, for £20 a year. In addition the Hall itself could be let for hire. But here the Council found itself in considerable difficulties because it had to decide what was a proper and an improper use of the

263 PCC Minute Book, January, 23 June 1871.
264 PCC Minute Book, 5 June, 7 August 1868.
265 PCC Minute Book, January 1875; 3, 17 March, 15 September 1871.

Hall. At the time of the Hall's opening, speakers stressed that the Hall symbolised the harmony of interests in the colony. But one of the first requests for the use of the Hall for a public meeting came from a free-trade anti Corn Law League which wished to protest against the Government's decision to impose import duties in foodstuffs. After heated discussion the request was granted.[266]

Another problem concerned the arches of the Hall. These were open arches originally, but Council decided to enclose them in order to allow market gardeners to hold a daily market. This led Council into a verbal war with the *Inquirer* journal which regarded the extra cost as not in the best interests of the city.[267] Even the leading gardeners like Richard Gallop, Fred Backshall, Waldeck, Wylde and Williams were reluctant to rent stalls unless Council abolished hawking or made hawkers' fees so high that gardeners would opt to take out stalls instead.[268] The gardeners did not get their way, but early in December they agreed that 'for the present a general daily market for Resale of Colonial Produce, shall be opened under the arches, on 1 February 1872'.[269] The rate struck was 5 s a month per 100 square feet. But the reconstruction work went slowly in the absence of convict labour, and in any case by mid-January only two applications had been received. It was only later that the market opened and even then it never supplanted the usual means of distribution.

To open or to close the arches of the Town Hall?: *a problem for the councillors.*

In the midst of these problems over the use of the Town Hall, Glyde called the annual electors' meeting. That inveterate watcher of Council affairs, Terence Farrelly, detested corruption. He rose to deplore the practice of councillors tendering for and getting Perth City Council contracts. But the game was open to all who wanted to play; indeed the Municipalities Act of that year had expressly permitted the practice. For a brief moment it seemed that Glyde would be challenged for the Chairmanship, but Edmund Birch, fit and proper person as he was, declined Joseph Hardey's kind invitation to make a contest of it.[270]

Nor would it have been fair for Glyde to face a challenge. He had proved to be an able successor to J. G. C. Carr. He had even begun to consider seriously those matters of importance raised by the Inspector of Nuisances in 1869—not out of a general interest in the welfare of the poorer members of the community however, though Glyde was a man of compassion who on one occasion persuaded Council to pay £5 towards the funeral expenses of a Council day labourer whose widow and children were destitute.[271] Council had raised the level of Lord Street north of St George's Terrace. In the heavy rains of June 1871 the Master of the Supreme Court, Mr A. H. Stone, found that a cottage he owned (C8) at the foot of Lord Street received the entire street's water, garbage and anything else that happened to be floating along. Mr Roe and J. W. Hardey, both respected senior citizens, were equally alarmed by the sanitary consequences of the existing arrangements for the immediate vicinity and for the city at large. Hardey pressed for a deeper culvert to be laid across the street, with a large grating. Council resolved to increase the size of the well hole and grating and to allow Mr Hardey to lower the trunking at his own expense.[272] The winter of 1871 was extremely severe.

266 PCC Minute Book, 2 June 1871.
267 *Inquirer*, July 1871; PCC Minute Book, 7, 14 July 1871.
268 PCC Minute Book, 30 November 1871.
269 PCC Minute Book, 6 December 1871.
270 PCC Minute Book, 4 December 1871.   271 PCC Minute Book, 3 March 1871.
272 PCC Minute Book, correspondence, 16, 21, 24, 27 June 1871.

Men at work remaking Adelaide Terrace: A. H. Stone's house at left.

While parts of Adelaide Terrace were subject to minor flooding, other parts of town, especially the Murray Street, William Street, Wellington Street, and Roe Street areas were covered with water for long periods of time to the great discomfort of the less affluent people who inhabited the areas. It became apparent even to the Perth City Council that the Wellington Street drain ('Main Drain') was inadequate for the needs of the growing city. Following the great hurricane of March 1872, which unroofed houses, blew down others and generally left Perth totally waterlogged, the Council began to deal with the problem.

Glyde enjoyed a relatively uneventful 1872 and was rewarded by being unopposed at the Annual Meeting of Electors in December. In February 1873 he was called on to prevent 'persons being allowed to bathe from the several Perth jetties'.[273] The nature of the indecency of the persons was not specified, but it was sufficiently dreadful for Council to prohibit bathing 'off all the Perth jetties, except Barrack Street, and from that as well between the hours of 7 a.m. and 7 p.m.'. A decision taken by Council later in 1872 made swimming from the jetties dangerous to health and probably did as much to discourage swimming as restricting hours for it. In September the Chairman stated that the citizens were desirous of having some waste land set apart for depositing the dirt and rubbish constantly accumulating from the sweeping and cleaning of houses, yards, shops and warehouses in the city. 'Council agreed that this was a serious problem and accordingly set aside a portion of ground midway between Barrack Street and the town jetties—100 feet of river frontage extending 50 feet inland.' It was the city's first official rubbish tip.[274]

The new Town Hall continued to be a source of trouble for Council. By July the citizenry had tired of entering the Hall from the rear or east end. Mr Jewell was asked to draw up plans for two staircases at the Barrack Street end, and inside the Hall the platform was moved to the south side, this work being done by the city's paupers. The letting of the Hall's rooms was proceeding slowly and the opening of the market in June was a non-event,[275] for most vegetable sales continued to take place on front-door steps in the traditional way. Then in December, Council received the unwelcome news from the Inspector of Nuisances that the stench and filth arising from the water closets in the rear of the Town

[273] PCC Minute Book, 16 February 1872.
[274] PCC Minute Book, 20 September 1872.
[275] PCC Minute Book, 15 August 1873; 'it was evident that many of the citizens never attended it'.

166

Hall were a major source of grievance to users, passers-by and local residents. Council had no choice but to remodel them.[276] The Hall itself was used infrequently—indeed the most regular booking was the Union Troop of Mounted Volunteers for sword practice twice a week! In November, however, Council made a symbolic gesture of its appreciation of the gift of the Hall. For yet another official opening a brass plate was prepared, naming the councillors and the architect, Mr Jewell, who graciously requested that James Manning's name be added 'as one of the architects of the building'.[277]

In other respects Council prospered. The Government granted it all the lands of the Town Hall and vicinity and in January 1873 vested in Council the river frontage between William Street and Mill Street. In such ways did the Government seek to increase the responsibilities of the Council. Council's paid staff was also increased, including the appointment of an Assistant Inspector of Nuisances. This appointment, made in December 1872, was partly a result of the grumbles of the citizens and councillors about 'the great nuisance of Cattle being allowed to stray all over the city'. Not only did cattle roam at will through the city, but the town herd was driven by Joseph Perry down Wellington Street to the Common west of the city, to the great annoyance of the residents of that unhappy street. (Some time previously he had been advised not to drive the herd down Hay Street.)[278]

In September 1872 Council received a request from the Surveyor-General to examine and report on which allotments Council wished to see reserved for drainage and other purposes.[279] The places nominated by Council in response to this request were to become important in the city's subsequent history. Apart from the Town Hall land, Council wanted the Tea Tree Lagoon (Sub. 32, 33, Sub.a) for a Botanical Garden and a Cricket Ground. It wanted Lots E 97–100 and T61 for clay deposits; S35 for a cattle pen; third swamp to the north for a public garden; Lots N40 and 90 for draining of second and third swamps; Lots N45 and 50, Y248, 232 and 210 for draining of Henderson's Lake and district; Lots V61 for a public pound; Russell Square; reserved space on Mt Eliza and No. 432 for a public park; the reserve in between Lots 108 and 109 for drainage; and the whole of the river front from Government House Jetty to Mill Street Jetty. Nearly all these lands were subsequently vested in the Council.

Early in 1873 oil lamps began to be placed on the corners of Perth's shopping streets. The initiative came from city traders and institutions. In April Shenton and Marfleet offered to provide lamps and oil if Council would erect a post and lantern on the corner of Hay and William Streets. This was agreed to, as was the Mechanics' Institute request for the Howick/Pier Street corner.[280] By the end of the year several other lamp posts had been erected in the central city area. It was from this time that Perth people tentatively began to use the streets in the evening, especially for late night shopping on certain days of the week.[281] In August 1873 another city improvement was experimented with when George Randell persuaded Council to allow him to make a wooden

276 PCC Minute Book, 6 December 1872.
277 PCC Minute Book, 15 November 1872.
278 See page 108 for a brief account of Perry's career.
279 PCC Minute Book, 20 September 1872.
280 PCC Minute Book, 25 April, 7 May 1873.
281 See H. C. Prinsep 'Diary', Battye Library.

footpath from Dr Hora's to Marfleet's in Hay Street—5 by 2 timber lying on sleepers.

But the latter part of 1873 was dominated by discussions on the draining of the lakes of Perth. Lake Kingsford had been first drained in 1854[282] and the land used for market gardens. But gradually the lake had reasserted itself and in the winters of 1872 and 1873 severe flooding of the northern part of the town, including Murray Street, and affecting all but the highest parts of the city, necessitated a review of the drainage problem. In August Council debated the issue. Some councillors urged the need to drain Lake Kingsford southwards down William Street. Councillor Jewell contended that this would endanger the large buildings already built along that line. Others suggested that Barrack Street might be suitable, but Jewell pointed to the danger of damaging the Town Hall, and the high cost at £2 per yard of a drain passing through the ridge at Hay Street. Council decided to seek the advice of the Surveyor-General and to call a public meeting on the subject.[283]

On 10 October a poorly attended public meeting discussed the Perth drain. The Chairman called upon the citizens for a statement of opinion on the subject. He himself was in no doubt that the trunking at present laid down was inadequate to carry the accumulated water from the various lakes and streets of the city during the winter. He

> remembered the time when the lakes, at present laid out as beautiful and profitable gardens well stocked with vegetables and various fruit trees were swamps covered with bullrushes, and he should be sorry to see them return to their original condition.

Glyde was aware that the owners would benefit directly from a new drain; but, he contended, 'that in a sanitary point of view, and for the promotion of the health of the citizens generally, a better system of drainage had become imperative'. Glyde then instructed the Supervisor to read a report prepared by Mr Jewell, the Government's Clerk of Works. The report recommended the construction of a barrel drain running eastwards from the lakes to Claise Brook. But how was this to be financed? Jewell had 'made some calculations'. The city's rateable value was £20,000, realizing £1000 at 5%. In addition, revenue from dog, cattle and other licenses realized £300. The drain would cost about £2000 which would have to be borrowed at 6% interest. This could be repaid in nine years by deducting £200 a year from the general revenue and imposing an additional tax of $1\frac{1}{2}d$ in £1 for the nine year period. It seemed reasonable enough.

But some ratepayers were not satisfied with Jewell's scheme. Mr Vincent, a councillor, was of the view that Perth had 'professional gentlemen [who] had had a great deal of practical experience in England and elsewhere' and that they ought to be encouraged to draw up alternative plans. Vincent stressed that the new drain should 'serve for the next generation as well as for the present'. He thought it should be linked to the provision of a supply of pure water, much needed as 'most of the wells of the city were more or less impregnated with a poisonous matter, injurious to health'. William Sloan, a publican, had different worries. He thought that it would be unfair to ask all the citizens to pay for the benefit of a section of the community, namely the private owners of the 'swamp gardens'. Perhaps the garden owners could bear 50% of

[282] *Government Gazette*, 7 November 1854.
[283] PCC Minute Book, 23 August, 5 September 1873.

the cost, and the ratepayers the other 50%. Mr Green thought that as the Government had sold the allotments for building purposes, it was 'bound to assist in defraying the expenses of draining them'. Glyde responded by assuring Mr Green that Council had already asked the Governor for aid and had been told by His Excellency that convict labour, if available, could be used on the work, although the Government did not accept that it had a responsibility to assist. R. C. Loftie agreed with Sloan that the drain must benefit the whole city, not just the owners of swamp property. As to the routes of the drain he favoured the one to Claise Brook as being the most natural and the least expensive. Mr Cumming, an auctioneer, thought the meeting was a waste of time—they had been there an hour and nothing had been resolved. Sloan then criticised Mr Vincent. The meeting had all the technical information it required, he said: 'The ratepayers would not get better if they paid another Mr Doyne £1000 for it'.[284] The Rev. Meadowcroft stressed the urgency of the matter—if effectual drainage was not adopted quickly then 'the city would probably be visited by some dire epidemic'. Terrence Farrelly proposed and Edmund Birch seconded that Council be empowered to undertake the general drainage of the city and that it provide funds for the same, not to exceed £2000. Two amendments were defeated and the resolution was carried by a majority. For Glyde the evening was a triumph.[285]

Glyde's victory was made complete at the follow-up meeting of Council on 25 October. Council was divided evenly over the alternative routes (William Street or Claise Brook), and Glyde gave his casting vote in favour of Jewell's plan for Claise Brook. Probably an important consideration for Glyde was his knowledge that the Government favoured the Claise Brook route. At the end of 1873 George Glyde resigned, having served six years as a councillor and four years as Chairman. At the annual election meeting in December, George Randell defeated J. T. Reilly for the Chairmanship by 121 votes to 78.[286]

Randell strove hard to get Council to reverse its decision and to commission local professional engineers, Victor and Brooking, but in March 1874 the decision was taken to approve of Jewell's plans for a drain running from Coombs corner in Wellington Street to Lord Street bridge and thence to Claise Brook via Water Street. Jewell's brick barrel-drain was estimated to cost Council £1899. Jewell himself received £20 for his plans. In August 1874 the contracts for the drain were let—Thomas Smith successfully tendered for the contract of 210 000 bricks; Joseph Perry provided the 1000 bushells of lime; and Fred Platt won the contract to construct the drain.[287] Construction began in November 1874, with some of the eastern parts of Wellington Street still under water.

In December 1874 George Randell resigned because of family bereavements and 'afflictions' in the past twelve months. Perhaps one of the 'afflictions' was the drain, for it was disclosed at the Annual Meeting that Council had a deficit of £400, due apparently to increases in the cost of the drain.[288]

[284] Doyne had earlier been associated with a scheme of doubtful propriety.
[285] PCC Minute Book, 10, 25 October 1873.
[286] PCC Minute Book, 25 October, 1 December 1873.
[287] PCC Minute Book, 7 August, 14 July 1874.
[288] PCC Minute Book, 7 December 1874.

Randell was succeeded by young George Shenton who defeated Terrence Farrelly by 116 votes to 64. At the same election the number of councillors per ward was increased from three to four. Shenton's immediate concern was the drain. At the 1874 Annual Meeting it was resolved to respectfully request the Commissioner of Crown Lands 'to set apart such lands as may be necessary for continuing the line of drain from Lake Henderson to the Island Lake, in order to secure the best flow of water possible, being conducted into the city, for sanitary as well as domestic purposes'.[289] This seems to have been agreed to. Shortage of finance led Council in February 1875 to discontinue all macadamising of roads in the city. In the first week of March 1875 convict labour was withdrawn from the roads—there were then 12 miles of macadamised roads and 25 miles of footpaths—and maybe the drain as well. On 11 June 1875 Council was told that the drain had already cost £2142 (of which 2½% went to Jewell as Supervisor—£54) and that a further £500 was needed to complete the job. In August 1875 it was reported that the Council's special tax of 6d in the pound was not being paid by the citizens. The 'Drain' had indeed become a drain on the city's resources,[290] but at least it was now operational.

Meanwhile the impurity of the water in the wells of the city continued to cause concern. In July 1874 the Council's Chairman (Randell) referred to complaints made about the impurity of the water belonging to the Town Hall, and believed by some people to be caused by drainage in wet weather from the cess-pit and urinal close by. Randell said that he had examined the site and believed that the pit and urinal ought to be moved some distance further down the yard, 'and if this did not improve the water complained of, it would at least remove a great deal of prejudice against the water'. Accordingly, the cess-pit and urinal were moved further away from the well.[291] In fact the general sanitary condition of the city was causing greater concern. Citizens and councillors complained of butchers slaughtering calves and pigs in the city precincts, contrary to the by-law. And some thought that Council should be given greater powers to cope with the situation. In July 1875 Shenton received from the Colonial Secretary a copy of a despatch from the Secretary of State, together with a medical report on the sanitary condition of the city prepared by Dr Shaw. Council agreed with the burden of Shaw's report, but claimed that the Municipalities Act was defective in that Council did not have the power to rectify the abuses. The report of this important meeting was a follows:

> The Chairman called attention to a leading article which appeared in the West Australian Times relating to Dr Shaw's report on the sanitary condition of Western Australia. The extracts printed in the Times, and the comments of the Editor would lead strangers to suppose that the sanitary condition of Perth was as bad as the most unhealthy parts of Africa, but it should be borne in mind that the year 1874 referred to by Dr Shaw was one of the most unhealthy seasons we ever had since the Colony was established and was no criterion of the general condition of the Public Health. Besides, it must be remembered that a large proportion of the deaths referred to took place among the invalid pensioners, whose constitutions had been injured by crime and debauchery before coming here. This death rate had been further swelled by the mortality among the aged pensioners sent out by the

[289] PCC Minute Book, 4 December 1874.
[290] PCC Minute Book, 7, 11 June, 6 August 1875.
[291] PCC Minute Book, 3 July 1874.

Home Government in every convict vessel... the Chairman... referred to the Municipalities Act in force in South Australia, and one which might be useful in framing and improving our local Municipalities Act here so as to give the Council power to deal more effectually with sanitary affairs in this Colony.[292]

A letter was sent to the Colonial Secretary seeking amendments to the Municipalities Act to allow the Perth City Council to have power over the keeping of pigs in the city and to enable the Perth City Council to borrow more money for sanitary purposes, especially if the dry-earth system was to be introduced. There the matter rested until the Parliamentary session of 1876 when amendments were made to the Act.

In 1875 too there were other issues of concern to the Council. At a meeting early in July, Councillor J. Chipper had severely criticised the Supervisor, George Lazenby, for not attending to his duties as efficiently as he ought. Lazenby promptly tendered his resignation. At a subsequent meeting of Council, Chipper was urged to withdraw his remarks. It was also pointed out by several councillors that it was well known that the Supervisor was vastly overworked. As the city's government had increased in complexity so too had the Supervisor's duties. As Bernard Smith observed:

Mr Lazenby was Supervisor of the city, Clerk of the Council, Clerk of the Market, Caretaker of the Town Hall, Inspector of Nuisances (it seems that a deputy had not in fact been appointed), Inspector of Weights and Measures, Receiver of Allotments belonging to the Council, keeps labourers' accounts and pays their wages daily.

Chipper duly apologised. Lazenby seems to have continued as Supervisor while Council resolved to effect a division of labour. On 9 July it moved to appoint a Secretary to assist the Supervisor.[293]

In September 1875 Council dealt with another problem created by the city's physical growth over the last decade. It commented on 'numerous shanties erected in some of our principal streets (being) a disgrace to the city and ought to be removed'. Councillor Jewell pointed out that under existing legislation Council could not act on the subject. He urged Council to seek from the Government a Building Act. In 1876 another Municipal Institutions Act was passed, but it did not tackle the problem of the 'disgraceful shanties'.[294] On a happier note, Council agreed to assist the Volunteers to erect a Drill Hall between Government House and the Commissariat in the south-west corner of the Public Gardens. The Hall would also be used by the Horticultural Society. This was duly erected and paid for by public subscription (£150).[295]

The city's defence against fire received a boost when late in 1875 the new fire engine arrived. Financed partly by the Council and partly by public subscription (£140), it was housed in the east part of the Market Place in Howick Street. Captain Hillman, formerly a councillor, was in charge of it, and his Volunteers were to staff it. Alas, it turned out to be a most inefficient machine.[296]

1876 was a quiet year. Other than grumbles about the 'disgraceful shanties' being erected in parts of the city, and participation in the erection of more oil lamps in the streets, Council seems to have been relatively untroubled. In December 1876 George Shenton was elected for his third term. By now the Municipalities Act had been amended to create a new ward, to be known as north ward—this ran from Roe Street

[292] PCC Minute Book, 5 July 1875.   [293] PCC Minute Book, 5, 9 July 1875.
[294] PCC Minute Book, 5 September 1875; 21 September 1875; also 40 Vic. No. 13, 1876.
[295] PCC Minute Book, 5, 27 July 1875.   [296] PCC Minute Book, 25 October 1875.

northwards and took in the area known as 'Perth Newtown' where many ex-convicts lived. Whereas for the past few years each of the three wards had returned four councillors, the amended Act prescribed three councillors for each of the four wards.[297]

1877 was more eventful. To begin with, Council's debt to the Western Australian Bank stood at £850, only a third of which was on the Main Account.[298] Council had to conserve its revenue and increase it where possible. In the belief that prevention was cheaper than cure, it used a watering cart in the principal streets to keep the top surface from blowing away in the hot winds of summer. When residents of Howick Street complained that a nuisance was caused by small boys congregating outside the Town Hall during the practice sessions of the Volunteers' Band, the Band was ordered to use a back room, and the front room was let to a solicitor, Howell, for £12 a year. In this year too the Government ceased shilly-shallying on the issue and withdrew prison labour once and for all. Council decided that it would be cheaper to have all work done by contract than to employ free labour themselves.[299]

In February 1877 the sanitary problem was revived when J. G. Lee Steere wrote to Council 'complaining of the unhealthy and dilapidated condition of the block of houses at the rear of his premises, near the river'. Shenton, a friend of Lee Steere's, got Council to agree that steps should be taken 'to enforce the sanitary provisions of the Municipal Act'. In the same month Council appointed its first Health Officer—the Colonial Surgeon, Alfred Waylen. This was done despite Councillor Letch's concern that a conflict of interest might arise. (In fact Waylen's appointment was simply the product of the smallness of the Western Australian community.)[300]

From August 1877 until well into 1878, the Perth City Coucil sought to influence the Government to run the proposed new railway line from Fremantle to Perth on the north side of the river.[301] In February 1878 this was formalised in the following resolution:

> having in view the general welfare of the Metropolis and its inhabitants, the projected railway from Fremantle to Guildford and Eastwards should pass through a central part of the city and to effect this, that a committee be appointed to obtain signatures to a petition, to be addressed to His Excellency the Governor [Ord].[302]

This was necessary, for the local engineer, W. E. Victor, was drawing up plans for the Fremantle municipality which showed the railway line on the south side of the river. This may also have been true of the plans being prepared for the Government by W. Brown. By April the clashes between the municipalities had become so intense that a resolution of the differences seemed unlikely and the Perth City Council withdrew from the rounds of talks. In July it forwarded a last request to the Government. It won the fight for the line to pass on the north side of the river. Now it was concerned that the line should 'least interfere with general traffic and mutilation of the streets' and it petitioned the Government accordingly.[303] In 1880 the railway from Perth to Fremantle was opened. It ran through the northern quarter of the town where the poorer people lived, and thus in the view of the fit and proper councillors

[297] PCC Minute Book, 4 December 1876.   [298] PCC Minute Book, December 1876.
[299] PCC Minute Book, 5 January 1877.
[300] PCC Minute Book, 2, 20 February 1877.
[301] PCC Minute Book, 3 August 1877.   [302] PCC Minute Book, 6 February 1878.
[303] PCC Minute Book, 4 April, 7 July 1878.

mutilated neither traffic nor lives. Henry Haynes was one whose backyard ran down to the railway line.

Late in 1877 Shenton had two pleasing duties to perform. One was to receive from the Government the land known as Victoria Park near Claise Brook, to be used as a recreation area by the people of Perth. The second was to read the farewell address to Governor Robinson, who had given the land to the Council. 'Government House', said Shenton, 'has been the centre of a refined and genial hospitality'. While wondering perhaps whether more might be said of his governorship, Robinson had some thoughts of his own which he wanted to leave with the citizens of Perth. He looked ahead to an Australian federation in which Western Australia would be politically united 'with those splendid colonies to the Eastward with which your own true interests are identical'.[304] Shenton had little time in which to dwell on the prospect of a federation, for in November 1877 he was challenged for the Chairmanship of the Perth City Council.

The challenge came from a 33-year-old lawyer, Stephen Henry Parker. Parker had achieved notoriety in 1870 when he was fined for publicly criticising Chief Justice Burt. He was a vibrant, assertive and popular young man in the city. The public election turned out to be a farce. Parker asked the Returning Officer if, in accordance with Section 30 of the Act, he had received notice in writing from the candidates. Councillor George Budd, the Returning Officer, said that he had not. Another lawyer (and councillor), Edward Stone, entered a written protest against the election on the grounds that the Returning Officer was not appointed by the Governor as required by Section 29 of the Act, and also because the candidates had not nominated in writing. Parker then claimed that he had nominated in writing 'To the Returning Officer seven days ago as required by the Act. If no Returning Officer had been appointed at the time then that was not his fault.' Stone then asked the Returning Officer if he'd received any notices. Budd said stolidly that he had not. Another ratepayer asked Budd who appointed him and when. Budd replied that Shenton had appointed him on the 12th. Yet another lawyer, Septimus Burt, asked Budd if he thought the election could proceed as there were no official candidates. Poor Budd, a genial storekeeper and publican, said despairingly 'the lawyers seem to have it all their own way here today'. Amid laughter Parker said cheerfully that if there was no Council then there'd be no one to pay the overdraft to the Western Australian Bank. At this point Shenton sent the Clerk off to his office to see if the nominations were there. They were, or at least Parker's was. Parker claimed that Shenton had already served for three years and was disqualified under Section 28 of the Act and that he had not sent in nomination papers. Shenton countered with the same criticism of Parker, namely that he had not sent nomination papers to the Returning Officer. By this time Budd, a down-to-earth man, had had enough of these legal niceties and said soundly 'let us proceed to business'. After the usual show of hands (which showed a slight majority for Parker), Shenton's supporters demanded a formal poll. When held, the election resulted in a victory for Parker by 172 votes to 151. The *West Australian Times* claimed that several of Shenton's supporters did not vote, as they were under the impression that the election was illegal. Certainly there was room for doubt as to the legality of the election, but

George Shenton Jnr: *Chairman and Mayor of the Perth City Council, 1875–77, 1880–84, 1886–88.*

---

[304] PCC Minute Book, August, September 1877.

in the event Shenton did not protest to the Governor. And in any case his position was compromised by the fact that the Attorney-General and the Crown Solicitor had voted at the election.[305]

Parker came into office because he successfully persuaded enough voters to believe that the Council under Shenton's Chairmanship had been wasteful of ratepayers' money. He had claimed at the annual meeting of ratepayers, held a week before the election, that the Western Australian Bank overdraft of £600 ought to be regarded as an unauthorised loan.[306] At the first meeting he chaired, he called for severe retrenchment, and when the Estimates were prepared he budgeted for a surplus. He also reminded councillors that under the new Act, Section 27, councillors could not hold Council contracts: the old practice would have to cease. Shenton, a merchant himself, had not been troubled by the old ways. At his final Council meeting he told the councillors that things had gone well for the city during his administration. A Chairman, he said, 'must be ruled by the majority of his Council'. He was pleased to note that out of twelve councillors elected for the ensuing year no less than ten were members of the present Council 'who, he apprehended, would uphold the policy which had been pursued heretofore'. Stephen Parker was not at this meeting, but Shenton's speech was printed in the *West Australian Times*. It could be read only as a challenge to the new Chairman.[307]

During the debates on the Municipal Institutions Bill in August 1876 George Shenton applauded the sanitary provisions of the Bill. He said that 'The atmosphere, both of Perth and Fremantle, was undergoing a process of poisoning, by reason of the nuisances injurious to public health which were allowed to accumulate, the Municipal Councils being powerless to deal with them.'[308] The Bill as enacted gave Council power to recover expenses following an enforced improvement of a property's sanitary arrangements. As for pig sties—regarded by Medical Officer as injurious to health in the municipalities of Perth and Fremantle—no specific action was taken. The Drafting Committee's wish to see pigs kept from 'the aristocratic quarters' of the town was opposed by the Attorney-General, who wished to see an amendment to the effect that no one could keep a pig within fifty yards of the dwelling place of a neighbour: 'Surely honourable members with an Irish element in their Constituencies would be very cautious about this clause!' Lee Steere and Shenton felt that this would prevent 'the poor man—the owner of a small grant' from owning a pig: 'We are not here to legislate for one class more than another. Who is there among the poorer classes who could keep a pig fifty yards from any other person's dwelling?' While it is possible that the Committee's recommendation may have passed, the issue was clouded by the Attorney-General's amendment, which seemed to members to be over-regulatory in character. Burt's motion that the clause be struck out was accordingly agreed to. Henceforth pigs only became a nuisance when they became a nuisance!

But the Act, while silent on pig sties, did allow the Perth City Council to borrow ten times its annual income, calculated upon the average ordinary annual income of the Municipality for the three years

---

[305] PCC Minute Book, 19 November 1877; *West Australian Times*, 20 November 1877.

[306] PCC Minute Book, 14 November 1877.

[307] PCC Minute Book, 30 November, 7, 21 December 1877; *West Australian Times*, 2 December 1877.

[308] *WAPD* (o.s.) Vol. 1, August 1876, pp.83, 114–5

Perth, north of Hay Street in the 1880s:
(1) A two-storey house under construction, the property of Mr O. P. Stables, civil servant. (2) The Perth Gaol. (3) Government Girls' School, James Street. (4) The railway station with engine centre right. (5) Mr Harry McGlew's iron foundry, Murray Street. (6) Mr John Liddelow's butchery, corner Murray and Barrack Streets. (7) Mr Kenworthy's blacksmith's shop. (8) Mr Hartshotl's printery and shop. (9) Sheds and warehouse of Mr J. H. Monger, merchant.

preceding the loan. In the case of Perth City Council, the way was open to borrow about £10,000. This was to be of the greatest importance to the city from 1878 onwards. Shenton had in mind the construction of waterworks, for concern about health had provided the context of the Bill. But in the event the borrowing clauses of the Bill were used to raise money for street improvements throughout the late 1870s and 1880s. Overall, the Bill did not have overly draconian clauses, such as the enforced introduction of the dry-earth closet system. In part this must have been because of the much healthier conditions of 1875 and 1876 and the Report of Colonial Surgeon Waylen for the first-named year. Waylen had noted that while the cess-pit was still the rule in Perth, the water in wells remained drinkable because of the 'very excellent [natural] filtering medium through which the sewage [had] to pass', namely light sandy soil, with a 'highly oxidising nature'. The Governor had seized on this in his report to the Secretary of State for Colonies. Perth might be backward as regards sewerage, but it was relatively healthy and free from disease and a dry winter in 1876 confirmed this view. The parliamentary debate on the health clauses of the Municipal Institutions Bill was low key, as were the provisions of the Act.[309]

Waylen's reports for the years 1876, 1877 and 1878 all expressed thankfulness for dry winters and a decreased incidence of zymotic disease; but he continued to express his concern for the sanitary condition of the city. He continued to press for the planting of eucalypts—for health as well as aesthetic reasons—in the most low-lying and thickly populated parts of the town. By 1878, however, his reports were gaining an urgency of tone about the sanitation of Perth. This in part reflected the widespread and growing concern among the leaders of Perth society. In mid-1877 Dr Barnett, Colonial Surgeon for Fremantle, published in the *West Australian Times* a series of articles on the sanitary condition of the city and country. These he later printed as a pamphlet, 'Suggestions respecting sanitary improvement in Western Australia'.[310] In recommending the introduction of the dry-earth closet system, Barnett wrote despairingly of 'the dull apathetic inertia of ignorance' which he feared would frustrate his and others' efforts to improve the sanitation of Perth and Fremantle. In September 1877 the Director of Works, Mr J. H. Thomas, addressed a long memorandum to the Colonial Secretary on the same subject. He gave graphic descriptions of polluted wells (including that at the Girls' and Infants' School), and urged the Government to make cess-pits watertight by law, and to introduce Goux's or Moule's dry-earth closet system as recommended by Dr Barnett. Thomas urged the Perth City Council to remove night soil in properly constructed carts with air-tight lids. The night soil, some 2400 tons a year at present, he calculated, would make splendid manure and render useful thousands of acres of presently valueless land round Perth. Waylen wrote to the Colonial Secretary a week later, like Barnett and Thomas deferring to the high opinion of Dr Buchanan of the United Kingdom.

By the end of 1877 the Colonial Secretary, Waylen, and Thomas had succeeded in persuading the Bishop of Perth, the Speaker of the Legislative Council and other Government Officers and leading citizens, including two members of the City Council, to requisition a public meeting on the sanitation of the city. The meeting, attended by about

309 *Votes and Proceedings of the Legislative Council*, 1876–79, and Act.
310 *West Australian Times*, May–June 1877.

eighty people and chaired by Parker, the Chairman of the City Council, took place on 16 January 1878.[311] The reformers had enlisted a letter of support from the Surveyor-General who proclaimed that the 'two great wants of the city were, first, earth closets and, second, a supply of good water' (artesian water rather than water from the Canning River, which would be too costly). His Lordship the Bishop claimed an imperfect knowledge of the state of affairs, but said that 'He had been struck with the want of cleanliness in the streets and the absence of any necessary sanitary arrangements in private houses'. The reports of Thomas and Waylen were then read to the meeting. The Colonial Secretary then addressed the meeting:

> The term dunghill had been applied to the city of Perth, and he asserted that they were living on a dunghill. They must not consider the outlay of a few pounds: they must look to the future . . . Their children might now be healthy, but if some steps were not taken, the future would find them weak and sickly, and they must remember that they were to form the future Western Australians.

He put a resolution calling for amendments to the Municipal Act 'to remedy the evils so clearly demonstrated to exist'. His resolution was carried unanimously. Another resolution urging the introduction of a dry-earth closet system was put after Councillor Jewell had presented recommendations from a Melbourne Committee in favour of the dry-earth system. Mr H. E. Victor and Dr Johnston spoke from Indian experience in recommending dry-earth closets to the people of Perth. George Walpole Leake thought that 'the measures proposed were specially devised for the poorer classes who resided in the back streets of the city'. He pointed to the value of the Adelaide experience. Mention of the poorer classes (who were absent from the meeting) led to Councillor Summers informing the meeting that the installation of a dry-earth closet would cost 7s 6d. The meeting recognized that the Government would have to assist the Perth City Council in introducing the scheme, for it would be too much to ask ratepayers alone to bear the full cost.

The meeting appointed a Sub-Committee, including two councillors, to present recommendations to the Perth City Council. This it did in late February. It urged the appointment of scavengers, and the compulsory introduction of earth closets. On 12 April 1878 the Perth City Council considered the report of the Sub-Committee and resolved that 'Sections 62 and 69 of the Municipal Institutions Act, 1871, be strictly enforced, and that the dry-earth closet system be fostered as far as possible'. The note of qualification at the end of the resolution was deliberate for Parker had insisted that while dry-earth closets were beneficial, he 'was convinced that poor people were not in a position to bear the expense'. Among the councillors only the ardent reformer R. R. Jewell was unmoved by his plea and dissented from the resolution as put.[312]

And there the matter rested. In November 1878 Governor Ord received a despatch from Hicks Beach, the Secretary of State for Colonies, dated 24 August 1878, in which the Colonial Surgeon's report for 1877 was cited in a demand 'to learn, at your convenience what you have been able to effect in the way of improvement'. Ord responded by appointing a Committee composed of the Colonial Secretary, the

[311] *Inquirer,* 23 January 1878.
[312] PCC Minute Book, 12 April 1878. The heavy cost lay less in the installation of the closet, than in its maintenance.

Governor Ord, 1878–80: his sensitive nostrils directed an interest in cess-pits and dry-earth closets. Local noses, such as those on the Perth City Council, did not accept that Perth was a dunghill.

Director of Works (Thomas) and the Colonial Surgeon (Waylen) to report on the subject. They, and Ord in his despatch to Hicks Beach, grumbled about the inactivity of the Perth City Council:

> It was admitted that with the exception of the power of compelling the exclusive use of earth closets, for which legislation (which could be had for the asking) might be necessary, ample and efficient powers are vested in the Council for ensuring the health of the city, and yet, with its eyes fully open to the fact that nothing but the introduction of earth closets would avail, the Council actually decided not to enforce their adoption.

The Governor reminded the Secretary of State that 'the gentlemen who form the Municipal Council of Perth are of the same class as those usually found in the Councils and Vestries of our small towns at home'. He should not be surprised, therefore, to learn that Perth councillors were unwilling to carry out a scheme 'which was spoken of as likely to cost £1000 a year':

> As one of them with commendable candour observed 'the assessment was quite sufficiently high already, and an additional £1000 a year would hardly be acceptable to the ratepayers!'

Given this attitude, added Ord, 'it is hopeless to expect any improvement in the sanitary condition of Perth'. Ord intended to bring the matter before the Legislative Council in the hope of prompting executive action 'even though it be at the cost of some curtailment of the rights of self-government'.[313]

The report of Ord's Committee merely gave a brief history of the subject. Indeed the only new piece of information it contained was that in his report for 1875, Waylen examined only three wells. His report comment, that he found only one well polluted by the 'presence of animal organic matter', takes on a significance and meaning altogether different from that of the report itself. Waylen, in fact, was always ambivalent on the issue; not until the pressure came from above did he commit himself entirely to the dry-earth closet idea. Even after the public debates in 1878, Waylen wrote in March 1879 that for Newcastle and York, where there was severe illness and disease, the dry-earth system of sewage disposal was of more importance than it was in Perth. Perth in 1878, as in 1875, 1876 and 1877, had been relatively disease-free. Waylen might swipe occasionally at the Perth City Council for not enforcing some of the public health clauses of the Municipal Act, but he knew, and so did the Perth City Council, that for the present the dunghill was more myth than reality.[314]

Parker's handling of the city's affairs was rewarded when in November, at the annual election, he was returned unopposed as Chairman. Little had happened in sanitation matters in the second half of 1878. At the Annual General Meeting on 11 November 1878 Parker had read a letter from 'their old friend and fellow citizen', Mr Padbury, on the water supply of Perth. Writing from England, Padbury had urged Council to run water from the Canning to Perth. He had priced the piping and he wrote eloquently of the benefits to the city's principal streets. Parker expressed doubt on the adequacy of the Canning as a water supply and the matter was dropped. Early in 1879 Waylen resigned as City Health Officer, perhaps in frustration at Council inactivity.[315]

313 *Votes and Proceedings of the Legislative Council* 1879.
314 *Votes and Proceedings of the Legislative Council* 1879.
315 PCC Minute Book, 11 November 1878, 7 February 1879.

It was not until after the winter of 1879, and following receipt of a letter on the subject fom the Colonial Secretary, that the Perth City Council renewed its interest in sanitary matters. Goldsworthy feared that the near approach of the summer heat made it imperative or rather 'a matter of mere human prudence to diminish, as far as possible, in towns, the risk of fever visiting their inhabitants'. Goldsworthy reminded the Perth City Council of its powers under the Act. He then suggested 'that a rigid investigation of every tenement in your Municipality for the discovery of nuisances should be, without delay, set on foot'. The Governor offered the Council one or more members of the police force to assist with the investigation. The Perth City Council resolved to act as the Governor directed.[316] Nor did the Governor ease up after this. Throughout October he harassed the Council. Under the Act it was required of householders that their cess-pits be watertight. On 10 October Parker reported that the Inspector had examined one hundred tenements 'and out of all that number there were only four where the state of the cess-pits was such as to comply with the requirements of the Act'. Here was a dilemma. It cost 7s6d to install an earth closet system, and a year before Parker had considered this to be too expensive for poor people. But cementing a cess-pit was a still greater expense—at least three times as great. In addition, as Councillor Stone observed, a cemented cess-pit would pollute the air, and a 'tainted atmosphere was as injurious to health as polluted water'. The Government wished the Council to introduce 'some effectual system of scavenging . . . to induce the citizens to adopt the dry-earth system'. Only then would the Government be prepared to assist financially. Council agreed to advertise for a night soil remover to collect within a three-quarter mile radius of the GPO.[317] And there again the matter rested.

In November 1879 Shenton replaced Parker as Chairman of the Perth City Council, and in March 1880 Governor Ord left the colony, as did Shenton who went to England for several months. It was not until late April 1880 that the Perth City Council considered tenders for a night soil remover.[318] The contract seems to have gone to Joseph Wylde, a gardener of Bulwer Street. But perhaps no one was appointed, for the monthly financial return shows no such payments. And in June Ord's replacement, Governor Robinson, who had interested himself in sanitary questions when previously Governor (1875-1877), questioned the Perth City Council as to whether Perth was 'in a better condition than it was during the time of his former administration of the city'. In reply the Perth City Council assured the Governor that the Inspector of Nuisances had visited

> every tenement in the more thickly populated part of the city and, in all cases where nuisances were found to exist, steps were taken to abate them.

Some councillors like Edward Stone and George Vincent thought that the Government was obsessed with cess-pit sanitary problems. In fact, as Stone pointed out, the Inspector had found only one instance of a cess-pit being close to a well. In Stone's view it was better to have an uncemented cess-pit, for a cemented one drove the 'foul exhalation and offensive effluvia' into the atmosphere and this was 'a more dangerous and fertile source of disease'. Vincent, who had examined tenements himself, had found that the greater danger came from the emptying of

316 PCC Minute Book, 18 September 1879; correspondence, 19, 23 September 1879.
317 PCC Minute Book, 17 October 1879.   318 PCC Minute Book, 20 April 1880.

179

slops on the ground in proximity to wells, particularly in wet weather. Clearly the debate was becoming better informed, but still little was being done.[319]

Indeed Council rejoiced to turn the tables on the Government, when at the same meeting a letter was read from four householders in Wellington Street complaining of the

> disgraceful nuisance which has been long existing nearly opposite our doors, caused by a drain, issuing from the Government Poor House, consisting of all sorts of filth, and which drain has broken out and overflown the street. The effluvium from this drain is so bad at times that we are obliged to keep our houses closed, especially when a heavy shower comes.

The Government, rejoiced councillors, 'are the only sinners'. The nuisance had not been abated in July or August and, until it was, then Perth City Council found no reason to set its own house in order. However at the annual elections in November, west ward was won by a young doctor, Edward Scott. Scott was an enthusiast for health reform, and within a month of his election he had persuaded Council to establish a Sanitary Committee composed of himself, Jewell (who had long favoured a dry-earth system), and Edward Stone. It was a talented Committee.[320]

But by 1880 the sanitation issue was only one of several major concerns of Council. Throughout the 1870s the Perth City Council had been paying off a large loan on the main drain; it had also had an overdraft of several hundred pounds at the Western Australian Bank. Thanks to Parker's economy measures in the late 1870s, these debts were all but wiped out by the end of 1880 (only £600 was left on the main account). The time seemed right to act on the loan provisions of the amended Municipal Institutions Act and seek a loan of £6000 for needed city improvements. And here the parsimony of the Government determined Council priorities. In 1877 the Imperial Government had granted Western Australia £50,000 for road and bridge construction. Despite the expectations of the Perth City Council,[321] none of this money was allocated for city road construction. In the meantime the northern part of the city continued to develop rapidly, while Parker's economy drive had reduced the amount of money available for repairs and maintenance of existing roads. In addition, the Perth City Council had been given responsibility for lands previously a charge on the Government, such as Victoria Park, the Mulberry Plantation, the riverside and the new Recreation Ground on reclaimed land between William and Barrack Street jetties on Bazaar Street. Furthermore the Perth City Council had to bear part of the cost of installing oil lighting in the principal streets of Perth. In October 1880 the Perth City Council agreed that top priority should be given to the macadamization of the streets in the northern and eastern parts of the city, and the improvement of the new Recreation Ground.[322] At the annual election in November 1880, Shenton, who had been made Mayor in September, was defeated by Parker (404 to 301). At the December meeting of Council, Parker proposed another set of road improvements with less emphasis on the back streets. Neither did the estimates for 1881 include money for needed road improvements in the back streets. This led to a full-scale revolt by

[319] PCC Minute Book, 25 June 1880.
[320] PCC Minute Book, 8 November, 3 December 1880.
[321] PCC Minute Book, November 1877.   [322] PCC Minute Book, 29 October 1880.

Left: *Looking towards north ward, the most troublesome ward for members of the Perth City Council.* Top: *Council road maintenance worker with wheel barrow in Murray Street, 1880s.*

the north ward members, especially Waldeck who opposed all Perth City Council expenditure for 1881, causing Parker to describe him as 'Western Australia's Parnell' in his policy of obstruction.[323] In particular the north ward members resented the proposed expenditure of £1000 on the new Riverside Recreation Ground. But, as Dr Scott argued, it was not a matter of roads versus recreation; it was rather a matter of 'health versus disease', for if left as it was, the Recreation Ground would be a sanitary risk to the residents. The loan proposal, put by Shenton originally, was confirmed by Council 5 votes to 4.[324]

If sanitation and water supply issues did not loom large in Council debates and expectations in the early 1880s, it is also true that the Sanitary Committee was not inactive. It carried out an efficient watching brief on city nuisances. For example, it supervised the filling in of the pond near the Pound in William Street and gained Council support for the planting of Tasmanian Blue Gums in the east ward; also for a new rubbish tip. It supported the Inspector of Nuisances in prosecuting offenders. In August 1881 Dr Scott pressed for changes in the method and times of night soil removal. The existing practice of removing the soil in the early evening, often the stillest part of the day, was both unsightly and left a tainted atmosphere. He also urged the increased use of disinfectants. In December 1881 Septimus Burt went on to the Sanitary Committee with Jewell and Scott. Perhaps never again was Council to have so talented a Committee. In March 1882 by-laws controlled the disposal of night soil. In May 1882 Dr Scott drew Council's attention to the state of the drain running through the gardens in west ward—it seemed to be polluted by the practice of owners depositing night soil in the gardens. By October, following a wet winter during which Murray Street was again flooded with tainted water, Scott declared roundly that

> the question of drainage was one which was becoming more and more pressing every day, and it was absolutely necessary in the interests of public health that some steps should be taken to introduce an efficient system, especially in some parts of the city.

[323] PCC Minute Book, 10 December 1880.
[324] PCC Minute Book, 14 December 1880.

181

It was an eloquent plea, but Council and ratepayers were to agree to raise another £6000 for road improvements, so large scale drainage works were out of the question.[325] The light sandy soils and generally mild winters lessened the need for the latter. Scott was becoming frustrated, and 1883 and 1884 passed too quietly for him. He was a young man who would accomplish much in the town in the future.

But to men like Shenton, Carr, Cole, Glyde, Bernard Smith, George Lazenby, S. H. Parker and others, the years to 1884 had seen the Perth City Council establish itself as a major institution in the life of the community. Its members had isolated and defined issues of importance to people like themselves and even, on some occasions, of importance to the other three-quarters of the population. It had become the forum and power centre of the 'fit and proper persons' of Perth. It was a means of maintaining a spiritual sense and a physical reality of the proper order of Perth society. It defined the interests of Perth in relation to Fremantle and to the country. Its short history demonstrated the constraints and freedoms of the people in Perth in relation to the Government. It was a social bonding agent not unlike the Perth Building Society, the Churches, the Temperance associations and the Mechanics' Institute. It was in the last-named only that the governance of fit and proper persons was challenged.

Social Dissidents: the Case of Joseph Chester

In Perth there were a few mechanics who refused to show a becoming deference to the gentry and officialdom, who did not seek representation on the Perth City Council, and who wished to control the fortunes of their own class. One such man was Joseph Chester, a cabinet-maker and upholsterer, who in the 1850s and 1860s struggled to make the Mechanics' Institute a forum for political and religious controversy. As a young man Chester had read his Tom Paine, and in the debate over the great reform bill of 1832, he had followed Lord Brougham in his campaign for a radical reallocation of parliamentary power in Britain, a campaign which men like Chester believed had been thwarted and defeated by the House of Lords and the monarchy. In the early 1850s Chester, Harry Hughes (a carpenter) and Thomas Allmond (a clerk in the Commandant's office) sought to establish the principle that lectures in the Institute should be delivered by the mechanics themselves and not by 'gentlemen'; but other, more influential, members, like George Lazenby, Bernard Smith and Terrence Farrelly, as well as the president, Septimus Roe, himself a gentleman, disagreed, and henceforth the lectures were given by clergymen (Anglican and non-conformist only), a Colonial Secretary or two, and some resident-officials of long standing, such as Alfred Durlacher, the colony's first historian. The mechanic's role was to listen, learn, and believe, whether the subject was the temples of Ninevah, ecclesiastical architecture, the poetry of Longfellow, 'self-culture' (or 'self-help' or 'self-improvement'), or British Liberty. The gentlemanly character and high social purpose of the lecture meetings were enhanced still further on those occasions when the Institute's patron, His Excellency the Governor, attended, sometimes in the company of his wife.

[325] PCC Minute Book, 4 March 1881; 23 December 1880; 5 August 1881; 3 March, 5 May, 4 October, 13 November 1882.

Defeated on this issue, and believing in a self-help of their own defining, Chester and his friends used the Institute's discussion classes to advantage. These classes were usually attended by ten to twenty members, whereas the lectures drew over 200 on many occasions. But the mechanics themselves could choose the topics for discussion, even though the constitution of the Institute forbade discussion of contemporary political and religious issues. In a debate in 1855 on whether or not a man was ever justified in shooting another, Chester launched an attack on the men who began wars: 'It is the great and noble that are the guilty parties . . . There will be shooting and killing so long as these nobles have relations to provide for.' In an attack on the Crimean War, worthy of a Roebuck or a John Bright, Chester urged his hearers to 'witness the devastation and obscenity of a pillaged village'. (Not until the Vietnam War over a hundred years later would some people of Perth speak in this way again). In a debate on the greatest statesman of modern times, Wellington, Pitt and Fox emerged as the leading contenders, with a majority going to Fox; but Chester thought that 'Lord Brougham had done more for his country than Pitt and Fox put together', and that Brougham had fought 'the battle of the People'. In a debate on the best means to develop the resources of the colony and advance its prosperity, Chester risked censure by arguing that

> the ruinous condition of the Colony was attributable to misgovernment, who when they could not make free slaves they introduced Chain Slaves.

A year later, in 1856, in a debate on British civil liberties since Magna Carta, most discussants argued that British law could 'not be altered for the better' or that 'the laws are at present as good as could be desired', and that

> There is nothing to prevent a man rising in the world . . . he [George Lazenby] felt a pride as an Englishman in living under such a Constitution.

Chester, with some support from Farrelly, contended that the people were as much slaves in 1856 as they were in the times of King John: 'We are governed by a set of tyrannical nobles'; the people of Scotland and Ireland were still in the greatest destitution; while in England 'it is the policy of the government to keep the people poor . . . see the degraded beings that are in the manufacturing towns'. In his final address to the group Chester sailed close to the wind:

> the government of the present day [is] a complete tyranny. We have a Queen, but she possesses no power . . . what use was she to her people; She seems to occupy that place merely to hug Prince Albert; it is the Lords by whom we are governed, and until we have vote by ballot we shall never be clear of their corruptions.

But a majority believed that there was 'ample opportunity now for every member of the community to improve and cultivate his mind', 'that it is impossible for all men to become equals', and that 'there has always been rich and poor, and it is wisely ordained by Providence that there should be'.

Chester lost that debate, but he was now chairman of the committee and introduced as the next topic, 'That the Republican form of government is superior to the British'. In the vigorous and prolonged debate which followed, the participants were charged with meddling too much in local politics; but the resolution was carried by one vote.

Roe: not an idle man in his generation. He believed that Chester impeded the growth of 'harmony and brotherly love'.

Chester: 'The government of the present day (is) a complete tyranny.' He believed that John Septimus Roe was 'out of order'.

JOSEPH CHESTER,
Upholsterer and Cabinet Maker, Perth,

BEGS respectfully to acquaint his friends and the public generally, that he is prepared to execute any orders that he may be favored with in the above line, in any of its various branches.

Sofas and Couches made to any design and repaired, re-stuffed, and covered. Palliasses made to order.

PAPER-HANGING in the best manner.

J. C. takes this opportunity to remark that there is a great superiority both in the wear and appearance of paper when put up on the walls properly, which he engages to do at no greater charge than usually paid for inferior workmanship.

Spring Stuffing in the seats of Sofas, Couches, Easy Chairs, Carriages and Gigs.

Venetian Blinds.—These blinds are very pleasant for warm climates, for while they darken the rooms they admit the air.

PIANOFORTES re-silked.

☞ Workshop for the present next door to Mr. B. Mason's Store, Hay Street, Perth.

The annual report of the Swan
River Mechanics' Institute for
1876.

Chester, it seemed, was losing his Don Quixote image and was emerging as a spokesman for, and leader of, a radical movement in Perth. But such fears were dispelled when, with a sudden burst of activity, the clergymen and Government officials, as well as the more sober mechanics, won the discussion group over to less controversial (and fewer) subjects and increased the number of public lectures by gentlemen. Their task was made easier when Chester moved to Guildford and no longer attended the Perth meetings. The gentry's grip on the Institute tightened, and few members, if any, would have disagreed with Governor Kennedy when in February 1862 in his farewell address he told them

> The day has gone by, when imaginary distinctions between classes can weigh with thinking men. I know of but two classes—one distinguished by industry and truth, and the other distinguished by the want of them.

By 1866 Chester was back in Perth. At the annual general meeting of the Institute he ruled the president, Septimus Roe, out of order for saying that the Institute had taken a step forwards, when in fact it had 'become a Reading Room for Gentlemen, and could not now be considered to be a "Mechanics' Institute"'. Chester was reproved by Bernard Smith and others. However, with William Ryan, an accountant who was a political radical, Chester revived the discussion group, and in April 1866 both men were elected to the Institute committee. Not for long however. Within a fortnight a special meeting of the Institute was convened, and, with Roe in the chair, Chester and Ryan were ousted by 20 votes to 10. The pair continued to participate in the discussions: Chester described Wellington as 'the most contemptible man in the world', while Ryan reminded members that 'the people had to take matters into their own hands' over the corn laws, a subject not without relevance to the ongoing debate in Perth over protection and free trade. Another debater, Richard Wynne, had the temerity to describe Western Australia as 'This poor, wretched, maimed limb of the British Empire'. All this was too much for Roe who had spent nearly forty years trying to make Swan River a jewel in the British Empire. ('I have not been an idle man in my generation' he wrote in his diary that year.) At the annual general meeting he spoke feelingly of the value of an institution where man could meet man 'on common ground, without any political, social or other feelings to sway them from a common brotherhood'. To this end he instituted changes to the rules of the Institute whereby it became even more a book club than before. And when in 1870 Chester complained that the committee was made up almost entirely of Government officials and that lectures and classes were not being held, Roe retorted that 'with regard to the Discussion Classes the Honourable Objector was as much to blame as anyone'. He urged Chester and other discontented mechanics (one of whom, Keaughram, had suggested that the few mechanics left on the Committee were 'under coercion') to withdraw from the Institute, for their presence impeded the growth of 'harmony and brotherly love'. As was his way Chester did not show a becoming deference and stayed on. Or rather hung on. After a short burst of debates in 1874 and 1875, in most of which Chester argued on the losing side, the discussion group closed down forever. The Mechanics' Institute became solely a literary and entertainment society, largely for men who moved in the best social circles, like H. C. Prinsep, Octavius Burt, Edward Stone, and Samuel Pole Phillips, and the builders and merchants of Perth. They sponsored such anodyne entertainment as the Lyons' Rocky Mountains Wonders, in which Miss Lyons sang *Up in a Balloon Boys, Up in a Balloon!* More books were borrowed by the gentry women of Perth than by the workers for whom the Institute was founded.

Joseph Chester seems to have died in 1886. John Septimus Roe died in 1878. In their twenty-five year war they had been as Paine versus Burke, as Washington versus George III, as Lord Brougham versus the Duke of Buckingham, as Francis Place versus Lord Liverpool, and as John Bright versus Lord Palmerston. Chester believed that the seed of crime lay in the flower of the aristocracy and that the noblest and best men of England were to be found in the Workhouses. Roe knew this to be demonstrable nonsense. But he knew also that if not contained, such ideas could take hold of the hearts and minds of more men, as they had done in Europe in 1848 and again in 1870. If 'internal peace' and brotherly love were to prevail then the Chesters of Perth, few in numbers as they were or seemed to be, would have to be contained or even expelled, just as Mead and McKail had been in the first decade of settlement. After all, nearly one-fifth of the adult males of Perth were members of the Institute in the 1870s. Roe won the battle for the minds of the members in the Institute. He had served his class well. In the minds of many people in Perth he had served the community well.[326]

Political Order and Social Order

The terms of political debate in Swan River were defined by the Governor, the officials, and the non-official gentry. No ex-convict ever became a member of the Perth City Council or of the Legislative Council. Indeed legislation specifically excluded them from the list of citizens eligible for office. In short, over two-thirds of the men of Perth, and all the women, took little part in the formal experience of colonial politics, including voting.[327] The politics of the Legislative Council tended to revolve around clashes between the Governor and his officials, and some of the nominated non-official members like Lionel Samson and Marshall Waller Clifton. In the early 1850s Clifton tried to win Council support for the introduction of representative government. He believed that Swan River was affluent enough to maintain a civil establishment. No other member of the Legislative Council shared his belief, though some felt, with the editor of the *Perth Gazette*, that

> on all occasions in which Australia has been spoken of at home, we have invariably found that New South Wales, Victoria, Tasmania, and South Australia have alone been referred to, and, that Western Australia has been tacitly considered as out of the Australian pale.[328]

More support was forthcoming from the York farmers and merchants like the Burges' and Monger,[329] and in mid-1856 they were joined by the leading town merchants like George Shenton, Mark Dyett, Robert

[326] All quotations in this section come from the Minute Books of the Swan River Mechanics' Institute: March, 4, 18 June, 25, 29 October 1855; 11, 12, 19, 26, 30 May, 10 November 1856; 18 February 1862; 29 January, 5 March, 9, 30 April, 25 June, 2 July, 10 September 1866; 7 January 1867; 3 February 1868; 10 January 1870; 15 June 1874.

[327] Electoral Roll for Perth in 1870, Battye Library Acc. No. 63.

[328] *Perth Gazette*, 15 April, 20 May 1853; the matter in question was Lord John Russell's despatch concerning self-government for the eastern colonies.

[329] *Perth Gazette*, 29 February 1856.

this is owing to the December accounts being paid and brought to account in 1876, contrary to the custom which has hitherto prevailed, and thus causing 13 payments to appear in 1876. The only increase has been a gratuity of £4 to the Librarian for extra work entailed by the letting of the hall so continuously of late. No additions of any consequence have been made to our exhibits in the Museum. A very fine collection of pearl and other shells, corals and sponges, star fish, &c., from the north-west coast, kindly presented by our indefatigable President, Capt. J. S. Roe, are the only ones we have to report. We can only reiterate our surprise that an institution of the kind is not more fully appreciated by the colonists generally, and some little effort made by them to collect more of the natural products of the colony, which abound in the several districts (animal, vegetable, or mineral), and forward them to the Museum for exhibition; thus affording strangers and visitors to the colony an opportunity of seeing at a glance all the products of the colony of Western Australia, and acting as an advertising medium to the colony at large. The thanks of the committee and members are due to the Local Government for the annual grants in aid, also to our respected President, Capt. J. S. Roe, R.N., and to our Vice-presidents, for their services, always cheerfully accorded when required.

B. SMITH, Chairman.

Statement of Receipts and Expenditure for the year ending 31st December, 1876.

RECEIPTS:

	£	s.	d.
Government Grant	50	0	0
Do. Museum	50	0	0
Subscriptions—Hon. members, £36; Ordinary, do., £92 2s. 6d.	128	2	6
Rent of Hall from various services	37	13	0
Legacy by the late Mr. C. King	10	0	0
Proceeds of sales, waste paper, condemned books, pictures, and sundries	5	17	8
	£281	13	2

EXPENDITURE:

	£	s.	d.
Balance due W. A. Bank, 31st December, 1876	34	12	7
Salaries and commissions	81	17	6
Habgood, on account of periodicals, papers, &c., to August, 1876	62	10	0
Repairs and improvements	25	14	2
Lighting and cleaning	21	10	9
Compiling and printing 300 copies Catalogue	20	4	10
Subscriptions and advertisements, local and colonial papers	10	11	0
Books purchased, binding, and repairs	10	2	7
Premium on Fire Insurance	2	10	0
Postage and stationery	2	2	0
Overdraft on W. A. Bank	0	14	6
Sundries	0	19	0
Balance in W. A. Bank	8	4	3
	£281	13	2

Examined and found correct,
G. W. Dent, } Auditors.
F. L. Hussey, }

Habgood and the Birch brothers in a concerted display of opposition to 'the present inordinate power of the Government' and Governor Kennedy's exercise of it.[330] One letter writer signed himself 'John McArthur' and described Kennedy as another Bligh. A second compared Kennedy unfavourably with 'the ever memorable' Governor Bourke of New South Wales. But at a large public meeting in the Court House, the men of York who wished to see the abolition of official representation on the Legislative Council failed to carry the day, and a resolution moved by Lionel Samson and seconded by George Shenton for equal representation of official and non-official members was carried. As one writer put it:

> It was the most unmistakeable exposition of public opinion which has ever occurred in this Colony, yet perhaps never were speakers more temperate in their expression of dissatisfaction with the Government, and the constitution of the Legislative Council.

Criticism of the Governor was so strong partly because it was believed that he was hindering the quest for 'internal peace'. In particular, by amending the publicans' licence bill so as to exclude as licence-holders the conditional pardon men, Kennedy was thought to have introduced 'class legislation of a most invidious and reprehensible manner' into the colony. Besides this concern for the rights of Joseph Green, the proprietor of the Cricketers' Arms down by the Causeway, there was an even greater concern about Kennedy's decision to prevent masters from paying servants in grog, a decision which hit hard at the exploitative labour relations in the colony.[331] By February 1857 some leading colonists were calling on Kennedy to resign, and in mid-1857 they received the unwelcome news that the Secretary of State for Colonies had rejected their plea for a part-elected Legislative Council.[332] A year later the non-official members no longer attended the meetings of the Legislative Council;[333] indeed the Council itself was described as 'an engine of unconstitutional oppression'. Kennedy weathered this and other storms and did his best to develop a land policy which would enable ex-convicts to purchase land, despite strong opposition from merchants and pastoralists—a Bligh indeed. Neither he nor the Government he represented made any concessions to the representative government movement, and he left the colony in 1862 unloved and unappreciated.

The men who wanted representative government received very little encouragement from Kennedy's successor, Governor Hampton. Indeed it was not until 1867 that the Government agreed even to increase the number of non-official members to six, equal to the number of official members.[334] Hampton also agreed that the non-official members could be elected for a period of three years. But by now there were those who feared elections of any sort and wished to

> avert the possibility of the Colony being plunged into the anarchy and confusion of demagoguism, such as Victoria is now reaping the lamentable fruits of.[335]

The fear of 'mobocracy' was something which the men of Swan River

[330] *Perth Gazette*, 4, 25 July, 1, 8 August 1856.
[331] *Perth Gazette*, 11 January, 30 May, 8 August 1856.
[332] *Perth Gazette*, 13 February, 29 May 1857.
[333] *Perth Gazette*, 29 October 1858.   [334] *Perth Gazette*, 13 September 1867.
[335] *Perth Gazette*, 22 September 1867, commenting on the bitter political conflicts in Victoria over money bills.

learned partly from observation of the conduct of politics in the eastern colonies; but it was also something deeply rooted in the Western Australian past through familial experience of the post-Napoleonic War upheavals in Britain. In the first election for the seat of Perth, J. G. C. Carr comfortably defeated Walter Padbury and Luke Leake: only 305 men voted at the election, out of the 1900 or so men in Perth.[336] Only Carr had favoured an elective franchise for the Legislative Council. The Secretary of State for Colonies was not pleased with Hampton's experiment, and it was not until 1870 that Hampton's successor, Governor Weld, was able to announce that representative government had been granted to Western Australia, and that henceforth the colony would have a two-thirds elected legislature. Western Australia, said Weld, now joined 'the long list of FREE communities over which [our] illustrious lady is justly proud to reign'.[337] At the first elections in Perth under representative government, the successful candidates were Carr and Luke Leake. The election seems to have been fought partly on sectarian lines, and the two successful candidates were Anglicans, while Birch was a Congregationalist, and Farrelly, who finished at the foot of the poll, was a Roman Catholic.[338] But to men at the time it seemed that a new era was dawning:

> Too long indeed has this colony slumbered under the paternal care of an autocratic government—too long, in truth, has she been the ward of Downing Street.[339]

For Perth the new dawn wore the colours of the old. Luke Leake, free trader and conservative, the sceptic of representative government and opponent of responsible government, was the Member for Perth in the Legislative Council from 1870 to 1886. Leake was five years old when he arrived in Swan River in 1833. He learnt from his redoubtable uncle, George Leake, the business and social values which 'shaped' Perth and gave it a distinctive 'sense of place'. In the 1850s Leake prospered mightily for he won Government contracts for the supply of tea, sugar and flour, and for more than a decade his ship the *Guyon* traded profitably between Perth, Singapore, Calcutta and Mauritius. From 1854 to his death in 1886 he was a director of the Western Australian Bank. In the early 1850s he also acted as an independent money-lender to those who could 'furnish unexceptionable security'.[340] He was a vice-president of the Mechanics' Institute in 1863-64 and president in succession to Roe from 1879-86, and he served on the Central Board of Education from 1878 to 1886. In the Weld Club he was vice-president from 1878-82, and president from 1882 to 1886. He was Speaker of the Legislative Council from 1870 to 1886 and was knighted in 1876. A deeply religious man, he donated £2000 in 1878 for the building of a new Anglican Cathedral, one which in form would be more spiritual than the old St George's Church.[341] He was one of those men in Perth of whom Kimberly was to write later that they were 'conservative in everything'. Their power to do good and evil was limited only by the occasional whims of the Imperial Government.

Perth was represented in the Legislative Council by two members. Leake's colleagues in the 1870s were J. G. C. Carr, from 1870 to 1873,

Sir Luke Leake, merchant, banker, and Member for Perth in the Legislative Council, 1870-86: product of and promoter of the gentry's quest for 'internal peace'.

[336] *Perth Gazette*, 15 November 1867.   [337] *Perth Gazette*, 3 June 1870.
[338] For a comment on the importance of sectarianism see *Perth Gazette*, 26 August 1870; for the results of the election see *Perth Gazette*, 21 October 1870.
[339] *Perth Gazette*, 11 November 1870.   [340] *Perth Gazette*, 25 June 1852.
[341] *ADB* Vol. 2—entry for G. W. and L. Leake.

and Edmund Birch between 1873 and 1875. Both men were similar to Leake in outlook and practice. Birch too was a director of the WA Bank; he had also been a chairman of the Mechanics' Institute and a vice-president of the Perth Working Men's Association. All three served for a time on the Perth City Council. So too did George Randell who represented Perth from 1875 to 1878, and who later became a director of the WA Bank and chairman of the local AMP Society directorate. One way and another Randell remained in parliament for the next thirty-five years. But in the 1878 elections he was defeated by Stephen Henry Parker, a young Perth lawyer. This marked something of a break in the representation of Perth in the Legislative Council, for although Parker was colonial born, a lawyer, and a member of the gentry, he had a passionate interest in individual rights which occasionally brought him into conflict with the Government and even the Judiciary. In 1870 Parker took out an affidavit on behalf of a convict whom he believed to be wrongfully incarcerated by the Comptroller General. In the course of the hearing Parker won the censure of the Chief Justice who promptly fined him £25 for malpractice. Two much-respected journalists were imprisoned when they printed an inflammatory letter from Parker on the subject, which the Chief Justice ruled to be libellous.[342] From that time until the mid-1880s Parker was a popular figure among the middling and lower classes of Perth, earning for himself the ancient and heroic title of the 'people's Harry'. As such he was regarded with great suspicion by the gentry and the Government.

Compounding their worry about Parker was the fact that from early on he was an advocate of responsible government. Between 1870 and 1875 there was considerable Governmental interest in responsible government, for the Governor, Sir Frederick Weld, was a former premier of New Zealand, and the Colonial Secretary, Frederick Barlee, was a Gladstonian Liberal who probably saw himself as the person most likely to be the colony's first premier. But the Secretary of State for Colonies vetoed their self-government proposals, and in any case Weld retired in 1874, and Barlee was appointed Lieutenant Governor of British Honduras a year later. Parker remained active, and in the late 1870s he was joined by two other young lawyers, Septimus Burt and Edward Stone, and together they formed a Reform League. The League was partly an electoral registration society and partly a means of educating the 'respectable classes' about the virtues of self-government. The League received strong support from the *Morning Herald*, and almost equally enthusiastic support from the *Western Australian Times*. With Legislative Council elections due early in 1880, some conservative landowners and Perth businessmen took steps to ensure that the influence of the League was minimised. Edward Stone seems to have been bought off with Government assistance when in 1879 he was offered the position of Acting Attorney General. Stone was alleged to have said of the League, 'Oh that can slide'.[343] In September 1879 Charles Harper, a deeply conservative Anglican farmer, pastoralist, and company director (e.g. Perth Ice Company), bought the *Western Australian Times* outright for £1100, with the intention of making it the colony's leading organ of country and conservative opinion, and a voicepiece for the Government in the critical debate over responsible

342 J. S. Battye *History of Western Australia*, 1924, pp.302–3.
343 Harper Papers, Cockburn Campbell to Harper, 25 November 1879.

VOL. I. NO. I.   PERTH, WESTERN AUSTRALIA, TUESDAY, NOVEMBER 18, 1879.   PRICE THREEPENCE.

government. Harper and his partner, Sir Thomas Cockburn Campbell, sought to influence the 'second rate classes' (the phrase is Cockburn Campbell's) as well as their own class of people. They were an energetic and purposeful pair. They spent another £1000 on new equipment, made new staff appointments, and then produced by far the most attractive newspaper in the colony. It was called the *West Australian*. The title was carefully chosen. Nothing with 'Swan River' in it would have done, for 'Swan River' was linked inextricably with convictism (so Mrs Millett reported). The *Western Australian Times* left room for a *Western Australian Chronicle* and so on. But the *West Australian* could claim to speak authoritatively for Western Australia: town and country; all denominations and classes. Outside the poetry of Henry Clay, it represented the purest articulation of the quest for internal peace, the harmonious society. What was in the name was an entire field of vision of the nature of colonial society.

The conservatism of the *West Australian* ran deep in the Western Australians' experience of the past. Harper, colonial born, had spent his youth and young manhood in the company of the founders of Swan River. It was almost certainly by design rather than accident that within a year of establishing the *West Australian*, Cockburn Campbell and Harper printed in serial form the diary and letters of George Fletcher Moore, that keen shaper of Perth society from 1830 to the 1850s. The articles were popular. The right chord had been struck. The circulation of the *West Australian* rose quickly. By 1884 there were over 1000 subscribers and a circulation in excess of 1500.[344] Aided and abetted by the *West Australian*, neither Governor Robinson (January 1875–September 1877, April 1880–February 1883) nor Governor Ord (November 1877–March 1880) offered any encouragement to the advocates of responsible government, although Robinson was critical of representative government: 'Let no man take charge of such a form of government who is not as patient as Job, as industrious as a Chinaman,

The 'West Australian', 18 November 1879: what was in the name was an entire field of vision of the nature of colonial society.

---

[344] Not even the establishment in 1882 of a rival Perth paper, the *Daily News*, halted the *West's* spectacular growth, though the *News*, an evening newspaper, sold a thousand copies of each issue in the mid-1880s.

189

Charles Harper, pastoralist, company director, and proprietor of the 'West Australian': arch-exponent of Perth's sense of place.

and as ubiquitous as a provincial Mayor in France'. Ord too would have preferred to do without interference from the non-official members of the Legislative Council, but he welcomed the support of several, like Sir Thomas Cockburn Campbell and Charles Harper. And in any case at successive general elections anti-responsible government candidates were returned in large numbers, even after the Council was increased in size in 1882. Even the few responsible government proponents possessed an 'inviolable conservatism of mind', and in the actions of lawyers like Parker there was more than a little of the young men's desire for public notice and opposition to expressions of their parents' conservatism, than a rejection of that conservatism. Perhaps this was especially true of Parker, for his father, a nominated member of the Legislative Council from 1876 to 1885, was a staunch ally of Harper in the latter's defence of the Government in the late 1870s.[345] It was around the time of his father's resignation from the Legislative Council that Stephen Henry Parker's flirtation with liberalism came to an end and he lost his reputation as the 'people's Harry'.

In 1883 a small black cloud (seen as such by Parker no less than Harper) appeared on the horizon, when a few members of the Working Men's Association threatened to create a Labor League. They met with little success for bishops and governors had done their work well over the years; but Donnelly, the ring-leader, had recently come from the eastern colonies—that, asserted the *West Australian*, was sufficiently damning. Hopefully, few like him would come to Western Australia.[346] In 1868 Arthur Shenton, the editor of the *Perth Gazette* for twenty years, observed approvingly that convictism had changed little of the character of Swan River, and that

> The theories and sciences which were important at the foundation of the Colony may be said still to preserve their sway.[347]

Five years later, in an address to the Bombay Chamber of Commerce, which was reported fully in the Perth press, Anton Helmich, a respected senior public servant and citizen, stated proudly that Perth was 'very far from being a democratic community'.[348] Vigilence of the Harper sort would ensure that it remained so. And in January 1884 the 'second rate classes' and the wielders of power in Perth society read in the columns of the *West Australian* an account of the trial, conviction, and hanging of Henry Haynes. For Haynes and Harper were the twin images of conservatism in Perth.[349]

[345] See letters from S. S. Parker to Charles Harper, Harper Papers, Battye Library.
[346] For a brief account of the incident, see H. J. Gibbney 'Western Australia', in D. J. Murphy (ed.) *Labor in Politics*, 1975, p.343.
[347] *Perth Gazette*, 16 October 1868.
[348] *Perth Gazette*, 18 April 1873.
[349] *ADB* Vols. 3-6—entries for Barlee, Robinson, Ord, Cockburn Campbell; *West Australian*, 8, 10 January 1884.

Perth at the end of the convict years: a part of, if not yet a jewel in, the British Empire.

St George's Terrace after the goldrushes: *Post Office and Treasury Buildings at right, Stirling Gardens and Moir's Buildings at left and middle distance. (John Campbell, artist.)* .

Chapter Four: 'Forrests in the City' — Perth 1884 to 1918

Perth after the Goldrushes

In Perth in 1911 there were about 100 people who had arrived in Swan River before 1850. There were a further 2000 who had come to Western Australia before 1871. In all they constituted 1.8% of the population of Perth and suburbs. In 1911, 95% of the population of Perth and suburbs had arrived after or been born in Western Australia since 1884. In 1884, the population of the district of Perth was just over 6000; by 1891 it was just over 9500; in 1901 it was nearly 44 000; and by 1911 Perth and suburbs had almost doubled to reach 87 000. In 1884 Perth had no suburbs. By 1911 it was ringed by them. In 1884 it was a market town; in 1911 it was a city. Even the municipality of Perth contained almost 36 000 people. Perth in 1911 had comfortably overtaken Hobart in size, and had reached half of Brisbane's size. Adelaide, which in 1884 was twelve times bigger than Perth, was now only twice its size.

The demography of Perth had been changed by the massive immigration of the goldrushes and their aftermath. The first wave of migrants came with the Kimberley goldrushes of the mid-1880s; the second with the great strikes in the Murchison, Yilgarn and Kalgoorlie regions from the late 1880s to the mid-1890s; and the third with the government-funded, less significant, emigration land-schemes of the late 1900s. In the early 1880s nearly 6 out of 10 of the people of Perth had been born in the colony; by 1901 this had slumped to 3 in 10; and by 1911 it had risen to 4 in 10 as the goldrush generation produced its babies. But even in 1911 no less than 4 in 10 people in Perth had been born and raised in the eastern colonies (states after 1901), especially Victoria, New South Wales, and South Australia. Twenty years before, in 1891, less than 1 in 10 Perth people were eastern colonial born. In the early 1880s, 4 in 10 Perth people had been born in the old country (mainly England and Ireland); by 1901 this had slumped to just over 2 in 10 and did not exceed this in 1911. In its demography Perth was now an Australian city.[1]

It was an Australian city in other ways. In 1890 a beneficent Imperial government had granted Western Australia self-government, such as the eastern colonies had received thirty-five years previously. Throughout the 1890s Western Australia had been governed by a Ministry headed by Sir John Forrest. When in 1901 Western Australia joined the Commonwealth and became an Australian State, and Forrest entered federal politics, a Labor Party contested the State Election, thereby heralding the emergence of party politics along eastern colonial lines. In 1904 a Labor Government held office for a year, and regained it

A page fom May Vivienne's Travels in Western Australia, 1902.

---

[1]   As the next census was not until 1921, the following paragraphs draw on the 1911 census information. Commonwealth Census of Australia, 1911; Census of Western Australia, 1891.

in 1911. The Governor, all powerful in 1884, had been stripped of many of his powers and functions, although he remained much more than a ceremonial figure. By 1911, too, not only did all adult males have the right to vote but the women did as well. In short, in 1911 Western Australia had most of the characteristics of a modern democratic political system.

Perth had also become a modern commercial city. Its economy was now far more complex and even included a sizable manufacturing industry. The colony had been linked by submarine cable to London, Fremantle had overhauled Albany as the colony's principal port (thanks to the Forrest Government's decision to enlarge the harbour), and Perth was the centre of a radial network of railway lines exceeding 2300 miles in length compared with less than 100 in 1884. In the early 1880s Western Australia had had a public debt of £360,000. By 1911 this had reached £24 million. In the early 1880s there were about 1300 savings bank accounts. In 1911 there were 97 150. All this development had been made possible by the discovery of gold. In 1890 gold to the value of £87,000 had been exported. In 1900 this had risen to nearly £4 million, and even in 1911 stood at £1,300,000. But Western Australia was not entirely dependent on the company drill. In 1911 exports of greasy wool were valued at about £1 million, towards which figure they had steadily moved after about 1900. And very late in the period—from about 1907—Western Australia began to export wheat in large quantities, the return in 1911 being almost £400,000. The number of acres under crop had risen from about 28 000 in 1881 to 612 000 in 1911, an increase due in part to the Forrest Government's Homestead Act (1893) and the establishment of an Agricultural Bank. For most of this period, however, the demand for food outstripped its production and Western Australia remained a net importer of foodstuffs. In this period of unprecedented growth the face of the city of Perth was transformed. The old and familiar cottages, warehouses and stores were pulled down and replaced with larger, more elaborate structures which, despite some rebuilding in the 1920s, gave Perth an architectural character which survived to the mineral boom of the 1960s and 1970s.[2]

At first glance these demographic, economic and political changes were so great that it would seem that little of the old ways could survive. A second look suggests otherwise. The men of 1884 steered Perth through the 1890s and early 1900s. Perth in 1911 was still basically a service city for its rural hinterland and the pastoral lands of the north; it remained the centre of administration—and the men at the centre of administration were the men of 1884. The men of 1884 were well placed to take maximum advantage of the gold discoveries, possessing as they did access to funds, information and so on, while being able to profit from the sale of produce to miners and those who came in their train, as well as through the sale and resale of urban land. And if, in 1911, control of the Legislative Assembly had passed to 't'othersider' Labor men, then the Legislative Council, with its massive power of veto, was still securely in the hands of the old Western Australians—indeed Labor would never ever control the Legislative Council and in time adopted a role in recognition of that. And while the mayoralty of the city of Perth could fall occasionally to a 't'othersider' adventurer, the dominant mayors in the period were George Shenton, Alexander Forrest and Thomas

[2]   Information from *WA Year Book*, 1965 ed.

Molloy, 'sandgroper' entrepreneurs to a man. Even Harry Brown, Mayor between 1903 and 1905, had arrived in Western Australia from South Africa in the late 1880s and worked for the old legal firm of Stone, Burt & Coy. before becoming secretary to the long-established Perth Building Society. Reflecting on the transformations of political life in Western Australia in the mid-1890s an experienced student of international politics, Henry de R. Walker, prophesied that the democratic movement would be 'checked by the conservative instincts of the native population'.[3] While wrong in some of his examples, the general thrust of his observation was undoubtedly correct. Writing in the early 1900s another visitor, May Vivienne, observed that 'Perth has now settled down and become quite a quiet city again, whereas a few years ago, when the gold fever was at its height, the state of the town was very different. Then the excitement was tremendous.'[4] A central task of this chapter is to describe the 'excitement' and the 'settling down'.

Freedom, progress, youthfulness, and fealty — The Town Hall

On 1 June 1870 the Perth Town Hall had been officially opened by Governor Weld. It was the same day on which he had announced that Western Australia had been granted representative government and joined 'the long list of FREE communities over which our illustrious lady The Queen, is justly proud to reign'. The day was uncharacteristically fine. Over Barrack Street near the Town Hall was an arch in evergreen on which was written the word 'PROGRESS'. During the opening ceremony there was much speech-making. Convict labour had built the hall. But convictism could now be relegated to the dustbin of history. James Lee Steere, a colonial gentleman, employed a different image:

> the progress of a country may be aptly compared to the growth of a human being; hitherto we have been a baby in swaddling clothes . . . we have now arrived at the age of youth . . .[5]

Men and women stood shoulder to shoulder and sang the national anthem, some managing with ease the newly added verse:

> Britain! Though here we stand
> On our Australian land
>   Thy sons are we.
> By all on earth we love,
> By all our hopes above
> We vow to death to prove
>   Faithfull to Thee.

Freedom, progress, youthfulness, and fealty—the Town Hall symbolised all these. What happened in the hall thereafter would be an index to the values of the colony. Bishop Hale took as his text the 127th Psalm, 1st verse:

> Except the Lord built the house,
> They labour in vain that build it;
> except the Lord help the city, the
> watchman watches in vain.

[3]   H. de R. Walker *Australasian Democracy*, 1897, p.169.
[4]   May Vivienne *Travels in Western Australia*, 2nd ed., 1902, p.39.
[5]   Lee Steere added that he hoped to live to see the day when Western Australia assumed the garb of a man. On his own reckoning he did so and spoke again when Western Australia received self-government in 1890. He remained in parliament until his death in 1903.

His prayer was simple:

> Help this building we beseech you in its future use. May it ever be devoted to purposes befitting a Christian land and be made largely useful in promoting the healthy enjoyment of the people and the social advancement of the community (so that no rash words be here spoken to stir up strife and angry passions); in all assemblies, may goodwill and harmony ever prevail.[6]

Hale, Roe, Harper, Shenton, Lee Steere, O'Grady Lefroy, the Stones and others, including the governors, had ensured that goodwill and harmony would prevail, and not until 1886 did the Town Hall witness rash words, strife, and angry passions on a scale so great that the quest for internal peace seemed threatened, and the very hall which symbolised goodwill and harmony in the colony became linked with mobocracy and demagogic urban politics.

The Case of John Horgan

It was in 1886 that John Horgan first addressed the people of Perth from the platform of the Town Hall at an election. The election had been occasioned by the death of the venerable Member for Perth, Sir Luke Leake. The three candidates were Edward Scott, a popular doctor who was a member of the Weld Club; William Traylen, Wesleyan preacher and temperance leader; and John Horgan, an Irish Catholic solicitor. Scott and Traylen were less conservative than Leake, but their style of politics was akin to his. Horgan's was entirely different. He stood for a radical programme which included the immediate introduction of responsible government, payment of members, manhood suffrage, a land tax, and a single chamber legislature. Moreover he indulged in acrimonious criticism of the Government and its supporters. The Weld Club he described as a 'Pot House'. Bishop Salvado was described as the colony's largest land grabber and squatter. Horgan described the ruling families of the Swan River as the 'Six Hungry Families'—hungry for land, money, and power. He castigated the *West Australian* for its reactionary political stance. He even attacked his opponents. In short Horgan did not play the electoral game in the traditional fashion. His Town Hall meeting delighted the workers present, particularly the Irish among them; and it outraged the respectable classes. At the election in June, Scott was returned with a handsome majority, but to the surprise of all but his most enthusiastic supporters Horgan scrambled into second place, relegating to third position the Rev. Traylen. To some it seemed a bad omen indeed. In the short term all was well however, for Scott was now Member for Perth, and Horgan was successfully sued for slander by the respected Police Magistrate, George Walpole Leake (a member of one of the 'Six Hungry Families') and fined £500. This would have deterred most men from further abuse of the Establishment, but Horgan was made of sterner stuff and promised his supporters that at the first opportunity he would nominate again.

Horgan had to bide his time for two years. But who was Horgan? If the Governor was putting the question it behoves the historian to do likewise. Horgan was born in July 1834 in Maroon, County Cork, in Ireland. His father was a Roman Catholic farmer with sufficient means to give John a good education. In the 1860s and 1870s John practised as

---

[6]   *Perth Gazette*, 3 June 1870.

a lawyer in Cork—indeed he became secretary to the County Cork Law Society. He was also active in local and parliamentary politics, and in the 1874 British general election he campaigned actively on behalf of one of his clients, a Home Ruler called Joseph Ronayne, who was elected to the House of Commons with a large majority. But in Britain and Ireland the 1870s were years of great economic hardship, particularly in rural areas like County Cork, and even middle class people like John Horgan found it difficult to make a decent living. Thousands of families emigrated to the 'golden lands of Australasia', for the Australian colonies were advertised as a veritable garden of Eden, an earthly paradise, in which even the humblest of mankind could live like 'The Lords of Olden Days'. In 1876, at the age of 42 years, John Horgan decided that his children should not have to suffer the ills of Old Ireland as they grew to maturity, and he emigrated with them to New South Wales, where for five years he practised law with moderate success.

But New South Wales in the late 1870s was also a place of turmoil. The trouble was less economic (although New South Wales did experience an economic recession in 1877–79) than social—or more specifically, religious. Roman Catholics in Australia had always had a difficult time of it, but in the late 1870s New South Wales was governed by that scourge of Catholics, Henry Parkes, then at the peak of his power as politician and platform orator. Parkes proposed to introduce a full system of free, compulsory and secular education, thereby threatening the existence of the Catholic schools. The issue tore the colony apart, but Parkes carried the day after some momentous clashes with Archbishop Vaughan. Vaughan had warned his flock that if Parkes' legislation was carried then New South Wales would become a den of iniquity. Perhaps Horgan, who was a devout Catholic, took Vaughan's words to heart, for on the passing of Parkes' legislation the Horgans moved to the calmer waters of Western Australia. The family, now ten in number, arrived in January 1881. Thus there settled in Perth a free Irish-Catholic Home-Ruler with a history of radical political activity and experience of the rough and tumble of eastern colonial political life.

Horgan found that in some ways life in Western Australia was even more repressive than in New South Wales. Irish-Catholic workers had no political rights whatsoever, and the Master and Servant Act was almost mediaeval in its power to control and suppress the workers. And even though a Roman Catholic governor, Frederick Weld, had ameliorated the condition of the Roman Catholic Church and its schools, the social establishment in Western Australia was strongly Anglican and pro-England. But Horgan was now fifty years of age. He seems to have decided to stay in Western Australia and take a strong stand for those things in which he believed. In his law practice he took working men's cases at little or no cost to them. He joined the Perth Working Men's Club (rather than the Mechanics' Institute or the Perth Club) and there he encouraged working men to air their grievances publicly. Although not in the Legislative Council he was one of those men in Perth who helped to get limited reforms made to the Master and Servant Act (1883–84). In 1886, in concert with another newly arrived lawyer, R. S. (Dickie) Haynes, Horgan formed Western Australia's first Eight Hours Association—a sorely needed organization, for some employers, including William Traylen who sweated his printery labour, worked their men up to seventy and even eighty hours per week. Then in mid-1886 came Luke Leake's death and the Perth by-election. Already some men

The end of an era: *the funeral of Sir Luke Leake, Perth, 1886.*

had trickled back to Perth from the Kimberley goldfields; already some independent labourers were at work on railway construction in the colony. In time many of them would become £10 householders in Perth. But even in 1886 Horgan managed second place in the poll.[7]

Throughout 1886 and 1887 the population of Perth was increased by an inflow of free labourers from the Kimberley field and as railway construction jobs were completed. A number of these men enrolled in 1887 as £10 householders. Early in 1888 the colony experienced a severe depression. Many firms went into liquidation, including The WA Manufacturing Coy., while even The Stanley Brewery found itself in financial difficulties. Unemployment was high:

> trade is dull, our markets are paralysed,
> The working man is to be seen on every side
> crying for work, and
> The prospects at present are as black as ever they can be.

The 'general public,' it was added, 'are railing against a Government who has brought the colony to such a disastrous position'.[8] One of the criticisms levelled against the Government was that it had tended to withdraw support for responsible government, thereby alienating Parker's Reform Party and men like Horgan who championed workers' rights. In addition the Government had decided not to accept a recommendation from a Select Committee of the Legislative Council to proceed with the construction of the Busselton-Bayswater railway. Many people in Perth had seen this line as easing the unemployment problem. A series of public meetings in the Perth Town Hall, addressed by Haynes, Horgan, and the former Attorney General, A. P. Hensman, condemned the Governor and all his supporters. Some of the more respected citizens like Alexander Forrest had attended the early meetings, but their absence from the later meetings was commented upon derisively by those who did attend. But all the meetings were attended by over 1000 people—over one-third of the adult male population of Perth. The *West*

7   The above paragraphs have been drawn substantially from C. T. Stannage 'Electoral Politics in Western Australia 1884–97', MA thesis, University of Western Australia, 1967. A £10 householder was an elector who lived in a house worth £10 annual rental.
8   *Southern Advertiser*, 8 May 1888.

Australian, which itself had been criticised at the meetings, was moved to comment that

> Public meetings have steadily deteriorated in this city, chiefly since various late arrivals from the other colonies have apparently sought to bring themselves into prominence by indulging in that style of invective common under the institutions to which they have been used but utterly out of place in Western Australia.[9]

But worse was to come. On 12 May the colony received the momentous news that the British Government had reinstated Chief Justice A. C. Onslow. The 'Onslow affair' as it was popularly known, had its origins in a personal and legal clash between Governor Broome and his Chief Justice in 1887. The upshot of the clash was that Broome suspended Onslow from his high office. It was widely felt, even for a time by the *West Australian*, that Onslow's suspension was a grave infringement of the independent status of the judiciary and of the rights of the people. At the time of the suspension there had been a public demonstration and torchlight procession. Governor Broome had been burnt in effigy and a band had played the 'Dead March' outside Government House in St George's Terrace. When on 12 May 1888 the city learnt that Onslow had been reinstated, the proprietors of the *West Australian* pleaded that the hatchet should be buried, for 'a small community must not be divided against itself'.[10] But many people in Perth, particularly among the workers, felt otherwise, and over 2000 people marched in yet another procession which gave three groans for Mayor Shenton (described as the 'Governor's stooge'), three for the *West Australian*, three for S. H. Parker who by supporting Broome forfeited his claim to be the 'People's Harry', and three for Governor Broome. Haynes told the crowd that 'it [is] the first time in the history of the colony that the people have secured a victory'. The city correspondent for the Geraldton *Victorian Express* told his country readers that

> they have no conception of the degraded condition to which political and public welfare has been reduced in their fair city.

Others shared his viewpoint. The principal bankers, pastoralists and merchants of Perth and Fremantle, including the Mayors (Shenton and D. K. Congdon), waited on His Excellency the Governor to express their disapproval of the goings on of the populace and to assure him that the saner elements had every confidence in his administration now and in the future. Broome, in his turn, expressed his gratitude to the 'large and influential class' represented. But by now he and they were on the defensive:

> it has been stated that the crowd was composed of the lower orders, but this is all fudge, for the numbers present would disprove the fact. The population of the city is estimated at seven thousand souls, and as upward of 4000 took part in the proceedings . . . it is hard to follow the dictum of one newspaper that the city is composed of so many roughs.[11]

It was around this time that the city was plunged into another by-election. Parker, as director of a company which had gone into liquidation, was forced to resign his seat in the Legislative Council. Only two candidates came forward to contest the seat. One was Septimus Burt, son of the former Chief Justice, a lawyer, an Acting Attorney

---

9   *West Australian*, 13 April 1888.
10   *Western Mail*, 19 May 1888.   11   *Eastern Districts Chronicle*, 19 May 1888.

General in Broome's Government, and a pillar of the Anglican Church. Burt was also a pastoralist and a member of the Weld Club. His candidature was sponsored by George Shenton, the Mayor of Perth, who got up a requisition of support in the traditional way. The requisition, which was published in the *West Australian*, included the names of most of the prominent businessmen of the town, as well as many senior civil servants. It was, to all intents and purposes, the membership lists of the Weld Club and the Mechanics' Institute. In the course of getting names for the requisition one of Burt's canvassers approached a well known Perth solicitor:

> "Will you sign this," said the gentleman who was canvassing. "Will I do what?" replied the solicitor, with a voice full of the rich brogue of the Emerald Isle. "Faith and I won't: Sure and I'm coming forward meself."

John Horgan was keeping the promise he had made in 1886.

The 1888 Perth by-election campaign was the most exciting in the history of Western Australia. There were never less than 1000 people at the Town Hall meetings, which were reported fully, indeed passionately, in the metropolitan and country newspapers. Horgan opened up with a public meeting on the evening of Friday 18 May. One of his committeemen, Dr Adam Jameson, who had arrived in the colony as recently as 1884, opened the meeting with a fiery address attacking the Government and deploring Burt's failure to welcome the reinstatement of Chief Justice Onslow, and for not declaring himself to be in favour of the immediate introduction of responsible government. Stirred by Jameson the big audience cheered noisily as the heavily bearded and rather grandfatherly figure of Horgan rose to his feet to address them. He did not let them down. First he attacked Governor Broome, whom he described as 'Czar' Broome, and as a 'bird of passage' who was damaging the colony yet would receive a 'fat pension' for his unworthy efforts. Broome, he said, had treated the artisans and workers of Perth most shamefully, especially by not proceeding with the construction of the Bayswater-Busselton railway line at a time of high unemployment. As for the *West Australian* it was nothing other than a 'reptile rag' and a 'doormat' for the Government. And behind the Government and the *West Australian* were the 'Six Hungry Families', all of whom were 'shoddy, mean and conceited' and kept from the working men what was rightfully theirs. Mayor Shenton he described as 'Warwick, The Kingmaker'. His opponent, Septimus Burt, was the creation of the Governor, the *West Australian*, and the likes of George Shenton—'the ideal champion of the six hungry families'. All this was greeted with tremendous enthusiasm by the huge audience which gave loud cheers for 'Honest' John Horgan. Horgan was followed by Hensman who delivered a reasoned attack on the Government, Burt, and on Shenton 'and his brother storekeepers'. He urged voters not to fear intimidation from employers, for the secret ballot would protect them. The meeting concluded with a loud and prolonged ovation for Horgan and his Committee.

Horgan's meeting had a mixed reception from the press. The *West Australian* thought that he had given an absurd display, but it acknowledged the power and subtlety of Hensman's address by devoting an editorial to his role. The Fremantle *Evening Times*, which had advocated Burt's return, now feared that Burt would rue the day when

Governor Broome had announced that 'Mr Burt unreservedly placed himself in my hands'—Burt would fail unless he lost his Government tag. The radical Perth journal, the *WA Bulletin*, expressed its delight at seeing that Burt only favoured an amendment to the present constitution while Horgan favoured the immediate introduction of self-government.[12] Burt's meeting was eagerly awaited.

On the evening of 21 May the Town Hall was again filled to capacity. Burt opened his speech with some rather superior remarks about Horgan having a free flow of adjectives 'like all his countrymen'. The Irishmen present booed heartily. Burt then explained that he did not oppose the introduction of responsible government but he wished to stress the hurdles to be jumped before it would be achieved. He declared his neutrality over the Onslow affair. He opposed the construction of the Busselton-Bayswater railway. He agreed with the Governor that the economic recession was a 'natural phenomenon' which would come to an end in due course. It was a low key speech and received a low key response from the audience. But not from one member of the audience. John Horgan rose and delivered himself of another anti-Government and anti-Burt tirade; but this time he had overstepped the mark and was howled down amid cries of 'Shut up about Mr Burt and let us have politics'. Horgan, however, took part in question-time and at the end of the meeting sought to have a resolution passed in favour of his return. Burt contested this and the meeting broke up in considerable disorder with the matter unresolved.

During the very wet week which followed, both candidates held meetings on street corners and in hotels, an extraordinary departure from accepted electoral practice. On one stormy night Burt failed to turn up at the Beaufort Arms Hotel, and the fifty or so electors there promptly resolved to vote for Horgan. Horgan's committee booked the Town Hall for a second large public meeting on Saturday 28 May, only two days before the election. At this meeting 'moderation' was the key word. Horgan even delivered a policy speech in which he said that he would strive to gain justice for the working man. Hensman showed how Burt had opposed the reform of the Master and Servant Act in 1884, and how he had benefited from the Governor's patronage earlier in the year to become a trustee of the Victoria Public Library. He concluded by noting that Burt's chief supporters like George Shenton and Sir Thomas Cockburn Campbell (part-owner of the *West Australian* and a member of the Legislative Council) had 'long been opponents of responsible government'. It was a statesmanlike performance and was well-received by the audience. Even the *West Australian* could see that Horgan's candidature had to be taken seriously. In a reflective editorial the *West*'s weekly, the *Western Mail*, had sensed the meaning of the demographic changes:

> Those whose business it is to sound the feeling of the metropolitan electors in respect of the filling up of the vacancy occasioned by the resignation of Mr S. H. Parker, realize, more vividly than it has ever been realized before, how great a change the last year or two has brought about, how great a reconstitution of the community, owing to the large influx of population from the other side. Past entirely are the days when such a canvass could be made as that of the late Speaker, Sir Luke Leake, who as an election approached, personally acquainted

John Horgan: *Irish Catholic politician, 1888. He described the* **West Australian** *as a 'reptile rag', the Weld Club as a 'pot house', and Septimus Burt as 'the ideal champion of the Six Hungry Families'.*

Septimus Burt: *Anglican politician, 1888: He was supported by the* **West Australian**, *was a foundation member of the Weld Club, and believed that Horgan possessed a free flow of adjectives 'like all his countrymen'.*

12 *West Australian*, 22 May 1888; *Evening Times*, 21 and 23 May 1888; *WA Bulletin*, 19 May 1888.

201

'The State of the Poll', or 'Weight Will Tell': the Perth By-election, 1888.

with almost every elector, could speak to each as an old friend, knowing his history, knowing his views . . . the old times we repeat are past; now old associations, friendly feelings, the ties of long acquaintance, play but a small part where previously they were all powerful. Views rather than persons govern the result of an election and all sorts of new elements, all sorts of fresh combinations, all sorts of previously unknown prejudices and predilections have to be reckoned with, propitiated and satisfied. In the old days, a good and honest man whom the people knew, whose career they had watched for years, was secure against any other whom they did not know, however much more popular might be the expressed opinion of the latter. Now, on the other hand, in the capital, population and politics are in a transition state, in which the electioneer must work almost in the dark with little certainty of what result may be in store for him.[13]

Perth was seen to be the colony's blue ribbon seat and its electors were charged with the responsibility of returning a worthy representative—someone like Leake or Parker or J.G.C. Carr or Edward Scott. In short, Perth electors must elect Burt, so contended the *West Australian.* But Burt was a 'Tory in politics' at a time when Toryism should be set to one side; and Horgan lacked political experience, but his cause was good. So contended the *WA (Catholic) Record* and the *WA Bulletin.* The lines were drawn.[14]

On Monday 28 May the colony held its breath as some of the men of Perth went to the polls. There were 1775 names on the roll: 566 were freeholders, each worth £100 in freehold land; 1249 were householders who paid £10 or more annually in rent. All 1775 had resided in the colony for at least 6 months. The roll used was the 1887 one, for the updated roll for 1888 did not come into effect until 4 June, a week after the by-election. Many people did not know this and turned up to vote. When turned away some of them stayed near the Town Hall and pressured

13   *Western Mail,* 19 May 1888.
14   *West Australian,* 26 May 1888; *WA (Catholic) Record,* 26 May 1888; *WA Bulletin,* 26 May 1888.

others to vote for Horgan. The electoral roll used therefore was out of date. Many £10 householder electors had left Perth in the early months of 1888 during the economic recession. In addition some names were entered twice; and some whose names were still on the roll were no longer qualified, as the 1888 list would reveal.[15] On the morning of the poll it was drizzling and promised to be wet all day. At 10 a.m. the booths (Town Hall, Perth Boys' School, Perth Girls' School, Canning Police Station) were opened and the drenched electors made their way in. Burt's people were bedecked in red and white ribbons, while Horgan's supporters wore blue ribbons. The whips of the city's cabbies were adorned with their favourite's colours. About noon the weather cleared a little, and lunch-time voters streamed into the booths, especially the Town Hall. There they were met by canvassers, including the gigantic proprietor of the Victoria Hotel, John Guilfoyle, who insisted on roaring all day:

> Vote for Horgan, begorra, and wipe out the Six Families and the rest of their belongings.

In the afternoon Burt had a band rallying support throughout the city. The booths closed at 6 p.m. amid rumours that the police and civil servants had voted for Horgan, but that Burt had got the proxy vote and was just ahead. From 7 p.m. the crowd began to mill around the Town Hall. At 9 p.m. the doors were opened and in streamed over 1200 people. Burtites and Horganites exchanged witticisms until 9.45 p.m. when the Returning Officer rose to declare the result of the poll. As silence fell he read:

Horgan	420 votes
Burt	417 votes
Spoilt	37 votes
Total	874 votes cast

Burt had been beaten. Amid tremendous excitement the stunned Horgan rose shakily and said:

> 'I do not value the victory so much for myself as for the people.'

It was Hensman who expounded more fully the meaning of the result:

> 'This victory will go through the length and breadth of the colony and will show that the time is coming when the will of the people will prevail.'

Burt did not speak. The crowd surged from the Hall. Horgan, Jameson, Haynes and Hensman were placed in a carriage and man-dragged heroically through the main streets of Perth. It was well after midnight before silence returned to the city.

In the morning following and for weeks thereafter the people of Perth considered the meaning of their action. For conservatives like Shenton the meaning was perfectly clear: if ever a case could have been made for responsible government, it had been killed forever—no sane community would risk a parliament of Horgans. Governor Broome's response differed slightly but significantly. He reported to the Secretary of State for Colonies that the electors of Perth had rejected the claims of Mr Burt, a 'respected colonist'. Instead they had voted into office a Mr Horgan,

> a lawyer, belonging to what may be called the extreme radical party. He has been lately cast in damages in an action for libel; but continues to

---

15 *West Australian*, 31 May 1888; *Evening Times*, 28 May 1888.

deal considerably in personal abuse. His politics and conduct are scarcely such as to inspire confidence in any thinking and dispassionate mind. But he is a politician of a type and character which have to be reckoned with for he has many supporters among the working classes.[16]

Perhaps even some of Horgan's supporters would have agreed with the Governor's assessment.

Certainly Horgan's victory was regarded at the time as a turning point in the history of working men's political activity. Even the *West Australian* congratulated the workers on assuming their responsibilities as electors, though it urged them to exercise those responsibilities more wisely in the future. The Avon Valley's *Eastern Districts Chronicle* had written that:

> there has been in past years and there is even now too much of the master and bondsman style of things not only in the country districts of which it has been the curse but also in the towns, and men have been so ground down and kept under that they have been afraid to vote according to their own inclinations, but have had to follow the dictates of their masters . . .[17]

The radical Perth journal, the *WA Bulletin*, wrote:

> Even the worm will turn if trod upon and at last the artizan classes have . . . stood on their dignity with the result that for the future the "working man" must be regarded as a potent factor in all elections.[18]

And the Perth *Daily News* concluded roundly that:

> The result has forever destroyed the impression that the electorate of Perth is a "close" or "pocket" borough of the Six Families.[19]

That the election had a liberating effect on the minds of the workers, analogous to the victory of Robert Lowe in Sydney forty years previously, cannot be doubted. That the 'Six Families' had been dished forever was far more debatable.

The result of the election led to a marked estrangement of town and country. It was felt that for the first time since 1870 Perth had elected a man who could in no way be regarded as a spokesman for country as well as town. As the *Western Mail* put it:

> Mr Horgan goes into Parliament as the representative of the democratic and urban influences of the town, influences for which few of the country constituencies feel much tenderness.[20]

In this respect Western Australia was becoming more like the eastern colonies—so argued Hackett, Harper and Cockburn Campbell. Henceforth the countrymen would have to be on their toes for

> The towns have a natural advantage in the stimulation of energy, and greater vitality of political action which are the essential characteristics of concentrated population. In addition, the metropolis, being the seat of Government and the meeting place of the Legislature, is able by demonstrations of opinion and through its more immediate intercourse with its members, to quadruple its ordinary influence.

In short, henceforth the influence of the metropolis would have to be contained. The countrymen must form political organizations and otherwise participate more fully in political life. The city had fallen to

---

16 *Governors' Despatches*, Despatch No. 141, p.371, 30 May 1888. In the same Despatch Broome warned the Secretary of State to deal 'most carefully with the settlement of the Responsible Government question'.
17 *Eastern Districts Chronicle*, 26 May 1888.
18 *WA Bulletin*, 2 June 1888.
19 *Daily News*, 30 May 1888.   20 *Western Mail*, 2 June 1888.

mob-rule and could no longer be accepted as the premier constituency.[21] The Bunbury *Southern Advertiser* made a clear connection between the result of the election and the forthcoming discussions over the nature of self-government:

> we believe that increased country representation would have a check on the aggrandisement of those more populous parts where so much money has already been spent and prevent the evil of centralization which would seek to advance the Capital City . . . at the expense of the country districts, which latter are really the backbone and mainstay of the Colony.[22]

In the past the country districts had been relatively indifferent to responsible government. But Horgan's return acted as a catalyst. By late 1888 when the Constitution Bill was debated, the country districts knew what kind of constitution they wanted and especially were they determined to prevent the political dominance of Perth.

Proclaiming the new Constitution

Between October 1888 and May 1889 the Legislative Council debated the contents of a Constitution Bill and an Electoral Bill. When Edward Scott, the Member for Perth, attempted to get a fourth seat for the city he was roundly abused by country members who formed a majority of the elected representatives, and some Government members who wanted 'a decent respectable conservative bill'.[23] Edward Keane, Scott's city colleague (after the January 1889 elections at which Horgan was defeated), was moved to comment that

> when the members of Perth or Fremantle attempted to get anything for either of these two towns, it had become the fashion for country members to set upon them.[24]

Metropolitan representation in the new Legislative Assembly was one-fifth of the elected members, whereas in the 1870 Act it had been one-third. Nor were the urban MP's able to secure the abolition of a property qualification for the members of the new Legislative Assembly. The merchant/pastoralist William Thorley Loton, who a decade later would become Mayor of Perth, said roundly that

> it is possible that people in the towns of Perth and Fremantle . . . may be opposed to a property qualification; but the country at large is in favour.[25]

And so it went on. An elected upper house was rejected, at least for six years or until the population reached 60 000. Scott and Parker tried unsuccessfully to get the franchise householder qualification reduced from £10 to £5, and the freehold qualification from £100 to £50. When the urban MP's sought a triennial parliament, the countrymen opted for five years. Cockburn Campbell, quoting Lord Bryce, traced the degeneracy of American politics to the frequency of elections. The 'martyrdom of public life' he said.

> would become so unsupportable that the better class of politicians would drop out of it, and their place would be taken by men of coarser fibre and less scrupulousness.

21 *Victorian Express*, 2 June 1888.
22 *Southern Advertiser*, 10 July 1888.
23 Attorney General C. N. Warton in *WAPD* Vol. 14 (o.s.), 1888, p.224.
24 *WAPD* Vol. 15 (o.s.), 1889, p.136.   25 *WAPD* Vol. 15 (o.s.), 1889, p.46.

Harry Venn, the member for Wellington, said roundly:

> I am not in favour of short parliaments. They lead to political agitation and turmoil.[26]

Both sides gave a little and the Constitution Bill included provision for four year parliaments! When the townsmen sought to extend the franchise to lodgers, who included 'all respectable mechanics and workingmen', the country members saw this as an attempt to strengthen the town vote. John Forrest spoke against 'revolutionising' the electoral system in this way.[27] The reform was squeezed through, but when the Electoral Bill was considered the lodger franchise was so hedged around with residence qualifications and separate forms that it was rendered inoperative.

It must not be thought that Keane and Scott were at all radical. They were far less so than Horgan. But in the minds of the countrymen the city had become identified with mobocracy and radicalism and anything that emanated from it was thought to be bad. The constitution which emerged from these discussions was deeply conservative, far more so than any of those in force in the eastern colonies of Australia. The Constitution and Electoral Acts of 1890 formed the framework of political life in Western Australia in the 1890s and early 1900s. They gave the 'sandgropers'—the 'ancient colonists'—a firm defence against the winds of change which were shortly to blow in strongly from the east. Poor Horgan. All he had achieved was to alert his enemies to the dangers of democracy, and to give them experience in combating the forces of change. Burt's, not his, was the political voice of the 1890s. And he died in 1908, a bitter old man, knowing that the 'Six Families', the Weld Club, and the *West Australian* had gone from strength to strength.

THE FIRST LEGISLATIVE COUNCIL UNDER RESPONSIBLE GOVERNMENT.

26 *WAPD* Vol. 15 (o.s.), 1889, p.38, 31 respectively.
27 *WAPD* Vol. 15 (o.s.), 1889, pp.142–4.

On 21 October 1890 the new Constitution of Western Australia was inaugurated—henceforth the day would be a public holiday known as Proclamation Day. The first Proclamation Day—21 October 1890—was celebrated in Perth. It was a day to remember. Despite the inclement weather the town was gay and colourful. The main streets were decorated with small banners suspended by ropes attached to painted masts. At the Town Hall corner there was a triumphal arch of palms, ferns, eucalypts and other foliage, and decorated with flowers, flags and inscriptions. The four faces of the arch were inscribed 'God Bless Our Western Land', 'Success to the New Constitution', 'Welcome Thrice Governor' (a tribute to Robinson who had brought back the new constitution), and 'Thanks to our Delegates'. A similar arch at the corner of Hay and William Streets bore the following inscriptions: 'God Save Our Queen', 'God Bless the Prince of Wales', 'Advance United Australia', and 'Union is Strength'. There were other arches at the Perth Railway Station, where Robinson had arrived the previous day. In Barrack Street below St George's Terrace, the Swan River Rowing Club and the WA Rowing Club had erected two more arches decorated with flowers, flags, shields, crossed oar-blades, and surmounted by a boat. The buildings of St George's Terrace and Hay Street were also decorated with foliage and flowers, flags and shields. The National Bank had the letters 'VR' over the porch, and above this the inscription 'Progress and Prosperity', in white on a red ground. From the roof of the Union Bank floated three Union Jacks. The Bank's balcony was draped with orange and red flags, the centre having a swan and two clasped hands. The WA Bank was smothered with whole palms and two enormous festoons of greenery knotted at intervals with everlastings. The NSW Bank had along the front '1890' with a swan between, in black on an orange ground. The Weld Club offered a 'charmingly draped verandah', and the AMP Offices deserved commendation, if not description. Shenton's cornerstore had an artistically decorated front, lots of foliage and flowers and two inscriptions: 'Prosperity to our Colony' and 'Welcome to our New Constitution'. Somewhat inexplicably Snowball and Coy, which was to prosper in the 1890s, surmounted their inscription 'Success to our Constitution' with a fine picture of St George and the Dragon. Courthope and Drummond's Offices (agents for The Phoenix Insurance Coy) bore the remarkable inscription 'Arise West Australia from the Hashes of the Past', but wit like this was unusual on the day. A streamer across Hay Street (between Mrs Wimbridge's coach factory and J. R. North's store) bore the words 'Australia Rejoices Today', which may have been true but only the City of Adelaide sent a telegram of best wishes. But the most striking display was that of Edward Keane's offices in St George's Terrace. Keane, the Member for Perth, director of the Midland Railway Coy, director of the newly formed Perth Waterworks Coy, and a thoroughly enterprising citizen, had employed Mr J. M. Lapsley to decorate his offices. Lapsley had excelled himself. Besides being festooned with native evergreens and adorned with flags, two stars were formed on the walls with picks and shovels. On the outer side of each was a wheelbarrow, over a pick and shovel, and between them ran a miniature pilot engine on rails, bearing the words 'Walkaway, E. K., No. 1' in gilt letters on its green side, and in front of these the inscription 'E. K. Midland Railway' was formed with gas jets for illumination. Beneath this device were the words 'At Last She Moves', and on the ground against the wall were stationed a number of pipes similar to those

Arouse, Westralia!
(Written for Proclamation Day, October 21 1890.)

Arouse, Westralia! Awake
From thy 'Swan's nest among the reeds';
Cast they broad shadow on the lake,
And strongly glide where Fortune Leads!

Let eaglets o'er their quarry scream,
The Vulture's brood may tear and slay,
Thou wakest from prophetic dream
Of offspring goodlier than they.

Thy sturdy cygnets from they side
With glancing feet scull fast and far,
They press their bosoms to the tide,
And stretch bold wings beyond the bar.

Their pennons with the breezes float,
And follow fast where Fortune leads,
Till by green holms and bays remote
Are found new nests among the reeds.

Their song (for onset, not for dirge)
Shall flood the creeks of broader ways,
And, with the music of the surge,
Swell the full chant of better days.

Thy seas have pearls; from reef and mine
Flash jewels and the pride of gold;
But goodlier far those sons of thine,
Famous in story yet untold.

God and the Right thy watchword be;
Patient—Yet strong to do and dare;
And thine Assessors, brave and free,
Labour and Vigilance and Prayer.

Henry Clay

Western Australia's Proclamation Day, 21 October 1890: 'At Last She Moves', thanks to Edward Keane?

being used by Keane in the construction of the Perth Waterworks. Passers-by could be forgiven for thinking that the colony moved at last because of Mr Keane and Mr Keane only. A year later Keane became Mayor of the City of Perth. He had caught perfectly the mood of the people.

The great day began well. If the wind was high, the showers were light and would in no way interfere with the proceedings. First there were the religious services. The new St George's Cathedral, designed in confused gothic by the aging Edmund Blackett, was the pride and joy of the Anglican congregation. It had not been completed in time for the Queen's Jubilee celebrations in June 1887, but now it would be the centrepiece of the morning's celebrations, for the Governor himself would be in attendance. For the occasion the interior had been decorated to the design of J. Talbot Hobbs, then at the commencement of his illustrious career as architect and soldier. He had erected a chancel screen of greenery and everlastings, 25 feet in height, surmounted in the centre by a magnificent cross of lavender, banksia flowers, shields, flags, wreaths, stars, sacred monograms . . . and then the glitter of the many uniforms, the colours of the ladies' dresses, the white robes of the choristers, and the varied tints of the East window in the background—'all served to enhance the beauty and impressiveness of a scene which will live in the memory of West Australians'. His Excellency arrived punctually at 9 o'clock. There was a little unsteadiness at the commencement of the Processional Hymn, but after a few bars all went excellently. The great features of the service were the Te Deum (set to music by Mr W. Stephens), a Proclamation Hymn (written by the Registrar General, Mr W. A. Gale, and composed by Mr W. Stephens), and the Domini Salvam fae reginam sung in the garrison chapels of England. 'The whole rendering of the service would have done the utmost credit to any cathedral in Australia.'

But well before the Anglicans fell to their knees in praise of the coming colony, the Roman Catholics had celebrated a Solemn High

208

Mass in the presence of His Lordship Bishop Gibney. A full choir sang Erst's Mass in A, which was then a popular work on days of high festivity. The service was over by 8.30. Perhaps Gibney, no lover of Anglicans and Englishmen, was a little less enthusiastic about Proclamation Day than was Bishop Parry. After all, many of Gibney's flock were not eligible to vote at the forthcoming general election for the Legislative Assembly. His solicitor, John Horgan, had tried to make the new Constitution one in which Roman Catholics could participate fully. But he had failed. Still, the Church must look to the future and at 9.30 the boys and girls from his schools in Perth, Fremantle, Guildford and Subiaco were marshalled on the hill of St Mary's Cathedral, provided with banners and streamers, and given directions for the march on Perth.

Back down in St George's Terrace, opposite Government House, the Rev. David Shearer preached to the Presbyterian Congregation, after singing the Anthem 'The Righteous Shall Be Glad'. Shearer's address was brief and to the point. He thanked

> Almighty God for His goodness to this Colony, in crowning with success the efforts put forth to obtain the privilege of self-government . . . Let us remember, however, that although we pass today from one form of Government to another, we still remain as much as ever the loyal subjects of our Gracious Queen Victoria . . . Our prayer now should be that God will raise up amongst us, for the Government of this Colony, men who will honour Him, guard the sanctity of the Lord's Day, and make His Word the rule of their lives in public and private. Those that honour God, He will honour. Righteousness exalteth a nation; the act of the rulers will be the act of the Colony; and God blesses or punishes nations for their public acts. The Lord prosper this Colony.

Further west in St George's Terrace, the Rev. E. Tremayne Dunstan delivered a similar message in the Trinity Congregational Church. His large congregation had already sung the 'Old Hundredth' and 'God bless our Native Land' when Dunstan, a great hater of Roman Catholics, expressed his hope that the note of thanksgiving struck that morning might be the dominant note of the national life.

Round the corner in William Street, in packed Wesley Church, the Rev. J. Young Simpson rose above the mass of lilies and palms to preach to his text—Isaiah 58:12, 'Thou shalt raise up the foundations of many generations.' 'Today,' he told them,

> We feel our obligation to shape society and its institutions by that ideal whose outlines and plan are drawn from the Gospels of our Blessed Lord . . . The faith of Christ can alone deal with and restrain and exalt, the mighty passionate life of these Australian lands.

What was also needed was the institution of the 'family home',

> a foundation which ensures the surest resistance to the vices which dense populations encourage. It heals the disorders of the prodigal. It forestalls crimes that the law is helpless to forbid. It opens Bibles . . .

And a third foundation was an educational system worthy of the colony: for 'the hearts of the children—so tender in impression, yet so mighty in the germination of their energies—are foundations of the land'. It was indeed a memorable sermon on a memorable day. But it was time for the churchgoers and their more numerous non-church-going brethren to gather for the grand procession.

By 10.30 all was in readiness for a start. The children from Fremantle, Guildford and Newcastle had arrived by train and were now in line with their Perth cousins carrying banners of every colour of the rainbow. Behind the children came the Volunteer Band, still under the baton of a member of the Bryan family. Then came over 200 Volunteers, mounted infantry and cadets. Sandwiched between the Volunteers and the temperance societies, the Hibernian Society and the several Protestant lodges, were the Fremantle and Perth fire brigades. Then came the Sons of Australia Benefit Society, almost as old as the colony itself. Members of the Perth Working Men's Association walked with them. The Swan River Mechanics' Institute had lost its separate identity and was not represented in the procession. Senior civil servants, bankers and merchants came next, followed by the councillors of Guildford, Fremantle and Perth. They in their turn were followed by the clergy of all denominations, including the Bishops Parry, Gibney and Salvado, the last-named having come down from New Norcia especially for the occasion. Then marched six selected 'old colonists', the equivalent of the Boer War veterans in the 1960s: F. F. Armstrong, T. Drummond, J. Nairn, Richard Gallop, Walter Padbury and Bernard Smith. Behind them came the members of the Legislative and Executive Councils, several more old colonists being in their ranks. And Sir Henry Wrensfordsley, the Acting Chief Justice, Judge Stone, Dr Scott, Sir Thomas Cockburn Campbell and Stephen Henry Parker, together with the Perth Town Clerk, Mr W. E. Victor, brought up the rear. The procession was 600 yards long, far and away the longest in the colony's history. The general public and the children of the government schools occupied balconies (allowed since 1885), verandahs and every open space in Hay Street, St George's Terrace, and Barrack Street heading down to the Recreation Ground. On the Recreation Ground the marchers from the senior civil servants back to Parker and Campbell took their places with the Governor in the Pavilion. Between the marchers and the general public, nearly 6000 citizens and children heard (or at least saw) Sir Henry Wrensfordsley read the Proclamation. Governor Robinson called for three cheers for the Queen, the Artillery fired the Royal Salute, and the schoolchildren, under the baton of Mr Andrew Boult, sang a verse of 'God Save the Queen'. After this the band played 'Unfurl the Flag', and the Union Jack was run up. Western Australia was an independent, self-governing colony.

The speechmaking went on for an hour or so, after which the Governor, the members of the Executive Council and other gentlemen were entertained to a cold luncheon at the Perth Yacht Club. The 2500 children set off to the Domain where they demolished 3000 lb of cake, 3000 sausage rolls, seven hogsheads of ginger beer, 3500 oranges, and 1 cwt of sweets. There were games, swings, a swingboat, a circus and exhibitions of skating down a toboggan slide. Meantime, back on the west end of the Recreation Ground, wave upon wave of citizens attacked a 300 ft-long table piled high with vegetables and potatoes, beer from four hogsheads, and the meat of an ox, four sheep, three pigs, as well as 300 loaves of bread, 600 lb of cake and 80 lb of cheese. The ox had been cooking since 8 p.m. the previous evening under the careful and experienced eye of old John Liddelow. After lunch the People's Sports were held: allcomers, maiden, quarter-horse, hurdle, old man's obstacle, and bicycle races (the last from George Shenton's house at Crawley, round Mounts Bay Road to the Recreation Ground), climbing the greasy pole, and catching a pig with greasy tail. There was also an Aboriginal race but it elicited little interest. The prizes ranged from 10s to £2. 'The

races were watched with interest and enthusiasm, and the gayest good humour as a rule prevailed, although in some instances there was rough behaviour, wholly inexcusable.'

In the evening central Perth became, for the first time, a city of light, as business places and private residences were illuminated with Chinese lanterns and transparencies, and there were features like Mr Lapsley's illuminated fountain in Barrack Street. The fire brigades led a torch-light procession, and public and private parties and balls were held throughout the city. A 'people's ball' was held in the Mechanics' Institute Hall, while the people who mattered attended a formal ball in the Town Hall. For the publicans of Perth, Proclamation Day was a bonanza, and so it continued to be up to the Great War.

But by the time of the Great War, Proclamation Day had undergone several transformations. From the early 1890s Perth was populated by 't'othersiders' who cared little for Proclamation Day and who, when they thought about the constitution, regarded it less an achievement than a hindrance to a better life in the West. By 1894 the *West Australian* observed with some alarm that Proclamation Day was being taken over by the Eight Hours Association: 'The local Eight Hours gathering is fast growing to be an important event in many respects.' That year thirteen societies took part in a procession and then took part in sports, sideshows, an art union drawing of prizes, followed by a 'cold collation' in the Mechanics' Institute. But the 'Proclamation' side of the Day's celebrations was being lost. The *West Australian* wrote that:

> The character and ambitions of a nation may justly be judged by its commemorations, and when it is careless about those it is to be feared that its spirit or its public feeling is decaying.

In 1895 the Eight Hours meeting was addressed by the fiery Irish leader, Michael Davitt, on the 'Question of the Living Wage'. This was not what the gentry wished to hear on Proclamation Day, for a 'living wage' could threaten the quest for 'internal peace'. But the WA Turf Club meeting on Proclamation Day holiday was proving to be extremely popular. In 1898 the *West Australian* devoted a half-column to the Eight Hours meeting, and two and a half columns to the race meeting, including an extensive coverage of the dresses of the gentry ladies:

> Lady Forrest, silk in a small brown check, with blue chiffon epaulettes, a draped front and peculiarly shaped belt cut into a sharp peak . . .

And in the following year the workers of Perth and Fremantle fell out and held separate demonstrations. Perhaps all would be well after all. Then in 1901 Henry Daglish, the leader of the Labor Party, speaking on the same platform as the Premier, told the crowd that his Party's 'aim' was 'not to pull down the higher classes but to uplift the lower'. Thus even as early as 1904 the *West Australian* knew that the dual celebration of Proclamation Day and Eight Hours Day was 'not incongruous'. In 1905 the *West* announced that the Eight Hours movement transcended the 'political ebb and flow'. By 1910 the workers of Perth and Fremantle had buried their old feud and were marching shoulder to shoulder again. But the Day was now an anodyne entertainment only, close in spirit and meaning to the old Foundation Day celebrations:

> Although Monday's holiday primarily honoured a turning point in the history of the state, its importance in that direction was almost forgotten in the glamour cast over the city by the great festival which annually presents the happiest and most potential features of manual labour.

In 1919 the Day became Labour Day and was celebrated 'in customary style'.[28]

'The air in Perth is full of the yellow fever'

What was it like to arrive in goldrush Perth? Of the many contemporary observers and participants perhaps none put it as well as Albert Calvert, an experienced explorer, author, and mining entrepreneur, who visited Western Australia for the fourth time in the summer of 1895–96. First there was the port of Albany, 'hot with the press of the inrush of people'. Then there was the crowd at Albany's railway station, 'rushing about in search of luggage and a window seat in the stuffy train', everyone 'signalling wildly with small branches cut from the green shrubs' in a desperate attempt to ward off 'the persistent attention of the myriads of flies'. With the packed passengers sitting on each other's laps, 'or like trussed fowls, without room to move their elbows', the train made its 'unlovely journey' to Perth 300 miles away. At the Katanning refreshment station 'our supper . . . is neither grateful nor comforting'. At Beverley it was even worse. 'Every room at the hotel shows traces of having been used as a sleeping apartment. A few people are still wrapped in their blankets, others are waiting their turn at the washbowl, and the bar is full.' Later that day the train steamed into Perth Central Station. But in Perth 'the hotels are besieged; the boarding houses are crammed'. But the people who keep the boarding houses are ingenious:

> They began by 'double-banking' the beds in each room, and all the wire mattress makers worked night and day to meet orders. Then, when

[28] *Daily News*, 23 October 1890; *West Australian*, 20 and 22 October 1890; *West Australian*, 20 and 22 October 1894, 23 October 1895, 23 October 1898, 24 October 1899, 22 October 1901, 24 October 1904, 23 October 1905, 25 October 1911, 27 October 1919.

from four to eight beds jostle each other for standing place in an attic, the verandahs and odd corners become resting places, (as do) the backyards . . .

Out in the streets

> The air in Perth is full of the yellow fever. Its germs, in the shape of talk of reefs, leases, claims, yields, trial crushings, camels, syndicates, stocks and Company flotations, are as thick as a London fog. In the smoking room, the bar, the club, the exchange, the bank, and even in the drawing room, the chorus goes up in praise of Mammon, of the bright yellow metal that is to be won . . . It is impossible to speak for two minutes with anybody, from a Cabinet Minister to a cow-minder, without referring to the omnipotent subject that lies closest to the hearts of all. The bar tender, as he passes a drink towards you with one hand, produces from under the counter a handful of specimens from a claim in which he is interested; the barber pauses with the razor poised in mid air, to offer you, at a price, his share in some mine of which he is part proprietor, and every railway porter and cab driver has either been on the fields or is on the point of starting out to make his fortune there . . . The few men in Perth who have no properties to dispose of, are touts for those who have, and every shop window in the town contains its complement of specimens of the coveted metal . . . the whole of the business of Perth is in one way or another connected with or resulting from the goldfields, and . . . every businessman in the city is bound, body and soul, to the new industry.

Once outfitted, especially with 'the modest canvas water-bag', it was back to the railway station and away to the fields. And then, for many, it was back to Perth and its suburbs.[29]

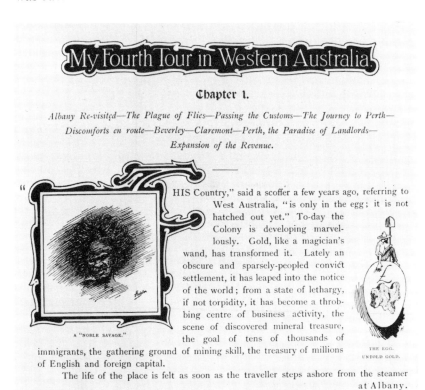

My Fourth Tour in Western Australia.

Chapter 1.

Albany Re-visited—The Plague of Flies—Passing the Customs—The Journey to Perth—Discomforts en route—Beverley—Claremont—Perth, the Paradise of Landlords—Expansion of the Revenue.

A "NOBLE SAVAGE."

"THIS Country," said a scoffer a few years ago, referring to West Australia, "is only in the egg; it is not hatched out yet." To-day the Colony is developing marvellously. Gold, like a magician's wand, has transformed it. Lately an obscure and sparsely-peopled convict settlement, it has leaped into the notice of the world; from a state of lethargy, if not torpidity, it has become a throbbing centre of business activity, the scene of discovered mineral treasure, the goal of tens of thousands of immigrants, the gathering ground of mining skill, the treasury of millions of English and foreign capital.

THE EGG.
UNTOLD GOLD.

The life of the place is felt as soon as the traveller steps ashore from the steamer at Albany.

---

29 A. F. Calvert *My Fourth Tour in Western Australia*, 1897, pp.10, 14, 20.

The Hon. W. G. Brookman, MLC, Mayor of Perth, 1900–01: 'I will make this city a fairer Athens and a freer Rome.'

One month's output from Brookman's Great Boulder Mine.

Winning Life's lottery: 't'othersiders' and 'sandgropers'

In the hectic economic life of Perth in the 1890s and early 1900s fortunes were won and lost in gold mining by many men, but none quite on the scale of William Gordon Brookman. Brookman was born in South Australia where in the 1880s he owned a jam and pickle manufacturing business. In 1890, as a result of strikes and down-turn in the economy, his company collapsed and in 1892 he was declared bankrupt. His brother, an affluent merchant, sent him to the eastern goldfields of Western Australia—he reached Kalgoorlie in mid-1893 a few weeks after Paddy Hannan's discoveries. The Brookman syndicate pegged many leases and floated several companies in Australia and in Britain. In 1895 Brookman went to London. By then he was a very wealthy man, and when he returned to Perth in December 1896—travelling by private train from Fremantle—he was director of thirty mining companies. He may also have been a millionaire. Certainly he successfully speculated in urban real estate, and in the grand manner owned a country estate (at Cannington), a seaside cottage at Mandurah, a yacht, a landau and a motorcar. His huge home in East Perth on Adelaide Terrace, complete with liveried servants, was, as his biographer puts it: 'the delight of goldrush immigrants and the envy of the old families'.[30] While thought by goldfield people to be an opponent of John Forrest's Government, Brookman did not accede to popular demand that he stand for the mayoralty of Perth until Alexander Forrest's term of office had expired. In August 1900 Brookman entered the Legislative Council as the Member for Metropolitan Province, and in November the same year he won the mayoralty of Perth, despite bitter opposition from many older families who raised the matter of Brookman's Adelaide bankruptcy and questioned whether the Brookmans were indeed married. Brookman defeated Quinlan, the favourite of the 'ancient colonists', by 4150 votes to 2161.[31] Brookman's election-leaflet was one of the longest ever presented to the electors. It was also one of the most reasoned—indeed many of the things he advocated, such as a bridge over the Narrows, Riverside Drive on the city foreshore, and deep sewerage, came into being in the course of the twentieth century.[32] In January 1901, on the occasion of the celebrations of the inauguration of the Commonwealth, Brookman concluded his speech with the noble words: 'Citizens of Perth, follow me and I will make this city a fairer Athens and a freer Rome.' Some, perhaps many, of the ratepayers thought that Brookman would put £20,000 of his own money into municipal improvements in his first year. But alas, his first year as Mayor was also his last.

By the middle of 1901 Brookman's financial empire was wrecked by the collapse of the London stock exchange. He was removed from his London directorates, and on 26 June he resigned the mayoralty with little achieved other than a new loan for the wood-blocking of footpaths. He had rarely attended Council meetings; his Council was both inexperienced and divided; and he was without an experienced town clerk. He was also faced with the unrelenting hostility of the old families

---

[30]   *ADB* Vol. 7, 1979—the entry is by R. O. Giles.
[31]   PCC Minute Book, 19 November 1900.
[32]   It is thought that the leaflet was composed by F. C. Vosper, the t'othersider editor of Perth's *Sunday Times*.

of Western Australia. He retired to Mandurah to live, and began to sell his Perth and suburban real estate in an effort to meet his debts. In 1904 he left Western Australia, and in 1910 he died of tuberculosis in his father's home in Adelaide. He was 51 years of age. His estate in South Australia was valued for probate at £7 10s and in Western Australia at £127. In his time he had established over fifty mines, with an investment value of £35 million.[33]

Left: Brookman's residence, 'Great Boulder', in Adelaide Terrace, 1900. Top: **Cottages in East Perth, 1900**: part of Brookman's real estate empire.

If Brookman was the prince of 't'othersider' mining magnates and urban speculators, there were many more knights and barons. Another who represented the Metropolitan Province in the Legislative Council (from 1903 to 1908) was Zebina Lane. Lane was born in Bendigo, the cradle of Australian mining. As early as 1870 he was a mine manager in the town. Then for a time he worked at Kyneton for the Intercolonial Smelting Coy, overseeing the smelting of lead and silver. Later he joined the rush to Broken Hill where he managed Broken Hill North and several other companies. He became the town's first mayor. In October 1893 he responded to the call of the golden west, and by the end of 1896 he had visited London twice in connection with the flotation of several mining companies, including the Great Boulder, the Perseverence (which he owned) and Boulder South. In 1899 he also leased a coalfield and floated in London the Collie Pty Coal Mining Company. As Newcastle supplies were wayward, and as the burgeoning railway system and the several power plants needed coal, Lane's investment was shrewdly calculated.[34] So too were his land speculations in Perth. From the late 1890s, his company, Zebina Lane and Coy, was rapidly developing the land in the northern part of East Perth called originally location 4. By 1904 the Norwood, Westralia and Zebina estates had been opened up between Summers Street, East Parade, Gardiner Street and Joel Street. One of the streets he engagingly called Zebina Street. Many of the small houses

---

[33] W. E. Bold 'Civic Reminiscences 1896–1943', unpublished typescript, 1944; Thiel & Coy *Twentieth Century Impressions of WA*; ADB-Vol. 7, entry for Brookman; PCC Minute Books, 1900–01.

[34] *Twentieth Century Impressions of WA*, p.331, 318—includes photo of Lane; Bolton and Mozley, p.105.

215

were sold, but even in 1904 construction was still going on and he was renting out seventeen houses (two of them in Adelaide Terrace), as well as a hospital in Stirling Street, a shop in Summers Street, and offices in Howick Street. His properties were to the north of the polluted main drain and the sites of noxious industries, so he attracted a 'better class' of tenant. The smallest of his houses were occupied by a house-gardener, a printing hand and an iron foundry worker, but most of his houses were rented by clerks and lesser Goverment officials, a journalist, a grocer, a builder, a coach-builder, a spirit merchant, a financier and a lawyer, with the two latter paying high rents, as did Mrs Mouritz who ran the private hospital.[35] Lane had diversified his interests sufficiently to weather the stock exchange collapses and he lived in comfort until his death in Perth in 1912.

Not all the men who made money from gold and invested in Perth real estate were from the eastern colonies. The British not only played an important investment role in the mining industry,[36] but some also came to Perth and became prominent urban landowners and politicians. One such man was Alfred E. Morgans, a Welsh-born engineer who had spent eighteen years working for British gold mining companies in southern Mexico. Morgans came to Western Australia in March 1896 at the age of 46. Within a year his company owned the fabulously wealthy Westralia Mount Morgan Gold Mining Company, on the Coolgardie fields. He was a powerful advocate of free enterprise, and strove unsuccessfully to persuade the Forrest Government to let men like himself provide economic infrastructure like railway lines, waterworks and roads. The United States was his model. These views were popular among the mining fraternity and in April 1897 he was elected MP for Coolgardie, which position he held until 1904. In the period of political instability following Forrest's departure for federal politics, Morgans became Premier of WA for a month. From the turn of the century he lived in a large double-storied house in St George's Terrace, directly opposite Government House. With an annual rateable value of £300 it was one of the most valuable properties in Perth's most prized residential street. Morgans also built shops and offices in central Hay Street (next to the Metropole Hotel) and in Barrack Street north of Murray Street. Occupied by merchants, tailors (including Parker & Coy, one of the largest tailors in Perth), a saddler, jewellers, grocers (Gilbert and Sharp), restaurants, Wigg & Coy's publishing house, the General Electric Coy and Lindrum's sporting goods and rooms, these properties netted Morgans a large rental. They also won him some trouble when in 1900 some were condemned by the city's health inspectors. He retired from public life in 1904 but lived in comfort in Perth until his death in 1933.[37]

While such men as Brookman, Lane and Morgans played extremely important roles in the redevelopment of Perth in the 1890s and 1900s, it is interesting to note that in the three major cyclopaedias published in this period almost half the biographical entries are of men—women appear only in occasional family photographs—who were in Western Australia before the Murchison and Eastern Goldfields were opened

[35] C. T. Stannage, unpublished computer printout of 'Owners of Perth Property 1884–1904', based on PCC ratebooks.

[36] See J. W. McCarty 'British Investment in Western Australian Goldmining 1894–1914', *University Studies in History* Vol. 4, No. 1, 1961–62, pp.7–32.

[37] Kimberly, pp.218–20; *Twentieth Century Impressions of WA*, pp.33, 229; Bolton and Mozley, p.136; Stannage printout 'Owners of Perth Property'.

up.[38] Perhaps this even under estimates the role of the pre-rush entrepreneurs in the growth and rebuilding and economic life of Perth in these years.

Before the goldrushes of the 1890s George Shenton was probably the wealthiest man in Western Australia, with a large merchandising and pastoral empire. When he died in 1909 it is likely that this Westralian-born entrepreneur was still the State's wealthiest man. Shenton was Mayor of Perth for most of the 1880s. In the 1890s he was Colonial Secretary in Forrest's first ministry and then became president of the Legislative Council, which position he held until 1906. Powerful in the political, economic and social life of Perth, Shenton was poised to take full advantage of the gold discoveries. In 1893 he was the leading member of the syndicate which sent L. A. Menzies to the eastern goldfields. Menzies discovered a rich field, which they called the Lady Shenton (George had been knighted in 1893). Shenton's Lady Shenton and Gold Estates Mining Companies had produced three tons of gold by 1901, a good result at about £3 12s an ounce. Indeed £104,000 had been paid in dividends to the holders of the £1 shares. But this was only one way in which Shenton benefited from the goldrushes, for he also held the agency for the Glasgow Nobel Explosive Company, the most important provider of explosives for the goldmining industry.[39] He also bought urban real estate in gold towns, and his family carried on merchandising for prospectors and mining companies as they had done (and continued to do) for pastoral and farming interests. This explains why in the 1890s George Shenton could exercise a plural vote in nearly all electorates in the colony. In fact the Yilgarn (Southern Cross) constituency roll in 1894 had almost as many old families' names on it as it had miners' names. Shenton also prospered as companies of which he was a director or shareholder prospered during the rush and its aftermath. His Lloyds Insurance agency benefited from the increased flow of shipping through Fremantle, and his Singapore trading business with the large steamship company Trinder Anderson and Coy prospered greatly in the 1890s.[40] As will be shown, the Perth Gas Company strengthened its monopolistic

The Lady Shenton Mine at Menzies, on the eastern goldfields, 1890s.

---

[38] The three books are: Kimberly *History of Western Australia: a Narrative of her Past with Biographies of her Leading Men*, 1897; Thiel & Coy *Twentieth Century Impressions of WA*, 1901; and Battye *Cyclopaedia of WA*, 2 vols., 1912–13.
[39] See *Twentieth Century Impressions of WA*, p.506.
[40] *Twentieth Century Impressions of WA*, p.505.

Sir George Shenton, 'ancient colonist' investor and philanthropist: also known as *'Warwick the Kingmaker'.*

Shenton's 'Crawley Park': 'this mansion is one of the finest in the colony'.

position in the 1890s, providing gas and electricity to vastly increased numbers of domestic premises and business houses, as well as to the Perth City Council.

Shenton was also a director and shareholder of the WA Bank. The WA Bank, although in keen competition with three eastern colonial and two British banks, increased its share of the total trading business from 30% to 40% between 1892 and 1901, and quadrupled its assets; and as late as 1911 it was in almost as strong a position. Between 1901 and 1911 it increased its paid up capital from £100,000 to £250,000. Throughout the 1890s and 1900s it returned between 17½% and 20% half yearly dividends, double those of the other banks. It handled half the gold and coin in WA, and it took up half the Government securities issued in the greatest period of expansion in the colony's history.[41] Shenton and several other members of old WA families profited greatly from their bank investments. Shenton was also chairman of the local boards of the Commercial Assurance Company and the Colonial Mutual Life Assurance Company, the latter being one of the big four operating in Western Australia.

Shenton also profited from the boom in Perth real estate from the mid-1890s. In the 1870s Shenton owned not only F11 and 12 in William Street, from where his merchant business was conducted, but he also had a warehouse in Bazaar Street on the river, a few cottages in Roe Street, and many blocks of land in the northern part of the town. In the 1880s he lived in the Terrace, but he had also bought land on the river at Crawley, adding to it in the 1890s. It was on this land that he erected

a beautiful residence, Crawley Park . . . Surrounded by 200 acres, well laid out, this mansion is one of the finest in the colony.[42]

In addition he bought the Nedlands Estate in 1893.

In the 1870s the Shenton family had let seven houses and one shop in Barrack and Goderich (Murray) Streets on Q17 in central Perth, just

41 *Statistical Registers of Western Australia,* 1897, 1901, 1911.
42 Kimberly, p.12.

*The **Western Australian Bank**, a **Shenton** interest: 20% half-yearly dividends throughout the goldrushes.*

north of the Town Hall. His tenants were a dressmaker, a carpenter, a shoemaker, two general dealers, a grocer and a painter (William Drabble, who became a large hardware businessman during the gold rushes). In the 1880s the value of this land increased but several of the 1870s tenants were still in occupation, although most of the premises were now identified as shops with houses attached. George Drabble had joined his brother William on the site. In the early and mid-1890s the Shentons sold this valuable block. George Shenton also sold F19/20 in central Barrack Street which he had leased at a profit to rival merchants J. H. Monger and J. F. Read in the 1870s and 1880s. In the late 1890s he sold his houses in Roe Street, but he invested in more land in the growing north ward area and in 1904 was leasing six houses in Lincoln Street. But his most valuable property in 1904, as in the 1870s, was the block of land running down William Street between Hay and Murray Streets. In that year the buildings housed thirty tenants (including his brother Ernest) in shops and offices with an annual rateable value in excess of £3500, compared with less than £300 in 1889.[43] In the late 1880s John Horgan had described Shenton as 'Warwick the Kingmaker'. By the early 1900s there were grounds for believing that Shenton had made himself King. Perhaps it was fortunate for the people of Perth that Shenton was also a profoundly religious and philanthropic man who returned much to the community which had made him and his family so wealthy. In 1909 his quest for internal peace came to an end. His estate was valued at over £200,000, larger even than Alexander Forrest's. He and his fellow WA entrepreneurs had weathered the storm of the goldrushes and guided the State into calmer waters. The old order had not changed, giving place to new.[44] Shenton knew that God fulfilled himself in many ways; but he

43 Stannage 'Owners of Perth Property'.
44 Compare A. F. Calvert *My Fourth Tour in Western Australia*, 1897, p.4: 'The old order is quickly changing and giving place to the new.' Also Tennyson 'le Morte d' Arthur'. Shenton's Will shows metropolitan real estate valued at £120,000. His WA Bank shares were valued at £16,000, and his Perth Gas Coy shares at £5600.

also destroyed the business and private papers accumulated over the decades.

Shenton had been Mayor of Perth in the 1880s. His son-in-law, Henry John Saunders, was Mayor from late 1895 to the end of 1897, key years in the growth of Perth. Saunders had arrived in Perth in 1884. He became chief engineer for the Midland Railway Company and then formed an engineering partnership with James Barrett. It was this firm which designed the Perth Waterworks. In the early 1890s Saunders made use of his experience and connections to become one of the largest gold mine entrepreneurs. His West Australian Goldfields Company, floated in London in 1894, returned a dividend of nearly 40% in its first year of operation. On a capital of £100,000, the company returned a nett profit of £232,000 in 1895–96. With Sir George Shenton he floated the Lady Shenton and Florence gold mines at Menzies, with equal success. By the mid-1890s, 'his name was familiar to the stock exchanges of the world', as a contemporary put it. He floated at least five other viable mines and advised other men about more. He also floated Town Properties of Western Australia which speculated in Perth real estate. In addition, in 1896 he bought location 42 which in 1914 he subdivided to form part of Como. His St George's Terrace office was the largest and most important mining bureau in the city. Other than company urban real estate Saunders owned little land in the city, although his Market House in central Pier Street was undoubtedly profitable. He held extensive pastoral leases in the Murchison, and in 1895 he purchased from the Brookman family one of the colony's oldest and finest farming properties, Henley Park, founded in 1829–30 by Captain Irwin and Judge Mackie, on the banks of the Swan near Guildford. In appearance the estate resembled an English park with its 5400 acres of pasture, orchards and vineyards. Saunders also bred race horses, and enjoyed considerable success on metropolitan tracks. He also maintained a large house in fashionable Adelaide Terrace. He was MLC for Metropolitan province from 1894 to 1902, and again in 1918 and 1919. He died in 1919.[45]

Alexander Forrest, Mayor of Perth 1893–95, 1898–1900: 'Man of Property'.

In May 1901, shortly before his death, Alexander Forrest said at a banquet held in his honour that the pastoral stations of the Kimberley region were 'gold mines', and that he had made them so.[46] Forrest, already a celebrated explorer, the affluent owner of several pastoral runs, and Mayor of Perth, also speculated in gold companies during the 1890s. One of his company's first mines, the Wealth of Nations outside Coolgardie, was sold by him to 'Colonel North, the nitrate king' for £147,000. It was a timely sale, for North found that the reef petered out just below the section already worked. Forrest then invested successfully in Murchison mines and another Coolgardie mine—the Golden Hole at Londonderry. This last resulted in a *cause célèbre* for it seemed that Forrest and his partner, the Minister for Mines (W. E. Marmion), had bought the mine from a claim-jumper. When they were challenged publicly, a Government Committee, on which sat Marmion and Alexander's brother, found in the Forrest syndicate's favour, and retrospective legislation was introduced protecting them.[47] These and his

---

45 Kimberly, pp.42–3; Battye *Cyclopaedia of WA* Vol. 2, p.248; *Twentieth Century Impressions of WA*, p.27; Bolton and Mozley, pp.166–7; Stannage 'Owners of Perth Property'.
46 *Twentieth Century Impressions of WA*, p.751.
47 See G. C. Bolton *Alexander Forrest*, 1958, pp.120–5.

pastoral investments enabled Alexander to purchase in 1895 a mansion in St George's Terrace, the former home of G. W. Leake, another old WA settler.

Forrest was a tough entrepreneur. When it suited his pastoral interests he had introduced and steered through a stock tax, and he defended it almost right through to its 50% reduction in 1898 when local demand for meat far outstripped local supply. And he did not let it go without first getting the Government to agree to grant 30 year leases on existing pastoral holdings. If for the northern pastoral industry he sought to protect monopolistic control, in the south-west timber industry he urged greater competition in order that his own small company could better its operation. By 1896 Forrest had become less concerned about the stock tax, for not only was his company selling in Perth all the meat it could produce, but it had also secured the agency for the importation of meat from Kidman's runs in South Australia and elsewhere.[48] During the second term of his mayoralty (November 1897 to 1901) Forrest was repeatedly charged with being the head of a 'meat ring' which kept up the price of meat for consumers in the metropolitan area and on the goldfields. At the mayoral elections of 1899 he only narrowly avoided defeat, so fast had his popularity declined. From 1899 until his death in 1901 Forrest had to contend with charges of corruption in connection with his Perth Ice Company and Railway Department contracts, as well as allegations that he was 'keeping' several of the pro-government politicians. While cleared by Government-appointed committees, Alexander Forrest was perhaps the unhappiest of Perth's successful entrepreneurs of the 1890s.

Already directors of many pastoral, mining, finance, timber, and manufacturing companies, both Alexander and John Forrest speculated

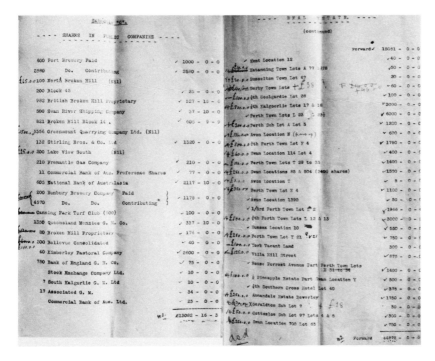

Some assets of an 'ancient colonist' entrepreneur: papers filed with Alexander Forrest's Will.

48 Bolton *Alexander Forrest*, p.146.

221

in Perth real estate. Alexander bought many urban lots in mining towns (which enabled him to hold a vote in all thirty constituencies in 1894). In 1891 Alexander (with George Leake) bought a riverfront part of Peppermint Grove, and in 1896 he bought and subdivided part of Dalkeith.[49] In the city proper, Alexander Forrest and Company owned a few houses in Parry Street north of the railway line and some more in East Perth, one of which was hard against the railway line and was a cheap three room cottage. More importantly, in partnership with E. G. Lacey, a prominent timber man with extensive land holdings in northern Perth—mainly shops and houses—Alexander owned offices in St George's Avenue in central Perth. Their tenants included lawyers, land agents and contractors. At the time of his death he owned 14 more houses in East Perth and the Aberdeen Street area, as well as a market garden in Railway Parade, East Perth, leased by Hop Lee. And he owned valuable vacant residential land in the north-west of the city off Newcastle Street. In the course of the 1890s he sold several properties in Fitzgerald Street. Both he and his brother were local directors of large insurance companies.[50]

John Forrest had bought land in Wittenoom, Water, and Brown Streets, East Perth, in the 1870s and 1880s. As late as 1895 he had not developed this land, nor odd blocks owned in Mount Street and Hay Street. Some of these properties were on the city's main drain in the least salubrious parts of East Perth. Forrest seems to have sold them late in the 1890s or early 1900s, when they were subdivided and built upon with cheap working class accommodation. Ironically, from 1904 Water Street was called Royal Street, a fine piece of advertising for the most polluted street in Perth.[51] But John Forrest's wealth derived from his wife's inheritance and pastoral concerns on the Ashburton and Murchison Rivers, and directorships of finance companies. Despite the East Perth properties he was anxious to give Perth, as the capital city, a 'pleasing appearance'. Certainly his Hay Street home, the Bungalow, was an ornament to the city, with its old-fashioned charm, croquet lawn and tennis court and 'garden of sweet flowers . . . most restful to the eye'.[52] It was also the centre of social rounds so important in securing the personal loyalties on which his ministry depended. The Forrests did not simply survive the goldrushes. Rather they directed and contained its anarchic energy, shaping its force into a mould created by still earlier generations of Western Australians who had nurtured them.[53] And they ensured that pastoral, trading and farming wealth would always be strongly represented in the counsels of the city and the State.

Stephen Henry Parker, lawyer and politician, was another colonial-born entrepreneur who flourished during the goldrushes.[54] He had been an energetic chairman of the Perth City Council in the late 1870s. He was

[49] Bolton *Alexander Forrest*, p.162 (for mining-town interests); Nomenclature Section of Lands and Surveys Department, 'Origins and Histories of Perth's Suburbs', unpublished mss, 1975. Forrest's assets were valued at £202,000, including valuable urban real estate.

[50] Alex was a director of Equitable Life Assurance and South British Fire and Marine Insurance, and John of the National Mutual Life Association of Australia.

[51] See M. Thomas 'East Perth 1884–1904', honours dissertation, University of WA, 1974. The properties were X14-20 E60-62 Wickham Street, East Perth.

[52] May Vivienne *Travels in Western Australia*, 2nd ed., 1902, p.45.

[53] See F. K. Crowley 'Sir John Forrest', in L. Hunt (ed.) *Westralian Portraits*, University of WA Press, 1979; also F. K. Crowley *Forrest 1847–1918* Vol. 1, 1971, pp.192, 106, 198, 277.

[54] For Parker see *Twentieth Century Impressions of WA*, p.393 (photo), p.40 (biography).

Perth comes of age: *Sir John Forrest opens the Perth Stock Exchange, 1896.*

Mayor briefly in 1881, in 1892 and in 1901, before being elevated to the bench of the Supreme Court of Western Australia. He was Chief Justice of Western Australia from 1906 to 1913. In the 1890s he was the MLA for Perth from 1890 to 1892; a member of the nominated Legislative Council from 1892 to 1894; and MLC for Metropolitan Province 1894 to 1897. Between 1892 and the end of 1894 he was Colonial Secretary in Forrest's ministry, but from then until 1897 he was in opposition to Forrest. At the 1897 general election he contested the Legislative Assembly seat of Perth, but the Forrests put up a Perth City councillor and real estate agent, Lyall Hall (who developed the North Perth estate), who pipped Parker by five votes.[55] Described by a hostile witness as belonging to the 'jellyfish order of politicians' Parker nevertheless left his impression on colonial politics and law.[56]

   He also made his mark in the commercial life of gold-rush Perth. In the mid-1890s he invested in gold mines and became a director of the London and Perth Exploration Company. He was also a director of the Mutual Life Assurance Company and a local director of the huge English merchant firm of Dalgety and Company which had extensive trading interests in the Australian colonies.[57] In the 1870s he bought a house on the corner of Irwin Street and St George's Terrace (A5). He still owned a house on the site at the end of the gold-rush years. In the 1880s, like so many of his affluent contemporaries, he bought several blocks of land in the northern part of the town under regulations which permitted purchase only by free-holders worth £500 or more. These he mostly sold at a profit in the late 1890s—the peak boom-time. He also sold the

[55]   The Forrests had chosen a good candidate in Hall. He was a recently arrived Victorian, responsible for a number of sub-divisions in the city's north ward where many newcomers were settling. In 1896 the electors of that ward returned him as their Council representative and as such he had helped them through the waterless summer of 1896–97 by having pumps put in the ward. See J. G. Wilson *Western Australia's Centenary,* 1929, pp.323–4.

[56]   *Victorian Express,* 6 December 1890.   [57]   Kimberly, p.18.

Stephen Henry Parker: lawyer, politician, Mayor of Perth, and speculator in urban real estate.

Beaufort Arms Hotel which he had owned since before 1889. But he bought other property in the same area and in 1904 leased five shops and factories in Beaufort Street. He also leased out five shops and a bakery in William Street just north of the railway bridge (1903). Even in those days it was a rough quarter. Indeed the houses on the other side of the road were brothels. The annual rateable value of this land rose from £75 in 1895 to £275 in 1904. In the early 1890s Parker bought several small (three room) cottages on L18 which ran from St George's Terrace to Bazaar Terrace. These too he sold during the boom, prompted perhaps by the fact that one of them was condemned as unfit for human habitation.[58] One of his best boom-period purchases was the Grosvernor Hotel (bought before 1900) on the corner of Hill and Hay Streets. This was rated at £425 in 1904. For Parker the goldrushes were golden indeed.[59]

They were also golden for Thomas George Anstruther Molloy, Mayor of Perth in 1908-9, and 1911-12. Molloy was the son of a Pensioner Guard who had served in the Crimea and in India at the time of the Mutiny (1857). The Molloys arrived in Western Australia in 1862. Thomas, after attending a Roman Catholic school, became manager of Cooperative Stores in central Perth. In 1875 he established himself as a baker on free-hold land in Goderich Street (Q6). He also owned ten, 2-room cottages for his workers and others. In the 1880s and 1890s he bought many blocks of land in West Perth—in Hay, Douro, Havelock and Ord Streets. In the 1890s he bought the interests of James Graves in various hotel ventures (in Fitzgerald Street and Hill Street) and built the Metropole Hotel in central Hay Street. He built the Royal Theatre next to the hotel in 1897. This combination proved very profitable and in 1904 he built His Majesty's Theatre and Hotel on the corner of King and Hay Streets, at a cost of £46,000. The rateable value of His Majesty's Theatre and Hotel alone was nearly £2000. In 1910 Molloy was responsible for establishing a new occupation for women—as barmaids.[60] As land values rocketed in fashionable West Perth, Molloy sold his lands—in Hay

The labourers who built Molloy's 'His Majesty's Theatre', 1903-04.

58   PCC Minute Book, 7 May 1900.
59   Stannage 'Owners of Perth Property'.   60   *West Australian*, 28 October 1910.

Street from Harvest Terrace to Thomas Street—at a great profit. As the councillor for west ward for many years he had ensured that the area would be well-serviced. In the 1890s and 1900s he was one of Perth's fiery particles, looked at askance by labor and non-labor politicians—the nearest thing Perth had to a populist politician.[61] But as an 'ancient colonist' he had survived the rushes magnificiently. He lived on in style until his death in 1938.

T. G. A. Molloy: from a single shop baker to an urban real estate king, and Mayor of Perth.

While some families have been singled out in order to show how the more prosperous of the 'ancient colonists' responded to the goldrushes and the effect their investments had on Perth's economic life and physical appearance, plenty of other families could have been treated in some way, although overall their impact may have been less marked. Forrest's Attorney General and political crutch, the lawyer/pastoralist Septimus Burt, prospered in the 1890s, less through speculation in urban real estate than through company directorships, his legal work, and the continued prosperity of north-west pastoralism with its captive labour force and equally captive market in the metropolis.[62] Burt bought Rossmoyne in 1882 and sold it for redevelopment in 1914. Burt also owned a fine house in Adelaide Terrace. Since that terrible moment in 1888 when 'honest' John Horgan had reviled and dished him in the Perth by-election, Burt had weathered other storms (including the hostility of some goldfields men, one of whom wrote a scathing poem called 'The Sneer of Septimus Burt') and turned into the twentieth century a wealthy and much respected man. During the Great War, two of his sons were killed. As the people of Subiaco would erect a monument in honour of Bartholomew Stubbs and other local men who died in action, so Burt donated to the Anglican Church a 'Burt Memorial Hall', close to the cathedral on St George's Terrace. In 1919, less than a year after the death of his old school-mate, political colleague, and fellow investor—John Forrest—Burt died and was buried at Karrakatta cemetery. His estate, valued for probate at nearly £150,000, was left mainly to his family. In 1888 he had written:

> I endeavour to make the motives of my actions the Glory of God, the welfare of my fellow-man, the honour of my Sovereign and the good of this country. If I can keep to these lines I do not think I can go far wrong.[63]

In 1919 there would have been few indeed who believed that Burt had gone far wrong.

A few years before Burt's death another old pastoralist and shaper of Perth, Charles Harper, died (1842–1912). In his time Harper had built many monuments, including his palatial home, Woodbridge, at Guildford, and the *West Australian* newspaper, which from 1896 was housed in grand new premises on the old site, still in use in 1979, the 100th anniversary of the paper's rebirth. Throughout the 1890s the *West* was both critic and supporter of the Forrest Government, but in general it did much to reconcile the general public to Forrest's actions. It was also a bridge between town and country, perhaps especially through its

61 Battye *Cyclopaedia of WA* Vol. 1, 1912, p.539–40; also Bolton and Mozley, p.130; and Stannage 'Owners of Perth Property'.
62 Like Forrest, Burt sold off land in a low-lying part of East Perth. This had probably been bought originally with an eye to resale to the Railways Department or to the PCC for drainage purposes.
63 *ADB* Vol. 7—entry for Burt, by B. K. de Garis and C. T. Stannage. The quotation comes from Burt's letterbook, in the possession of Chief Justice F. T. P. Burt, Cottesloe, WA.

weekly companion the *Western Mail* (1885), which enjoyed a wide country circulation in the goldrush years and after. Miners who in the 1890s read only goldfields' journals, like the *Western Argus* and *Kalgoorlie Miner*, read the *West* in the suburbs in the 1900s, and the *Western Mail* on new rural homesteads in the 1900s. The history of the *West Australian* offers another level of meaning to the epithet 'Forrests in the City'. In the 1890s, too, Harper sought to ensure that the old and good values of the pioneers and of his own generation would be perpetuated into the twentieth century. His vehicle was a school at Guildford which he sold to the Anglican Church in 1911. It then became known as Guildford Grammar and its products would continue Harper's work in Perth and the country, some indeed in the Country Party, for it too was a Harper creation. Harper's achievement was worth defending, and two of his sons were killed at Gallipoli.[64]

One of the largest landowners in central Perth in the 1890s, and one of the few wealthy Irish Catholics, was the family firm of Connor and Quinlan. Daniel Connor had arrived in Swan River colony in 1853 to work as a farm labourer. In the 1850s he operated as a hawker in the Toodyay district

> with a bundle of small goods, such as needles, pins and cottons, tied up in a red handkerchief, dangling from a stick over his shoulder.

But he made more money dealing in unbranded cattle than in hawking and by 1860 owned 60 acres of land near Guildford. In the 1860s he bought a store and other allotments in Newcastle, which grew quickly to become the principal town of the western Avon Valley. By the 1870s, through merchandising, milling and speculating in farming land, he had become the wealthiest man in the district. In 1883 his daughter Teresa married Timothy Quinlan, a young Irishman who had been orphaned in Swan River in the mid-1860s. Quinlan brought little capital to the family, but he had considerable commercial experience as a former employee of J. H. Monger. In the year of their marriage the Quinlans bought the Shamrock Hotel in central Hay Street, Perth. It was a successful venture and in 1889 Quinlan entered the Perth City Council, retaining his seat until 1902. In 1900, in the 'ancient colonist' interest, he contested the mayoralty with W. G. Brookman who beat him convincingly. Between 1890 and 1894 Quinlan represented West Perth in the Legislative Assembly, and from 1897 to 1911 he held the family borough of Toodyay for the Forrest and Liberal Party interest. In the 1890s he was a director of the Stanley Brewery and the South British Insurance Company. It was in the 1890s that old Dan Connor came to Perth to live and to invest in urban real estate. By the late 1890s they owned three blocks of land adjacent to and including the Shamrock Hotel, with Hay Street, Barrack Street (block length) and Murray Street frontages. The first purchased was the corner block F20. In 1895 it contained twenty-four shops and the Grand Hotel, with a rateable value of nearly £1500. Nine years later the same block had an annual rateable value of £4400, while the adjacent blocks F19 and F18 were rated at £2450 and £2230 respectively. In 1904 the blocks were tenanted by over eighty shop-keepers, businesses and hoteliers. They owned a few more shops further east in central Hay Street. In the 1890s they sold some houses they owned in Wellington Street. Quinlan owned additional land on F1, also in

---

[64] *ADB* Vol. 4—entry for Harper; also Kimberly, p.5; *Twentieth Century Impressions of WA*, pp.168–74; and F. R. Mercer *The Life of Charles Harper*, Perth, 1958.

Barrack Street, tenanted by the properous tailors and drapers, James Coultas and William Jones. Quinlan died a wealthy man in 1927. Old Dan Connor had died in Perth in 1898. At the time he was a large shareholder in the National Bank of Australasia and an investing member of the AMP. He'd had no need for insurance and no money in the bank in his hawking days.[65]

Farming and pastoral wealth gave a marked character to parts of the inner suburbs like southern East Perth and the high land to the west of the city. Two of the grandest homes built in West Perth in the boom years belonged to the de Pledge family, northern pastoralists, and to the Hassell family, southern farmers. Thomas de Pledge owned a one million acre run—'Yanrey'—in the Onslow district, acquired in lots between 1898 and 1904. De Pledge had arrived in Western Australia in the 1880s and had worked on the properties of Alexander Forrest, Septimus Burt and Charles Harper. Set in the midst of 'charmingly designed flowerbeds and extensive lawns' his King's Park Road residence, Craigmore, was one of the most beautiful homes in Perth, complete with several domestic servants and gardeners. Even grander was J. F. T. Hassell's, Kendenup, in Hay Street west, a block away. Hassell was the son of an Albany pioneer from the 1830s. By the late 1880s he was sole owner of an extensive farm in the Plantagenet region. A Forrest Government supporter, he was an MLC in 1893-94 and the MLA for Albany in 1900-01. His brother Albert was also a parliamentarian. The goldrushes and big export orders had provided

The Shamrock Hotel in central Hay Street, 1919: Timothy Quinlan's property before and during the goldrushes. (John Campbell, artist.)

[65] The quotation and some of the detail of Connor's story comes from R. Erickson *Old Toodyay and Newcastle*, 1974, especially pp.184, 227, 322; Kimberly, pp.84-5; Bolton and Mozley, p.157; Stannage 'Owners of Perth Property'. Given Quinlan's anti-Chinese tirades at a meeting of the PCC it is curious that he should have leased one of his Murray Street premises to Sing Hing, a laundryman.

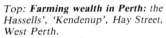

Top: **Farming wealth in Perth:** the Hassells', 'Kendenup', Hay Street, West Perth.
Right: Shearers at work on J. F. T. Hassell's property at Katanning.

huge new markets for their produce, and the West Perth houses reflected and symbolised their eminent place in Perth and Westralian society.[66]

H. J. Saunders was not the only engineer-contractor from pre-goldrush days to prosper during the goldrushes. Neil McNeil was 26 years of age when he arrived in Western Australia. He was already an experienced engineer and railway contractor, having built the Colac to Camperdown railway in Victoria; another line in Tasmania; and the Lilydale to Healesville line, back in Victoria. While engaged on this last job he undertook the construction of extensive waterworks in connection with the Metropolitan Water Supply Scheme. After completing several more railway lines in Victoria he came to Western Australia to construct the Jarrahdale to Bunbury line. With William McLean (later McLean Bros and Rigg) and John Whittingham he took over the Jarrahdale Timber Company and opened up the WA timber trade in the London markets (including timber for the streets of London). McNeil later merged this company with a London-based firm. He took over from Saunders the promotion of the Perth Waterworks Scheme in 1889 (again with McLean and Whittingham), leading to the construction of Perth's waterworks in 1890–91. With Shenton, Saunders and others he financed the prospector Menzies on the Coolgardie and Murchison fields. He seems to have had a large holding in the Star of the East Mine in the Murchison in the mid-1890s. With Alex Forrest he had a hand in the Wealth of Nations and Londonderry Mines. Perhaps he was less successful as a mining investor than Saunders, but in the course of the 1890s he 'became a very large owner of real estate, both in the metropolitan and rural districts being proprietor of Surrey Chambers and McNeil's Buildings (in central Perth), and Phillimore Chambers, Fremantle, and many other of the principal buildings between the coast

66 Battye *Cyclopaedia of WA* Vol. 2, 1913, pp.212–3, pp.268–9.

and the goldfields, to which in 1908 he added the famous Mt Barker Estate, upon which one of the two leading orchards in the State has since been developed'.[67]

In this time McNeil built for himself a magnificent home in Peppermint Grove, called The Cliff, an appropriate name as the house was on high ground overlooking the Swan River. Surrey Chambers, which McNeil built in the late 1890s on the corner of Howard Street and St George's Terrace, was one of Perth's largest buildings until the 1960s when it was pulled down. There was a hotel on the site, and nearly forty offices, all of which had a high annual rating because of their prestigeous siting. Indeed the annual rateable value of the Chambers in 1904 was nearly £2000. McNeil's other large central Perth holding was in Barrack Street, just off St George's Terrace near the Weld Club. His tenants were bankers, financiers, insurance companies, lawyers and so on. One of his largest tenants was the Government's Detective Department! But like so many affluent contemporaries McNeil also speculated in residential land north of the railway line. He bought and sold houses in the Roe Street area throughout the 1890s. His tenants were labouring and skilled trades-people. By 1904 several of his tenants were women, one a masseuse, another a widow, a third a nurse or midwife. The land may have been valuable despite its low rating, but the houses were mostly small three room cottages with little earning capacity. Perhaps McNeil expected that the State Railways Department would eventually buy the land, for it is difficult otherwise to understand why he held on to the properties.[68] McNeil was one of the State's wealthiest men. He had arrived in Western Australia in the early 1880s not as a mendicant refugee from the old world, but as the affluent son of an affluent father who had made his fortune in goldrush Ballarat in commercial and pastoral development. McNeil's, like Shenton's, was a precious inheritance, which contributed to the reshaping of Perth in the boom years.

Contracting wealth in Perth: Neil McNeil's, 'The Cliff', at Peppermint Grove, 1911.

[67] Battye *Cyclopaedia of WA* Vol. 2, 1913, pp.289–91.
[68] Stannage 'Owners of Perth Property'.

Pastoral and farming wealth, merchandising, contracting, mining wealth, and urban real estate wealth were thus all represented in Perth. So too was timber wealth. One of the most impressive homes in Adelaide Terrace (D3) belonged to James Cornish Port. Called Collieville, it had a morning room, drawing room, kitchen, pantry, scullery and office on the ground floor, with a ballroom and dining room. Upstairs were five bedrooms, a bathroom, and a tower. Behind his own house he built a row of terrace houses, Bicester Terrace. As with Neil McNeil, Port began his working life in his father's timber and construction business in Victoria. In the early 1880s he came to Western Australia to supervise the erection of the National Bank in Perth. Backed by some South Australian interests, Port founded one of Perth's largest timber yards (the Lion) and one on the Eastern Railway. He then bought timber land in the south-west, near Collie, and after ten years' successful enterprise floated the Jarrah Timber and Wood Paving Corporation in Perth and London, with a capital of £250,000. By 1900 the company owned 80 000 acres of the best timber country in the south-west. It met large sleeper contracts for the West Australian, South Australian, Ceylon and Natal Governments. It provided the piles and sawn timber for the Fremantle Harbour Works, and it supplied the jarrah blocks for the paving of Hay and other streets in Perth. Little is known of Port's career, but certainly it gives another level of meaning to the phrase 'Forrests in the City'.[69]

The man who designed Harper's new *West Australian* offices in St George's Terrace was Joseph Talbot Hobbs. An English-trained architect, Hobbs had arrived in Western Australia in 1887. In 1890 he married the daughter of J. Hurst, a builder and Perth City councillor with shops and houses in Hay Street, East Perth. By 1901 he had designed and overseered the construction of buildings in WA, especially in Perth, to the value of £750,000. Among his goldrush buildings were Moir's Chambers on the corner of St George's Terrace and Barrack

The Anglican Cathedral of St George, and Church Offices:
Joseph Talbot Hobbs prayed in the former and designed the latter, 1900s.

[69] *Twentieth Century Impressions of WA*, pp.366–7; see also M. Thomas, 'East Perth, 1884–1904', for transcript of an interview with Port's daughter.

230

Street, the Weld Club on the same block, Sandover's premises in Hay Street (with Alfred Lee), Surrey Chambers (for Neil McNeil), warehouses in Wellington Street, Prince's Buildings, the Masonic Hall, the new Swan Brewery, Saw's Buildings in Hay Street, and Church offices nearby. He was architect for the Anglican Church and also for the AMP and other insurance companies.[70] He owned and let several shops on the corner of Hay and Pier Streets and several houses further east along Hay Street. By 1904 he also owned nine houses in the northern part of the town, off Charles and Law Streets. Most lucrative, however, were the offices he leased on his Pier Street property, his tenants being the Woods and Forests Department, the Government Labour Bureau, and the Government Savings Bank Department. In 1904 he founded the architectural firm of Hobbs, Smith and Forbes. By 1911 he was a Lieutenant Colonel in command of the 2nd Infantry, having been a soldier and officer for nearly thirty years. In the Great War he won distinction as a military leader.[71]

Joseph Talbot Hobbs in 1901: architect, landowner, and Christian soldier who designed the new Swan Brewery. (John Campbell, artist, 1904.)

Hobbs was one of only a handful of architects in Western Australia before the goldrushes. Most of the prominent architects of Perth in the 1890s and 1900s arrived in the mid-1890s from Britain or the eastern colonies. In this way came Charles Oldham, architect of the £30,000 Emanuel Buildings in St George's Terrace, and G. & O. Wills' warehouse, and the man who replaced pillars with steel girder spans across shop fronts. Edwin Summerhayes arrived in 1894, worked for a time at Coolgardie, and returned to Perth where he designed many buildings, including Sir John Forrest's 'Forrest Chambers'. Michael and James Cavanagh came to WA from the eastern colonies in 1896 and 1900 respectively. By 1911 they had designed department stores like Foy and Gibson, Brennans', and Bairds' Arcade; the Fire Brigade Station in

70 *Twentieth Century Impressions of WA*, pp.424–5.
71 Battye *Cyclopaedia of WA* Vol. 1, pp.398, 624; Stannage 'Owners of Perth Property'.

231

Murray Street; the Esplanade Hotel; and several buildings for the Roman Catholic church, including Christian Bros College in St George's Terrace and St John of God's Hospital in Subiaco. Another goldrush architect was James Hine, who from 1895 built St Andrew's Presbyterian Church in St George's Terrace, Methodist Ladies College in Claremont, and many 'cosy suburban homes'. A late starter, but one whose career in Perth would be unparalleled, was Harold Boas. Boas arrived from South Australia in 1905 to build some houses for his brother Lionel, then establishing himself at Subiaco. Boas stayed in WA and by 1911 he was well-established, having built the Nedlands Hotel, and many houses in Subiaco, West Perth, East Perth and Mt Lawley where he was closely linked to the development of Copley and Robinson's Mt Lawley 1000 acre estate. He married in 1911 and lived in the more prosperous part of West Perth. Boas was an early advocate of orderly town planning and one of the founders of the Town Planning Institute a few years later. In his time he would design many buildings in central Perth and elsewhere, in a career spanning the first three-quarters of the twentieth century.[72]

Doctors had always enjoyed a high status in Perth society, as much for their education and social gifts as for their medical skill. Some, like Waylen and Ferguson, had owned valuable rural estates. In the 1890s there was a rapid increase in the number of doctors practising in Perth and the suburbs and a Medical Board was established to register them. It was from this time that doctors began to speculate in urban real estate. One who did so profitably was Dr Daniel Kenny. Kenny had arrived in Western Australia from Ireland in 1885. He did moderately well at first, but in the 1890s he became chief medical examiner for the colony's largest insurance company, the AMP. He became well-known for his land speculations, and by 1904 he owned thirty-five houses and shops north of the railway line in Beaufort, William, James and Fitzgerald Streets. He had also invested wisely in the growing suburbs of Cottesloe and Buckland Hill. His home was in St George's Terrace opposite Government House. Dr Adam Jameson, the sanitary reformer, was Kenny's investment partner in the suburbs. None of the other Perth doctors speculated on Kenny's scale, but several like Dr Tratman, Dr Lovegrove, and Dr Kelsall owned shops or houses to let, or vacant land for residential development.[73] Doctors were among the earliest purchasers of motorcars.

Many of Perth's old artisan families also prospered in the goldrushes. In 1842 Thomas Britnall, a shoemaker and leather-cutter, arrived in Swan River Colony from England. He successfully practised his trade in Perth for many years, passing the skill on to his son William who was born in the colony in 1843. By the 1890s there were four generations of Britnalls living in Perth. Thomas himself died in 1893 and William in 1902. The family, like the Birçhs, were prominent in the life of the Congregational Church. In the 1870s or earlier the Britnalls began to accumulate Perth real estate. William seems to have become a real estate agent. By 1879–81 they owned 12 three and four bedroom cottages in working class Wellington and Moore Streets near the railway line in

72 See Battye *Cyclopaedia of WA* Vol. 1, pp.623–630. For Temple Poole, the Government Architect, see J. White and M. Pitt Morrison (eds.) *Western Towns and Buildings,* 1979.
73 See Battye *Cyclopaedia of WA* Vol. 1, pp.597–8. There is an account of Jameson's municipal career in H. S. G. Downey *Mosman Park,* 1971; also Stannage 'Owners of Perth Property'.

Pier Street. They also had two blocks in Murray Street west of William Street, on which were five cottages, occupied by labourers and small artisans who paid minimal rents. They also owned a block in central Hay Street (F16). In the late 1880s Britnall sold his Wellington Street houses to the Perth Gas Coy which let them right through the period. By 1889 they owned more valuable land in Milligan Street and had held on to their 1879 houses. They had extended their holdings in west Murray Street and moved into East Perth (three houses) in Howick/Hay Street. Their old Murray Street blocks now had 20 rented houses on them. They had another eight cottages in central King Street, another six houses in Lake Street, and four in Roe Street. In 1904 the family had sold off all but the Roe and central Hay Street properties. The latter, occupied by Potts the bootmaker, and Sands and McDougalls, the stationers, now had an annual value of £500 compared with £47 in 1879 and £205 in 1895. In the 1870s Thomas was still practising his craft in the central Hay Street shop. He lived in one of his Wellington Street cottages, moving to one of his Murray Street cottages in 1881 where he was still living ten years later, but was then describing himself as an absentee landlord. He seems to have still been living in the Murray Street house on his death in 1893. William's family lived in a cottage on the same block until the 1890s when they moved across to the Roe Street houses where they lived until William's death in 1902.

For fifty years, Thomas had laboured in Perth. He had found respectability and comfort for his family. He may also have found an internal peace, for prayer was at the centre of his life's work. But internal peace may have eluded him at the last. Even as in a single day of his old age the past would wing its way to the forefront of his mind and brilliantly erase the present, however momentarily, he might think sometimes of that Wellington Street tenant of his, the tailor Haynes, who battered his wife to death and then asked if he could be buried alongside her. Perhaps, just perhaps, he Thomas shouldn't have prosecuted the man for stealing a roll of cloth. What was a roll of cloth to him now? What had it been to him then? Hadn't the State law encouraged him to act against what he knew to be God's law? In any case he had sold the man's house to the Perth Gas Company. But could his own life's experience be disposed of as easily? Thomas Britnall, an upright citizen and a loving family man, knew that the answer would be found in prayer to the all-forgiving Lord.

Several other older families like the Cockrams, Kings, Snowballs, Brittains (builders and brickyard owners), Churchyards and Chippers prospered in much the same way as the Britnalls. The Cockrams had arrived in 1850—farmers from Devonshire. Richard took up land in Wanneroo and Gingin, but his sons Edmund and Edwin became urban and rural hoteliers. Edmund developed land in Perth from the 1860s. By the time Edmund died in the 1890s the family owned houses and, more usually, shops in central Hay Street, Murray Street, James Street, Roe Street and Beaufort Street. Their most lucrative property—central Hay and Murray Streets—was used by restauranteurs like Albany Bell and Mrs Musson, and was kept by the family throughout the goldrushes.

The Churchyards arrived in Perth in 1853. John King Churchyard was a carpenter. He did well in the convict years and by 1870 was on the Perth City Council. He became an experienced valuer of city property and (with Stephen Chipper) was employed by the City Council for many

Albany Bell's chain of tea rooms was well patronised by the people of Perth throughout and after the goldrushes. (Central Hay Street, 1911.)

years for valuation purposes. In his time he was one of Perth's largest builders, but he was not a speculative builder like the Britnalls. From the 1870s until his death in 1906, Churchyard owned blocks W8 and 9, bordered by Beaufort Street, James Street and Stirling Street. He put ten houses on the block, all of them returning a higher rental than Britnall's! Many of his tenants were women. His cheapest house in 1904 was tenanted by a dressmaker. The most valuable building on the block was the Court Hotel which he erected in the late 1880s. Alas, the Court was moved back to central Perth, and while the hotel was not exactly a white elephant, Churchyard leased it and then sold it in the late 1890s. Like the Britnalls, Churchyard initially lived in one of his own cottages and described himself as a carpenter. Later he described himself as a builder, and once, in an uncharacteristic burst of pride, as of independent means and a landlord. Like old Thomas Britnall he stayed on the block until his death in 1906.[74]

Another who prospered as a result of Perth's rapid growth was Alfred Lee. Lee was born in Toodyay in 1860, the son of a Pensioner guard. After attending a Roman Catholic school in Fremantle, Lee was apprenticed to the Perth carpenter, James Halliday, who built the Barracks at the top of St George's Terrace. Lee then branched out on his own and in the late 1870s won a contract for the tea-rooms of the Legislative Council. He later won larger contracts and in the early 1890s profited from the construction of Sandover Buildings in central Hay Street, and the complex of buildings owned by Connor and Quinlan along Barrack Street. He enjoyed their patronage in other ways—for two years he managed their Grand Hotel. He then developed some East Perth properties and in 1895 was elected to represent East Perth on the Perth City Council. Lee held firm views about labour relations, but he was an undeniably successful builder of goldrush Perth. His aging father lived on into the 1890s to witness his son's rise to prominence in the affairs of the city.[75]

The builders of central Perth in the goldrush years tended to come from the ranks of the 'ancient colonists'. Apart from those discussed above, there were men like Robert Law who in the early 1900s did much of the contract work for the sewerage system of the city, as well as build Harry Boan's grand new emporium in Wellington Street (so superbly placed opposite the railway station), Perth Boys' School, and Surrey Chambers for Mr Neil McNeil. Henry Guthrie was another local builder. Guthrie worked for a time with Alfred Lee and then went on to build Brennans' department store and the Central Coffee Palace. More typical of an inner Perth suburb speculator-builder was George Smeddles. Smeddles had graduated from boot-making to house-building in the 1890s. He bought cheap land in low-lying Brown Street in East Perth, created Smeddles Terrace out of some vacant land, and by 1904 was letting sixteen very small houses at low rentals. Smeddles owned another twelve small houses in northern Perth. George Taylor began with a single block of land in East Perth in 1879. In the 1880s he built and leased out a few houses in Wellington Street, but in the 1890s he expanded rapidly as the town's population increased. He shrewdly catered for two rental levels: very cheap in Bronte Street; more expensive in Goderich Street. In 1904 he owned in all about twenty-three houses.

74 For the Britnalls, Brittains, Churchyards *et al.* see *WA Biographical Index*, 1979; also Stannage 'Owners of Perth Property'.
75 Kimberly, pp.231–2.

Harry Boan's 'The People's Store', in Wellington Street opposite the city railway station: founded in 1896 and rebuilt in the early 1900s.

But some newcomers were also prominent. Shirley White, who became president of the Master Builders' and Contractors' Association, came from Victoria with the first eastern goldfields' rush in 1893. Simon Alexander arrived from Sydney as late as 1897, but through his ownership of the Donnybrook Freestone Quarries, which provided much of the stone for Perth's office and shop construction, he became a wealthy man and a member (east ward) of the Perth City Council. Another prominent 'recent arrival' was Frederick Liebe who from 1896 built office blocks, hotels, banks, as well as His Majesty's Theatre for Tom Molloy, and the Art Gallery for the State Government. Overall, however, builders who arrived during the goldrushes were far more important in suburban construction than in the rebuilding of the city proper. Scots, Victorians and South Australians like Arthur Nelson, Joseph Richardson, William Fairweather, and the Henderson brothers, were responsible for a great deal of the building stock of Subiaco to 1911, and for many years after. Two of the families were still in the trade in Subiaco in the 1970s, and another dealt in real estate in Subiaco and adjacent suburbs. The land agents, too, tended to be 'recent arrivals', like Joseph Charles (perhaps the most flambuoyant) and Purkiss and Owtram; but older firms like Mosey and Britnall continued to be prominent and won Government valuation work as well as free enterprise work.[76]

A number of families benefited from investments made by their forebears. The land held in the Birchs' name in central Hay Street on the Barrack Street corner increased in annual value from £155 in 1879 to £1625 in 1904—from two shops to thirteen shops and offices. The Hardey family profited from an early investment in Murray and Wellington Streets. Ignatius Boladeras' land in Murray Street, bought in

[76] Battye *Cyclopaedia of WA* Vol. 1, pp.648–60; also Stannage 'Owners of Perth Property'; and M. Thomas 'East Perth 1884–1904', p.35.

the 1850s and 1860s, was switched entirely from one room cottages occupied by ex-convicts, washerwomen, boatmen, and domestic servants, to shops tenanted by engravers, restauranteurs and bootmakers. His estate, like that of his fellow Benedictine artisans, Rodoreda and Oriel, benefited the family greatly during the goldrush years. Not all the estates were local in origin. In the 1880s Anthony Hordern, the eastern colonial railway king, had bought F8, a block running between St George's Terrace and Hay Street in central Perth. Between 1895 and 1904 the two frontages appreciated in annual rateable value from £450 to over £2000, and were in use as shops and offices.[77]

But the 1890s also heralded the arrival of large urban land companies. One representative land company was the Colonial Finance Corporation which built an estate off north Lake Street, with streets named after two of the investors, Brookman and Moir. The seventy-five houses built on the estate seem to have been well-made for their annual rateable value was high. This was not always the case with the land companies. Other investors in central city land were the insurance companies, especially the South British Insurance Company with thirty-five offices in Barrack Street in 1904; the National Mutual Life Association in St George's Terrace; and the AMP Society, also in St George's Terrace. The insurance companies also underwrote much of the mining and urban development in these years. Among the AMP's assets in 1901 were WA Government Securities, municipal debentures, mortgages and house property. The value of the AMP's 16 800 policies in WA in 1911 was nearly £4 million, or double what it had been in 1891.[78] Although the AMP was by far the largest insurance company in WA before and after the goldrushes, all the companies experienced extremely rapid growth.

Certainly it was an age in which it was believed that insurance was something which most people should have. The AMP's policy total tripled between 1901 and 1911, although the State's population increased by only two-thirds. Families had more to lose in 1911 than they had had in 1890. One index to this is home-ownership. Another is the penetration downwards of an improved standard of living, an index to which is savings accounts. In 1892 the Government Savings Bank had 4443 depositors. This represented 7.5% of the population, and the average deposit per head of population was £1 1s 2d. In 1901 the figures were 39 318, 21% and £8 11s 8d. By 1911 they were 87 569, 30.5% and £14 3s 6d.[79] The trading banks enjoyed equally spectacular growth rates in their respective sphere.

Another financial institution deeply involved with Perth real estate in the goldrush era was the Perth Building Society which remained in the hands of the 'ancient colonists'. Among the Society's directors in the 1890s and 1900s were George Glyde, merchant, landowner, and a former chairman of the Perth City Council; George Shenton; W. T. Loton, Mayor of Perth 1901–1902; Alexander Forrest; Timothy Quinlan; and Major R. A. Sholl. The manager of the Society from 1892 to 1918 was Harry Brown, Mayor of Perth from 1903 to 1905. The Society's solicitors were Stone and Burt, while the Western Australian Bank

A customer's view of the National Mutual Life Insurance Company offices in St George's Terrace, 1890s.

---

[77] For the Birchs see *WA Biographical Index*, 1979; also Stannage 'Owners of Perth Property', especially for the Hardey family.

[78] *WA Statistical Register*, 1901, 1911. The AMP held nine-tenths of the total Government Securities held by insurance companies.

[79] *WA Statistical Register*, 1897, 1901, 1911.

handled its banking from 1862 to 1927. The shareholders too were predominantly Westralian. In the 1880s the Society financed the construction of 176 buildings. In the 1890s this figure almost doubled to reach 300; and between 1900 and 1911 about the same number of buildings was financed. These accounted for about 70% of the Society's total loans. The implied average housing price of the loans suggests strongly that the Perth Building Society catered for fairly affluent borrowers (£300 in the 1880s; £400 in the 1890s; and £500 in the 1900s). The Society's resources tripled between 1884 and the eve of the Great War.[80]

A different sort of land company which prospered from the rise in urban real estate values in these years was the churches. The prince of clerical entrepreneurs was Bishop Salvado of the Nullius Abbey of New Norcia. By the 1890s Salvado was not only one of the largest rural landowners in Western Australia, he also owned valuable urban real estate, especially N6-10 off Goderich Street not far from the Roman Catholic Cathedral. He had eight cottages on this site. Closer to the city centre he owned A11, the corner block on Pier/Howick and Goderich Streets. This block contained the offices of Bowra and O'Dea, Roman Catholic funeral directors. One of Salvado's house tenants was Hugh McKernan, a Roman Catholic politician. From the late 1890s the Roman Catholic Church owned shops and offices in Murray Street, Hay Street and James Street, houses in Adelaide Terrace (S22) which were tenanted by John Horgan and F. W. Moorhead, both Catholic MP's in their time (Moorhead for Murchison 1899-1901). The Church had also acquired valuable land in Irwin Street on which were built lodging houses. In Wellington Street Bishop Gibney owned the Federal Hotel, leased to Michael Mulcahy. In 1898 Salvado had subdivided his East Perth property, pushed through a street called Salvado Row, and built about forty small cottages—that is, semi-detached houses on quarter-acre blocks. In 1900 some of these houses were condemned as unfit for human habitation, probably in association with the bubonic plague scare which produced an intensive burst of demolition and renovation in the central city area, then and again in 1903.[81]

The Anglican Church, led by Bishop C. O. L. Riley throughout the goldrush days, owned valuable land on the historic central square site as well as developmental land in northern Perth. The Cathedral Avenue buildings were tenanted by lawyers (the beginnings of an association on the site which has continued through to the present day), land agents, merchants, and restauranteurs. In 1901 the land had a rateable value of £1200. Other land in Mount Street and St George's Terrace had been sold in the course of the 1890s. Back along Hay Street in the central shopping block the Congregational Church owned the frontages of large stores like A. W. Dobbie and Coy, Sandover and Coy (sold in the late 1890s), and Sloans; while down the block in St George's Terrace, land was leased to the Commercial Union Bank and other finance dealers. In 1904 the rateable value of the land exceeded £1000. Wesley's central city block was also a valuable investment in the boom years, for in the Lord's name the churches, no less than the Charles Harpers of Perth, let money make money for the greater good of mankind.

New Trinity Church in St George's Terrace, built 1896.

[80] R. M. C. Lourens 'The Perth Building Society', PhD thesis, University of WA, 1973. The paragraph was drawn substantially from tables 32, 40, 53, 54, and Appendix F.
[81] PCC Minute Book, 27 August 1900; also Stannage 'Owners of Perth Property'.

Presenting a fine facade to the people of Perth: rebuilding the National Bank of Australasia in St George's Terrace, 1896.

Not everyone did as well out of the boom of the 1890s as they'd hoped to. The Rev. William Traylen, an ancient colonist printer, temperance advocate, politician and Perth City councillor, hoped to make a fortune out of urban real estate. In the hectic years of 1895 and 1896 he wrote numerous letters to overseas and intercolonial friends, politicians, and finance companies, offering his services as agent for prospective mining, water-supply, and land companies. Always he knew of someone or some group with money and someone else or some other company with things to dispose of. But he never seems to have been able to get sellers and buyers together, and so missed out on that most lucrative experience—receipt of an agent's commission. It was not that Traylen's fortunes declined during the boom. Far from it. Six shops in Hay Street—owned jointly with the Hardey family—which in April 1894 were let for £1 10s a week, were let twelve months later for £2; to be raised to £2 5s in June 1895 and to £2 10s by the end of the year. From the rental of his Central Buildings he was grossing £850 annually, and his land on the corner of Beaufort Street and Roe Street was valued at £2500 even in 1894, before the best of the boom times. A year later his Barrack Street/Wellington Street corner block (130-foot frontage) was returning £383 per year. As for agencies, he pulled off a minor one with J. B. Were and Son of Melbourne to purchase bank shares for them. But he could induce neither Were nor Fred Illingworth, both Victorian land-boomers from the 1880s, to form a company to supply Northam with water: 'I ask (for myself) £500 in cash and 1000 shares in the Company.' After several more careers Traylen died in Guildford in 1926. But in the 1890s and 1900s Perth had many men like William Traylen who never quite realized their dream of great wealth.[82]

The activities of the land and mining speculators, the builders, architects, storekeepers and the like had transformed the face of central

[82] Letterbook of William Traylen, 1895–96, given to the author by Mr N. G. Traylen and lodged in Battye Library; also Stannage 'Owners of Perth Property'.

The National Bank of Australasia rebuilt in time for the Queen's Diamond Jubilee celebrations, 1897.

Perth by the Great War. Office 'blocks' or 'towers' had replaced shops and houses, and shops and offices had replaced cottages. There were very few vacant blocks left in the city. Theatres, clubs and hotels were now far more numerous. The average height of the buildings of Perth had doubled, while several buildings in St George's Terrace were three or more times higher than the structures demolished to make way for them. From the riverside Perth even had a building 'skyline', a term imported from the United States of America. The value of land in central Perth had risen 1000% since the mid-1880s. Even so, Perth was like a palimpsest, and there were still pockets of convict Perth to comfort or dismay the oldtimers. Even the Town Hall had survived the goldrushes. It had always been a financial liability to the Perth City Council which on several occasions tried to sell it to the Colonial Government. Forrest, wily politician that he was, offered the Council half what they asked for, so the Hall stayed in the hands of the people of Perth. In the 1900s a new generation of 'fit and proper' persons viewed it with equal displeasure, but none of the several governments which shuffled across the political stage in those years could be trapped into buying it. The Perth Town Hall had always been more of a symbol than a success, but by the end of the goldrush years it had lost even its symbolic value. It was not until the late 1920s when the city councillors launched yet another attack on it that it began its career as an historical relic, for by then pre-goldrush Western Australia had become an object of historical curiosity and an Historical Society had been formed. Composed largely of the older families of Western Australia, the Royal WA Historical Society became the custodian of the Westralian past, providing an essential educational link back to the gentry's quest for 'internal peace'. The goldrushes had changed the physical face of Perth but the old values preserved their sway.

Suburbanization and suburb makers

In the 1890s and 1900s, the enormous increase in population in Western Australia led to the suburbanization of Perth and the construction of thousands of family homes and lodging houses. In the municipality of Perth the growth was remarkable. In 1881 there were 932 houses in Perth. In the mid-1880s a minor surge of population had led to there being 1700 houses in the municipality by early 1891. Nearly four years later—that is, by the end of 1894—the number of houses had risen to about 2500, an annual increase of only 200. Then came a spectacular increase between 1895 and 1897. Building licence approvals (domestic and lodging houses and businesses) leapt to 1064 in 1896, rising to 1405 in 1897, before falling equally dramatically to 420 in 1898, and in 1899 dwindling to a lower figure than for 1893. But by 1901 the number of houses in the municipality of Perth had reached 5126. Thereafter house construction was less spectacular in Perth. Until about 1904 there was considerable construction of domestic dwellings in West Perth, but thereafter the rate of construction was sluggish, and in 1911 when the total was 6858 there were still very few signs of a building revival. It was in this period that the Perth City Council building surveyors reported that many people were extending and renovating their homes, and that speculation in house construction had waned considerably.[83]

The slower residential growth of the municipality of Perth after 1901 was caused partly by the extremely rapid development of

A suburb of transients and battlers: East Perth north of Hay Street, 1900s.

---

[83] PCC, City Surveyor's annual reports, 1898–1911; Censuses of WA, 1881, 1891, 1901; and Commonwealth Census of 1911.

commercial premises in streets formerly used for residential purposes. Murray Street, for instance, lost entirely its historic residential character, as did Wellington Street, William Street and much of Hay Street. But another factor was the willingness of immigrants from the eastern colonies to take advantage of cheap land available in districts adjacent to the city proper. The fifteen years after 1895 saw the suburbanization of Perth. For the period 1901 to 1911 the transformation can be seen in the following table:

Municipality	Population		Houses	
	1901	1911	1901	1911
Perth (includes North Perth in 1901)	27 553	35 767	5126	6858
Leederville (gazetted 1896)	2555	5457	664	1246
Subiaco (gazetted 1897)	2055	8926	720	2055
North Perth (gazetted 1901)	1200 (est. 1901)	4391	400 (est. 1901)	1018
Victoria Park (gazetted 1897)	546	2267	335	546
Claremont (gazetted 1898)	2015	4222	458	860
Cottesloe (gazetted 1907)	1383	2704	300 (est. 1901)	541
Helena Vale/ Midland Junction (gazetted 1893) Called Midland Junction from 1901.	1568	3483	315	739

Two other municipalities—South Perth and Guildford—grew only slowly by comparison. South Perth's population increased from 796 to 1197 with 272 houses; and Guildford's population increased by only 210 to reach 1669 in 1911. Outside the gazetted municipalities population growth was equally rapid. In 1911 the populations of metropolitan road boards (excluding the Fremantles) were as follows:

Road Board	Population 1911	Houses 1911
Perth (including Maylands and Mt Lawley)	5066	854
Claremont	1230	184
Cottesloe Beach	1704	381
Peppermint Grove	1043	204
Melville	565	123
Bayswater	1790	417
Bassendean	981	211
Belmont Park	1088	271
Greenmount	2716	688

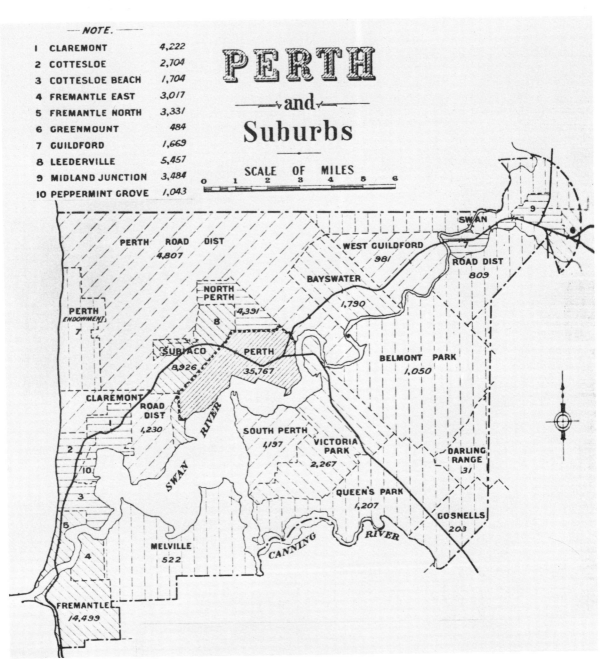

PERTH
and
Suburbs

SCALE OF MILES

Most of these places scarcely existed in the mid-1890s. Further out on the Albany line, Armadale with 1327 people was growing rapidly, as was the Swan area on the northern line with 1829 people. Wanneroo, although gazetted a road board, had only 197 inhabitants in 1911. In short, Perth in these hectic years developed a pattern of suburbs which remained largely unaltered until after the Second World War. The port of Fremantle had also increased its population, but not to the same extent as Perth and its suburbs—in 1891 Fremantle had been about two-thirds the size of Perth. In 1901 its population had reached 14 700, just over half Perth's size. In 1911 the municipality of Fremantle contained 14 500 people, to which should be added East and North Fremantle's 5500. Thus Perth's status was enhanced considerably in relation to that of its port.

The pace of change in Perth and its suburbs in the first decade of the twentieth century is evident from land-use analysis.[84] Even as late as 1904, 10% of central Perth was vacant land; by 1911 there was no vacant land left. As late as 1904 one-third of the land of the central ward was used for residential purposes. By 1911 this had shrunk to one-fifth, while commercial premises (offices, not shops) increased from 23% to 43% of the land in use. By 1904 Perth had reached saturation point in its shop and hotel requirements and there was no change in land usage for these industries (approximately 30% in 1904 and 1911). West Perth, which formed the Perth City Council's south ward, was 90% developed by 1904, as was Perth's east ward, better known as East Perth. In other respects these 'suburbs' differed quite markedly from each other, West Perth being largely residential (75%) and East Perth far less so (55%) with rather more factory and industrial activity. Outside the municipality of Perth the chief characteristic was the decrease in vacant land in the gazetted municipalities and road boards. Subiaco, which experienced large and even growth rates, increased its built-up area from 3% to 44%. Indeed the area under housing rose from 27% to 40%. If the largely vacant south ward is removed from the analysis, central and north Subiaco had less than 25% of land left vacant. In North Perth the changes were equally spectacular. In 1904 only 12% of the municipality had been built on, but by 1911 the area under housing had trebled—and for the central and east wards (those close to Central Perth) over half the land was used for domestic purposes. For Claremont the same story could be told. Vacant land decreased from two-thirds to two-fifths, and housing rose from 35% to 52% of land in use. Like West Perth, Claremont in these years attracted many storekeepers to service its stabilising populations (from 3% to 8% of the population for West Perth and from 1% to 6% for Claremont).

Evidence of the rate books and censuses shows fairly clearly that between the late 1890s and 1911, Perth's suburbs developed in such a way that it could be said that some were more desirable to live in than others. Differences in topography, accessibility of transport, location of industries, the cheapness of land, and people's perceptions of a hierarchy of suburbs all tended to give each suburb a fairly distinctive appearance and character. Elderly people reminiscing on their youth in the late 1890s and early 1900s spoke of their own and other families as 'being social' or 'having a good position' or 'people we would never have had the chance of meeting' or 'not in the Lady Forrest group'. They would say

> the people of Adelaide Terrace were the bosses and all that sort of thing . . . the working man lived somewhere else.

West Perth would be remembered as 'a nice area' with a 'better class' of house and 'wealthy people, doctors and . . . live up the top of King's Park'. In Cottesloe the people were 'higher up I suppose you would say'. One person remembered that for Adelaide Terrace, Cottesloe and West Perth, 'If you went to the front door they would say "tradesmen's entrance please"'. Neighbouring Claremont had a 'sort of middle

[84] The following paragraphs are drawn substantially from Ms D. Robinson's MA thesis 'Social Status in Perth 1901–11', University of WA, 1979.

A suburb for 'ordinary people':
Subiaco from the railway station,
1900s.

class–upper class people', and in South Perth there were 'decent houses . . . very nice, very nicely dressed and spoken people'—Mr Shenton's Haddon Hall (1898) being mentioned. Other suburbs were described differently or given a different emphasis. Subiaco contained 'ordinary people . . . a good working class with a high standard of living . . . there was no money in Subiaco in those days: most of the men worked at Whittaker's (timber yard)'. There were larrikins in York Street near the railway line. North Perth and Leederville were seen as mixed suburbs but generally having 'a good class of working man'. North Perth was connected in some people's minds with Mt Lawley 'but not quite as nice'. Closer to the town centre, James Street was 'not a nice locality', having Chinamen and larrikins, and the Brisbane Street/north Lord Street area had 'poor people'. South along Lord Street into East Perth there were 'nearly all working people', many living on small blocks—'a slummy place', and 'very damp'. Across the Causeway lay Victoria Park—'a cheaper part'.

These reminiscences correspond quite closely with contemporary perceptions. In *Twentieth Century Impressions of WA*, a huge cyclopaedia prepared for the Duke of York and Cornwall when he visited WA in July 1901, Subiaco is described as follows:

> Being so handy to the town, Subiaco is much affected by the artisan class, many of whom have been able to acquire the freeholds of their residences.

In Leederville too, 'like Subiaco, many of its residents, who belong to the working class, have been able to acquire their own homes'. Claremont was described as

> a pleasantly situated suburb . . . a prosperous municipality, containing a number of handsome villas and residences erected by professional and businessmen, whose means enable them to live in comfort in a locality possessing the charms of a rural district, which is yet within easy distance of town. Adjoining Claremont are Peppermint Grove and Cottesloe, which have also been taken up by the well-to-do classes. These are particularly well-favoured localities, in close proximity to river and sea, and contain some fine residences.[85]

And in *Travels in Western Australia* (1901), May Vivienne described these suburbs in the same way—'fashionable' with 'elegant villas and

85   *Twentieth Century Impressions of WA*, pp.396–7.

244

mansions'.[86] Neither Vivienne nor the authors of *Twentieth Century Impressions* mentioned the less salubrious districts. But a few years later (1902–04, 1905) the *WA Year Book* described Midland Junction in terms of its industries (brick-making and railway workshops); Claremont in terms of its 'handsome well-built houses' and public facilities; Leederville was described as 'flourishing' and having 'very low rates'; and Subiaco had its hospitals, industrial schools and so on. And the independent *Year Book of Western Australia* wrote that 'the district between Hay Street west and the King's Park, the high land of the city, has become a very fashionable residential resort'.[87] Guide books, commercial packets of photographs, and newspaper supplements on Perth (for example Nixon and Merrilies, *One Hundred Glimpses of Western Australia*, 1898), all tend to confirm the impression that the suburbs had differing status characters.

So too does analysis of land values, types of housing, occupations, home-ownership, house size; also land use, as has been shown. Those suburbs identified as 'artisan' in social composition tended to have proportionately more houses built of weatherboard with an iron roof. In the early 1900s, 75% of the homes of Subiaco and Leederville were wooden, while in Claremont less than 50% were made of weatherboard. Weatherboard homes could be bought as cheaply as £95 (plus the cost of the land), which helps explain why both these suburbs had high rates of home-ownership and low municipal rates; indeed the rate of home-ownership in Subiaco was higher than for Claremont during this period. Single or detached brick homes could cost just under £200. Brick was the traditional building material for Perth and this changed little in the goldrush years, partly because the Building Act discouraged wooden housing in the central area. Although quite a few wooden homes were erected in the low-lying parts of East Perth, West Perth and North Perth, brick remained the popular building material—there were two brickworks in North Perth and four in East Perth;[88] and in 1901, after the building boom had worked itself out in much of the city proper, over 85% of the homes were built of brick. (Comparison with 1911 is not possible as the 1911 Commonwealth Census does not give figures for building materials for the local government areas.)

Whatever the construction material, the houses of Subiaco, Leederville, Victoria Park and Midland Junction (where 7 in 10 homes were built of the brick made locally), tended to be smaller than those of Claremont, Cottesloe, West Perth (above the railway line), Adelaide Terrace, and South Perth. For the first named group 50–60% of houses had 3–4 rooms, and 12–16% had only two rooms. Claremont had scarcely any two room cottages, 33% had 3–4 rooms, 33% 5–6 rooms, and 17% 7–10 rooms. In West Perth 23% of the houses had 7–10 rooms and 34% had 3–4 rooms. West Perth tended to have two clusters of house values: one from £125 to £250 (those nearer the railway line), and another from £350 to £600 for those houses south of Hay Street west. North Perth, which in 1901 shared some of Claremont's characteristics, particularly in its central ward, declined in social status markedly between 1901 and 1911 as its east ward became populated with workers. In 1911 85% of the homes of North Perth were rated below £200,

Suburban weatherboard house, Subiaco in the 1890s.

[86] May Vivienne *Travels in Western Australia*, 2nd ed., 1902, p.70.
[87] *WA Year Books*, 1902–5; *Year Book of Western Australia*, E. S. Wigg & Son, 1906, p.202.
[88] *WA Statistical Register*, 1901, Pt. VI, p.7.

A respectable suburban family: the Caporns in the 1900s.

whereas in Claremont (where valuations were similar as recently as 1904) 80% were rated at above £200. This sort of evidence corresponds with occupational variation from suburb to suburb. Noxious trades tended to be absent from southern West Perth, Cottesloe, Claremont, Mt Lawley, Highgate Hill and Peppermint Grove; while pastoralists, Stock Exchange members, leading bankers and insurance company directors tended to be over-represented in these suburbs. Though they were also present in Adelaide Terrace, Subiaco's north ward and North Perth's central ward, there were proportionately more professional men in Claremont, Cottesloe, West Perth and central North Perth. Artisans and labourers tended to predominate in East Perth, Victoria Park, Leederville, North Perth and, of course, Midland Junction (40–48% in 1904), though as an occupational category they lost ground to commerce and transport in all these suburbs by 1911.[89]

Home ownership, aspired to by all classes of people in Perth in the 1890s and 1900s, was less easy to achieve than popular opinion, as expressed in guide books, booster literature and land agents' advertisements would have it. Round the turn of the century home-ownership levels hit 50–60% in some suburbs, such as Subiaco, Claremont and North Perth and perhaps others. This was a high figure, especially in comparison with those eastern colonial cities still pulling out of the depression of the 1890s. Perhaps the surprising thing for Perth is that the rate of home-ownership does not seem to have increased by 1911—indeed there is some evidence to suggest that it declined between 1901 and 1911. This is surprising because in 1911 the Perth statistical region had the highest rental rates of all the Australian cities for all sizes of house except for two-room cottages in Sydney. An unfurnished room cost on average 5s per week; a 3-room unfurnished house 8s 6d; 10s 7d for a 4-room house; 13s 11d for a 5-room house and so on.[90] Average weekly incomes ranged between £2 and £3, so one's rental was a sizeable expenditure. High though 1911 rentals were, they were still lower than in the late 1890s when home-ownership appealed powerfully to the people.

[89] Ms D. Robinson 'Social Status in Perth 1901–11', Chapter 3.
[90] Commonwealth Census 1911, Vol. 3, pp.1974–5.

For Perth and suburbs in 1911, of nearly 22 000 dwellings only 7500 were owner-occupied. Even allowing for about one-fifth of the population living in lodging houses and hotels, the rate of owner-occupation in Perth would not have exceeded 45% — smaller than the booster literature would suggest, but larger still than nearly all cities of the Empire.

There were some people who aspired to home-ownership in a salubrious area in the long term, but who in the short term were content to rent a house in that same area for the status the address brought with it. This helps to explain why in the higher, more desirable parts of West Perth, home-ownership was less than in those parts of West Perth closer to the railway line. In other 'suburbs' like East Perth in the 1890s there were many transients who rented for a time and then moved on, often to Subiaco where they became home-owners. Not until the early 1900s did East Perth lose its character as a 'transients'' suburb. In the early 1900s North Perth (east ward) seems to have had a high tenancy rate with some people moving across to central ward or out of the suburb and into Subiaco or Leederville. In addition there was an intermediate group which does not show up as 'almost' home-owners in the rate books. These were what the 1911 census taker called the 'rent purchasers', those renting a house but buying it on an instalment basis. Six per cent of houses were identified in this way in the 1911 census, and time-payment was usually to a land company (e.g. the Woodville Estate in North Perth or the Westralia and Norwood Estates in East Perth), or to a builder. Several of East Perth's builders let up to ten or more houses; indeed 50% of the housing stock of East Perth was owned by such men and smaller builders. People paying off homes to the banks and building societies tended to be identified as home-owners. This probably helps to inflate the home-ownership percentage of the population, for at least some of these houses would have been resumed for non-repayment.

For many families—perhaps more than one-half—home-ownership remained always an unfulfilled dream. Many families moved from suburb to suburb and within a suburb, always moving from one rental level to a lower one in a desperate attempt to hold the family together and to make a limited and often irregular income stretch further. In one such 1890s family, the husband was a tailor. First he rented a house and shop in central Hay Street, but the rapid increase in land values there from the mid-1890s drove him out to Subiaco where first he lived in a tent and then in one of a row of wooden terrace houses, in Hay Street west:

> you'd see everyone going to bed right along the terrace of houses,
> because of their poor construction.

But Hay Street west too increased in value and he moved to a side street—Townshend Road—then across to Rokeby Road where, defeated again when Subiaco's main shopping street increased in value, he moved to Barker Road, another side street. Eventually, he and his family came to rest in Chester Street, well up the sandy hill away from the twin shopping and business arteries of Rokeby Road and Hay Street west. In most of the houses he rented on his odyssey there was no piped water (and no bathroom), no drainage and no electric light (even though from 1903 the Subiaco municipality had its own electric power plant). He seems eventually to have bought his Chester Street house. But life had not been easy for him.[91]

91 Ms D. Robinson 'Social Status in Perth 1901–11', Chapter 4.

In any assessment of the extent of upward social mobility in Perth, a major factor to be taken into account would be the circumstances of the 70% of non-Western Australians in the population. The conjunction of economic depression in the eastern colonies and the discovery of huge goldfields in Western Australia had precipitated the largest permanent internal migration in Australian history. Between 1891 and 1901, 81 292 people left the colonies of Victoria (63 978), South Australia (16 660) and Tasmania (654) for other colonies. Of this number 69 657 or 86% came to Western Australia. In 1901 just over 50% of the people of Perth and its suburbs had been in the colony less than five years. In the decade 1901 to 1911, 60 688 people left the colonies of Victoria (38 589), South Australia (11 149) and Tasmania (10 950). Of this number 34 248 or 56% came to Western Australia.[92] In the following decade the decline in the number of people engaged in mining and quarrying in Western Australia (from 18 200 employed men in 1911 to 9000 in 1921) caused an outward movement of 20 000 people to the Eastern States, especially Victoria and New South Wales, the loss being particularly heavy from the mining districts. It seems clear therefore that the great bulk of eastern colonial-born people who came to Western Australia between 1891 and 1911 stayed to build homes and build families in the metropolitan area and in the new agricultural districts opened up by the Government. Indeed a central demographic fact for the post 1900 period is the increase in the percentage of eastern colonial-born women, who came west to join husbands and fiancées. Male population growth in Western Australia between 1901 and 1911 was 40%; for women it was 76%.[93] And there was a corresponding decrease in the number of money orders sent from Western Australia to families in the Eastern States.

In the magisterial district of Perth in 1891, 52% of the population had been born in Western Australia. By 1901 only 27% were Westralian-born, while 20% were Victorian-born, 8% NSW-born, and 7% South Australian-born. English-born people accounted for a further 16%. By 1911 the proportion of Westralian-born in the metropolitan area (the statistical area employed by the Commonwealth Statistician) had risen to 38%, but of course many of these people were young and were the children of eastern colonial migrants of the 1890s and 1900s. The eastern colonial-born in the metropolitan area was almost as great in number (37%), while the English-born component was down a little to 13%. (For the United Kingdom as a whole the percentages are 24% and 20%.) Some suburbs of Perth had very few Westralian-born people in them at all. In Subiaco in 1901 only 20% had been born in Western Australia, and as late as 1911 one-third of the population had been born in Victoria. This was also true of Victoria Park and probably North Perth as well. Midland was almost exclusively British and eastern colonial. In the other suburbs the colonial mix was greater. Claremont and Cottesloe contained proportionately more Englishmen and Westralian-born people. Leederville, with a longer history than Subiaco, also contained fewer eastern colonial people, as did Guildford and South Perth.[94] In the city of Perth, central and northern East Perth was largely (recent) immigrant, as was northern West Perth. But in Adelaide Terrace, West

92 D. T. Rowland *Internal Migration in Australia*, Census Monograph Series, Australian Bureau of Statistics, Canberra, 1979, pp.20–3.
93 *WA Statistical Register*, 1911, Pt. I.
94 Census of Western Australia, 1901, Pt. I, pp. 117, 119; and Commonwealth Census, 1911, Vol. 2, Pt. II, p.218.

Perth south and Highgate Hill there were a disproportionately great number of locally born inhabitants.

The permanency of the shift to Western Australia for so many eastern colonial-born people suggests strongly that they believed that they could do better for their families by staying in the west than by returning from whence they came. If in the short-term some stayed simply because they could not afford to return, their number overall must have been remarkably small. As in Victoria in the 1850s and 1860s, so in Western Australia in the 1890s and 1900s, the economic activity generated by gold—in the manufacturing, commercial, transport and service, and building industries, as well as the administrative and clerical industries and in the professions—provided better employment prospects for the dispossessed migrants than anywhere else in Australia. They came to put the eastern colonial crash of the 1890s behind them and to start afresh in Western Australia. Perhaps they did so more cautiously than they or their parents had done in the 1880s, but it is also true that they did so no less determinedly.

They did not come, like Lane's refugees to Paraguay, to create a socialist Utopia. Rather they came in a spirit of individualism and free enterprise, and at the same time hoping to ensure that the grosser abuses of capitalism which they had experienced in Victoria and New South Wales would be reduced and even eliminated.[95] Only two of Perth's several banks had closed their doors in the 1890s, and the local WA Bank was not one of them. And neither had the Perth Building Society collapsed in the 1890s. Nor was it strange that Western Australia should be the first State to establish an arbitration court for the settlement of industrial disputes (1902), for the quest for internal peace, which had been so prominent a feature of WA colonial life since the 1830s, had been furthered, not weakened, by the goldrushes. Populist politics of the Horgan sort held little appeal to the people of Perth from the 1890s until the Depression of the 1930s. Rather such differences of political opinion as existed were institutionalised into the Labor and non-Labor parties. And although 80% of the workforce was in receipt of wages, Labor never got 80% of the vote. Indeed so peripheral was politics that only 40–50% of enrolled electors voted in 1901, 1904, 1908, and 1911. And Labor's first important leader, Henry Daglish, was a conservative ex-Victorian civil servant who lived in Subiaco where after a period of renting houses, he gained for his family the security of their own house. Daglish, like most of the eastern colonial migrants, was not a man to turn the world upside down. But neither was he a man to allow the grosser injustices of capitalist society to prevail. Historians have seen in the Australia of the 1900s a powerful impulse 'to assert the dignity of the ordinary man through a new Australian social order'.[96] Universal suffrage, free education, an arbitration system, a fair wage based upon 'the normal needs of the average employee regarded as a human being in a civilized community,' as Justice Higgins of the Commonwealth Court of Conciliation and Arbitration put it in his famous judgment of 1907—these were at the heart of the new social order. And while great inequalities continued to exist in Western Australian society then and later, it may also be the case that the rhetoric and reality of a new social order were closer in Perth than in any other Australian city. Men went to

95 Michael Cannon *The Land Boomers*, 1966; for a more sober account, despite its title, see G. Davison *Marvellous Melbourne*, 1978.
96 G. Greenwood (ed.) *Australia: a Social and Political History*, 1955, p.207.

Suburban streetscape: Subiaco's Rokeby Road, 1905.

the Great War of 1914–18 for many reasons, but among the more important was a belief in the reality of the achievement of a new social order and a belief that it was worth fighting for. Western Australia (with Queensland) enjoyed the highest rate of home-ownership in the Commonwealth, and Perth the highest of the Australian cities, with all that meant in relation to employment and family life; and the quality and availability of education, church life, and recreational life was splendid for many. Western Australia sent proportionately more volunteer-soldiers to the Great War than any other Australian State, and twice it voted overwhelmingly in favour of conscription (1916, 1917). And the commemorative tablets and monuments erected to the fallen in each of Perth's goldrush suburbs after 1918 were an affirmation of the value of suburban and family life in their adopted State in the British Empire.[97]

And the suburban grip often remained extremely tight as a result of community experience of peace and war. For example, as late as the 1920s and 1930s even the more affluent people of Subiaco stayed in the suburb, though they might send their children to private or church schools in districts such as Claremont-Cottesloe. Many people lived and died in the suburb into which they had moved during the goldrushes. Their children usually went to the local schools and eventually married into other local families, buying or renting a house in the same suburb. In 1894 Bartholomew Stubbs fled Victoria and settled on the Kalgoorlie goldfields. Late in the 1890s he came down to Perth, moving into Subiaco. In Subiaco, Stubbs plied his trade as a tailor and in time bought a house. An active though conservative union man, Stubbs was elected as the local MLC in 1911. His children went to the local Roman Catholic school. In 1913 his step-daughter married a local man called Jones who worked as a clerk at the Swan Brewery. With the aid of a grant from the Workers' Homes Board (created in 1912) they bought a block of land in the bush along the sandy track known as Heytesbury Road, a mile from the shopping centre. A local builder named Henderson designed and built for them a brick and iron house. Despite financial stringency they

[97]   Commonwealth Census of 1911, Vol. 1, p.418; for WA's contribution to the Great War see Suzanne Welborn 'The Spirit of Place and Anzac' in C. T. Stannage (General Editor), *A New History of Western Australia*, 1979.

250

raised a family and were active in church and community affairs. As Mrs Jones was to put it:

> We put a deposit on a workers' home and paid 15s per week and reared a family of eight. At £4 a week we had no luxury.

One of their children married into the Henderson family. Some members of the family still live in Subiaco (1979), as does the aging Mrs Jones. In February 1916 Mrs Jones' father, Bartholomew Stubbs, MLC, ordered his son-in-law to stay in work and care for his daughter and the children. He then volunteered for service overseas. He was 46 years of age. In September 1917 he was killed in action on the Western Front. Stubbs had won 'freedom and honour' for his family in Subiaco. He believed that their achievement was worth fighting for—even to death.[98]

Living Conditions and Social Institutions

Not everyone prospered in the boom years. Henry Haynes' friends and acquaintances failed to prosper. And in 1891 a young miner called Ernest Maurice fell ill in Perth while living cheaply in a Brisbane Street boarding house. He had come to make a fortune on the Yilgarn field, but he contracted typhoid and died. His gifts to posterity included a picture card of the divine Sarah Bernhardt, a pencilled diary documenting his movements and illness, some letters and a revolver.[99] He too was a prototype for the boom years. In the course of the 1890s many thousands of men would come into Perth, some hundreds of them carrying the dreaded typhoid bacillus. Other men, infected in Perth, would lose their jobs as they battled against a disease which often took six months to recover from. Without a bread-winner their families suffered greatly. It was not for nothing that typhoid was known as 'the pauperising fever'.

Ernest Maurice's last diary entry, together with his cigarette card of the 'divine' Sarah Bernhardt.

---

[98] Interview with Mrs Jones, 1974—transcript lodged in Subiaco Museum; also Bolton and Mozley, p.183.

[99] Maurice's belonging were found by the author in the vaults of the Supreme Court of Western Australia. They are now on display in the Old Gaol at the WA Museum.

Typhoid was always present. In 1897 the Wesleyan Sisters of the People, whose object was to do all they could 'for the poor, sick, and needy, in the name of Him "who came not to be ministered unto but to minister" ', nursed many typhoid victims in Perth. A typical account of the scenes they found is as follows:

> Last summer I was called to a case where a mother was caring for her only boy who was to all appearances dying. She had just nursed her second child who was a typhoid case. I was called to the house at 9 p.m. to find that the doctor had also ordered her to bed ill. The sick boy, 10 years old, was delirious. Between the delirium of the sick boy and the anxiety of the mother, I . . . was completely exhausted when I returned to the Sisters' Home, at 10 a.m. next morning. The next day the mother was taken to hospital . . . Twice did the doctors hold consultations so grave was the case. Typhoid, pneumonia and complications all were centred in one little mortal of ten. But for the kindness of the neighbour I also should have been ill. She took care of the boy's two sisters and brought me food . . . The sick lad never spoke for two weeks. The father came back from the goldfield but as there was so little room in their home he stayed with a friend.

After a further crisis on one of the hottest days of the summer, Sister Grace's patient regained consciousness and slowly recovered.[100] About one in three victims did not do so.

Doctors spoke of an epidemic when the number of reported cases rose from 566 in 1895 to 663 in 1896 and then to 1408 and 800 in the two succeeding years. And governments and councils heeded their view and ordered the demolition of many cottages in the less salubrious parts of the city, the clearance of some ethnic minorities, and the introduction of more sanitary drainage systems, and rubbish and night-soil removal arrangements. And in truth there had been an epidemic. But there had also been a massive population increase in Perth and hence more cases of typhoid. No doubt the improved sanitary arrangements promoted the general well-being of the population, and men like Dr William Pope Seed, the City Council's Medical Officer, believed that 'if an efficient scheme of disposing of the sewage is completed, we may expect typhoid to disappear from Perth at an early date'; and a few years later the improvement in typhoid case numbers was 'plainly due to the deep drainage system'.[101] But only where the sewers transported human excreta could they reduce the potential spread of disease, and this was for less than one-fifth of households in Perth by the Great War. Septic tank systems also helped in this regard. Typhoid was not in fact related to the inhalation of noxious effluvia as doctors and administrators believed. It was communicated directly through contact with contaminated water, excreta, or food.[102] As Perth's water became cleaner and more plentiful, as excreta was removed in sealed pans, as checks on food supplies became more systematic, and as personal hygiene came to be practised in schools and homes, so typhoid began to wane. One pupil recalled of school, 'You had to be clean. It started in the "Babies" that you had to show your hands.'[103] During the goldrushes, the disease was so little understood that it is likely that the many more recorded cases of

---

[100] W. Lutton *The Wesley Story*, 1970.

[101] Annual Report of the PCC, 1912, p.60; Annual Report, 1915, p.69.

[102] I am indebted to Dan Coward for permitting me to read in typescript his pioneering article 'The Myth of the Great Life Saver: Sewers and Mortality in Sydney c. 1870–1900', in *Community Health Studies* (forthcoming issue).

[103] The quotation comes from M. Thomas 'East Perth 1884–1904', p.354.

Smallpox epidemic in Perth, 1893:
quarantine tents at Subiaco.
Typhoid was only one of the
serious epidemics in goldrush
Perth.

dysentery were in fact typhoid cases. Had this been known Perth might
have got a deep sewerage system far sooner than it did. As it was, for the
poorer classes the social costs of remedial action were extremely high.
Noxious industries were pushed away from well-to-do sub-districts into
working areas (Adelaide Terrace residents formed an energetic
'community action' group in this regard), sewer main drains were run
through working class streets, and workers were sometimes dispossessed
as zealous and well-intentioned government and municipal officials
condemned their houses as being unfit for human habitation.

Perhaps the problem was most acute in central East Perth, which
bore the brunt of the mid-1890s population influx. Two large open
drains, with the city as their catchment area, flowed into East Perth
where they joined together to form the Claise Brook drain. In the 1880s
gilgies were caught in the drain, but even they could not survive the
1890s. Then the stench became notorious. In East Perth alone the drain
received refuse from a tannery, soap factory, brickworks, factories,
stables, laundries, four saw mills, foundries, and so on. By the turn of
the century the drain was regarded as 'a disgrace to the Council', and
local children were warned not to go near it. One of the open drains, in
Coolgardie Street, was known as the 'fever drain'. By 1901 the
dangerous clay hole east of Plain Street had been transformed into
Queen's Gardens, but directly across the road was the East Perth rubbish
tip. 'Filled with water, overflowing with rubbish and surrounded by mud
and decay, it was "a standing disgrace",' as a contemporary put it. If
children were out late in the evening or late home for lunch, the young
working class mothers of the area would rush around to the tip fearing
the worst for their children. Not until 1904 was the tip covered with sand.
As if all this was not enough, central East Perth was selected as the site of
the city's gasometer. Its construction in the late 1890s led to the decline
and fall of Kensington Street.[104] Finally, from 1906 the new sewage filter
beds were located on Burswood Island off East Perth's river bank. The
hot summer easterly winds off the Darling Scarp carried the stench into
the crowded, ill-ventilated, semi-detached premises which predominated
in all but the higher land near Highgate, and the Adelaide Terrace area.
East Perth, in short, was Perth's Collingwood.

[104] The above paragraphs are drawn from M. Thomas' 'East Perth 1884–1904', pp.21–2.

East Perth in 1900.

254

Perhaps surprisingly, few of its parliamentarians and councillors were social and municipal reformers. From 1894 until 1904 the MLA for East Perth was Walter James, a locally born barrister who had been heavily influenced by Joseph Chamberlain's 'unauthorised programme' of political and social reform while in England in the mid-1880s. In parliament and on the Perth City Council (1891–1896) James did his best to ameliorate the living conditions of his constituents, but it would be true to say that the market and governmental forces were too strong for him, and the electors' frustrations surfaced in the formation of a ratepayers' association in 1899. But at least he tried. East Perth was too often prey to adventurers and developers like Thomas Draper (later more at home as the MLA for West Perth) and Joseph Charles. But it was not mere accident that the third east ward Perth City councillor in 1901, Thomas A. Shafto, was also Chairman of Council's Health Committee. Shafto later built the Shaftsbury Hotel and Shaftsbury Gardens, a semi-open air theatre used largely for picture shows. 'He had in addition large interests in real estate in all parts of the metropolis'.[105] Curiously, of east ward's three representatives in 1911, two were pre-goldrush Westralians. One of these men, J. C. Foster, the proprietor of the Royal Hotel in central Perth, let several houses in Wittenoom and Water Streets, close to the Wellington Square reserve. Most of East Perth's representatives were connected one way or another with real estate development. For those with a little land and capital it was a condition difficult to avoid in goldrush Perth.

The residents of northern East Perth, especially those over the railway line, had closer links with Highgate where St Albans Church was located, than with central and southern East Perth. Socially they looked to William Thorley Loton's huge residence at the corner of Bulwer Street and Lord Street. Loton, a landowner and pastoralist, was Mayor of Perth from 1901 to 1903. In the southern sector the Adelaide Terrace residents held out against factories, tramlines (directed down narrow Hay Street instead of the natural line down the Terraces), and lodging houses, of which there were several in East Perth in Goderich Street and elsewhere. (Indeed in the late 1890s the Perth City Council was issuing nearly 150 lodging house licenses annually, while hotels and 'informal' lodging houses took in thousands more tenants.) But even the Roes, Burts, Parkers, Stones, Wittenooms and other old families could not keep out the 'new wealth' of Brookman, Port and a few others. And from about 1895 for a couple of years they had to tolerate the presence of tent-dwellers at the river end of the Terrace, though some owners, like James B. Roe, leased vacant land to them, thereby turning a socially undesirable crowd into a financial asset.[106] Still, the genteel residential character of Adelaide Terrace was not unduly disturbed until the inter-war years.

There were several Hocking families in goldrush Perth. A Herbert Hocking was president of the Stock Exchange, and an E. W. Hocking was a Perth City councillor. Neither lived in East Perth. But another family of Hockings did so. This Hocking family came to live in East Perth because they couldn't afford to go anywhere else. Hocking was a Cornishman who had done well enough in Melbourne in the booming 1880s to own a small business. But he lost his small business and his

[105] Battye *Cyclopaedia of WA* Vol. 1, p.545.
[106] PCC Health Committee Minutes, 27 January 1897.

house in the great bank crash of 1893. In East Perth he found employment as a carter with the large timber merchants, Coombe Wood and Coy. He rented a five-room cottage in Royal Street in one of the swampiest parts of the suburb. This done he sent to Victoria for his wife and their eight children. In time Mrs Hocking found part-time employment as a midwife (usually for Dr Kenny). The oldest girl cleaned offices in the city from 5 a.m. to mid-morning, thus supplementing the family income. In time two of the girls would become tailoresses. The weatherboard house did not have piped water, so the girls had to cart water from a well. There was no gas, so cooking was done on a wood stove, and candles were generally used for lighting, as they were cheaper than kerosene.

The Hocking family had embraced the new Salvation Army faith, and with a Bible reading every Sunday evening before dinner, they could be said to be a religious family. One of the daughters became a full-time worker for the Salvation Army, which from the 1890s held considerable appeal to working class families. Adherents of the Salvation Army increased from 0.5% of Perth's population in 1891 to 5% by 1901. The church, or rather fortress, was also the centre of their social life, including a New Year's Day excursion to Cottesloe Beach and picnics at Armadale or Swanview.

In time Mr Hocking struggled his way out of Royal Street into Wellington Street close to the old recreation ground, still called 'the Rec', even though it was now graced by the title Wellington Square. The urge to be independent was still strong within Hocking, and in the early 1900s he moved again, this time to a house in Lord Street with a bakehouse attached to the back of the premises. There he became a part-time confectionery-maker. But across the city in West Perth the firm of Plaistowe was mass producing sweets, and the age of the backyard manufacturer was starting to wane. Hocking would never keep his family on the proceeds of his confectionery-making. But carting offered him steady employment and he managed to keep out of 'poorly regarded' Kensington and Brown Streets. Even in Royal Street they had got by. Most of the family's foodstuff requirements were bought at the front door: vegetables from the Chinaman (probably Ah Sue, whose garden was off Hill Street); milk from either Dan Keane's dairy in Summers Street or Murphy's at the bottom of Adelaide Terrace; bread and meat were delivered as well; the rabbit seller called; and there was a general store nearby. Eggs, however, came from the backyard fowl run.

As with most families of their socio-economic status the Hockings only called in the doctor for very serious illnesses. Until 1909 Perth did not have a Children's Hospital, so children suffering from infectious diseases were treated at home. When one of the Hocking children contracted that terrible child-killer, diphtheria, Mrs Hocking nursed her son in a room of their own house. During her fourteen day vigil Mrs Hocking did not leave the room. Her older girls passed food and drink in to her, these being the only times when the big carbolic-impregnated sheet covering the door was drawn aside. When one of the other children had his adenoids and tonsils removed, Dr Kenny operated with the child lying on the kitchen table.

Life was hard for the Hockings, but they stuck it out in Perth and eventually broke out of East Perth and rented a house in Vincent Street, Mt Lawley. Mrs Hocking even had a holiday—a week's stay under tent on the Como foreshore. For the Hockings the gamble of moving west had proved worthwhile. Perhaps their standard of living had been improved only marginally; but that was enough. Hocking's son fought at Gallipoli and Flanders. The father died in 1918, too soon to see his son gain secure employment with the Government.[107]

Across in Victoria Park a not dissimilar family history was being enacted. In the early 1890s Mr Robinson had arrived in Perth from New South Wales and gone on to Southern Cross where he worked for a time as a storekeeper. By 1898 he had saved enough money to return to New South Wales, gather up his wife and children and return to Western Australia. Robinson had several storekeeping jobs in Leederville, Victoria Park and South Perth before buying his own house in Victoria Park in 1903. It was a three-room weatherboard house, lacking piped water, and gas and electricity. They erected two 1000 gallon water tanks and made do with oil lamps and candles. There was little they could do initially about overcrowding in the bedrooms, but in time Robinson built extra rooms, verandahs and a bathroom. His children were educated at a local government school, where they also happily played hide and seek, staghorn, drop the hankie, and rounders. The neighbours were people like themselves, poor but just keeping their heads above water. Robinson's hard-won move from the floating, unstable, property-less sector of the working class to a settled, respectable, property-owning working class was the most significant experience of upward social mobility in the goldrush period.[108]

It was in response to a massive increase in demand for medical care in the goldrush years that the people of Perth developed a hospital system which would endure for several generations. The Perth Public Hospital, situated in Goderich/Murray Street, was enlarged considerably in the 1890s. It was under the management of a Board chaired (until 1909) by Sir George Shenton. The Board was composed of several doctors and pro-Forrest Government and Liberal politicians including W. T. Loton, Timothy Quinlan, J. G. G. Foulkes, and Harry Brown; there was also Herbert Hocking, the president of the Stock Exchange. The hospital had a staff of about 60 in the early 1900s, including 32 probationer nurses whose annual salaries varied from £30 to £12. Senior nurses received between £50 and £70. Male orderlies earned about £1 per week, housemaids, wardsmaids and the sculleryman rather less. The six casual laundry hands received 5s per day. The hospital dealt with 7847 patients in the year 1904–05, including 335 typhoid cases and 57 diphtheria cases. Over half the hospital's patients were out-patients.[109]

Until the mid-1890s the incurable and dying elderly people of Perth were cared for in the Government-subsidised Home of the Good Shepherd, an Anglican charity. When in 1895 state aid to religion was abolished, the Anglican Church was unable to carry on the institution. In 1898 Lady Onslow and Dr A. Saw convened a public meeting in the Perth Town Hall at which resolutions were passed affirming the need for a home for the dying and incurable, conducted on undenominational lines. The Government agreed to put up £1000 for building purposes and up to £1000 a year for running expenses. The churches launched a successful appeal, but farmers and pastoralists could not be induced to

Albany 'highway' through Victoria Park, 1900s and 1920s: *a suburb of New South Welshmen and Victorians.*

107 M. Thomas 'East Perth 1884–1904', transcript of an interview with Mr H. Hocking.
108 PCC clippings file 'History of Victoria Park School', being in part the reminiscences of Miss Dora Robinson.
109 *WA Year Book* (Wigg & Son), 1906.

An end to the quest for 'internal peace': The Old Men's Home at Perth, 1900.

donate money. The first site chosen was in a residential part of Subiaco. After protests from residents and the Subiaco Council, the Home of Peace was built in the bush further south at Hamersley Road. Opened in 1902, it had forty-two patients in 1912. The Home had a special cancer wing. There was also a smoke-room for men. With the exception of Bishop Riley, all the Home's presidents were 'ancient colonists'.

The people who ended their days in the Home of Peace tended to come from the more affluent classes, a legacy of its Anglican foundation. But some poorer old men eked out a living in shanties near the Causeway, and many aged of the less privileged in Perth society tended to find their way to the Old Men's Home under Mt Eliza on the banks of the Swan, or to the Home for Women in Central Perth. From 1897 the Government Inspector of Charities was James Longmore, who had worked with Dr Barnardo's in the East End of London. Longmore found that 'no matter how wealthy a nation may be, poverty and privation will be found to exist to a greater or lesser degree'. In a single year, 1900, Longmore issued food rations to 560 destitute men and women in Perth, most of them in their forties and fifties. Longmore's Department also administered the Old Men's Home. In 1900 the Home had 265 inmates. Some of the men who pottered around the river's edge chatting, day-dreaming, feeding the swans and fishing, were ex-convicts—the ones who had never made the break from Swan River and who had never managed to pull themselves up to respectability and comfort. Some people called them old reprobates and voted against any increase in State expenditure on them. Others, like Vosper, understood the fragility of existence and that the whole social system was marred if all the people in it were not cared for adequately. Shortly after Vosper's death, the State Government decided to move the old men from their beautifully sited 'Home' to the bush at Dalkeith, where from their new quarters they could look down on a ruined convict depot, the crumbling walls of which bore witness to the tragedy of their youth and old age. And back at the Government's women's home there was need for a

Holding out against institutionalization: old man down by the Causeway.

maternity wing with a midwife constantly in attendance. Since 1884 the Government had brought out young women to work as domestic servants. There would always be Catherine Kellys' in Perth and Matron Annear was still there to care for them.[110]

In 1900 a children's ward was added to the Perth Hospital, but it looked out on the morgue, and the exercise ground was dominated by the chimney stack of the Gas Company's works. In 1909, after a ten year delay, the first stage of a Children's Hospital was erected on land on the edge of Subiaco and West Perth. The creation of a children's hospital was a triumph for a Perth storekeeper Charles Moore, a businessman E. J. Bickford, and the children of Perth. In 1897 Moore encouraged children to donate pennies for a hospital. Within a couple of months he had raised £100. That same year the Government agreed to create three hospitals as part of the Queen's Diamond Jubilee celebration. They included a children's hospital, the Victoria Institute for the Blind, and the Home of the Good Shepherd (called the Home of Peace from the early 1900s). One of the fund-raising activities for the Children's Hospital was an 'Olde Englyshe Fayre', held in April 1898, which raised £1200. But the lowest tender for the construction of a Children's Hospital was well in excess of the money raised, and for some extraordinary reason no Government subsidy was forthcoming. It was not until Charles Moore, whose Hay Street store had flourished during the goldrushes, offered several thousand pounds for the hospital that Newton Moore's Government agreed to a State subsidy of £1000 for the building and £ for £ up to £1250 annually for maintenance. In 1909 the first wing was opened, and so heavy was the demand that further wings were added before the Great War. In 1912 over 15 519 out-patients were treated. The death-rate was 15%, high to modern eyes, but lower than most countries in the world at the time. In 1911 the Hospital appointed the State's first specialist children's doctor. It had been a long struggle for Moore and his friends who at times must have despaired of gaining

[110] *Twentieth Century Impressions of WA*, pp.99–100; also V. Courtney *Perth and All This*, 1962, pp.4–5; see also J. Watson (ed.) *Catalpa '76*, 1976, pp.65–70, which discusses the last days of several Fenians. Matron Annear was still alive in the centennial year, 1929—see J. G. Wilson *WA's Centenary*, 1929, pp.220-22.

259

Goldrush Perth's finest achievement: the Hospital for 'The Relief of Poor and Suffering Children'.

government assistance. Certainly there were very few donations from affluent townsmen and politicians. Several prominent doctors opposed the scheme; and Sir John Forrest (despite Lady Forrest's interest) was lukewarm and seems to have donated only £2 2s (the same amount as Sam Lee, a Perth laundryman). Sir George Shenton gave generously (indeed he bequeathed £1000 to the Hospital), but it was the effort of thousands of ordinary families which supplemented Moore's generosity. 'Uncle Tom' of the *Daily News*, on behalf of his 'nieces and nephews' of the 'Sunshine League', raised the cost of two wards and a 'Sunshine Cot'. In December 1908 a school-children's 'Penny Christmas Box Fund' produced 200 000 pennies. Earlier, at the 'Englyshe Fayre', the Trades and Labour Council had sold unionist-made goods on a 'labour stall'. At a crucial moment in 1909 Harry Boan of the 'People's Store' helped out, as did the Subiaco and Leederville Councils whose children stood to benefit greatly from the new hospital. It was the greatest achievement of the people of Perth in the goldrush years, not least because it fulfilled the purpose for which it was called into being, namely 'the Relief of Poor and Suffering Children'—'the children of those who are not in a position to pay for skilled treatment in their own homes or in private hospitals, and for the waifs and orphans'.[111]

It was in the late 1890s that the Deaf and Dumb Institution and the Victoria Institute and Industrial School for the Blind were founded. For several years the former was simply a house in East Perth, but in 1900 the Institution was moved to a new building at Cottesloe Beach. There the children were taught speech and lip-reading and the usual school subjects, supplemented by manual training for the boys and dressmaking and cookery for the girls. From 1898 blind children were able to attend a school at Maylands. The aim of the Institution was to provide a sound primary education for blind children and training for trades like brush-making, mat-making, and hair-curling. By 1912 some forty children attended the school, which was supported largely by voluntary contributions.

The early 1900s saw what was almost a rediscovery of children in Perth. The children of the 1880s were few in number, and to the mid-1890s the influx of young men and women largely intent on earning a living did not add greatly to the number of children in Perth. From the mid-1890s, however, there was a baby-boom, as the pioneers in city and suburbs produced their families. In 1900 there were 18 000 children in

[111] 'History of the Children's Hospital, Perth, Vol. 1, 1897–1910', compiled by the Administrator's staff, 1978; Children's Hospital First Report June 1909, and Annual Report 1910; also Battye *Cyclopaedia of WA* Vol. 2, pp.102-9.

government schools alone; by 1911 this had risen to 44 000. Add the children attending Catholic and private schools as well as pre-schoolers and it can be seen readily enough that a central task for the people of Perth in these years was to educate and care for children.[112] For the children of affluent parents and for the children of the 'respectable' working class, life in Perth was zestful. For the children of struggling families the quality of life was too often extremely low. In the early 1900s baby-farming was a widespread practice in Perth—'Person, kind, wanted to adopt babygirl, two years old, this office'[113]—and there were numerous cases of neglect and cruelty, the most infamous being the Mitchell baby-farming case. By 1906 the condition of many of Perth's children had become so bad that the problem could no longer be ignored. A Children's Protection Society was formed to help those parents and children whose precariousness of existence created the baby-farming industry. The Child Protection Society introduced a foster-mother system:

> through the system of foster homes the parents are held to the children. There is in modern life so much loosening of the parental tie that any agency which seeks to keep them firm and vibrant with affection . . . deserves every encouragement from both public and Government.

Not until the return of Scaddan's Labor Government did money come from the State; and in the interim some 450 children were boarded out. The Society also pressured the Government to pass a 'State Children's Act' under the terms of which the State cared for children who were 'criminally inclined' or orphaned or whose parents were 'morally, mentally, or physically unfit for their parental duty'. No doubt some overzealous officers caused more familial hardship than had existed previously, and the Acts could in no way alleviate the economic condition of poor working class families; but in that it retarded the growth of baby-farming, it was a major social reform.

So too was the creation of the Waifs' Home at Parkerville. Founded in 1902 by the Sisters of the Church, the Home cared for as many as fifty infants 'saved . . . from surroundings of unspeakable wretchedness', even in prosperous Perth.[114] Another institution founded in these years was the House of Mercy. Located first in Lake Street (1892) and then in Lincoln Street in northern East Perth (1901), the House of Mercy was a gentry women's charity which 'reclaimed' young unmarried mothers. Reclamation of the girls was achieved in part by having them work in a laundry which did sufficiently well for the House to become self-supporting. Dr Roberta Stewart (Jull), Western Australia's first woman doctor, was closely associated with the House of Mercy after 1898, by which time nearly seventy girls had been 'reclaimed'.[115] In Perth too there were also the industrial schools for poor and convicted children. In the early 1900s the Government's Industrial School and Receiving Depot at Subiaco had over forty children, ten girls among them. The other four

[112] Compare N. Hicks 'This Sin and Scandal': Australia's Population Debate 1891–1911, 1978. In Western Australia the high rate of migrant inflow disguised the fact that WA families were having fewer children in the early 1900s. The 'population debate' was therefore less fierce in WA than in all other Australian states except perhaps for Queensland.
[113] West Australian, 15 March 1901, cited in R. Campbell 'Aspects of Perth, 1901', honours dissertation, University of WA, 1972.
[114] Battye Cyclopaedia of WA Vol. 2, pp.112–4.
[115] See A. Porter ' ''A Mangle, Wringer, Bowl, Scissors, a Bible and a Prayer Book'': The House of Mercy, Perth, 1890–99', Time Remembered No. 2, 1978, pp.35–46.

industrial schools belonged to the churches. The Orphanage Industrial School for Roman Catholic Girls (at Subiaco), housed nearly eighty girls in 1901; while the Anglicans' industrial school, attached to the Orphanage in Adelaide Terrace, had nearly fifty girls. The Roman Catholics ran two industrial schools for boys—at Subiaco and Victoria Park. Girls learnt domestic duties, and boys crafts like bootmaking, carpentry, tailoring and farming (at Clontarf).[116]

In the 1890s and 1900s there were still young girls and boys who suffered as grievously as ever children had suffered in Perth. Mostly they came from poor working class families. There were still eleven-year-old girls with records of several thefts behind them, their enforced lifestyle making them vulnerable to sexual abuse from men unwilling to pay the many prostitutes of Perth. And young women, some experiencing the 'freedoms' of a housemaid's job in a hotel, still had cause to seek an abortionist who would do his work cheaply in the back room of a Murray Street boarding house. Some of the women of Perth struggled to survive while their husbands went to the fields in search of gold. When jobs were lost or the will to remain independent weakened they might seek the support of another man and eventually be subject to a divorce petition, following the shaming report of Mr George Gurney or Mr Alfred Parnacott or any other of the private detectives of Perth.

Still other women found their way to the brothels of Louisa Chawker and Mrs Dyson in Stirling Street, or to Annie Hughes' Monte Carlo brothel back in Murray Street. In 1900 about forty-five houses were used as brothels, some having been in use for several years (including Ada Monroe's in the 'Cowyard' behind Sir John Forrest's residence). In 1911 seventy-five houses were used by prostitutes, or at least were so identified by policemen. They tended to be located in William, Roe, James, Murray, Fitzgerald and Aberdeen Streets, as well as in tents on vacant land in East Perth. Often they were identified as 'tobacconists' or 'laundries'. In the early 1900s some of the coffee palaces like the Duke of York, the Prince of Wales and the Windsor were fronts for brothels. Many of the girls were professionals from the eastern colonies, France and Japan, and bore names like Annie Ah Long, Blanche d'Abigny, or, less exotically, Mabel Grey and Kate Hamilton. The evidence suggests that Perth had few *belles de jour*, but certainly the brothels contained some women (and their children) who could not stand the conditions of life in isolated timber mill settlements or on the goldfields. Like all cities, Perth could offer anonymity and refuge for the socially dispossessed and needy. For the women and men who contracted venereal disease there was little relief available. Indeed not until the passing of the 1911 Public Health Act did doctors and the Perth Hospital begin to come to terms with such contagious diseases. Most who contracted venereal disease suffered in silence, and the social *mores* of the time were such that at least one son of a well-respected and religious family shot himself rather than reveal his condition.[117]

---

[116] See Campbell 'Aspects of Perth, 1901', p.67.

[117] The principal sources for these two paragraphs are the Supreme Court's individual criminal case files and divorce case files for the 1890s, as well as the Health Committee Minute Book of the PCC. Ms Raelene Davidson provided much of the detail of the second paragraph. Davidson's work on prostitution in Perth from the 1890s to the 1930's (MA thesis in progress), is an important contribution to Westralian social history. See also V. Courtney *Perth and All This*, 1962, pp.256–7.

The Case of Martha Rendall

There were some occasions on which poverty, ignorance, immorality, and child abuse surfaced in sensational ways. Few if any of Perth's elderly people of the 1970s would not remember the sensational case of Martha Rendall. In the mid-1900s Martha Rendall, who was separated from her husband and children (in South Australia), lived with a Mr Morris in Robertson Street, East Perth, close by the railway line. Morris, a carpenter, had beaten and then kicked out his wife following a series of disastrous domestic conflicts between 1903 and 1906. Mrs Morris successfully applied for maintenance of 1s6d per week, which amount she supplemented by cleaning and by taking in sewing and washing. She lived with a Mrs Hedley in Subiaco. Morris had kept their several children. Martha Rendall moved in with him and cared for his children. Then in July 1907 Annie Morris, aged nine, died of a throat affliction; and in October 1907 Olive Morris, aged seven, died of a similar illness. A year later one of the older children, Arthur, aged fifteen, also died of a throat affliction. Not until after April 1909 when another child became ill and ran away to his mother at Subiaco did anyone begin to suspect foul play. In August 1909, following exhumation and examination of the bodies, a Coroner's Court found that Martha Rendall had administered spirits of salts (hydrochloric acid) to the children thereby causing their deaths. A month later a Supreme Court jury found Martha Rendall guilty of murder of the boy Arthur, and she was hanged at Fremantle Gaol on 6 October 1909. She had left a signed statement protesting her innocence.

There were those at the time and some (perhaps many) since who regarded Martha Rendall as a sadist and a pervert. The evidence for this view was the recollection by a neighbouring woman of looking through a window, the blind of which was not completely drawn, and seeing Mrs Rendall apparently in a paroxysm of merriment as she applied a swab to the throat of the screaming child. Rendall may well have been a sadist and a pervert, but the deaths of the children and Rendall's hanging raise more important matters relating to the nature of Perth society after eighty years of settlement. In 1909 Rendall was a married woman, in her late 40s, with several children of her own in South Australia. In her life she had had several miscarriages and two of her children had been still-born. Her own marriage had broken up and she was the catalyst for the breakdown of the Morris' marriage. In the cheap rented premises in Robertson Street, East Perth, she had cared for Morris' six dependent children, ensuring that they went to school, feeding them well, within the limits of a restricted income (as one of the children deposed at her trial). The family doctor, Dr Cuthbert, found no fault with her.

In mid-1907 four of the children became ill with diphtheria. Cuthbert was called in by Mrs Rendall and the children recovered. He was called in again in July and August with Annie died and Olive, George, and Arthur were ill again. Annie and Olive had severe bowel haemorrhage, and Olive and Arthur (when he died a year later) had the same membraneous condition of the throat. Cuthbert could not explain the cause of the deaths. He added that when Arthur was ill a second time, he hadn't called in another doctor at once because 'I felt that they could not bear the expense'. Doctors who attended later did not charge for their services. He had prescribed a swab for the throats of the children, though not spirits of salts. At the post-mortem of Arthur, Dr Cumpston was irritated because 'the woman [Mrs Rendall] insisted on being present throughout the operation'. Cumpston must have been quite rattled because he said that it was an unsatisfactory examination. Dr Cleland, who was also at the post-mortem, was so fascinated by Arthur's death that he read a paper on the subject to the WA Branch of the British Medical Association. When the three bodies were exhumed several months later (April 1909), Dr Tymms said that Arthur's death was consistent with death from some irritant, but because of decomposition he couldn't say the same for Annie and Olive. At the Coroner's Court Mr E. A. Mann, the Government Analyst, said that it was impossible to prove the use of spirits of salts directly: 'the summary of my research, therefore, is that while affording no proof of the use of hydrochloric acid, it, on the other hand reveals no facts inconsistent with such use'. The Coroner reported that 27 ounces of spirits of salts were found in the Morris' house. Dr Donald Steele, bacteriologist and pathologist at the Government laboratory, reported that in July 1909 he had conducted tests on guinea pigs with spirits of salts. This was enough for the Coroner's jury which found that death had been caused by poison administered by Rendall. The boys, Willie and George, had both deposed that Willie brought spirits of salts into the house for experiments in connection with his work. Martha too had referred to this, and asserted that she had painted Arthur's throat with medicine prescribed by the doctor; and that as a disinfectant on the brush she had used Condy's fluid. She denied having used spirits of salts.

At the murder trial the doctors again gave evidence, as did Detective Sergeant Mann who seems to have believed that Rendall was a pervert. Counsel for the prosecution spent much time speaking of Mrs Morris' good regard as a mother (Mrs Morris was a prosecution witness). The evidence for Mrs Rendall's action was circumstantial but conclusive. Mr Clydesdale, for Rendall, seems to have believed that Barker had to establish a motive for murder, but as this had not even been attempted then there was no case to answer. Clydesdale did not call a single witness on Mrs Rendall's behalf. In his summing up Justice McMillan referred to the press publicity during the hearings. He concurred in the view that 'at the time when the offence was alleged to have been committed they [Morris and Rendall] were living A Life of Immorality', but the jury should not 'be led away from the case by a very natural dislike for conduct to which he had referred'. He ignored Clydesdale's point about motive and said that the case for Mrs Rendall was that she never used spirits of salt at all. When the jury sentenced her to death (and found Morris not guilty) Justice McMillan, in sentencing her to death, let his feelings get the better of him:

> Nobody had suggested that she was mad. If she was in her senses, she must be a moral deformity. She had shown little emotion; her demeanour annoyed him.

Perhaps the issue of Rendall's 'moral deformity' was the heart of the matter. She had offended against the teachings of the churches; she had flouted the social conventions about 'family'. In comparison with the 'wronged' Mrs Morris she was evil incarnate. Perhaps it would have been different had Morris divorced his wife and Mrs Rendall had divorced her husband. But people who could not afford the opinion of a second doctor could not afford the costs associated with divorce cases, of which in any case there were still few in Western Australia, for divorce was very much a socially divisive topic. Perhaps too if she had shed a tear or two in a becoming manner the press and jury may have warmed to her a little. But a woman with her experience of life would not easily turn to water. Perhaps too if she had been petite and frail things might have gone better for her. But she was a large and strong looking working woman who, as was implied often, looked capable of wrong-doing. Perhaps if she had been younger her actions may have been put down to inexperience and foolhardiness. But she was middle-aged and therefore alleged to know right from wrong, and what could be administered safely and what could not. Perhaps too the timing of the death was unfortunate for her. The case was heard in the year of the opening of a children's hospital and within a couple of years of the establishment by affluent people of the Children's Protection Society and the passing of legislation on the safety and well-being of poor children—in short it was a period of intense social nervousness and worry about the children of the less well-to-do, something that police and people could turn against her. Perhaps too she suffered because she and the dead children embarrassed and confused the medical profession, still struggling to understand the nature of disease and uncertain about the value of a children's hospital. Perhaps too a lawyer did not probe as deeply as he might have done in her defence. Perhaps the deaths were accidental—that the Condy's fluid reacted with the bismuth medication or, unbeknown to Rendall, the disinfectant brush had become impregnated with Willie's spirits of salts. Despite expression of concern by some people, the *West Australian*, Hackett's paper, knew for certain that Martha Rendall was 'stolid and brazen':

> the woman herself . . . was a physical and mental abnormality.

Perth in 1909 was one of the most civilized and affluent cities in the history of the world, but it was not a city of light.[118]

Aborigines and Colonists: 'only a matter of time'?

The period 1884 to the early 1900s represents one of the most wretched chapters in the history of black-white relations in Western Australia. If the 'dark underside of the Australian mind—the violence, the arrogant assertion of superiority, the ruthless, single-minded and often amoral pursuit of material progress'[119] was most evident in the pastoral areas of the Kimberleys and the north-west where the Westralian Aborigines were enslaved and denied 'life, liberty and the pursuit of happiness,' it is also true that the powerful influence of pastoralism in the affairs of Perth implicated the city in the social consequences of Aboriginal dispossession and humiliation. It was a Perth annual journal *The Golden West* which printed the following in its first issue:

> the West Australian Aborigine stands right at the bottom of the class to which we belong. The native black has no intelligence . . . He is as a general rule . . . brutish, faithless, vicious, the animal being given the fullest loose, a natural born liar and a thief . . . The Australian black

---

118 *West Australian*, 11, 12, 13, 17 August 1909, 8–11, 13–15, 28 September 1909, 4–6, 9 October 1909; *Truth* 11 and 25 September, 2 and 9 October 1909. Unlike The *West Australian*, *Truth* was sympathetic towards Rendall and believed that she did not get a fair trial. Throughout the hearings *Truth* employed the headline 'The Toxiological Tragedy'.
119 H. Reynolds (ed.) *Aborigines and Settlers: The Australian Experience 1788–1939*, 1972, p.xii.

Christmas card, early 1900s.

may have a soul, but if he has, then the horse and dog are infinitely the superior in every way of the black human—[120]

Even the author of *Twentieth Century Impressions of WA* castigated the Aborigine for being 'indolent in the extreme' and for lolling and hanging about towns begging for food,[121] while Battye's *Cyclopaedia* of 1912–13 wrote of the

> deficient quality of his [the Aborigine's] intelligence. The absence of a reflective faculty is shown by their improvidence and want of forethought, as well as by the apparent inability to connect cause and effect.[122]

It added that 'from the stand-point of morality there is little to be said for them' while 'towards the whites they are often treacherous'. Battye's authors also found that the Aborigines were hospitable, and that they showed reverence for old age, as well as parental and filial love. As for their future, well, in the opinion of most experts and citizens 'their extinction is only a matter of time'.[123] This was the climate of opinion which led ultimately to what Professor Stanner has termed 'the Great Australian Silence'.[124]

In Western Australia one who was not silent was the Rev. J. B. Gribble. In the mid-1880s Gribble exposed the abuses of pastoralism, especially the rounding up of bush Aborigines, their enslavement in an assignment system, their torture and chaining if they attempted to escape. The pastoralists and their Perth mouthpieces, including the *West Australian*, Governor Broome, and Bishop Parry (then in need of funds for his new Cathedral), turned on Gribble and portrayed him as a

[120] *The Golden West* Vol. 1, 1906, p.50.
[121] *Twentieth Century Impressions of WA*, 1901, pp.179–80.
[122] Battye *Cyclopaedia of WA* Vol. 1, p.51.
[123] Battye *Cyclopaedia of WA* Vol. 1, p.60.
[124] W. E. H. Stanner *After The Dreaming*, 1968, pp.18–29.

slandering trouble-maker. Gribble, wrote the *West*, was not a 'gentleman'.[125] Even the radical press agreed that the settlers of the Gascoyne were 'true Britishers' who had only shot a few Aborigines in order to prevent greater bloodshed in the future.[126] Bishop Parry speedily packed Gribble off to the eastern colonies. Gribble wrote a powerful indictment of pastoralism which he called *Dark Deeds in a Sunny Land* (1886). For nearly twenty years there was a conspiracy of silence, broken only intermittently by eastern colonial reports of atrocities in Western Australia, and some reports in WA mining newspapers and the *Sunday Times*.

Until the mid-1890s legal control of the Aborigines was vested in the Imperial Government. In 1896, however, John Forrest's Government took over the Aborigines' Protection Board. The first Chief Protector appointed under the new regime was Henry Charles Prinsep who knew little about Aborigines (he never travelled to the Kimberleys or the north-west to see them) and was probably chosen for his pliancy and weakness than for any other possible qualities he may have had for the job.[127] Forrest kept expenditure at £5000, as did his successors, until in 1904–05 the Roth Commission exposed the scandalously low figure. It was doubled at once, and quadrupled within five years. In 1899–1900 Forrest refused to institute an inquiry into the treatment of Aborigines in Western Australia. When Dr Roth was appointed by the James Government, following further disclosures of abuse of Aborigines, the *West Australian* and others strove to discredit the Commission's findings, which included an indictment of the labour system prevailing in the north.[128]

The Aboriginal problem was fiercely debated in Perth only when there were 'incidents' such as the Gribble affair and the Roth Report. The Aborigines actually seen by the people of Perth were the families living at Third Swamp (until it was converted into Hyde Park), Mongers Lake, the Guildford area, Victoria Park and East Perth. Numbers present in the vicinity of Perth are difficult to determine. The 1911 Commonwealth Census counted 110 Aborigines in the metropolitan area, but this figure is almost certainly too low. There were many more half-castes in the camps, partly because over the period 1884 to 1911 half-castes lost their status as 'whites'. Some of the Aborigines came in from a Welshpool settlement, created in 1901 by Prinsep. At the settlement each Aboriginal family was to grow vegetables, fruit and flowers for the Perth market. But even before his resignation in 1907 Prinsep's scheme had failed.[129] Other Aborigines brought clothes props into Perth for they were always in demand, as was rabbit meat. In 1909 an Aboriginal orphanage was opened in East Perth.[130] Some Aboriginal girls worked as domestics in Perth, but little is known about them.[131]

Aboriginal children at Lake Monger camp, 1920s.

125 *West Australian*, 14 January 1886.
126 *Victorian Express*, 13 February 1886; for Gribble see also C. M. H. Clark *A History of Australia* Vol. 4, 1978, pp.323-4; also Gribble to the Archbishop of Canterbury, 1886–87, in Lambeth Palace Archives, London.
127 See P. Biskup *Not Slaves Not Citizens: The Aboriginal Problem in Western Australia 1898-1954*, 1973, pp.54, 67.
128 Biskup *Not Slaves Not Citizens*, pp.59–65; for the situation in the Kimberleys see A. Gill 'Aborigines, Settlers and Police in the Kimberleys 1887–1905' *Studies in Western Australian History*, No. 1, June 1977, pp.1–28. See also B. T. Haynes, G. Barrett, L. and A. Brennan (eds.) *WA Aborigines 1622-1972*, 1972.
129 Biskup *Not Slaves Not Citizens*, p.53.
130 Biskup *Not Slaves Not Citizens*, p.121
131 Biskup *Not Slaves Not Citizens*, p.147.

After 1883 Aboriginal prisoners were no longer incarcerated in Perth Gaol. It was in 1907 that Daisy Bates wrote 'we buried Jaobaitch, the last of the Perth tribe of Aborigines'. She was right only on the narrowest of definitions, for the Aborigines would return to Perth in ever increasing numbers, in defiance of the social Darwinians' theories.[132] And East Perth would become for them an urban hell, a sanctuary, a fortress, and the headquarters of the black-power movement decades later.

Social mobility in goldrush Perth

The pattern of economic life which emerges from the study of individual entrepreneurs and workers is fairly clear. Those well off or comfortably off before the goldrushes profited greatly from the increased tempo of economic activity and distanced themselves still further from the rest of the 'ancient colonist' population. This population, at least as indicated by property development and physical mobility, did not share significantly in the general prosperity of the boom years, and suffered greatly in the years of economic recession such as 1892–93, 1897–98, and 1908–10—they had too little to fall back on in times of economic stress. As for the 't'othersiders', those with business experience and support from 'home' tended to do well in the goldrush years—as agents, storekeepers, builders and the like. For them Western Australia proved to be a relatively open society—that is to say, the rate of expansion of economic opportunity was so great that it could not be completely dominated by the local establishment. Some 't'othersider' men even found their way on to the membership list of the Weld Club, and several were members of the Stock Exchange and the Chambers of Commerce and Manufacturers. With the creation of several new municipalities quite a few of these men gained access to and representation on decision-making bodies. The Perth City Council was also open to them, although the old hands tended to hold the balance of power. For the unskilled 't'othersider' labourer, employment prospects were good for much of the period, but like their 'sandgroper' counterparts, the thing most difficult to achieve was to move from the unstable, floating property-less sector of the working class to the settled, respectable property-owning working class groups. To make the latter group was the best that such men could aspire to, and it was an aspiration difficult to meet. The city had thousands of people who lacked respectability and comfort. They could be found doing odd jobs for householders, temporary work on factory floors, in brickyards and tanneries and breweries—the transport sector was full of such men, as was the service sector when gardeners, barmen, municipal employees like roadmakers, night-soil removalists, garbage cleaners, warehouse workers and the like would drift back to lodging houses and hotels as their masters and respectable work-mates went on to their homes. And there was still great hardship in even the most respectable of working class families. And the Aborigines of Perth suffered whether times were booming or depressed.

But even for the Hockings, and the Robinsons, WA society had proved to be more open and less susceptible to disaster than had Victorian society. Probably the most oppressed Victorians, New South

---

[132] Cited in V. Courtney *Perth and All This*, 1962, p.176.

268

Wales men and South Australians stayed in the inner city areas of those states, lacking the will and the cash to make the trip to Perth. It was the marginal men who made the move, and while many stayed close to that condition in Perth, others clawed their way upwards and won respectability. The evidence suggests that the majority did so. It would be the next generation which would experience blocked mobility and even a descent to economic and social disaster greater than that known by their parents.

The needs of the people: cess-pans, water, gas, drains, sewers, roads

From the mid-1880s the tasks of the Perth City Council were manifold. It had to extend and maintain the roads of the rapidly developing city; to ensure that the city had a reliable and pure water supply and that sanitary arrangements were adequate; to foster the growth of public facilities like gas lighting, electric lighting, tramways; and to create parks and recreation facilities. In this the experience of local government since 1858 proved invaluable, and several long-standing councillors like Molloy and Quinlan provided continuity of effort and vision for much of the period. Until the 1890s the councillors tended to be drawn from 'ancient colonists', men who had been in Western Australia for many years or had been born in the colony. Thereafter the colonial and Imperial mix was greater, although residents of long standing continued to be prominent. Perhaps one of the most striking changes in the social composition of the Perth City Council in these years was the decline in professional representation. There was a time in the 1880s when over one-third of the councillors were lawyers and doctors. In 1901 only one architect and one lawyer were on Council. The remaining thirteen members were real estate agents (3), hoteliers (3), dealers, storekeepers, and other businessmen. Two major city companies—the Swan Brewery and the Perth Building Society—had their managers on the Council. About five of the fifteen councillors had been in Western Australia for less than ten years. In the 1911–12 Council there were no lawyers and only one architect (Mr Ochiltree, who was an early advocate of orderly town planning). At least four councillors were builders, while there were several land agents, manufacturers and traders. Over one-third of the councillors had been born in Victoria, but all of them had been in the State for fifteen years or longer. Well over half the councillors were Freemasons. In 1901 there were at least five parliamentarians on Council, all of them non-Labor. In the 1911–12 Council, there were very few parliamentarians and only one of them, Ebeneezer Allen, was a Labor man. The pattern established by 1911 would persist for several generations. Though internal strife was frequent and unsettling, if Council faltered, as it did sometimes, it must be remembered that the demands of Perth's growth seemed insatiable and that Council was prey to the whims of Forrest's ministry and the succession of ministries which shuffled across the political stage between 1901 and 1911. Some councillors used their position to further their own ends and increase their personal fortunes. Such evidence as is extant suggests that they were few in number. Most councillors were self-made men, proud of their own achievements and determined to make life in

Perth efficient and healthy, and the city itself a place of beauty. As fit and proper persons they were loyalists and patriots.[133]

The mid and late 1880s were dominated by discussions about the city's water supply and sanitation. In June 1884 Governor Broome, alerted by Dr Waylen's report for 1883, persuaded the Legislative Council to establish a commission of inquiry into the sanitation of the city. The Commission found that despite population increases, there had been few sanitary improvements in the city; it also found some appalling cases of filth and disease in the poorer quarters. It recommended the creation of a Central Board of Health and several local boards. The municipalities, including Perth, would be represented on the Board but they would not control it. While the Legislative Council considered these recommendations the Perth City Council moved to forestall them by upgrading its Sanitary Committee to include a councillor from each ward plus the Mayor. (Indeed it established the practice whereby Council Committees included a representative of each ward.) But in 1886 the Government did establish the Board of Health, which thereafter was a source of friction between the Council and Government. Nevertheless it did spur on Council to set its own house in order. In the course of 1886 several councillors, notably J. S. Christie, drew attention to the 'amount of sickness prevalent in the City'—impure water and the absence of 'sanitary precautions' were thought to be the causes of sickness. And there were still the pigs! In mid-1886 the Council at last deprived the families of Perth of their resident pigs in the belief, probably false, that disease spread from domestic pig sties. But the problems of unclean closets and impure water supply remained unresolved.

The question of the water supply was becoming increasingly pressing. In mid-1886 Mayor Shenton reported that the Government intended to bring water from the Canning River at a cost of £25,000. But by the end of the year no action had been taken. In that year the Perth City Council lost a case in the Supreme Court and henceforth was liable for repairs of drains in the city, even where they crossed private property. This was an unexpected and costly burden which effectively killed Council's interest in water supply for 12 months. Not until October 1887 was a public meeting held on the water supply question. Shenton favoured the Canning River scheme as proposed by Barrett and H. J. Saunders, civil engineers. So too did the Director of Public Works. Only a Government guarantee could get the project off the ground, but Shenton wanted the full backing of the ratepayers. At his bidding, William Traylen, veteran editor of the *Temperance Advocate*, moved that

> In the opinion of this meeting, it is highly desirable that the city should be provided with a sufficiency of pure water for drinking and culinary purposes.

The motion was seconded by a recently arrived working man with a large family who

> believed that it would be cheaper for the ratepayers of Perth to pay for a pure water supply than to pay their doctor's bills.

It was R. S. Haynes, lawyer and political radical, and now a councillor, who proposed that the Government be urged to introduce a Waterworks

---

[133] Councillors' occupations, dates of arrival in WA, etc are drawn from *Twentieth Century Impressions of WA*; Kimberly; Battye's *Cyclopaedia*; Bolton and Mozley; and PCC records.

Bill. Haynes was supported by another Horgan supporter, Dr Adam Jameson, who expressed the hope that the scheme would not only supply Perth with fresh drinking water but would also include an efficient sewerage system. The older hands, like Traylen, Shenton and Scott, were not impressed with the latter suggestion. Dr Scott, who of course strongly favoured the water supply proposal, said roundly that the sewerage scheme was unnecessary because of the 'sandy nature of the soil (which) operated largely as a filtering and deodorising agent'. Accordingly Haynes' resolution was carried, but not the matter about sewage.[134] Shenton was re-elected to the Mayoralty for 1888.

1888 was a difficult year for Shenton. The immediate problems of the city tended to be submerged by the political clashes over the economic recession, the non-construction of the Busselton-Bayswater railway, responsible government, and the by-election for the seat of Perth. Several of Shenton's political opponents, like Haynes and Neelands, were members of the Perth City Council, while at the half-yearly and annual general meetings other opponents harassed him. Some did so on a personal basis. John Elliot, the working man, charged Shenton with corruption. Shenton, he said, had directed a Council contract to one of his tenants as well as ensuring that a company of which he was a shareholder, namely the Perth Gas Company, won the right to light the Town Hall and several of the streets of Perth.[135] Other fierce critics were Walter James, Lewis Hasluck and Edward Courthope, all well known figures in the life of the city. Shenton resigned at the end of the year and the Mayoralty went to the Member for Perth, Edward Scott, who defeated William Traylen narrowly.

Scott immediately convened a public meeting on the water supply question. To the surprise of the sceptics he won taxpayer approval for the introduction of a special water levy of 1s in the £ which would raise £3150 in a single year. Perhaps they were determined not to be seen to be backward, for Dr Waylen had stressed that the new towns of western America and the suburbs of Melbourne received piped water. Perhaps they could see that the present scheme of street watering was costing £400 a year—easy money and water down the drain, as it were. Jameson had again raised the question of sewerage; after all, he said 'if they brought water into the town they ought to have some means of carrying it out'. Others weren't satisfied that the proposed supply would cover the entire city, particularly the northern sections. Still others were anxious to see the scheme financed by the municipality and not given to a private company. One who did not agree with this latter suggestion was the new Member for Perth, the entrepreneur Edward Keane. Scott skirted around most of these issues, though he did suggest that the area to be covered would extend to George and Charles Street in the west, Newcastle, Ellen and Mangles Streets in the north, and Cemetery Road in the east, which would indeed have met the demands of about 75% of the inhabitants of Perth. Scott forwarded the resolutions and results of the referendum to the Government. But Broome's was a 'mark-time' administration, and in August 1889 the Perth City Council was informed that the Government would not underwrite the cost of a water supply for the city. Scott was undeterred. Perhaps he even welcomed the opportunity to proceed

---

[134] For Christie's comment see PCC Minute Book, 5 March 1886; for Haynes' resolution, PCC Minute Book, October 1887.
[135] PCC Minute Book, 12 November 1888.

Piped water for the people of Perth: Edward Keane's Waterworks Board in 1896.

independently. On 21 October 1889 the Perth City Council signed a contract with Edward Keane for Neil McNeil and Company of Melbourne to provide a water supply from Munday's Creek on the Canning, in the area of Keane's timber mills.[136] Council had the right to purchase the scheme at capital value of £120,000 plus one-third at any time after 1909. One of the members of the Council's committee which recommended the McNeil scheme was H. J. Saunders, who had become a councillor earlier the same year. Saunders had previously sold his waterworks specifications to McNeil. He had also opposed the idea that the Perth City Council should raise a loan to construct the waterworks as a municipal enterprise.

In mid-1891 Scott, who had favoured Keane's scheme, resigned from the Mayoralty which passed to Edward Keane. Keane was thus Mayor of Perth when the reservoir, called appropriately the Victoria Reservoir, was opened in October 1891. A day before the opening Keane announced that he had disposed of all his financial interests in the Perth Waterworks Scheme.[137] The contract had been met. Plumbers from England and the eastern colonies were arriving to lay the service pipes to the boundaries of the properties. All seemed well.

Within a few weeks, however, it was clear that all was not well. At a well-attended public meeting on 14 October many ratepayers criticised the Company and the Perth City Council. It was argued that the contract had not been fulfilled (indeed Council itself had only reluctantly returned the contractor's deposit of £5000 on 9 October) and that the Company was charging too much both for the household connection and for the water. Elliot returned to the attack, attributing the 'muddle' to the dominance of 'family influence'. Timothy Quinlan, councillor and parliamentarian, read a letter from the Company

> to a poor man for connecting his premises with the mains in which they stated they would charge him £8 15s—this being for 60 feet of half-inch piping laid in the surface and one tap.

The meeting expressed its anger and dismay at this and other revelations and resolved not to pay a water levy until the abuses had been rectified. Council was forced to renegotiate with the Company, but found to its chagrin that Neil McNeil had sold out and that the Company was in the hands of another company of which W. McLean and J. Whittingham of Melbourne were the principals. Not until early December did Council win the Company's agreement to connect the mains to all ratepayers' dwellings at slightly lower charges, but in doing so they had to consider a higher capital valuation for eventual purchase.[138] In October 1891 Edward Stone had resigned from the Council because his law firm was acting for the Waterworks Company. In 1889 he had supported the scheme proposed by Keane. In March 1892 Keane resigned from the Mayoralty, after a period of illness. By now many ratepayers were feeling ill about the origins of the contract. There were even those who said that there had been graft and corruption.

Some people felt the water itself made them ill. In April 1892 the Council expressed concern about the possibility of water in the reservoir on Mt Eliza being polluted;[139] and at about the same time, William Traylen claimed in the Legislative Assembly that he had evidence that

[136] PCC Minute Book, 21 October 1889.   [137] PCC Minute Book, 2 October 1891.
[138] PCC Minute Book, 16 November, 4 December 1891.
[139] PCC Minute Book, 7 April 1892.

Munday's Brook was being polluted by Keane's Canning Jarrah Mills. The evidence was compelling—there had been typhoid cases at the mill and the watercourses had been polluted by human and animal excreta. Traylen's attempt to give the Council's Board of Health power over the catchment area was defeated in the Legislative Council on this and other occasions in 1892 and 1893. But in July 1892 the Mt Eliza reservoir had at least been emptied and drained. Pollution aside, the plain fact of the matter was that the Company was extremely tardy in extending its mains into the eastern, western, and northern parts of the city, and only under pressure from the Council did the Company make some effort to meet its obligations.[140] In August 1893 the ratepayers voted overwhelmingly in favour of a proposal to purchase the waterworks, but in September the Forrest Ministry refused to guarantee the debentures as required by Council.[141] Meantime Perth in 1892 and 1893 experienced a severe economic recession which probably reduced the profitability of the Company and encouraged speculation about the possible sale of the waterworks, at the same time as it affected the ratepayers' ability to pay increased water charges. For 1894 the Council reduced the general rates by 10%, though the radicals, James and Haynes, had sought to relieve the pressure on ratepayers by up to $33\frac{1}{3}\%$, so difficult were the financial circumstances of many residents.[142] Many residents, particularly in the growing suburbs of Leederville, Woodville (North Perth), Highgate, Victoria Park, and Subiaco, but also in East Perth and parts of West Perth suffered the long hot summers without piped water at all or with water available for only an hour or so per week. By early 1894 the Health Officer, Dr O'Connor, was cautioning people about the impurity of the piped water (among other pollutants a dead bullock had been found floating in the reservoir). The Mayor, Alex Forrest, took little interest in these matters—indeed, as often as not, he was absent from Council meetings, seeing to his business interests on the goldfields and elsewhere. Towards the end of 1894 William Traylen again stressed the need for a government instrumentality to deal with water and sewerage. Sir John Forrest was not sympathetic largely because he believed that Traylen's views were in advance of public opinion. Traylen was undeterred. In a powerful speech to the Legislative Assembly he linked the high rate of infant mortality in Perth to the impure and inadequate water supply and surface pollution:

> My good friends who live in their splendid houses, with their pleasant gardens and happy surroundings, and who know nothing about these troubles I have referred to, forget to sympathise with those who haven't such surroundings and who have troubles enough.[143]

Those who lacked such surroundings suffered greatly during 1895 and the extremely hot summer of 1895–96. In mid-1895 the Perth City Council received a petition from 'The Ladies of Perth' 'expressing concern about sanitary conditions in the City'. By 1895 the city was badly overcrowded—shanties were being thrown up on vacant lots; there were tent settlements in East Perth, at Third Swamp (Hyde Park), and Subiaco; stables and other outbuildings were being used as lodging houses; and lodging house construction and the issue of lodging house

---

[140] PCC Minute Book, 7 October 1892.
[141] PCC Minute Book, 4, 6, 7 July, 4 August, 17 September, 6 October 1893.
[142] PCC Minute Book, 1 and 16 December 1893.
[143] *WAPD* (n.s.) Vol. 6, pp.188–203, August 1894.

licences had accelerated greatly. By late 1895 the Perth City Council's Building Surveyors could not keep up with building applications. Leederville and Subiaco had grown so quickly that each had petitioned the Government to be given municipal status.

As early as February 1894 the City Health Officer, Dr O'Connor, had advocated the construction of a 'fever hospital' to cope with the rapidly increasing number of typhoid cases 'which had been brought down from the Yilgarn line'.[144] The lack of an adequate water supply and adequate sewerage were thought to be responsible for the 566 cases of typhoid reported in Perth in 1895—70 deaths. Some looked to reputed carriers of disease. In July 1895 Timothy Quinlan drew Council's attention

> to the existence of certain premises in King Street which were overcrowded with hordes of Chinese and used as a gambling den and that the same were in an unsanitary condition.[145]

Some time earlier a group of Chinamen had been caught depositing rotten potatoes in the river. For a time the Chinese were made a scapegoat—indeed, when in 1898 the renovated Perth Baths were reopened, the Chinese (and the Aborigines) were specifically excluded from using them. But perhaps the bad odour on the river, complained of earlier, was due to refuse from the Weld Club, which at that time employed Chinese servants and cooks.[146] In 1897, acting on a complaint from the residents of Station Street (Forrest Place), Council officers found the sheds and rooms occupied by Chinese as laundries and gambling dens 'reeking with filth'. These, and other Chinese laundries in Mackie and Hutt Streets, were ordered to be pulled down.[147] But to most rational men the apparently increasing incidence of disease could not be attributed solely to the alleged characteristics of the Asiatics in Perth. After all the Chinese comprised less than 2% of the population.

In November 1895 Alexander Forrest retired from the Mayoralty. His only achievement—a not inconsiderable one—had been to induce his brother to increase the Government subsidy to the Council from 10s to £1 for each £1 collected by Council from rates. His record on the water supply of the metropolis was as disappointing as his brother's. At the November 1895 general elections H. J. Saunders, a man with a past interest in waterworks companies, defeated Councillor Molloy quite comfortably, though Molloy did very well in the northern and eastern districts where the poorer people lived. In the north ward election a Labor man, Charles Oldham, defeated a sitting councillor. Oldham was a building contractor who won North Perth in the Legislative Assembly elections of April 1897.

Saunders became Mayor at a critical time. In December 1895 the Water Supply Company's threat to cut off water altogether was only narrowly averted, after Council had threatened in return not to pay rates to the Company. Clearly the pressure was beginning to tell on both parties.[148] Throughout January 1896 Council dealt with many grumbles from ratepayers about the water mains not reaching outlying areas, water being cut off at night, poor pressure outside the central city area, and so on. At a public meeting that summer, Council was again urged to

---

144 PCC Minute Book, 2 February 1894.   145 PCC Minute Book, 14 July 1895.
146 T. S. Louch *The First Fifty Years: The History of the Weld Club 1871–1921*, Perth, 1964.
147 PCC Health Committee Minute Book, 2, 25 February 1897.
148 PCC Minute Book, 11 December 1895.

Betwixt two definitions: Harry Armstrong (St George's Terrace) as sanitary engineer and plumber.

approach Premier Forrest about purchasing the scheme from the Company. Forrest continued to procrastinate. Perhaps it was only a very severe outbreak of typhoid in June and July which caused him to agree on 30 July to take over the waterworks from the Company. In September 1896 the Council's contract with the Company was formally handed over to the Government. That same month the Government created a nominated Metropolitan Waterworks Board, with the Mayor of Perth an *ex officio* member. The first chairman of the Board was none other than Mr Edward Keane, emerging from bankruptcy and as chirpy as ever he'd been in the late 1880s and early 1890s when he'd launched the Waterworks Company. Keane found that the main pipe from the Victoria Reservoir to Perth was too small for the needs of the city, and in the course of 1897 he overseered the construction of a 21-inch main as well as authorising the sinking of bores in the town.[149] But in the short term he could do little other than introduce a water cart service.

Perth was never to suffer again as it did, in the summer of 1896–97, as the following complaints indicate:

> We, that is the residents of Highgate Hill, have only had water twice during the last three weeks and then only for an hour or two at most . . . It was bad enough when the Company had it, but there is simply no water at all now.

or

> There would be quite a famine in our neighbourhood, but for the existence of two or three wells, from which troops of women and girls can be seen daily carrying water.

Sometimes, to the great inconvenience of families, the water cart did not reach a locality until midnight; and in mid-January one water carter operating in a depressed part of East Perth was stoned by the local inhabitants. And these people knew that 'the people in the Terrace are never without a strong supply' and that 'if we had only been lucky enough to have the management living in this street . . . I think they would soon see a way to get water here'. Even Keane agreed with them, for in an interview he showed that of nearly 700 000 gallons consumed in 24 hours on one summer day in Perth, 191 800 gallons were accounted

[149] PCC Minute Book, 20 October 1896.

275

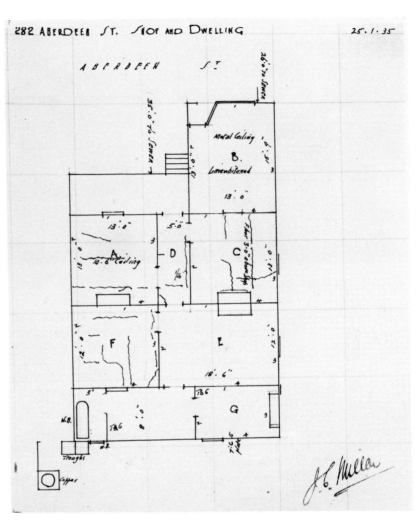

282 ABERDEEN ST. SHOP AND DWELLING   25·1·35

Public Works Department plan of a house in Aberdeen Street, indicating the placement of taps: the house was built in the goldrush years, and shows signs of age by the mid-1930s.

for by 195 users. Among the selfish users he listed were Sir John and Alexander Forrest, and other politicians and senior civil servants. Despite criticism from some of the selfish users of water Keane held on for nearly two years, until Sir John Forrest found cause to induce him to resign—Keane, although improving the water supply greatly, had overspent his budget and had used contractors with whom he had a vested interest. In a decade characterised by extravagance and shady dealings Keane's misdemeanors seem petty enough. But Keane had also bribed the official receiver in his bankruptcy case, and this was about to become public knowledge. In short, from Forrest's point of view, Keane had to go.[150]

Keane had vastly improved the water supply of central Perth, including East and West Perth and the Highgate area. But it was his successor as Chairman of the Board, the redoubtable William Traylen, who over the next five years extended the mains to parts of the municipalities of Subiaco, Leederville, Victoria Park and North Perth,

[150] The incidents cited in this paragraph are drawn from Sue-Jane Hunt and G. C. Bolton 'Cleansing the Dunghill: Water Supply and Sanitation in Perth, 1878–1912', *Studies in Western Australian History* No. 2, March 1978, pp.12-14.

and even beyond Highgate Hill to the new estate of Mt Lawley. In addition, Traylen took over the administration of the water supply of Fremantle and suburbs between, like Peppermint Grove and Claremont. Also, the catchment reservoirs were increased in size, and the introduction of an aeration process helped to purify the domestic water supply. In 1904 the Labor Government abolished the Board and placed water supply under the direct control of the Minister for Works. After 1897 the Perth City Council had played little part in the water supply saga. Alexander Forrest (Mayor from 1898 to 1900), who had never taken an interest in the question, did not attend the meetings of Traylen's Board, and nor did his successors. Henry Brown, Mayor in 1904, supported the abolition of the Board, but did so in his capacity as a member of the Legislative Assembly. Some of Traylen's decisions had occasioned dismay in Perth. In December 1898 at a ratepayers' meeting S. H. Parker and Thomas Molloy steered through a resolution urging the Council to regain control of the water supply of the city. This was in protest against the Board's decision to extend the water mains to Subiaco.[151] Nothing came from the protest.

Although by 1911 Perth and its suburbs were connected to piped water, it must not be thought that all households received scheme water. Usually scheme water came well after the major flurry of building activity in all suburbs, and it came first to the more affluent households. For many people in Perth itself, but more particularly in the suburbs, the well remained an important source of supply, and by 1911 too the household galvanised iron water tank was becoming an important supplementary supply system, although the 'better class' (as Inspector Halliday put it) had begun to install them as early as 1885.[152] Piped water was always expensive for, and a source of dismay to, the working people of Perth, as even Alexander Forrest admitted in his Mayoral report for 1899–1900. By 1903 the position had worsened still further when the Board increased the cost to private consumers to 2s per thousand gallons, or double the cost of water to the citizens of Melbourne and Sydney. By 1911, despite high costs to the consumer, the demand for water was rapidly outstripping its supply, and the Government dithered over whether to build a dam on the Canning (as the Perth City Council wanted) or to resort to expediencies such as bore water. Already in 1911 several bores were in use. The suburb of Subiaco was dependent on bore water. Eventually the dam was built, but debate about Perth's supply would recur often in the next sixty-five years. But by 1911 the people of Perth were at last using pure water, though it was as late as 1908 when the Government Bacteriologist proclaimed Perth's water to be almost entirely free of injurious micro-organisms.[153] In 1911, 15 075 of Perth and suburbs' 22 000 houses had piped water. The rest made do with tanks, wells and neighbours' taps.

For drinking purposes, most families usually filled daily a canvas water-bag which, with a tin mug attached by a piece of string, was hung under the verandah to be cooled by such movement of air as there was. This too was a practice which was continued until well after the Second

[151] PCC Minute Book, 15 December 1898.
[152] Report of Commission into the Sanitary Condition of Perth, 1885: *Votes and Proceedings of the Legislative Council*, 1885, No. 20, evidence of the Inspector of Nuisances.
[153] Perth City Council Health Inspector's Report, November 1908. Year Book of the Commonwealth of Australia No. 2, 1901–08, p.1040; No. 5, 1901–11, p.1025.

World War. From the 1890s the availability of piped water encouraged the construction and use of bathrooms. For a time bathrooms were restricted to the houses of upper and middle class people who in consequence tended to bathe at least twice weekly in their iron, claw-footed baths. Some even used hot water, provided by gas heating. By 1911 most houses being built, even those for workers, included a bathroom, but many working class families lived in houses built earlier which lacked the facility.[154] The conjunction of piped water and the building boom of the late 1890s and 1900s virtually created a new occupational group, the plumbers, who became identified as such, instead of using the old term of sanitary engineers.

The provision of cheap, plentiful, and clean water was far and away the most important public need which the Perth City Council had to deal with in the period 1884 to 1911. It was often linked in the public mind with the issue of sanitation and sewerage. Between 1886 and 1891, the sanitation of the city was the responsibility of the Perth Board of Health (created under the Public Health Act of 1886), the membership of which overlapped greatly with the Perth City Council. From January 1892, however, the Perth City Council was given major responsibility in this area. From 1893 the Perth City Council was enabled, by act of parliament, to introduce a system of double-pan collection by sanitary contractors. Some members of parliament like William Traylen and Winthrop Hackett advocated a deep drainage and sewerage scheme, but most politicians and Perth City councillors believed that the great expense (estimated in 1894 at £200,000) was unwarranted and that the people did not want sewerage. Thus for most of the 1890s the excreta of the people of Perth either went into the (often rarely cleaned) cess-pits or dry-earth closets as these latter were installed. Increasingly, people were cajoled and brow-beaten into changing over to the double-pan system. In 1897, there were 1408 cases of typhoid in Perth, doubling the 1896 figure of 663; and the number of deaths rose from 89 to 134. Several sewerage schemes were considered that year but no immediate action resulted, at least partly because the projected cost was now a mammoth £500,000. In 1898 Perth's doctors petitioned parliament on the need for a deep sewerage system.[155] Again no action was taken. Not until well after Forrest's departure for federal politics did the State Government commit itself to the introduction of deep drainage. In 1902 experimental tanks and filter beds of a new and cheaper bacterial process were installed in Government House. In 1903 the Under Secretary for Public Works in NSW recommended that the bacterial process be adopted for Perth, and parts of North Perth and Leederville, using the Claise Brook outlet. The estimated cost was £112,000.[156] In 1904 legislation was introduced and then withdrawn. But this system was slowly installed throughout central Perth and into the inner suburbs north of the river between 1906 and 1920. The main outlet was at Claise Brook on the Swan River, outlets at North Beach[157] and Crawley having been rejected. Some wealthy households installed their own septic tanks. Most made do with the double-pan system and dry-earth closets until the sewerage pipes reached them.

[154] H. Sorenson's Quote Book, 1897–99, cited in Ms D. Robinson 'Social Status in Perth'.
[155] *Votes and Proceedings*, 1898, No. A4.
[156] Mayor's Annual Report, 1902–03, p.4.
[157] PCC Minute Book, 27 November 1899—C. Y. O'Connor favoured a sea outlet.

The greatest pressure for reform had come from the Perth City Council. From 1887 the ratepayers had had to pay a special health rate for the local board of health. At 3*d* in the £1, it was not an insignificant amount.[158] It paid for a medical officer and an inspector. But advocates of a clean and plentiful water supply did not always advocate sewerage schemes. Probably until the late 1890s most people agreed with Dr Scott's view, expressed in October 1887, that 'the sandy nature of the soil operated largely as a filtering and deodorising agent'. Even Traylen did not change his mind about this for another seven years. In 1892, following the enactment of the Public Health Act Amendment Act, the Perth City Council established a Health Committee which overseered sanitation issues in these years.[159] The night soil removal service was run by private contractors. By March 1893 several councillors, including Molloy and Walter James, wished to see the service run by Council servants, as many ratepayers complained that the contractors came irregularly, in the stillest part of the day, and were slovenly in their work.[160] No action was taken. In the same year William Traylen presented Council with a report on the refuse practices of eastern colonial cities. Again no action followed, though a Committee considered Traylen's report.[161] He had better luck in January 1894 when Council accepted his report on night soil removal and invited tenders for a more efficient removal scheme, namely the double-pan system.[162] In August 1894 the Health Officer deprecated the double-pan system of the Sanitary Company and urged the introduction of deep sewerage. Traylen spoke against this in Council.[163] It was not until 1900 that the double-pan system operated throughout the city with a twice weekly service. By 1895 the citizens of Perth were objecting to the presence of the night soil depot (884 Reserve) in their midst and the search for a new site was on. Perth Commonage beyond Subiaco seemed a likely choice, but the high costs of a railway line from Subiaco Station to the proposed site deterred the Government. Not until 1903 was the old site closed down completely, but between 1899 and 1903 processed matter was pumped from 884 to a new site at 954 in what was to become the Mt Lawley area, near Walcott Street. From 1903 the night soil was carted by road direct to this site.[164]

In 1896 another consequence of the growth of the city manifested itself. The city faced its first strike by the workmen of the sanitary section. Although some councillors described them as 'anarchists' and 'agitators', and Councillor Lee urged his followers not to recognise a combination of employees, it was clear that the nature of their work and the increased cost of living justified their claim for 10*s* a day. In a tied voting situation Mayor Saunders turned down the claim and a strike seemed imminent. But in fact the men had not formed a 'combination'; indeed lacking union strength, they had no choice but to return to work. Some of these men carried the so-called 'fever-pans' during the typhoid 'epidemic' of 1897 and 1898, again without an increase in their pay. It was the typhoid 'epidemic' which induced the Perth City Council to create a systematic scavenging or rubbish disposal service. Sited in working class districts of North and East Perth, the rubbish tips were a

---

158 PCC Minute Book, 4 March 1887.
159 PCC Minute Book, 4 March 1892.
160 PCC Minute Book, 10 March 1893.   161 PCC Minute Book, 20 September 1893.
162 PCC Minute Book, 3 January 1894.   163 PCC Minute Book, 5 August 1894.
164 PCC Minute Book, 5, 17 May, 7 June 1895; 5 March 1897; Mayor's Reports 1897–98 and 1902–03.

health hazard to workmen and residents alike. Not until 1903 was the East Perth tip closed. Children who grew up there in those years recall in old age the stench of the tip. In 1899 the Perth City Council sacked nearly all its sanitary workers, and it was a new team which received the 10s a day introduced in October 1901. Throughout the nineteenth century the Perth City Council had treated its workers well, giving compensation to the sick or injured well before the Forrest Government passed a Workers Compensation Act (1898). But the early 1900s were years of adjustment to the growth of unionism and a considerable amount of industrial legislation, and there were occasions on which some councillors persisted with an individualism no longer touched by common humanity. But such councillors and such occasions were few in number.[165]

In 1896, at the time of the creation of the Metropolitan Waterworks Board, the Perth City Council again recommended the establishment of a deep drainage system, but to no avail. In the absence of a deep drainage system, the surface drainage system had to be maintained and extended. This was a large task for the pressure on the drains had increased enormously in the 1890s, as the amount of water pouring into them probably tripled in the course of the decade. In 1897–98, £20,000 (paid by the Government) was expended on upgrading the system. Then in mid-1899 the City Engineer reported that the main drain (in Wellington Street) was about to collapse. Had this occurred the city could have been flooded as it had been in former times.[166] With the aid of a grant of £10,000 the Council drained the Sutherland Street area and rebuilt a large section of the Wellington Street drain—it was set seven feet lower than the old drain and had three times the capacity. These works were still in progress in May 1901 when the Duke of York visited Perth, and

Men at work on the Wellington Street drain, 1901.

[165] PCC Minute Book, 6 November 1896; 24 September 1892; City Engineer's Report, November 1899; November 1903.
[166] PCC Minute Book, 5 June 1899.

*The installation of the city's septic
sewerage system, Burswood, 1905.*

although Council was proud of its drain, the royal personage was kept
away from Wellington Street.[167] From this time many private households
were given permission (at a price) to connect their drains to the Council
street drains. If deep drainage was introduced these people would have to
pay a second connection fee. By 1905 the Perth City Council was fed up
with the several State Governments with which they had had to deal since
1900—six ministries in five years. By 1905 storm water drainage funds
were required urgently, and still no decision had been taken on the
sewerage question. Only in 1906 were funds forthcoming, and a new
main drain was run through the city from north to south with an outlet at
Mounts Bay Road. In 1906 a new refuse destructor was built and
construction was begun on the septic tanks in East Perth. In 1907 the
filter beds on Burswood Island in the middle of the river were in danger
of being flooded, and construction of only one sewerage main had been
commenced.[168] Even as late as November 1908 reticulation had not been
proceeded with, although some mains had been laid. And even at this
late date many households and businesses were still being connected to
the storm-water drainage scheme, while in the same year Sir John Forrest
had a septic tank installed in his Hay Street home, and Timothy Quinlan
installed a septic tank for his Moanna Cafe and thirty-three shops in Hay
Street.[169] Emanuel's Buildings in St George's Terrace also had a septic
tank. At the end of 1911 only 700 premises were connected to the sewer.
Even as late as 1920 less than one-third of the houses of Perth and
suburbs had been sewered, and the pan system was still widely used.[170]

While the provision of a plentiful and pure water supply was the
single most important activity of the Perth City Council in the goldrush
period, and while the twin problems of night soil removal and sewerage
occupied much of Council's attention, the growing city had other needs

[167] PCC Minute Book, 20 May 1901.
[168] PCC Annual Report, 1906–07.   [169] City Engineer's Report, November 1908.
[170] Year Book of the Commonwealth of Australia No. 5, 1901–11, p.1031; No. 14,
     1901–20, p.888; also PCC Health Officer's Report, 1 November 1915.

281

which required action by the councillors. In particular the councillors had to provide adequate communications, power and lighting in Perth.

In 1883 the Perth Gas Company had been formed with a view to winning a contract with the Perth City Council to supply the city with coal gas. Agreement between the Council and the Company (the memberships of which overlapped) was reached in 1885, and by late that year, mains pipes were being laid in some of the central streets and the power plant was under construction.[171] The agreement was ratified in parliament by the Perth Gas Company Act, 1886, which empowered the Company to manufacture and supply gas within a radius of five miles from the General Post Office in Perth. The agreement provided for the purchase of all the Company's assets by the Council at any time after December 1906, the price to be determined by arbitration in the event of non-agreement by Council and Company. In 1886 gas lighting was installed in the Town Hall, but the installation of gas in domestic households proceeded very slowly indeed, and as late as 1889 only St George's Terrace and central Hay Street had been connected. General street lighting had proceeded rather more quickly and by mid-1889 there were 117 gas lamps in the city, an increase of 37 over the previous year.[172] Oil lighting, however, remained the most used form until the mid-1890s.

In 1891 some of the more progressive councillors recommended the introduction of electric lighting. Late in that year Council advertised for tenders for the provision of an electricity supply.[173] Shortly after, the Perth Gas Company announced its intention to tender; indeed it sought permission to erect poles for electric wire in Perth, a request which was refused.[174] By this time a rival company had been formed. Called the Electric Lighting & Power Company it opened negotiations with the Council in April 1892.[175] In June 1892 Council refused to negotiate with the Perth Gas Company and the way seemed clear for its rival.[176] At the half-yearly meeting of the ratepayers, the Mayor, S. H. Parker, in observing that electric light 'was apparently the light of the age', suggested that Council should raise a loan to undertake the work itself and that

> before twelve months, the Council trusted to see the whole of the streets of the city, besides the Town Hall, lit with this light.[177]

Alas, it was not to be as simple as that. The Perth Gas Company, which had been charging Council 14s per thousand feet of gas, offered to supply gas at 10s per thousand feet. Councillors began to do some arithmetic but the additions did not tally. In the twelve month period 1891–92 one set of figures showed a cost to Council of £952, while another came to only £738. The manager of the Gas Company, Mr Wigglesworth, had asserted that the cost to Council would be £603.[178] While there was a small majority of councillors in favour of an agreement with the Electric Lighting and Power Company, some of the prominent councillors like Walter James and Thomas Molloy doubted if the agreement to supply electricity at £876 per annum was an improvement. Accordingly Council sought the ideas of the ratepayers at a public meeting held in August 1892. There it emerged that the city got

---

171 PCC Minute Book, 7 August 1885.
172 PCC Minute Book, 4 January, 13 May 1889.
173 PCC Minute Book, 4 December 1891.   174 PCC Minute Book, 8 January 1892.
175 PCC Minute Book, 7 April 1892.   176 PCC Minute Book, 3 June 1892.
177 *West Australian*, 10 May 1892.   178 *West Australian*, 20 April 1892.

gas from sunset to midnight except on moonlight nights when the supply was cut off completely (about 65 nights in a year); and that when there was a strike in the Newcastle coalfield, the Company used 'colonial gas' from Collie which produced an inferior light. Timothy Quinlan claimed to have paid £140 for gas in the past year, though it was not clear whether he was speaking of his house, his hotel or both. Quinlan himself had become a shareholder in the Electric Light Company. The chairman of the Perth Gas Company, Mr F. T. Crowder, met with a hostile reception, as did the manager, Mr Wigglesworth.[179] The meeting voted to proceed with the Electric Lighting and Power Company, whose spokesman at the meeting was the manager, C. J. Otte. The meeting also decided to conduct a poll on the question. This took place later in the month and drew a voting response of 617 out of 1500 ratepayers. Never before or after in Perth's history was there to be the sight of two companies haranguing the public at a poll as to the relative merits of their wares. Each Company had an electoral committee which prepared and distributed 'dodgers' and placards, hired cabs to collect electors and carry them to the Town Hall booth, and so on.

> Sometimes it was the elevating influence of gas which affected the crowd; at other times it was the electrical influence at work . . . Singularly enough, the transition from gas to Gladstone; from electricity to Erin seemed an easy one, and thus the crowd was treated to disquisitions, not only on street lighting, but also to addresses on the Grand Old Man and Home Rule.

The election was conducted on a one-man-one-vote principle and resulted in a majority vote in favour of electric light—375 votes to 242.[180] The way seemed clear for the introduction of electricity. The Perth Gas Company had been discredited.

Or had it? At the Annual General Meeting of Ratepayers, the Mayor, S. H. Parker, casually announced that some difficulties had arisen in the negotiations between the Council and the Electric Lighting Company, and that in the event of negotiations being broken off, then he was confident that the Perth Gas Company proposed to get statutory power to enable it to supply electric light to the ratepayers and inhabitants of Perth.[181] In February 1893, following the City Council's refusal to sign an agreement at once, the directors of the Electric Lighting Company pulled out of the negotiations. The City Council then asked the Perth Gas Company to light the streets with gas for a further two years.[182] As the Gas Company had lost interest in electricity temporarily, a Mr Alex McKenzie began to negotiate with Council on the subject.[183] By August 1893 McKenzie had contracted with Mr McNeil (of Waterworks fame) to supply poles, wires, etc, and it seemed that Council would proceed with him.[184] A month later McKenzie pulled out, following the collapse of his bank. A Mr Moyle took up the negotiations, but the tide was running in the Perth Gas Company's direction.[185] Throughout 1893 it had extended its mains very slowly indeed, fearing over-capitalization at a time of economic recession in Perth. As late as September 1894, Beaufort Street residents were still without gas

---

[179] *West Australian*, 12 August 1892.   [180] *West Australian*, 23 August 1893.
[181] *West Australian*, 16 November 1892.
[182] PCC Minute Book, 3 February 1893.
[183] PCC Minute Book, 10 March, 7 April 1893.
[184] PCC Minute Book, 4 August 1893.
[185] PCC Minute Book, 26 September, 6 October 1893.

lighting.[186] Yet the recession was also keeping out competitors, and in 1894 it was the Perth Gas Company which acted upon its statutory right and began to erect light poles and wires for the electrification of business houses and some private residences. It also re-entered into negotiations with the Perth City Council. But in fact the enthusiasm for electricity was on the wane. R. S. Haynes, one of its foremost advocates, was no longer on Council; and S. H. Parker, was no longer the Mayor. And Alexander Forrest took little interest in the subject, perhaps because several of his friends and political allies like Sir George Shenton and Sir James Lee Steere were directors or shareholders of the Perth Gas Company. It was not until mid-1894 that the Gas Company had to provide gas at the lower rate of 10s per thousand, and it also provided electric light for the Town Hall. Messrs Wigglesworth and Crowder had won through.[187]

Not that relations between the Council and the Company were always good. Ratepayers continued to grumble about the lack of lamps once out of the central city area, and the cost of the gas supply to residents remained high. In 1896 Council sought the approval of the Government to borrow money for electric lighting of the city and the introduction of tramways, but to no avail. By the end of 1897 gas lamps had been established as far north as Brisbane Street and as far west as Colin Street. Perth was slowly but surely becoming a gas city, as other Australian cities were as surely turning to electricity. Melbourne streets were lit by electricity from 1894.[188] In mid-1898 Alexander Forrest, Mayor a second time, voted down an attempt by some councillors to have the Council undertake the electrification of the city.[189] In the meantime several private businesses such as hotels (J. Chipper's Court Hotel, for example), and the offices of the *Daily News* (Stirling Bros), as well as some Government Departments like the Railways Department, had installed their own electric lighting power plants.[190] By the turn of the century pressure for electrification was coming from the newly created road boards of North Perth and Victoria Park, especially the latter which wished to see the Causeway ablaze with electric light.[191] Yet in mid-1899 the Perth City Council again rejected tenders for electric lighting—this time from the Electric Tramways Company as well as the Perth Gas Company.[192] In 1900–01 Council again resolved to establish its own plant, but at a poll on the subject the ratepayers overwhelmingly rejected the scheme and favoured the issue of a licence to a Company.[193] Alerted by the experience of other colonies, the Council called for tenders for an underground system of electric wiring; but no tenders were received.[194] In May 1901 there was yet another poll on electric lighting—this time on the advisability or otherwise of its municipalization. The anti-municipalization vote of 880 was double the pro-vote of 421.[195] Council doggedly stuck with municipalization.[196] All this came to naught. In October 1902 the Perth City Council came to an agreement with the Gas Company to provide a further 300 lamps in the streets of the city.[197] Only the corners of streets along which ran the electric trolley trams (after 1900) were illuminated by electric light, under

186 PCC Minute Book, 29 December 1893.   187 *West Australian*, 15 May 1894.
188 G. Davison *Marvellous Melbourne*, 1978, p.173; PCC Minute Book, 4 June 1897.
189 PCC Minute Book, 27, 30 May 1898.   190 PCC Minute Book, 11 October 1898.
191 PCC Minute Book, 1 May 1899.   192 PCC Minute Book, 2 June 1899.
193 PCC Minute Book, 1 October 1900.   194 PCC Minute Book, 1 April 1901.
195 PCC Minute Book, 7 May 1901.   196 PCC Minute Book, 9 September 1901.
197 PCC Minute Book, 13 October 1902.

*An electric tram on
Beaufort/Barrack Street bridge:*
*linking the northern suburbs to
central Perth.*

an agreement with the Electric Tramways Company—this included the
Causeway, as well as Hay Street. Not until 1912 when the Perth City
Council purchased the Perth Gas Company did the electrification of the
street lighting begin on a comprehensive scale.

It should not be thought that the introduction of gas lamps in the
streets of Perth in the mid-1880s led to a sudden decrease in kerosene
lamps. Indeed for many years the increase of kerosene lamps matched
that of gas. As late as December 1899 there were 100 kerosene lamps,
mainly in East Perth and West Perth. At that time there were 410 gas
lamps, mainly in central Perth but extending north to Brisbane Street.
Hay Street with 49 gas lamps, and St George's Terrace and Adelaide
Terraces with 38, were easily the best illuminated streets. Until the
agreement with the Gas Company in mid-1902, the increase in lighting
after 1899 was almost entirely of the kerosene type. By the end of 1904,
however, Perth had nearly 800 incandescent gas lamps and the kerosene
lamps had been almost entirely phased out (and only 130 oil lamps
remained). The lamps were set about 60 yards apart, some in the centre
of the roads to avoid the foliage of kerbside trees. The lamps were lit for
all but eight or nine nights per month. This was a practice deplored by
many citizens who complained that in the centre of the city, where the
tall buildings threw heavy shadows, moonlight could not penetrate.[198]
On the eve of the purchase of the Perth Gas Company, the number of gas
lamps in the city had risen to nearly 1200.[199] There were still 80 kerosene
lamps in the city. There would be little change from this for many years,
even after the purchase of the Gas Company. What would increase
enormously would be the number of metered houses in Perth. Between
1911 and 1914 the number of meters (pre-payment and pay as you use)
almost doubled, reaching 2772 on the eve of the Great War. In addition
the number of gas cookers and grillers on hire from the Perth City
Council had reached 1769 which was double the October 1912 figure.

198 City Engineer's Report, 1 November 1904.
199 City Engineer's Report, November 1910.

Electricity in the service of the people of Perth.

And to produce the gas, work was commenced on the construction of a power plant at Trafalgar Road in East Perth. The gas works would be sited there for more than sixty years.

Electricity had made considerable inroads by the Great War. The first use was in telephones, one of which was installed at the Perth City Council in 1888. Expensive at first, the telephone was the preserve of businessmen, just as the telegraph had been previously. By the late 1890s there were about 500 subscribers, paying £7 a year (commercial subscribers) or £5 a year (private subscribers). By 1914 the growth in telephone subscriptions had led to the opening of an automatic exchange. Not until after the Second World War, however, did the telephone come within the financial reach of most of the people of Perth. Electric street lighting grew very sluggishly—indeed in 1914 there were only 131 electric lamps in the streets of Perth. Another 95 had been established in the suburbs of Mt Lawley and Maylands, and Subiaco had its own electric light and power plant in 1903. The great advance was in domestic lighting, for by 1914 nearly 5000 meters were connected to the city power supply system.[200] This represented nearly 50% of the houses of Perth. For the suburbs the percentage was probably higher.

Important as was the issue of the provision of gas and electricity, it did not equal in importance the upgrading and extending of the town's roads and footpaths, at least as measured by Council's expenditure over the years. From the first loan taken up in 1881–82 (total £2000)—to the twelfth loan, taken up in 1909—(total £11,000), some £234,000 was borrowed from individuals and insurance companies and banks. The great bulk of this money was spent on drainage and road construction and maintenance.

By the late 1870s only the central streets had been macadamised and then only in narrow and shallow strips. Even Irwin Street lacked such a strip. But pressure to extend the macadamised road system was coming from the north ward members, as the following exchange indicates:

> Cr E. Stone: 'Irwin Street was the only thoroughfare in the city proper which had not yet been macadamized.'
>
> Cr MacKenzie: ' "City proper!" What do you mean by "city proper"? I suppose we who don't reside in your "city proper" are not proper citizens. We are not going to stand that!'

On a close vote the £50 at issue went to Stirling Street for a stone top dressing.[201] Irwin Street had to wait until 1881 when the Perth City Council, having met its debt on the main drain, was able to take out a loan, largely for road construction.[202] The successful tenderers for debentures at 5% were Miss Bunbury (Francis Lochee was her agent) and the Mayor, George Shenton, the former taking 25 debentures at £100 each, and the latter taking six debentures at the same price. Four other old families, the Helms and the Habgoods, the Purkis, and the McKails took the remainder of the £6000 loan. Shenton was still receiving the interest on his loan at the time of his death in 1909. One of the successful contract tenderers was R. H. Hester, a descendent of the unfortunate Thomas Hester. Hester's contract was for the macadamization of Roe Street at a value of £1023.[203] With the town's finances in a healthy state,

200 PCC City Electrical Engineer's Report, October 1914.
201 PCC Minute Book, 30 December 1878.
202 PCC Minute Book, 14 December 1880.
203 PCC Minute Book, 14 February, 1, 7, 29 April, 19 August, 4 November 1881.

the Council decided to press on with road construction in the north ward, especially James Street, and in March 1882 floated a second loan—of £4000. This second loan was taken up more slowly, but as with the first the debentures were bought by individuals. At the same time a rather drastic revaluation of properties in Perth was undertaken and the rates were increased to 1s 6d in the £, which included 6d for the two loans.[204] This flurry of activity meant that by the end of 1883 there were 18 miles of macadamized roads in the town, and 27 miles of made (dredged shell) footpaths.[205]

In the next three years the rateable value of the town increased rapidly—from £45,366 in 1885 to £70,338 in 1887. Thereafter to 1890 the increase was more sedate, due to the economic recession of 1888 and part of 1889, but by the beginning of 1891 the rateable value exceeded £80,000. In 1885 Council took out a third loan—for £8000—but the money was largely expended on maintenance and reconstruction of roads, especially Wellington Street in the Railway Station area.[206] One innovation was a decision to import flag-stones for the footpaths of Perth. Another was to experiment with the use of blue metal from the Parkerville quarry. By now some contractors like Alfred Deardon—who for years had made a living (at least in part) by watering the streets of Perth—were doing extremely well from road construction contracts. Others who did well were J. Elsegood, Thomas Statham, the Bunning Bros, and William Drabble, the two last named families lasting in their businesses through to the 1970s. In 1888, undeterred by the prevailing economic depression, Council took out its fourth loan in eight years—this time for £10,000. By now the tenders for the debentures were coming from banks: indeed the fourth loan went entirely to the Commercial Bank.[207] This fourth loan was used for the blue-metalling of Wellington Street, part of Beaufort Street, and Duke Street in the west of the town, for the large settlement to the west was now as disadvantaged as had been the James Street–Brisbane Street population of a few years earlier.

But by mid-1891 it was clear that the Council could not keep up with the rate of development of the town. Unless the rating system was extended to include Government or church property or the Government provided Council with a subsidy, or the loan arrangements were altered to allow for a bigger percentage against rates collected, then the Council could do little beyond repairing roads already made. Within the municipality were 50 miles of roads, but only 27 miles were even made partially—that is up to 18 feet wide. The remaining 23 miles were merely sand-tracks which were well nigh impassable in all seasons. The flagging of footpaths had proceeded so slowly that not one block in the city was fully flagged. In desperation the Perth City Council, headed by Edward Keane, turned to the Forrest Government for assistance. Their memorial requested Forrest to follow the example of the eastern colonies, in several of which the Government supplemented by an equivalent sum each pound raised by the general rates.[208] In reply to the memorialists Forrest agreed that 'the streets and paths of the City of Perth are not what they should be'. He grumbled about the state of roads and paths in winter time. But he would not agree that the Government property and church

[204] PCC Minute Book, 3 February, 12 March, 10 May, 15 December 1882.
[205] PCC Minute Book, 12 November 1883.
[206] PCC Minute Book, 19 December 1885.
[207] PCC Minute Book, 6 April 1888.   [208] Memorial dated July 1891.

property should be rated. Nor did he believe that his Government had neglected the needs of the city; and, as was his way, he listed his Government's achievements, the most notable of which was to reserve 1000 acres on the top of Mt Eliza for a public park. However, he had been struck by the beauty of eastern colonial cities and of the part played in their beautification by the respective governments. He thought that his Government might be able to assist the Perth City Council, for the economic outlook for the colony was very bright.[209] Within the next eighteen months a new Municipalities Act was passed and the Perth City Council received a Government subsidy of 10s for each £1 raised by rates. This meant that in 1892 alone, the Perth City Council was able to spend an additional £1935 on road improvements. In April 1892 Council agreed to take out its biggest loan ever—£15,000. The loan was not fully taken up until 1893, and then all but £3000 of it was taken up by the Post Office Savings Bank.[210]

In the same period it began an active programme of taking over many streets still in private hands, such as Queen Street, north Hutt (William) Street (which belonged to Henry Anstey), and several other streets belonging to the Intercolonial Land and Building Company.[211] More Government money was forthcoming for further reclamation of the Esplanade, the establishment of a market, and so on. Thus by the time Alexander Forrest became Mayor—November 1892—the principle of Government subsidization of Council's work had been firmly established. And although the rate revenue collected in 1893 fell below that of 1891 and 1892 because of recession in the economy, the Council was able to press ahead with road and footpath construction.[212] In 1894–95 under pressure from his brother Alexander and a newly formed

The new Market in Wellington Street, built in 1897, photographed in the 1920s. It was demolished in 1927.

[209] *West Australian*, 19 July 1891.
[210] *West Australian*, 14 November 1893; PCC Minute Book, 11 April 1892.
[211] PCC Minute Book, 11 May, 1 July, 1892.
[212] See Alexander Forrest's First Mayoral Report, 13 November 1893.

Municipal Association, John Forrest agreed to increase the subsidy to councils from 10s in £1 to £1 for £1.[213] This ensured that in the years of most rapid growth to the turn of the century, the Perth City Council was able to meet most of the demands for new roads and footpaths.

In the mid-1890s there were several other advances in transport facilities. In 1894, after protracted negotiations with the Government, a new bridge was built over the railway line at Beaufort Street. In the course of construction of the bridge, the Working Men's Institute was pulled down, as the bridge was brought into alignment with Barrack Street, rather than Beaufort Street as in the past. By the mid-1890s businessmen and private residents in the William Street/Hutt Street area were being adversely affected by the rapid expansion of railway lines. In 1894 no fewer than seven lines lay between a pedestrian, rider or carrier travelling on the north-south road.[214] It was estimated that because of rail traffic, the road crossing was closed nearly 50% of each working day. Despite representations to the Government, little was accomplished until the turn of the century when a start was made on what became known as the Horseshoe Bridge. Completed in 1903 the Horseshoe Bridge led to a revitalization of business and residential interest in the northern quarter. It was in the late 1890s that the Stirling Street and Havelock Street crossings, in the east and west of the city respectively, were closed to the public.[215]

The mid to late 1890s saw a flurry of street renaming and the introduction of street name signs and numbering of houses, churches, business establishments, etc. One of the streets renamed was Cemetery Road. In February 1895 this historic transverse road, leading from the city north-east to the East Perth Cemetery and St Bartholomew's Church, was renamed 'The Avenue'. This was indeed appropriate for by the 1890s, the gum shade-trees planted for the benefit of pall-bearers in the 1860s had grown into a splendid avenue. But the cemetery itself was about to be closed as such, and after considerable community debate, in the course of which a Subiaco site (reserve 2852) was used for a short time, a large new cemetery site was established at Karrakatta, south of the main area of settlement at Subiaco, and well away from the growing suburb of Claremont.[216] While the matter of the cemetery was still unresolved, the Perth City Council had a change of heart about 'The Avenue' and renamed it 'Forrest Avenue'—in honour of either Sir John Forrest or Mayor Alexander Forrest. Other changes were about to occur. In 1896, at the instigation of the Post Office, the Perth City Council began the tasks of street house-numbering and fixing direction plates. In the course of simplifying the knowability of Perth it was also decided to rename Hutt, part of Goderich and all of Howick Streets. In 1897 they became extensions of the equally historic William, Murray and Hay Streets. One Imperial hero was additionally honoured in the course of these changes. The ancient (1830s) 'Old Recreation Ground', off Wellington Street in East Perth, was given the official title of Wellington Square. It was about this time that the training and exercising of horses was forbidden on the square. In July 1899, James Brittain's clay-pits, which had been used for brick-making since the 1850s, were taken over by the Council and transformed into Queen's Gardens. At the same time

Forrest Avenue, Perth, 1896: the eucalypts had been planted thirty years before as an act of faith in the future of Perth.

213 PCC Minute Book, 4 May 1894.
214 PCC Minute Book, 2 November, 7 December 1894.
215 PCC Minute Book, 18 June 1897.
216 PCC Minute Book, 1 February, 1 March 1895.

Third Swamp, where the surviving Perth Aboriginal encampment was, and where the tents of transient miners had been erected, was renamed Hyde Park and placed in the care of the city's Gardening Inspector. Late in 1897 Howard Street was punched through private land between St George's Terrace and the Esplanade. In the late 1890s and early 1900s, the Perth City Council took over this and several other private streets, including Queen Street, St George's Court, and the streets of the East Norwood Estate and other estates in East Perth. By 1911 there was scarcely a private street left in Perth.[217]

In 1896 the creation of the Leederville Roads Board slightly reduced resident pressure on the Perth City Council. But there were still plenty of deputations from disgruntled residents, especially from the northern and western parts of the city. By 1895 West Perth (south ward) had its own railway station and, but for the rapid development of neighbouring Subiaco, may have become a separate municipality. (However, a poll on the subject revealed much apathy and an easy majority in favour of the *status quo*.)[218] The Perth City Council tightened its hold on the district when the Building Act was amended to apply to Perth generally and not just to the central city area. The amendment meant that many of the wooden houses erected in the less salubrious parts of West Perth, especially near the railway station, were now legally sub-standard. As the provisions of the Act did not cover the Subiaco area, that suburb contained many wooden dwellings. The difference can be shown statistically. In 1901, of 5126 buildings in the City of Perth, 3930 were made of brick and only 730 of wood. But in the Perth magisterial distict, which since 1897 included new suburbs like Subiaco, Victoria Park, North Perth (1901) and South Perth, of 9149 buildings, 4583 were brick and 3271 were made of wood. Put another way, of 1930 houses in the magisterial district of Perth in 1891 only 7% were made of wood; in 1901 in the same area about 36% were made of wood.[219] From the mid-1890s too, the Perth City Council had to grapple with the rapid growth of 'temporary dwellings', usually tents. It did so by licensing them, charging a fee of 5s per month, rising to 10s a month in 1896, and by restricting their erection to certain parts of the city, such as the Mulberry Plantation and Moore Street in East Perth, Third Swamp (Hyde Park) in the northern quarter, and Perth Commonage at Subiaco.[220]

But while the regulation of housing was an increasingly important function of the Perth City Council and led to the creation of several new positions on Council's staff, road construction continued to absorb the bulk of Council's income. In 1896 a loan of £30,000 was taken out. Of this amount no less than £16,000 was spent on road construction in the north, west and east of the city.[221] In December 1896, following a drastic revaluation of city property and an equally dramatic updating of the city's ratebooks, the annual rateable value of Perth rose by 90% to £204,000. A rate of 1s6d in the £ netted over £15,000. This level was easily bettered for 1898 (£20,000), (and for 1899 the capital value of Perth was about £4 million, with an annual value of £289,104) and in that year Council took out its seventh loan—for £80,000, an amount far

217 PCC Minute Book, 1 March, 1895; 10 January 1896—a number plate cost 6d.; 6 June, 15 August 1898; 5 March 1900; 14 October 1901.
218 PCC Minute Book, 2 October 1896.
219 Censuses of WA, 1891, p.101; 1901, Pt. 1, pp.16–7.
220 PCC Minute Book, 6 November 1895; 10 June 1896.
221 PCC Minute Book, 5 June 1896.

greater than the combined value of loans one to six.[222] These loans were taken up largely by the Post Office Savings Bank, the WA Bank (of which Sir George Shenton was director), and the Colonial Mutual Life Association (of which Sir George Shenton was also a director). It was the largest loan taken out by the Perth City Council in the pre-war era, although six additional loans for lesser amounts were taken out between 1899 and 1914. With these two large loans the Council, on the recommendation of the City Engineer, began to remake all the existing roads, for it was felt that patching would no longer suffice.[223] New roads were built to join West Perth to Subiaco (including extensions of Coghlan and Douro Roads), the most important of which was Brooking Road which was extended down the back of Mt Eliza to Thomas Street. With Hay Street west, it formed a major link between the town centre and West Perth and Subiaco.[224] In 1901, on the occasion of the Duke of York and Cornwall's visit to Western Australia, Brooking Street was renamed King's Park Road, a fitting change for at about the same time Perth Park on the top of Mt Eliza was renamed King's Park.

Workers lay Mr J. C. Port's jarrah blocks in Hay Street, 1898-99.

In the central city area St George's and Adelaide Terraces were remetalled—probably about the tenth time these streets had been remade. Wellington Street was also remetalled in conjunction with the laying of the huge new drain. Between 1898 and the end of 1899, Hay Street was torn up and rebuilt with a jarrah block base overlaid with asphalt. This was done as part of the contract to lay tracks for the overhead electric tramway which commenced passenger carriage in September 1899.[225] By 1900 the line had been extended west to Subiaco, east to Victoria Park, and north along Barrack and Beaufort Streets to Highgate Hill. By 1911 the electric tramway system reached Leederville and North Perth. In addition there were several east-west lines in the north of the city. Of course horse carriages were still in use, but the electric tramway had meant the end of the horse-tram along Hay Street, so prominent a feature of Perth life for most of the 1890s. At least one omnibus company, Mr J. Conigrave's, was as early as 1898 seeking permission to introduce motorcars, an innovation which would be resisted by Perth Cabmen's Union over the next decade, but to no avail.[226] The upsurge of road usage in the 1890s had caused the Perth City Council to appoint a Traffic Inspector. By the late 1890s Perth had become the bicycle capital of Australia. In 1901 Armstrong's cycle factory and shop alone sold 1500 bicycles, and there were many more production and retail outlets in Perth and suburbs. The cyclists required regulation for they were a hazard to pedestrians. From October 1899 it was an offence to ride a bell-less bike in the city.[227] With the wood-blocking of the footpaths after 1901, more pedestrians abandoned the roads to men on and in machines.[228] Hay Street, however, then and until its rebirth as a pedestrian mall in the 1970s, was a narrow congested melange of people and vehicles.

In the early and mid-1890s the Premier, John Forrest, and all the Mayors of Perth had often expressed their desire to see Perth offering a 'pleasing appearance' to visitors: as Edward Keane put it in 1891, 'It is by the capital that strangers and visitors are accustomed to judge a

222 PCC Minute Book, 11, 31 October, 5 December 1898.
223 PCC Minute Book, 4 June 1897.   224 PCC Minute Book, 19 December 1898.
225 PCC Minute Book, 9 October 1899.   226 PCC Minute Book, 10 October 1898.
227 PCC Minute Book, 24 October 1899.
228 PCC Minute Book, 7 January, 27 March 1901; Mayor's Report 1900–01.

A moment of transition: horses, cars, trams and pedestrians, 1900s.

A revolution in road surfacing: the Perth City Council's tar truck, 1910s.

colony'. In 1907 it was another Mayor, Sydney Stubbs, who proudly reprinted in his Annual Report an article from the London *Standard* for December 1906:

> To use an expressive but horrible Americanism "There are no flies on Perth!" Its citizens are obviously full of go, and they have called to their aid all the most modern appliances for expediting communication either by road or car. The electric trolley car hums along the beautifully graded streets, alongside which run a very forest of telegraph poles supporting a shimmering network of telegraph and telephone wires. I take off my hat metaphorically to those responsible for the roadways of Perth [which] put to utter shame the roadways of many far more pretentious and incomparably older towns and cities ... both in the motherland and in the United States.[229]

Certainly the achievement was not inconsiderable. In 1907 Perth had 90 miles of made roads, many now sealed with tar, compared with only 25 partially made ones in 1891. This was 23 miles more than Ballarat, and only 12 less than Adelaide. The roads were well-made and were well-maintained by regular, though costly, street-watering, which was also an important agent for the good health of the citizens.

All this improvement came in the nick of time, for from about 1904 there was an increasing number of motorcars using the roads. At first only motorcar cabs were licensed. In 1903 Mr S. W. Copley's motor

[229] Mayor's Annual Report, 1906–07; the journalist-visitor was Frank T. Bullen.

buses ran from the GPO to Victoria Park.[230] Private cars increased in
number, and they could and did exceed speed limits with impunity. But
not until the 1920s did suburban bus services become general. In 1908 the
Government agreed to allow the Councils to license private cars. At the
end of that year 95 cars had been licensed. By the end of 1909 the amount
of money received by the Perth City Council for horse-cab licences was
lower than that for 1899. The Traffic Inspector, Henry Ward, attributed
this to 'the dullness of the times and the advent of the motor taxi-cab'. In
1913 the Perth City Council bought its first motor lorries—two five-ton
lorries, and one two-and-a-half-ton lorry—following consideration of
the matter by a 'Special Committee re Motor Traction'. The lighter lorry
was used for night-soil removal, doing in two hours what a two-horse
cart did in an entire night. Indeed it replaced three double-horse carts.
The larger machines were used for street-watering.[231] Motor vehicles
were now almost as prominent as carts and carriages in the streets of
Perth. In 1915, 1400 licences were issued for the latter and 835 for the
former. And Perth now had motor dealers (12 by 1915), some of whom,
like Mr Winterbottom, had graduated from bicycle dealerships. And
when cattle were driven up St George's Terrace on their way to the
slaughter yards at Subiaco, the car drivers of Perth slowed down for
them, for the town depended on the country as it had always done.

*The country in the town: cattle in
St George's Terrace, on their way
to the Subiaco Abattoir, 1920s.*

*Mr Winterbottom advertises Dodge
motorcars, 1929.*

'Greater Perth'

The rapid development of suburbs around the city of Perth had
caused administrators of the Government, companies, and several
municipalities many problems. Agreement had to be reached about
tramways, gas and electricity, water and sewerage services, night soil and
garbage removal, road construction, building regulations and so on. In
the early 1900s some people began to suggest that perhaps the
municipalities should be amalgamated to form a Greater Perth
Authority. The impetus for this came from a man with a Peelite-

---

[230] Mayor's Annual Report, 1902–03.   [231] Mayor's Annual Report, November 1913.

*W. E. Bold, Town Clerk
Extraordinary, 1901–44: 'The boss
Panjandrum'.*

Gladstonian passion for high efficiency in administration—the Town Clerk for the City of Perth, W. E. Bold. Bold was a Lancashire man with engineering and clerical experience who arrived in Western Australia in 1896 at the age of 23 years. Late that year he gained employment as clerk-typist to the Town Clerk of the City of Perth, H. E. Petherick. It was the beginnings of an association with the Council which would end with his retirement in 1944–45. Bold's senior, H. E. Petherick, had overseered a rather haphazard growth of Council's staff in the 1890s. Petherick, however, was a fairly inefficient man and a poor manager who sought the support of the bottle during office hours and after. In 1900 Petherick was forced to resign and—after eighteen months of Council infighting—Bold was offered the Town Clerkship in November 1901. Bold had survived the difficult time of Brookman's Mayoralty, and as the mayoralty went to less troublesome men, and as Council (thanks to a rapid turnover of personnel) became less faction-ridden, Bold began to boost his staff's morale and efficiency in all the key areas—engineering, building, health, sanitation and clerical. His model was the Birmingham of Joseph Chamberlain, so advanced in municipal reform and administrative efficiency. Cool under fire, persuasive in conversation and in written reports, Bold became a powerful driving force in Council affairs. By 1905 a hostile witness wrote that Bold

> comported himself like the boss Panjandrum: [he was] the real mayor and [Mayor] Brown merely his easy-going factotum.[232]

In part it was Bold's dress and manner which annoyed those in Perth who spoke for that 'temper democratic; bias, offensively Australian', for he was a stiff, priggish sort of person who always wore a top hat and morning coat with a very high-collared shirt. He also affected a tightly twirled moustache. In Council he was always bewigged. This in itself was a source of wonder to the self-made men he served. Bold even attracted the notice of WA's most celebrated versifier and bohemian, 'Dryblower' Murphy, who characterised him as 'Beau Brummel Bold' and a 'toffy young spark'.[233] But the rather unbending, abstemious and deeply religious Town Clerk was already forming a vision about the future development of the capital city which over the next thirty years he saw realized—a 'boss Panjandrum' indeed.

In his quest for high technical efficiency Bold wanted one authority—the Perth City Council—to control most of the city's public facilities. A key to his thinking is the title of his presidential address to the Municipal Officers' Association in September 1906 (Bold was a foundation member of the Association): 'Municipal Socialism—Some of its Advantages'. In the course of this speech he referred favourably to Bernard Shaw's Fabian writings on the value of municipal trading. A year before, he had delivered an address on 'The Modern Municipality', in which he spoke favourably of municipal socialism, including the need for the municipality to provide good housing for workers, pure milk for nursing mothers and children, as well as parks ('lungs') for the city. Two of his inspirations seem to have been Adna Weber's *The Growth of Cities* (1899), and the London *Municipal Journal* which was already beginning to advocate town planning and the need for garden cities.[234]

---

[232] *Sunday Times*, 17 September 1905.
[233] *Sunday Times*, 30 August 1903.
[234] *Morning Herald*, 28 August 1905, the relevant article being contained in Bold's voluminous 'Scrapbooks', lodged in the Battye Library at PR2073.

Bold's first opportunity came in 1905 when the East Ward Ratepayers' Association of North Perth requested the Perth City Council to take over the ward from the North Perth Municipality. A PCC committee met with the Ratepayers' Association, but the Ratepayers' Association decided not to go ahead with its plan.[235] However, the North Perth Council itself approached the Perth City Council about amalgamation, and Bold suggested that perhaps the Councils of Subiaco and Leederville should also be invited to take part in a Conference on what was now described as 'Greater Perth'. This Conference took place on 24 October 1906. A proposal to amalgamate, put by North Perth Council, was successfully amended at the instance of the Subiaco Council to

> that quarterly conferences between these municipalities be held for the purpose of discussing matters of common interest, such as tramways, sewerage, lighting etc.

From the outset it was not intended that South Perth and Victoria Park would participate. A further meeting of the Conference was held in January 1907, but the discussion did not get beyond a recognition of the need to standardise hawking licences and the administration of the Weights and Measures and Bread Acts.[236] The Conference did not meet again for three years.

Bold's influence on the Mayors of Perth was increasing, however. In his 1906–07 Annual Report, Sydney Stubbs put his name to what was certainly Bold's Report—in tone as well as content:

> The City requires the services of men of attainments and experience in the Council, owing to the number of complicated questions before them for consideration. Unfortunately, Perth is suffering today from many mistakes which were made in past years. The gas and electric light concessions were given away before the City had attained to any importance. This mistake did not prevent the tramway service being placed in the hands of a private company at a later date. The markets were given back to the Government. And the installation of the sewerage system was delayed for so many years that house drainage connections were made to the storm-water drains . . . It is, of course, no use crying over spilt milk, but one cannot help reflecting that if these City monopolies, which have been placed in the hands of private companies, had been retained by the Municipality, the City would now be practically rate-free.

In 1908 and 1909 Bold had in Tom Molloy a Mayor who in the 1890s had favoured the municipalization of public facilities. Molloy wanted Council to purchase the gas and electricity works from the Company; to gain municipal control of the city's abattoirs; to have Council strongly represented on a water and sewerage board; to establish a municipal milk depot, and so on. Despite some opposition in Council, Molloy and Bold pushed through the purchase of the gas and electric light works in 1909. Perhaps their most convincing argument was that

> the lighting of the City is a service which is created by the people, and the people should have the profits which accrue therefrom,

and the Company's profits since January 1907 had reached about £90,000![237] In 1909 too the General Municipal Conference discussed

---

[235] Mayor's Annual Report 1904–05.
[236] Greater Perth Conference Minutes, 1906–12, PCC; also Mayor's Annual Reports, 1905–06, 1906–07.
[237] Mayor's Annual Report, 1908–09, p.9.

several important pieces of legislation, including the Consolidating Health Bill, the Fire Brigades Bill, and the Municipal Amending Bill. But amalgamation of Councils seemed as distant as ever.

At the November 1909 mayoral elections, R. P. Vincent, a builder and hardware wholesaler, campaigned almost exclusively on the 'Greater Perth' issue. As Mayor he reconvened the Greater Perth Conference and ensured that South Perth, Victoria Park and the Perth Roads Board took part. The conference, held on 15 June 1910, affirmed the desirability of initiating a scheme for the amalgamation of the city and suburbs. In the course of half-a-dozen committee meetings in July, principles of representation on the enlarged Council and disposal of assets, etc, were agreed upon; but when the Committee's report was considered by the full Conference in August, its general recommendation in favour of amalgamation was agreed to only after the Chairman, Mayor Vincent, gave a casting vote for the Ayes after a 10–10 tie.

In October 1910 Subiaco withdrew from the Conference, even though its rights to the assets of the Subiaco Electric Lighting Plant had been secured. Local patriotism in Subiaco was too strong for the Greater Perth advocates. Nevertheless, in February 1911 a referendum was held in the other municipalities which resulted in strong ratepayer endorsement of the Greater Perth scheme: 82% in favour in Perth; 84% in Leederville; 81% in North Perth; and 80% in the Maylands and Mt Lawley wards of the Perth Roads Board. Later that year a Greater Perth Bill was introduced as a private bill into the Legislative Assembly. The Bill was largely the work of Bold and R. T. Robinson (joint owner of the Mt Lawley estate and later Liberal MP for Canning), the two greatest enthusiasts for the Greater Perth movement, following Vincent's departure from office at the end of 1910. Had a Liberal Government been in office the Greater Perth Bill may have been steered through parliament, but in October 1911 Jack Scaddan's Labor Government had taken office. For a brief time in his career Scaddan was an enthusiast for state socialism. It seemed to him and to his Attorney-General, Thomas Walker, that a Greater Perth Council might well be an alternative power-centre of such magnitude that it would jeopardise the plans of the Labor Government. In particular, Scaddan and Walker wanted the State Government to purchase the tramway system (and it did so in 1912) and to institute a state bus service (or at least prevent Molloy from purchasing motor buses, as he had proposed to do).[238] Robinson was told that despite the Government's objections to the Bill it could become law before too long. This seems to have meant that if the proposed powers of the Greater Perth Council were reduced then the Scaddan Government would not object to the principle of Greater Perth.[239] In the event the Government delayed for so long that the North Perth and Leederville Councils decided to unite with the Perth City Council within the provisions of the Municipal Corporations Act of 1906. This union was validated in retrospect by the City of Perth Act of 1914. The enlarged Council had no increased powers under this arrangement, so the Scaddan Government was well satisfied. In 1917 Victoria Park joined the Perth City Council under the terms of the 1914 Act as amended. Thus by the end of the Great War the number of councillors for Perth was 24 with

238 See Mayor's Annual Report 1911–12, p.5.
239 Minutes of the Greater Perth Conference and Committees, and the reports of Robinson on his conversations with the Premier and the Attorney General, June 1910 to 28 June 1912; PCC Archives; also Mayor's Annual Reports, 1910–13.

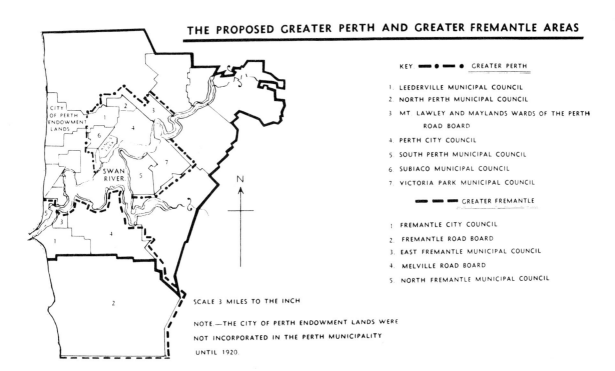

KEY ▬●▬● GREATER PERTH

1. LEEDERVILLE MUNICIPAL COUNCIL
2. NORTH PERTH MUNICIPAL COUNCIL
3. MT. LAWLEY AND MAYLANDS WARDS OF THE PERTH
   ROAD BOARD
4. PERTH CITY COUNCIL
5. SOUTH PERTH MUNICIPAL COUNCIL
6. SUBIACO MUNICIPAL COUNCIL
7. VICTORIA PARK MUNICIPAL COUNCIL

▬▬▬ GREATER FREMANTLE

1. FREMANTLE CITY COUNCIL
2. FREMANTLE ROAD BOARD
3. EAST FREMANTLE MUNICIPAL COUNCIL
4. MELVILLE ROAD BOARD
5. NORTH FREMANTLE MUNICIPAL COUNCIL

SCALE 3 MILES TO THE INCH

NOTE.—THE CITY OF PERTH ENDOWMENT LANDS WERE
NOT INCORPORATED IN THE PERTH MUNICIPALITY
UNTIL 1920.

one mayor, as against 45 councillors and four mayors under the arrangements which had prevailed from the mid-1890s.[240]

It seems likely that the Greater Perth movement of 1906–12 was, at least in its latter stages, an attempt by leading Liberal politicians and councillors to combat what was perceived to be the growing menace of the Labor Party. Mayor Richard Vincent was a founder of the National Political League which was formed in the interests of the Liberal Party, and which by 1911 had merged into the Liberal League of Western Australia. Vincent in fact was on the League's Executive Council.[241] Most of the Perth City councillors probably would have preferred to see public facilities in private hands, but if the choice was between municipal control and state control then the former was distinctly preferable, especially after Labor's success at the 1911 elections. Of the Perth City councillors in 1911, only one (Ebeneezer Allen) was a Labor politician, and one other (J. Gibson—a former goldfields unionist) may have been a Labor man. None were labouring employees (among other factors, Council met in the daytime!). Certainly Molloy enlisted the support of non-Labor politicians in the Legislative Council. But this was to no avail, as in regard to the tramways purchase Scaddan had met the legal obligations to the Perth City Council, and the Legislative Council's hands were tied. The issue however had been between 'municipalization' and 'nationalization', as the Perth City Council put it in a pamphlet issued to ratepayers. And councillors, architects and developers were strongly opposed to 'state trading'.[242]

[240] See J. R. H. Johns Metropolitan Government in Western Australia, 1950, pp.59–65—map, p.60. There is also a detailed account of the Greater Perth Movement in R. E. Robertson 'W. E. Bold, CBE, an analysis of his administrative contribution, community interest and social influence', MA thesis, University of WA, 1970, pp.129–75.   [241] Battye Cyclopaedia of WA Vol. 1, p.544.
[242] For the views of one of them see H. Boas 'Bricks and Mortar', unpublished autobiography, 1971, p.82, Battye Library.

Bold's role is less easy to categorise. Probably the power-play of the people with whom he had to deal annoyed him as an impediment to good order and bureaucratic reform. He seems to have believed in municipal socialism as something separate from political activity, although it is difficult to see him other than as a non-Labor supporter. He had failed to achieve a Greater Perth, but he remained very active in pursuit of those ends which he'd hoped to achieve with a Greater Perth Council. In November 1911 he drew up a most comprehensive Town Planning Report in which he urged the adoption of a City Improvement Plan. It read in part, 'We can now appreciate in Perth... the grave disadvantages of the rectangular or draught-board system of town planning' and went on to reveal the influence of the 'national efficiency' movement in Great Britain, then generating enthusiasm for town planning, well ventilated modern school design, children's gymnasiums, national defence and so on.[243] Later he elaborated on these ideas in an article, 'Perth in the Making', printed in the *WA Mining, Building and Engineering Journal* (November 1912). Scaddan's Government agreed to discuss the idea but no progress was made before the outbreak of the Great War. It was Bold, however, who in 1913 instituted the first children's playground—on the reserve at the corner of Lake and Stuart Streets. It had a sandpit and an enclosure for games, as well as swings and see-saws. It was also Bold who in 1913 successfully recommended the purchase and reclamation of inner city market gardens as parks and reserves, such as Robertson Park in northern Perth.[244]

In 1914 the Perth City Council underwrote some of the expenses of Charles C. Reade, who had been sent to Australia by the Garden Cities and Town Planning Association of Great Britain: Bold and a Perth architect, Harold Boas, were deeply involved in Reade's visit. One outcome of the lecture tour was a meeting attended by Reade, the Government Architect, the President of the Institute of Architects, the Surveyor General, Bold and the Mayor of Perth, at which the likely nature of a Town Planning Bill was discussed. Bold was sent on a world trip to acquaint himself with town planning practices in Britain and America.[245] This trip (and that of Boas to England in 1916) was to have profound consequences for the history of Perth after the Great War. In London, Bold attended two major conferences: the Imperial Health and Town Planning Conference, and the Garden Cities and Town Planning Association Conference. At these conferences he heard papers delivered by the garden city publicist Ebeneezer Howard (author of *Garden Cities of Tomorrow*, 1902); by Raymond Unwin who designed Letchworth, outside London; by Seebohm Rowntree (author of *Poverty: A Study of Town Life*, 1901) on housing reform; and by Basil Holmes on the value of open spaces in cities. Bold visited Letchworth Garden City, and the garden suburbs of Hampstead, Wembley Hill, Bournville and others, as well as Birmingham and Liverpool which had pioneered municipal reform. Crossing to the United States of America Bold saw many cities, being particularly impressed by Kansas with its new tree-lined boulevard-type arterial roads, and by the replanned city of Washington. On his return to Perth Bold presented the Council with a 57-page report in which he refined his Greater Perth concept to embrace a redeveloped

[243] See G. R. Searle *The Quest for National Efficiency*, 1973.
[244] Mayor's Annual Report, November 1913, p.10.
[245] Mayor's Annual Report, November 1914, p.12.

civic centre, like Chicago's, and satellite garden and sea-side suburbs. The central thrust of his report was the need for planning on 'City Beautiful' lines: 'the keystone of the arch of successful municipal effort'.

In 1917, on Bold's recommendation, the 1300-acre Limekilns Estate was bought by the Perth City Council from old Joe Perry.[246] The Estate was adjacent to western seaside endowment lands already held by the city. Despite opposition from Works Minister, W. George, an old PCC enemy of Bold's, Sir James Mitchell's Government passed the City of Perth Endowment Lands Act in 1920, by the terms of which the Perth City Council was empowered to develop and sell the land in its trust. In the mid-1920s the Council, at Bold's suggestion, invited the architects Hope and Klem to design satellite towns on the new lands. Floreat Park,

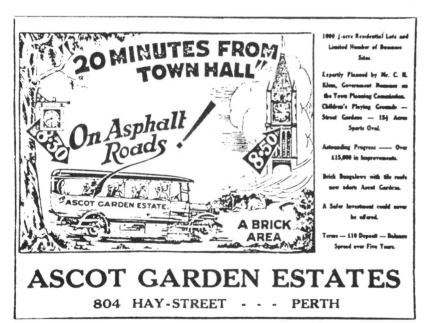

[246] This sale, and one a little earlier to the Federal Government for the site of the new GPO in what became Forrest Place, helps explain why on his death Joe's personal cash worth exceeded £200,000.

An interest of W. E. Bold: the children's playground at Robertson Park, 1933.

Wembley Park and City Beach, built and peopled over the next forty years, clearly owed much to Raymond Unwin's writings and the 'City Beautiful' and 'Garden Suburb' movements. Bold even managed to create a Boulevard, west of Leederville out to the sea at City Beach. It was in 1928 that the Western Australian parliament passed Australia's first Town Planning Act. Bold, Boas, Klem and a handful of others were the prime movers of the legislation, but Bold was the pivotal figure. The first two were also responsible for the creation in 1930 of a Town Planning Committee of the Perth City Council. From the Great War to the Second World War the physical shape of Perth owed much to the work of Bold. It was only on the eve of his death in 1953 that a major new inquiry into planning for Perth and its suburbs was instituted by the State Government and Perth City Council. When Stephenson and Hepburn settled down to their task, the Perth under their microscope owed much in inspiration and form to W. E. Bold, Town Clerk extraordinary.[247]

Town and Country

Because Perth was not a spontaneous creation as were the goldfields' cities of Southern Cross, Coolgardie and Kalgoorlie, the influences exerted by the new arrivals did not wipe out the previously dominant (rural dominated) modes of human association; but neither was the new completely grafted on to the old, and what had emerged by the end of the century was something rather different from, perhaps more typically 'urban' than, what had existed in the 1870s and early 1880s. This can be evidenced in several ways.

[247] See *ADB* Vol. 7—entry for Bold by C. T. Stannage; R. Clark, 'the City Beautiful', and 'Garden City Movement', *Architect* Vol. 10, No. 2 and 4, 1969; M. Webb 'Planning and Development in Metropolitan Perth to 1953', in *Perth City and Region*, Australian Planning Institute Congress, Perth, 1968; Harold Boas 'Bricks and Mortar'; PCC Annual Reports, 1911–31; Bold Scrapbooks Vols. 1-3, Battye Library; G. Stephenson and J. A. Hepburn *Plan for the Metropolitan Region: Perth and Fremantle, Western Australia*, 1955. Readers interested in comparisons with the eastern states will find much of value in L. Sandercock *Cities for Sale: Property, Politics and Urban Planning in Australia*, 1975, Pt. I 'Laissez-faire in the Cities 1900–45'.

Firstly, there was an increasing intellectuality in city politics at the end of the 1880s and into the 1890s. This is seen most clearly in the formation and activity of the WA Liberal Association (formed 1888) whose members, on the whole, lacked the market-town mentality of pre-1880s Perth: they were young, well-educated (several were lawyers), inspired by the political activity of Joseph Chamberlain in Britain and eastern colonies' town liberals like Deakin and Higgins, and were pledged to destroy what they saw as the political dominance of a social clique, which in this instance was perceived to be non-urban in composition.[248] In the words of the young Liberal Association activist, Walter James (Premier of WA in 1902–04):

> One of our greatest objects is to destroy the cliquism that has so long ruled the colony, and to enforce the rule that the legislators ought to take their views from their constituents, and feel responsible to the electors rather than to any social coterie.[249]

But the 'old order' was too strong initially and the Liberal Association was stigmatised as a group of young irresponsibles and as a city creation with no appreciation of the virtues of country conservatism. But the 'religion of the springtime' had come to stay with the increasing urbanization of Perth and it was not confined to the middle class. It has been observed that 'intellectuality' 'extends in many directions with the specialization of the urban environment';[250] and from the mid-1880s the urban intellect operated among the city workers, particularly the artisans, who formed organizations which supplanted the old working men's associations which had been ordained by the pillars of an organic view of colonial society—the landed gentry. By the early 1900s trade unions played an important role in the political life of Perth. Sometimes they exercised their role through arbitration and negotiation. At other times they resorted to direct action, as in the builders' labourers' strike of 1897, or in the Tramways Union strike of 1910.

No formal political organizations existed until the late 1880s: their emergence from that period is intimately related to the growth of urbanism. In this context Louis Wirth's comment is apt:

> The bonds of kinship, of neighbourliness and of sentiments arising out of living together for generations under a common folk tradition are likely to be absent, or, at best, relatively weak in an aggregate the members of which have such diverse origins and backgrounds. Under such circumstances competition and formal control mechanisms furnish the substitutes for the bonds of (folk) solidarity.[251]

Whereas Sir Luke Leake in the 1870s and early 1880s had been able, as an election approached, to canvass 'personally acquainted with almost every elector, [speaking] to each as an old friend, knowing his history, knowing his views, and certain at any rate of a friendly reception . . .'[252] this was no longer feasible in the changed conditions of the 1890s—'folk

---

[248] 'Intelligence originates in resistance to the feudal powers of blood and tradition against which the bourgeoisie as an intellectual class becomes conscious of its own existence. As it develops the urban intellect becomes the religion of the springtime and sets aside the old religion of noble and priest for the new religion of the Tiers Etat, liberal science.' Spengler, quoted in M. Weber *The City*, Glencoe Free Press, 1958, p.35. Clearly WA in the 1880s was not a feudal society; there were present, however, elements of an organic view of society.

[249] *West Australian*, 21 January 1889.

[250] M. Weber *The City*, p.3. The quotation comes from Georg Simmell.

[251] L. Wirth 'Urbanism as a Way of Life', in *American Journal of Sociology* Vol. 44, 1938, p.11.

[252] *Western Mail*, 19 May 1888.

bonds' were inadequate for both electors and candidates. Indeed the growth of urbanization and urban attitudes had made it necessary 'to communicate through indirect media', to articulate individual interests through delegation in the case of electors; and to develop platform oratory and cultivate the support of organized groups in the case of candidates. And, as in the city, interests were made effective through representation, and the voice of a representative was heard with a deference roughly proportional to the number for whom he spoke, organized registration of voters was seen as a primary task.

Furthermore, where in the past the whole electorate had known Sir Luke Leake intimately—the man as well as his views—the urban environment of the 1890s increasingly segmented human relationships in all spheres of life, the political being no exception. This meant that from the late 1880s the full personality of an urban electorate candidate was not known to the electors. The result of this was an increasing emphasis on the nature of the candidate's views, rather than on his personal morality, the 'goodness' or 'badness' of his reputation.

It is possible to view the politics of Perth from the late 1880s in terms of Durkheim's 'city as a social dust heap'. In Perth in these years no single group controlled all of a person's actions (as in the country), but the increasing division of labour had produced 'an unstable unity in which consensus and solidarity [were] partial and problematic'.[253] This instability produced a viewpoint which did not accept the concept of an organic society, which in practice was seen as a notion to buttress the political and economic dominance of a social coterie. The partial breakdown of consensus in the city was an essential condition for the anti-*status-quo* agitation which characterised the late 1880s and 1890s.

Initially the country reaction was conditioned by the proximity of the inauguration of responsible government which, it was feared, would place additional power into the hands of the central towns.[254] Thus when the Liberal Association sponsored candidates in country constituencies it was viewed by rural men as a city plot to secure an urban majority in the Legislative Council which was to deliberate on a Constitution Bill at its next session; and the country reacted in a flurry of organization which was untypical to say the least. The venerable Samuel Pole Phillips, the squire of Culham (situated in the heart of the eastern districts), was moved to contrast the activity preceding the 1889 election with a general election held several years earlier at which 'not twenty in one hundred (voters) could give a political reason for voting'.[255] Certainly from 1889 onwards the country districts exerted themselves in order to retain political power, and with the formation of constituency political associations in 1890, had clearly heeded the *West Australian*'s caution that 'old standing, social influence and established reputations' no longer held undisputed sway in the fast-changing conditions of the colony.[256] In regard to popular registration, group organization, and streamlined electioneering techniques, the city was the pacemaker and the country the imitator. It has already shown how effective the country conservative reaction was in the debates on the Constitution and Electoral Bills, which, when enacted, formed the electoral framework for

[253] Quoted in Greer's *The Emerging City: Myth and Reality*, Glencoe Free Press, 1962, p.14.
[254] See e.g. *Eastern Districts Chronicle*, 10 March 1888, and the *West Australian*, 29 December 1888, 9 January 1889.
[255] *West Australian*, 21 March 1889.   [256] *West Australian*, 8 February 1889.

302

the politics of the 1890s. In these years the town–country dialectic was intense as the urban democrats strove to dislodge rural conservatism from the dominant position it had secured in 1889. This can be shown by consideration of a variety of issues.

Firstly, it was an urban stimulus which produced the movement for free, compulsory, and secular education. At the 1894 general election all three Perth constituencies returned men who were opposed to a continuation of state aid to religion and to church schools. The *West Australian* commented that 'there will not be many to deny that the metropolitan elections strike the knell of the present dual system'.[257] Country centres like York, Toodyay and Nelson returned men committed to a defence of the dual system of government-financed state and church schools; and when the Legislative Assembly reconvened, such men were initially in a majority. But under pressure from urban representatives their resistance wilted, and by the end of 1895 Western Australia had free, compulsory, and secular education. In that the Westralian urban centres provided the original stimulus and most of the drive to reform the education system, they parallel developments in the United States of America and the eastern colonies of Australia.

The urban stimulus was felt in other directions, principally in social justice reform demands. It has been written of American cities that

> the new conditions of city life begat a social conscience on the part of townsfolk which would be lasting of effect and which increasingly differentiated them from their brethren on the farm . . .[258]

Thus the 'urban intellect' men like James, Simpson, Molloy, Neelands (of the Perth City Council), and Canning, not only effectively pursued social reform through their membership of the City Council, but also carried their 'social consciences' into the colonial/State legislature. Such reforms of the early 1890s as the Public Health Acts Amendment Act, the Master and Servant Act Amendment Act, the abolition of the Imported Labour Registry Act, and the Married Women's Property Act were due largely to the agitation and concern of products of an urban environment and were reluctantly agreed to by the Forrest Government. The major opposition to the Acts listed tended to come from rural areas, if not necessarily from members of rural constituencies; and also from one or two urban members like Marmion who had retained the old 'market-town' mentality.

The demand for political reform came principally from urban centres, both metropolitan and goldfields.[259] Public debate over the vexed questions of plural voting and the introduction of payment of members, for example, invariably separated urban and rural interests, as did discussions on the redistribution of seats. Country conservative reaction to an urban demand for a redistribution on a population basis was to grant an extra urban-type seat, but also to keep all other constituencies intact or create further rural seats; but by the end of the nineteenth century, repeated concessions had undermined the ability of country conservatism to counter urban demands. Federation, the most

Secular education for the people: the new Boys' School, James Street, 1896.

Secular education for the people: Perth Modern School, 1911.

---

[257] *West Australian*, 15 June 1894.

[258] A. M. Schlesinger, *Paths to the Present*, New York, 1949, Chapter 3 'The City in American Civilization', p.220.

[259] See C. T. Stannage 'The Composition of the Western Australian Parliament, 1890–1911', *University Studies in History* Vol. 4, No. 4, 1966, pp.9–11. I have considered that what goldfields men called their 'Australianism' was in reality the dominance of urban values in their political attitudes.

Celebrating Federation in the streets of Perth, 1900.

important political question at the turn of the century, was a triumph in Western Australia for urban aspirations—and, indeed, one aspect of urban support for federation was a desire for intercolonial free-trade. This would bring about the abolition of food duties which in the popular mind were equated with the high cost of living. Earlier, the most important single issue of the 1897 general election was the cost of living. Without exception, the urban centres returned men pledged to abolish duties on the necessities of life; and once again country conservativism opposed an urban demand. The success of many 'urban oriented' candidates at the 1897 election foreshadowed urban success over federation and the return of an 'urban oriented' Legislative Assembly at the 1901 general election.

Several further political consequences of urbanization merit attention. Firstly, there was a rapid increase in non-conformist groups in the metropolitan area, and a consequential breakdown of Anglican dominance in comparison with country areas. Between 1870 and 1891 the number of Anglicans in Perth increased one and a half times from 2640 to 4350; the number of Roman Catholics also increased one and a half times, from 1570 to 2424 persons. But there was a nine-fold increase in Presbyterians, from 59 to 552 persons and a two-fold increase in Wesleyans, from 499 to 1076. At Fremantle the relative increases of Anglicans and Roman Catholics were similar to Perth, and there was a similar advance in non-conformism: the number of Wesleyans increased eleven-fold, while the number of Presbyterians increased some five and a half times. Whereas in 1891 the combined numbers of Roman Catholics, Wesleyans and Presbyterians almost equalled the number of Anglicans in

*'Yes' for Federation: poll figures outside the offices of the **West Australian**, 1900.*

the metropolitan area, in representative country districts, Wellington, Williams and Blackwood, the numbers of Anglicans doubled the combined figure of the other denominations. As a rider to this, Wesleyans and Presbyterians accounted for between 17 and 20% of the metropolitan population, whereas in the three country districts considered they accounted for 9, 4 and 5% respectively. During the 1890s (to 1901) the number of Anglicans and Roman Catholics doubled, while Methodists increased some four and a half times and Presbyterians some six and a half times. While in 1901 Presbyterians and Methodists accounted for 25% of the Perth and Fremantle populations, and between 30–35% of the populations of East Coolgardie and Dundas, they only accounted between 5 and 10% in York and Toodyay, representative country districts.[260]

This disproportionate metropolitan increase in non-conformism meant of course a corresponding increase in the influence of non-conformist values and attitudes. One manifestation of the increasing influence of non-conformism has already been discussed, namely the success of urban centres in getting the Assisted Schools and Ecclesiastical Grant Acts abolished in the course of the 1890s. A second manifestation was the three-way relationship of non-conformism, the temperance movement and liberal political groups in the early 1890s. A third manifestation was an outgrowth of the second, namely that the early 1890s agitation against Asiatic labour in Western Australia was strongly supported, perhaps spearheaded, by non-conformist artisans and Liberal Association activists. In the first Commonwealth Parliament in 1901 it was a Westralian Labor Senator, George Pearce, who declared roundly that a White Australia policy was necessary on racial grounds.[261]

Another political consequence of the rapid urbanization of the metropolitan area and port towns in the late 1880s and 1890s was the withdrawal of 'market-town' men from city electoral politics. This withdrawal took two forms: firstly, some men sought havens in the country rather than participate in the hurly-burly of city politics—William Traylen, S. H. Parker, and Timothy Quinlan were three such men; secondly, some men sought havens in the Upper House (nominated to 1894, elected on a propertied franchise thereafter)—George Shenton, Sir Thomas Cockburn Campbell, George Randell (after 1897), W. D. Moore, T. Burges, and D. K. Congdon were some such men. Contemporary country opinion believed that there was something 'low' about city politics, something distasteful in which 'gentlemen' should not participate.[262] This was an extension of the widespread notion that cities tended to be morally corrupting societal influences—witness the *West Australian*'s observation, made late in 1890:

> The flocking of population into the town can scarcely be called desirable from the point of view of the general public morality of the people.[263]

[260] Percentages calculated from figures in *Census of WA 1891*, pp.120–3; and from *Census of WA 1901*, Pt. IV, pp.24–8.

[261] In all three manifestations of non-conformist influence in the early 1890s comparisons can be found in the eastern colonies. See particularly A. A. Morrison 'Religion and Politics in Queensland in 1881', *Journal of the Historical Society of Queensland* Vol. 4, No. 4, December 1951, pp.455–70. For Pearce see A. T. Yarwood *Asian Migration to Australia*, 1964, p.25.

[262] Country members talked of 'Berryism' which they equated with city mob rule. See *WAPD* Vol. 40 (o.s.), 1889, p.35.

[263] *West Australian*, 27 September 1890.

Regardless of whether or not there was in fact something 'low' about city politics one thing is clear; there was an element of uncertainty about the return of an urban-centre candidate from the 1880s which was virtually absent in the country; and men unused to factious electoral contests were ill-at-ease in city politics and preferred the relative tranquillity of a country or Upper House haven. The *Eastern Districts Chronicle* described this uncertainty in the following manner:

> In large centres of population there is always an appreciable restless element on the lookout for change, and members representing such mixed constituencies are never too sure of their return to Parliament. With rural or sparsely peopled constituencies it is different. [There are] no organized elements to foster a spirit of opposition.[264]

When city politics were abandoned to 'agitators and adventurers', country conservatism trusted towns even less than it did before.

With the gradual withdrawal of country gentlemen from participation in electoral politics, political leadership tended to be supplied increasingly from the urban centres. In the 1870s when Perth was but a market-town, leadership of the elected members of the old Legislative Council was in the hands of James Lee Steere, who represented a rural constituency. During the 1880s political leadership of the elected members was taken away from Lee Steere and placed in the hands of Stephen Henry Parker, a town liberal. However, with the growth of town radicalism late in the 1880s, country conservatives came to regard Parker as 'much safer' than the Hensman–Haynes–Horgan led radical party. Parker, increasingly dependent on country support, deserted his city seat for Vasse, a south-west farming constituency; but nevertheless he continued to be far more urban-orientated than his principal parliamentary supporters. On the inauguration of responsible government, Parker declined to contest the premiership with John Forrest, who then became the automatic choice.[265] With his stolidly held belief in the superior virtues of those who tilled the soil, Forrest could hardly be considered 'urban'. Nevertheless as a consensus politican he paid due regard to urban demands, if not sharing urban values and attitudes; and in this respect he was well in advance of his principal supporters, the rural members. Forrest maintained control for a decade, a feat unprecedented in Australian colonial politics; but on his departure his old group, then led by George Throssell of the eastern districts, fell away and was absorbed into the town liberal group led by the urban men, Leake and James.[266] Indeed in Leake's first ministry there was not one minister from a rural constituency.[267] The same was true of the James ministry of 1902–04, and was certainly true of the first Labor Government which gained office in 1904 under the leadership of a Metropolitan Member, Henry Daglish. A resurgence of country power was evident in the Wilson and Newton Moore ministries from 1905 to

---

[264] *Eastern Districts Chronicle*, 26 May 1894.

[265] See his comments in his election speech to the York electors: 'In the near future he would sit on the Opposition side . . . he had not expressed himself as a candidate for (the position of premier). He could not help thinking that as Mr Forrest held a position in the Executive Government at the present time, if he expressed a desire to form a government, it was only right and proper that he should have the opportunity.' *Eastern Districts Chronicle*, 1 December 1890.

[266] See B. K. Hyams 'Political Parties 1901–16', honours dissertation, University of WA, 1954.

[267] A country member, Layman, was moved to observe publicly that 'He had never heard Mr Leake say a single word in favour of the farmer', *West Australian*, 3 May 1901.

1911, but Labor's success under Scaddan in October 1911 was a triumph for metropolitan interests.

That it would be a pyrrhic victory would become apparent only with the passing of the years, for the changes of the goldrush years—substantial though they were—disguised to some extent the persistence of rural influence in the political life of the colony. The political and social reforms of the 1890s and 1900s, however unthinkable they had been in the 1880s and however unwelcome later, had in fact been contained and channelled by 'ancient colonist' power in the Legislative Council, the Perth City Council, and the financial institutions of the city. In Perth one symbol of the alliance between urban and rural wealth was the Weld Club.

Social Control: religion, sport and recreation

In the 1890s and 1900s Perth had its Tattersalls' Club, Perth Club, West Australian Club, Travellers' Club, Exchange Club and so on. But the club of clubs was the Weld Club. Already well-established before the boom, the Weld Club in 1896 moved into sumptuous quarters in Barrack Street, just off St George's Terrace (in which street most of its members had offices and some of them their homes). Phillip Mennell, author of *The Coming Colony*, 1892, wrote of the Weld Club as

> unique as a centre of sociability and once admitted to its somewhat exclusive portals you are admitted into pleasant contact with everybody who is anybody in the small capital of the largest colony.

And Gilbert Parker, with the keen sensibility of the expert salesman, compared it favourably with the Australia Club in Sydney.[268]

During the goldrushes the entrance and subscription fees were raised several times, the former reaching £40 in 1894 (later reduced to £25). Even this high figure did not deter affluent mining men, though the Club kept an eye on the *bona fides* of prospective members. The goldfields' members formed a progressive lobby within the Club, but it could not be said that they exerted an influence equal to that of 'ancient colonist' members. By the late 1890s (1898), the Weld Club had snared even that most progressive of the *enfants terrible* of the 1880s, Walter Hartwell James. The Club members were served by indentured Singapore Chinese who worked as cooks, bedmakers, yardmen, waiters, butlers and billiard-makers. With the introduction of the Commonwealth Immigration Act (1901), the Weld Club had to begin employing white servants, but even as late as 1924 there were still six Chinese servants on the staff. Some, like King See, the head bedroom boy, worked for the Club for thirty years. Not until 1927 did the Club employ female staff. For Club members there was good accommodation, billiards, fine food, bowls and tennis. There was also a reading room which took the *Tatler* but not the Sydney *Bulletin*. If most of the people of Perth could not afford a yacht for sailing on the Swan, there were some members of the Weld Club who could afford to go to London for the Derby, and hold court on a superb house-boat, *The Golden Grasshopper*, on the Thames.[269]

---

[268] Gilbert Parker *Round the Compass in Australia*, 1892, p.387.
[269] The material in this paragraph comes from T. S. Louch *The First Fifty Years: The History of the Weld Club 1871–1921*, 1964.

From the early 1890s the Weld Club's immediate neighbour in Barrack Street was the Women's Christian Temperance Union (1892), then at the commencement of its career in the furtherance of women's rights. In the mid and late 1890s the Union strove hard to gain votes for women, a movement much deplored by many of the men next door. One Weld Club member, Alexander Forrest, said roundly in Parliament that 'Members of our family have been brought up to believe that man should be the breadwinner and that his wife's place is in the home, and not in the rough and tumble of politics'.[270] Probably a more congenial neighbour would have been the Karrakatta Club, a gentry women's club formed in 1894. Its headquarters were in St George's Terrace. Far more radical in the early 1900s was Mrs Jean Beadle's Women's Labor Organization. Just as the Weld Club stayed close to the heartland of finance and Liberal and Country Party politics, so the Working Men's Institute stayed close to the men it served. When the Barrack Street railway bridge was rebuilt, the Institute was moved across to Beaufort Street where in the early 1900s the Trades and Labour Council erected its premises. The Institute of Railwaymen was nearby. This spatial separation of capital and labour interests would persist in Perth right through to the 1970s.[271]

Perth in 1918 was still a profoundly religious society. The 1890s and early 1900s saw much church-building in Perth and the suburbs, though church construction tended to occur after hotels and progress halls were erected. Church-going continued to characterise the population, with people walking or driving considerable distances to reach the chapel or church of their choice. Family prayer and Bible readings were still popular. And the respect for the dead, shown by the closure of shops as a hearse carriage went by, and the bowing of heads, had a religious foundation. Perhaps the depression of the 1890s in the eastern colonies had caused a renewed commitment to religious practice. Certainly much of the social life of the city and suburbs revolved round the churches—church picnics, social evenings, and the general fellowship of involvement in church life. It was specified in some Wills that inheritance was possible only if the children professed their parents' faith. Religion also lay at the heart of the business life of Perth. Certainly the Roman Catholic business community was 'exclusive', in the sense that a Catholic landowner would tend to lease property to other Catholics, employ a Catholic lawyer, like Moorhead or Horgan, and deal with a Catholic builder.[272] The builder would tend to employ Catholic labouring men. Catholic housewives tended to purchase goods from Catholic traders wherever possible, and their children usually attended Catholic schools. In the suburbs, neighbourhoods often had a denominational base. All this applied equally to Wesleyanism, Presbyterianism and non-conformist groups like the Congregationalists and Baptists. At the highest levels of society it was true of Anglicanism as well. This was perhaps the greatest period of freemasonry in the history of Western Australia.

This denominational cohesion is also evident in politics, for at no time in the 1890s and 1900s did two Catholics contest the one seat. And some Anglicans prominent in municipal and political life were great

[270] V. Courtney *Perth and All This*, 1962, p.36.
[271] See Justina Williams *The First Furrow*, 1976.
[272] The 'exclusiveness' of Catholic business life is seen most clearly in the papers of Timothy Quinlan, 1896–1902, in the possession of Mr A. D. Quinlan of Dalkeith; the files of the *WA (Catholic) Record* are also invaluable.

haters of Catholicism. Municipal and parliamentary elections were often fiercely contested on denominational lines.[273] At the 1894 general election the central issue was whether or not state aid to churches and church schools should be continued. A defender of the system, T. G. Molloy, blamed his defeat on 'the religious bitterness which had existed', while an abolitionist, B. C. Wood, who defeated the Catholic spokesman and sitting member for West Perth, Timothy Quinlan, believed that his win was due to the temperance (largely non-conformist) and Orange (radical Anglican) votes.[274] The Catholic Vicar General of Perth, Father Bourke, had even mobilised the smallish Catholic proxy vote, for he wrote to Bishop Salvado of New Norcia that

> Mr Quinlan is for West Perth, Mr Canning is for East Perth, and Mr Molloy, Central Perth. They are all of course in favour of the Assisted Schools, and the way your Lordship can help is by sending a proxy each in their behalf.[275]

In an earlier election, the Perth by-election of 1888, Catholics had voted *en bloc* for John Horgan, and the prominent Anglicans *en bloc* for Septimus Burt.[276] Wesleyans too had voted for Burt, for George Shenton had willed it so. Bishop Gibney, the spiritual, social, and political leader of the Roman Catholic congregation, believed that his flock 'must fight or fail'. His activities in the 1890s and early 1900s can be explained in part by a letter he wrote for his people in 1890:

> To my own knowledge the advancement of the country under Constitutional Government has been retarded for twenty years by the opposition of the upper class and now they have hampered the Constitution with conditions which will render the New Constitution nugatory for the vast majority of the people . . .[277]

And while it was to be expected that the Protestant Loyal Orange Lodge would oppose Catholics at each and every instance, it was perhaps more surprising that the liberal Anglican lawyer and political reformer, Walter James (Premier 1902–04), who disliked the Constitution as much as Gibney, could write

> I believe the majority of Roman Catholics are selfish and intolerant . . . Roman Catholics have made and are constantly making deliberate and organized attempts to acquire political power.[278]

That such a man could write in this way suggests the depth of sectarianism in the life of Perth.

Nor did the coming of formal political parties bring to an end this basis to politics, for the Labor Party, although racked by ideological and regional divisions, attracted proportionately more Roman Catholics than

[273] Regrettably, this is not discussed in B. K. de Garis' chapter 'Western Australia' in P. Loveday *et al. The Emergence of the Australian Party System*, 1977, pp.298–354; but see C. T. Stannage 'The Composition of the Western Australian Parliament 1890–1911', *University Studies in History* Vol. 4, No. 4, 1966, pp.32–3.

[274] For Molloy's assessment, see *West Australian*, 15 June 1894. For Wood's comment, see *West Australian*, 15, 16 June 1894.

[275] Father Bourke's letter is in the *Salvado Papers*, Nullius Abbey of New Norcia; it is dated 8 June 1894. His request may have fallen on deaf ears for Salvado, a Spanish aristocrat, usually supported Anglican and non-conformist candidates from the Westralian gentry rather than Irish Catholic candidates. See C. T. Stannage 'Bishops Gibney and Salvado and Electoral Politics 1884–97', *Journal of Religious History*, June 1971, pp.274–85.

[276] The ballot papers and counterfoils for the 1888 Perth by-election are in the Supreme Court of Western Australia.

[277] For Gibney's letter see *WA Record*, 27 November 1890.

[278] James' letter to the Geraldton lawyer, F. Whitcombe, was printed in the *Victorian Express*, 8 January 1892; also *West Australian*, 7 January 1892; *WA Record*, 31 December 1891.

did the Liberal Party, which was dominated by Anglicans. But party politics did reduce tensions between Catholics and non-conformists. Indeed, in the 1901–1911 period the parliamentary Labor Party contained about an equal number of Catholics and non-conformists. This suggests that for many adherents of those faiths, class base had become more important in politics than the religious base. However, in times of great social stress, the religious factor could reassert itself, as in the conscription crises of 1916 and 1917 which divided and broke the Labor Party.

In Perth in the 1890s and 1900s organized sport 'helped shape and sustain the city's social structure as well as relationships within it'.[279] The most prestigeous sporting club in Western Australia was the Western Australian Turf Club (WATC). It was also the oldest, having been formed in 1852. Membership of the Club had always been restricted to members of the gentry—leading pastoralists and farmers, senior civil servants, lawyers, doctors, and merchants. Nor was the qualification for membership relaxed during the goldrush decade and its aftermath. It was, and continued to be, the sporting branch of the Weld Club (after 1871). Indeed at least one of the Weld Club's founding members, Stephen Henry Parker, rode one of his horses at WATC meetings. Appropriately enough—for its rider was an advocate of responsible government—the horse was called 'West Australian'. In 1872 'West Australian', with Stephen Henry's lawyer brother George in the saddle, won the colony's most important race—the Queen's Plate. Indeed Stephen Henry Parker's horses won the event from 1872 to 1876. The Parkers remained active members of the Weld Club and WATC right through the 1890s. In the 1880s another of Perth's MLC's and Mayor, Dr Edward Scott, was known as the 'sporting doctor' because of his interest in racing. Alexander Forrest was an active member of both clubs for many years. In 1887 he won the first Perth Cup with 'First Prince'. Nor was his successor as Mayor, H. J. Saunders, lacking in interest in horse-racing. His stables at Henley Park were among the finest in the colony, and as late as the 1904–05 season he led in ten winners on metropolitan tracks.[280] Other prominent members of the Weld Club who were active in the WATC were Robert Frederick Sholl, pastoralist and politician, and George Leake, lawyer and politician, who was Premier of Western Australia in 1901–02. Old William Strickland, WA born and well-respected in financial circles, was president of the WATC throughout the 1890s. In short, the 'ancient colonists' of the WATC successfully maintained and even extended their authority over the colony's largest spectator-sport, which was also one of the important means of maintaining social distance, so imperative a need of the old order.

This was not achieved without experiencing some anxious moments. In the 1880s and 1890s the city race-goers enjoyed the successes of George Towton, a Perth hotelier and livery owner who was not a gentleman. The lower orders called him 'King' George. Towton won the second Perth Cup (1888) with 'Telephone', and for a time in the early

[279] B. Stoddart 'Sport and Society in Perth 1890–1940', in C. T. Stannage (General Editor) *A New History of Western Australia*, 1979. Stoddart's pioneering study has been drawn on in this section. So too have two honours dissertations in the Department of History, University of Western Australia: L. Joll 'Perth Society in 1891', 1972; and R. Campbell 'Aspects of Perth and its Society, 1901', 1972.
[280] *Year Book of Western Australia*, 1906, E. S. Wigg & Son, p.131.

Carbinier wins the 1900 Perth Cup:
The Western Australian Turf Club
was the sporting arm of the Weld
Club.

1890s his stable seemed unbeatable, though the Dempsters did their best to keep the major races in the hands of the gentry. A more serious cause for concern was the propensity of the people of Perth to bet on races. It was not that the gentry frowned on betting. Even the genteel ladies, like May Vivienne, enjoyed a 'flutter' on the races. Having commented on the many pleasant afternoon tea parties in evidence and the excellence of the band, she added:

> When we left to return to Perth I felt quite charmed with the pretty course, and also with my good luck, for I had won two dozen pairs of gloves and ten golden sovereigns!

A final comment—'quite a run of luck for me'—suggests that Vivienne, who mixed with the elite of Perth, indulged in betting with some frequency.[281] But in 1898 the enterprising newcomer land agent, Joseph Charles, launched WA Tattersalls, with a 'consultation' of 5s on the Perth Cup which netted him nearly 12 000 subscribers. By 1900 he was operating on Victorian and British races and enjoyed an overseas and intercolonial clientele. For the 1900 Melbourne Cup his 5s subscribers numbered 100 000. He had just installed an 'electrical apparatus' to ensure 'speedy drawing and perfect fairness' when the Government (headed by WATC member, George Leake) closed down his operation.[282] Off-course betting could not be suppressed entirely, but in that it took total control away from the WATC, it was perceived to be a threat to the good order of society, and was represented as such to the Select Committee on Racing in 1905. And it could not be denied that on-course betting was worth protecting, for in 1904 alone, £90,000 was invested on the WATC totalizer. But more was at stake than mere money.

The WA colonial elite succeeded in keeping horse-racing as the premier sporting experience of the people of Perth and they maintained their authority over the game. They did so also with cricket. Cricket had always been played by the gentry, though occasionally games were played by them against the mechanics. But in 1885 the Western Australian Cricket Association was formed. In 1890 when Governor Broome agreed to vest fourteen acres of foreshore land at East Perth in the WACA, he chose as trustees John Forrest, the Hon. J. Amherst

281 May Vivienne *Travels in Western Australia*, 2nd ed., 1902, p.46.
282 *Twentieth Century Impressions of WA*, p.444.

(MLC, 1890–1894), and George Parker of racing fame. In the 1890s the WACA Committee included J. C. H. James, a senior civil servant who had married into the Clifton family; Bush and Darlot, both northern pastoralists; Robert Sholl of the WATC; and the redoubtable Edward Scott. By 1901 the WACA controlled six senior clubs and was fostering the game in state and public schools. Darlot was active in the public schools, and their inter-school competition later honoured his name. Perhaps because of the 't'othersider' presence the *West Australian* reported fully the England-Australian games in 1901. From the reports it is difficult to establish which side the *West* wished to see win.[283] Perhaps the game was the thing. But cricket in Perth, a 'manly and healthy' sport, was a game sponsored by the ancient colonists right through to the Great War and maybe beyond it. In that the clubs came to be regionally based, it was also a way of keeping in touch with the suburbs. They thought it worth their while, for the values of the game were the values of the ordered society they knew and sought to conserve in the turbulent years of the goldrushes.

Cricket was played by most classes in Perth society. But tennis was restricted to the affluent, at least until the creation of public courts in the 1900s. By definition a poor family did not possess a tennis court. But the Forrests did, and so did many of the wealthier families in West Perth and in the Claremont/Cottesloe/Peppermint Grove area.[284] Competition tennis was played on the courts of Government House until the mid-1890s. In 1895 a club was formed and a championship instituted. The social composition of the proposed membership could be inferred from the newspaper notice:

> The co-operation of the leading residents of Perth has been invited to form a club, such as exists in England and in the other colonies, not only to provide healthful and desirable exercise for both ladies and gentlemen, but also to furnish that which is absolutely lacking in Perth—a place of general resort where members can readily meet their friends.[285]

—a sort of Weld Club with women admitted to membership. The leading figures in the WA Lawn Tennis Association were Sir Edward Stone—'ancient colonist' lawyer and politician, who succeeded Parker as Chief Justice of Western Australia—and leading bankers and managers of the insurance companies, and other respectable financiers. Tennis gradually increased in popularity, due to the construction of municipal tennis courts as well as the Association's own courts at Mueller Park in Subiaco. Eventually the Association would have its headquarters in King's Park, and the Royal King's Park Tennis Club membership would be as exclusive as the Weld Club from whence it sprang. Even more exclusive than tennis in the pre-Great War years was golf.[286]

Even Australian Rules football was not immune to the influence of the WA gentry. In the 1880s the game had been promoted by several young men who at that time were tilting against the authority of the Governor and his senior gentry colleagues. The most important figure was Walter Hartwell James. James, as secretary of the Metropolitan Football Club, had to work very hard to get the 'fit and proper' persons

[283] *West Australian*, 12, 19 November 1901, cited in Campbell 'Aspects of Perth', p.26.
[284] See notes and photographs in Vivienne *Travels in Western Australia*; Battye's *Cyclopaedia*, and *Twentieth Century Impressions of WA*.
[285] *West Australian*, 8 April 1895, cited Stoddart 'Sport and Society'.
[286] Battye *Cyclopaedia of WA* Vol. 2, p.396.

Tennis on the Esplanade: not yet a sport for all the people of Perth.

of the Perth City Council to agree to allow the players to use the recreation ground. Already there was concern about the disorderly character of the game. In 1885 James formed the WA Football Association and gradually the game made headway, though faster in Fremantle where gentry influence was less marked. In 1890 the fears of the gentry seemed realized when, at a Fremantle versus Perth match, the barrackers invaded the field in a display of violence without precedence in the sporting annals of the colony.[287] There was talk of football fostering juvenile larrikinism. In the following season another West Perth–Fremantle match was kept in order only by the arrival of six policemen.[288] Nor was violence restricted to the working class spectators of the game. In 1895, the years in which enclosed grounds were first used, a player was charged with violence and fined by the Perth court. It was the ubiquitous George Parker who gave evidence against the player, for the fact of the matter was—and even James, who was shortly to become a member of the Weld Club, was uneasy about this and sided with Parker—that Australian Rules was not as subject to 'ancient colonist' influence as it ought to be. In part this was because the popularity of the game increased dramatically in the 1890s with the influx of Victorians into WA. Indeed the ranks of clubs like South Melbourne, Essendon, Geelong, Carlton and Collingwood were almost depleted by the exodus to the west:

> some of the best men who ever played the Australian game—notably Albert Thurgood, Irving, Watson, Grecian, the Duggans, Rolfe, Marmo, McKenzie, 'Les' Jones, Robertson, and dozens of others, were playing either metropolitan or goldfields football.[289]

By 1900 Aussie Rules was firmly established in Perth. Old clubs like Rovers, Centrals, and Railways were now known by suburban names. In the 1901 season, won by West Perth, the five other teams in the

287 *West Australian*, 17 June 1890, cited Stoddart 'Sport and Society'.
288 *Western Mail*, 7 August 1891.
289 *Twentieth Century Impressions of WA*, p.159.

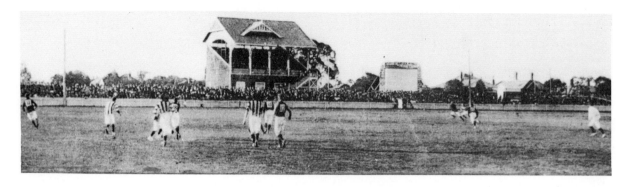

Australian Rules Football: brought 't'othersider' and 'sandgroper' together and produced men of 'nerve and courage'.

From 1893 the bicycle took youths on excursions and men to work: cycling became Perth's most popular and democratic sport.

competition were Perth, East Fremantle, North Fremantle, South Fremantle, and Subiaco. At the end of each season a metropolitan team played a goldfields team, a tradition which lasted through to the Great War. Round about 1900 the State primary schools, which had been sturdily British in orientation, adopted Australian Rules as an optional sport in school hours.[290] When the Great War broke out, the very qualities of the game which had won it the disapproval of the gentry—namely, overtones of social disorder—became a State and national asset, although it was not John Forrest, but Jack Scaddan, Labor Premier and Subiaco follower, who said that football produced men of 'nerve and courage'.[291]

There were other organized sports which were not controlled by the 'ancient colonists' and which owed their popularity to the influx of 't'othersiders'. One was cycling. By the mid-1890s the Perth and Fremantle Cycling Clubs were well-established. Indeed throughout the goldrush years cycling ranked with football and cricket in popularity. Most towns in Western Australia had a cycling track, which usually ran around the local cricket oval. At the turn of the century the Western Australian League of Wheelmen had a track round the WACA ground; but the League itself was run by 't'othersiders'. Cycling seems to have enjoyed a considerable spectator following. The only cause for alarm was the gambling associated with it. But in general it seems to have been regarded as an anodyne form of entertainment.[292]

Cycling was a young man's sport, but probably the fastest growing sport in Western Australia in the early 1900s was lawn bowls. In 1901 five clubs were affiliated with the WA Association. This had risen to twelve in 1904. By 1911 there were thirty affiliated clubs. In Perth there was a green on the Esplanade and another at the WACA, while the King's Park Club was established in 1903-04.[293] In the early 1900s the president of the Association was Lawrence Alexander, the Mayor of Fremantle. Alexander was a merchant who had been in Western Australia since 1888. Bowling clubs, then and later, were informal arenas of local municipal and parliamentary politics, and many members of councils and parliament and aspirants to office found that it was imperative to be known to club bowlers.[294] Not until the introduction of

290 M. Thomas 'East Perth 1884–1904', 1974, p.218; also Battye *Cyclopaedia of WA* Vol. 2, p.394.
291 Cited Stoddart 'Sport and Society'.
292 *Twentieth Century Impressions of WA*, 1901, pp.160–3.
293 *Year Book of Western Australia*, 1906, p.141.
294 *Twentieth Century Impressions of WA*, 1901, pp.163, 455; Battye *Cyclopaedia of WA* Vol. 2, 1913, p.396; John K. Ewers *The Western Gateway*, rev. ed. 1971, p.109.

old-age pensions was it possible for elderly workers to play bowls, and even then the game did not become popular in working class districts until after the Second World War.

Other sports were played in Perth. The WA Athletics' Association enjoyed vice-regal patronage and held carnivals on the Esplanade. In the late 1890s hockey was beginning to be played by women. It was also fostered in high schools as a girls' sport. Lacrosse was also played, but it had very few adherents. Soccer (British Association) and rugby had their devotees, the first named being more popular, but even in the 1890s both were well behind football as participant and spectator sports. For the affluent there was yachting. Yachting was almost as prestigeous as horse-racing, for ownership of a yacht was a symbol of one's high status in Perth society. In 1891 the Perth Yacht Club received the royal warrant. Entry to the Club was only marginally less difficult than to the Weld Club. But there was also the Perth Flying Squadron, the Mounts Bay Sailing Club and the Perth Dinghy Club. In time the yachts on the Swan River formed part of the romanticism of the King's Park–Perth Water view. Even the poorer residents of East Perth could come to the foreshore and see the more affluent Westralians at play on the water. Rowing was also a popular sport with both the leisured classes and those workers who could afford the £1 13s entrance fee and £2 5s subscription. Workers and others could and did bet on races conducted by the WA Rowing Association, and the achievements of some of the famous Australian scullers were followed in the local press. But participation was limited to those who did not have to work long hours at tiring assignments. Social distance increased still further in the 1900s with the appearance of privately owned motor-launches.

The leisure activities of the people of Perth were not confined to organized sports, though the institutionalization of sports is a central characteristic of the period. A sport like roller skating was open to all people, for entrance to the several halls of Perth (the East Perth Exhibition Hall, the central Hay Street rink and, on occasions, the Town Hall rink) was cheap and the skates could be hired. Skating was enjoyed by both girls and boys. Indeed the rinks, like the city's dance halls, were important meeting places for young lovers and friends out on the town free of parental supervision. With the extension of the tramway system more 'teenagers' could get into the city centre. Even the daughter of a strict Wesleyan household, which frowned on dancing and the like, could sometimes slip away with a girlfriend to St George's Hall for dancing and Molloy's Royal Theatre for a film. But it would be church and a Sunday school picnic (perhaps at Sir George Shenton's residence at Crawley) the next day.[295]

Despite its ancient lineage boxing was not much encouraged by the gentry. There was a boxing academy in Perth—but boxing was most popular in the working class districts such as East Perth, and gambling took place with only slight harassment from the law. Women were not allowed at boxing matches, but in the early 1900s the young Effie Fellows, later a celebrated male impersonator, slipped in dressed in boys clothes and was caught and reprimanded by the Court.[296] There was even cock-fighting in some suburban backyards. This probably survived to the Great War, even though the Perth City Council tried to stamp it out.[297]

Saturday night for the young: a film at the Royal or the Queen's Theatre.

Sunday for the young: a picnic at Sir George Shenton's 'Crawley Park'—after church or Sunday school.

295 Interview with Mrs Maud Riley, nee Caporn, 1975.
296 Thomas 'East Perth 1884–1904', Appendix; also PCC Minute Book, 2 March 1894.
297 PCC Minute Book, 3 November 1893.

315

Family bathing and picnicking by
the Swan River at Peppermint
Grove, 1900s.

The Swan River was the scene of much of the recreational life of
Perth. An activity like crabbing was open to all classes. Even the elite
enjoyed it:

> there were plenty of Blue Manna crabs and you used to wade out with a
> pair of boots on your feet for fear of glass or crabs, and you would
> wade out nearly up to your middle with a half kerosene tin with a bit of
> water out on a string floating alongside you, and a big crab net. As you
> caught your crabs you dropped them into the tin . . . came ashore and
> tipped the whole lot into a big kerosene tin of boiling water and that was
> the end of the crab and you had a good feed.

Even the great Nellie Melba went crabbing during her visit in 1902.[298]

If yachting was not open to the working class, other forms of river
tripping were available. Indeed some unions, like the railway employees'
union, organized river cruises to Peppermint Grove, Point Walter and
South Perth. So too did Church Sunday schools. A typical experience
was that of the Congregationalist Sunday school in the late summer of
1891:

> Shortly after 8 a.m. a procession was formed by a band and marched to
> a jetty where the steamers were waiting . . . Arriving at Crawley they
> lunched and then races and games were indulged in. The group returned
> at 7.30 p.m.[299]

In the hot weather the children and young men and women would swim
in the municipal baths, off the Perth jetty. This was the scene of
occasional horse-play and general high spirits. But admission was not
free. The youngsters of East Perth preferred to swim in the river near the
Bunbury Bridge; the Victoria Park families would travel to Como; and
the western suburbs' families would go to Crawley or back overland to
Mongers' Lake at Leederville. Some groups, like the Asians and the
Aborigines, were not allowed to swim in the public baths, and probably
the cost, low though it was, deterred working class children from making
regular use of the baths in summer.

There were also the parks of Perth. From the late 1890s Perth Park
(King's Park from 1901) had been terraced down to the river. It had
pleasant walks, benches for parents to rest while their children played,
and summerhouses to which one could retreat from the sun of high

Family recreation at Lake Monger,
west of the city, 1912.

---

298 Bishop C. L. Riley 'Early Perth'—talk given to the Karrakatta Club, 31 July 1962, pp.
14–5, Battye Library, PR 4614; also Dr J. Summers *Music and Musicians*, 1910, p.29.
299 *West Australian*, 4 March 1891, cited Joll 'Perth in 1891'.

316

summer. Several tea houses offered light refreshment. In short, by 1911 a visit to the Park was something most people did on at least one of the thirteen public holidays of the year. For some of the people of West Perth a stroll in the Park could be a daily occurrence.

There were other parks in the city. Even East Perth from 1899 had a park—Queen's Gardens, an eight-acre reserve of lily ponds and grass-walks. There was also Wellington Square not far away, while on the north side of the city there were Weld and Russell Squares, and Hyde Park. North of Havelock Street was Delhi Square, a tribute (as were several streets in the area) to the glorious suppression of the Indian Mutiny and the later crowning of Queen Victoria as Empress of India. Sometimes the use made of the parks was not altogether to the liking of the Perth City councillors—Weld Square, in particular, seemed to attract drifters and young people out for an evening's larking.[300]

Across the river at South Perth were the Zoological Gardens. In 1897 Winthrop Hackett, then president of the Acclimatization Committee, persuaded the Forrest Government to establish a zoo. The Gardens were opened to the general public on October 1898 and were popular at once, having nearly 200 000 visitors in the first three years, and one million by 1912. Families would catch a ferry from the Perth side, arrive at Mends Street Jetty, and make the short walk to the 'Zoo'. There the children, most of whom had never seen wild animals other than in picture books, could hear the Director, Mr Le Souef, lecture on the animals in his charge. But there was far more to the Zoo than Mr Le Souef's lectures. There was a lion and a rather bad-tempered lioness, a baby (in 1900) tiger, bears, buffalos, pythons, a sacred Indian cow from Singapore, a monkey, leopards and, most popular of all, a white kangaroo. There were also dingoes, koala bears and tiger snakes in the Australian collection, for from the outset Le Souef (whose father was Director of the Victorian Zoological Society) had been determined to include Australian fauna. And even though the Gardens did not bear her name, Queen Victoria presented it with eight red and fallow deer from the herd at Windsor. Le Souef loved animals and children. He instituted donkey and camel rides, goat-carriages and cattle chariots for the children of Perth, as well as swing-boats, climbing bars and other play facilities. He even provided free hot water for the parents' luncheons and tea, and by 1911 cricket, tennis, croquet and bowls could be played in the grounds.[301]

One of the most popular societies in Perth was the Horticultural Society. In February each year it held a show of fruit, vegetables and flowers. In September it held a wildflower show in the Perth Town Hall.[302] May Vivienne drove in from Claremont to see the show in 1900:

> The drive over the bloom-covered slopes of the Park, the sweet odours of the pretty flowers of the Bush mingling with that of the golden wattle, was most enjoyable. I can never ride or drive through that park, and gaze on the beautiful scene below, without feeling that God has indeed given us a lovely world to live in. It was a holiday, and consequently many little parties (frequently of two) were exploring the flower-scented knolls and enjoying the breeze from the water. Perth was quite gay, all the carriages of the elite seemed engaged in carrying their fair owners to the flower-show. On entering the Town Hall a

'Sand Pies': anyone could enjoy the beaches of Perth. (Florence Fuller, artist, 1900s.)

---

[300] PCC Minute Book, 17 February 1902.
[301] *Twentieth Century Impressions of WA*, pp.190-2.
[302] *West Australian*, 24 February 1891, cited Joll 'Perth in 1891'.

317

perfect blaze of beauty in the shape of wildflowers met the eye. The silver and golden wattle, laden with fragrant perfume, drew me immediately to the spot where they were. In the 'Salyang Mia-Mia' (wattle-house) a most refreshing cup of tea was to be procured. Sitting in this fragrant bower and sipping tea brought to mind the lines:

All the world is turning golden,
         turning golden,
Gold buttercups, gold moths upon the wing,
Gold is shining thro' the eyelids that
         were holden,
Till the Spring.[303]

In the Spring also there was the Royal Agricultural Show, gentry in origin, but an increasingly popular event with the people of Perth. In the early 1900s the Society acquired grounds at Claremont where the annual 'Show' has been held ever since.

Picking wildflowers in the bush of Perth and its hinterland, or strolling in King's Park, were two popular recreations for many families.

[303] May Vivienne *Travels in Western Australia*, 2nd ed. 1902, p.58.

318

Every now and again there would be some extraordinary event to excite the people. In January 1891 there was the Great Australian Circus: 3s in dress circle—1s in the pit. In 1891 also there was Professor J. W. Price's balloon ascent. At first bad weather and then a puncture delayed the fantastic sight, but in March the professor made it, if only to 150 feet. Almost twenty years later a huge crowd turned out to Loton's Park (recently acquired by the Perth City Council from the estate of the late Mayor, William Thorley Loton) to welcome the first of the magnificent men in their flying machines, who landed safely to great applause.

Not all the drama was in the air, however. Government House patronage (Sir William Robinson fancied himself as a composer and performer) ensured the success of the Amateur Operatic Society, which gave annual peformances of Gilbert and Sullivan operettas, including *Iolanthe*, *The Yeomen of the Guard* and *The Sorcerer*. In Nellie Wiggleworth, fair of face and form, the Society had a star attraction.[304] For the more earnest music lovers there was the Musical Union, which even before the goldrushes had over 150 members. They sang Handel's *Messiah*, *Aeis and Galatea* and other classical pieces.[305]

It was in 1891 that Perth was host to Miss Janet Achurch and her drama company. The *West Australian* welcomed her warmly:

> Her arrival cannot under any circumstances fail to be an event of great interest. A few years ago it would have belonged to the region of the impossible. But times have changed since then and if Miss Achurch's enterprise proves the success that is anticipated, financially as well as artistically, we may expect from time to time some of the wandering constellations of the theatrical world will make Western Australia one of their halting places.[306]

Perhaps the most amazing thing about Miss Achurch's Company was the playwright whose works were performed, for she played Ibsen's *Hedda Gabler* and *The Dolls' House*, both of which were revolutionary in their exploration of social relationships and congenital disease. By the early 1900s drama was being put on at the Cremorne Gardens, the Queen's Hall and the Theatre Royal. Films were also beginning to compete as popular entertainment.

In 1891 the *West Australian* had written that

> as the years roll on and the Community becomes larger as well as richer we shall have more varied and complete means of enjoyment.[307]

A decade later it was clear that the prophecy was correct, though the means of enjoyment were less varied and less complete the further one went down the social scale, and it applied far less to women than to men. Certainly increasing size and wealth had enabled the councils and the colonial/state governments to provide more recreational facilities for the people, such as parks, playing fields, swimming baths, bands, the Zoo and so on. The Government had also been able to extend the city's cultural facilities. The most important of these was the Victoria Public Library. In 1886 the old Legislative Council voted £5000 for the celebrations in connection with Queen Victoria's Golden Jubilee in 1887. It was decided that £2000 should be sent to the Colonial Institute in London and that £3000 should be spent on the construction of a free public library in Perth. On 21 June 1887 Governor Broome laid the

304 See A. H. Kornweibel *Apollo and the Pioneers*, pp.76–81.
305 See F. Hart *Western Australia in 1891*, p.129.
306 *West Australian*, 23 April 1891, cited Joll 'Perth in 1891'.
307 *West Australian*, 2 April 1891.

foundation stone on the site of old Perth Boys' School in St George's Terrace. And there it remained for a decade. Books to the value of £1000 were purchased and placed in the WA Bank's old premises which served as the public library. In June 1897, Queen Victoria's Diamond Jubilee was celebrated in Perth; and in the more prosperous late 1890s the Forrest Government at last built a new library, on a new site over in Beaufort Street. The old foundation stone was carried to the new site, a second stone (with appropriate wording for the Diamond Jubilee) was also laid, and the Victoria Public Library was erected without further delay. In 1903 a second section was erected, and a year later the name of the Queen in whose honour the buildings had been erected was removed from the title of the library, which was henceforth known as the 'Public Library of Western Australia'. A third major section was added in 1911–12.

When the library opened in 1887 it had only 1796 volumes. It grew slowly until 1894 when James Sykes Battye became Principal Librarian. With enlarged funds Battye increased the library's holdings to 23 500 volumes in 1897–98, the period of the move to the new site, and to 102 815 in 1912. Battye introduced a travelling library scheme whereby books were loaned to mechanics', miners' and agricultural institutes. The average number of library visitors per year rose from 20 000 in the early 1890s, to 100 000 by 1901, and to 190 000 in 1912. Battye collected not only reference books, newspapers and periodicals, but also documentary material on Western Australian history. He himself wrote on Western Australian history, and in 1912–13 compiled and published the massive two volume *Cyclopaedia of Western Australia* (from which in part this account of the library's history comes). He may also have written the historical sections, as well as the library sections, of Thiel and Co's *Twentieth Century Impressions of WA* (1901). In Battye's first decade and a half (he did not retire as Principal Librarian until 1953), the library had served the people of Perth well. Evening visits to the library were popular, as were Sunday afternoon visits. Battye was a conservative man as were the members of his management committee, including the chairmen Sir James Lee Steere (1890–1903) and Winthrop Hackett (1903–1913). Septimus Burt was one of the early trustees. Probably the library's collection of books differed somewhat in kind from that of the Swan River Mechanics' Institute (which in 1898 moved into magnificent new premises on the corner of Pier and Hay Streets) in that the emphasis of the latter was increasingly on fiction. But in social tone and morality the two libraries had the same sort of people ordering the books. No radical political journals were purchased; nor were books by Hyndman or even by the Fabians. Sensational literature, whether in book form or of the newspaper variety (*Truth* for example), or the literary-cum art journal sort (*The Yellow Book* by Beardsley and others) could not be seen in the Victoria Public Library and the Mechanics' Institute Library, though it might be found on the goldfields or at Geraldton.

By the early 1900s the people of Perth were visiting in great numbers the Museum and Art Gallery. In 1887 the Perth Gaol had its last hanging and the remaining prisoners were taken to Fremantle Gaol. It was the end of an era. (The Gaol was used briefly as a court house, but the court was then moved back to Stirling Gardens. In 1903 a grand new Supreme Court was erected near the 1837 Court House.) The ethnological and other collections of the Swan River Mechanics' Institute, together with the Rev. Nicolay's geological collection and the Police Department's collection of Aboriginal weapons, were lodged in the old gaol. In the course of the 1890s several galleries were added (one of which was used by the Victorian Public Library), and in 1901 the Duke of York laid the foundation stone of a two-storey art gallery. After years of delay the Art Gallery was completed in 1908. The Museum and Art Gallery, like the Victoria Public Library, represented an immense achievement for the leaders of WA society and Sir John Forrest in particular. It was the last fulsome burst of that impulse to mould the people in the image of gentryism. What the Mechanics' Institute had done for the 1850s–70s, so the Library and Museum would do for the twentieth century. Prosperity and 'sound' education had removed the need for the coercive art of the gothic.

Interior of the Art Gallery of Western Australia, 1900s: the Director, Bernard Woodard, had a passion for sculpture.

Frederick McCubbin's 'Down on his Luck' has been one of the WA Art Gallery's best known and most loved paintings since its acquisition in 1896. (Painted in Victoria, 1889.)

And as the view from King's Park fostered a pastoral myth, so too did the paintings in the Art Gallery. The collection was aristocratic, rural, sentimental and romantic: Gainsborough, Lawrence, Bonington's 'Lugarno', Richard Wilson's 'Yacht Racing on the Solant', La Thangue and George Clausen among British painters—and among the Australian paintings, McCubbin's 'Down on his Luck' and the domestic landscapes of Buvelot, Pitt-Morison (who was assistant to the Director, Mr Bernard Woodward), and Ford Paterson. Sir Edward Poynton, a Victorian Olympian, had assisted with the selection of British paintings. As the poetry of revolt was absent from the Library, so the disturbing and disorderly art of Whistler, and that of the early Impressionists would not grace the walls of the WA Art Gallery, though Whistler's friend and biographer Joseph Pennell actually purchased some drawings for the gallery. These paintings, invaluable as they were, would be all the people of Perth would see for thirty or so years, for from 1911 the Library, Art Gallery and Museum were brought under one committee, which was dominated by the Librarian, J. S. Battye. Between 1896 and 1911, £11,380 was spent on paintings. Between 1911 and 1927 only £32 was spent on art; and for the years 1911 to 1953 only £7400 worth of paintings was bought. Thus it can be seen that the impulse to be a fine Victorian city was strong within the governments of Western Australia in the goldrush years.[308] Far more popular with the general public was the natural history section of the Museum. And the most popular item in the natural history section was the skeleton of the whale, stranded near Busselton in 1897. Nearly 80 feet in length it was housed in a special shed where several generations of WA school children viewed it.

'The Nursery' (detail), presented to the Art Gallery of Western Australia by Sir Winthrop Hackett in 1911. (Sir Ernest Albert Waterlow, British artist, 1893.)

'The Whale': surely the best known whale skeleton in the world—a nightmare for curators and a thing of wonder to the children of Perth.

308 *Twentieth Century Impressions of WA*, pp.93–7; Battye *Cyclopaedia of WA* Vol. 2, pp.531–3; 'The Western Australian Museum and Art Gallery, Perth', by Bernard Woodward *The Museum Journal* Vol. 3, No. 6, December 1903; the WA Art Gallery Catalogue *Acquisitions 1975–77*, pp.2–3; the WA Art Gallery Catalogue *The First Fifteen Years*, 1979.

'If Jesus Comes to Jarrahland'

To concentrate exclusively on the roles of the State Library, Museum and Art Gallery, and the mechanics' institutes, and the various art, theatre and music societies in Perth, would be to miss one of the most vital areas of cultural and educational activity, namely the press. The period from the late 1880s to the early 1900s was probably the most brilliant passage of journalism in the history of Western Australia. The outstanding newspaper man of the time was Winthrop Hackett, part-proprietor and editor of the *West Australian* from 1887 to 1916. At Trinity College, Dublin, where he studied law, Hackett was thought to be a democrat. And in Victoria from the late 1870s to 1882 he wrote for David Syme's liberal newspaper, the *Age*, and stood (unsuccessfully) for the Victorian Legislative Assembly as an advanced liberal. But in 1883 he formed a business partnership with Charles Harper, the deeply conservative Anglican parliamentarian and pastoralist; and from the mid-1880s he was identified in the public mind with the local gentry establishment. This was a fair assessment, for Hackett was a governor's man and was always extremely cautious about political reform. In addition he was a stalwart Anglican churchgoer, a member of the Weld Club, and a trustee/committeeman on nearly all the educational instrumentalities—library, museum, zoo etc—of Broome's and Forrest's administrations, and only at the eleventh hour did he come out in favour of federation. But the federation issue also reveals that he was not as conservative as many of the Forrest Government supporters, including Charles Harper, who opposed federation to the last. And at another important moment in Perth's history, Hackett opposed the Forrest Government's desire to retain state aid to church schools and religion, thereby allying himself with some liberal politicians like George Leake and Walter James. Hackett seems to have been motivated by a belief that state education (with religious instruction) should be available to all children. This view also undergirded his major achievement—namely the establishment of a University which would be free and open to all with the necessary academic qualifications. He achieved this in 1911, the same year which saw the opening of Perth Modern School, another of Hackett's interests. On Hackett's death in 1926 his estate included a £425,000 benefaction for the University of Western Australia, to be used for buildings (Winthrop Hall, constructed between 1931 and 1933, being the most notable) and to assist students of limited means. The Church of England received £138,000, much of which it used to build St George's College at the University of Western Australia. He also left money to the Art Gallery, which purchased Streeton's 'Barron Gorge' and Longstaff's 'Breaking the News', to the delight of many thousands of Western Australians over the years.[309]

Hackett's fortune was built on the success of the *West Australian*. In 1885 the *West* had established a weekly companion called the *Western Mail*, the editorship of which passed to the talented 'ancient colonist', Alfred Carson, in 1897. In 1885 the *West Australian* became a daily newspaper. It was an eight page paper by 1891 and reached 12 pages in 1901—nearly half the columns of which were advertisements, the source of Hackett's great wealth. In 1898 a linotype machine replaced hand

---

[309] Details of Hackett's career are drawn from Kimberly; Battye's *Cyclopaedia*; and Bolton and Mozley *WA Legislature*.

composition. By the late 1890s the *Mail* was a 50 page journal with several pages of illustrations and a cartoon by Ben Strange. In December each year a Christmas Supplement of 100 pages was issued 'which commanded the most flattering notices everywhere'.[310] This was the opinion of the authors of *Twentieth Century Impressions of WA*, and the popularity of the *Mail* suggests that it was shared by many readers. But the stories printed in the *Mail*, even those with local settings, tended to shy away from realism and highlight the sensational and the romantic. The *West Australian* never encouraged local writing and looked always to Britain for literary inspiration. It praised literary craftsmanship, however fantastic the theme, and would have nothing to do with a literature which reflected working class life and attitudes.[311] Nevertheless Hackett recognized union labour and became one of the first employers of labour to introduce an eight-hour working day, perhaps because of the considerable strength of the Typographical Union.

Hackett's and Harper's *West Australian* was not the first daily newspaper in Perth. In 1882 Stirling's evening *Daily News* was established. From 1886 Alexander Forrest was a shareholder in the company but he seems to have regarded his holding as an investment only, for in the 1880s, and from 1896 when the new morning daily, the *Morning Herald*, was established, the editors generally ran a more liberal political line than did either of the Forrests. This should not be exaggerated, however. The *Morning Herald* strongly opposed federation, and when in 1896 it had attacked duties on food, Alexander Forrest was busy gaining the agency of Kidman for the importation of meat, and in the same year the *Herald*'s attacks on inefficiency in the Railway Department almost certainly helped John Forrest to get rid of a troublesome cabinet colleague in Harry Venn. The *Herald* was an extremely profitable enterprise for its 'ancient colonist' directors and shareholders, as Arthur Lovekin declared proudly on his retirement as managing director in October 1900. It was a year later that the *News*' weekly companion, the *Inquirer*, ceased publication. It had been issued continuously since 1840. In the early 1900s, however, the Roman Catholic Church bought a large holding in the *Morning Herald*, and Bishop Gibney's nominee became chairman of directors. The paper lost circulation and advertising and went into liquidation in 1904. Its demise hastened Gibney's resignation as Bishop of Perth and thus forms a curious interlude in the city's church history.[312]

In the 1890s Hackett, the Forrests, Harper, Burt and other Westralian leaders of opinion had to contend with the goldfields' press and the values espoused in the numerous regional journals. Press espousal of views opposed to local gentryism had begun in Perth in the late 1880s with the publication of the *WA Bulletin*, which had supported Horgan in his election contest with Septimus Burt. In the early 1890s the focus of hostility to the Forrest Government was Geraldton's *Victorian Express*, edited by John Drew. In 1894 the Government sued the *Express* for £3000 for refusing to name a correspondent who had cast aspersions on a Government doctor in the district. On his return to Geraldton after a fourteen day spell in gaol for contempt of court, Drew mocked the

[310] *Twentieth Century Impressions of WA*, pp.168–74.
[311] See B. Smith 'Western Australian Goldfields Literature' *University Studies in History* Vol. 4, No. 2, 1963–64, pp.136–8.
[312] Battye *Cyclopaedia of WA* Vol. 1, pp.584–7; *Twentieth Century Impressions of WA*, pp.163–8.

Attorney-General, Burt, who had described the *Express* as a 'scourge'. Drew said:

> It is a scourge of injustice, the scourge of inhumanity, the scourge of the oppressors of the poor, and of public robbers in every degree.

Drew also spoke of 'the undesirable servility of some of the colony's principal journals'. Septimus Burt was often quoted as being representative of a 'sandgroper' and gentry viewpoint. Burt's words—'Miners are birds of passage . . . who are they to have a vote and maybe upset the settled policy of the Government? Enough of pick and shovel representation'—deeply angered miners—indeed workers generally. One of their spokesmen wrote 'The Sneer of Septimus Burt':

> 'Tis a voice that has rung aforetime, since the
>   days when the world was new,
> Wherever the sweating thousands have toiled for
>   the favoured few,
> 'Tis the horsehair wig that is speaking to the
>   roofing of cabbage tree
> Stiff broadcloth and speckless linen to moleskin
>   and dungaree,
> The puny quill to the pickaxe, the gown to the
>   clay-stained shirt,
> The man of the words to the worker—the voice
>   of Septimus Burt.
>
> For a murmur rose from the goldfields and some
>   grew grave at the cry,
> (Like cattle chafe at the thunder in the calm
>   of a cloudless sky),
> 'A vote is a free man's birthright; ye have
>   fooled us long with your tricks,
> Let the will of the people govern and not the
>   will of the Six.'
> So some in high places hearkened and sprung to
>   their feet alert
> For they knew that the storm was on them—not
>   such was Septimus Burt.
>
> Quoth he, ' 'Tis a senseless clamour, you fight
>   with a hopeless cause
> Your work is to ply the pickaxe and ours to frame
>   the laws
> Get back to the shaft and windlass, with your
>   tools in your horny clasp,
> Nor trouble your wits with matters too deep for
>   your wits to grasp;
> Go scratch in the dirt like rabbits; go, tunnel
>   like moles in the dirt,
> Thank God for heaven-sent rulers like me,' cried
>   Septimus Burt.
>
> Will an epigram, think you, daunt them? Will
>   they swerve from the path at a breath?
> The men who have laughed at peril and closed
>   in his lair with death?
> Now a little reckoning awaits you, and short
>   shrift will be yours at our hands
> Who have sneered at the rights of Labour and
>   mocked at our just demands.
> Too late you may rue your folly, too late to
>   recant or revert
> You may find that your lips have spoken—the
>   knell of Septimus Burt.

The author of 'The Sneer of Septimus Burt' was Andree Hayward, an Englishman more highly educated (Rugby, Oxford and the law) than Septimus Burt, but one who respected workers as equals. He arrived in WA in 1894 and worked on Drew's newspaper from 1894 to 1898. The Sydney *Bulletin* was the inspiration of much of his own verse and the general attitude of the *Express*. In the minds of people like Hayward, Perth was identified with the Forrest Government, the 'Six Families' and social servility. As 'Dryblower' Murphy put it in the *Coolgardie Miner* in 1896:

> that spud patch long and wide
>   Whose owners all reside
> In the small but smellful village where the
>   Swannee River flows . . .
> And the grovelling yokel lifts his hat
>   as Premiers pass him by.

Others wrote of 'The will of politicians Prostituting high positions Keeping up the old traditions'.[313]

Through ownership and staff appointments, the Perth *Sunday Times* was nourished by its contact with the goldfields and '. . . did a great deal to carry this political and social influence into the city—especially the homes of the working class'.[314] The *Daily News*, the *West Australian* and *Morning Herald* newspapers were all owned and run by men who had been in the colony in the pre-goldrush days. This was not true of the *Sunday Times* which was issued first in 1897 under the editorship of Frederick Vosper. Vosper was an ex-Queensland journalist who had had a spell in prison during the Charters Towers' strikes of 1891–92. He came to WA in 1892 and made his local reputation on the goldfields as editor of the *Coolgardie Miner*. A great hater of the Forrest Government, he was MLA for North-East Coolgardie from 1897 to his early death in 1901. In his turn this long-haired radical inspired great hate among the Perth gentry, for his *Sunday Times* (a 'Journal for the People') was unsparing in its criticism of the Government and individual leaders of Perth society. His paper was widely read, especially by workers. The *Sunday Times* was always in financial difficulties for it won little advertising, and towards the end of 1900 Vosper wrote despairingly to his father that:

*Two sketches of F. C. B. Vosper, 't'othersider' journalist in Perth: top: by Ben Strage, from **Clare's Weekly**; bottom: by Walker Hodgson, from Calvert's **My Fourth Tour in Western Australia**.*

> Here I have had a long fight against the old ruling clique, and was no use to myself, much less to others, so far as influence went.

Vosper was ill for much of 1900, and in January 1901 a neglected appendix caused his death. He was just thirty-three years of age.[315] In the funeral oration the Roman Catholic priest, Father Duff, spoke of how Vosper had used his great intellect in defence of the poor and helpless: 'when anybody had a grievance, he was told "Go to Vosper" '.[316]

Vosper was an extreme individualist—with a venomous pen. In Perth's history he has an unenviable reputation as the man whose criticisms of C. Y. O'Connor's Coolgardie Water Scheme apparently caused that great engineer to commit suicide.[317] But Vosper should also

---

[313] Smith 'Goldfields Literature', p.123.

[314] Smith 'Goldfields Literature', p.97.

[315] Vosper Correspondence, Battye Library 817A. See also his Will in the Supreme Court. His assets amounted to £110; his liabilities to £106.

[316] Cited in J. Bastin and J. Stoodley 'F. C. B. Vosper: An Australian Radical' *University Studies in History* Vol. 5, No. 1, 1967, p.52.

[317] See M. Tauman *The Chief: C. Y. O'Connor*, 1978, p.229.

Ten Years Ago
(*Written September, 1902.*)

Ten years ago Westralia slept,
  A Cinderella lone and shy,
Within whose veins no ardour
    leapt,
For whom Hope gilded not the
    sky;
Ten years ago she waked and
    yawned
Unconscious of her destined fate;
Ten years ago her hey-day dawned
To lift her to her high estate,
Her wond'rous wealth bewitched
    the world,
Towards her turned the human
    flow,
When Bayley back the curtain
    hurled,
  Ten years ago.

Ten years ago—a wondrous ten—
Two mates rode east from South'rn
    Cross,
Where lie the bleaching bones of
    men
Among the granite, grass and
    moss.
A hundred followed in their
    tracks—
A thousand more, and still they
    came—
Their little all upon their backs,
Their hearts with lust of gold
    aflame.
A month of work—and wak'ning
    Perth
Stared dazzled at a golden show,
A show that staggered half the
    earth,
  Ten years ago.

Ten years ago we tramped the East
That promised much and gave us
    nought,
Until at last it even ceased
To promise what we vainly sought.
Ten years ago we crossed the Bight
Towards a famous, far-off find;
Ahead, an El Dorado bright,
A starved and bankrupt land
    behind.
Our dishes rang, our 'anchors'
    swung
When Bayley rooted round his
    blow,
When hopes were high and hearts
    were young,
  Ten years ago.

"Dryblower" Murphy

be remembered as an important penal and political reformer.[318] The *Sunday Times* and its goldfields companion, the *Sun*, wanted to 'remove injustice and wrong and to establish just conditions for all'. Beverley Smith has observed of the *Sunday Times* in the 1900s that 'there was recurring criticism of the urban landlord and the land monopolist, of sweating in the clothing industry, maltreatment of the Aborigines by pastoralists, and of bad conditions in various state institutions, such as the homes of the aged. The effects of poverty—prostitution, outbreaks of bubonic plague and the high incidence of death through abortion—were freely discussed'.[319] In 1908 the *Sunday Times* printed 'Dryblower's' collection of verse, *Jarrahland Jingles*, in which the poet wrote in praise of workers and of their exploitation by the rich. In 'If Jesus Comes to Jarrahland', 'Dryblower' has Jesus saying to the rich of Perth:

Yea, he said, your hearts are hollow and your
  Lord you will deny
While mingling with your carols comes a
  hungry helpless cry,
For in city, slum and highway and upon the
  mulga tracks
You have human Christs among you bearing Crosses
  on their backs.

But even 'Dryblower', hostile witness to gentryism as he was, could see that a fine city had been 'created' during the goldrushes ('Ten Years Ago'); and in the same year (1908) a colleague on the *Sunday Times*, J. E. Webb, commenced a series of articles on 'The Land We Live In: An Appreciation of Wonderful Western Australia'. Another of the *Sunday Times*' contributors, 'Bluebush' (John Bourke), wanted to experience mateship and the brotherhood of men, but he disliked social conflict and so wavered between 'spasmodic desire for action to right wrongs and ultimate dependence on passing delights and the bottle'.[320] Perhaps many became disillusioned when Daglish's Labor Government of 1904–05 achieved so little:

Oh brother workers, we have dreamed in vain
Who saw Utopia in a Labor reign.

By 1910–11 the *Sunday Times* was almost indistinguishable in its world view from the *Western Mail* and the *West Australian*, and central to this decline was a retreat from the literature of humanity to the literature of art, with all that implied for the triumph of elitism. As usual the poets were one step ahead in their perception of this, and those people who hailed Scaddan's landslide victory in 1911 as the beginning of a new political and social order had misread the signs. Scaddan's victory was the last kick of a movement in Perth which was vulnerable in the extreme. Scaddan too misread the signs and pressed ahead with a nationalization programme of sorts which won his Government such universal censure that Labor never again had the will to do more than ameliorate the condition of workers in a quietist manner. Henceforth the means of gaining office would be to appear more Westralian than the other side. That too was foreshadowed by the transformation of the *Sunday Times*, and apotheosized in the first *Westralian Gift Book* of 1916, which contained little or nothing about the real world of city and

318 See E. Jaggard 'Frederick Vosper', in L. Hunt (ed.) *Westralian Portraits*, 1979.
319 *The Sun*, 1903, cited in Smith 'Goldfields Literature', p.97.
320 Smith 'Goldfields Literature', p.99.

country life.[321] A. C. Chandler, whose career from goldfields editor through to the days of the *Sunday Times*' rejection of the literature of humanity and easy collaboration with the *Western Mail* and academicism, ended his days as a contributor to the conservative *Argonaut* in the interwar years.[322] Even 'Dryblower', the arch-nonconformist and progressivist, urged the unemployed in the Great Depression to endure hardship without complaint. Perth's journalism would never again be as vital as it was in the 1890s and early 1900s. That too was a triumph of the old order. The defiant, argumentative, and social reformist character of much journalism of the 1890s and 1900s was also suppressed in WA historical writing for the next two generations, perhaps most determinedly and influentially by that arch-shaper of Westralians' perceptions of their past, James Sykes Battye, friend of and collaborator with Winthrop Hackett and John Forrest in the testing years, and custodian of their achievement.

Vosper's *Sunday Times* may have been vitriolic on occasions, but for sheer sensationalism it could not compete with John Norton's paper, *Truth*, first sold on the streets of Perth in January 1903. Norton's journalists found much of their news in the court rooms of Perth and in sporting clubs. *Truth* may not have been taken by the Weld Club, but it very rapidly gained a large circulation in Perth, for it had an entertainment value lacking in the *West* or even the *Sunday Times*. It also had a common touch and a domestic scale which appealed to many lower class families—perhaps especially the men, for it was a paper which could be talked about at work and more acceptably read in the hotel and boarding house than in the family home. Like drink, sport and religion it helped men to put to one side the cares and routines of labour. And for John Norton, *Truth*'s Sydney proprietor, it was as golden as any nugget found on the WA fields.[323]

Forrests in the City: a sense of place

Since the beginning of the settlement of Swan River local people and visitors walked, rode, or drove up to the top of Mt Eliza and looked back down on the town and the river. Painters and photographers have portrayed the scene thousands of times. The portrait is always the same—not in detail of course, but in mood and inspiration. The river is still, the day is clear (with a haze over the Ranges to the east), the foreshore is tree-lined and the buildings rise prettily above the foliage. In the immediate foreground are trees and shrubbery providing a frame for the composed scene. The scene itself is an arcadia—a statement of the ancient pastoral of Virgil and the landscapes of Claude and his British and colonial romantic followers through to the city planners of the last quarter of the twentieth century. As Stirling had described Swan River in the picturesque language of the romantic era, so Perth has been described in word and picture ever since. In short, Swan River forms part of the great western tradition of the pastoral idyll, a tradition which was central to the gentry's quest for internal peace and belief in a harmonious society where men were at one with each other and with nature.

May Vivienne: 'Poetess of the Pastoral'.

[321] Smith 'Goldfields Literature', p.111.
[322] Smith 'Goldfields Literature', p.145; also F. G. Clarke 'The Argonauts Civil and Political Club' *Labour History*, No. 18, May 1970, pp.32–39.
[323] See Battye *Cyclopaedia of WA* Vol. 1, p.591.

'All Joy Befall Your Grace': His Royal Highness the Duke of York and Cornwall in Perth, 1901—the entrance to King's Park.

The Bushmen's Contingent leaving for the Boer War in South Africa, 1900: 'painting in glowing red the pride and pomp of war'.

Mt Eliza itself forms part of the pastoral mystique. There was a time when Mt Eliza was home to the Aborigines and the animals and plants of the wilderness. But in the course of the nineteenth century it was cleared of Aborigines and animals and entered its career as a river and city-viewing point and a rifle range for the Volunteers. From the turn of the century it was cleared of the Volunteers too, or rather of their rifle range, for from 1901 Mt Eliza became not simply Perth Park (the Forrest Government's gift to the people of Perth), but King's Park, a symbol of the unity of Empire and a focus for the hearts of the loyal men and women of Perth. This was a different but complementary myth. In July 1901 the citizens of Perth welcomed H.R.H. the Duke of Cornwall and York, who renamed the Park in his father's honour and opened a new roadway along the top of the park, which he called Princess May Drive after his Royal bride. The ceremony was notable for the singing of the National Anthem and 'Rule Britannia' by a choir of 6000 children—a choir as large as the entire population of the city not fifteen years previously. In the city proper, triumphal arches had been erected on many street corners, and the streets, the houses and the business premises were decorated with bunting and appropriate words of welcome. Although worded simply, the messages sprang from the deepest convictions of a loyal people. Even the Irish Catholics took part in the proceedings. Some of the phrases used were: 'One People: One Destiny'; 'All Joy Befall Your Grace'; 'Trade Follows The Flag'; and so on. A visiting journalist wrote of the people's 'generous patriotism and an intense pride in the Great Empire'.[324]

But the Duke did more than rename the Park and open a drive-way. He also laid the foundation stone of the 'Fallen Soldiers' Memorial', in honour of the Western Australian soldiers (some of them the Volunteers who had practised their shooting on the park range) who had lost their lives during the South African War. Some forty soldiers from Western Australia had been killed in South Africa. Among the honoured dead was Lieutenant A. A. Forrest, whose father, Alexander Forrest, had died in June while mourning the death of his son. In September 1902 the completed memorial was unveiled by Alexander Forrest's friend, Sir Edward Stone, then Chief Justice and Acting Governor of Western Australia. The memorial itself was one of the largest and most impressive erected in Australia. It consisted of a bronze group on a stone pedestal, with four bronze panels depicting scenes from the War. Until the Great War of 1914–1918 it was Perth's most important symbol of sacrifice for community and Empire. For some men in Perth it would remain so until the 1970s when the last Boer War veteran died. Not everyone in Perth had approved of British action in South Africa, and many a labourer working on construction sites around the city, as well as countrymen, felt that the Boer was a fine fellow. And at least one Education Department examiner noted in 1902 that some pupil teachers rather too readily 'painted in glowing red the pride and pomp of war'. But West Australian men had lost their lives in South Africa, and West Australian nurses had also served there. The plaque in St George's Cathedral, and the memorial in King's Park, honoured them. In time, too, the memorial would be flanked by one old cannon used during the War. Generations of Perth children would be lifted up on and clamber over the gun, firing on

---

[324] E. F. Knight *With the Royal Tour*, 1902, p.99. See also *Twentieth Century Impressions of WA*, pp.55–9 for a detailed account of the Royal Tour.

unsuspecting passersby, and reading haltingly the odd place names engraved on the bronze plaques.[325]

In 1903 the Governor, Sir Frederick Bedford, unveiled a very fine marble statue of Queen Victoria, placed only a short walk away from the 'Fallen Soldiers' Memorial'. It was a noble site for a tribute to Queen Victoria, whose death in January 1901 had occasioned universal dismay in Perth and been the subject of countless sermons and speeches. The *West Australian* wrote then of the

> expressions of sorrow which overspread the faces of all, and the words of the saddest regret that fell from their lips, testified to the loyal and loving regard for their deceased sovereign.

For the people of Perth, immigrant and local, were 'not only citizens of the Empire, but also subjects of a Queen'.[326] In time, too, Queen Victoria's statue would be surrounded by four old cannons mounted on wheels, and not until they had clambered over all four would the boys of Perth allow their parents—who had taken tea in the rooms nearby—to lead them home. Some stayed to read the plaque to the Great White Queen. Others went home and read the Rev. Fitchett's *Deeds That Won the Empire* or the stories of Kipling, Henty, and others. Many joined the Boy Scouts (1905) or the British Empire League of Youth. And there were always the Empire Day (24 May) celebrations on the Esplanade below King's Park, with reviews of cadets, the unfurling of the Union Jack, and the singing of the National Anthem; and later there would be Empire pictures and songs in His Majesty's Theatre. Behind the stirring stories of modern times stretched the full length of British history. As Mr Murdoch put it in his school primer *The Struggle for Freedom* (1906):

> There are few in Australia, we may hope, who are not proud of their connection with Britain. There are few who can read unmoved the heroic history of that land, who can hear without a thrill the story of the invincible Armada, or think without pride of Nelson, or of Gordon, of Hampden or of Chatham.[327]

Imperial Loyalty in Perth:
Top: Nurse Elizabeth Bole, 'well known and loved by many soldiers': served at Mooi River, Natal, 1900; Great War service 1914–19. Below: the Fallen Soldiers' Memorial, King's Park, 1900s. Left: a small citizen leads the Empire Day March on the Esplanade, 1909.

325 The sculptor was J. White of Annandale, New South Wales.
326 *West Australian*, 24 January 1901. Queen Victoria died on 22 January. Thanks to the submarine cable the people of Perth could mourn in unison with the people of the Motherland and the Empire. Thus the social respose to the news (as with news of British defeats and victories in the Boer War) was far more emotional than news of similar happenings in earlier times. The sculptor was F. J. Williamson of England, and the statue was the gift of a London businessman with WA interests, Allen H. Stoneham.
327 W. Murdoch *The Struggle for Freedom*, first published in 1906; the quotation comes from the eleventh edition, 1911, p.231.

The sorrow and the sacrifice of Mrs Munro, mother of Perth.

In time some of the youngsters who looked on the bronze plaques of the Boer War memorial and on the face of the Queen in whose name the war was fought, would themselves be looked at as names on lists of those who fell in the Great War of 1914 to 1918. 1914 was a year of depression and drought in Western Australia. Unemployed men in Perth queued for soup and other rations, while in the country some farmers walked off their lands and still more dismissed their labourers. These men were among the 4444 recruited within twenty-four hours of the opening of the recruiting halls on the declaration of the War in August 1914. Other men were motivated to enlist from love of hearth and homeland. The WA quota was exceeded by three and a half times, so enthusiastically did the families of the State commit their sons to the European War. And even in the dark days of 1916 and 1917, Western Australians voted in favour of overseas conscription when a majority of their eastern states' compatriots turned down conscription. In the dry hills of the Middle East and in the mud of France the Western Australian soldiers fought with great gallantry. Wherever they served they were used as shock troops. And they suffered accordingly. The first AIF experienced the appallingly high casualty rate of 66% wounded and dead. By the War's end in November 1918 the number of Westralian dead had risen to 6000, with another 11 000 wounded. In these figures lie the explanation for the use of the expression 'The Great War'. The men of Perth (and sometimes the women of Perth who nursed them) suffered from gun-shot wounds, enteric fever, dysentery, shell-shock, and poisoning by gas. They discovered, as one wrote after the terrible slaughter at Gallipoli on 25 April 1915, that

> If all war is like that then it's worse than any picture I've saw.

And many a grieving mother cradled a damaged watch, a few coins, and maybe a photo of a son who had died for 'Freedom and Honour'. In time the people of Perth would erect in their honour a monument on the most prominent point of King's Park, overlooking the city. The names of still others would be recorded on plaques pinned to the trees which lined the drives of the beautiful park. Thus King's Park was a beauty spot of almost incomparable charm:

> The scene is so exquisite that I cannot bear to go on, but must pull up the horse and stop for a few minutes, that the mind may drink in the sight.[328]

But above all the Park became a sacred place; and the view which never

---

[328] See May Vivienne *Travels in Western Australia*, 2nd ed. 1902, p.35. For other descriptions of the Park in these years see *Twentieth Century Impressions of WA*, pp.55–9, and Battye *Cyclopaedia of WA* Vol. 1, pp.534–5.

failed to excite the imagination was seen through the filter of social experience.[329]

In 1903 the people who admired Alexander Forrest most deeply, commissioned the sculptor Porcelli to create in bronze a life-size statue of their friend. The patrons and the artist decided that Alexander should be garbed, not in the suit of the 1890s businessman, politician and Mayor, but in the rougher clothes of the 1860s and 70s explorer. This was appropriate, for despite his approachability Alexander Forrest had become a legendary figure to the people of Perth. In the swirl of urban growth and suburbanization he was a bridge across the years to the pioneering days, and the erection of the statue was an act of faith—faith in the value of the Westralian past as a guide and comforter for the future. For the 't'othersider' majority of the population, well, it was just the Westralians being 'sandgroperish'. Or was there more to it? If it was, Alexander's old friend the Mayor, Harry Brown, who overseered the removal of the statue from St George's Terrace near Mount Street to the corner of Barrack Street and St George's Terrace, it was also true that the 't'othersider' councillors joined with the 'sandgroper' councillors in approving the new site. Like Forrest, they themselves were 'fit and proper persons' and entrepreneurs to a man. Forrest's statue today, whose tomorrow?

As it happened, the next statue erected in the capital city was of Alexander's brother. After a distinguished career in federal politics, Sir John Forrest had been honoured with the nation's first peerage. He had been on his way to Britain to take his seat in the House of Lords as Baron Forrest of Bunbury when an illness worsened suddenly, and he died in great pain at sea. It was the State Government of Forrest's protégé and friend, Sir James Mitchell, which commissioned the statue. The site chosen was not in the city centre but on one of the highest points of Mt Eliza, not more than five hundred yards from the marble statue of the Queen he revered. Forrest and his people had passed through too intense an experience of Empire for the patrons to garb him in the simple clothes of the explorer. Instead the sculptor, Sir Bertram MacKennal, portrayed him as Baron Forrest of Bunbury, complete with the robes of Imperial distinction.[330] Statues, street names, parks, buildings, portraits, school texts and history books—the Forrests would be in the city forever.

Alexander Forrest, forever in the centre of Perth. (Porcelli, sculptor, 1903.)

Left: **Queen Victoria:** held in 'loyal and loving regard' by the people of Perth. Right: **Baron Forrest of Bunbury:** 'I gave (the people) great beneficent works and devoted all my energies to liberal and progressive legislation.'

[329] The quotation and much of the detail of this paragraph is drawn from Ms Suzanne Welborn 'The Spirit of Place and Anzac', in C. T. Stannage (General Editor) *A New History of Western Australia,* 1979. But see also H. Colebatch *A Story of a Hundred Years,* 1929, and J. G. Wilson *WA's Centenary,* 1929.

[330] See G. C. Bolton *Alexander Forrest,* 1958; F. K. Crowley 'John Forrest', in L. Hunt (ed.) *Westralian Portraits,* 1979.

Return to the promised land: *the troopship 'Konigen Luise' at Fremantle, 1919.*

Chapter Five: 'The Past in the Present' — Twentieth Century Perth

The Centennial Celebrations, 1929

The next history of Perth—of twentieth century Perth—will be complex and interesting, in part because of the great increase in population, as the following table indicates:

Date	City of Perth	Metro Area	Houses in City of Perth
1911	36 000	120 000	6 858
1933	82 000	143 600	18 358
1947	99 000	170 000	26 663
1961	95 000	420 000	26 845
1971	97 500	703 000	31 101
1976	87 600	805 000	30 073

The next history of Perth will also revolve around the seminal social and economic experiences of all the people in the city and its suburbs. Some of the rhythms of public life are already clear to us. In 1929 the people of Perth celebrated the one hundredth anniversary of the foundation of Western Australia. In 1929, as in 1911, about one-third of the State's population lived in the metropolitan area; but by 1929 the city's population had more than doubled. By 1929 much of the housing stock of the city was over thirty years' old, and was showing signs of wear. But the State was in a prosperous condition with wheat production expanding greatly. For many of the people of Perth, life was sluggish and comfortable. Phillip Collier (Labor) and James Mitchell (Nationalist) had swapped the premiership a couple of times, but in practice there was little which separated them. Certainly both men were Western Australian patriots.[1] 1929 was an interesting year for them, as for all Western Australians. In April, talkies were introduced in the cinema. In June 1929 interstate air-mail services commenced. But, above all, there were the centennial celebrations.

It was James Mitchell who in November 1927 called a public meeting to discuss plans for the centennial celebrations. In February 1928, and throughout that year, various schemes were considered. Some were rejected.[2] One was Canon Henn's suggestion that Western Australia should be renamed 'Kingsland':

> it would be a compliment to the only King of Great Britain who had visited the country, and a true description of a land so royally endowed with ample territories and rich resources.

[1] See G. C. Bolton *A Fine Country to Starve In*, 1972, chapter I; also S. Glynn *Government Policy and Agricultural Development*, 1975.

[2] The account of the 1929 celebrations is drawn largely from Ms Ruth Allender's unpublished research essay, 'Western Australia at its Centenary'. All references have been cited with her permission.

Another rejected proposal was that for a 'Palace of the Golden West', incorporating a concert hall, exhibition hall, and so on—a sort of Cultural Centre, in fact. The 'Palace' was to be erected in King's Park, overlooking the river. Most Perth people believed that the 'Palace of the Golden West' was already in existence—in the centre of town.[3] In the event, the Committee settled for less ambitious things. Each school child was given one shilling. The Shenton Mill site was taken over as a public recreation area. There were centennial balls. A National (later John Forrest National) Park was created. A centenary stamp was issued. In 1929, too, Perth became a Lord Mayoralty, the first incumbent being J. T. Franklin, an aging builder who had served on the Perth City Council since the goldrush years. One popular item was an historical film, called *The Golden West*. It was reported that viewers cheered the closing lines:

> Out of the West a mighty voice is calling,
> Unto the east its tone reverberate,
> Out of the West a prospect looms enthralling,
> The vision splendid of a mighty State.[4]

At the heart of the celebration was the colony's history. In the Spring of 1929 a Centennial Procession and historical pageant was held in the streets of Perth. Watched by 60 000 people, it

> presented a picture, deeply etched in firm bold strokes, of Western Australia's present condition of hopeful optimistic prosperity, and it gave some idea, moreover, of what men mean when they talk about the soul of a nation.[5]

Another attempt to capture the soul of the nation was the official *A Story of a Hundred Years*, edited by Senator Sir Hal Colebatch, a former non-Labor premier. In a fine display of party unity, the then Labor premier, Phillip Collier, praised the editor and the past and present people of Western Australia. Collier's 'Foreword' read in part:

> The story of our hundred years cannot fail to be inspiring. Few colonising enterprises have been embarked upon in the face of greater natural difficulties—none has resulted in more complete success... Western Australia has become the home of a happy and prosperous people, full of love and patriotism for their country and of confidence in its resources.

There were other voices, however. Surfacing from a reading of 279 centennial odes, Walter Murdoch noted wryly that 'This nonsense about pioneers gets, after a time, on one's nerves'.[6]

Few people in Perth questioned that the man on the land was the real pioneer. As the Governor, William Campion, said:

> I have watched the advancing tide of conquest of the virgin bush with feelings akin to those with which one watched the gallantry of our fellows in the front line during the war. Many of the same qualities are needed in the bush pioneer, and whenever I have met him, I have found him a splendid chap—quite often an ex-Imperial Service man.[7]

At the opening of the Centenary Pavilion at the Royal Agricultural Show, the State's foremost historian, James Sykes Battye, (whose own

---

[3]   *Daily News* 29 February 1928: Premier's Department file 143/28.
[4]   Premier's Department file 560/28.
[5]   *West Australian* 3 October 1929
[6]   W. Murdoch, *Collected Essays of Walter Murdoch*, 1938, p.77.
[7]   *West Australian* 5 January 1929.

PERTH CITY COUNCIL
· 1929 ·

The Right Hon. the Lord Mayor.   (J.T.Franklin, C.M.G., M.L.C., J.P.)

(Back Row.) Councillors. J.M.Fraser,   H.S.Raphael,   A.Todd,   J.J.Lloyd J.P.,   E.R.Cuddy,   J.B.Farr J.P.,   W.A.Leilier J.P.,   H.Boas.

(Mid. row.) Councillors, J.W.Burgess J.P., H.H.Stunts, J.L.Hardwick, J.George J.P., A.W.Bergman J.P., H.J.Singer, P.Menzies J.P., W.R.Read J.P., A.Collins *(Town Clerk)*

(Front row.)   H.Baker J.P.   T.A.Shafe,   C.Harper J.P.,   C.H.Bull,   W.E.Bold J.P., F.A.I.S., A.T.P.I. *(Town Clerk)* Clr.' C.E.C.Gould, O.C.Lyons J.P., C.J.B.Veryard, H.O.Howling.

Western Australia: A History, 1924, had been drawn on by the compiler of *A Story of a Hundred Years*) sounded the official note when he said:

> we will continue the work of the pioneers so that Western Australia will become one of the greatest, proudest, most prosperous and most loyal possessions of the British Empire.[8]

Certainly loyalty in 1929, as throughout Perth's history, was central to the people's self-identity. Almost all the centenary publications commenced with photographs of King George V and Queen Mary, while 'Long Live the King' and 'God Bless the Queen' were heard more than any other lines in 1929. The King responded with a telegram in which he desired to

> congratulate my loyal people in Western Australia on the wonderful progress made in these hundred years.[9]

That Perth was the home of a happy and contented people seems clear enough. It is a view most persuasively put in two brilliant reconstructions of the interwar years, namely G. C. Bolton's *A Fine Country to Starve In*, and Sir Paul Hasluck's autobiography, *Mucking About*. It is also true, as both authors were aware, that behind the 1929 Western Australian looking glass, there was a less visible Perth—people suffering from stunted ambitions, inadequate housing, and inadequate employment. One unemployed man said of 1929:

> The only sustance we got was collecting the crusts from Boans . . . We got a four gallon tin of soup from the Crystal Hotel and that used to be distributed on the Esplanade.[10]

In July, 1929, several hundred unemployed men marched through the streets of Perth in protest against their condition: fourteen of them were

8   *West Australian* 10 September 1929.
9   Premier's Department file 234/29: telegram 1 June 1929.
10 Foxley, S.G. 'Interview', p.2 (Battye Library, PR 6361).

337

gaoled for disorderly behaviour. By mid-winter, some 300 bed tickets were being issued nightly in Perth by the Trades Hall, and many of the city's charitable organizations were stretched to the limit of their resources. One of the first acts of the newly created Lord Mayor was to open an Unemployment Relief Fund. In December 1929, the Lord Mayor ran a Christmas Cheer Fund for the children of the unemployed. And the obverse side of the British coin revealed itself when the political parties blamed southern Europeans for the unemployment situation. In Miss May Holman's words:

> The number of foreigners coming into the country is a dastardly shame.[11]

She, like most Western Australians, blamed (and usually with good cause) the Commonwealth Government for the State's problems in relation to unemployment.

If many migrants and workers in Perth were experiencing life on harsher terms than the 1929 speechifiers would allow, this was even more true of the Aborigines. In September, a truck load of Aborigines had been brought to Perth to take part in the Centenary Parade—but only in order to remind the crowd about the dangers faced by Stirling and the pioneers. And the Parade was held only a few years after the most appalling massacre of Aborigines by white men in the history of Western Australia—at Oombulgurri, near Forest River in the far north. But at least one 1929 writer was certain that

> Western Australia is not ashamed of her treatment during her hundred years of the original lords of the soil.[12]

Only the General Conference of the Methodist Church entered a caveat—in the spirit of Joseph Hardey—by resolving to

> enter a strong protest against the treatment being meted out to the unfortunate Aborigines of this country.[13]

Perhaps rather more people believed that all would be well before too long, for Professor Porteus and Mr Childs were heading north-west on an expedition 'to show, for scientific purposes, the general life of the Aborigine before he died out'.[14]

The children of Sister Kate's Home on holiday at Fremantle.

[11] *WAPD* (n.s.), Vol. 82, 25 July 1929.
[12] *Civil Service Journal*. Centenary Number, 1929, p.83.
[13] *Western Methodist* 1 July 1929.   [14] *West Australian* 30 May 1929.

For many of the people of Perth, the Aborigines were 'out of sight and out of mind'. Far more important to their lives was the unveiling of the State War Memorial in King's Park in November, a ceremony watched by nearly 10 000 people. The Governor General, Lord Stonehaven, put their view succinctly:

Unemployed men march through the streets of Perth in protest against an economic depression not of their making.

> We, who went through the War, have a special position in the community. We must see to it that the rising generation should realize to what they owe their freedom, and all the proud privileges which are their birthright as members of the British Empire.[15]

Depression and War

As 1929 turned into 1930, the peoples of the world experienced the full horrors of the greatest economic depression of the twentieth century. By 1933 nearly one in four men in Perth was unemployed, and another one in four was on short-time. Their families suffered in ways which serious research is only beginning to reveal. Many unemployed families were told by governments, employers of labour, and charitable institutions, that if they stayed quiet, all would come right for them. Many men did as they were told, and waited patiently and unprotestingly, bearing their suffering in proud and dignified silence. Others did protest vigorously—in marches along the streets of Perth, culminating in demonstrations outside the Treasury Buildings in Barrack Street. Throughout the Depression, the Perth City Council did what it

15 Premier's Department file 458/29.

The Town Hall in 1935: *more of a symbol than a success. (Portia Bennett, artist.)*

Going to the War, 1939.

could for the unemployed. A number of relief-works were undertaken, including the construction of Riverside Drive. But even on the eve of the Second World War, over one in ten men in Perth was unemployed, and many more lived in slums, as identified by a series of scandals in the mid-1930s.[16]

During the Second World War, the men and women of Perth served in nearly all the major theatres of war, often with great gallantry, as in the Great War. In the war with Japan, Perth, for the first time in its history, felt the proximity of invasion. Air-raid shelters were prepared, and alerts were rehearsed. Children in schools were provided with gas masks. Throughout the War, the Lord Mayor, Thomas Meagher, and his Council worked hard to maintain the city's services; and by their example they helped to keep high the morale of the people of Perth. The traditional tie with Great Britain, which had been eroded considerably during the 1930s, was strengthened during the Second World War, even though it was realized that Britain could no longer defend Western Australia as she had done for over one hundred years.[17]

'Internal Peace'?: Perth 1945 to 1979

After the Second World War, the Federal Government's Department of Post-War Reconstruction, in co-operation with the State Government, began the awesome task of building thousands of houses, creating employment, and so on. But the immediate post war years saw also an enormous growth in self-help activities, as witnessed in the thousands of 'extra rooms', often in asbestos, put up in the suburbs. And to the suburbs, both old and new, came the European migrants, survivors of the holocaust of western and eastern Europe. The migrants fought tenaciously to carve out decent lives for themselves and their families in a social environment which could be, and too often was, hostile. Migrant children often suffered terrible indignities at the hands

---

16 There are accounts of the Depression in G.C. Bolton *A Fine Country to Starve In*, 1972, and G. Snooks *Depression and Recovery 1929/29–1938/39*, 1974.

17 For the war period see F. K. Crowley *Australia's Western Third*, 1960.

A Naturalization Ceremony at the Perth City Council, 1950s.

of Western Australian children and some teachers, and carried with them for years the scars of their troubled youth. That the migrants contributed greatly to the life of modern Perth is beyond dispute.

For a great many people in Perth in the 1950s, life was fairly comfortable. Processed frozen foods, plastics, consumer durables, television (from 1959), cars (especially the Holden), drive-in-cinemas, all testified to an improving standard of living for many. For much of the period, Western Australia was governed by a Labor Government, while in the federal sphere, Mr Menzies' Liberal Government remained in office throughout the 1950s and for much of the 1960s. Both governments encouraged the work of the schools, of which there were now many, for the baby boom after the war had put great pressure on educational services in both state and private school systems. These years were sometimes described as an 'age of affluence'. But, as always in the history of Perth, while some families were very affluent and powerful, many more made ends meet readily enough, without having investments or power other than at the local suburban level. And there were still those for whom 'watching the pennies' was a way of life.

In 1962, Perth was host to the Empire Games. In some ways the Games were an affirmation of the old Imperial connection, as were the Royal visits and the holiday on the Queen's birthday. But the Empire Games had a greater significance than this. Perth had won the right to hold the Games. It could at last be said that the city was a jewel in the British Empire. And at a more popular level, the Games celebrated Western Australia's rise to prominence in international athletics—John Winter, and then Shirley Strickland, had become household names throughout the country, the Empire, and the international sporting community.[18]

From the mid-1950s the young people of Perth, with pennies—and even shillings—in their pockets, were experiencing life in the city through

18   There is an account of Shirley Strickland's career in L. Hunt (Ed.) *Westralian Portraits*, 1979.

the filter of American and British popular culture. Pop songs like *I see the Moon*, *She Wears Red Feathers*, *Tell Me a Story*, and *How much is that Doggie in the Window* were very popular; and many a parent was anxious about bodgie or widgie sons and daughters. In the mid-1950s, rock and roll hit Perth, as it did round the world. In the Hay Street theatres, the more exuberant youngsters jived in the aisles to the beat of *Rock Around the Clock*. If Bill Haley and his Comets were big, even bigger (and more threatening to parents) was Elvis Presley, whose gyrations ushered in what became known as the age of permissiveness. *Heartbreak Hotel*, *You ain't nothin' but a Hound Dog*, and a string of other songs, became as much part of the fabric of Perth life as the train to school, shopping in Bairds or Boans, Friday night at the open air cinema, or the Saturday arvo matinee or football. There were even 'delinquents' who, on motorbikes, scooters, and even as car owners (mostly on hire purchase), ventured into the 'Snake Pit' at Scarborough, for Scarborough then, as today, was a refuge for the wilder youngsters of Perth. Many a young man in Perth looked as if he'd stepped out of James Dean's *Rebel Without a Cause*; and many a girl looked for the world like a Connie Francis or any of the other American bobby sox film and pop stars. In the early 1960s all eyes switched to Britain, for four mop haired youths from 'The Cavern' in Liverpool, were sweeping up the Charts with *I Want to Hold Your Hand* and *She Loves You, Yeah, Yeah, Yeah*. Beatlemania, Carnaby Street, the mini-skirt . . . and for the angrier young, there were the 'Stones' and the 'Animals'.

And in time the revolt of youth began to assume a social content and purpose—evident in the songs of protest sung by people like Bob Dylan and Joan Baez, and by the Beatles themselves in their beautiful and moving lines of spiritual and social alienation, such as

> Ah, look at all the lonely people
> Where do they all come from? . . .
> Where do they all belong?   (Eleanor Rigby)

and

> Lady Madonna, children at your feet
> Wonder how you manage to make ends meet.
> Lady Madonna, baby at your breast
> Wonder how you manage to feed the rest.

The songs of protest against the wars of old people, against racialism, against colonialism, and against poverty in the midst of affluence, came together in the late 1960s in the moratorium marches in Perth against the Vietnam War. It came together in the feminist movement, with its powerful assertion of the rights of women in Australian society. It came together also in the increased concern for the physical and social environment of the city: indeed 'environmentalism', as expressed in such well-known books as George Seddon's *Sense of Place* and *Swan River Landscapes*, came to form part of the everyday discourse, in the media, in parliament, in colleges, in schools, and in homes in Perth.[19] It came together in the increased concern for Aboriginal welfare, and the renewed determination on the part of Aborigines themselves to insist on their voice being heard, even in the most apathetic and hostile corners of political and social life. The publication in Perth of a journal called *Aboriginal and Islander Identity*, was as poignant and meaningful an expression of this as could be found.

[19]   G. Seddon *Sense of Place*, 1972; also *Swan River Landscapes*, 1970

Television reaches the people of Perth: from the West Australian, *17 October 1959.*

A moratorium march in the streets of Perth, late 1960s.

And the context for all this was the massive industrial and commercial development of Western Australia from the mid-1960s to the mid-1970s. In the course of this development, the city of Perth was altered physically, as the old and familiar building landmarks were torn down and replaced by skyscraper office blocks. Fortunes were made by some people in the great mineral booms, such as the nickel boom; or in the surge of real estate development in the city and new suburbs. By the mid-1970s, the number of Perth suburbs had doubled in just over a decade; and the town of Wanneroo, to the north-west of the city, became a juggernaut municipality, experiencing the problems of rapid growth which the City of Perth had experienced during the goldrushes.

Just as in 1870 the opening of the Perth Town Hall was of great significance to the people of Perth, so too was the opening of the Perth Concert Hall in 1973. The Hall was the product of the confident years. In speaking at the opening of the Hall, the Leader of the Opposition, Sir Charles Court, spoke with the vigour and purpose which characterised his work in the field of industrial and mining development. He embodied the confidence of those years. Of equal significance was the speech made by the Premier, Mr John Tonkin. Mr Tonkin spoke with a sense of wonder that Perth should be so privileged as to have such a beautiful concert hall. He spoke from the depths of the years of deprivation: he spoke for the generation of the Great Depression. Six years on, both men would be involved in the sesquicentenary celebrations of the foundation of Western Australia.

For the people of Perth, 1979 is a year of celebrations and of reflection. It is also the international year of the child. As in 1929 there are pageants, balls, books, pictures, albums, and a thousand and one other ways of celebrating the occasion. Once more there is an emphasis on the pioneers, and this time Stirling was honoured in metal. Stirling also found his way into the State Government sponsored book, *Westralian Portraits*, as he did with *A Story of a Hundred Years* in 1929; but in *Westralian Portraits* he had to take second place behind the Aboriginal patriot, Yagan. This too was a foreshadowing of changes, as was the concluding entry in the same book—Mr Ken Colbung, the Perth

Aboriginal leader. As the Government's 'Plaques Committee' settled down to its task of naming 150 Western Australians who should be set in stone and walked upon by the people of Perth, some less well known Perthians were to be juxtaposed with the men and women who have predominated in historical writing to the present time. This too was a sign of the times. Even more striking is the preparation of the *Dictionary of Western Australians 1829–1914*, for it will democratically list everyone who lived and worked in the colony. But as the school children streamed through the beautiful Old Gaol Museum in Perth—some clutching their 150th gifts from the Government, like the *Album* or the *Diary* or the *Historical Atlas* (called *Atlas of Human Endeavour* rather than the more pompous *Atlas of Achievement*, as originally suggested)—they passed before the massive figure of John Forrest. For in looking at Perth's history, despite some changes, the Forrests, in 1979, as in 1929 and 1879, embodied the spirit of place. It might even be so in the bicentennial year of 2029.

Perth as Pastoral Myth: *a town planner's testimony, 1975.*

Bibliography

NOTE: Readers should also consult J. Gentilli and D. Rumley *A Bibliography of Metropolitan Perth*, Department of Geography, University of Western Australia, 1977.

Official Records—Unpublished

Colonial Secretary's Office. Correspondence (WA State Archives Acc. No. 36).

General Road Trust. Minutes 1838–47 (WA State Archives Acc. No. 491).

Governor's despatches (WA State Archives Acc. No. 390).

Greater Perth Conference and Committees. Minutes 1906–12 (Held in the Perth City Council).

Lands and Surveys Department. Description books. (WA State Archives Acc. No. 660).

Perth City Council. Health Committee Minutes.

Perth City Council. Minute Books.

Perth City Council. Rate Books.

Perth Electoral Roll 1870 (WA State Archives Acc. No. 63); also Perth Electoral Roll 1887 (Held in Supreme Court of WA).

Supreme Court Records (Held in Supreme Court of WA).

Swan River Papers Vol. 1–16 (WA State Archives Acc. No. 58).

Official Records—Published

Census of Western Australia. 1848–1901.

Children's Hospital, Perth. Annual Reports.

Commonwealth Census of Australia, 1911.

Commonwealth of Australia. Year Books, 1901–11.

Historical Records of Australia. Series III, Vol. VI, Syd., Library Committee of the Commonwealth Parliament, 1923.

House of Commons. Select Committee on Transportation together with the Proceedings of the Committee, Minutes of Evidence, Appendix and Index, 1861. British Parliamentary Paper No. 286.

Perth City Council. Mayor's Annual Reports, 1898 — (These include reports of senior council officials.)

Statistical Registers of Western Australia.

Statutes of Western Australia.

Victorian Year Book, 1881–82.

Western Australian Blue Books.

Western Australian Government Gazettes.

Western Australian Parliamentary Debates.

Western Australian Votes and Proceedings of Parliament.

Western Australian Year Books.

Private Papers and Interviews

ALLENDER, R. 'Western Australia at its Centenary', (Unpublished research essay held by the author).

BOAS, H. 'Bricks and Mortar'. Unpublished autobiography, 1971 (Battye Library Acc. No. 881A/41).

BOLD, W. E. Civic Reminiscences, 1893–1943 (Battye Library).

BOLD, W. E. Scrapbooks. Vols. 1–3 (Battye Library Acc. No. PR2073).

BURT, S. Letterbook (In possession of Chief Justice F. T. P. Burt, Cottesloe, WA).

GALLOP Family Papers 1829–95 (Battye Library Acc. No. 1862A).

HARDEY, J. Diary 1830–39 (Battye Library Acc. No. 566A).

HARPER, C. Papers 1872–1910 (Battye Library Acc. No. 1973A).

JONES, Mrs Interview with the author, 1974 (Typescript in Subiaco Museum, WA).

MITCHELL, Mrs W. Diary (Mitchell Library, 5-82A, B1148-49).
MOORE Family Papers 1830s-70s (Battye Library, Acc. No. 1075A, 1150A).
Perth City Council. Clippings File (Held in the Perth City Council).
Perth Gas Company. Minute Book 1883-93 (Battye Library Acc. No. 476A).
PRINSEP, H. C. Diaries 1866-1922 (Battye Library Acc. No. 499A).
QUINLAN, T. Papers 1896-1902 (In possession of Mr A. D. Quinlan, Dalkeith, WA).
RILEY, M. Interview with the author, 1975 (Notes in author's possession).
SALVADO, R. Papers (Held in Nullius Abbey, New Norcia).
SANFORD Letters (Mitchell Library, mss 759).
STANNAGE, C. T. 'Owners of Perth Property 1879-1904'. Unpublished computer print-out based on Perth City Council Rate Books.
Stone, James & Co. Legal papers (Battye Library Acc. No. 711A).
Swan River Mechanics' Institute. Minute Books (Held in Perth City Council).
TAYLOR, S. 'An investigation of the concept of pauperism among women in mid-nineteenth century Western Australia, with particular emphasis on the institution of the Perth Poor House 1862-1969.' (Unpublished research essay held by the author).
THOMSON, Mrs J. G. (nee Emma Roe) Diary 1853-55 (Battye Library Acc. No. 752A).
TRAYLEN, W. Letterbook 1895-96 (Battye Library Acc. No. 1458A).
TRIGG, H. Correspondence 1829-30 (Battye Library Acc. No. HS/591).
VENN, Mrs H. Diary 1888-89, 1892-97 (Battye Library Acc. No. 1193A).
VOSPER, F. C. B. Letters (Battye Library Acc. No. 817A).

Newspapers and Periodicals

Civil Service Journal
Daily News
Eastern Districts Chronicle
Evening Times
Golden West
Inquirer
Morning Herald
Perth Gazette
Southern Advertiser
Swan River Guardian
Sunday Times
Truth
Victorian Express
West Australian
WA Bulletin
WA Record
Western Australian Times
Western Mail

Books, Articles and Theses

ALEXANDER, F. (ed.) *Four Bishops and Their See*, Nedlands, UWAP, 1957.
ANDERSON, P. 'Economic Aspects of Transportation to Western Australia', BA Hons thesis, UWA, 1950.
Anonymous 'A Letter from a Convict in Australia to a Brother in England', *Cornhill Magazine* Vol. XIII, January-June 1866.
ARMSTRONG, A. *The Church of England, The Methodists and Society 1770-1850*, Lond., Uni. of Lond. P., 1973.
Australian Dictionary of Biography Vols. 1-7, Carlton (Vic.), MUP, 1966-79.
Australian Planning Congress. *The City and Region of Perth.* Papers and proceedings of the 10th Congress, 1968. [Perth, Australian Planning Institute, 1969.]

BACKHOUSE, J. A. *A Narrative of a Visit to the Australian Colonies*, Lond., Hamilton, Adams, 1843.

BASSETT, M. *The Hentys: An Australian Colonial Tapestry*, Lond., OUP, 1954.

BASTIN, J. AND STOODLEY, J. 'F. C. B. Vosper: An Australian Radical', *University Studies in History*, Vol. V, No. 1, 1967.

BATE, W. *Lucky City: The First Generation at Ballarat: 1851-1901*, Carlton (Vic.), MUP, 1978.

BATTYE, J. S. (ed.) *Cyclopaedia of Western Australia*, 2 vols., Perth, Cyclopaedia Co., 1912-13.

BATTYE, J. S. *Western Australia: A History from its Discovery to the Inauguration of the Commonwealth*, Oxford, Clarendon P., 1924.

BERGER, J. *Ways of Seeing*, Harmondsworth, Penguin, 1972.

BELL, C. AND NEWBY, H. *Community Studies: An Introduction to the Sociology of the Local Community*, Lond., George Allen & Unwin, 1971.

BISKUP, P. *Not Slaves, Not Citizens: The Aboriginal Problem in Western Australia, 1898-1954*, St Lucia (Q), QUP, 1973.

BOLGER, P. *Hobart Town*, Canberra, ANU, 1973.

BOLTON, G. C. *A Fine Country to Starve In*, Nedlands, UWAP, 1972.

BOLTON, G. C. *Alexander Forrest: His Life and Times*, Carlton (Vic.), MUP, 1958.

BOLTON, G. C. 'The Idea of a Colonial Gentry', *Historical Studies* Vol. 13, No. 51, October 1968.

BOLTON, G. C. AND HUTCHISON, D. 'European Man in Southwestern Australia', *Journal of the Royal Society of Western Australia* Vol. 56, 1973.

BOLTON, G. C. AND MOZLEY, A. *Western Australian Legislature 1870-1930*, Canberra, ANU, 1961.

BRIGGS, A. *The Age of Improvement*, Lond., Longmans, 1959.

BROOME, N. 'Western Australia', *Royal Colonial Institute Proceedings* Vol. XVI, 1884-85.

BROOMHALL, F. H. *The Veterans: A History of the Enrolled Pensioner Force in Western Australia 1850-80*, 2 vols., typescript, 1975.

BUNBURY, W. S. AND MORRELL, W. P. (eds.) *Early Days in Western Australia: Being the Letters and Journal of Lieutenant H. W. Bunbury*, Lond., OUP, 1930.

BURSTOWE, H. *Reminiscences of Horsham*, 1911 (reprinted Flocrost, 1975).

BURTON, A. *Church Beginnings in the West* [Perth, The Author], 1941.

BURTON, A. 'A Diary of Joseph Hardey', *RWAHS* Vol. I, Pt. VI, 1929.

BURTON, A. AND HENN, P. U. (eds.) *Wollaston's Picton Journal 1841-44*. Reprint, Nedlands, UWAP, 1975.

BUTLIN, S. J. *Foundations of the Australian Monetary System 1788-1851*, Carlton (Vic.), MUP, 1953.

BUXTON, G. L. *The Riverina 1861-91: An Australian Regional Study*, Carlton (Vic.), MUP, 1967.

CALVERT, A. F. *My Fourth Tour in Western Australia*, Lond., Heinemann, 1897.

CAMERON, J. M. AND JAGGARD, E. K. (eds.) *WA Readings*, 2nd edition, Perth, Churchlands College, 1977.

CAMMILLERI, C. 'Walter Padbury 1820-1907', *RWAHS* Vol. VII, Pt. III, 1971.

CAMPBELL, R. 'Aspects of Perth and its Society, 1901', BA Hons thesis, UWA, 1972.

CANNON, M. *The Land Boomers*, Carlton (Vic.), MUP, 1966.

CHAMBERS, J. D. AND MINGAY, G. E. *The Agricultural Revolution 1750-1880*, Lond., Batsford, 1966.

CLARK, C. M. H. *A History of Australia* Vols. 1-4, Carlton (Vic.), MUP, 1962-78.

CLARK, G. K. *The Making of Victorian England*, Lond., Methuen, 1962.

CLARK, R. 'The City Beautiful', *Architect* Vol. 10, No. 2, 1969.

CLARK, R. 'Garden City Movement', *Architect* Vol. 10, No. 4, 1969.

COBB, R. C. *A Sense of Place*, Lond., Duckworth, 1975.

COHEN, B. *A History of Medicine in Western Australia*, Perth, Paterson Brokensha [1965].

COLEBATCH, H. (ed.) *A Story of a Hundred Years: Western Australia 1829-1929*, Perth, Govt. Print., 1929.

CORNISH, H. *Under the Southern Cross*, 2nd edition, Madras, Higginbotham, 1880.

COURTNEY, V. *Perth and All This: A Story about a City and its Society*, Syd., Halstead P., 1962.

COWARD, D. 'The Myth of the Great Life Saver: The Sewers and Mortality in Sydney 1870-1900', *Community Health Studies* (forthcoming issue).

CROWLEY, F. K. *Australia's Western Third: A History of Western Australia from the First Settlements to Modern Times*, Lond. Macmillan, 1960.

CROWLEY, F. K. *Forrest 1847-1918* Vol. I, 1847-91, St Lucia (Q), QUP, 1971.

CROWLEY, F. K. 'Master and Servant in Western Australia', *RWAHS* Vol. IV, Pt. VI, 1954.

DAVISON, G. *The Rise and Fall of Marvellous Melbourne*, Carlton (Vic.), MUP, 1978.

Dictionary of Western Australians 1829-1914 (also known as *WA Biographical Index*), Nedlands, UWAP, 1979. Several volumes.

DOWNEY, H.S.G. *Mosman Park*, Mosman Park (WA), Town of Mosman Park [1971].

DURACK, M. *To Be Heirs Forever*, Lond., Constable, 1976.

EASTON, L. A. *Stirling City*, Nedlands, UWAP, 1971.

EDWARDS, R. D. AND WILLIAMS, T. D. (eds.) *The Great Famine: Studies in Irish History 1845-52*, Dublin, Brown and Nolan, 1956.

ELLIOT, I. *Moondyne Joe: The Man and the Myth*, Nedlands, UWAP, 1978.

ERICKSON, R. *Old Toodyay and Newcastle*, Toodyay, Toodyay Shire Council, 1974.

ERICKSON, R. 'T. N. Yule Esq.: A Gentleman of Misfortune', *RWAHS* Vol. VII, Pt. III, 1971.

EWERS, J. K. *The Western Gateway: A History of Fremantle*, 2nd edition, Nedlands, UWAP, 1971.

FALL, J. 'Crime and Criminal Records in Western Australia 1829-55' *Studies in Western Australian History* No. 3, November 1978.

GERTZEL, C. J. 'The Convict System in Western Australia', BA Hons thesis, UWA, 1949.

GILL, A. 'Aborigines, Settlers and Police in the Kimberleys 1887-1905', *Studies in Western Australian History* No. 1, June 1977.

GREEN, V. H. H. *Religion at Oxford and Cambridge*, Lond., SCM Press, 1964.

GREENWOOD, G. (ed.) *Australia: A Social and Political History*, Syd., Angus and Robertson, 1955.

GREER, S. *The Emerging City: Myth and Reality*, Glencoe, Ill., The Free Press, 1962.

GRIBBLE, J. B. *Dark Deeds in a Sunny Land: Blacks and Whites in North West Australia*, Perth, Daily News, 1905 (Preface dated 1886).

HAMMOND, J. E. 'The Builders of Perth', *RWAHS* Vol. I, Pt. IX, 1931.

HART, F. *Western Australia in 1891*, Perth, Govt. of WA [1891].

HARVEY, D. *Social Justice and the City*, Lond., Edward Arnold, 1973.

HASLUCK, A. *Thomas Peel of Swan River*, Melb., OUP, 1965.

HASLUCK, A. AND LUKIS, M. *Victorian and Edwardian Perth*, Syd., Ferguson, 1977.

HASLUCK, A. *Unwilling Emigrants: A Study of the Convict Period in Western Australia*, Melb. OUP, 1959.

HASLUCK, P. 'Guildford and the Swan', *RWAHS* Vol. I, Pt. II, 1928.

HASLUCK, P. *Mucking About: An Autobiography*, Carlton (Vic.), MUP, 1977.

HAYNES, B. T. *et al.* (eds.) *WA Aborigines 1622-1972: An Extract from Themes from Western Australian History: A Selection of Docments and Readings*, Perth, History Association of WA, 1972.

HENN, P. U. (ed.) *Wollaston's Albany Journals 1848-1856*, Perth, Paterson Brokensha [1954].

HICKS, N. *'This Sin and Scandal': Australia's Population Debate 1891-1911*, Canberra, ANU, 1978.

HIRST, J. B. *Adelaide and the Country 1870-1917: Their Social and Political Relationship*, Carlton (Vic.), MUP, 1973.

HOUGHTON, W. E. *The Victorian Frame of Mind 1830-70*, Lond., OUP, 1957.

HUNT, L. (ed.) *Westralian Portraits*, Nedlands, UWAP, 1979.

HUNT, S. AND BOLTON, G. C. 'Cleansing the Dunghill: Water Supply and Sanitation in Perth 1878-1912', *Studies in Western Australian History* No. 2, March 1978.

HYAMS, B. K. 'Western Australian Political Parties 1901-16', BA Hons thesis, UWA, 1954.

INGLIS, B. *Poverty and the Industrial Revolution*, Lond., Panther, 1972.

JOHNS, J. R. H. *Metropolitan Government in Western Australia*, Nedlands, UWAP [1950].

JOLL, L. 'Perth Society in 1891', BA Hons thesis, UWA, 1972.

JOSKE, E. P. 'Captain Graham: Colonist and Coroner of Fremantle', *RWAHS*, Vol. VII, Pt. VI, 1974.

JOSKE, E. P. 'Health and Hospital: A Study of Community Welfare in Western Australia 1829-55', MA thesis, UWA, 1973.

KENNEDY, J. 'Perth in my Boyhood', *RWAHS* Vol. I, Pt. I, 1927.

KIMBERLY, W. B. *History of West Australia: A Narrative of her Past together with Biographies of her Leading Men*, Melb., F. W. Niven, 1897.

KNIGHT, E. F. *With the Royal Tour*, Lond., Longman's Green, 1902.

KORNWEIBEL, A. H. *Apollo and the Pioneers* [Perth], Music Council of WA, 1973.

LA NAUZE, J. A. 'Merchants in Action', *Economic Record* Vol. 31, May 1955.

LAWSON, R. *Brisbane in the 1890s*, St Lucia (Q), QUP, 1973.

LOUCH, T. S. *The First Fifty Years: The History of the Weld Club 1871-1921*, Perth, Weld Club, 1964.

LOURENS, R. M. C. 'The Perth Building Society: A Study in Institutional Growth', PhD thesis, UWA, 1973.

LOVEDAY, P. *et al.* (eds.) *The Emergence of the Australian Party System*, Syd., Hale and Iremonger, 1977.

LUKES, S. *Power: A Radical View*, Lond., Macmillan, 1974.

LUTTON, W. *The Wesley Story: A Centenary of Wesley Church, Perth, Western Australia 1870-1970* [Perth, Wesley Church, 1970].

MCCARTHY, P. 'The Foundations of Catholicism in Western Australia 1829-1911', *University Studies in History* Vol. II, No. 4, 1956.

MCCARTY, J. W. 'British Investment in Western Australian Gold Mining 1894-1914', *University Studies in History* Vol. IV, No. 1, 1961-62.

McCARTY, J. W. AND SCHEDVIN, C. B. (eds.) *Australian Capital Cities: Historical Essays*, Syd., SUP, 1978.

MacDONAGH, O. 'Highbury and Chawton: Social Convergence in "Emma" ', *Historical Studies* Vol. 18, No. 70, April 1978.

McGREGOR, O. R. *Divorce in England: A Centenary Study*, Lond., Heinemann, 1957.

MARKEY, D. *More of a Symbol than a Success: Foundation Years of the Swan River Colony*, Perth, Mt Lawley Teachers' College, 1976.

MARX, L. *The Machine in the Garden: Technology and Pastoral Ideal in America*, Lond., OUP, 1974.

MERCER, F. R. *The Life of Charles Harper of 'Woodbridge' Guildford, Western Australia*, Perth, Westralian Farmers Co-operative Printing Works, 1958.

MILLETT, E. *An Australian Parsonage, or, the Settler and the Savage in Western Australia*, Lond., E. Stanford, 1872.

MOORE, G. F. *Diary of Ten Years Eventful Life of an Early Settler in Western Australia*, Lond., M. Walbrook, 1884.

MORRISON, A. A. 'Religion and Politics in Queensland in 1881', *Journal of the Historical Society of Queensland*, Vol. IV, No. 4, December 1951.

MOSSENSON, D. *State Education in Western Australia 1829-1960*, Nedlands, UWAP, 1972.

MURDOCH, W. *The Struggle for Freedom: Lessons in English History*, 6th edition, Melb., Whitcombe and Tombs, 1911.

MURPHY, D. J. (ed.) *Labor in Politics: The State Labor Parties in Australia 1880-1920*, St Lucia (Q), QUP, 1975.

NAPIER, K. D. 'New Holland in Europe', *RWAHS* Vol. VII, Pt. VII, 1975.

NEWBOLT, M. 'The Sisters of Mercy', *RWAHS* Vol. VII, Pt. VI, 1974.

OBELKEVICH, J. *Religion and Rural Society: South Lindsey 1825-75*, Oxford, Clarendon P., 1976.

OLDHAM, R. 'The Reminiscences of William Wade', *RWAHS*, Vol. VI, Pt. II, 1963.

OLDHAM, R. AND J. *Western Heritage: A Study of the Colonial Architecture of Perth, Western Australia*, Perth, Paterson Brokensha [1961].

O'REILLY, J. B. *Moondyne*, 1879; Rigby ed., 1975.

PARKER, G. *Round the Compass in Australia*, Lond., Hutchinson, 1892.

PARRY, A. (ed.) *The Admirals Fremantle*, Lond., Chatto and Windus, 1971.

PIKE, D. *Paradise of Dissent: South Australia 1829-57*, Carlton (Vic.), MUP, 1957.

PORTER, A. ' "A Mangle, Wringer, Bowl, Scissors, a Bible and a Prayer Book": The House of Mercy, Perth 1890-99', *Time Remembered* No. 2, 1978.

Princess Margaret Hospital for Children, Perth. 'History of the Children's Hospital, Perth' Vol. 1, 1897-1910, Perth, PMH, 1978.

PRINT, M. AND ZANI, L. (eds.) *Local History in Schools*, Perth, History Association of WA, 1976.

REECE, R. H. W. *Aborigines and Colonists: Aborigines and Colonial Society in New South Wales in the 1830s and 1840s*, Syd., SUP, 1974.

REYNOLDS, H. (ed.) *Aborigines and Settlers: The Australian Experience 1788-1939*, Melb., Cassell Australia, 1972.

REYNOLDS, H. 'Racial Thought in Early Colonial Australia', *Australian Journal of Politics and History* Vol. 20, 1974.

RILEY, C. L. 'Early Perth'. Talk given to the Karrakatta Club, 31 July 1962 (Battye Library Acc. No. PR4614).

ROBERTSON, R. E. 'W. E. Bold, C. B. E.: An Analysis of his Administrative Contribution, Community Interest and Social Influence', MA thesis, UWA, 1971.

ROBIN, A DE Q *Mathew Blagden Hale: The Life of an Australian Pioneer Bishop*, Melb., Hawthorn P., 1976.

ROE, J. B. 'Some Old Time Memories', *RWAHS* Vol. 1, Pt. I, 1927.

ROWLAND, D. T. *Internal Migration in Australia*, Canberra, Australian Bureau of Statistics, 1979, Census Monograph Series.

ROWNTREE, B. S. *Poverty: Study of Town Life*, Lond., Macmillan, 1901.

RUSSO, G. 'Bishop Salvado's Mission to Christianize and Civilize the Aborigines', MA thesis, UWA, 1974.

SANDERCOCK, L. *Cities for Sale: Property, Politics and Urban Planning in Australia*, Carlton (Vic.), MUP, 1975.

SCHEDVIN, C. B. AND McCARTY, J. W. (eds.) *Urbanization in Australia: The Nineteenth Century*, Syd., SUP, 1974.

SCHLESINGER, A. M. *Paths to the Present*, New York, McMillan & Co., 1949.

SEARLE, G. R. *The Quest for National Efficiency: A Study in British Politics and Political Thought*, Oxford, Blackwell, 1973.

SEDDON, G. *Swan River Landscapes*, Nedlands, UWAP, 1970.

SEDDON, G. *Sense of Place*, Nedlands, UWAP, 1972.

SHAW, A. G. L. *Convicts and the Colonies: A Study of Penal Transportation from Great Britain and Ireland to Australia and Other Parts of the British Empire*, Lond., Faber, 1966.

SKINNER, M. L. *The Fifth Sparrow: An Autobiography*, Syd., SUP, 1972.

SMITH, B. 'Early Western Australian Literature: A Guide to Colonial Life', *University Studies in History* Vol. IV, No. 1, 1961–1962.

SMITH, B. 'Western Australian Goldfields Literature', *University Studies in History* Vol. IV, No. 2, 1963–64.

SNOOKS, G. *Depression and Recovery, 1928–29 to 1938–39*, Nedlands, UWAP, 1974.

SPEARRITT, P. *Sydney Since the Twenties*, Syd., Hale and Iremonger, 1978.

STANNAGE, C. T. 'Bishops Gibney and Salvado and Electoral Politics 1884–97', *Journal of Religious History*, June 1971.

STANNAGE, C. T. 'The Composition of the Western Australian Parliament 1890–1911', *University Studies in History* Vol. IV, No. 4, 1966.

STANNAGE, C. T. 'Electoral Politics in Western Australia 1884–97', MA thesis, UWA, 1967.

STANNAGE, C. T. 'The Records of the Supreme Court of Western Australia', *Studies in Western Australian History* No. 3, November 1978.

STANNAGE, C. T. (ed.) *Local History in Western Australia*, Perth, the editor, 1975.

STANNAGE, C. T. (Gen. Ed.) *A New History of Western Australia*, Nedlands, UWAP, 1979.

STANNAGE, C. T. 'Uncovering Poverty in Australian History', *RWAHS* Vol. VII, Pt. VIII, 1976.

STANNAGE, C. T. 'Western Australian History 1964–74: Retrospect and Prospect', *Teaching History* Vol. 8, Pt. 2, August 1974.

STANNER, W. E. H. *After the Dreaming: Black and White Australians—an Anthropologist's View*, Syd., ABC, 1969 (Boyer Lecture, 1968).

STAPLES, A. C. 'Henry Charles Prinsep', *RWAHS* Vol. V, Pt. 1, 1955.

STAVE, B. M. *The Making of Urban History: Historiography Through Oral History*, Cal., Sage Publications, 1977.

STEDMAN JONES, G. *Outcast London: A Study in the Relationship Between Classes in Victorian Society*, Oxford, OUP, 1971.

STEPHENSON, G. AND HEPBURN, J. A. *Plan for the Metropolitan Region: Perth and Fremantle, WA*, Perth, Govt. Print., 1955.

STEPHENSON, G. *The Design of Central Perth*, Nedlands, UWAP, 1975.

STONE, C. H. 'The Diary of Alfred Hawes Stone', *RWAHS* Vol. I, Pt. VI, 1929.

SUMMERS, J. *Music and Musicians: Personal Reminiscences 1865–1910*, Perth, Galway Printing Co., 1910.

TAUMAN, M. *The Chief: C. Y. O'Connor*, Nedlands, UWAP, 1978.

TAYLOR, S. 'The Convicts of Western Australia 1850–68', BA Hons thesis, UWA, 1978.

THOMAS, M. 'East Perth 1884–1904', BA Hons thesis, UWA, 1974.

THOMPSON, E. P. *The Making of the English Working Class*, Harmondsworth, Penguin, 1968.

TROLLOPE, A. *Australia and New Zealand, Vol. 2, Tasmania, WA and SA*, Lond., Chapman and Hall, 1873.

TWOPENY, R. E. N. *Town Life in Australia*, Lond., Elliot Stock, 1883.

TUCKFIELD, T. 'Early Colonial Inns and Taverns' *RWAHS* Vol. VII, Pt. III, 1971.

Twentieth Century Impressions of Western Australia, Perth, P. W. H. Thiel & Co., 1901.

UREN, M. J. *Land Looking West: The Story of Governor James Stirling in Western Australia*, Lond., OUP, 1948.

UREN, M. J. *The City of Melville: From Bushland to Expanding Metropolis*, Perth, Melville City Council, 1975.

VIVIENNE, M. *Travels in Western Australia*, 2nd edition, Lond., Heinemann, 1902.

WALKER, H. DE R. *Australian Democracy*, Lond., Unwin, 1897.

WARNER, S. B. *The Urban Wilderness: A History of the American City*, N.Y., Harper & Row, 1972.

WATSON, J. (ed.) *Catalpa '76, 100 Years Ago: A Special Collection of Papers on the Background and Significance of the Fenian Escape from Fremantle, WA, Easter, 1876*, Nedlands, UWA, 1976.

WEBER, M. *The City*, Glencoe, Ill., The Free Press, 1958.

Western Australian Almanacs.

Western Australian Art Gallery. *Acquisitions 1975–77*, Catalogue, Perth, WA Art Gallery, 1977.

Western Australian Art Gallery. *The First Fifteen Years*, Catalogue, Perth, WA Art Gallery, 1979.

Western Australian Education Department. *Swan River Settlement*, Perth, Govt. Print. [1968].

WHITE, J. AND PITT MORISON, M. (eds.) *Western Towns and Buildings*, Nedlands, UWAP, 1979.

WHITELEY, E. S. 'The Birth and Progress of Insurance', *RWAHS* Vol. III, Pt. IX, 1947.

WILLIAMS, A. E. AND JONES, A. B. *Western Wakening*, Perth, Carroll's Pty Ltd, 1975.

WILLIAMS, J. *The First Furrow*, Perth, Lone Hand P., 1976.

WILSON, J. G. *Western Australia's Centenary 1829–1929: First Century's Progress with Antecedent Records*, Perth, Historic P., 1929.

WIRTH, L. 'Urbanization as a Way of Life', *American Journal of Sociology*, Vol. XLIV, 1938.

WOODWARD, B. 'The Western Australian Museum and Art Gallery, Perth', *The Museum's Journal* Vol. 3, No. 6, December, 1903.

YARWOOD, A. T. *Asian Migration to Australia: The Background to Exclusion 1896–1923*, Carlton (Vic.), MUP, 1964.

Year Book of Western Australia, Perth, E. S. Wigg & Son, 1906.

Your Museum, Vol. 4, No. 3, September 1976 (Issue contains various articles on the Old Gaol, Perth).

Index

Page numbers in *italics* refer to illustrations; also ff, subject mentioned extends over two or more pages.

Photographic sources

The following individuals and organisations provided photographs and gave their permission for them to be reproduced.

Position of photograph: t-top, b-bottom, l-left, r-right.

Front cover, WA Newspapers Ltd. Front endpaper, Battye Library. Back endpaper, Perth City Council. Page 10, Art Gallery of WA. 11, Ernest Polis. 12, *Civil Service Journal*, 1929. 13t, Mitchell Library. 13b, Battye Library. 18, Battye Library. 21, *Australian Heritage*. 23, Battye Library. 25, Battye *Cyclopaedia of WA*. 27, Art Gallery of WA. 28, WA Newspapers Ltd. 31, *Civil Service Journal*, 1929. 32, D. Markey *More of a Symbol than a Success*. 35, Perth City Council. 36, Battye *Cyclopaedia of WA*. 37, Carroll's Pty Ltd. 38, Lutton *The Wesley Story*. 40, Battye Library. 45, Battye *Cyclopaedia of WA*. 47, Battye Library. 50, Battye Library. 51, Battye Library. 53, Battye Library. 55, Battye Library. 59, Battye Library. 61, WA Museum. 62, Art Gallery of WA. 63, WA Newspapers Ltd. 64, Perth City Council. 67, Supreme Court of WA. 68, Battye Library. 70, Supreme Court of WA. 76, Supreme Court of WA. 79, Battye Library. 80, WA Newspapers Ltd. 81, WA Newspapers Ltd. 82, Art Gallery of WA. 84, Battye Library. 92, Supreme Court of WA. 93, WA Newspapers Ltd. 100, Supreme Court of WA. 101, Battye Library. 102, WA Museum. 105, Battye Library. 106t, Battye Library. 106b, Perth City Council. 107t, Battye Library. 107b, Perth City Council. 108, Battye Library. 109, Battye Library. 110, Perth City Council. 111, Woodham Smith *The Great Famine*. 112, Battye Library. 115, Supreme Court of WA. 117, Battye Library. 118, Perth City Council. 122, Art Gallery of WA. 123, Art Gallery of WA. 124, Battye Library. 128 (2 prints), Battye Library. 129t, Battye Library. 129b, Mrs White. 130, Perth City Council. 131, Perth City Council. 133, WA Newspapers Ltd. 134t, Perth City Council. 134b, Battye Library. 135, Battye Library. 136, Battye Library. 137, Battye Library. 138, Perth City Council. 142 (2 prints), WA Newspapers Ltd. 143, Battye Library. 144, Art Gallery of WA. 145, WA Newspapers Ltd. 146, Battye Library. 147 (2 prints), Perth City Council. 148, Battye *Cyclopaedia of WA*. 150, Battye Library. 151t, Perth City Council. 151b, WA Newspapers Ltd. 152, Battye Library. 153, Lutton *The Wesley Story*. 155, Battye Library. 157, WA Newspapers Ltd. 160, Perth City Council. 163, WA Museum. 164, WA Newspapers Ltd. 165, Perth City Council. 166, WA Museum. 173, WA Newspapers Ltd. 175, Perth City Council. 178, Battye *Cyclopaedia of WA*. 181 (2 prints), Perth City Council. 183t, Perth City Council. 183b, Battye Library. 184–5, Perth City Council. 187, Battye Library. 189, *Twentieth Century Impressions of WA*. 190, Battye Library. 191, Perth City Council. 192, Mrs A. D. McGeorge, per Art Gallery of WA. 193, Ernest Polis. 198, Battye Library. 201t, *WA Bulletin*, June 1888. 201b, Battye Library. 202, *WA Bulletin*, May 1888. 206, *Twentieth Century Impressions of WA*. 208, Perth City Council. 211, Perth City Council. 213, Calvert *My Fourth Tour in Western Australia*. 214, *Twentieth Century Impressions of WA*. 215 (2 prints), *Twentieth Century Impressions of WA*. 217, *Twentieth Century Impressions of WA*. 218 (2 prints), Battye Library. 219, Battye *Cyclopaedia of WA*. 220, Perth City Council. 221, Supreme Court of WA. 223 (2 prints), Perth City Council. 224 (2 prints), Battye Library. 225, Perth City Council. 227, Keith Sinclair. 228 (2 prints), Battye *Cyclopaedia of WA*. 229, Battye *Cyclopaedia of WA*. 230, Battye *Cyclopaedia of WA*. 231, Keith Sinclair. 233, Battye *Cyclopaedia of WA*. 235, Battye *Cyclopaedia of WA*. 236, Battye *Cyclopaedia of WA*. 237, Battye *Cyclopaedia of WA*. 238, Perth City Council. 239, Perth City Council. 240, Perth City Council. 242, Commonwealth Census 1911. 244, Perth City Council. 245, Perry 'Architecture in Subiaco'. 246, Mrs White. 250, Subiaco Historical Society. 251, WA Museum. 253, Battye Library. 254, Battye Library. 257, Perth City Council. 258, *Twentieth Century Impressions of WA*. 259, WA Newspapers Ltd. 260, Battye *Cyclopaedia of WA*. 266, Mrs White. 267, Perth City Council. 272, Perth City Council. 275, Perth City Council. 276, PWD Plan Book. 280, Perth City Council. 281, Perth City Council. 285, Perth City Council. 286, Perth City Council. 288, Perth City Council. 289, Calvert *My Fourth Tour in Western Australia*. 291, Perth City Council. 292 (2 prints), Perth City Council. 293t, WA Newspapers Ltd. 293b, *Civil Service Journal*, 1929. 294, Perth City Council. 297, Johns Metropolitan Govt. 299t, Perth City Council. 299b, Clark 'City Beautiful'. 300, Perth City Council. 303 (2 prints), Mossenson *State Education in Western Australia*. 304t, Perth City Council. 304b, *Twentieth Century Impressions of WA*. 311, *Twentieth Century Impressions of WA*. 313, WA Newspapers Ltd. 314t, WA Newspapers Ltd. 314b, *Twentieth Century Impressions of WA*. 315 (2 prints), WA

Newspapers Ltd. **316**t, Perth City Council. **316**b, Battye Library. **317**, Art Gallery of WA. **318**t, Battye Library. **318**b, F. J. McNamara. **321**, Art Gallery of WA. **322**, Art Gallery of WA. **323**t, Art Gallery of WA. **323**b, WA Museum. **327**t, *Westerly*. **327**b, Calvert *My Fourth Tour in Western Australia*. **329**, Vivienne *Travels in Western Australia*. **330** (2 prints), *Twentieth Century Impressions of WA*. **331**t, WA Newspapers Ltd. **331**lb, Perth City Council. **331**rb, Battye Library. **332**t, Battye Library. **332**b (three prints), Ernest Polis. **333**b (three prints), Ernest Polis. **334**, Battye Library. **337**, Perth City Council. **338**b, WA Newspapers Ltd. **339**, Battye Library. **340**, Robert Vallis. **341**, Battye Library. **342** (2 prints), Perth City Council. **343**, WA Newspapers Ltd. **344**, WA Newspapers Ltd. **345**t, G. Stephenson *The Design of Central Perth*. **345**b, WA Museum.

Mr Ernest Polis, ARPS, photographed or re-photographed over two-thirds of the illustrations used in this book. The author wishes to place on record his debt of gratitude to Mr Polis for his cheerful and expert co-operation.